What Is Work?
Gender at the Crossroads
of Home, Family, and Business
from the Early Modern Era to the Present

International Studies in Social History

General Editor: Marcel van der Linden, International Institute of Social History, Amsterdam

Published in Association with the International Institute of Social History, Amsterdam

Published under the auspices of the International Institute of Social History, Amsterdam, this series offers transnational perspectives on labor and working-class history. For a long time, labor historians have been working within national interpretive frameworks. But interest in studies contrasting different national and regional experiences and studying cross-border interactions has been increasing in recent years. This series is designed to act as a forum for these new approaches.

For a full series listing, please see back matter.

WHAT IS WORK?

*Gender at the Crossroads
of Home, Family, and Business
from the Early Modern Era to the Present*

Edited by
Raffaella Sarti, Anna Bellavitis, and Manuela Martini

berghahn
NEW YORK • OXFORD
www.berghahnbooks.com

First published in 2018 by
Berghahn Books
www.berghahnbooks.com

© 2018, 2020 Raffaella Sarti, Anna Bellavitis, Manuela Martini
First paperback edition published in 2020

All rights reserved. Except for the quotation of short passages for the purposes of criticism and review, no part of this book may be reproduced in any form or by any means, electronic or mechanical, including photocopying, recording, or any information storage and retrieval system now known or to be invented, without written permission of the publisher.

Library of Congress Cataloging-in-Publication Data

A C.I.P. cataloging record is available from the Library of Congress

British Library Cataloguing in Publication Data

A catalogue record for this book is available from the British Library

ISBN 978-1-78533-911-0 hardback
ISBN 978-1-78920-802-3 paperback
ISBN 978-1-78533-912-7 ebook

Contents

List of Figures and Tables — vii

Introduction
What Is Work? Gender at the Crossroads of Home, Family, and Business from the Early Modern Era to the Present — 1
Raffaella Sarti, Anna Bellavitis, and Manuela Martini

I. SETTING THE SCENE: THE FEMINIST CHALLENGES TO THE "DELABORIZATION" OF HOUSEHOLD WORK — 85

1 Family Work: A Policy-Relevant Intellectual History — 89
Nancy Folbre

2 Productive and Reproductive Work: Uses and Abuses of an Old Dichotomy — 114
Alessandra Pescarolo

3 The Home as a Factory: Rethinking the Debate on Housewives' Wages in Italy, 1929–1980 — 139
Alessandra Gissi

II. THE CUNNING HISTORIAN: UNVEILING AND OVERCOMING THE GENDER BIAS OF SOURCES — 161

4 The Statistical Construction of Women's Work and the Male Breadwinner Economy in Spain (1856–1930) — 165
Cristina Borderías

5 Toiling Women, Non-working Housewives, and Lesser Citizens: Statistical and Legal Constructions of Female Work and Citizenship in Italy — 188
Raffaella Sarti

6 The Complexities of Work: Analyzing Men's and Women's Work in the Early Modern World with the Verb-Oriented Method 226
Maria Ågren

7 The Visibility of Women's Work: Logics and Contexts of Documents' Production 243
Margareth Lanzinger

III. THE VALUE OF CARE AND UNPAID HOME-BASED WORK: THE ROLE OF THE LAW 265

8 Regulating Home Labors: The ILO and the Feminization of Work 269
Eileen Boris

9 Family-Relations Law between "Stratification" and "Resistance": Housework and Family Law Exceptionalism 295
Maria Rosaria Marella

10 Could Family (Care) Work Be Paid? From French Agricultural Inheritance Law (1939) to Legal Recognition of Excessive Filial Duty (1994) 326
Florence Weber

IV. CONCLUSION

Conclusion
Can We Construct a Holistic Approach to Women's Labor History over the *Longue Durée*? 349
Laura Lee Downs

Index 368

Figures and Tables

Figures

Figure 3.1. Daniela, "Salario alle casalinghe?" (*Effe*, no. 3 [1974]: np).   150

Figure 3.2. Daniela, "Salario alle casalinghe?" (*Effe*, no. 3 [1974]: np).   151

Figure 3.3. "Salario alle casalinghe?" (*Effe*, no. 3 [1974]: 21).   152

Figure 3.4. Collettivo Internazionale Femminista, *Le operaie della casa* (Venezia: Marsilio, 1974). Cover of the book.   153

Figure 5.1. Percentages of housewives and economically active women among women, Italy, 1861–2011. Sources: Italian population censuses, 1861–2011 (original census data).   199

Figure 5.2. Percentage of women in the Italian male and female active population, 1881–1961. Source: Ornello Vitali, *Aspetti dello sviluppo economico italiano alla luce della ricostruzione della popolazione attiva* (Roma: Failli, 1970).   201

Figure 5.3. Percentage of economically active women among women and percentage of domestic workers among economically active women, Italy, 1861–2001. Sources: Italian population censuses, 1861–2011 (original census data).   205

Tables

Table 4.1. Categories and classification of (unpaid) domestic work in the national population censuses. Sources: Spanish national censuses.   174

Table 5.1. Classification of women whom we would define as "housewives" in the Italian population censuses. Sources: Italian population censuses, 1861–2011. 194

Table 6.1. All work activities grouped according to category and gender, Sweden 1550–1799 (absolute numbers). Source: Maria Ågren ed., *Making a Living, Making a Difference: Gender and Work in Early Modern European Society* (Oxford: Oxford University Press, 2017), 30. 230

INTRODUCTION

WHAT IS WORK?
Gender at the Crossroads of Home, Family, and Business from the Early Modern Era to the Present

Raffaella Sarti, Anna Bellavitis, and Manuela Martini

1. What is work? A fresh perspective from the (alleged) margins

What is work? The question chosen as a title for this volume is an ambitious one. We are obviously aware that a huge body of literature on work exists, and we certainly do not pretend we can give a definite answer to the question,[1] which may not even be possible.[2] Instead, we will use this question as a tool to interrogate history, the social sciences, and also politics. Such a question prompts us in fact to adopt a critical and diversified view of work and, consequently, of economic and social policies, too. On the other hand, establishing the boundaries, implications, and stakes of a new characterization of work is a crucial issue in the contemporary debate, and is obviously also motivated by the ongoing dramatic economic, technological, organizational, social, and cultural changes affecting the world of work.

Let us start with a telling example. "Italy is a Democratic Republic, founded on work," article 1 of the Italian Constitution, written after the Second World War and enforced in 1948, authoritatively states[3]: this implied and still implies a kind of overlap between enjoying citizenship and working. When the Italian Constitution was enforced, according to the Italian population censuses as many as three-quarters of adult Italian women were not working or, more precisely, were economically "inactive." What did they do? About 60 percent of them were housewives:

they were therefore likely to actually work very hard. Moreover, some of them were working (either part time or full time) in the family business but without any remuneration. Yet statisticians and economists did not consider housewives' activities as work, something that continues to happen even today. This exclusion obviously represented, and largely still represents, a serious gender bias in the political and economic construction of the Italian Republic.[4]

While the Italian case is particularly illuminating, it is not unique. Work was and still is defined in statistics such as the official calculations of GDP in such a way that it marginalizes female activities, especially those performed at home for free. Prostitution, the production and trafficking of drugs, as well as the smuggling of alcohol and tobacco have recently been officially included in the calculation of GDP in all EU countries,[5] whereas this is not yet the case with unpaid care- and domestic work. Therefore, according to the official GDP calculations, if we order a pizza that is delivered to us at home by a pizzeria, we contribute to GDP, but we don't if we prepare a pizza at home, except for the ingredients, electricity, etc., that we pay for; similarly, if we hire a babysitter, we increase our country's wealth, but we don't if we care for our children ourselves, whereas we would contribute to the wealth of the nation if we sold heroin to the young (a rather paradoxical calculation, indeed, even more so if we think that drug pushers do not pay taxes on their income).

Nonetheless, things have radically changed since the 1940s and 1950s. By the 1960s and 1970s, increasing criticism had been leveled against the rather simplified notion of work that had been developed by political economists and statisticians in the late eighteenth and nineteenth centuries and that (though never completely uncontested) had become hegemonic.[6] Female and feminist scholars and activists have played (and still play) a crucial role in questioning that notion, for instance by highlighting women's role in economic development[7] or by campaigning for wages to housewives that would make the economic value of care and housework visible,[8] to quote but two examples. However, other people, too, such as the scholars who have elaborated the so-called "new home economics,"[9] have called for a more complex and inclusive notion of work. As a consequence, today there is large consent on the need for such a revision and "complexification" of that very notion. Not only feminist scholars but also official statistics agencies produce statistics that include unpaid domestic and care work and calculate its economic value, though generally in "satellite accounts." Scholars who calculate the economic value of unpaid care- and housework conclude that it is likely to significantly alter the evaluation of the wealth of each single nation and the ranking of different countries, as the quantity of this type of work is not the same everywhere.[10]

Approaching the question "What is work?" from a historical perspective allows us to analyze the transformations and assess the achievements of the last decades. Moreover, it allows us to unveil the variety of historical forms of work, thus contributing to the aforementioned "complexification" of the very concept of work.

As a vantage point for our analysis, we have chosen the household, convinced that it offers a particularly fruitful perspective. We will therefore present the multiple forms of labor performed within the household economy, assessing whether or not they were considered proper work by different actors in different contexts and periods. Households were and still are more than just the sites of female, unpaid, and/or (allegedly) unproductive activities. Both women and men, girls and boys performed and perform a wide range of tasks within the household, though often highly gendered ones: home-based work, care work, unpaid market work, domestic service, waged labor, housekeeping, etc. Our ambitious plan has grown from a more limited project titled *Family Work, Unpaid Work: Forms and Actors of Productive Domestic Work in Europe (15th–21st Centuries)*. This project aimed to investigate different forms of unpaid work and production for the market performed within family-run economic activities. Both unpaid and paid care and housework (respectively performed by family members and domestic workers) have been the objects of burgeoning research in the last decades,[11] and paid industrial home work has also attracted attention.[12] Much less interest has been devoted to unpaid work for the market carried out within family enterprises;[13] thus the project's intent was to gather empirical studies dealing with women's and children's unpaid work for the market, especially in urban domestic production.[14]

The research developed within this project, however, has led us to analyze any type of work performed at home: the more we discovered about the importance of unpaid work for the market, not only in the Middle Ages or in the early modern era but also in present times, the more we were pushed to include in our analysis any form of home-based productive work (unpaid, paid, hybrid, and intermediate) as well as any other type of work carried out at home, both paid and unpaid, for self-consumption and care. In other words, in addition to paid and unpaid work for the market, this book will also deal with family non-market work. Yet the very notion of "non-market work" needs to be clarified. As stated by Nancy Folbre, a wide range of care work activities can be measured according to their market value. But some of the activities related to care do not have market substitutes. The definition of family work that she suggests includes both of these and aims to "refer to them as what they are, rather than what they are not," i.e., positively as "family work" and not negatively as "non-market work."[15]

Rather than a social and economic history of work especially focusing on home-based activities, the book provides readers with an analysis of the (often controversial and changing) value attributed to those activities by people belonging to different classes and social groups; by different religions and cultures; and by various philosophers, economists, policymakers, statisticians, political activists, feminists, international agencies, and organizations. In order to obtain a broad picture of what was and is (considered) work, nobody can ignore its gendered dimension; to develop a gendered perspective, we have, therefore, taken into account meanings and practices associated in past and present societies with female and male activities.

All the types of work addressed in the following pages have, over time, experienced specific transformations as for their practical organization and ideological evaluation, though each with peculiar features, as this book will show, thanks to its gendered, long-term perspective (sixteenth to twenty-first centuries) and thanks to its multidisciplinary approach. The contributors, who specialize in gender history, economic sociology, family history, civil law, and feminist economics, focus on women's work, family obligations, and household economies in European and North American countries, discussing continuities and discontinuities on gender-related tasks and forms of labor.

Today the ongoing transformations are radically modifying opportunities and implications of home-based work. The internet in particular, but also 3D printers and other devices, are making new forms of work at home (not only unpaid and non-market, but also paid and market work) possible, and a lively discussion is taking place on these new opportunities, on their advantages and disadvantages.[16]

By contrast, for a long time households had been increasingly *considered* as marginal places of economic activity in comparison to factories, shops, offices, etc., while many of the activities performed at home were ever more insistently deemed as non-work, as several chapters of this book will show in detail. Therefore, looking at work from the vantage point of the household allows us to discover the changing and often contested boundaries of what was/is regarded as (proper) work in different Euro-American contexts, from early modern times to the present. In practically any social context there are/were, in fact, different and often concurrent ideas (explicitly expressed or implicitly assumed) about what work is/was and who must or might be considered a worker, and these very ideas have changed over time, as a wealth of literature has shown.[17] More particularly, our approach allows us to uncover the ambiguities and biases—especially the gender ones—of the mainstream conceptions of work embedded in laws, population census categories, national and international statistics on labor forces, economic statistics on GDP, etc. Looking at work from its (alleged) margins therefore makes possible a fresh perspective on it, with implications that are important (at least so it seems to us) for both scholars and policymakers.

2. Changing and conflicting words and ideas

Labor, *lavoro, travail, trabajo, trabalho,* work, *Arbeit,* and so forth: the vocabulary of work is rich and interesting to analyze.[18] It expresses both positive and negative values: etymologically, "work" expresses the ideas of an "accomplished task"; the first meaning of the Old English term *weorc, worc* is "something done, [a] discreet act performed by someone, [an] action (whether voluntary or required), [a] proceeding, [a] business; that which is made or manufactured, products of labor."[19] By contrast, labor and *lavoro*, as well as *Arbeit* and maybe even more *travail, trabajo, trabalho,* express toil, suffering, and pain. Labor and *lavoro* derive in fact from the Latin *labor*, which primarily means "toil";[20] as for *Arbeit,* the Germanic words from which it derives signified toil, need, and hardship, in addition to work,[21] while the French *travail* (derived from the Latin *trepalium,* an instrument of torture) may have originally described a device to subjugate animals (now called *travail à ferrer* or *travail de maréchal*); from the twelfth century, the word is attested with the meaning of labor in childbirth, labor pain, torment, toil.[22] The positive or negative value attributed to work cannot be associated with a particular national culture, as argued by Hannah Arendt in the 1950s. "Every European language, ancient and modern, contains two etymologically unrelated words" to express those different concepts, she wrote, even though over time their meaning changed and intermingled: "The Greek language distinguishes between *ponein* and *ergazesthai,* the Latin between *laborare* and *facere* or *fabricari*... , the French between *travailler* and *ouvrer,* the German between *arbeiten* and *werken.* In all these cases, only the equivalents for 'labor' have an unequivocal connotation of pain and trouble."[23]

Even in such an influential book as the Bible we find both positive and negative connotations of work: in Genesis (2:2), God is described as a worker, and one who rested after finishing his work, on the seventh day. But work is also the punishment for the original sin: "By the sweat of your brow you will eat your food" (Gen. 3:19).[24] According to Jacques Le Goff, three themes developed from the biblical vision of the curse that followed the original sin, before which human beings joyfully participated in the work of the Creator: first, the theme of human beings collaborating with God in the completion of the creation; second, the theme of work as a physically degrading yoke for a sinful mankind; and, finally, the theme of a mankind redeemed by Christ using work as a form of mortification in order to do penance so as to regain its original splendor.[25]

The monastic world in particular developed an idea of work as an ascetic exercise and redemptive penance, well summarized in the motto *ora et labora*, "pray and work." The meaning of this Benedictine formula (dating from after Benedict), according to Le Goff, is the following: "Work to transform matter, witness of your baseness, to elevate yourself."[26] This concept of work had therefore two different sides: on the one hand, work appeared as tiring and thankless toil; on the other, it appeared as a spiritual, inventive, redeeming activity that played an important role in opening the doors of salvation for human beings.

Significantly, Mathieu Arnoux has recently suggested that the demographic and economic growth that took place in Europe from the eleventh to the thirteenth centuries, unaccompanied by any important technical change, was due not only to increasing peasants' work but also to the success of the ideological model of the three-orders society—*bellatores, oratores, laboratores*. This model appeared in the tenth century and spread in the following period. For about three centuries, i.e. until the great crisis that shook Europe from the 1300s, it made field work a socially and religiously valued activity and the peasant a respectable member of society, contributing to economic development and social stability.[27]

In medieval but also early modern times, we find a rather positive evaluation of work in the world of urban crafts, too. In this case, work was an essential trait of individual and collective identities, a basic component of many social bodies of urban society. As Anna Bellavitis writes, "One of the most frequent representations of urban identity in medieval and early modern times is based on the complementarity between the citizens' body [*corpo cittadino*] and trades [*corpi di mestiere*]."[28] As such, work played a crucial role in the access to citizenship and to the political and/or economic rights connected with it (citizenship was constructed in a huge variety of ways in the complex medieval and early modern world).

Conversely, the European medieval and early modern aristocracies, despite their deep-seated differences, all by and large considered the capacity of living without exercising any "mechanical arts" firsthand a requirement to belonging to their ranks, and this capacity implied the access to rights and privileges foreclosed to the other classes. In a sense, they had to be able to escape the biblical curse, "by the sweat of your brow you will eat your food": they should afford leisure, live on income, or at least devote themselves to activities far from the world of crafts and mechanical arts.[29]

Actually, in the Western world, the upper classes' disdain toward manual work had a long tradition, going back to the Greeks and Romans. In ancient times the figure of the independent farmer and artisan had certainly been prized (think of Ulysses who built his own bed or Cincinnatus who went back to his fields after leading the Roman army). Yet dependent manual activities had been considered as base, slave work (though free men, too, carried out such activities, and not all slaves performed manual work or were condemned to the lowest social position). Moreover, contempt for manual work had increased over time among the upper classes. Significantly, in Roman culture, a crucial notion was that of *otium*, the leisure enjoyed by the most fortunate, while the activities of those who had to work to earn a living were defined as *negotium, nec-otium*, the absence of leisure: the central concept was not work but its absence.[30]

In the light of these statements, one could conclude that in medieval and early modern European societies the clergy, the aristocracy, and the third state all had their own concept of work. Yet this would be too simplistic, since those societies—despite their efforts to distinguish, separate, and rank social groups—were actually complex, interrelated, chaotic. Our statements are schematic generalizations that, however, help us to stress the presence of several concurrent concepts of work in those societies.

While trying to make a rough list of different interpretations of work, we should also remember that within the Christian world other reasons to praise work, in addition to those already mentioned, had been suggested especially by St. Paul and had been circulating since his times. Paul had in fact warned Christians to work so as to avoid being an idle burden to others (2 Thess. 3:7–12). Additionally, he had warned thieves to stop stealing and to work honestly in order to earn their living and the means to help people in need (Eph. 4:28). Jumping to the early modern times, in the fifteenth and sixteenth centuries we find humanists influenced by Stoic philosophy highlighting the value of labor.[31] The Catholic humanist Juan Luis Vives, too, had a positive view of Stoicism, as he considered the Stoic sage the truer Christian.[32] Concern toward growing poverty and vagrancy led him to write the well-known treatise *De subventione pauperum* (1526), where he suggested a kind of disciplinary welfare system that implied a concept of work as a remedy to poverty and to its dangers: while the poor who were unable to work because of age or illness should be assisted by public authorities, those able to work should work, and if they refused, they should be forced to do it.[33] On the other hand, the Protestant Reformation, with the notion of *Beruf*, introduced another positive meaning of work, if and when it was and is performed according to God's calling. In Lutheran milieus, the *Hausväterliteratur* played an important role in developing such a view.[34] Significantly, as Mary Ågren writes in this book, in early modern Lutheran Sweden, "those who did not work were branded as 'time-thieves'—a concept suggesting that work was the normal and recommended way of spending one's time." Here, too, there was a convergence with ideas brought about by humanism, despite the fact that Lutherans frequently rejected humanist ideas: Leon Battista Alberti, for instance, in his dialogue *I Libri della Famiglia* (1433–40) had stigmatized idleness, arguing that time was very precious and should not be wasted.[35]

As is well known, rivers of ink have already been used to discuss Max Weber's hypothesis that the Reformation ethics prompted the capitalist development, so we will not delve into this issue here.[36] However, we want to highlight that between the eighteenth and nineteenth centuries the idea of work as toil to be avoided was increasingly criticized by thinkers who stigmatized the (alleged) idleness of the aristocracy and (in part) of the clergy, stressing the importance of work for the economic growth and well-being of the nation. Yet, work was not only increasingly seen as a welcome source of wealth. When the balance between the negative and positive connotations of work resolutely shifted toward the latter, work became less associated with painful and degrading activities, being conversely seen increasingly as a source of dignity. Furthermore, people shared more and more the idea that work was or must be a source of rights.[37] A society was emerging where—according to Adriano Tilgher—"work seems the summing up of all duties and virtues. It is in work that man of capitalistic civilizations finds his nobility and worth. His whole code of ethics is contained in the one precept, 'Work!'. Labor, for him, is no longer the expiation of the sins of his father, nor is it a contact with something necessarily contaminating. It is through work that he embodies in himself the sacred principle of activity."[38] "The modern age has carried with it a theoretical glorification of labor and has resulted in a factual transformation of the whole of society into a laboring society," Hannah Arendt confirmed.[39] Labor became the "mediator between the individual and the collective" and was codified as social status "providing access to citizenship within the welfare state."[40]

This does not mean that other concepts of work ceased to exist: in a sense, work continued to be like both sides of a coin. This is particularly clear in Marx's view, despite its complexity and change over time.[41] On the one hand, especially in his earlier writings, he associated labor with alienation (*Entäusserung*). "What, then, constitutes the alienation of labor?" he asked in *The Economic and Philosophical Manuscripts of 1844*, answering as follows:

> First, the fact that labor is *external* to the worker, i.e., it does not belong to his essential being; that in his work, therefore, he does not affirm himself but denies himself, does not feel content but unhappy, does not develop freely his

physical and mental energy but mortifies his body and ruins his mind. The worker therefore only feels himself outside his work, and in his work feels outside himself.[42]

Yet, in Marx's view, not all labor was alienating; on the contrary, he argued that "it is just in the working-up" of the world that "man first really proves himself to be a species being": "through and because of this production, nature appears as *his* work and his reality." As a consequence, alienated, estranged labor, "in tearing away from man the object of his production . . . tears from him his *species life*." This also means "that man is estranged from the other, as each of them is from man's essential nature."[43] According to Marx, who increasingly refused any essentialism, the alienated labor with such dehumanizing consequences was represented by waged labor under capitalism. Communism, the suppression of private property,[44] and the reduction of necessary labor time[45] would allow humans to overcome alienation.

The tension between the notion of work as a source of alienation and self-realization is still present today.[46] Nonetheless, from the late eighteenth century onward, as mentioned, the positive views of work gained much ground, and for the last couple of centuries Europeans have belonged to societies (mainly) based on work.[47] While the fundamental questions remain of whether work still is, will be, and must be the basis of our societies,[48] if we look at work in a historical perspective, a crucial issue is whether the positive views of work that spread from the eighteenth century onward encompassed any type of toil. In the following pages, we will try to answer this question, which is decisive also to understand some of the limits and problems of labor-based societies as well as some of the reasons of their current crisis. We will address the issue in relation to the manifold forms of work performed at home. Let us therefore first of all illustrate their features in medieval and early modern households, i.e. before the "glorification" of work.

3. The medieval and early modern households as a site of multiple activities

The biblical curse against Adam and Eve and their eating of the forbidden fruit not only condemned men to procure their food by the sweat of their brows, it also established that women would suffer when giving birth to their children.[49] Interestingly, in many languages the same word can be used to identify both work and the pains of childbirth,[50] as if the two activities—named production and reproduction in modern socioeconomic language—belonged to the same domain and were two different but equally painful gendered ways to reach the same goal, i.e. making sure that both human life and mankind would live on.

In a sense, such a view of labor expressed the reality of a large share of preindustrial European households. Many of them were not only kin groups but also work groups,[51] and they were often sites of all those activities today defined as production, consumption, reproduction, transmission, and care respectively, as shown by a rich body of literature.[52] Significantly, the word "economy," which nowadays indicates something different from the household activities, originally referred precisely to households: in ancient Greek, the word literally meant "household management" and kept this meaning for centuries, with the current definition starting to emerge as late as the mid-seventeenth century.[53] Household members, men and women, adults and children, would in normal circumstances all cooperate in some way to ensure their own survival, often producing goods and services for larger circles, too.

This does not mean that every family was a cooperating working team.[54] At the bottom of the social ladder there were people who were certainly too poor to have a house and/or who lived from hand to mouth or on charity, not involved in any common work.[55] On the other hand, as a cause or consequence of poverty, the destitute often had rather weak family ties or no family at all.[56] Additionally, there were differences among households due to the activities performed by each individual or family, as well as to the peculiar economic features of each place: the households of day laborers, for instance, were likely not to be, or only marginally to be, sites of production; therefore in those places where day labor was very common, many households were not productive units.[57] Furthermore, not every house was a place of activities such as cooking: the poor, especially in the cities, might not be able to afford a dwelling equipped with a fireplace and might eat food obtained as alms or bought in inns, in shops, or from street sellers[58] who were largely women.[59] Especially in certain regions, however (particularly, it seems, in Mediterranean Europe), eating on the streets or in taverns or in open-air working places such as fields or construction sites was very widespread and not necessarily a sign of poverty.[60]

While these differences have to be stressed to avoid misleading generalizations and to appreciate the complexity and variety of medieval and early modern societies, it remains true that, as mentioned, many urban and rural households were places of production (both for themselves and for the market) as well as consumption, reproduction, transmission, and care. This was also the case with the households of the aristocratic families who despised manual work. A wealth of literature has proposed a model of self-sufficient noble households where, under the wise and expert direction of the family head, live-in staff, outdoor servants, and peasants dealt with almost all everyday needs, also ensuring the production of victuals and even textiles for the family.⁶¹ This was certainly an ideal model that overvalued self-sufficiency while undervaluing the recourse to the market.⁶² Nevertheless, noble households, too, were to a certain extent places of production, although this was normally thanks to the manual work of servants rather than that of their masters,⁶³ if we exclude the manual activities performed (especially by noblewomen) to prevent the vices brought about by idleness, as prescribed by sermons and conduct literature.⁶⁴

In peasants' as well as in artisans' families, generally all members who were able to work contributed to the household economy. Recent research, as illustrated in the next pages, is revealing that the division of work might have been more or less rigid but usually was more complex than was previously assumed. However, one's status within the family (head of the family/dependent, husband/wife, parent/child, master/servant) resulting from the intersection of gender (men and women), generation (parents and children, birth order), marital status (unmarried, married, separated, [divorced], widowed), age (adults, children, the elderly), economic and legal (in)dependency, social position, etc., contributed in defining the tasks that he or she carried out.⁶⁵

Early modern Sweden was, for instance, a society with a relatively low degree of specialization, as shown by Maria Ågren in this volume. As for gender, on the basis of sixteen thousand statements on work activities drawn from Swedish sources spanning from 1550 to 1799, she concludes that in such an example of a mainly rural society, no category of work was "all-male or all-female, with military work as the only exception": although rare, there were also women fishers and hunters. In other contexts, the degree of specialization along gender lines was often higher than in Sweden, especially (but not only) in the cities. Women were barred from many activities, to the point that cross-dressing might (also) be a strategy used by some of them to carry out male jobs—for instance, to become soldiers or even, for unmarried women, to keep a tavern.⁶⁶ Additionally, their work, if paid, was normally remunerated at a lower rate than men's. Furthermore, among artisans, they generally had no or only limited access to ruling roles within the guilds.⁶⁷

On the other hand, however, women did not work less than men, as also maintained by the Venetian writer Lucrezia Marinella in her book on women's excellence (1600–1601).⁶⁸ Everywhere they normally and actively contributed to the family economy in manifold ways. Examining as many as 13,500 answers to the question asking what they were "worth" and how they supported themselves, given by witnesses to the ecclesiastical courts judges of seven English dioceses, two archdeaconries, and the Cambridge University courts between 1550 and 1728, Alex Shepard has, for instance, recently concluded that marriage was normally an economic partnership and married women played a crucial role in household economies: significantly, the word "wife" had not only a legal but also an occupational dimension.[69] In this context, housekeeping was work connected to marital status and was crucial to the household economy.

A longstanding tradition, going back to Xenophon's Οἰκονομικός (a dialogue on household management), stressed the importance of preserving the family assets: according to innumerable early modern conduct manuals, preserving the household's possessions was a wife's responsibility, whereas the husband was in charge of acquiring goods for the family. Such a rigid division of responsibilities was an ideal model, and everyday life was often far less neatly cut. Women, however, were often actually in charge (among other things) of preserving goods, and this was no minor task, especially at a time when preserving was considered as important as (or even more important than) acquiring. Possessions were indeed crucial to assess and keep one's status.[70] Sumptuary laws that, in late medieval and early modern towns, very often addressed women might contribute to this division of tasks. According to Martha Howell, when the so-called "commercial revolution" took place, men acquired the positive role of producers and women the negative one of consumers. Sumptuary laws, then, were conceived to keep women away from excessive consumption and to force them to keep and preserve the goods of the family.[71]

Household management was likely to be anything but simple. Significantly, Antonio Genovesi, who in 1765 was appointed to the first Italian chair in economics, noting that the entire economic management of middle-class households was in female hands,[72] argued in favor of better education for women (also) to improve their capacity to cope with this responsibility. In Paris and Holland—he recalled approvingly—girls from merchant families were schooled in writing and numeracy.[73] Not surprisingly, it has been argued that the very reason for improving women's education was to prepare wives to be good assistants for their husbands: in Denmark, the Copenhagen Dottreskolen, a school created in 1791 where male teachers gave girls a scientific education, was in fact intended to prepare good merchants' wives, capable of keeping account books.[74] In artisans', merchants', and shopkeepers' households all over Europe, wives were indeed likely, among other things, to serve as accountants for the family enterprise. Additionally, they might also have taken care of the relationships with customers, to mention but another task.[75] Noblewomen, too, however, might have kept account records.[76]

Households might also have been the site of other activities, to our eyes far less obvious, such as, for instance, schooling and even university teaching. We do not refer, in this case, to the fact that in late medieval and early modern Europe tutors were often hired by parents to educate their children at home. Rather, we would like to stress that in some contexts, such as Reformation Germany, university professors gave lessons at home and their wives (and other family members) were directly involved in the organization of teaching and of students' hospitality.[77]

This intermingling within the domestic space of multiple activities might give women unexpected chances, especially—as has often been maintained—when they were widows or otherwise alone and continued to manage the household and/or the family enterprise. In many cases, guild statutes, too, recognizing women's skills, officially gave widows the right to replace their dead husbands in the workshops.[78] Historians have in fact often considered widowhood as the period when women—no longer subjected to their husband's authority—could become heads of their families and were freer to control their possessions. At the same time, however, scholars have also stressed the very fact that widows' skills had often been developed during marriage, noting that guilds might "make it hard for widows to replace lost spousal labor" and denouncing the many risks of becoming poor attached to widowhood, as well as the differential impact of economic crises on different types of women.[79]

Earlier studies already suggested that women's relationship with work was highly influenced by their life cycle, stressing the differences among unmarried girls, married women, and widows.[80] Recent research, on the one hand, has highlighted the consequences of marriage—as for family status and type of work carried out—not only for women but also for men, though also showing the existence of social, regional, cultural, and historical differences, with marriage playing a more crucial role in northern than in southern Europe. At least in part, this was due to different legal contexts: under Roman law, a son, be he single or married, remained under parental authority for as long as his father was alive, unless he was emancipated through a legal act, whereas emancipation, in other legal systems, was generally linked to marriage and/or adult age.[81]

On the other hand, while confirming the importance of marital status for women, recent studies have shown that the gulf between unmarried singles and wives was often larger than that between wives and widows.[82] Research on England[83] and Scandinavia in particular has shown that, for women, marriage implied a transition to more authoritative and managerial roles, especially in households with servants to be governed by the family heads. In her contribution to this book, Maria Ågren shows that in early modern Sweden "the division of work was strongly structured by marital status, household position, and, implicitly, age. The work repertoires of unmarried people, who were often young, were radically different from that of married and widowed people": a major conclusion of the project whose results are illustrated by Ågren is "the paramount importance of marriage in early modern society. Marriage was important to both women and men because it provided them with possibilities of supporting themselves through their own work and through the work of those that they could govern": "early modern women did not get married to be supported by their husbands. They got married to be better able to support themselves. The same was true for men: marriage improved their chances of supporting themselves too." While this conclusion is undoubtedly very important, we must never forget the high diversity in European regions. Marriage certainly did not have the same role everywhere, both for men and for women. In contexts where marrying implied creating a new, independent household and becoming family heads, which, even in Mediterranean Europe, was the norm for the majority of urban families,[84] a couple's role and responsibility were different from those experienced in contexts where complex households prevailed and young people, after marriage, lived in the parental house of one of the spouses and were subject to the authority of an older couple. This was, for instance, the case in the large sharecroppers' households typical of the countryside of central Italy, rather strictly organized along gender and generation lines, to quote but one example.[85]

Italian sharecroppers' households were work units, as were many other types of households around Europe. This does not mean, however, that each household was a working group whose members were all toiling in and for the family trade, shop, or farm, with wives and children "assisting" the male family head. As mentioned above, in destitute families, each member often provided for his/her own survival.[86] Because of poverty, family distress, education and many other reasons, children might be sent to another household to work as servants or apprentices.[87] Certainly live-in servants often became members of a household, different from their parental one, which was a working group. Yet there were also families whose members, all or part of them, (mainly) worked *outside* their households—sailors who spent most of their lives away from their families are only an extreme case of a wide range of possibilities.[88] Furthermore, it is important to note that there were dual-earner families, with husband and wife engaged in different trades.[89] In some cases, even guild statutes recognized the women's right to work independently from their husbands; for example, in Nantes, the master butchers' wives could sell offal coming from their husbands' activities, but independently from them.[90] Lively debates have arisen about European diversity[91] as well as about historical change, discussing whether and how the organization and economic role of household work have changed over time because of growing commercialization, capitalist development, "industrious" and "industrial" revolution, (alleged) consumer revolution, etc.[92]

Before addressing those issues, it has to be stressed that in medieval and early modern Europe the multiple activities performed at home which today we would classify as production, reproduction, and care were normally and crucially all considered as work: it is true that on the whole they were neither recorded, nor praised, nor adequately rewarded with money, goods, or gratitude, as denounced by authors like the proto-feminist Moderata Fonte and François Poullain de la Barre.[93] Nevertheless, they were not considered leisure or something different from proper work. Yet things would change over time.

4. Productive, unproductive, reproductive work and the "delaborization" of household work

In any society, as mentioned above, different and even conflicting concepts of work can probably be discovered. Additionally, new concepts appear; some become more common, others decline or even disappear, and even the range of ideas on the subject changes over time. While in medieval and early modern Europe, as mentioned, several different concepts of work coexisted, philosophers and writers from the second half of the seventeenth century onward increasingly regarded work as an activity that created value[94]: in the eighteenth and the nineteenth centuries, scholars such as Adam Smith, David Ricardo, and Karl Marx would elaborate different labor theories of value, referring to value "as the amount of labor necessary to produce a marketable commodity."[95] Fated to prompt huge debates, those theories are today generally rejected by mainstream economists. While associating work with value, early modern and modern scholars considered as value-producing all those activities that were performed for pay or that generated income. In other words, work was increasingly seen as a commodity: "A man's Labour also is a commodity exchangeable for benefit, as well as any other thing," Hobbes argued in the *Leviathan* (1651).[96] The idea of work as a commodity sold and bought according to the laws of supply and demand was destined to gain credit,[97] and this would eventually lead to (proper) work being considered as (almost) only paid work.[98]

Such a change was not gender neutral: in a sense, it broke the unified meaning field suggested by the use of the same word, in many languages, to indicate the painful toil of childbirth to ensure the survival of the species and the similarly painful toil performed in the fields, workshops, or elsewhere to ensure subsistence. Labor in the sense of delivery was never a commodity exchanged for money (if we exclude recent implications of surrogate motherhood and womb-for-rent). Many other activities necessary to individual and collective survival and welfare were done for free or, more often, as part of complex networks of mutual duties and exchanges regulated by customs, solidarity norms and culturally constructed emotional ties rather than by the market. These activities—frequently performed at home and mainly by women—were increasingly seen as something different from (proper) work, as we will show.

The growing association of work with value and money was not the sole change that affected the way human activities were considered. Especially to the eyes of Enlightenment philosophers, "work came to appear as an active human intervention in nature for the purpose of assuring the ongoing existence of the human species": "man was seen as ruling over nature" and tools were increasingly considered the basis upon which the "human dominion over nature rested."[99] In fact, the idea of man as *Homo faber* and even as *Homo artifex* had a long tradition.[100] Yet, according to specialists, the emphasis on the ability of and legitimacy for mankind to intervene on nature (i.e., on what was still seen by most people as God's work) was new. Again, activities such as childbearing, breastfeeding, and caring for children were no longer considered as work inasmuch as they did not imply any particular dominion over nature nor the use of any particular tool; rather, in this new perspective they could and would be strictly associated with nature and seen as natural activities radically different from the (emblematically cultural) activity represented by work, which conversely implied to intervene and rule upon nature.[101]

This undervaluation of reproduction and care work also implied, as shown by Nancy Folbre in her chapter, that several intellectuals believed that human beings were not themselves "produced."

The aforementioned change intermingled with the gradual reduction in the plurality of meanings of the notion of work. Whereas many different human activities had usually been seen as work, in the eighteenth century only some of them were associated to the general and abstract concept of work that was then developing.[102] Seen as a "purposeful application of physical and mental forces in order to fulfil needs"[103] and as a commodity that everybody could sell at his/her wants on the basis of freely agreed contracts, work was indeed increasingly separated from single individuals. An abstract and general category of work (though also present in some contexts of the past, such as Ancient Greece[104]) was increasingly developed: in this way, work became something measurable in time and money, and was sold/paid accordingly.[105] With an only apparent paradox, the emerging general concept of work was more limited than the traditional one: specific to the Western world, it eventually "narrowed down to mean work for a living and for an earning, work and work-products to be sold," "market-related work," excluding domestic chores and family care.[106]

An important step along this route is represented by Adam Smith's distinction between productive and unproductive work. In a well-known page from the *Wealth of Nations* (1776), he wrote that

> there is one sort of labour which adds to the value of the subject upon which it is bestowed: there is another which has no such effect. The former, as it produces a value, may be called productive; the latter, unproductive labour. Thus the labour of a manufacturer adds, generally, to the value of the materials which he works upon, that of his own maintenance, and of his master's profit. The labour of a menial servant, on the contrary, adds to the value of nothing. Though the manufacturer has his wages advanced to him by his master, he, in reality, costs him no expence, the value of those wages being generally restored, together with a profit, in the improved value of the subject upon which his labour is bestowed. But the maintenance of a menial servant never is restored. A man grows rich by employing a multitude of manufacturers: he grows poor by maintaining a multitude of menial servants.[107]

Smith was aware that productivity could not be the sole criterion to measure the importance of an activity:

> The labour of some of the most respectable orders in the society is, like that of menial servants, unproductive of any value, and does not fix or realize itself in any permanent subject; or vendible commodity, which endures after that labour is past, and for which an equal quantity of labour could afterwards be procured.[108]

Even "the sovereign, for example, with all the officers both of justice and war who serve under him, the whole army and navy, are unproductive labourers," as well as "some both of the gravest and most important, and some of the most frivolous professions: churchmen, lawyers, physicians, men of letters of all kinds; players, buffoons, musicians, opera-singers, opera-dancers."[109] Additionally, he maintained that the servant's work, as well as that of the manufacturer, "has its value, and deserves its reward."[110]

Nevertheless, the distinction between productive and unproductive labor subtly lessened the activities now labeled as unproductive. As stressed by Nancy Folbre, Smith actually devalued domestic and care work. Significantly, explaining the "principle which gives occasion to the division of labour" and stressing the positive consequences of self-interest, he argued that "it is not from the benevolence of the butcher, the brewer, or the baker, that we expect our dinner, but from their regard to their own interest."[111] "Smith neglected to mention that none of these tradesmen actually puts dinner on the table, ignoring cooks, maids, wives, and mothers in one fell swoop," Folbre acutely comments.[112] He did not even take into account the obvious fact that unpaid family care work is crucial to ensuring the supply of labor to the market: "It is a necessary input into the production of a future generation of wage earners, as well as maintenance of existing wage earners in the face of the depreciation wrought by aging, morbidity, and death. It is a necessary input into human capital, and, more broadly, human capabilities."[113] Smith was not the only thinker to ignore that contribution; quite the opposite: Folbre argues that this was largely the case with the British and French liberal, political, and social theorists of the seventeenth and eighteenth centuries. In a sense, they shared Hobbes's approach that looked "at men as if they had just emerged from the earth like mushrooms and grown up without any obligation to each other."[114] Locke would argue that workers were not themselves produced, and this idea would be later developed by Ricardo and Marx. The latter conceived productive and unproductive work as notions historically variable according to the mode of production: within capitalism, only work that produces a surplus value for the capitalist can be considered productive.[115] Many other scholars discussed the categories of productive and unproductive work; Jean Baptiste Say, to mention but another one, considered as productive all those activities that were sold and paid for.[116]

Although different, all these economic theorists considered unpaid carework and domestic tasks as unproductive. They brought about a theoretical "delaborization" of that kind of work, which later would be (often) defined as reproductive. As explained by Alessandra Pescarolo in this volume, classical economists ignored such activities: "The concept of reproductive work does not exist in classical economics."

In her contribution, Pescarolo focuses precisely on the reproductive-productive work dichotomy, analyzing its elaboration and meanings and discussing whether it could and can help to give value to domestic and care work. She explains that the category of reproductive work was first conceived in the 1960s by Marxist feminists who tried to situate domestic activities within the Marxist theoretical framework and to pinpoint their connection with wage labor. The category was destined to be successful, mainly (according to Pescarolo) because of its proximity to the concept of social reproduction: a concept already used by Marx and very common in sociological literature. Yet, while the category of reproductive work originally referred to the reproduction of the working capacity, it would later also be used with different meanings by both Marxist and non-Marxist scholars and activists, sometimes encompassing only unpaid domestic and care work, at other times also paid domestic work and paid extra-domestic personal services. In this book, Eileen Boris defines as "reproductive labors" "those activities that exist as a counterpart, but also prior, to employment or income generation, what usually is considered production. Also referred to as social reproduction, such work is about the making of people through the tasks of daily life which are necessary to develop and sustain labor power. These activities are both material (like feeding), emotional (like love), and assimilative (like the transferring of norms and values), whether occurring in the family, school, church, or community."

The concept has recently been expanded to the global level by theorists who denounce the global division of reproductive labor, which implies an "extraction" of such labor from the South of the world by the North through the emigration of millions of people, especially women, from their impoverished countries to work as domestic workers and caregivers in affluent ones.[117]

While Rhacel Parreñas's comparative research on Filipina domestic workers in Rome and Los Angeles has played a crucial role in the development of the very concept of the international division of reproductive labor,[118] Italy had also been important for the elaboration of the category of reproductive labor by Marxist feminists in the 1970s. In both cases, this role by Italy does not seem casual: in the 1960s and 1970s, Italy had very high percentages of housewives among adult women compared to other European countries;[119] in the last decades, the recourse to (foreign) paid domestic workers and caregivers has become very common among Italian families.[120] Not surprisingly, Italian feminist theorists were influenced by the emergence of materialistic feminism elaborated between France and the United States by Christine Delphy in the seventies. According to her well-known critical analysis, in the domestic model, production is based on the household conceived as a socioeconomic institution.[121] The labor force of the household members—women, children, unmarried siblings—belongs to the head of the household, who takes advantage of this work for both market and non-market production. According to Delphy, there is a lack of analysis in Marx's theory on the sexual division of work in the patriarchal mode of production, which he "under-problematizes." This does not mean, in Delphy's words, that Marx's materialistic concepts cannot be applied to "women's oppression."[122] Nor that he completely ignored the sexual division of labor: "It is in fact not so much a matter of non-recognition as of non-problematization."[123] Marx, though disregarding domestic and care work, addressed the issue of reproduction work. He considered the part of factory work exchanged by workers for the salary necessary to guarantee their survival (the so-called "necessary work") as such, whereas he considered the other part of work, producing surplus, as productive: "Productive labour, in its meaning for capitalist production, is wage-labour which, exchanged against the variable part of capital (the part of the capital that is spent on wages), reproduces not only this part of the capital (or the value of its own labour-power), but in addition produces surplus-value for the capitalist."[124] The members of the Italian collective Lotta Femminista (Feminist Struggle), founded in Padua, Italy, in 1971,[125] contended, from a Marxist perspective, that unpaid work performed by housewives was reproductive work. At the same time, they questioned the idea that domestic work was unproductive, arguing that it actually produced the "strange commodity" represented by "the laborer himself,"[126] i.e., labor power. Thanks to the collaboration between the founder of the collective, Mariarosa Dalla Costa, and the American, Britain-based feminist Selma James, these elaborations intermingled with those of other feminists and launched the debate on domestic labor on an international level. Dalla Costa and James maintained that housewives' work guaranteed the reproduction and production of labor power (which was vital for capitalism):

> The ability to labor resides only in a human being whose life is consumed in the process of producing. First it must be nine months in the womb, must be fed, clothed and trained; then when it works its bed must be made, its floor swept, its lunchbox prepared, its sexuality not gratified but quietened, its dinner ready when it gets home, even if this is eight in the morning from the night shift. This is how labor power is produced and reproduced when it is daily consumed in the factory of the office. *To describe its basic production and reproduction is to describe women's work.*[127]

Their book *The Power of Women and the Subversion of the Community*, published in Italian in March 1972, in English in October of the same year, and soon translated into German (1973), French (1973), and Spanish (1975), was in fact destined to become a bestseller.[128] It offered the women's movement "a material foundation for 'sisterhood,'" as Dalla Costa and James wrote in the foreword to the third edition (1975). "That material foundation was the social activity, the *work*, which the female personality was shaped to submit to. That work was housework." The two authors were aware of the novelty of their approach:

> In singling out the work of the housewife as that for which women are trained and by which women are defined; in identifying its product as labor power—the working class—this book broke with all those previous analyses of capitalist so-

ciety which began and ended in the factory, which began and ended with men. Our isolation in the family while doing our work has hidden its social nature. The fact that it brought no wage had hidden its social nature. The fact that it brought no wage had hidden that it was work.[129]

Both to reveal the true nature of housework and to empower women, they invoked wages for housework: "If our wageless work is the basis of our powerlessness in relation both to men and to capital, . . . the wages for that work, which alone will make it possible for us to reject that work, must be our lever of power."[130] Their book, therefore, became the starting point of an international campaign for wages for housework. During a meeting held in Padua in 1972, Dalla Costa and James, together with Silvia Federici, an Italian woman living in the United States, and Brigitte Galtier, a French one, founded the International Feminist Collective to prompt discussion on the production/reproduction issue and to coordinate feminist actions, and shortly thereafter Wages for Housework groups and committees started to form.[131]

Issues of racial discrimination were soon joined to gender issues, thanks to the foundation of the International Black Women for Wages for Housework group by Margaret Prescod and Wilmette Brown in 1974, and in 1975 the Wages Due Lesbians organization campaigned for wages for housework because they wanted both the "unwaged work lesbian women have in common with other women, and the additional physical and emotional housework of surviving in a hostile and prejudiced society, recognized as work and paid" as such.[132] Despite the international spread of the campaign and the theoretical support of it by professional economists such as Antonella Picchio,[133] many feminists, however, did not advocate it, being afraid that wages for housework, if introduced, would make the gender division of labor more rigid.

These fears were not without reason. The idea that wages for housework would empower women had certainly circulated rather early among activists: as recalled by Nancy Folbre in her chapter, "in 1873, an article in *The Woman's Journal* explicitly demanded wages for housework," and "in 1878, the National Woman Suffrage Convention passed a resolution calling for the legal recognition of women's rights to 'the proceeds of her labor in the family.'" Nonetheless, as shown by Alessandra Gissi in her chapter on the Italian debate on housewives' wages, ideas on the need to pay for housework were not necessarily leftist, revolutionary, or women-friendly ones; proposals of this kind had indeed been suggested (without being realized) during Italian Fascism in the 1930s, within a program aiming to consolidate gender hierarchies, to configure motherhood as a patriotic duty, and to make the most of the resources of domestic work, rationalizing it according to the domestic Taylorism proposed by the American Christine Frederick and encouraging housewives' hard working.[134]

Conversely, from the point of view of the promoters and supporters of the campaign for wages for housework, the worries on the possible negative consequences of granting a payment to housewives might sound paradoxical: promoters and supporters called for wages also to "denaturalize" housework[135] and to contribute to a real revolution and empowering of women. As Silvia Federici writes,

> The wage at least recognises that you are a worker.... To have a wage means to be part of a social contract, and there is no doubt concerning its meaning: you work, not because you like it, or because it comes naturally to you, but because it is the only condition under which you are allowed to live. But exploited as you might be, you are not that work. Today you are a postman, tomorrow a cabdriver.... But in the case of housework the situation is qualitatively different. The difference lies in the fact that not only has housework been imposed on women, but it has been transformed into a natural attribute of our female physique and personality ... the unwaged condition of housework has been the most powerful weapon in reinforcing the common assumption that housework is not work.... Yet just how natural it is to be a housewife is shown by the fact that it takes at least twenty years of socialisation-day-to-day training.... By denying housework a wage and transforming it into an act of love, capital has killed many birds with one stone. First of all, it has got a hell of a lot of work almost for free.... At the same time, it has disciplined the male worker too, by making his woman dependent on his work and his wage, and trapped him in this discipline by giving him a servant after he himself has done so much serving at the factory or the office.... But if we take wages for housework as a political perspective, we can see that struggling for it is going to produce a revolution in our lives and in our social power as women.[136]

The naturalization of housework was indeed an issue that in the 1960s and 1970s all feminists and women's and gender historians had to tackle.[137]

5. Historicizing, deconstructing, and dismantling separate spheres

By the time second-wave feminisms developed, family and the domestic sphere were often seen as a space for "natural" relationships, i.e., those belonging to nature as opposed to culture and history. Many people believed that domestic tasks and care work were mainly performed out of natural instincts and love; as such, they were generally performed, and must be performed, for free. They were not regarded as proper work: as already mentioned, from the eighteenth century onward, paid work, especially individual waged labor, had increasingly been considered as proper work. The spreading ideology of separate spheres had been associating the private one (as opposed to the public) with nature, instincts, emotions, love, the family, the home, domesticity, women, femininity, care, protection, leisure, non-market activities, and, definitely, non-work. The public one had conversely been associated with history, culture, rationality, impersonality, men, masculinity, politics, bureaucracy, market, money, contracts, competition, factories and work, labor, employment, and the professions. While reality could not be reduced to those rigid dichotomies, they had contributed and were contributing to shaping people's ideas about proper roles and goals to reach, actually influencing their lives. Women had been and were largely encouraged to give up their waged employment to stay at home to care for their families, and this had become an ideal to pursue even in the eyes of many working-class men and women. People (especially women) who did not agree with the ideology of separate spheres and its implications had certainly always existed, as shown by several contributors to this book, as did families who were too poor to afford for the wife/mother to be a housewife. Nevertheless, the separate-spheres ideology had gained ground for a couple of centuries before becoming the target of increasing criticism—a milestone in this direction was represented by Betty Friedan's *The Feminine Mystique* (1963), which denounced the housewives' frustration and lack of fulfilment.[138] Before this happened, the separate-spheres ideology was shared not only by conservatives but also by many leftists.

Women's and gender history made a crucial contribution in destroying such an ideological construct. Recovering women's forgotten history and looking back to the past to discover the roots of the present was an important issue for feminists, both for those who were and those who were not professional historians—we would say for the entire feminist movement.[139] Inasmuch as research progressed, it unveiled the historical and cultural variability of allegedly natural and immutable realities such as the family and motherhood—feminists were obviously working in contexts where many other researchers, too, from anthropologists to historians of the family, to mention but two, had provided and were providing evidence of such variability.[140] Recovering women's history, therefore, implied expanding the historians' territory to include the family and the domestic sphere within the realm of history. This did not only shift and threaten the boundaries between the supposedly separate spheres, it also undermined the very foundations of the separate spheres. Showing their historical variability implied, in fact, the unveiling of the artificiality and therefore the changeability of such a social and ideological construct, normally presented as a natural and immutable fact.[141]

Crucial research would show when and how separate spheres had been constructed. Leonore Davidoff's and Catherine Hall's *Family Fortunes* (1987) was an especially important contribution to understanding both the development of the ideology of the separate spheres and the actual changes of family life and gender roles that took place in England between 1750 and 1850, even though the book was interpreted differently and sometimes criticized because it allegedly overemphasized the effectiveness of the public/private divide.[142] As shown by Davidoff and Hall, during that period, large sectors of the English middle classes moved to new houses with gardens in the elegant neighborhoods that developed away from the rapidly spreading factories and the unhealthy working-class quarters. This was cause and effect of the growing separation between enterprise and household in the age of developing capitalism that brought about the rise of the private company and the business corporation, the development of public accountability, and more formal financial procedures: a series of changes that contributed in shifting "the world of women ever further from the power of the active market." The family head was then increasingly seen as the sole breadwinner for the family, while as the nineteenth century progressed, "the view hardened that female relatives were and should be dependants."[143] In early modern times, adult men were the heads and leaders of a co-residing working team that included their wives, children, and servants and whose activities were all considered as work. In the nineteenth century, they remained family heads as they used to be, but their wives were increasingly considered responsible for managing the house, educating the children and directing the servants. Of course, especially in small family businesses or shops of the lower middle class, women and children continued to work unpaid both in care duties or by helping in the making and selling of craft products. At the same time, all these activities, especially care tasks, were less and less seen as proper work, or considered due as mutual marital help in the case of unpaid work for market production. As John Tosh would stress some years later, for men the home was increasingly constructed not as a workplace but as a refuge from the conflicts and hardship of the workplace, the market, and politics.[144] While Tosh referred particularly to middle-class men, this change was actually likely to affect the working class, too: the worker "is at home when he is not working, and when he is working he is not at home," Marx argued in the 1840s.[145]

But let us continue to focus on the English upper middle classes. According to Davidoff and Hall,

> Women's identification with the domestic and moral sphere implied that they would only become active economic agents when forced by necessity. As the nineteenth century progressed, it was increasingly assumed that a woman engaged in business was a woman without either an income of her own or a man to support her. But unlike a man whose family status and self-worth rose through his economic exertions, a woman who did likewise risked opprobrium for herself and possible shame for those around her. Structured inequality made it exceedingly difficult for a woman to support herself on her own, much less take on dependants. . . . At a time when the concept of occupation was becoming the core element of the masculine identity, any position for women other than in relation to men was anomalous.[146]

Not every middle-class woman became an "idle" housewife; yet, when women contributed to the family enterprises, their contribution, according to Davidoff and Hall, increasingly became a "hidden investment." The two authors saw the marginalization of women from the realm of economy as a further step down the lane described by Alice Clark for the seventeenth century and Ivy Pinchbeck for the eighteenth and early nineteenth centuries: in their pioneering works, published in 1919 and 1930 respectively, according to Davidoff and Hall, they had "outlined the slow shift from women's active participation in commerce, farming and other business pursuits."[147]

While both Clark and Pinchbeck had spoken of a declining women's employment opportunity, Clark's view was actually more pessimistic than Pinchbeck's. Focusing on the women's role in London textile crafts,[148] Clark argued that the progressive separation of the workplace from the family house, a consequence of the capitalist evolution of the English textile industry in the seventeenth century, had pushed women out of the production.[149] Clark mainly stressed the negative consequences of raising capitalism on women's work, whereas Pinchbeck (dealing with a different period), though maintaining that at the beginning of the Industrial Revolution women had suffered from declining employment opportunities, concluded that "the Industrial Revolution has on the whole proved beneficial to women. It has resulted in greater leisure for women in the home and has relieved them from the drudgery and monotony that characterized much of the hand labor previously performed in connection with industrial work under the domestic system. For the women workers outside the home, it has resulted in better conditions, a greater variety of openings and an improved status."[150]

In the last decades, innumerable studies have addressed the impact of capitalism as well as that of the Industrial Revolution on women's work. As for Clark's decline thesis, much research, especially on the German area, confirmed this decline, stressing the role played by the guilds in the whole process. In their books, both published in 1986, Martha Howell and Merry Wiesner attributed this decline to economic and cultural factors. Wiesner insisted at the same time on the increasing specialization of craftwork and on the competition between men and women in labor markets, in a context of demographic growth, but also on the emergence of new family models due to the Protestant Reformation.[151] For Howell, when production moved out of the family, women's work was gradually eliminated, as their work outside of the home threatened to undermine the patriarchal family. At the same time, in some German cities, the political role of guilds meant the immediate exclusion of women.[152] More recently, Sheilagh Ogilvie has proposed a different interpretation, seeing guilds as masculine societies that excluded women, as well as Jews, from their "social capital" and forced many women into marginal activities such as spinning or begging, as well as the black market "informal sector." Ogilvie draws a stark boundary between privileged insiders and dishonored and impoverished outsiders.[153]

The French case does by no means support the "decline thesis": female guilds that existed in the Middle Ages in Paris and Rouen continued to exist in the early modern period, like for example the "lingères en neuf" in Rouen, a guild that totally excluded men, even from the government offices.[154] In addition, and above all, new female guilds were created at the end of the seventeenth century, following a decree by Colbert imposing that all crafts be organized in guilds. This is the case, for example, of the Parisian guild of seamstresses.[155]

On the other hand, being a member of a guild did not necessarily involve just privileges, but also obligations, control, and tax imposition. This is the reason why craftswomen often *refused* to enter guilds, preferring to work on their own.[156] More generally, the "decline" movement was all but unidirectional, and in the seventeenth and eighteenth centuries, guilds were in most cases reopened to women as a means to lower production costs.[157]

As for the discussion on the impact of the Industrial Revolution on the gendered division of work and on women's work, it cannot be separated from the new views of the impact of the first industrialization wave itself. Since the early 1970s, historians have paid growing attention to the importance and features of "the industrialization before the industrialization," i.e. proto-industry,[158] and what has been called the "industrious revolution."[159] The term "rural proto-industry" has been coined to describe nonagricultural activities for the interregional and international markets performed, at home, by the rural population to supplement their earnings from agricultural work by producing items, generally textiles, for merchants who provided them with the raw materials. These activities often represented the start of industrialization, even though the areas in which they were highly developed did not always turn into industrialized areas and sometimes even experienced de-industrialization. Scholars of the phenomenon stressed the large increase in production that proto-industry made possible, thus proposing an interpretation of historical change that made the Industrial Revolution less revolutionary than generally accepted. They also highlighted that such an increase was reached in the absence of significant technological innovation boosting productivity, in contrast to what would happen with the Industrial Revolution. Proto-industrial activities might be carried out not only by landless rural populations who did not manage to work on a continuous basis but also by landed families, especially during the periods when work in the fields was not very demanding. In any case, a common and crucial feature of proto-industry was the exploitation of then (relatively) underused work capacities within the family. This implied a growing involvement of women and children into market-oriented work. To explain the demographic growth that characterized many proto-industrial populations, scholars suggested that the opportunity to earn offered by proto-industry and the rentability of children's work for proto-industrial families loosened the constraints to family formation that had traditionally led to late marriage and low fertility rates,[160] favoring early marriage and relatively high fertility rates. Empirical research has eventually shown highly diversified cases, thus partially undermining the strong links between economic and demographic behaviors suggested by this interpretation which has nonetheless contributed to make women's and children's work visible, as would also be the case with the category of the Industrious Revolution.[161]

This category, elaborated by Jan de Vries in the early 1990s to interpret some phases of the western European past by reworking the same definition proposed by the demographic historian Akira Hayami in relation to Japan,[162] has contributed to convince a growing number of economic historians to admit the economic importance of working women in pre-industrial times (until recently, economic historians generally considered women's work as complementary to adult men's work, dismissing it as if it were a phenomenon that had little impact on economy and society: an object to which they paid little attention).[163] De Vries's Industrious Revolution category deals with the economic changes that preceded, prepared, and flanked the Industrial Revolution. According to de Vries, from the mid-seventeenth century, households chose to reallocate their time and labor, hitherto devoted to recreation and to the production of non-market goods, toward the production of marketable goods in order to increase their purchasing power and consumption. One of the main ways to achieve this goal, according to de Vries, was the growing participation of (married) women and children in the wage labor market. Thus, a new allocation of resources within the households would have led to a joint increase in the supply and demand of market goods. On this, he suggests, lay the foundations of economic growth in the period preceding industrialization. The thesis is based primarily on the cases of the Dutch and English economies.[164]

This analysis has prompted a lively debate and new research. De Vries's conclusions have been challenged by several scholars: Gregory Clark and Ysbrand Van Der Werf have not found evidence of growing work rates in England and Wales,[165] while Robert C. Allen and Jacob Louis Weisdorf have pinpointed two "industrious revolutions" among English rural workers but both attributable to economic hardship and not accompanied by growing consumption; conversely English urban laborers displayed signs of industrious behavior not linked to economic hardship, which might imply higher consumption.[166] Sheila Ogilvie has stressed the institutional constraints to women's work and consumption in Germany.[167] As for the Low Countries, a group of Dutch historians (including Elise van Nederveen Meerkerk, Danielle van den Heuvel, and Ariadne Schmidt) has collected a large amount of empirical data as part of a research project titled "Women's Work in the Early Modern Northern Netherlands, c. 1500–1815" (2003–2009).[168] De Vries's thesis certainly has the merit of highlighting the utmost importance of work performed by married women and children. But in the case of the Low Countries, where we do see a strong increase in the participation of married women and children in the labor market in the seventeenth century, it is doubtful—according to the aforementioned historians—that consumption was the first motivation of the increased households' work effort. New consumption patterns really developed in the Dutch Republic on a large scale only in the eighteenth century, when the new colonial products (coffee, tea, tobacco) became accessible to part of the middle and lower classes. In the view of the aforementioned Dutch historians, it is therefore proletarianization and economic need, rather than new attitudes toward consumption, that comes into play to explain the Industrious Revolution, even though the work of wives in proletarian families could sometimes become an incentive for extra consumption. Nonetheless differences between periods and socioeconomic groups due to the labor market segmentation must be considered: from the early seventeenth century, emerging capitalist production relations were the cause of increasing proletarianization and, after 1650, of a growing shift of textile production to rural areas, where wages were lower. Consequently, both among the urban poor and in rural families, women and children were increasingly involved in production for the market, whereas the economic decline following the Dutch Golden Age (1600–70) affected artisans and traders in particular.[169]

While married couples traditionally often formed an economic partnership, especially among self-employed artisans and business people, the aforementioned transformations also implied a decreasing cooperation between husbands and wives.[170] Among pre-industrial but proletarianized Dutch textile workers, both spouses were increasingly waged workers,[171] and among the middling sort, where married couples used to cooperate in the same trade, women increasingly started independent businesses.[172] Guild regulations, by admitting or excluding married women as independent members, were certainly important in making this change possible; research carried out in the last few years shows, however, that large supply and demand of commodities gave women new opportunities to start and manage their own businesses.[173] New colonial products implied changing consumption attitudes and also brought about new types of shops where women, too, might be involved. In Leiden, for instance, hundreds of people entered into the booming tea- and coffee-selling trades during the eighteenth century. Interestingly, they were mostly women: women who were very often married and whose husbands worked in different economic sectors. Unfortunately, the available data does not allow us to know how many of them moved from the condition of unpaid housewives to that of independent traders; it does show, however, that at least one-third of them "did not withdraw from a typical family economy in which husband, wife and children worked together in the same trade," moving from the condition of (unpaid) assistant of their husbands to that of independent retailers. They were in fact married to men whose job was not normally carried out at home. Furthermore, contrary to the stereotypes according to which women stopped having extra-domestic work when they married and became mothers, most of the tea and coffee sellers started their businesses a couple of years after marriage and after the birth of their first children—a good example to challenge stereotypes but also to show how difficult it is to generalize about work and women's work in particular.[174]

If on the one hand the notion of Industrious Revolution as formulated by de Vries is not, or not completely, supported by the available empirical data, on the other hand it has turned out to be extremely useful in prompting research, especially on the issues at the very core of this book: family economy, paid and unpaid household production, women's work, etc. As mentioned, consumption—the desire to consume—plays a crucial role in de Vries's interpretation of historical change. Yet he rejects the idea that the new consumer demand was a "'consumer revolution,' an exploding volume of purchased goods."[175]

Such an idea had been suggested by Neil McKendrick, John Brewer, and J. H. Plumb in 1982 in their highly influential book *The Birth of a*

Consumer Society: The Commercialization of Eighteenth-Century England, whose first chapter, significantly entitled "The Consumer Revolution in Eighteenth-Century England," opens with the following statements: "There was a consumer boom in England in the eighteenth century. In the third quarter of the century the boom reached revolutionary proportions. . . . Just as the Industrial Revolution of the eighteenth century marks one of the great discontinuities in history, one of the great turning points in the history of human experience," so "does the matching revolution on consumption. For the consumer revolution was the necessary analogue to the industrial revolution." Though different from de Vries's Industrious Revolution, the Consumer Revolution had not only the focus on consumption but also the attention to the role of women in common with the latter: "Men, and in particular women, bought as never before."[176]

The author of the first chapter of the book, Neil McKendrick, had already started to stress women's and children's roles in previous years. In an essay published in 1974 on home demand and economic growth during the Industrial Revolution, he had highlighted the importance of women's and children's wages both for the survival of the family and for making new forms of consumption possible, contributing in creating demand for goods of central importance to the very development of industry. Yet waged work by women and children outside the home—badly paid but nevertheless paid—threatened traditional gender and generation hierarchies within the family. Exactly because of this, according to McKendrick, its economic value was not recognized and its negative aspects (which certainly existed) were overemphasized by a chorus of voices denouncing heartless exploitation, the removal of women from the family and their maternal role, the undermining of the paterfamilias's authority, and the new opportunity for women to have their own money with which they could indulge their vanity.[177]

McKendrick's arguments contributed to a wide-ranging debate on the importance of female and child labor in the growth of both production and demand for consumer goods. At the same time, they helped the development of studies into the reasons for the previous lack of interest in consumption among academics. While the last thirty years have witnessed a booming development of studies on the history of consumption, for a long time scholars had indeed focused on production, neglecting consumption.[178] According to several scholars, a crucial reason for such neglect was the establishment of theoretical positions contrasting production, which in its "proper" form was supposed to be an adult male activity, and consumption, seen as a fatuous female activity.[179]

In the light of recent research, briefly mentioned above, showing that it was not at all infrequent for women and children in pre-industrial societies to work and earn outside their families, it may be surprising to learn which tremendous anxieties and worries female and child waged factory work caused during the Industrial Revolution. Interestingly, as a reaction against such a disturbing contemporary reality, some people even rewrote the past. In spite of the fact that women and children had worked in pre-industrial society, too, it was argued that their labor was an unwelcomed novelty brought about by industrialization.[180]

Anxieties reached such a point that in a sense the woman worker became a product of the Industrial Revolution, as argued by Joan Scott: never before had working women been observed and described in such an obsessive way. The very fact that the relatively new types of working women emerging during industrialization were perceived as a problem gave them unprecedented visibility precisely in order to overcome the problem they represented.[181] Solving such a problem meant, for many people, emphasizing the distinction between private and public and pursuing individual, familial, national, etc., strategies to convince or force women to work for free at home caring for their families. In a sense, the discourse on separate spheres was a reaction to ongoing transformations more than a reflection of them.[182] According to some scholars, the breadwinner ideology, inextricably linked to the ideology of separate spheres, or even the breadwinner family model, was already a fact before the Industrial Revolution.[183] Nevertheless, the spreading of female and child factory work[184] certainly prompted the development of those ideologies: female factory workers, according to many thinkers, priests, politicians, social reformers, and the like, should be brought back home from the allegedly immoral and de-womanizing environment of the factory and educated to their "natural" role as wives and mothers, for both their well-being and that of their children and families.[185] While the anxieties caused by factory work contributed to giving women's workers, perceived as a problem, large visibility in the public discourses, the efforts to put men and women in their allegedly "right place," according to the dominant ideas on proper gender roles, were not without consequences on people's behavior and women's work. Among other things, they might also imply making working women invisible and "effacing" paid women's work, thus affecting the very production of documents that later would be used by historians precisely to study gender roles.

6. The cunning historian: unveiling and overcoming the gender bias

As long as women were associated with the allegedly immutable realm of nature[186] rather than with history and change, asking whether women had a history and whether women's history did exist was far from rhetorical, as stressed by Gisela Bock or Michelle Perrot. Such questions, asked from a feminist perspective, were provocative rather than trivial.[187] On the other hand, women were really absent from most historical narratives: there were "hardly any women at all," as already declared by Miss Morland in Jane Austen's *Northanger Abbey*.[188] For those (mainly feminist) historians who considered it obvious that women actually had a history, *how* to write their history making them visible was conversely far from obvious.[189] In other words: how could *her-story* be written? Finding sources on women was naturally crucial to writing such a history. Contrary to what one might expect, sources on women turned out to be not at all rare, also allowing historians to document the existence of women who were radically different from the housewives, spouses, and mothers who allegedly should have represented all our female ancestors. Italian historians, to quote but one example, were quick to document illegitimate mothers; women active in "public," from prostitutes to saints; and women who did not live in households headed by a man but in not-kin, all-female households, in institutions, and in convents.[190] Many sources also allowed historians to show that women had always worked, performing both paid and unpaid activities, both domestic and extra-domestic: their roles had changed over time, but paid extra-domestic work was not a novelty brought about by industrialization and/or modernization.[191]

Yet, while on the one hand sources turned out to be rather plentiful, on the other hand they often were heavily gender biased. This was also the case with supposedly gender-neutral documents such as statistics and population censuses, which were often presented as scientific tools for the knowledge and representation of a country. In fact, they were crucial weapons used within the political struggle to shape social reality: ideas on the proper place for men and women affected how data about the working population were collected and presented.[192] Unveiling the fact that these documents were (and still are) gender biased has been a major contribution by women's and gender historians.

By way of comparing different sources on the same individual[193] and analyzing how information was collected and reported in the documents, numerous scholars were able to show that women, especially married ones, were recorded in most sources only according to their marital status, therefore simply as "wife of," or as housewives. This was common practice both in the early modern age and in later times. Nonetheless, even the meaning of such classifications was radically different in different periods. Overseeing such a difference might imply and actually has implied anachronistic and misleading representations of the past. As mentioned above, in early modern times being a wife/housewife was a well-defined role with an economic content. Especially among people who had to work to survive, i.e. among the large majority of the population, being a wife and being defined as such did not imply being (considered) someone who did not work, but rather the contrary. This was even more so if the woman was described as a housewife, housewifery being a kind of work. To contemporary scholars interested in knowing what wives and housewives actually did, such definitions might certainly be useless, since they might imply many different activities, according to the context, the family business, the job of the husband. In order to know what early modern women actually did, historians have to use sources and methods allowing them to go beyond simple labels such as "housewife." This is the case with the verb-oriented method illustrated in this volume by Maria Ågren.[194]

As mentioned, while many early modern sources defined women as housewives and/or according to their (partially overlapping) marital status, this did not imply that their activities were deemed as economically irrelevant. Things went all the more differently when housewifery was increasingly seen as something other than proper work. The professional classification, not only of women but also of men, was a difficult task for the statistical authorities who, especially from the nineteenth century onward, were developing and were assuming increasing importance: many men had unstable jobs, worked irregularly, performed multiple activities, lived from hand to mouth, etc. Yet the classification of women turned out to be particularly difficult and ideologically laden. Ambiguities were in fact often overcome by classifying women according to what was considered to be their proper role, i.e. as housewives, even though they also performed other activities, sometimes even paid, extra-domestic ones. At the same time, housewifery was increasingly seen as something different from proper work, as explained above. In other words, in the nineteenth and twentieth centuries, women were often statistically constructed as dependent and unproductive, "whatever their productive functions."[195]

Nancy Folbre, who in the 1980s and 1990s wrote important contributions on the statistical construction of the unproductive housewife,[196] deals with that issue in this book, too. She shows, among other things, that in the 1851 Census for England and Wales wives, mothers and mistresses who did not work for pay were placed in a category by themselves, different from that of "dependents" (children, the sick, vagrants, etc.), whereas in 1881 housewives were classified as "unoccupied" and in 1891 as "dependents." The new classifications mirrored the developing categories of the political economy and strengthened a statistical representation of the country in line with the breadwinner ideology, according to which the male family heads provided for their wives and children (whereas, in fact, many families would not survive without the paid or unpaid work of women and children; yet this representation also justified very low female and children's wages). Similar decisions to classify wives and daughters not engaged in paid occupations as "dependents" were taken in Australia and in the United States.

However, the underrepresentation of women in statistics did not only depend on the classification of housewives as non-workers; nor did it simply depend on the fact that women were especially likely to engage in irregular and/or home-based activities that, although paid, easily escaped recording. Criteria used to classify women and men might be explicitly different. As shown by Raffaella Sarti in her chapter, the *General Report* referring to the 1901 Italian Census explained that individuals were classified according to their professions, not according to their conditions. This meant, for instance, that lawyer capitalists had been classified among lawyers and not among capitalists, without checking how much time they devoted to the activity of lawyers. On the contrary, as explicitly explained in the *Report*, if a woman had declared that she was in charge of domestic tasks and was also engaged in "secondary" activities such as spinning, weaving, sewing for herself or others, or worked as a temporary servant, she was classified as a housewife (which was considered being a "condition") among the "people supported by the family," while all the other occupations carried out, although paid, had been put "in the classification of accessory professions" (not even analytically sorted in the census). While adult men were often assumed by default to be workers, women might be underrecorded even when they performed paid extra-domestic work on a regular basis. Cristina Borderías, for instance, working on the women employed by the Spanish national telephone company, thanks to data from the company's archive, estimated an underrepresentation of about 35 percent in the municipal population census of Barcelona in 1930.[197] On the other hand, inasmuch as performing paid and/or extra-domestic jobs was stigmatized, women themselves were occasionally likely to hide their occupation when declaring their status to census officers or filling out census forms (but often such declarations were made by the male head of the family).[198]

Both Borderías and Sarti, in their contributions to this book, document a growing tendency to classify women as housewives in population censuses, in Spain and Italy respectively, between the late nineteenth century and the first decades of the twentieth. While single historical population censuses differ both because of peculiar national approaches and changes over time, to the point that each census almost has its own features, generally speaking huge research on these sources has revealed that they all had similar biases and often experienced similar changes over time. Many scholars from different countries would therefore subscribe, with reference to the country they analyze, to Borderías's claim that the statistical system "contributed decisively to the progressive invisibility of the labor activities of women."[199]

The long-term analysis of female participation to the labor force based on censuses and other similar sources has revealed a U-shaped trend: broadly speaking, female participation rates were shown to be falling during the nineteenth and the first half of the twentieth centuries, then recovering after the Second World War. According to the "classical" narrative by Claudia Goldin,

> When incomes are extremely low and when certain types of agriculture dominate (for example, poultry, dairy, rice, cotton, peanuts; generally not grains, livestock, tree crops, sugarcane), women are in the labor force to a great extent. They are sometimes paid laborers but more often are unpaid workers on family farms and in household businesses, often doing home workshop production. As incomes rise in most societies, often because of an expansion of the market or the introduction of new technology, women's labor force participation rates fall. Women's work is often implicitly bought by the family, and women then retreat into the home, although their hours of work may not materially change. The decline in female labor force participation rates owes, in part, to an income effect, but it may be reinforced by a reduction in the relative price of home-produced goods and by a decrease in the demand for women's labor in agriculture. Even when women's relative wage rises, married women may be barred from manufacturing employment by social custom or by employer preference.
>
> But as female education improves and as the value of women's time in the market increases still further, relative to the price of goods, they move back into the paid labor force, as reflected in the move along the rising portion of the U-shaped curve.[200]

In light of the biases shown in research conducted on censuses and other similar sources, a crucial issue is whether such a U-shaped participation to the labor force mirrors "reality" or is only a statistical illusion due, as for the declining part of the U-trend, to the growing underrecording of female work described above. The ideas on the proper role and right place of men and women that led to undervalue, underrecord, and even to efface women's work from such sources were actually real phenomena that deserve to be illustrated and understood. Such ideas certainly did not just cause census officers, family heads, and sometimes women themselves to make female work invisible; they also affected decisions, by men and women, on the actual activities performed by women, and induced some of them (how many?) to avoid entering the labor market or to withdraw from it when they could afford "not to work."[201] Much discussion has indeed addressed the question whether two clearly distinct spheres really existed, with some scholars stressing that for the lower classes it was impossible to separate the spheres,[202] and others arguing that middle-class women never stopped playing a crucial economic role and in the nineteenth century were able to exploit the new economic and financial opportunities opened up by economic development, to quote but two positions within a multifaceted debate.[203]

Establishing whether the aforementioned biases make those sources completely useless or whether ways actually exist to measure and deal with women's underrepresentation is therefore a crucial endeavor if one wants to know which changes affected the structure of the labor force, its composition by age and gender, the contribution of men and women to family budgets, and national domestic product.[204] It is true that a possible way to roughly calculate the total female economic contribution to GDP is to give housework the same market value as if it were performed by paid servants/domestic workers.[205] Yet ignoring how many, and which, women really were unpaid housewives and how many, and which, women performed paid activities (possibly paid at different rates than domestic service) producing goods or services in precise economic sectors instead represents a serious bias (even though *unpaid* housewives, too, might and may actually produce goods and services for the market).[206] Pinpointing how many, and which, women workers were underrecorded in censuses and similar sources is important to reconstruct long-term historical trends. While more recent and better estimates of the value of household production are based on more telling sources than censuses, such as time budgets,[207] the available sources on the use of time in past centuries are generally qualitative ones and difficult to compare with modern ones.[208] As a consequence, censuses, despite all their bias, remain rather important sources.

Efforts to evaluate the reliability of censuses and other similar sources and to correct female underrecording started rather early and have not only been pursued by feminist historians.[209] Women's and gender historians, however, have been especially active in this area. Some scholars have confirmed census biases and suggested possible corrections[210]; in Britain, some historians have even "rehabilitated" the censuses, showing, especially through comparisons with other sources, that the original data collected in the Census Enumerator's Books was much more accurate and reliable than the aggregate one published in the tables.[211]

Though with some exceptions,[212] the results of these efforts seem to confirm that long-term female participation to the labor force actually had a U-shaped trend, but with participation rates always significantly higher than previously calculated using original, uncorrected data taken from censuses and other similar sources.[213]

"Cunning" historians are thus not only able to document the biases of the sources but also to find ways to overcome them. A crucial method is to compare sources that, being written with different purposes, have a different "interest" in recording or omitting women's work. The very existence of such sources testifies that even within contexts where ideologies devaluing women's work were very strong, they did not permeate the entire society rigidly and homogeneously. According to the goal to be reached, reality could be described in different ways, often ignoring women's work, but sometimes highlighting it. In this book, the chapter by Margareth Lanzinger presents a particularly telling example of the potential of comparing sources aiming to reach different goals. Lanzinger focuses on applications for permission to marry submitted to the Catholic religious authorities in nineteenth-century Tyrol by men and women who, being blood relatives or related by marriage, could marry only if they obtained a special dispensation (marriages among kinfolk were forbidden). People had to justify their requests with arguments, which are likely to include detailed descriptions of women's activities and skills. This was often the case with brothers- and sisters-in-law, who—after the death of the man's wife and the woman's sister—wanted to marry, having often been living under the same roof for several years. In such cases the man was likely to describe the role of the woman in the family business, her contribution to the survival and well-being of the household in great detail, in order to present her as the best, not to say his only, possible wife. While these touching requests were often rejected, forcing people to resubmit them several times, the reiterated applications, forcibly enriched with new arguments, represent today a particularly rich source for historians, often revealing details of the multiple activities performed by women, too.

7. The value of home-based work and its regulation

The obscuring of women's work not only affected censuses and similar sources but many other documents as well: as shown by Eileen Boris in her chapter, this was long the case even with the documents and reports produced by the International Labour Office, even though this institution would also support research and campaigns that have been, and still are, crucial to recognizing the value of different types of home-based work.[214] This is the case, to quote but one example, of the ILO-sponsored book *Lace Makers of Narsapur: Indian Housewives Produce for the World Market* by Maria Mies (1982), a study examining "substantial household industry in Andhra Pradesh, India, in which secluded poor Christian and

Hindu women produce[d] lace which yield[ed] about 90 per cent of the State's handicrafts export earnings." These poor women produced "the lace through an extensive network of male agents, traders and exporters." The business was very profitable for most of those male actors, whereas the producers themselves, all females, became impoverished: they were not even "considered 'workers' but rather 'housewives,' in spite of a 6-8-hour day at lace work (in addition to about 7 hours of other productive work and housework)." To define this process, Mies introduced the very discerning concept of *housewifization*. What was at stake was not only scientific precision: "the illusion that the women produce lace in their leisure time" contributed in fact "to inhibiting the sole means of improving their lot—organisation."[215]

From a feminist perspective, the effort to identify exactly what women all over the world did and do, and to correct data taken from biased sources accordingly, does not aim to produce a more accurate picture of the work/non-work divide, but rather the contrary. Having more accurate data on women's roles is indeed necessary, not only to better evaluate the female contribution to GNP as is traditionally calculated but also, and mainly, to calculate the economic value of all those forms of home-based work that are not included in traditional GDP calculation's methods alongside those that are already included.

Recent research focusing on "unpaid" work performed within the household has contributed to disclose a nuanced continuum encompassing a wide variety of home-based activities: unpaid care for the family members, unpaid work for self-consumption, unpaid and paid market-oriented work for the family business, paid industrial homework, paid carework performed in one's household,[216] paid carework and paid domestic work in others' households.[217] It is a variety that challenges the "classical" dichotomy of unpaid vs. paid work,[218] as well as that of family vs. market. At the same time, observing such a multifaceted variety, neither a serious scholar nor a fair policymaker can avoid tackling the question of the economic value of all these forms of work. In other words, the question is not only to distinguish between "real" housewives and "housewifized" workers: though this distinction is important for the sake of precision, the crucial issue is to arrive at a much more complete calculation of the economic contribution of any type of work.

Interestingly, studies focusing on the medieval and early modern periods show that working within one's family normally gave people, especially adults,[219] some rights on the family revenues and assets, entitling them to some form of remuneration, even though the actual type of remuneration may be effective in the short or long term, and was likely to depend on age, gender, position within the family, etc.; therefore, according to the idea that all humans are equal, it was not necessarily fair but might be considered fair or at least acceptable in a world structurally based on inequality, where a different value was attributed to men and women, adults and children, masters and servants, etc.[220] Intermingling with moral and legal norms, this created complex networks of gendered and generational rights and duties, solidarities and obligations, credits and debts among family members,[221] which makes it impossible to reduce the unwaged activities performed at home to the category of "unpaid" work.[222] Such a category, though very useful to interrogate the sources, is too rigid, one-sided, and clearly misleading when historians look for appropriate interpretative frameworks. It runs the risk of obscuring the multiple ways of remunerating one's contribution to the family's survival, welfare, and wealth.

Yet, as explained above, especially from the nineteenth century, the domestic sphere was increasingly considered the site of unpaid, gratuitous, love-driven activities seen as the opposite of the paid, market-oriented activities performed in factories, companies, shops, and offices. Even domestic workers, who were actually paid, were generally no longer considered proper workers precisely because they were associated with the domestic sphere and carried out more or less the same tasks that wives and mothers carried out for fee.[223] These ideas, which obscured the economic value of home-based activities, solidified in laws. Many scholars, activists, and policymakers are aware, today, that the emphasis on love and gratuity actually implies a marginalization and a discrimination of those who perform care, domestic, home-based activities. Nonetheless, not only GDP calculation but also the law still contributes in preventing a fair appraisal of their economic value (such an appraisal would obviously not entail denying their emotional importance). As Maria Rosaria Marella writes in her chapter, "the results achieved by other social sciences in the analysis of housework have not been shared so far by legal analysis. Lawyers keep on ignoring the issue, projecting it in the background of a strict family/market divide." According to Marella, we cannot properly speak of a "legal irrelevance of housework; rather, it has a limited relevance, restricted to the field of family law, assumed in its exceptionalism." In Italy, a country whose constitution (article 29) defines the family as a "natural society" based on marriage, the courts assume that the relationship between family members is shaped by "a natural obligation" of solidarity that excludes any contamination with economic exchanges. Yet these apparently economically invaluable activities, done for free because of a "natural obligation," surprisingly become "economically relevant and valuable with market parameters" in relations with a third party. According to the law, their loss represents in fact a damage valued in pecuniary terms: a solution, according to Marella, that both the systems of common and of civil law share. In fact, the 1975 Italian reform of family law has tried to overcome such a naturalization of family relationships. Yet, as stated by Marella, the productive function of the family is still misunderstood; the recognition of productivity is limited to the regime of the family business, while for the rest the "rationale of family solidarity—and its 'natural' corollary of the gratuitousness of the work done in the domestic sphere" is dominant. Article 230bis of the Civil Code, regulating family businesses, states, in fact, that the family members who work for the family and those who work for the family business have the right to both be su pported according to the wealth of the family and to share in the business earnings, also making clear that "the work by a woman is considered equivalent to that by a man."[224]

In point of fact, recent research on Italian women involved in family businesses shows that, while their numbers are growing, they are often invisible, barred from decision-making and not rewarded fairly as for job titles and salaries, although, according to Francesca Cesaroni and Annalisa Sentuti, their minor roles are not always the result of gender discrimination.[225] Gender discrimination and gender stereotyping are conversely at work among French wine-grape farmers in the Cognac region who even nowadays normally pass on their farms, professional skills, and the status of business head to their male heirs assuming that, if there are sons and daughters, the latter are "not interested" in inheriting the farm.[226]

As in Italy, in France, too, state attitude toward the regulation of home-based work has turned out to be difficult and ambiguous. As noted by Manuela Martini, the French Parliament has been very slow in defining the legal status of family workers, despite the fact that family businesses are still widespread in the country. Although social rights in France are among the most advanced in Europe, in this case a law to grant occupational status to collaborating spouses as well as social security benefits to those carrying out unpaid work was eventually enacted as late as 1982; it implied a refashioning of the boundaries between the marital duty to assist one's spouse and the work that, exceeding this moral and legal obligation, gives legal right to compensation.[227] As illustrated by Florence Weber in her chapter, the French do have a legal obligation to support a family member in need (spouse, parent, child, grandparent, grandchildren, son-in-law, daughter-in-law, mother-in-law, father-in-law, but not siblings). Furthermore, the so-called *piété filiale* (filial devotion) is a moral duty and an absolute obligation. French law does not subject the children's duty to support their parents to any conditions: "For jurists, the reality, both past and present, of family relationships cannot justify the presence or absence of help to a parent nor the 'amount' of this help." As a consequence, all children have an identical obligation to care for their parents, and, if necessary, to pay for caring for them, independently from their emotional relationship and from the economic exchanges that might have been favoring one child and unfavoring another; conversely, the care they normally provide does not affect their share of the inheritance. Yet, in two cases the law considers the reality of family relations to compensate for an excessive burden instead. Already in 1939, a law was introduced to take into account the unpaid work carried out, in agriculture, by children who remain with their parents, becoming their "family workers," while their siblings no longer work on the family farms: in this case, the law calculates for them "deferred wages" (*salaires différés*) to be settled with a larger share of the inheritance (law 29 July 1939). Furthermore, a judgment of the French Supreme Court of 12 July 1994 introduced the notion of "unjust enrichment within family relations" (*enrichissement sans cause dans les relations de famille*), to grant an advantage at the time of inheritance to a child who took care of his/her elderly parents, who had become impoverished, to compensate him/her for the larger family work he performed in comparison with his sister.

These cases show that, at least in particular cases, the law assesses both the unpaid market-oriented work performed within the family business and the care work done for free, because of love or at least moral obligations, in economic terms, showing how ambiguous and blurred the boundaries between all those activities are. It is not just state authorities, however, who have tried and try to regulate home-based labor. In her chapter, Eileen Boris illustrates the difficult growth, within the International Labour Organization (ILO), of the consciousness of the numerous activities performed at home by women, of the importance of those activities, and of the need to consider them as proper work and to regulate them. The ILO's mainly male representatives initially considered only paid extra-domestic work performed in factories, shops, offices as work, being at the same time often afraid of the possible disruptive consequences, on the family, of the massive entry of women into such working contexts. Over time, however, especially thanks to clever and engaged women, the ILO has passed important conventions, such as Convention 177 on home work in 1995 and Convention 189, in 2011, on "Decent Work for Domestic Workers" in particular: with convention 177, "for the first time, the ILO valued work in the home as worthy of a labor standard of its own. Technical assistance and standard-setting on home work solidified institutional support for the informal sector, helping to redirect ILO efforts to the reproductive labor that occurs in that realm." Convention 189 "marks the worthiness of monetized reproductive labor" and became "conceivable because of the earlier victory of home-based pieceworkers."

8. Which future for home-based work?

The issue of assessing the value of any kind of home-based work, always important, is all the more crucial if we consider that such forms of work, far from being about to disappear thanks to technical and social modernization, as many people expected until some decades ago, are experiencing an expansion instead. This is precisely the case with paid domestic and care work as well as with home work. Paid domestic and care work is experiencing a real boom at the global level,[228] while home work and offshore production, as explained by Eileen Boris, "encouraged by favorable tariff and tax policies," "spread beyond their historical presence in garments and textiles to include the making of additional consumer goods, electronics, and plastics. With the computer revolution, telework and home assembly of components updated the practice of clerical homework in Australia, Canada, and other 'developed' nations, but also served as additional forms of offshoring from North to South and from expensive to cheaper labor markets."

A complex scene therefore unfolds before our eyes. Until some decades ago, many people expected economic and social modernization to lead to the spreading of "standard" paid extra-domestic work; to put it in the simplest terms, they expected, thanks to growing opportunities for work in "standard" sectors as well as expanding welfare and public services, that paid domestic work and home-based work would disappear, and that women would increasingly be freed from caring and domestic tasks and be all the more integrated in the standard labor force, gaining, in this way, not only a salary but also all the growing benefits, protections, and rights associated with proper work. In fact, things have gone differently: because of a variety of causes, in "developed" countries where "standard" work used to be common, it is increasingly a privilege, while multiple forms of "non-standard" work—poorly paid, irregular, insecure, not granting any or little social protection—are spreading. Domestic and care work, even live-in, is experiencing a revival, while multiple forms of home-based work, both "traditional" and "new" are spreading. The struggle to make home-based labor visible and to give it fair recognition happens at a time when "standard" labor is becoming less common: according to some scholars, as explained by Sarti in her chapter, there is a kind of feminization of work, in the sense that work today is becoming, for both men and women, more similar to traditional women's work than used to be in "developed" countries until a few years ago; i.e., it is becoming more irregular, less paid, less recognized, less associated with rights and status, less crucial for the foundation of one's identity. Furthermore, growing automation and robotization make the scenario of a spreading lack of work and unemployment all the more possible and threatening.

While, on the one hand, this landscape is rather disturbing, on the other hand, the idea that universal basic income could be introduced, guaranteeing at least a minimum for survival to everybody, independently from the fact of working and earning, is gaining momentum, counterbalancing, at least in part, the alarming scenery we broadly described above, even though in fact there is no agreement on the possible advantages and disadvantages of such an introduction, both in general and in particular on gender equality.[229] The world is rapidly changing, challenging the received social equilibriums as well as reality's interpretations: new disquieting problems, such as the aforementioned ones, climate change and ecological unsustainability, are arising and new imbalances are developing between rich and poor, North and South, West and East. Yet at the same time, new opportunities unfold. Avoiding the obscuring of the contribution made by a section of humanity—actually the largest—to the common survival and (potential) well-being is in any case a crucial premise to make the worst scenarios for the future less likely. This book aims to make a contribution to reach this goal.

Anna Bellavitis is professor of early modern history, director of the Groupe de Recherche d'Histoire at Université de Rouen-Normandie, and senior member of the Institut Universitaire de France. She is, or has been, responsible for many international research projects, on family history, gender history, and labor history of early modern Europe, in collaboration with European universities and institutions. Her recent publications include: *"Tout ce qu'elle saura et pourra faire." Femmes, droits, travail en Normandie du Moyen Âge à la Grande guerre*, edited with Virginie Jourdain, Virginie Lemonnier-Lesage, Beatrice Zucca Micheletto (Rouen: PURH, 2015); *Il lavoro delle donne nelle città dell'Europa moderna* (Roma: Viella, 2016); "Patterns of Transmission and Urban Experience: When Gender Matters," in *The Routledge History Handbook of Gender and the Urban Experience*, edited by Deborah Simonton (New York: Routledge, 2017), 11–20; "Workplace Cultures," in *A Cultural History of Work*, edited by Deborah Simonton and Anne Montenach, vol. 3, *1450–1650*, edited by Bert De Munck and Thomas Safley (London: Bloomsbury Academic, 2018), 89–100. For further details see http://grhis.univ-rouen.fr/grhis/?page_id=545.

Manuela Martini is professor of modern history at the Université Lumière Lyon 2. She has directed several international research projects on the history of work, family, and gender history and labor migrations. She belongs to numerous scientific organizations, commissions, and advisory boards and is a member of the editorial collective of *Gender & History*. She has published extensively in French, Italian, Spanish, German, and English and authored or edited sixteen books or journals' special issues on European economic history, gender history, and labor international migrations. Her more recent authored book is *Bâtiment en famille: Migrations et petite entreprise en banlieue parisienne au XXe siècle* (Paris: CNRS Éditions, 2016). Her publications on gender and labor issues include "When Unpaid Workers Need a Legal Status: Family Workers and Reforms to Labour Rights in Twentieth-Century France," *International Review of Social History* 59, no. 2 (2014): 247–78, the special issue titled "Households, Family Workshops and Unpaid Market Work in Europe from the 16th Century to the Present," *History of the Family* 19, no. 3 (2014), edited with Anna Bellavitis, and the special issue titled "Per una nuova storia del lavoro dell'età contemporanea: genere, economie, soggetti," *Genesis* 15, no. 2 (2016), edited with Cristina Borderías. For further details see http://larhra.ish-lyon.cnrs.fr/membre/506.

Raffaella Sarti teaches early modern history and gender history at the University of Urbino, Italy. She has also worked in Paris, Vienna, Bologna, and Murcia. She is a member of the editorial collective of *Gender & History*. Her studies address domestic service and care work; Mediterranean slavery; marriage and celibacy; family and material culture; gender and the nation; masculinity; graffiti. She is the author of approximately 150 publications in nine languages, including *Europe at Home: Family and Material Culture 1500–1800* (New Haven, CT: Yale University Press, 2002) and *Servo e padrone, o della (in)dipendenza: Un percorso da Aristotele ai nostri giorni* (Bologna: Alma Mater Studiorum Università di Bologna, 2015). She has edited "Men in a Woman's Job: Male Domestic Workers, International Migration and the Globalization of Care," with Francesca Scrinzi, special issue of *Men and Masculinities* 13, no. 1 (2010); "Men at Home: Domesticities, Authority, Emotions and Work," special issue of *Gender & History* 27, no. 3 (2015); *Familles laborieuses: Rémunération, transmission et apprentissage dans les ateliers familiaux de la fin du Moyen Âge à l'époque contemporaine en Europe*, with Anna Bellavitis and Manuela Martini, in *Mélanges de l'École française de Rome—Italie et Méditerranée modernes et contemporaines* 128, no. 1 (2016). For more details see http://www.uniurb.it/sarti/.

Notes

This essay is the product of the many discussions had by the editors of the volume. Nonetheless, section 1 was jointly written by the three editors; sections 2, 3, 4, 6 and 8 were mainly written by Raffaella Sarti (who has also written the short introductions to the first three parts of the book); section 5 was jointly written by the three editors, with large parts done by Anna Bellavitis; section 7 was mainly written by Manuela Martini. English revision by Clelia Boscolo, Universtity of Birmingham.

 1. A few years ago, Marcel van der Linden discussed some of the answers given to the question "What is work?"; see his article "Studying Attitudes to Work Worldwide, 1500–1650: Concepts, Sources, and Problems of Interpretation," *International Review of Social History* 56, S19 (2011): 25–43.
 2. As written by Jürgen Kocka, "A history of work would seem to be highly attractive, because it would have to integrate very different approaches, methods and aspects, ranging from straightforward economic history to cultural constructivism, including the analysis of institutional politics. But can it be done? There is reason for doubt, since the concept of 'work' is not very precise, [is] very changeable over time and between cultures and highly contested. Very often what it means is not easily separated from other human activities, but embedded, which makes its separate conceptualization appear a bit artificial and problematic. In addition, concepts like 'work' are highly aggregate and abstract; they comprise very different phenomena. This diversity makes it difficult to formulate observations valid for the whole aggregate, i.e. work in general"; see Jürgen Kocka, "Work as a Problem in European History," in *Work in a Modern Society: The German Historical Experience in Comparative Perspective,* ed. Jürgen Kocka (New York: Berghahn, 2010), 1. On the very existence of societies with/without a concept of work, see Marie-Noëlle Chamoux, "Sociétés avec et sans concept de travail," *Sociologie du travail* 36, Hors série, no. 4 (1994): 57–71.
 3. The official English translation of the Italian Constitution is provided on the website of the Camera dei Deputati of the Italian Parliament: http://en.camera.it/4?scheda_informazioni=23.
 4. See on this issue Raffaella Sarti's chapter in this book.
 5. Marianthi Dunn, "Annual National Accounts—How ESA 2010 Has Changed the Main GDP Aggregates," *Eurostat Statistics Explained,* January 2015.
 6. John Black, Nigar Hashimzade, and Gareth Myles, eds., *Oxford Dictionary of Economics* (Oxford: Oxford University Press, 2009).
 7. Ester Boserup, *Women's Role in Economic Development* (New York: Earthscan, 1970).
 8. Mariarosa Dalla Costa and Selma James, *The Power of Women and the Subversion of the Community* (1972; Bristol: Falling Wall Press, 1975). On the debate on wages for housewives, see below as well as the chapters by Alessandra Gissi, Alessandra Pescarolo, and Maria Rosaria Marella in this book.
 9. Gary S. Becker, *A Treatise on the Family* (Cambridge, MA: Harvard University Press, 1981).
10. On these issues see Nancy Folbre's chapter in this book. "We need to develop a better system of national income accounting that includes the 'human capital sector' of the economy as a part of a larger set of nonmarket accounts," she wrote some years ago; see Nancy Folbre, *Valuing Children: Rethinking the Economics of the Family* (Cambridge, MA: Harvard University Press, 2008), 7. On the problems and methods to measure and value unpaid household work, see John W. Kendrick, "Expanding Imputed Values in the National Income and Product Accounts," *Review of Income and Wealth* 25, no. 4 (1979): 349–63; Ann Chadeau, Annie Fouquet, Claude Thélot, "Peut-on mesurer le travail domestique?," *Economie et statistique,* no. 136 (1981): 29–42; Ann Chadeau, "Measuring

Household Activities: Some International Comparisons," *Review of Income and Wealth* 31, no. 3 (1985): 237–54; Marilyn Waring, *If Women Counted: A New Feminist Economics* (San Francisco: HarperCollins, 1988); Heinrich Lützel, "Household Production and National Accounts," *Statistical Journal of the United Nations Economic Commission for Europe* 6, no. 4 (1989): 337–48; Lourdes Benería, "Accounting for Women's Work: The Progress of Two Decades," *World Development* 20, no. 11 (1992): 1547–60; Nancy Folbre and Barnet Wagman, "Counting Housework: New Estimates of Real Product in the United States, 1800–1860," *Journal of Economic History* 53, no. 2 (1993): 275–88; Duncan Ironmonger, "Counting Outputs, Capital Inputs and Caring Labor: Estimating Gross Household Product," *Feminist Economics* 2, no. 3 (1996): 37–64; Meg Luxton, "The UN, Women, and Household Labour: Measuring and Valuing Unpaid Work," *Women's Studies International Forum* 20, no. 3 (1997): 431–39; Antonella Picchio, ed., *Unpaid Work and the Economy: A Gender Analysis of the Standards of Living* (New York: Routledge, 2005); Joseph Stiglitz, Amartya Sen, and Jean-Paul Fitoussi, *Report by the Commission on Economic Performance and Social Progress Revisited* (Paris: Sciences Po Publications, 2009), no. 33; Alberto Alesina and Andrea Ichino, *L'Italia fatta in casa: indagine sulla vera ricchezza degli italiani* (Milano: Mondadori, 2009); Gianna C. Giannelli, Lucia Mangiavacchi, and Luca Piccoli, "GDP and the Value of Family Caretaking: How Much Does Europe Care?," IZA (Forschungsinstitut zur Zukunft der Arbeit, Institute for the Study of Labor) Discussion Paper No. 5046, July 2010; Delphine Roy, "La contribution du travail domestique non marchand au bien-être matériel des ménages: une quantification à partir de l'enquête Emploi du Temps," *Document de travail*, no F1104, Insee, March 2011; Nadim Ahmad and Koh Seung-Hee, "Incorporating Estimates of Household Production of Non-market Services into International Comparisons of Material Well-Being," *OECD Statistics Working Papers*, 14 October 2011; Monica Montella, "La produzione domestica: il valore aggiunto generato dalle famiglie," working paper, Dipartimento di Economia e Diritto Sapienza Università di Roma, Roma, 2012; Kar-Fai Gee, "Development of Estimates for Household Production of Non-market Services in OECD Countries for the Index of Economic Well-Being," Centre for the Study of Living Standards, Research Report 2015; Andrea Brandolini and Eliana Viviano, "Accounting for Total Work in Labour Statistics," *Journal for Labour Market Research* 8, no. 26 (2016): 1–14.

11. For surveys of research on housework, see Beth Anne Shelton and John Daphne, "The Division of Household Labor," *Annual Review of Sociology* 22 (1996): 299–322; Scott Coltrane, "Research on Household Labor: Modeling and Measuring the Social Embeddedness of Routine Family Work," *Journal of Marriage and the Family* 62, no. 4 (2000): 1208–33; Mylène Lachance-Grzela and Geneviève Bouchard, "Why Do Women Do the Lion's Share of Housework? A Decade of Research," *Sex Roles* 63, nos. 11–12 (2010): 767–80. For a survey of research on paid domestic work, see Raffaella Sarti, "Historians, Social Scientists, Servants, and Domestic Workers: Fifty Years of Research on Domestic and Care Work," *International Review of Social History* 59, no. 2 (2014): 279–314, also published in *Towards a Global History of Domestic and Caregiving Workers*, ed. Dirk Hoerder, Elise van Nederveen Meerkerk, and Silke Neunsinger (Leiden: Brill, 2015), 25–60; see also the introduction to this book.

12. Eileen Boris, *Home to Work: Motherhood and the Politics of Industrial Homework in the United States* (New York: Cambridge University Press, 1994) and her chapter in this book; Alessandra Pescarolo and Gian Bruno Ravenni, *Il proletariato invisibile: la manifattura della paglia nella Toscana mezzadrile (1820–1950)* (Milano: Angeli, 1991); Eloisa Betti, "Lavoro a domicilio e relazioni di genere negli anni Cinquanta: Appunti sul caso bolognese," *Genesis* 14, no. 2 (2015): 107–33; Tania Toffanin, *Fabbriche invisibili: storie di donne, lavoranti a domicilio* (Verona: Ombre Corte, 2016).

13. As stressed by Lisa Phillips, "Silent Partners: The Role of Unpaid Market Labor in Fami-

lies," *Feminist Economics* 14, no. 2 (2008): 37, "unpaid market labor is conceptually distinct from both paid work and unpaid domestic labor."

14. The project was led by the three editors of this book and supported by the École Française of Rome and the Universities of Paris-Diderot (ICT laboratory), Rouen (GRHIS laboratory), and Urbino Carlo Bo. Seven research meetings/conferences have taken place, in Paris (2011), Glasgow (2012), Rouen (2012), Rome (2014), Turin (2015), Valencia (2016), and Madrid (2016). So far, the outcomes of the project are contained in the article by Manuela Martini, "When Unpaid Workers Need a Legal Status: Family Workers and Reforms to Labour Rights in Twentieth-Century France," *International Review of Social History* 59, no. 2 (2014): 247–78; the special issue "Households, Family Workshops and Unpaid Market Work in Europe from the 16th Century to the Present," edited by Manuela Martini and Anna Bellavitis, of the journal *History of the Family* 19, no. 3 (2014); and the special issue "Familles laborieuses: Rémunération, transmission et apprentissage dans les ateliers familiaux de la fin du Moyen Âge à l'époque contemporaine en Europe," edited by Anna Bellavitis, Manuela Martini, and Raffaella Sarti, of the journal *Mélanges de l'École française de Rome—Italie et Méditerranée modernes et contemporaines* 128, no. 1 (2016), including mainly articles in French especially focusing on artisan families from the Middle Ages to the present.

15. Folbre, *Valuing Children*, 97. See also Nancy Folbre, "Inequality and Time Use in the Household," in *Oxford Handbook of Economic Inequality*, ed. Wiener Salverda, Brian Nolan, and Timothy Smeeding (New York: Oxford University Press, 2008); Folbre and Wagman, "Counting Housework."

16. The issue started to be discussed in the 1980s: Margrethe H. Olson, and Sophia B. Primps, "Working at Home with Computers: Work and Nonwork Issues," *Journal of Social Issues* 40, no. 3 (1984): 97–112; Boas Shamir and Ilan Salomon, "Work-at-Home and the Quality of Working Life," *Academy of Management Review* 10, no. 3 (1985): 455–64; Sandra Burchi, *Ripartire da casa: lavori e reti dallo spazio domestico* (Milano: Angeli, 2014). For a review, see Diane E. Bailey and Nancy B. Kurland, "A Review of Telework Research: Findings, New Directions, and Lessons for the Study of Modern Work," *Journal of Organizational Behavior* 23, no. 4 (2002): 383–400. Today literature on the issue, which affects the very boundary between work and non-work, is huge; see for instance Julie B. Olson-Buchanan, Wendy R. Boswell, and Timothy J. Morgan, "The Role of Technology in Managing the Work and Nonwork Interface," in *The Oxford Handbook of Work and Family*, ed. Tammy D. Allen and Lillian T. Eby (Oxford: Oxford University Press, 2016), 333–48. On 3D printers, see the chapter by Alessandra Pescarolo in this book.

17. For a comprehensive survey, see Herbert Applebaum, *The Concepts of Work: Ancient, Medieval and Modern* (New York: State University of New York Press, 1992). For a short but useful overview, see Josef Ehmer, "Work, History of," *International Encyclopedia of the Social & Behavioral Sciences*, ed. Neil J. Smelser and Paul B. Baltes (Amsterdam: Elsevier, 2001), 24:16569–75. Josef Ehmer has also edited (with Catharina Lis) the book *The Idea of Work in Europe from Antiquity to Modern Times* (Farnham-Burlington: Ashgate 2009), while Catharina Lis and Hugo Soly have written *Worthy Efforts: Attitudes to Work and Workers in Pre-industrial Europe* (Leiden: Brill, 2012). Other important publications on the subject include, among others, Patrick Joyce, ed., *The Historical Meanings of Work* (Cambridge: Cambridge University Press, 1987); Kocka, *Work in a Modern Society*; Karin Hofmeester and Christine Moll-Murata, eds., "The Joy and Pain of Work: Global Attitudes and Valuations, 1500–1650," special issue of *International Review of Social History* 56, S19 (2011). See section 2 for further bibliographical references.

18. Still interesting is the article by Maurice Godelier, "Work and Its Representations: A Research Proposal," *History Workshop Journal* 10, no. 1 (1980): 164–74, which starts with an analysis of language.

19. Douglas Harper, *Online Etymological Dictionary*, retrieved 29 August 2016 from http://www.etymonline.com/index.php?term=work.
20. See for instance Charlton T. Lewis and Charles Short, *A Latin Dictionary*, Perseus Digital Library, Tufts University, retrieved 29 August 2016 from http://www.perseus.tufts.edu/hopper/morph?l=labor&la=la&can=labor1&prior=labor.
21. Gerhard Köbler, *Deutsches Etymologisches Wörterbuch*, 1995, retrieved 29 August 2016 from http://www.koeblergerhard.de/derwbhin.html.
22. "Travail," Centre National des Ressources Textuales et Lexicales, Portal Lexical, Etymologie, retrieved 29 August 2016 from http://www.cnrtl.fr/etymologie/travail; *Trésor de la Langue française informatisé* (TLFI), retrieved 29 August 2016 from http://atilf.atilf.fr/dendien/scripts/tlfiv5/advanced.exe?8;s=3459330510; Émile Littré, *Dictionnaire de la langue française*, online edition:
    Wallon, trava, travail de maréchal; provenç. trabalh, trebalh, trebail, fatigue; esp. trabajo, fatigue; portug. trabalho, fatigue; ital. travaglio, travail de maréchal et fatigue. Il est impossible de séparer travail des maréchaux et travail, peine, fatigue, pour la forme, ni même pour le sens; car, de travail qui assujettit les animaux, on passe sans peine à travail, gêne, sens primordial (travail de labors, Job. 454). Travail se tire du prov. travar, entraver, du lat. trabs, poutre.
    Retrieved 29 August 2016 from http://www.littre.org/definition/travail. Still valid is the article by Lucien Febvre, "Travail: évolution d'un mot et d'une idée," *Journal de Psychologie normale et pathologique* 51, no. 1 (1948): 19–28.
23. Hannah Arendt, *The Human Condition*, 2nd ed. introd. Margaret Canovan, (1958; Chicago: University of Chicago Press, 1998), 80. The English translations of Marx use the words "work" and "labor" with meanings different from those described here: "work" is used to refer to the simple process of producing, whereas "labor" means the process of creation of value; see Applebaum, *Concept of Work*, 437–38. For a questioning of this traditional translation, see Christian Fuchs, *Reading Marx in the Information Age: A Media and Communication Studies Perspective on Capital* (New York: Routledge, 2016), 1:28.
24. All Scripture citations are taken from the New International Version unless otherwise noted. In the Bible there are of course many other references to work.
25. Jacques Le Goff, *Un lungo Medioevo* (Roma: Edizioni Dedalo, 2006), 60.
26. Ibid.
27. Mathieu Arnoux, *Le temps des laboureurs: travail, ordre social et croissance en Europe (XIe–XIVe siècle)* (Paris: Albin Michel, 2012). On this representation of society, a groundbreaking contribution was provided by Ottavia Niccoli, *I sacerdoti, i guerrieri, i contadini: storia di un'immagine della società* (Torino: Einaudi, 1979). More recently see Ottavia Niccoli, "Immagini e metafore della società in età moderna: Lectio magistralis tenuta il 16 novembre 2010," *Quaderni del Dipartimento di Sociologia e Ricerca Sociale dell'Università degli Studi di Trento* no. 54 (2011): 5–29.
28. Anna Bellavitis, *Donne cittadinanza e corporazioni tra medioevo ed età moderna: ricerche in corso*, in *Corpi e storia: donne e uomini dal mondo antico all'età contemporanea*, ed. Nadia Maria Filippini, Tiziana Plebani, and Anna Scattigno (Roma: Viella, 2002), 87: "Una delle rappresentazioni più frequenti dell'identità urbana in epoca medievale e moderna si articola sulla complementarietà tra corpo cittadino e corpi di mestiere." Bellavitis also stresses the limitations of this representation.
29. Claudio Donati, *L'idea di nobiltà in Italia, secoli XIV–XVIII* (Roma-Bari: Laterza, 1988); Luca Mocarelli, "The Attitude of Milanese Society to Work and Commercial Activities," in Ehmer and Lis, *Idea of Work*, 101–21. Thorstein Veblen, *The Theory of the Leisure Class*, ed. Martha Banta (Oxford: Oxford University Press, 2009; originally published New York: Macmillan, 1899) still offers stimulating insights. Lis and Soly, *Worthy Efforts*, 169–70, 552, argue, however, that European aristocracies never perceived themselves as leisure classes.

30. Arendt, *Human Condition*, 80–84; Godelier, "Work and Its Representations," 171–72; Applebaum, *Concept of Work*, 3–175.
31. Lis and Soly, *Worthy Efforts*, 422.
32. In his work *De initiis, sectis et laudibus philosophiae*, Vives maintained that he did not believe "that there is any truer Christian than the Stoic sage" (III, 17), see Lorenzo Casini, "Juan Luis Vives [Joannes Ludovicus Vives]," *The Stanford Encyclopedia of Philosophy* (Spring 2017 edition), ed. Edward N. Zalta, retrieved 17 December 2017 from https://plato.stanford.edu/archives/spr2017/entries/vives/.
33. Juan Luis Vives, *De Subventione Pauperum sive De Humanis Necessitatibus, Libri II*, ed. Constant Matheeussen and Charles Fantazzi, with the assistance of Jeanine De Landtsheer, trans. Charles Fantazzi (Leiden: Brill, 2002) (Latin original and English translation). On this issue, see Robert Jütfe, "Poor Relief and Social Discipline in Sixteenth-Century Europe," *European History Quarterly* 11, no. 1 (1981): 25–52; Lis and Soly, *Worthy Efforts*, 474.
34. Lis and Soly, *Worthy Efforts*, 194.
35. Leon Battista Alberti, *I Libri della Famiglia*, ed. Alberto Tenenti and Ruggiero Romano, new edition by Francesco Furlan (Torino: Einaudi, 1994); for the English translation, see Leon Battista Alberti, *The Family in Renaissance Florence: A Translation of I Libri della Famiglia by Leon Battista Alberti*, trans. and introd. Renée Neu Watkins (Columbia: University of South Carolina Press, 1969). On this issue see Lis and Soly, *Worthy Efforts*, 257.
36. Max Weber, *Die protestantische Ethik und der Geist des Kapitalismus*, 1904–1905, English trans.: *The Protestant Ethic and the Spirit of Capitalism: With Other Writings on the Rise of the West* (New York: Oxford University Press, 2009), or *The Protestant Ethic and the Spirit of Capitalism*, trans. Talcott Parsons, with an introduction by Anthony Giddens (London: Routledge, 2001).
37. Febvre, "Travail"; Godelier, "Work and its Representations," 166; Patrick Joyce, "The Historical Meanings of Work: An Introduction," in Joyce, *Historical Meanings of Work*, 2.
38. Adriano Tilgher, *Work: What It Has Meant to Men through the Ages* (New York: Harcourt, Brace and Co., 1930), English trans. (by Dorothy Canfield Fisher) of *Homo Faber: storia del concetto di lavoro nella civiltà occidentale, analisi filosofica di concetti affini* (Roma: Libreria di scienze e lettere, 1929), 134.
39. Arendt, *Human Condition*, 4.
40. Benedicte Zimmermann, "Work and Labor: History of the Concept," *International Encyclopedia of the Social & Behavioral Sciences* 24 (2001): 16561.
41. See, from the more recent works on Marx, his biography by Gareth Stedman Jones, *Karl Marx: Greatness and Illusion* (Cambridge, MA: The Belknap Press of Harvard University Press, 2016).
42. Karl Marx, *The Economic and Philosophical Manuscripts of 1844*, trans. and ed. Martin Milligan (Mineola, NY: Dover Publications, 2007), unabridged republication of the work originally published by Moscow: Foreign Languages House, 1961, p. 72. We are grateful to Stefano Visentin and Luca Basso for their helpful suggestions on Marx.
43. Ibid., 76–77, emphasis in the original.
44. Ibid., 102.
45. Karl Marx, *Grundrisse: Foundations of the Critique of Political Economy (Rough Draft)* (1857–61), trans. Martin Nicolaus (London: Penguin Books in association with New Left Review, 1973), 625, retrieved 17 December 2017 from https://www.marxists.org/archive/marx/works/1857/grundrisse/; Karl Marx, *Capital: A Critique of Political Economy*, vol. 3: *The Process of Capitalist Production as a Whole* (1894, edited and completed by Friedrich Engels), Institute of Marxism-Leninism, URSS, 1959-New York, International Publishers, s.d., retrieved 17 December 2017 from https://www.marxists.org/archive/marx/works/1894-c3/index.htm:

In fact, the realm of freedom actually begins only where labour which is determined by necessity and mundane considerations ceases; thus in the very nature of things it lies beyond the sphere of actual material production. Just as the savage must wrestle with Nature to satisfy his wants, to maintain and reproduce life, so must civilised man, and he must do so in all social formations and under all possible modes of production. With his development this realm of physical necessity expands as a result of his wants; but, at the same time, the forces of production which satisfy these wants also increase. Freedom in this field can only consist in socialised man, the associated producers, rationally regulating their interchange with Nature, bringing it under their common control, instead of being ruled by it as by the blind forces of Nature; and achieving this with the least expenditure of energy and under conditions most favourable to, and worthy of, their human nature. But it nonetheless still remains a realm of necessity. Beyond it begins that development of human energy which is an end in itself, the true realm of freedom, which, however, can blossom forth only with this realm of necessity as its basis. The shortening of the working-day is its basic prerequisite (571).

Even though in this passage Marx associated freedom with the reduction of necessary labor, and despite the fact that he increasingly refused any essentialism, stressing the historical variability of working conditions, not only in earlier writings but also in the *Capital*, he considered labor as a crucial feature of humans. In the first volume, considering "the labour-process independently of the particular form it assumes under given social conditions," he maintained that

labour is, in the first place, a process in which both man and Nature participate, and in which man of his own accord starts, regulates, and controls the material reactions [*Stoffwechsel*, also translated with 'metabolism'] between himself and Nature. He opposes himself to Nature as one of her own forces, setting in motion arms and legs, head and hands, the natural forces of his body, in order to appropriate Nature's productions in a form adapted to his own wants. By thus acting on the external world and changing it, he at the same time changes his own nature. He develops his slumbering powers and compels them to act in obedience to his sway. We are not now dealing with those primitive instinctive forms of labour that remind us of the mere animal. An immeasurable interval of time separates the state of things in which a man brings his labour-power to market for sale as a commodity, from that state in which human labour was still in its first instinctive stage. We pre-suppose labour in a form that stamps it as exclusively human. A spider conducts operations that resemble those of a weaver, and a bee puts to shame many an architect in the construction of her cells. But what distinguishes the worst architect from the best of bees is this, that the architect raises his structure in imagination before he erects it in reality. At the end of every labour-process, we get a result that already existed in the imagination of the labourer at its commencement. He not only effects a change of form in the material on which he works, but he also realises a purpose of his own that gives the law to his modus operandi, and to which he must subordinate his will. And this subordination is no mere momentary act. Besides the exertion of the bodily organs, the process demands that, during the whole operation, the workman's will be steadily in consonance with his purpose. This means close attention. The less he is attracted by the nature of the work, and the mode in which it is carried on, and the less, therefore, he enjoys it as something which gives play to his bodily and mental powers, the more close his attention is forced to be." (Karl Marx, *Capital: A Critique of Political Economy*, vol. 1, book 1, *The Process of Production of Capital* [1867], first English edition of 1887 [fourth German edition changes included as indicated] with some modernization of spelling, translated by Samuel Moore and Edward Aveling, edited by Frederick Engels [Moscow, Progress Pub-

lishers, w.d.], retrieved 8 January 2017 from https://www.marxists.org/archive/marx/works/1867-c1/index.htm, 127)
46. Zimmermann, *Work and Labor*, 16562.
47. Dominique Méda, *Le travail: Une valeur en voie de disparition* (Paris: Aubier, 1995), 8.
48. As stressed for instance by Méda, *Le travail*, 15–16, almost paradoxically, while in the 1970s liberation from work (considered as a source of alienation) was seen as a goal by many thinkers and political activists, in the last decades growing unemployment due to different phenomena has been causing great concern and alarmed debates among policymakers, intellectuals, and ordinary people. Among the causes of such a growth, we can mention increasing productivity due to mechanization, digitalization and the internet, rapid population growth, the slowing down of economic development, financial and economic crises. On the liberation from work, see for instance André Gorz, *Paths to Paradise: On the Liberation from Work* (London: Pluto Press, 1985). For an early analysis of the crisis of labor-based societies, see Ralf Dahrendorf, "Im Entschwinden der Arbeitsgesellschaft: Wandlungen in der sozialen Konstruktion des menschlichen Lebens," *Merkur* 34, no. 8 (1980): 749–60; Joachim Matthes, ed., *Krise der Arbeitsgesellschaft? Verhandlungen des 21. Deutschen Soziologentages in Bamberg 1982* (Frankfurt: Campus, 1983); Jürgen Habermas, *The Philosophical Discourse of Modernity: Twelve Lectures*, trans. Frederick G. Lawrence (Cambridge, MA: The MIT Press, 1990), 79, original edition: *Der philosophische Diskurs der Moderne: Zwölf Vorlesungen* (Frankfurt a.M.: Suhrkamp, 1985).
49. Genesis 3:16: "I will make your pains in childbearing very severe; with painful labor you will give birth to children."
50. See the dictionaries mentioned above, notes 19–22. Marcel van der Linden ("Studying Attitudes to Work Worldwide," 26), referring to W. N. Evans, writes that "there are linguistic indications to suggest that work was originally associated with womanhood."
51. Peter Laslett, "Family and Household as Work and Kin Group: Areas of Traditional Europe Compared," in *Family Forms in Historic Europe*, ed. Richard Wall, Jean Robin, and Peter Laslett (Cambridge: Cambridge University Press, 1983), 513–63.
52. Among early studies, see for instance Jack Goody, *Production and Reproduction: A Comparative Study of the Domestic Domain* (Cambridge: Cambridge University Press, 1976); Louise A. Tilly and Joan W. Scott, *Women, Work and the Family* (New York: Holt, Rinehart and Winston, 1978). More recently, see Simonetta Cavaciocchi, ed., *La famiglia nell'economia europea, secc. XIII–XVIII, Atti delle Settimane di studio della Fondazione Istituto internazionale di Storia economica F. Datini di Prato* (Firenze: Firenze University Press, 2009). See also Bellavitis, Martini, and Sarti, *Familles laborieuses*. On the categories of productive, unproductive, and reproductive work themselves, see below and the chapters by Nancy Folbre and Alessandra Pescarolo in this book.
53. Douglas Harper, "Economy," *Online Etymology Dictionary*, retrieved 16 January 2017 from http://www.etymonline.com/index.php?term=economy.
54. See for instance the cases analyzed by Beatrice Zucca Micheletto, "Husbands, Masculinity, Male Work and Household Economy in Eighteenth-Century Italy: The Case of Turin," *Gender & History* 27, no. 3 (2015): 752–72.
55. Raffaella Sarti, *Europe at Home: Family and Material Culture, 1500–1800* (New Haven, CT: Yale University Press, 2002), 9–14, trans. (by Allan Cameron) of *Vita di casa: abitare, mangiare, vestire nell'Europa moderna* (Roma-Bari: Laterza, 1999).
56. For instance, ibid.; Sandra Cavallo, "Fatherhood and the Non-propertied Classes in Renaissance and Early Modern Italian Towns," *History of the Family* 17, no. 3 (2012): 309–25, also published in *The Power of the Fathers: Historical Perspectives from Ancient Rome to the Nineteenth Century*, ed. Margareth Lanzinger (New York: Routledge, 2015), 31–46.
57. Sarti, *Europe at Home*, 75–78; Raffaella Sarti, *Ländliche Hauslandschaften in Europa in einer Langzeitperspektive*, in *Das Haus in der Geschichte Europas: Ein Handbuch*, ed. Joachim Eibach and Inken Schmidt-Voges, together with Simone Derix, Philip Hahn, Elizabeth

Harding, Margareth Lanzinger, red. Roman Bonderer (Berlin: De Gruyter Oldenbourg, 2015), 175–94.
58. Sarti, *Europe at Home*, 95, 162–63.
59. See, for example, the case of Poland, Andrzej Karpinski, "The Woman on the Market Place: The Scale of Feminization of Retail Trade in Polish Towns in the Second Half of the 16th and the 17th Century," in *La donna nell'economia, secc. XIII-XVIII, Atti delle Settimane di studi dell'Istituto internazionale di Storia economica F. Datini di Prato*, ed. Simonetta Cavaciocchi (Firenze: Le Monnier, 1990), 283–92, and, more generally, Anne Montenach, *Espaces et pratiques du commerce alimentaire à Lyon au XVIIe siècle: l'économie du quotidien* (Grenoble: Universitaires de Grenoble, 2009); Deborah Simonton and Anne Montenach, *Female Agency in the Urban Economy: Gender in European Towns, 1640–1830* (New York: Routledge, 2013); Simonetta Cavaciocchi, ed., *Il commercio al minuto: domanda e offerta tra economia formale e informale, secc. XIII–XVIII, Atti delle Settimane di studio dell'Istituto internazionale di Storia economica F. Datini di Prato* (Firenze: Firenze University Press, 2015); Melissa Calaresu and Danielle van den Heuvel, eds., *Food Hawkers: Selling in the Streets from Antiquity to the Present* (New York: Routledge, 2016).
60. Melissa Calaresu and Danielle van den Heuvel, "Introduction: Food Hawkers from Representation to Reality," in Calaresu and van der Heuvel, *Food Hawkers*, 1–18: "A variety of 'street luxuries' were available on the streets to serve poor and rich alike" (2).
61. Otto Brunner, "Das 'Ganze Haus' und die alteuropäische 'Ökonomik,'" in Otto Brunner, *Neue Wege der Verfassungs- und Sozialgeschichte* (Göttingen: Vandenhoeck & Ruprecht, 1968, 2nd edition), 103–27 (an important but in our view correctly criticized essay); Daniela Frigo, *Il padre di famiglia: governo della casa e governo civile nella tradizione dell'"economica" tra Cinque e Seicento* (Roma-Bari: Bulzoni, 1985); Karen Harvey, *The Little Republic: Masculinity and Domestic Authority in Eighteenth-Century Britain* (Oxford: Oxford University Press, 2012); Raffaella Sarti, *Servo e padrone, o della (in)dipendenza: un percorso da Aristotele ai nostri giorni*, vol. I: *Teorie e dibattiti*, Series "Quaderni" of *Scienza & Politica*, Quaderno no. 2 (2015) (Bologna: Alma Mater Studiorum Università di Bologna, 2015), 48–64, open-access e-book available at http://amsacta.unibo.it/4293/1/Sarti_Servo_e_Padrone_1.pdf. Retrieved 17 December 2017.
62. Mauro Ambrosoli and Lorenzo Ornaghi, "Il Padre di famiglia," *Quaderni storici* 22, no. 64 (1987): 223–32.
63. This does not mean that nobles interested in manual work were absent. Lis and Soly (*Worthy Efforts*, 205), for instance, report that Gervase Markham, the son of a country gentleman and author of several books—the best known of which is *The English Huswife* (London: Roger Jackson, 1615)—spent several years living as a husbandman among husbandmen.
64. See note 61.
65. In addition to the texts mentioned in the following notes, see for instance Amanda Flather, "Space, Place, and Gender: The Sexual and Spatial Division of Labor in the Early Modern Household," *History and Theory* 52, no. 3 (2013): 344–60.
66. Carmen Sarasúa, "Leaving Home to Help the Family? Male and Female Temporary Migrants in Eighteenth- and Nineteenth-Century Spain," in *Women, Gender and Labour Migration: Historical and Global Perspectives*, ed. Pamela Sharpe (New York: Routledge, 2001), 29–59; Jane Potter, "Valliant Heroines or Pacific Ladies? Women in War and Peace," in *The Routledge History of Women*, ed. Deborah Simonton (New York: Routledge 2006), 259–98; Bridget Hill, *Women Alone: Spinsters in England, 1660–1850* (New Haven, CT: Yale University Press, 2001), 136–41.
67. The bibliography on women and guilds is large and dominated by the so-called "decline thesis": for a critical update on this debate, see Clare Crowston, "Women, Gender and Guilds in Early Modern Europe: An Overview of Recent Research," in *The Return of the Guilds*, ed. Jan Lucassen, Tine De Moor, and Jan Luiten van Zanden, supplement of *International Review of Social History* 53 (2008): 19–44. More generally, on women's work

in Early Modern Europe, see Anna Bellavitis, *Il lavoro delle donne nelle città dell'Europa moderna* (Roma: Viella, 2016).
68. Lucrezia Marinella, *La nobiltà et l'eccellenza delle donne, co' difetti et mancamenti de gli huomini*, 2nd ed. (Venezia: Gio. Battista Ciotti, 1601), 88–89 ("Le villanelle si adoprano ne gli essercitij rusticali, et in tutte quelle fatiche, che gli huomini altresì fanno. Nelle Cittadi quante opere laboriose sono fatte da loro? Infinite certo, et veggiamo notte, et giorno con grandissima patienza, et gran fatica"). The work has been translated into English: *The Nobility and Excellence of Women, and the Defects and Vices of Men*, ed. and trans. Anne Dunhill (Chicago: University of Chicago Press, 1999).
69. Alexandra Shepard, *Accounting for Oneself: Worth, Status, and the Social Order in Early Modern England* (Oxford: Oxford University Press, 2015), 257 (wives "were charged with managing, saving, and increasing household assets—and it is possible that these tasks, encompassed within the skills lumped together as 'housewifery,' lent an occupational dimension to the term 'wife,' which tends to be overlooked in approaches to marriage predominantly as a *legal* status determined by coverture. The logic that matched husbandry with housewifery extended to couples with means as well as those without"). See also Alexandra Shepard, "Crediting Women in the Early Modern English Economy," *History Workshop Journal* 79, no. 1 (2015): 1–24.
70. Frigo, *Il Padre di Famiglia*, 161–64; Shepard, "Crediting Women," 16.
71. Martha C. Howell, "The Gender of Europe's Commercial Economy, 1200–1700," *Gender & History* 20, no. 3 (2008): 519–38; Martha C. Howell, *Commerce before Capitalism in Europe, 1300–1600* (Cambridge: Cambridge University Press, 2010).
72. Genovesi may have overgeneralized the managerial responsibilities of middle-class Italian women; see Sarti, *Europe at Home*, 218.
73. Antonio Genovesi, *Lezioni di Commercio o sia di Economia Civile* (1765–67; Bassano: Remondini, 1769), 338.
74. Rebecca Rogers, "Learning to Be Good Girls and Women: Education, Training and Schools," in Simonton, *Routledge History of Women*, 93–133.
75. Corine Maitte, "Le travail invisible dans les familles artisanales (XVIIe–XVIIIe siècles)," *Mélanges de l'École française de Rome—Italie et Méditerranée modernes et contemporaines* 128, no. 1 (2016): retrieved 17 December 2017 from https:// mefrim.revues.org/2366; Juanjo Romero-Martín, "Craftswomen in Times of Change: Artisan Family Strategies in Nineteenth Century Barcelona," Ibid., http://mefrim.revues.org/2445; Bellavitis, *Il lavoro delle donne*, 91–92.
76. On noblewomen, see for instance Amanda Vickery, *The Gentleman's Daughter: Women's Lives in Georgian England* (New Haven, CT: Yale University Press, 1999), esp. 141–80; Jane Whittle and Elizabeth Griffiths, *Consumption and Gender in the Early Seventeenth-Century Household: The World of Alice Le Strange* (Oxford: Oxford University Press, 2012).
77. Paul Grendler, *Schooling in Renaissance Italy: Literacy and Learning, 1300–1600* (Baltimore: The Johns Hopkins University Press, 1989); Sara Mendelson and Patricia Crawford, *Women in Early Modern England 1550–1720* (Oxford: Clarendon Press, 1998); Elizabeth Harding, *Der Gelehrte im Haus: Ehe, Familie und Haushalt in der Standeskultur der frühneuzeitlichen Universität Helmstedt* (Wiesbaden: Harrassowitz Verlag, 2014); Elizabeth Harding, "The Early Modern German Professor at Home—Masculinity, Bachelorhood and Family Concepts (Sixteenth–Eighteenth Centuries)," in "Men at Home: Domesticities, Authority, Emotions and Work," ed. Raffaella Sarti, special issue of *Gender & History* 27, no. 3 (2015): 736–51.
78. Janine M. Lanza, "Les veuves d'artisans dans le Paris du XVIIIe siècle," and Daryl M. Hafter, "Les veuves dans les corporations de Rouen sous l'Ancien Régime," in *Veufs, veuves et veuvage dans la France d'Ancien Régime*, Actes du Colloque de Poitiers (11–12 juin 1998), Textes réunis par Nicole Pellegrin, présentés et édités par Colette H. Winn (Paris: Honoré Champion, 2003), respectively 109–20 and 121–33; Janine M. Lanza, *From*

Wives to Widows in Early Modern Paris: Gender, Economy, and Law (Aldershot-Burlington: Ashgate, 2007); Ariadne Schmidt, "Women and Guilds: Corporations and Female Labour Market Participation in Early Modern Holland," *Gender & History* 21, no. 1 (2009): 170–89; Sabine Juratic, "Marchandes ou savantes? Les veuves des libraires parisiens sous le règne de Louis XIV," in *Femmes savantes, savoirs des femmes*, ed. Colette Nativel (Genève: Droz, 1999), 59–68; Deborah L. Simonton, "Widows and Wenches: Single Women in Eighteenth-Century Urban Economies," in Simonton and Montenach, *Female Agency*, 3–115; Jane McLeod, "Printer Widows and the State in Eighteenth-Century France," in *Women and Work in Eighteenth-Century France*, ed. Daryl M. Hafter and Nina Kushner (Baton Rouge: Louisiana State University Press, 2015), 113–29; Bellavitis, *Il lavoro delle donne*, 93–96, 122–26.

79. Quotation from Sheilagh Ogilvie, "How Does Social Capital Affect Women? Guilds and Communities in Early Modern Germany," *American Historical Review* 109, no. 2 (2004): 340. On these issues, see for instance Olwen Hufton, "Women without Men: Widows and Spinsters in Britain and France in the Eighteenth Century," *Journal of Family History* 9, no. 4 (1984): 355–76 (highlighting the consequences of economic crises on single women); Maura Palazzi, *Donne sole: storie dell'altra faccia dell'Italia tra antico regime e società contemporanea* (Milano: Bruno Mondadori, 1997); Sandra Cavallo and Lyndan Warner, eds., *Widowhood in Medieval and Early Modern Europe* (Harlow: Longman, 1999); Manon van der Heijden, Ariadne Schmidt, and Richard Wall, eds., "Broken Families: Economic Resources and Social Networks of Women Who Head Families," special issue of *History of the Family* 12, no. 4 (2007).

80. For instance, Tilly and Scott, *Women, Work and the Family*; Natalie Zemon Davis, "Women in the Crafts in Sixteenth-Century Lyon," *Feminist Studies* 8, no. 1 (1982): 46–80.

81. Merry E. Wiesner, "Guilds, Male Bonding and Women's Work in Early Modern Germany," *Gender & History* 1, no. 2 (1989): 25–137; Merry E. Wiesner, "Wandervogels Women: Journeymen's Concepts of Masculinity in Early Modern Germany," *Journal of Social History* 24, no. 4 (1991): 767–82; John Tosh, *A Man's Place: Masculinity and the Middle-Class Home in Victorian England* (New Haven, CT: Yale University Press, 1999); Sandra Cavallo, "Bachelorhood and Masculinity in Renaissance and Early Modern Italy," *European History Quarterly* 38, no.3 (2008): 375–97; Sarti, "Men at Home"; Lanzinger, *Power of the Fathers*.

82. Shepard, "Crediting Women," 5; Jane Whittle, "Enterprising Widows and Active Wives: Women's Unpaid Work in the Household Economy of Early Modern England," *History of the Family* 9, no. 3 (2014): 283–300; Ariadne Schmidt, Isabelle Devos, and Bruno Blondé, "Introduction: Single and the City; Men and Women Alone in North-Western European Towns since the Late Middle Ages," in *Single Life and the City*, ed. Isabelle Devos, Julie De Groot, and Ariadne Schmidt (New York: Palgrave Macmillan, 2015), 1–24.

83. Shepard, *Accounting for Oneself*.

84. As written as early as 1984 by Marzio Barbagli referring to Italy: "From the fourteenth century onwards, the majority of urban population after marriage followed the neolocal residence rule and spent large part of their family lives in nuclear households"; see *Sotto lo stesso tetto: mutamenti della famiglia in Italia dal XV al XX secolo* (Bologna: Il Mulino, 1984), 238.

85. For instance Carlo Poni, "La famiglia contadina e il podere in Emilia Romagna," in Carlo Poni, *Fossi e cavedagne benedicon le campagne* (Bologna: Il Mulino, 1982), 283–356; Pier Paolo Viazzo, "What's So Special about the Mediterranean? Thirty Years of Research on Household and Family in Italy," *Continuity and Change* 18, no. 1 (2003): 111–37.

86. See notes 54–60.

87. Raffaella Sarti, "Who Are Servants? Defining Domestic Service in Western Europe (16th–21st Centuries)," in *Proceedings of the Servant Project*, ed. Suzy Pasleau and Isabelle Schopp, with Raffaella Sarti (Liège: Éditions de l'Université de Liège, 2005), 2: 3–59, retrieved 17 December 2017 from http://www.uniurb.it/sarti/Raffaella_Sarti_Who_are_

servants_Proceedings_of_the_Servant_Project.pdf; Raffaella Sarti, "Criados rurales: el caso de Italia desde una perspectiva comparada (siglos XVI al XX)," *Mundo Agrario* 18, no. 39 (2017), e065-e065: 1–32, https://doi.org/10.24215/15155994e065; Raffaella Sarti, "Rural Life-Cycle Service: Established Interpretations and New (Surprising) Data: The Italian Case in Comparative Perspective (Sixteenth to Twentieth Centuries)," in *Servants in Rural Europe, c. 1400–1900*, ed. Jane Whittle (Woodbridge: Boydell & Brewer, 2017), 227–254, all with further references.

88. Manon van der Heijden and Danielle van den Heuvel, "Sailors' Families and the Urban Institutional Framework in Early Modern Holland," *History of the Family* 12, no. 4 (2007): 296–309.
89. Danielle van den Heuvel, "Partners in Marriage and Business? Guilds and the Family Economy in Urban Food Markets in the Dutch Republic," *Continuity and Change* 23, no. 2 (2008): 217–36; Danielle van den Heuvel and Elise van Nederveen Meerkerk, "Households, Work and Consumer Changes: The Case of Tea and Coffee Sellers in 18th-Century Leiden," *Mems Working Papers* (2014); Andrea Caracausi, "Beaten Children and Women's Work in Early Modern Italy," *Past & Present*, no. 222 (2014): 95–128; Zucca Micheletto, "Husbands, Masculinity"; Hafter and Kushner, *Women and Work*.
90. Elisabeth Musgrave, "Women and the Craft Guilds in Eighteenth-Century Nantes," in *The Artisan and the European Town, 1500–1900*, ed. Geoffrey Crossick (Aldershot-Burlington: Ashgate, 1997), 151–71.
91. For instance, Tine De Moor and Jan Luiten Van Zanden, "Girl Power: The European Marriage Pattern and Labour Markets in the North Sea Region in the Late Medieval and Early Modern Period," *Economic History Review* 63, no. 1 (2010): 1–33; Tracy Dennison and Sheilagh Ogilvie, "Does the European Marriage Pattern Explain Economic Growth?," *Journal of Economic History* 74, no. 3 (2014): 651–93; Beatrice Zucca Micheletto, "Reconsidering the Southern Europe Model: Dowry, Women's Work and Marriage Patterns in Pre-Industrial Urban Italy (Turin, Second Half of the 18th Century)," *History of the Family* 16, no. 4 (2011): 354–70; Simonton, "Widows and Wenches."
92. In this book we have chosen to focus on commonalities and historical change more than on differences among regions. This does not mean, however, that we undervalue geographical diversity, rather the contrary.
93. Moderata Fonte [= Modesta Pozzo or Dal Pozzo], *Il Merito delle Donne: . . . ; Ove chiaramente si scuopre quanto siano elle degne, e più perfette degli huomini* (Venetia: Domenico Imberti, 1600), 24, 52–53, 114; for the English translation see: *The Worth of Women: Wherein is Clearly Revealed their Nobility and Their Superiority to Men*, ed. and trans. Virginia Cox (Chicago: University of Chicago Press, 1997); François Poullain [or Poulain de la Barre], *De l'égalité des deux sexes, discours physique et moral où l'on voit l'importance de se défaire des préjugez* (Paris: Jean du Puis, 1673), 89 and passim. The first English translation is the following: *The Woman as Good as the Man: Or, The Equality of Both Sexes*, trans. A. L. (London: N. Brooks, 1677); a recent one is included in the volume *The Equality of the Sexes: Three Feminist Texts of the Seventeenth Century*, trans. Desmond M. Clarke (Oxford: Oxford University Press, 2013). Shepard (*Accounting for Oneself*, 193–94) found that husbands generally did not mention any dependency on the work of their wives when they explained how they supported themselves. Stimulating insights on the ways men perceived their role in early modern Germany in David W. Sabean, *Property, Production, and Family in Neckarhausen, 1700–1870* (Cambridge: Cambridge University Press, 1990), 117–18.
94. Ehmer, "Work, History of," 16570.
95. Quotation taken from the particularly extensive entry "Labor Theory of Value," Wikipedia, retrieved August 2016 from https://en.wikipedia.org/wiki/Labor_theory_of_value.
96. Thomas Hobbes, *Leviathan* (1651), *Of the Nutrition and Procreation of a Commonwealth*, chapter XXIV, eBooks@Adelaide, University of Adelaide Library, retrieved 17 December 2017 from https://ebooks.adelaide.edu.au/h/hobbes/thomas/h68l/.

97. Antimo Negri, "Per una storia del concetto di lavoro nella cultura filosofica ed economica occidentale," in *Il lavoro come fattore produttivo e come risorsa nella storia economica,* ed. Sergio Zaninelli and Mario Taccolini (Milano: Vita e Pensiero, 2002), xiv–xv.
98. Ehmer, "Work, History of," 16570.
99. Ibid.
100. Tilgher, *Homo Faber*; Lis and Soly, *Worthy Efforts,* 14, 318, 322.
101. For instance, Gianna Pomata, "La storia delle donne: una questione di confine," in *Il mondo contemporaneo,* ed. Giovanni De Luna, Peppino Ortoleva, Marco Revelli, and Nicola Tranfaglia, vol. 10: *Gli strumenti della ricerca,* 2, *Questioni di metodo**,* pt. 2 (Firenze: La Nuova Italia, 1983), 1434–69; Carole Pateman, *The Sexual Contract* (Stanford: Stanford University Press, 1988).
102. Joyce, *Historical Meanings of Work*; Kocka, "Work as a Problem"; Karin Hausen, "Work in Gender, Gender in Work: The German Case in Comparative Perspective," in Kocka, *Work in a Modern Society,* 73–92; Josef Ehmer, "Work, History of," and Zimmermann, "Work and Labor."
103. Kocka, "Work as a Problem," 3. See also Keith Thomas, *The Oxford Book of Work* (Oxford: Oxford University Press, 1999), xiv, who states that in the eighteenth century work was an activity having "an end beyond itself, being designed to produce something," and was associated to a market value.
104. Leone Porciani, "Schiavi pubblici ad Atene: per una discussione sul rapporto fra amministrazione e politica," in *Revisiter l'esclavage ancien: méthodologies et nouvelles approches critiques,* forthcoming. We are grateful to the author for allowing us to read and quote his still unpublished essay; Leone Porciani, "Appunti sulla schiavitù greca: il caso dei *dēmosioi* ad Atene," in *Nuove e antiche forme di schiavitù,* ed. Mauro Simonazzi and Thomas Casadei (Napoli: Editoriale Scientifica, 2018), 37.
105. Zimmermann, "Work and Labor," 16562.
106. Kocka, "Work as a Problem," 8.
107. Adam Smith, *An Inquiry into the Nature and Causes of the Wealth of Nations* (1776), book II, chapter III, "Of the Accumulation of Capital, or of Productive and Unproductive Labour," II.3.1, retrieved 16 July 2018 from https://www.econlib.org/library/Smith/smWN.html?chapter_num=18#book-reader.
108. Ibid., 2.
109. Ibid.
110. Ibid., 1.
111. Ibid., book I, chapter II, "Of the Principle which Gives Occasion to the Division of Labour," in *The Wealth of Nations,* I.2.2, retrieved 16 July 2018 from https://www.econlib.org/library/Smith/smWN.html?chapter_num=5#book-reader.
112. Nancy Folbre, *Greed, Lust and Gender: A History of Economic Ideas* (Oxford: Oxford University Press, 2009), 59.
113. See Folbre's article in this volume.
114. The quotation is taken from the English translation of Hobbes's *De Cive*; see *On the Citizen,* ed. and trans. Richard Tuck and Michael Silverthorne (1998; Cambridge: Cambridge University Press, 2003), 102.
115. For instance, Marx, *Capital,* vol. 1, book 1, *The Process of Production of Capital,* pt. 5, *Production of Absolute and Relative Surplus-Value,* chap. 16, "Absolute and Relative Surplus-Value," 359: "That labourer alone is productive, who produces surplus-value for the capitalist, and thus works for the self-expansion of capital."
116. Jean Baptiste Say, *Traité d'économie politique, ou simple exposition de la manière dont se forment, se distribuent et se consomment les richesses,* cinquième édition, tome I (Paris: Rapilly, 1826), 145.
117. Rhacel Salazar Parreñas, "Migrant Filipina Domestic Workers and the International Division of Reproductive Labor," *Gender & Society* 14, no. 4 (2000): 560–80; Barbara Ehren-

reich and Arlie Russell Hochschild, eds., *Global Woman: Nannies, Maids, and Sex Workers in the New Economy* (New York: Macmillan, 2003); Rhacel Salazar Parreñas, "The International Division of Reproductive Labor: Paid Domestic Work and Globalization," in *Critical Globalization Studies*, ed. Richard P. Applebaum and William I. Robinson (New York: Routledge, 2005), 237–47; Nicola Yeates, "Changing Places: Ireland in the International Division of Reproductive Labour," *Translocations: The Irish Migration, Race and Social Transformation Review* 1, no. 1 (2006): 5–21; Eileen Boris and Rhacel Salazar Parreñas, eds., *Intimate Labors: Culture, Technologies and the Politics of Care* (Stanford, CA: Stanford University Press, 2010); Manoela Carpenedo and Henrique Caetano Nardi, "Brazilian Women in the International Division of Reproductive Work: Constructing Subjectivities," *Revista de Estudios Sociales* 45 (2013): 96–109; Ester Gallo and Francesca Scrinzi, "Introduction: Men and Masculinities in the International Division of Reproductive Labour," in *Migration, Masculinities and Reproductive Labour*, ed. Ester Gallo and Francesca Scrinzi (London: Palgrave Macmillan, 2016), 1–36.

118. In addition to the previous note, see Rhacel Salazar Parreñas, *Servants of Globalization: Migration and Domestic Work*, 2nd ed. (2001, with the subtitle *Women, Migration and Domestic Work* [Stanford: Stanford University Press, 2015]).

119. Actually, this is the case today, too: in 2014, Greece and Italy had the lowest and second lowest female employment rates respectively; see Eurostat, Employment Statistics, August 2015, retrieved 5 November 2016 from http://ec.europa.eu/eurostat/statistics-explained/index.php/Employment_statistics.

120. See note 117; Sarti's chapter in this book; and Raffaella Sarti, "Open Houses versus Closed Borders: Migrant Domestic Workers in Italy; A Gendered Perspective (1950s–2010s)," in *Gender and Migration in Italy: A Multilayered Perspective*, ed. Elisa Olivito (Farnham-Burlington: Ashgate, 2016), 39–59.

121. Christine Delphy, "Un féminisme matérialiste est possible," *Nouvelles Questions Féministes* 4 (Fall 1982) 50–86, originally published as "A Materialist Feminism is Possible," *Feminist Review*, No. 4, 1980, 79–105, trans. Diana Leonard; Christine Delphy and Diana Leonard, *Familiar Exploitation: A New Analysis of Marriage in Contemporary Western Societies* (Oxford: Polity Press, 1992); Christine Delphy, *L'ennemi principal* (Tome 1): *économie politique du patriarcat* (Paris: Syllepse, 1998); and Christine Delphy, *L'ennemi principal* (Tome 2): *penser le genre* (Paris: Syllepse, 2001).

122. "Ainsi il est clair que la non-reconnaissance de la division sexuelle dans l'analyse du Capital n'empêche nullement l'application de concepts matérialistes à l'oppression des femmes"; Delphy, "Un féminisme matérialiste est possible," 62; English version, "A Materialist Feminism is Possible," 87: "It is therefore clear that the non-recognition of sexual division in the analysis of *Capital* in no way prevents the application of materialist concepts to the oppression of women."

123. Delphy, "A Materialist Feminism is Possible," 87. French version, "Un féminisme matérialiste est possible," 62: "En effet, il ne s'agit pas tant d'une non-reconnaissance que d'une non-problématisatisation."

124. Karl Marx, *Theories of Surplus-Value* (1863) (Moscow, Progress Publishers, w.d.), 300, retrieved 17 December 2017 from https://www.marxists.org/archive/marx/works/1863/theories-surplus-value/ch04.htm; Ian Gough, "Marx's Theory of Productive and Unproductive Labour," *New Left Review* 1, no. 76 (1972): 47–72.

125. On the collective, see the chapters by Alessandra Pescarolo and Alessandra Gissi in this volume.

126. Selma James, "Introduction," in Dalla Costa and James, *Power of Women* (third edition), 10–11 (describing Dalla Costa ideas). "It is no accident that the Dalla Costa article has come from Italy. First of all because so few women in Italy have jobs outside the home, the housewife's position seems frozen," James wrote (14). A second reason, according to James, was that "the working class there has a unique history of struggle" (15).

127. Ibid., 11, emphasis in the original. On these issues, see also Maud A. Bracke, "Between the Transnational and the Local: Mapping the Trajectories and Contexts of the Wages for Housework Campaign in 1970s Italian Feminism," *Women's History Review* 22, no. 4 (2013): 625–42.
128. Mariarosa Dalla Costa and Selma James, *Potere femminile e sovversione sociale, con "Il posto della donna" di Selma James* (Padova: Marsilio, 1972); Dalla Costa and James, *Power of Women*. See the *Archivio di Lotta Femminista per il salario al lavoro domestico, Donazione Mariarosa Dalla Costa* (Archive of Lotta Femminista [Feminist Struggle] for wages for housework, Donation by Mariarosa Dalla Costa), retrieved 17 December 2017 from www.padovanet.it/sites/default/files/attachment/C_1_Allegati_20187_Allegato.pdf.
129. Foreword to the third edition of Dalla Costa and James, *Power of Women*, 3.
130. Ibid.
131. *Archivio di Lotta Femminista*, 3.
132. *The International Wages for Housework Campaign*, undated flyer, retrieved 17 December 2017 from http://freedomarchives.org/Documents/Finder/DOC500_scans/500.020.Wages.for.Housework.pdf.
133. Antonella Picchio, *Social Reproduction: The Political Economy of the Labour Market* (Cambridge: Cambridge University Press, 1992).
134. Christine Frederick, *The New Housekeeping: Efficiency Studies in Home Management* (Garden City, NY: Doubleday, Page & Company, 1913); Christine Frederick, *Household Engineering: The Scientific Management in the Home* (Chicago: American School of Home Economics, 1919).
135. Louise Toupin, *Le salaire au travail ménager: Chronique d'une lutte féministe internationale (1972–1977)* (Montréal: Éditions du Remue-Ménage, 2014), 102.
136. Silvia Federici, *Wages Against Housework* (Bristol: Power of Women Collective and Falling Wall Press, 1975), 2–3.
137. For instance, Gisela Bock and Barbara Duden, "Arbeit aus Liebe—Liebe als Arbeit: Zur Entstehung der Hausarbeit im Kapitalismus," in *Frauen und Wissenschaft. Beiträge zur Berliner Sommeruniversität für Frauen, Juli 1976*, edited by Gruppe Berliner Dozentinnen (Berlin: Courage Verlag, 1977), 118–99. Much later, work (*Arbeit*) and love (*Liebe*) were also the focuses of the posthumous book by Edith Saurer, *Liebe und Arbeit: Geschlechterbeziehungen im 19. und 20. Jahrhundert*, ed. Margareth Lanzinger (Wien-Köln-Weimar: Böhlau, 2014).
138. Betty Friedan, *The Feminine Mystique* (New York: W. W. Norton and Co., 1963).
139. Think, for instance, of the interest in witches and witch-hunting by nonprofessional historians such as Barbara Ehrenreich and Deirdre English, authors of *Witches, Midwives, and Nurses: Complaints and Disorders* (New York: Feminist Press, 1973), and Luisa Muraro, author of *La signora del gioco: episodi di caccia alle streghe* (Milano: Feltrinelli, 1976).
140. In 1960, for instance, Philippe Ariès suggested that even the parental love for children was a historical phenomenon whose advent could be placed around the seventeenth century; his conclusions were not confirmed by later research but prompted a lively debate lasting for decades; see Philippe Ariès, *L'enfant et la vie familiale sous l'ancien régime* (Paris: Plon, 1960), Engl. transl. *Centuries of Childhood: A Social History of Family Life*, trans. Robert Baldick, London: Jonathan Cape, 1962).
141. For instance: Natalie Zemon Davis, "'Women's History' in Transition: The European Case," *Feminist Studies* 3, nos. 3–4 (1976): 83–103; Pomata, "La storia delle donne." For a useful survey of the first studies also stressing the implications of the notion of separate spheres for the development of a more interpretative and less *evenementiel* historical approach, see Linda K. Kerber, "Separate Spheres, Female Worlds, Woman's Place: The Rhetoric of Women's History," *Journal of American History* 75, no. 1 (1988): 9–39.

142. Amanda Vickery, "Golden Age to Separate Spheres? A Review of the Categories and Chronology of English Women's History," *Historical Journal* 36, no. 2 (1993): 383–414; Kathryn Gleadle, "Revisiting Family Fortunes: Reflections on the Twentieth Anniversary of the Publication of L. Davidoff & C. Hall (1987) *Family Fortunes: Men and Women of the English Middle Class, 1780–1850* (London: Hutchinson)," *Women's History Review* 16, no. 5 (2007): 773–82; Susie Steinbach, "Can We Still Use 'Separate Spheres'? British History 25 Years after *Family Fortunes*," *History Compass* 10711 (2012): 826–37.
143. Leonore Davidoff and Catherine Hall, *Family Fortunes: Men and Women of the English Middle Class, 1780–1850* (London: Hutchinson, 1987), 279. A revised edition was published in 2002 by Routledge.
144. Tosh, *A Man's Place*. See also Sarti, "Men at Home."
145. Marx, *Economic and Philosophical Manuscripts of 1844*, 72.
146. Davidoff and Hall, *Family Fortunes*, 272.
147. Ibid.; Alice Clark, *Working Life of Women in the Seventeenth Century* (New York: George Routledge & Sons-Button & Co., 1919; London: Routledge & K. Paul, 1982); Maxine Berg, "The First Women Economic Historians," *Economic History Review* 45, no. 2 (1992): 308–29.
148. See, for an overview of the "decline thesis," Crowston, "Women, Gender and Guilds."
149. Clark, *Working Life of Women*.
150. Ivy Pinchbeck, *Women Workers and the Industrial Revolution, 1750–1850* (New York: Frank Cass, 1977; first edition, London: George Routledge, 1930), 4. For a discussion, see Joyce Burnette, "A Pioneer in Women's History: Ivy Pinchbeck's *Women Workers and the Industrial Revolution, 1750–1850*," retrieved 17 December 2017 from http://www.eh.net/?s=women+workers+and+the+industrial+revolution.
151. Merry E. Wiesner, *Working Women in Renaissance Germany* (New Brunswick, NJ: Rutgers University Press, 1986); Merry E. Wiesner, *Gender and the Worlds of Work*, in *Germany: A New Social and Economic History*, vol. 1, *1450–1630*, ed. Bob Scribner (New York: Arnold, 1996), 209–32.
152. Marta C. Howell, *Women, Production, and Patriarchy in Late Medieval Cities* (Chicago: University of Chicago Press, 1986); Martha C. Howell, "Citizenship and Gender: Women's Political Status in Northern Medieval Cities," in *Women and Power in the Middle Ages*, ed. Mary Erler and Marianne Kowaleski (Athens, GA: University of Georgia Press, 1988), 37–60.
153. Sheilagh Ogilvie, *A Bitter Living: Women, Markets, and Social Capital in Early Modern Germany* (Oxford: Oxford University Press, 2003).
154. Daryl M. Hafter, *Women and Work in Preindustrial France* (University Park: The Pennsylvania State University Press, 2007); Anna Bellavitis, Virginie Jourdain, Virginie Lemonnier-Lesage, Beatrice Zucca Micheletto, eds., *"Tout ce qu'elle saura et pourra faire": Femmes, droits, travail en Normandie du Moyen Âge à la Grande guerre* (Mont-Saint-Aignan: Presses Universitaires de Rouen et du Havre, 2015).
155. Clare Crowston, *Fabricating Women: The Seamstresses of Old Regime France, 1675–1791* (Durham, NC: Duke University Press, 2001).
156. Angela Groppi, *Une ressource légale pour une pratique illégale: les juifs et les femmes contre la corporation des tailleurs dans la Rome pontificale (XVIIe–XVIIIe siècles)*, in *The Value of the Norm/Il valore delle norme*, ed. Renata Ago (Roma: Biblink, 2002), 137–62.
157. Angela Groppi, ed., *Il lavoro delle donne* (Roma-Bari: Laterza, 1996); Marcello Della Valentina, "Il setificio salvato dalle donne: le tessitrici veneziane nel Settecento," in *Spazi, poteri, diritti delle donne a Venezia in età moderna*, ed. Anna Bellavitis, Nadia Maria Filippini, and Tiziana Plebani (Verona: QuiEdit, 2012), 321–35; Bellavitis, *Il lavoro delle donne*.
158. Franklin Mendels, "Proto-industrialization: The First Phase of the Industrialization Process," *Journal of Economic History* 32, no. 1 (1972): 241–61; Peter Kriedte, Hans

Medick, Jürgen Schlumbohm, with contributions by Herbert Kisch and Franklin F. Mendels, *Industrialisierung vor der Industrialisierung: Gewerbliche Warenproduktion auf dem Land in der Formationsperiode des Kapitalismus* (Göttingen: Vandenhoeck und Ruprecht, 1977), English translation: Beate Schempp, *Industrialization before Industrialization: Rural Industry in the Genesis of Capitalism* (Cambridge: Cambridge University Press; Paris: Editions de la Maison des Sciences de l'Homme, 1981).

159. Jan De Vries, "The Industrial Revolution and the Industrious Revolution," *Journal of Economic History* 54, no. 2 (1994): 249–70; Jan De Vries, *The Industrious Revolution: Consumer Behavior and the Household Economy, 1650 to the Present* (Cambridge: Cambridge University Press, 2008).

160. For instance, the need, for many people, to wait until they inherited a farm before marrying.

161. Jürgen Schlumbohm, *Lebensläufe, Familien, Höfe: die Bauern und Heuerleute des Osnabrückischen Kirchspiels Belm in proto-industrieller Zeit, 1650–1860* (Göttingen: Vandenhoeck & Ruprecht, 1994); Hans Medick, *Weben und Überleben in Laichingen 1650–1900: Lokalgeschichte als allgemeine Geschichte* (Göttingen: Vandenhoeck & Ruprecht, 1996).

162. De Vries, *Industrious Revolution*, xi, on Akira Hayami's inspiring role.

163. Sara Horrell and Jane Humphries, "Women's Labour Force Participation and the Transition to the Male-Breadwinner Family, 1790–1865," *Economic History Review* 48, no. 1 (1995): 89–117; Jane Humphries and Carmen Sarasúa, "Off the Record: Reconstructing Women's Labor Force Participation in the European Past," *Feminist Economics* 18, no. 4 (2012): 39–67.

164. See note 159.

165. Gregory Clark and Ysbrand Van Der Werf, "Work in Progress? The Industrious Revolution," *Journal of Economic History* 58, no. 3 (1998): 830–43.

166. Robert C. Allen and Jacob Louis Weisdorf, "Was there an 'Industrious Revolution' before the Industrial Revolution? An Empirical Exercise for England, c. 1300–1830," *Economic History Review* 64, no. 3 (2011): 715–29.

167. Sheilagh Ogilvie, "Consumption, Social Capital, and the 'Industrious Revolution' in Early Modern Germany," *Journal of Economic History* 70, no. 2 (2010): 287–325.

168. See http://www.nwo.nl/en/research-and-results/research-projects/i/01/201.html, last accessed on 17 December 2017.

169. Elise van Nederveen Meerkerk, "Segmentation in the Pre-Industrial Labour Market: Women's Work in the Dutch Textile Industry, 1581–1810," *International Review of Social History* 51, no. 2 (2006): 189–216; Elise van Nederveen Meerkerk, "Couples Cooperating? Dutch TextileWorkers, Family Labour and the 'Industrious Revolution,' c. 1600–1800," *Continuity and Change* 23, no. 2 (2008): 237–66; Elise van Nederveen Meerkerk and Ariadne Schmidt, "Reconsidering the 'First Male Breadwinner Economy': Long-Term Trends in Female Labor Force Participation in the Netherlands, c. 1600–1900," *Feminist Economics* 18, no. 4 (2012): 69–96.

170. Danielle van den Heuvel and Elise van Nederveen Meerkerk, "Introduction: Partners in Business? Spousal Cooperation in Trades in Early Modern England and the Dutch Republic," *Continuity and Change* 23, no. 2 (2008): 209–16.

171. Van Nederveen Meerkerk, "Couples Cooperating?; Amy Louise Erickson, "Married Women's Occupations in Eighteenth-Century London," *Continuity and Change* 23, no. 2 (2008): 267–307.

172. Van den Heuvel, "Partners in Marriage and Business?"

173. Ibid.; van den Heuvel and van Nederveen Meerkerk, "Introduction: Partners in Marriage and Business?," 212.

174. Van den Heuvel and van Nederveen Meerkerk, "Households, Work and Consumer Changes." The paper is based on a dataset of "831 individuals who held a permit to sell tea, coffee and chocolate in the Dutch city of Leiden during the long eighteenth-century."

Women made up 56.6 percent of new tea and coffee sellers in the first half of the century, 80 percent in the second half. Among women, married ones grew from 60 percent in the first half of the century to 77 percent after the 1750s.
175. De Vries, *Industrious Revolution*, 122.
176. Neil McKendrick, John Brewer, and J. H. Plumb, *The Birth of a Consumer Society: The Commercialization of Eighteenth-Century England* (London: Europa Publications Limited, 1982), 9. As many other scholars, we, too, believe that consumption grew over a long time span rather than experiencing a sudden revolution; see Sarti, *Europe at Home*, 4–5.
177. Neil McKendrick, "Home Demand and Economic Growth: A New View of the Role of Women and Children in the Industrial Revolution," in *Historical Perspectives: Studies in English Thought and Society in Honour of J. H. Plumb*, ed. Neil McKendrick (London: Europa Publications Limited, 1974), 152–210.
178. On the history of research on consumption, see for instance Hartmut Berghoff and Uwe Spiekermann, eds., *Decoding Modern Consumer Societies* (New York: Palgrave Macmillan, 2012); Janine Maegraith and Craig Muldrew, "Consumption and Material Life," in *The Oxford Handbook of Early Modern European History, 1350–1750*, vol. 1: *Peoples and Place*, ed. Hamish Scott (Oxford: Oxford University Press, 2015), 369–97.
179. Sarti, *Europe at Home*, 219, with further references.
180. McKendrick, "Home Demand and Economic Growth."
181. Joan Wallach Scott, "The Woman Worker in the Nineteenth Century," in *History of Women in the West*, ed. Georges Duby and Michelle Perrot, vol. 4: *Emerging Feminism from Revolution to World War*, ed. Geneviève Fraisse (Harvard: Harvard University Press, 1993; originally published in Italian and French, trans. Arthur Goldhammer), 399–426.
182. Robert Beachy, Béatrice Craig, and Alastair Owens, eds., *Women, Business and Finance in Nineteenth-Century Europe: Rethinking Separate Spheres* (New York: Berg, 2006).
183. Marion W. Gray, *Productive Men, Reproductive Women: The Agrarian Household and the Emergence of Separate Spheres during the German Enlightenment* (New York: Berghahn Books, 2000), 9, argues that norms about separate spheres that "came to characterize the nineteenth century were actually in place in German-speaking Europe before industrial capitalism, in conjunction with the increased power of the state, disrupted traditional living and working condition": in her view, "while the Industrial Revolution was responsible for the establishment of the roles of 'housewife' and 'breadwinner' as widespread social phenomena, the *ideals* fostering this development circulated widely before industry altered the social and economic landscape"; according to Jane Humphries, *Childhood and Child Labour in the British Industrial Revolution* (Cambridge: Cambridge University Press, 2010), 120, in Britain, "the male-breadwinner family" "preceded industrialization." "Whether its origins were in the sixteenth or seventeenth century, or even earlier in the medieval period, by the eighteenth century a male-breadwinner system appears established." See also Horrell and Humphries, "Women's Labour Force Participation"; Sara Horrell and Jane Humphries, "The Origins and Expansion of the Male Breadwinner Family: The Case of Nineteenth-Century Britain," in "The Rise and Decline of the Male Breadwinner Family?," ed. Angélique Janssens, special issue of *International Review of Social History* 42 (1997): 25–64. The whole issue is important for the history of the breadwinner family. A large conference on *Women, Work and the Breadwinner Ideology* took place in Salzburg, Austria, in 1999. For a report, see Marian van der Klein, "Women, Work and the Breadwinner Ideology, from the Fifteenth to the Twentieth Century," in *International Labor and Working-Class History* 58 (2000): 318–21. For more recent inquiries on the origin of the breadwinner model, see Laura L. Frader, *Breadwinners and Citizens: Gender in the Making of the French Social Model* (Durham, NC: Duke University Press, 2008), and Osamu Saito, "Historical Origins of the Male Breadwinner Household Model: Britain, Sweden and Japan," *Japan Labor Review* 11, no. 4 (2014): 5–20.

184. The phenomenon was stressed, with many others, even by Marx and Engels in the *Manifesto of the Communist Party* (1848): "Modern Industry has converted the little workshop of the patriarchal master into the great factory of the industrial capitalist. . . . The less the skill and exertion of strength implied in manual labour, in other words, the more modern industry becomes developed, the more is the labour of men superseded by that of women. Differences of age and sex have no longer any distinctive social validity for the working class. All are instruments of labour, more or less expensive to use, according to their age and sex." (Quote taken from the online version of the *Manifesto* available at https://www.marxists.org/archive/marx/works/1848/communist-manifesto/index.htm; source: *Marx and Engels Selected Works* [Moscow: Progress Publishers, 1969], 1:98–137; trans. Samuel Moore in collaboration with Frederick Engels, 1888; transcribed by Zodiac and Brian Baggins; proofread and corrected against the 1888 English edition by Andy Blunden 2004; copy left: Marxists Internet Archive [marxists.org] 1987, 2000, 2010; permission is granted to distribute this document under the terms of the Creative Commons Attribution-Share-Alike License).

185. As McKendrick writes in "Home Demand and Economic Growth," 163: "Whatever the truth of the matter, female and child labour was seen as a novel abuse which must be condemned." Not just politically conservative or reactionary people but also radical and revolutionary ones often argued that women should be "brought back" home from the factories. An interesting case is represented, for instance, by Jules Simon (1814–96), a radical French politician and prime minister (1876–77), who, though being aware that female extra-domestic work was not at all a novelty due to industrialization, maintained that any means permitted by freedom should be used to bring wives and mothers back home ("il faut user de tous les moyens que la liberté autorise pour ramener l'épouse et la mère dans la maison," Jules Simon, *L'ouvrière* [Paris: Hachette, 1861], vi). On Simon's book, see Joan Wallach Scott, "'L'ouvrière! Mot impie, sordide . . .': Women Workers in the Discourse of French Political Economy, 1840–1860," in Joan Wallach Scott, *Gender and the Politics of History* (New York: Columbia University Press, 1988), 138–63 (or. ed. in Joyce, *Historical Meanings of Work*, 119–42).

186. After Darwin, considering nature as immutable was obviously increasingly out of date.

187. For instance: Carl N. Degler, *Is There a History of Women? An Inaugural Lecture Delivered before the University of Oxford on 14 March 1974* (Oxford: Clarendon, 1975); Huguette Buchardeau, *Pas d'histoire, les femmes?* (Paris: Syros, 1977); Michelle Perrot, ed., *Une histoire des femmes est-elle possible?* (Marseille: Rivages, 1984); Gisela Bock, "Women's History and Gender History: Aspects of an International Debate," *Gender & History* 1, no. 1 (1989): 7.

188. Jane Austen, *Northanger Abbey* (London: John Murray, 1818), Planet eBook, 121, retrieved 17 December 2017 from https://www.planetebook.com/ebooks/Northanger-Abbey.pdf.

189. Sheila Rowbotham, *Hidden from History: 300 Years of Women's Oppression and the Fight Against It* (London: Pluto Press, 1973); Renate Bridenthal and Claudia Koonz, eds., *Becoming Visible: Women in European History* (Boston: Houghton Mifflin, 1977).

190. Gianna Pomata, "Madri illegittime tra Ottocento e Novecento: storie cliniche e storie di vita," *Quaderni storici* 15, no. 44 (1980): 497–542; Lucia Ferrante, "L'onore ritrovato: donne della Casa del Soccorso di S. Paolo a Bologna (secoli XVI–XVII)," *Quaderni storici* 18, no. 53 (1983): 291–316; Lucia Ferrante, "Pro mercede carnali . . . Il giusto prezzo rivendicato in tribunale," *Memoria* 3, no. 17 (1986): 42–58; Gabriella Zarri, "Pietà e profezia alle corti padane: le pie consigliere dei principi," in *Il Rinascimento nelle corti padane: società e cultura*, ed. Paolo Rossi et al. (Bari: De Donato, 1977), 201–37; Gabriella Zarri, "Monasteri femminili e città (secoli XV–XVIII)," in *Storia d'Italia, Annali*, vol. 9: *Chiesa e potere politico dal medioevo all'età contemporanea*, ed. Giorgio Chittolini and Giovanni Miccoli (Torino: Einaudi, 1986), 357–429; Maura Palazzi, "Vivere a com-

pagnia e vivere a dozzina: gruppi domestici non coniugali nella Bologna di fine Settecento," in *Ragnatele di rapporti: Patronage e reti di relazione nelle storie delle donne*, ed. Lucia Ferrante, Maura Palazzi, and Gianna Pomata (Torino: Rosenberg & Sellier, 1988), 344–81. For more details, see Raffaella Sarti, "Oltre il gender? Un percorso tra recenti studi italiani di storia economico-sociale," in *A che punto è la storia delle donne in Italia*, ed. Anna Rossi-Doria (Roma: Viella, 2003), 93–144.

191. Alice Kessler-Harris, *Women Have Always Worked: A Historical Overview* (New York: Feminist Press, 1981); Gisela Bock, *Geschlechtergeschichten der Neuzeit: Ideen, Politik, Praxis* (Göttingen: Vandenhoeck & Ruprecht, 2014), 47 (the chapter was originally written in 1989); Cristina Borderías, Cristina Carrasco Bengoa, and Carme Alemany, eds., *Las mujeres y el trabajo: rupturas conceptuales* (Barcelona: Icaria, 1994); Groppi, *Il lavoro delle donne*; Silvie Schweitzer, *Les Femmes ont toujours travaillé: Une histoire du travail des femmes aux XIXe et XXe siècles* (Paris: Odile Jacob, 2002).

192. An early inspiring study on statistics is Joan Wallach Scott's chapter "Statistical Representations of Work: 'The Politics of the Chamber of Commerce's Statistique de l'Industrie à Paris,' 1847–48," in *Work in France: Representations, Meaning, Organization, and Practice*, ed. Stephen Laurence Kaplan and Cynthia J. Koepp (Ithaca, NY: Cornell University Press, 1986), 335–63, republished as "A Statistical Representation of Work: La Statistique de l'Industrie à Paris, 1847–1848," in Scott, *Gender and the Politics of History*, 113–38.

193. For instance, Margherita Pelaja, "Mestieri femminili e luoghi comuni: Le domestiche a Roma a metà Ottocento," *Quaderni storici* 23, no. 68 (1988): 497–518; Raffaella Sarti, "Servire al femminile, servire al maschile nella Bologna sette-ottocentesca," in *Operaie, serve, maestre, impiegate*, ed. Paola Nava (Torino: Rosenberg & Sellier, 1992), 237–64.

194. A similar method was suggested as early as 1990 by Margherita Pelaja, "Relazioni personali e vincoli di gruppo: il lavoro delle donne nella Roma dell'Ottocento," *Memoria* 10, no. 30 (1990): 44–52.

195. Desley Deacon, "Political Arithmetic: The Nineteenth-Century Australian Census and the Construction of the Dependent Woman," *Signs: Journal of Women in Culture and Society* 11, no. 1 (1985): 27–47; Edward Higgs, "Women, Occupations and Work in the Nineteenth Century Censuses," *History Workshop*, no. 23 (1987): 59–80.

196. Nancy Folbre and Marjorie Abel, "Women's Work and Women's Households: Gender Bias in the US Census," *Social Research* 56, no. 3 (1989): 545–69; Nancy Folbre, "The Unproductive Housewife: Her Evolution in Nineteenth-Century Economic Thought," *Signs: Journal of Women in Culture and Society* 16, no. 3 (1991): 463–84.

197. Cristina Borderías, "Women's Work and Household Economic Strategies in Industrializing Catalonia," *Social History* 29, no. 3 (2004): 380.

198. Such a case of women ashamed to declare their occupation was mentioned, for instance, in the 1899 Dutch Census; see Schmidt and van Nederveen Meerkerk, "Reconsidering the 'First Male Breadwinner Economy,'" 80.

199. E.g. ibid., 86 ("This under-recording was apparently more serious in 1899 than in 1849"); Elise van Nederveen Meerkerk and Richard Paping, "Beyond the Census: Reconstructing Dutch Women's Labour Market Participation in Agriculture in the Netherlands, ca. 1830–1910," *History of the Family* 19, no. 4 (2014): 447–68.

200. Claudia Goldin, "The U-Shaped Female Labor Force Function in Economic Development and Economic History," in *Investment in Women's Human Capital*, ed. T. Paul Schultz (Chicago: University of Chicago Press, 1995), 62; see also page 88:

> In sum, I have demonstrated that the labor force participation of women is generally U-shaped over the course of economic development. The reasons for the downward portion of the U are probably found in a combination of an initially strong income effect and a weak substitution effect, and a change in the locus of production from the home to the factory. It was the rising portion of the U that concerned most of this essay. Why the function changes direction holds the key to

why women enter the labor force at higher stages of economic development and why their social, political, and legal status generally improves with economic progress. The reasons were sought in the change in the education of females relative to males as educational resource constraints are relaxed, and in women's ability to obtain jobs in the white-collar sector after school completion. Their increased education and their ability to work in more prestigious occupations both increases the substitution effect and decreases the income effect. As the substitution effect begins to swamp the income effect, the upward portion of the U is traced out, and women's labor force participation enters the modern era.

201. E.g. Wiebke Schulz, Ineke Maas, and Marco H. D. van Leeuwen, "When Women Disappear from the Labour Market: Occupational Status of Dutch Women at Marriage in a Modernizing Society, 1865–1922," *History of the Family* 19, no. 4 (2014): 426–46.
202. E.g. Andrew August, "How Separate a Sphere? Poor Women and Paid Work in Late-Victorian London," *Journal of Family History* 19, no. 3 (1994): 285–309.
203. Beachy, Craig, and Owens, *Women, Business and Finance*.
204. A wrong evaluation of women's work may significantly alter our understanding of the past, as Maxine Berg writes in relation to the Industrial Revolution:
    Failure to take account of gender divisions may also have affected macro-economic indicators of the Industrial Revolution. If it was the case that higher proportions of women than men were occupied in the newer progressive manufacturing sectors, then the distribution of the labour force between different industries would be changed, and with this productivity estimates based on these. We can, indeed, ask to what extent our views of the low productivity of British industry in the crucial years of the Industrial Revolution have been distorted because we have been looking at the industrial distribution of the wrong workforce. It was the female not the male workforce which counted in the new high-productivity industries. Women's labour was, on the other hand, also heavily concentrated in traditional labour-intensive activities. As the relative significance of traditional and dynamic industries changed, so too did distributions within the female workforce."
    See Maxine Berg, *The Age of Manufactures, 1700–1820: Industry, Innovation and Work in Britain* (1994; New York: Rouledge, 2005), 117.
205. On estimates of the economic value of housework made in this way, see Folbre's and Boris's contributions in this book.
206. The fact that *unpaid* housewives might and may actually produce goods and services for the market (better addressed below) obviously makes things even more complicated. On this issue, see Manuela Martini and Anna Bellavitis, "Household Economies, Social Norms and Practices of Unpaid Market Work in Europe from the Sixteenth Century to the Present," *History of the Family* 19, no. 3 (2014): 273–82.
207. See Folbre's contribution and note 10.
208. See, for instance, Lorna Weatherill, *Consumer Behaviour and Material Culture in Britain 1660–1760* (New York: Rouledge, 1988), 143, to quote but one example.
209. The census officers themselves often discussed reliability and underrepresentations, as shown in this volume by Sarti. Among scholars who tried to correct censuses, see Ornello Vitali, *Aspetti dello sviluppo economico italiano alla luce della ricostruzione della popolazione attiva* (Roma: Failli, 1970); Olivier Marchand and Claude Thélot, *Deux siècles de travail en France* (Paris: Insee, 1991).
210. Van Nederveen Meerkerk and Paping, "Beyond the Census."
211. Sophie McGeevor, "How Well Did the Nineteenth Century Census Record Women's 'Regular' Employment in England and Wales? A Case Study of Hertfordshire in 1851," *History of the Family* 19, no. 4 (2014): 489–512; Edward Higgs and Amanda Wilkinson, "Women, Occupations and Work in the Victorian Censuses Revisited," *History Workshop Journal* 81, no. 1 (2016): 17–38.

212. Richard L. Zijdeman, Marco H. D. van Leeuwen, Danièle Rébaudo, and Jean-Pierre Pélissier, "Working Women in France, Nineteenth and Twentieth Centuries: Where, When, and Which Women Were in Work at Marriage?," *History of the Family* 19, no. 4 (2014): 537–63, maintain that female labor force participation between 1860 and 1950 was rather stable, about 60 percent.
213. Humphries and Sarasúa, "Off the Record."
214. The ILO, for instance, very early on, beginning in 1937, included the category of "unpaid family workers" in family businesses among the active population in the tables of its Yearbook of Labour Statistics, Martini, "When Unpaid Workers," 248.
215. Maria Mies, *The Lace Makers of Narsapur: Indian Housewives Produce for the World Market* (North Geelong, Victoria: Spinifex Press, 2012; first edition London: Zed Books, 1982), 200, on the concept of *housewifization*; the quotes are taken from the preface by Dharam Ghai, chief, Rural Employment Policies branch, ILO, xviii–xix.
216. For instance, breastfeeding carried out at home in the past, *maman de jours* in the present.
217. In addition to all the chapters in this book, see also the other publication by our research group: Martini and Bellavitis, *Households, Family Workshops*; Bellavitis, Martini, Sarti, *Familles laborieuses*; on servants see Sarti, "Who Are Servants?"
218. For some case studies see the special issue on "Households, Family Workshops and Unpaid Market Work," ed. Martini and Bellavitis, for instance the articles by Beatrice Zucca Micheletto, "Only Unpaid Labour Force? Women's and Girls' Work and Property in Family Business in Early Modern Italy," 323–40, and Céline Bessière, "Female and Male Domestic Partners in Wine-Grape Farms (Cognac, France): Conjugal Asymmetry and Gender Discrimination in Family Business," 341–57.
219. Children working at home were generally supposed to work for free. This might lead someone to create ambiguous adoption-like relationships with young apprentices and servants that might turn out to be highly exploitative; see Christiane Klapisch-Zuber, "Disciples, fils, travailleurs: Les apprentis peintres et sculpteurs italiens au XVe et XVIe siècle," *Mélanges de l'École française de Rome—Italie et Méditerranée modernes et contemporaines* 128, no. 1 (2016): retrieved 17 December 2017 from http://journals.openedition.org/mefrim/2469?lang=it#text. Furthermore, a father had full rights over the earnings of his children legally dependent on him if they had gainful employment; see for instance Cavallo, "Fatherhood and the Non-propertied Classes."
220. See for instance Maitte, "Le travail invisible dans les familles artisanales"; Àngels Solà, "Apprentices, Women and Masters in the Silk Weavers' Guild of Barcelona, 1790–1840," *Mélanges de l'École française de Rome—Italie et Méditerranée modernes et contemporaines*, 128, no. 1 (2016): retrieved 17 December 2017 from http://journals.openedition.org/mefrim/2449.
221. See, for instance, Angela Groppi, *Il welfare prima del welfare: assistenza alla vecchiaia e solidarietà tra generazioni a Roma in età moderna* (Roma: Viella, 2010); Angela Groppi, "Le Tribunal du Vicariat et les obligations alimentaires intrafamiliales dans la Rome des Papes (XVIIIe–XIXe siècles)," in *La justice des familles: autour de la transmission des biens, des savoirs et des pouvoirs (Europe, Nouveau monde, XIIe–XIXe siècles)*, ed. Anna Bellavitis and Isabelle Chabot (Rome: École Française de Rome, 2011), 245–62.
222. Bellavitis, Martini, and Sarti, *Familles laborieuses*.
223. Sarti, *Servo e padrone*, 195–201, and Sarti's contribution to this volume.
224. "Il lavoro della donna è considerato equivalente a quello dell'uomo," see http://www.normattiva.it/uri-res/N2Ls?urn:nir:stato:regio.decreto:1942-03-16;262. But on the economic duties of children toward their parents, in early modern Italy, see Groppi, *Il welfare prima del welfare*.
225. Francesca Maria Cesaroni and Annalisa Sentuti, "Women and Family Businesses: When Women Are Left only Minor Roles," *History of the Family*," 19, no. 3 (2014): 358–79. In some cases, especially in past years, legal requirements for managing a business, such

as educational qualifications, made even women who, in fact, were extremely active officially almost invisible; see Anna Badino, "Lavoro femminile e imprese familiari in anni di mobilità interna: Torino 1960–1980," *Mélanges de l'École française de Rome—Italie et Méditerranée modernes et contemporaines* 128, no. 1 (2016): retrieved 17 December 2017 http://journals.openedition.org/mefrim/2458.
226. Bessière, "Female and male domestic partners."
227. Martini, "When Unpaid Workers."
228. Sarti, "Historians."
229. Addressing the lively discussion on universal basic income and other possible solutions to cope with current problems is beyond the scope of this Introduction. For a useful anthology see Karl Widerquist, José A. Noguera, Yannick Vanderborght, and Jurgen De Wispelaere, eds., *Basic Income: An Anthology of Contemporary Research* (Chichester: Wiley Blackwell, 2013). The anthology also has a section on "Feminism" that "examines whether Basic Income enhances gender equality. It shows how feminists are deeply divided on the issue. Some believe Basic Income will enhance women's ability to challenge the gendered division of labor. Others believe it will perpetuate traditional women's gender roles by making it easier for them to fall into household care work" (xx).

References

Ahmad, Nadim, and Koh Seung-Hee. "Incorporating Estimates of Household Production of Non-market Services into International Comparisons of Material Well-Being." In *OECD Statistics Working Papers*, 14 October 2011.

Alberti, Leon Battista. *I Libri della Famiglia*, edited by Alberto Tenenti and Ruggiero Romano, new edition by Francesco Furlan. Torino: Einaudi, 1994. For the English translation see: Leon Battista Alberti. *The Family in Renaissance Florence: A Translation of I Libri della Famiglia by Leon Battista Alberti*, translated and with an introduction by Renée Neu Watkins. Columbia: University of South Carolina Press, 1969.

Alesina, Alberto, and Andrea Ichino. *L'Italia fatta in casa: indagine sulla vera ricchezza degli italiani*. Milano: Mondadori, 2009.

Allen, Robert C., and Jacob Louis Weisdorf. "Was there an 'Industrious Revolution' before the Industrial Revolution? An Empirical Exercise for England, c. 1300–1830." *Economic History Review* 64, no. 3 (2011): 715–29.

Ambrosoli, Mauro, and Lorenzo Ornaghi. "Il Padre di famiglia." *Quaderni storici* 22, no. 64 (1987): 223–32.

Applebaum, Herbert. *The Concepts of Work: Ancient, Medieval and Modern*. New York: State University of New York Press, 1992.

Archivio di Lotta Femminista per il salario al lavoro domestico, Donazione Mariarosa Dalla Costa (Archive of Lotta Femminista [Feminist Struggle] for wages for housework, Donation by Mariarosa Dalla Costa). Retrieved 17 December 2017 from www.padovanet.it/sites/default/files/attachment/C_1_Allegati_20187_Allegato.pdf.

Arendt, Hannah. *The Human Condition*. 2nd edition. Introduction by Margaret Canovan. Chicago: University of Chicago Press, 1998. Originally published 1958.

Ariès, Philippe. *L'enfant et la vie familiale sous l'ancien régime.* Paris: Plon, 1960. English translation: *Centuries of Childhood: A Social History of Family Life*, translated by Robert Baldick. London: Jonathan Cape, 1962.

Arnoux, Mathieu. *Le temps des laboureurs: travail, ordre social et croissance en Europe (XIe–XIVe siècle).* Paris: Albin Michel, 2012.

August, Andrew. "How Separate a Sphere? Poor Women and Paid Work in Late-Victorian London." *Journal of Family History* 19, no. 3 (1994): 285–309.

Austen, Jane. *Northanger Abbey.* London: John Murray, 1818. Planet eBook. Retrieved 17 December 2017 from https://www.planetebook.com/ebooks/Northanger-Abbey.pdf.

Badino, Anna. "Lavoro femminile e imprese familiari in anni di mobilità interna: Torino 1960–1980." *Mélanges de l'École française de Rome—Italie et Méditerranée modernes et contemporaines* 128, no. 1 (2016): retrieved 17 December 2017 from http://journals.openedition.org/mefrim/2458.

Bailey, Diane E., and Nancy B. Kurland. "A Review of Telework Research: Findings, New Directions, and Lessons for the Study of Modern Work." *Journal of Organizational Behavior* 23, no. 4 (2002): 383–400.

Barbagli, Marzio. *Sotto lo stesso tetto: mutamenti della famiglia in Italia dal XV al XX secolo.* Bologna: Il Mulino, 1984.

Beachy, Robert, Béatrice Craig, and Alastair Owens, eds. *Women, Business and Finance in Nineteenth-Century Europe: Rethinking Separate Spheres.* New York: Berg, 2006.

Becker, Gary S. *A Treatise on the Family.* Cambridge, MA: Harvard University Press, 1981.

Bellavitis, Anna. "Donne cittadinanza e corporazioni tra medioevo ed età moderna: ricerche in corso." In *Corpi e storia: donne e uomini dal mondo antico all'età contemporanea*, edited by Nadia Maria Filippini, Tiziana Plebani, and Anna Scattigno, 87–104. Roma: Viella, 2002.

———. *Il lavoro delle donne nelle città dell'Europa moderna.* Roma: Viella, 2016.

Bellavitis, Anna, Virginie Jourdain, Virginie Lemonnier-Lesage, and Beatrice Zucca Micheletto, eds. *"Tout ce qu'elle saura et pourra faire": Femmes, droits, travail en Normandie du Moyen Âge à la Grande guerre.* Mont-Saint-Aignan: Presses Universitaires de Rouen et du Havre, 2015.

Bellavitis, Anna, Manuela Martini, and Raffaella Sarti, eds. "Familles laborieuses: Rémunération, transmission et apprentissage dans les ateliers familiaux de la fin du Moyen Âge à l'époque contemporaine en Europe." Special issue of the *Mélanges de l'École française de Rome—Italie et Méditerranée modernes et contemporaines* 128, no. 1 (2016): retrieved 17 December 2017 from http://journals.openedition.org/mefrim/2366.

Benería, Lourdes. "Accounting for Women's Work: The Progress of Two Decades." *World Development* 20, no. 11 (1992): 1547–60.

Berg, Maxine. "The First Women Economic Historians." *Economic History Review* 45, no. 2 (1992): 308–29.

———. *The Age of Manufactures, 1700–1820: Industry, Innovation and Work in Britain.* New York: Routledge, 2005. First published in 1994.

Berghoff, Hartmut, and Uwe Spiekermann, eds. *Decoding Modern Consumer Societies.* New York: Palgrave Macmillan, 2012.

Bessière, Céline. "Female and Male Domestic Partners in Wine-Grape Farms (Cognac, France): Conjugal Asymmetry and Gender Discrimination in Family Business." *History of the Family* 19, no. 3 (2014): 341–57.
Betti, Eloisa. "Lavoro a domicilio e relazioni di genere negli anni Cinquanta: appunti sul caso bolognese." *Genesis* 14, no. 2 (2015): 107–33.
Black, John, Nigar Hashimzade, and Gareth Myles, eds. *Oxford Dictionary of Economics*. Oxford: Oxford University Press, 2009.
Bock, Gisela. "Women's History and Gender History: Aspects of an International Debate." *Gender & History* 1, no. 1 (1989): 7–30.
———. *Geschlechtergeschichten der Neuzeit: Ideen, Politik, Praxis*. Göttingen: Vandenhoeck & Ruprecht, 2014.
Bock, Gisela, and Barbara Duden. "Arbeit aus Liebe—Liebe als Arbeit: Zur Entstehung der Hausarbeit im Kapitalismus." In *Frauen und Wissenschaft: Beiträge zur Berliner Sommeruniversität für Frauen, Juli 1976*, edited by Gruppe Berliner Dozentinnen, 118–99. Berlin: Courage Verlag, 1977.
Borderías, Cristina. "Women's Work and Household Economic Strategies in Industrializing Catalonia." *Social History* 29, no. 3 (2004): 373–83.
Borderías, Cristina, Cristina Carrasco Bengoa, and Carmen Alemany, eds. *Las mujeres y el trabajo: rupturas conceptuales*. Barcelona: Icaria, 1994.
Boris, Eileen. *Home to Work: Motherhood and the Politics of Industrial Homework in the United States*. New York: Cambridge University Press, 1994.
Boris, Eileen, and Rhacel Salazar Parreñas, eds. *Intimate Labors: Culture, Technologies and the Politics of Care*. Stanford, CA: Stanford University Press, 2010.
Boserup, Ester. *Women's Role in Economic Development*. New York: Earthscan, 1970.
Bracke, Maud A. "Between the Transnational and the Local: Mapping the Trajectories and Contexts of the Wages for Housework Campaign in 1970s Italian Feminism." *Women's History Review* 22, no. 4 (2013): 625–42.
Brandolini, Andrea, and Eliana Viviano. "Accounting for Total Work in Labour Statistics." *Journal for Labour Market Research* 8, no. 26 (2016): 1–14.
Bridenthal, Renate, and Claudia Koonz, eds. *Becoming Visible: Women in European History*. Boston: Houghton Mifflin, 1977.
Brunner, Otto. "Das 'Ganze Haus' und die alteuropäische 'Ökonomik.'" In Otto Brunner, *Neue Wege der Verfassungs- und Sozialgeschichte*. 2nd edition, 103–27. Göttingen: Vandenhoeck & Ruprecht, 1968.
Buchardeau, Huguette. *Pas d'histoire, les femmes?* Paris: Syros, 1977.
Burchi, Sandra. *Ripartire da casa: lavori e reti dallo spazio domestico*. Milano: Angeli, 2014.
Burnette, Joyce. "A Pioneer in Women's History: Ivy Pinchbeck's Women Workers and the Industrial Revolution, 1750–1850." Retrieved 17 December 2017 from http://www.eh.net/?s=women+workers+and+the+industrial+revolution.
Calaresu, Melissa, and Danielle van den Heuvel, eds. *Food Hawkers: Selling in the Streets from Antiquity to the Present*. Abingdon: Routledge, 2016.
Caracausi, Andrea. "Beaten Children and Women's Work in Early Modern Italy." *Past & Present*, no. 222 (2014): 95–128.
Carpenedo, Manoela, and Henrique Caetano Nardi. "Brazilian Women in the International Division of Reproductive Work: Constructing Subjectivities." *Revista de Estudios Sociales* 45 (2013): 96–109.

Casini, Lorenzo, "Juan Luis Vives [Joannes Ludovicus Vives]." *The Stanford Encyclopedia of Philosophy* (Spring 2017 Edition), edited by Edward N. Zalta. Retrieved 17 December 2017 from https://plato.stanford.edu/archives/spr2017/entries/vives.

Cavaciocchi, Simonetta, ed. *La famiglia nell'economia europea, secc. XIII–XVIII, Atti delle Settimane di studio della Fondazione Istituto internazionale di Storia economica F. Datini di Prato.* Firenze: Firenze University Press, 2009.

———, ed. *Il commercio al minuto: domanda e offerta tra economia formale e informale, secc. XIII–XVIII, Atti delle Settimane di studio dell'Istituto internazionale di Storia economica F. Datini di Prato.* Firenze: Firenze University Press, 2015.

Cavallo, Sandra. "Bachelorhood and Masculinity in Renaissance and Early Modern Italy." *European History Quarterly* 38, no. 3 (2008): 375–97.

———. "Fatherhood and the Non-propertied Classes in Renaissance and Early Modern Italian Towns." *History of the Family* 17, no. 3 (2012): 309–25. Also published in *The Power of the Fathers: Historical Perspectives from Ancient Rome to the Nineteenth Century*, edited by Margareth Lanzinger, 31–46. New York: Routledge, 2015.

Cavallo, Sandra, and Lyndan Warner, eds. *Widowhood in Medieval and Early Modern Europe.* Harlow: Longman, 1999.

Cesaroni, Francesca Maria, and Annalisa Sentuti. "Women and Family Businesses: When Women Are Left only Minor Roles." *History of the Family* 19, no. 3 (2014): 358–79.

Chadeau, Ann. "Measuring Household Activities: Some International Comparisons." *Review of Income and Wealth* 31, no. 3 (1985): 237–54.

Chadeau, Ann, Annie Fouquet, and Claudee Thélot. "Peut-on mesurer le travail domestique?" *Economie et statistique*, no. 136 (1981): 29–42.

Chamoux, Marie-Noëlle. "Sociétés avec et sans concept de travail." *Sociologie du travail* 36, Hors série, no. 4 (1994): 57–71.

Clark, Alice. *The Working Life of Women in the Seventeenth Century.* New York: George Routledge & Sons-Button & Co., 1919. Republished: London: Routledge & K. Paul, 1982.

Clark, Gregory, and Ysbrand Van Der Werf. "Work in Progress? The Industrious Revolution." *Journal of Economic History* 58, no. 3 (1998): 830–43.

Coltrane, Scott. "Research on Household Labor: Modeling and Measuring the Social Embeddedness of Routine Family Work." *Journal of Marriage and the Family* 62, no. 4 (2000): 1208–33.

Crowston, Clare. *Fabricating Women: The Seamstresses of Old Regime France, 1675–1791.* Durham, NC: Duke University Press, 2001.

———. "Women, Gender and Guilds in Early Modern Europe: An Overview of Recent Research." In *The Return of the Guilds*, edited by Jan Lucassen, Tine De Moor, and Jan Luiten van Zanden, 19–44. Supplement of *International Review of Social History* 53 (2008).

Dahrendorf, Ralf. "Im Entschwinden der Arbeitsgesellschaft: Wandlungen in der sozialen Konstruktion des menschlichen Lebens." *Merkur* 34, no. 8 (1980): 749–60.

Dalla Costa, Mariarosa. *Potere femminile e sovversione sociale, con "Il posto della donna" di Selma James.* Padova: Marsilio, 1972; English edition: Mariarosa Dalla

Costa and Selma James. *The Power of Women and the Subversion of the Community*. Third edition. Bristol: Falling Wall Press, 1975. Originally published in 1972. Retrieved 17 December 2017 from https://libcom.org/library/power-women-subversion-community-della-costa-selma-james.

Davidoff, Leonore, and Catherine Hall. *Family Fortunes: Men and Women of the English Middle Class, 1780–1850*. London: Hutchinson, 1987.

Davis, Natalie Zemon. "'Women's History' in Transition: The European Case." *Feminist Studies* 3, nos. 3–4 (1976): 83–103.

———. "Women in the Crafts in Sixteenth-Century Lyon." *Feminist Studies* 8, no. 1 (1982): 46–80.

De Moor, Tine, and Jan Luiten Van Zanden. "Girl Power: The European Marriage Pattern and Labour Markets in the North Sea Region in the Late Medieval and Early Modern Period." *Economic History Review* 63, no. 1 (2010): 1–33.

De Vries, Jan. "The Industrial Revolution and the Industrious Revolution." *Journal of Economic History* 54, no. 2 (1994): 249–70.

———. *The Industrious Revolution: Consumer Behavior and the Household Economy, 1650 to the Present*. Cambridge: Cambridge University Press, 2008.

Deacon, Desley. "Political Arithmetic: The Nineteenth-Century Australian Census and the Construction of the Dependent Woman." *Signs: Journal of Women in Culture and Society* 11, no. 1 (1985): 27–47.

Degler, Carl N. *Is There a History of Women? An Inaugural Lecture Delivered before the University of Oxford on 14 March 1974*. Oxford: Clarendon, 1975.

Della Valentina, Marcello. "Il setificio salvato dalle donne: le tessitrici veneziane nel Settecento." In *Spazi, poteri, diritti delle donne a Venezia in età moderna*, edited by Anna Bellavitis, Nadia Maria Filippini, and Tiziana Plebani, 321–35. Verona: QuiEdit, 2012.

Delphy, Christine. "Un féminisme matérialiste est possible." *Nouvelles Questions Féministes* 4 (Fall 1982): 50–86. Originally published as "A Materialist Feminism is Possible," *Feminist Review*, no. 4, 1980, 79–105, translated by Diana Leonard.

———. *L'ennemi principal* (Tome 1): *économie politique du patriarcat*. Paris: Syllepse, 1998.

———. *L'ennemi principal* (Tome 2): *penser le genre*. Paris: Syllepse, 2001.

Delphy, Christine, and Diana Leonard. *Familiar Exploitation: A New Analysis of Marriage in Contemporary Western Societies*. Oxford: Polity Press, 1992.

Dennison, Tracy, and Sheilagh Ogilvie. "Does the European Marriage Pattern Explain Economic Growth?" *Journal of Economic History* 74, no. 3 (2014): 651–93.

Donati, Claudio. *L'idea di nobiltà in Italia, secoli XIV–XVIII*. Roma-Bari: Laterza, 1988.

Dunn, Marianthi. "Annual National Accounts—How ESA 2010 Has Changed the Main GDP Aggregates." *Eurostat Statistics Explained*, January 2015.

Ehmer, Josef. "Work, History of." *International Encyclopedia of the Social & Behavioral Sciences*, editors in chief Neil J. Smelser and Paul B. Baltes, 24:16569–75. Amsterdam: Elsevier, 2001.

Ehmer, Josef, and Catharina Lis. *The Idea of Work in Europe from Antiquity to Modern Times*. Farnham-Burlington: Ashgate, 2009.

Ehrenreich, Barbara, and Deirdre English. *Witches, Midwives, and Nurses: Complaints and Disorders*. New York: Feminist Press, 1973.

Ehrenreich, Barbara, and Arlie Russell Hochschild, eds. *Global Woman: Nannies, Maids, and Sex Workers in the New Economy.* New York: Macmillan, 2003.
Erickson, Amy Louise. "Married Women's Occupations in Eighteenth-Century London." *Continuity and Change* 23, no. 2 (2008): 267–307.
Eurostat. Employment Statistics, August 2015. Retrieved 5 November 2016 from http://ec.europa.eu/eurostat/statistics-explained/index.php/Employment_sta tistics.
Febvre, Lucien. "Travail: évolution d'un mot et d'une idée." *Journal de Psychologie normale et pathologique* 51, no. 1 (1948): 19–28.
Federici, Silvia. *Wages Against Housework.* Bristol: Power of Women Collective and Falling Wall Press, 1975.
Ferrante, Lucia. "L'onore ritrovato: donne della Casa del Soccorso di S. Paolo a Bologna (secoli XVI–XVII)." *Quaderni storici* 18, no. 53 (1983): 291–316.
———. "Pro mercede carnali . . . Il giusto prezzo rivendicato in tribunale." *Memoria* 3, no. 17 (1986): 42–58.
Flather, Amanda. "Space, Place, and Gender: The Sexual and Spatial Division of Labor in the Early Modern Household." *History and Theory* 52, no. 3 (2013): 344–60.
Folbre, Nancy. "The Unproductive Housewife: Her Evolution in Nineteenth-Century Economic Thought." *Signs, Journal of Women and Culture in Society* 16, no. 3 (1991): 463–84.
———. *Valuing Children: Rethinking the Economics of the Family.* Cambridge, MA: Harvard University Press, 2008.
———. "Inequality and Time Use in the Household." In *Oxford Handbook of Economic Inequality,* edited by Wiener Salverda, Brian Nolan, and Timothy Smeeding, 342–63. New York: Oxford University Press, 2009.
———. *Greed, Lust and Gender: A History of Economic Ideas.* Oxford: Oxford University Press, 2009.
Folbre, Nancy, and Marjorie Abel. "Women's Work and Women's Households: Gender Bias in the US Census." *Social Research* 56, no. 3 (1989): 545–69.
Folbre, Nancy, and Barnet Wagman. "Counting Housework: New Estimates of Real Product in the United States, 1800–1860." *Journal of Economic History* 53, no. 2 (1993): 275–88.
Fonte, Moderata [= Modesta Pozzo or Da Pozzo]. *Il Merito delle Donne, Scritto da Moderata Fonte in due giornate. Ove chiaramente si scuopre quanto siano elle degne, e più perfette degli huomini.* Venetia: Domenico Imberti, 1600; for the English translation see: *The Worth of Women: Wherein is Clearly Revealed their Nobility and Their Superiority to Men,* edited and translated by Virginia Cox. Chicago: University of Chicago Press, 1997.
Frader, Laura L. *Breadwinners and Citizens: Gender in the Making of the French Social Model.* Durham, NC: Duke University Press, 2008.
Frederick, Christine. *The New Housekeeping: Efficiency Studies in Home Management.* Garden City, NY: Doubleday, Page & Company, 1913.
———. *Household Engineering: The Scientific Management in the Home.* Chicago: American School of Home Economics, 1915.
Friedan, Betty. *The Feminine Mystique.* New York: W. W. Norton and Co., 1963.
Frigo, Daniela. *Il padre di famiglia: governo della casa e governo civile nella tradizione dell'"economica" tra Cinque e Seicento.* Roma-Bari: Bulzoni, 1985.

Fuchs, Christian. *Reading Marx in the Information Age: A Media and Communication Studies Perspective on Capital.* New York: Routledge, 2016.

Gallo, Ester, and Francesca Scrinzi. "Introduction: Men and Masculinities in the International Division of Reproductive Labour." In *Migration, Masculinities and Reproductive Labour,* edited by Ester Gallo and Francesca Scrinzi, 1–36. London: Palgrave Macmillan, 2016.

Gee, Kar-Fai. "Development of Estimates for Household Production of Non-market Services in OECD Countries for the Index of Economic Well-Being." Centre for the Study of Living Standards, Research Report 2015. Retrieved 17 December 2017 from http://www.csls.ca/reports/csls2015-09.pdf.

Genovesi, Antonio. *Lezioni di Commercio o sia di Economia Civile.* Bassano: Remondini, 1769. First edition 1765–67.

Giannelli, Gianna C., Lucia Mangiavacchi, and Luca Piccoli. "GDP and the Value of Family Caretaking: How Much Does Europe Care?" IZA (Forschungsinstitut zur Zukunft der Arbeit, Institute for the Study of Labor) Discussion Paper No. 5046, July 2010.

Gleadle, Kathryn. "Revisiting Family Fortunes: Reflections on the Twentieth Anniversary of the Publication of L. Davidoff & C. Hall (1987) *Family Fortunes: Men and Women of the English Middle Class, 1780–1850* (London: Hutchinson)." *Women's History Review* 16, no. 5 (2007): 773–82.

Godelier, Maurice. "Work and Its Representations: A Research Proposal." *History Workshop Journal* 10, no. 1 (1980): 164–74.

Goldin, Claudia. "The U-Shaped Female Labor Force Function in Economic Development and Economic History." In *Investment in Women's Human Capital,* edited by T. Paul Schultz, 61–90. Chicago: University of Chicago Press, 1995.

Goody, Jack. *Production and Reproduction: A Comparative Study of the Domestic Domain.* Cambridge: Cambridge University Press, 1976.

Gorz, André. *Paths to Paradise: On the Liberation from Work.* London: Pluto Press, 1985.

Gough, Ian. "Marx's Theory of Productive and Unproductive Labour." *New Left Review* 1, no. 76 (1972): 47–72.

Gray, Marion W. *Productive Men, Reproductive Women: The Agrarian Household and the Emergence of Separate Spheres during the German Enlightenment.* New York: Berghahn Books, 2000.

Grendler, Paul. *Schooling in Renaissance Italy: Literacy and Learning, 1300–1600.* Baltimore: The Johns Hopkins University Press, 1989.

Groppi, Angela, ed. *Il lavoro delle donne.* Roma-Bari: Laterza, 1996.

———. "Une ressource légale pour une pratique illégale: Les juifs et les femmes contre la corporation des tailleurs dans la Rome pontificale (XVIIe–XVIIIe siècles)." In *The Value of the Norm/Il valore delle norme,* edited by Renata Ago, 137–62. Roma: Biblink, 2002.

———. *Il welfare prima del welfare: assistenza alla vecchiaia e solidarietà tra generazioni a Roma in età moderna.* Roma: Viella, 2010.

———. "Le Tribunal du Vicariat et les obligations alimentaires intrafamiliales dans la Rome des Papes (XVIIIe–XIXe siècles)." In *La justice des familles: autour de la transmission des biens, des savoirs et des pouvoirs (Europe, Nouveau monde, XIIe–*

XIXe siècles), edited by Anna Bellavitis and Isabelle Chabot, 245–62. Rome: École Française de Rome, 2011.

Habermas, Jürgen. *The Philosophical Discourse of Modernity: Twelve Lectures*. Translated by Frederick G. Lawrence. Cambridge, MA: The MIT Press, 1990. Original edition: *Der philosophische Diskurs der Moderne: Zwölf Vorlesungen*. Frankfurt a.M.: Suhrkamp, 1985.

Hafter, Daryl M. "Les veuves dans les corporations de Rouen sous l'Ancien Régime." In *Veufs, veuves et veuvage dans la France d'Ancien Régime*, Actes du Colloque de Poitiers (11–12 juin 1998), Textes réunis par Nicole Pellegrin, présentés et édités par Colette H. Winn, 121–33. Paris: Honoré Champion, 2003.

———. *Women and Work in Preindustrial France*. University Park: The Pennsylvania State University Press, 2007.

Harding, Elizabeth. *Der Gelehrte im Haus: Ehe, Familie und Haushalt in der Standeskultur der frühneuzeitlichen Universität Helmstedt*. Wiesbaden: Harrassowitz Verlag, 2014.

———. "The Early Modern German Professor at Home—Masculinity, Bachelorhood and Family Concepts (Sixteenth–Eighteenth Centuries)." In "Men at Home: Domesticities, Authority, Emotions and Work," edited by Raffaella Sarti, special issue of *Gender & History* 27, no. 3 (2015): 736–51.

Harper, Douglas. *Online Etymology Dictionary*. Retrieved 16 January 2017 from http://www.etymonline.com.

Harvey, Karen. *The Little Republic: Masculinity and Domestic Authority in Eighteenth-Century Britain*. Oxford: Oxford University Press, 2012.

Hausen, Karin. "Work in Gender, Gender in Work: The German Case in Comparative Perspective." In *Work in a Modern Society: The German Historical Experience in Comparative Perspective*, edited by Jürgen Kocka, 73–92. New York: Berghahn Books, 2010.

Higgs, Edward. "Women, Occupations and Work in the Nineteenth Century Censuses." *History Workshop*, no. 23 (1987): 59–80.

Higgs, Edward, and Amanda Wilkinson. "Women, Occupations and Work in the Victorian Censuses Revisited." *History Workshop Journal* 81, no. 1 (2016): 17–38.

Hill, Bridget. *Women Alone: Spinsters in England, 1660–1850*. New Haven, CT: Yale University Press, 2001.

Hobbes, Thomas. *On the Citizen* (English translation of *De Cive*, first published in 1642). Edited and translated by Richard Tuck and Michael Silverthorne. Cambridge: Cambridge University Press, 2003. First edition published in 1998.

———. *Leviathan* (1651). eBooks@Adelaide, University of Adelaide Library, Retrieved 17 December 2017, from https://ebooks.adelaide.edu.au/h/hobbes/thomas/h68l/.

Hofmeester, Karin, and Christine Moll-Murata, eds. "The Joy and Pain of Work: Global Attitudes and Valuations, 1500–1650." Special issue of *International Review of Social History* 56, S19 (2011).

Horrell, Sara, and Jane Humphries. "The Origins and Expansion of the Male Breadwinner Family: The Case of Nineteenth-century Britain." In "The Rise and Decline of the Male Breadwinner Family?," edited by Angélique Janssens, special issue of *International Review of Social History* 42 (1997): 25–64.

———. "Women's Labour Force Participation and the Transition to the Male Breadwinner Family, 1790–1865." *Economic History Review* 48, no. 1 (1995): 89–117.
Howell, Martha C. *Women, Production, and Patriarchy in Late Medieval Cities*. Chicago: University of Chicago Press, 1986.
———. "Citizenship and Gender: Women's Political Status in Northern Medieval Cities." In *Women and Power in the Middle Ages*, edited by Mary Erler and Marianne Kowaleski, 37–60. Athens: University of Georgia Press, 1988.
———. "The Gender of Europe's Commercial Economy, 1200–1700." *Gender & History* 20, no. 3 (2008): 519–38.
———. *Commerce before Capitalism in Europe, 1300–1600*. Cambridge: Cambridge University Press, 2010.
Hufton, Olwen. "Women without Men: Widows and Spinsters in Britain and France in the Eighteenth Century." *Journal of Family History* 9, no. 4 (1984): 355–76.
Humphries, Jane. *Childhood and Child Labour in the British Industrial Revolution*. Cambridge: Cambridge University Press, 2010.
Humphries, Jane, and Carmen Sarasúa. "Off the Record: Reconstructing Women's Labor Force Participation in the European Past." *Feminist Economics* 18, no. 4 (2012): 39–67.
The International Wages for Housework Campaign. Undated flyer. Retrieved 17 December 2017 from http://freedomarchives.org/Documents/Finder/DOC500 _scans/500.020.Wages.for.Housework.pdf.
Ironmonger, Duncan. "Counting Outputs, Capital Inputs and Caring Labor: Estimating Gross Household Product." *Feminist Economics* 2, no. 3 (1996): 37–64.
James, Selma. "Introduction." In Mariarosa Dalla Costa and Selma James, *The Power of Women and the Subversion of the Community*. Third edition, 10–11. Bristol: Falling Wall Press, 1975. First published in 1972.
Joyce, Patrick. "The Historical Meanings of Work: An Introduction." In *The Historical Meanings of Work*, edited by Patrick Joyce, 1–30. Cambridge: Cambridge University Press, 1987.
Joyce, Patrick, ed. *The Historical Meanings of Work*. Cambridge: Cambridge University Press, 1987.
Juratic, Sabine. "Marchandes ou savantes? Les veuves des libraires parisiens sous le règne de Louis XIV." In *Femmes savantes, savoirs des femmes*, edited by Colette Nativel, 59–68. Genève: Droz, 1999.
Jütfe, Robert. "Poor Relief and Social Discipline in Sixteenth-Century Europe." *European History Quarterly* 11, no. 1 (1981): 25–52.
Karpinski, Andrzej. "The Woman on the Market Place: The Scale of Feminization of Retail Trade in Polish Towns in the Second Half of the 16th and the 17th Century." In *La donna nell'economia, secc. XIII–XVIII, Atti delle Settimane di studi dell'Istituto internazionale di Storia economica F. Datini di Prato*, edited by Simonetta Cavaciocchi, 283–92. Firenze: Le Monnier, 1990.
Kendrick, John W. "Expanding Imputed Values in the National Income and Product Accounts." *Review of Income and Wealth* 25, no. 4 (1979): 349–63.
Kerber, Linda K. "Separate Spheres, Female Worlds, Woman's Place: The Rhetoric of Women's History." *Journal of American History* 75, no. 1 (1988): 9–39.
Kessler-Harris, Alice. *Women Have Always Worked: A Historical Overview*. New York: Feminist Press, 1981.

Klapisch-Zuber, Christiane. "Disciples, fils, travailleurs: Les apprentis peintres et sculpteurs italiens au XVe et XVIe siècle." *Mélanges de l'École française de Rome— Italie et Méditerranée modernes et contemporaines* 128, no. 1 (2016). Retrieved 17 December 2017 from http://journals.openedition.org/mefrim/2469.

Köbler, Gerhard. *Deutsches Etymologisches Wörterbuch*, 1995. Retrieved 17 December 2017 from http://www.koeblergerhard.de/derwbhin.html.

Kocka, Jürgen. "Work as a Problem in European History." In *Work in a Modern Society: The German Historical Experience in Comparative Perspective*, edited by Jürgen Kocka, 1–15. New York: Berghahn Books, 2010.

Kocka, Jürgen, ed., *Work in a Modern Society: The German Historical Experience in Comparative Perspective*. New York: Berghahn Books, 2010.

Kriedte, Peter, Hans Medick, and Jürgen Schlumbohm, with contributions by Herbert Kisch and Franklin F. Mendels. *Industrialisierung vor der Industrialisierung: Gewerbliche Warenproduktion auf dem Land in der Formationsperiode des Kapitalismus*. Göttingen: Vandenhoeck und Ruprecht, 1977. English translation: Beate Schempp. *Industrialization before Industrialization: Rural Industry in the Genesis of Capitalism*. Cambridge: Cambridge University Press; Paris: Editions de la Maison des Sciences de l'Homme, 1981.

"Labor Theory of Value." Wikipedia. Retrieved August 2016 from https://en.wikipedia.org/wiki/Labor_theory_of_value.

Lachance-Grzela, Mylène, and Geneviève Bouchard. "Why Do Women Do the Lion's Share of Housework? A Decade of Research." *Sex Roles* 63, nos. 11–12 (2010): 767–80.

Lanza, Janine M. "Les veuves d'artisans dans le Paris du XVIIIe siècle." In *Veufs, veuves et veuvage dans la France d'Ancien Régime*, Actes du Colloque de Poitiers (11–12 juin 1998), Textes réunis par Nicole Pellegrin, présentés et édités par Colette H. Winn, 109–20. Paris: Honoré Champion, 2003.

———. *From Wives to Widows in Early Modern Paris: Gender, Economy, and Law*. Aldershot-Burlington: Ashgate, 2007.

Laslett, Peter. "Family and Household as Work and Kin Group: Areas of Traditional Europe Compared." In *Family Forms in Historic Europe*, edited by Richard Wall, Jean Robin, and Peter Laslett, 513–63. Cambridge: Cambridge University Press, 1983.

Le Goff, Jacques. *Un lungo Medioevo*. Roma: Edizioni Dedalo, 2006.

Lewis, Charlton T., and Charles Short. *A Latin Dictionary*. Perseus Digital Library, Tufts University. Retrieved 29 August 2016 from http://www.perseus.tufts.edu/hopper/morph?l=labor&la=la&can=labor1&prior=labor.

Lis, Catharina, and Hugo Soly. *Worthy Efforts: Attitudes to Work and Workers in Pre-industrial Europe*. Leiden: Brill, 2012.

Littré, Émile, *Dictionnaire de la langue française*. Retrieved 29 August 2016 from http://www.littre.org.

Lützel, Heinrich. "Household Production and National Accounts." *Statistical Journal of the United Nations Economic Commission for Europe* 6, no. 4 (1989): 337–48.

Luxton, Meg. "The UN, Women, and Household Labour: Measuring and Valuing Unpaid Work." *Women's Studies International Forum* 20, no. 3 (1997): 431–39.

Maegraith, Janine, and Craig Muldrew. "Consumption and Material Life." In *The Oxford Handbook of Early Modern European History, 1350–1750*. Vol. 1: *Peoples* and *Place*, edited by Hamish Scott, 369–97. Oxford: Oxford University Press, 2015.

Maitte, Corine. "Le travail invisible dans les familles artisanales (XVIIe–XVIIIe siècles)." *Mélanges de l'École française de Rome—Italie et Méditerranée modernes et contemporaines* 128, no. 1 (2016): retrieved 17 December 2017 from http://journals.openedition.org/mefrim/2436.

Marchand, Olivier, and Claude Thélot. *Deux siècles de travail en France*. Paris: Insee, 1991.

Marinella, Lucrezia. *La nobiltà et l'eccellenza delle donne, co' difetti et mancamenti de gli huomini*. 2nd edition. Venezia: Gio. Battista Ciotti, 1601; for the English translation see *The Nobility and Excellence of Women, and the Defects and Vices of Men*, edited and translated by Anne Dunhill. Chicago: University of Chicago Press, 1999.

Martini, Manuela. "When Unpaid Workers Need a Legal Status: Family Workers and Reforms to Labour Rights in Twentieth-Century France." *International Review of Social History* 59, no. 2 (2014): 247–78.

Martini, Manuela, and Anna Bellavitis. "Household Economies, Social Norms and Practices of Unpaid Market Work in Europe from the Sixteenth Century to the Present." *History of the Family* 19, no. 3 (2014): 273–82.

Martini, Manuela, and Anna Bellavitis, eds. "Households, Family Workshops and Unpaid Market Work in Europe from the 16th Century to the Present." Special issue of *History of the Family* 19, no. 3 (2014).

Marx, Karl. *The Economic and Philosophical Manuscripts of 1844*. Translated and edited by Martin Milligan. Mineola, NY: Dover Publications, 2007. Unabridged republication of the work originally published by Moscow: Foreign Languages House, 1961.

———. *Theories of Surplus-Value* (1863). Moscow: Progress Publishers, w.d. Retrieved 17 December 2017 from https://www.marxists.org/archive/marx/works/1863/theories-surplus-value/.

———. *Grundrisse: Foundations of the Critique of Political Economy (Rough Draft)* (1857–61). Translated by Martin Nicolaus. London: Penguin Books in association with New Left Review, 1973. Retrieved 17 December 2017 from https://www.marxists.org/archive/marx/works/1857/grundrisse/.

———. *Capital: A Critique of Political Economy*. Vol. 1, book 1: *The Process of Production of Capital* (1867). First English edition of 1887. Translated by Samuel Moore and Edward Aveling, edited by Frederick Engels. Moscow: Progress Publishers, w.d. Retrieved 8 January 2017 from https://www.marxists.org/archive/marx/works/1867-c1/index.htm and vol. 3: *The Process of Capitalist Production as a Whole* (1894, edited and completed by Friedrich Engels), Institute of Marxism-Leninism, URSS, 1959-New York, International Publishers, s.d., Retrieved 17 December 2017 from https://www.marxists.org/archive/marx/works/1894-c3/index.htm.

Marx, Karl, and Friedrich Engels. *Manifesto of the Communist Party* (1848): online version of the *Manifesto* available at https://www.marxists.org/archive/marx/works/1848/communist-manifesto/index.htm. Source: *Marx and Engels Selected Works*. Vol. 1. Moscow: Progress Publishers, Moscow, 1969, 98–137. Translated by Samuel Moore in collaboration with Frederick Engels, 1888; transcribed by Zodiac and Brian Baggins; proofread and corrected against the 1888 English edition by Andy Blunden 2004; copy left: Marxists Internet Archive (marxists.org) 1987, 2000, 2010.

Matthes, Joachim, ed., *Krise der Arbeitsgesellschaft? Verhandlungen des 21. Deutschen Soziologentages in Bamberg 1982*. Frankfurt: Campus, 1983.

McGeevor, Sophie. "How Well Did the Nineteenth Century Census Record Women's 'Regular' Employment in England and Wales? A Case Study of Hertfordshire in 1851." *History of the Family* 19, no. 4 (2014): 489–512.

McKendrick, Neil. "Home Demand and Economic Growth: A New View of the Role of Women and Children in the Industrial Revolution." In *Historical Perspectives: Studies in English Thought and Society in Honour of J. H. Plumb*, edited by Neil McKendrick, 152–210. London: Europa Publications Limited, 1974.

McKendrick, Neil, John Brewer, and J. H. Plumb. *The Birth of a Consumer Society: The Commercialization of Eighteenth-Century England*. London: Europa Publications Limited, 1982.

McLeod, Jane. "Printer Widows and the State in Eighteenth-Century France." In *Women and Work in Eighteenth-Century France*, edited by Daryl M. Hafter and Nina Kushner, 113–29. Baton Rouge: Louisiana State University Press, 2015.

Méda, Dominique. *Le travail: Une valeur en voie de disparition*. Paris: Aubier, 1995.

Medick, Hans. *Weben und Überleben in Laichingen 1650–1900: Lokalgeschichte als allgemeine Geschichte*. Göttingen: Vandenhoeck & Ruprecht, 1996.

Mendels, Franklin. "Proto-industrialization: The First Phase of the Industrialization Process." *Journal of Economic History* 32, no. 1 (1972): 241–61.

Mendelson, Sara, and Patricia Crawford. *Women in Early Modern England 1550–1720*. Oxford: Clarendon Press, 1998.

Mies, Maria. *The Lace Makers of Narsapur: Indian Housewives Produce for the World Market*. North Geelong, Victoria: Spinifex Press, 2012. First edition London: Zed Books, 1982.

Mocarelli, Luca. "The Attitude of Milanese Society to Work and Commercial Activities." In *The Idea of Work in Europe from Antiquity to Modern Times*, edited by Josef Ehmer and Catharina Lis, 101–21. Farnham-Burlington: Ashgate 2009.

Montella, Monica. "La produzione domestica: il valore aggiunto generato dalle famiglie." Working paper, Dipartimento di Economia e Diritto Sapienza Università di Roma, Roma, 2012.

Montenach, Anne. *Espaces et pratiques du commerce alimentaire à Lyon au XVIIe siècle: l'économie du quotidien*. Grenoble: Presses Universitaires de Grenoble, 2009.

Muraro, Luisa. *La signora del gioco: episodi di caccia alle streghe*. Milano: Feltrinelli, 1976.

Musgrave, Elisabeth. "Women and the Craft Guilds in Eighteenth-Century Nantes." In *The Artisan and the European Town, 1500–1900*, edited by Geoffrey Crossick, 151–71. Aldershot-Burlington: Ashgate, 1997.

Negri, Antimo. "Per una storia del concetto di lavoro nella cultura filosofica ed economica occidentale." In *Il lavoro come fattore produttivo e come risorsa nella storia economica*, edited by Sergio Zaninelli and Mario Taccolini, xii–xl. Milano: Vita e Pensiero, 2002.

Niccoli, Ottavia. *I sacerdoti, i guerrieri, i contadini: storia di un'immagine della società*. Torino: Einaudi, 1979.

———. "Immagini e metafore della società in età moderna: Lectio magistralis tenuta il 16 novembre 2010." *Quaderni del Dipartimento di Sociologia e Ricerca Sociale dell'Università degli Studi di Trento*, no. 54 (2011): 5–29.
Ogilvie, Sheilagh. *A Bitter Living: Women, Markets, and Social Capital in Early Modern Germany*. Oxford: Oxford University Press, 2003.
———. "How Does Social Capital Affect Women? Guilds and Communities in Early Modern Germany." *American Historical Review* 109, no. 2 (2004): 325–59.
———. "Consumption, Social Capital, and the 'Industrious Revolution' in Early Modern Germany." *Journal of Economic History* 70, no. 2 (2010): 287–325.
Olson, Margrethe H., and Sophia B. Primps. "Working at Home with Computers: Work and Nonwork Issues." *Journal of Social Issues* 40, no. 3 (1984): 97–112.
Olson-Buchanan, Julie B., Wendy R. Boswell, and Timothy J. Morgan. "The Role of Technology in Managing the Work and Nonwork Interface." In *The Oxford Handbook of Work and Family*, edited by Tammy D. Allen and Lillian T. Eby, 333–48. Oxford: Oxford University Press, 2016.
Palazzi, Maura. "Vivere a compagnia e vivere a dozzina: gruppi domestici non coniugali nella Bologna di fine Settecento." In *Ragnatele di rapporti: patronage e reti di relazione nelle storie delle donne*, edited by Lucia Ferrante, Maura Palazzi, and Gianna Pomata, 344–81. Torino: Rosenberg & Sellier, 1988.
———. *Donne sole: storie dell'altra faccia dell'Italia tra antico regime e società contemporanea*. Milano: Bruno Mondadori 1997.
Parreñas, Rhacel Salazar. "Migrant Filipina Domestic Workers and the International Division of Reproductive Labor." *Gender & Society* 14, no. 4 (2000): 560–80.
———. "The International Division of Reproductive Labor: Paid Domestic Work and Globalization." In *Critical Globalization Studies*, edited by Richard P. Applebaum and William I. Robinson, 237–47. New York: Routledge, 2005.
———. *Servants of Globalization: Migration and Domestic Work*. 2nd edition. Stanford: Stanford University Press, 2015. First published in 2001 with the subtitle *Women, Migration and Domestic Work*.
Pateman, Carole. *The Sexual Contract*. Stanford: Stanford University Press, 1988.
Pelaja, Margherita. "Mestieri femminili e luoghi comuni: le domestiche a Roma a metà Ottocento." *Quaderni storici* 23, no. 68 (1988): 497–518.
———. "Relazioni personali e vincoli di gruppo: il lavoro delle donne nella Roma dell'Ottocento." *Memoria* 10, no. 30 (1990): 44–52.
Perrot, Michelle, ed. *Une histoire des femmes est-elle possible?* Marseille: Rivages, 1984.
Pescarolo, Alessandra, and Gian Bruno Ravenni. *Il proletariato invisibile: la manifattura della paglia nella Toscana mezzadrile (1820–1950)*. Milano: Angeli, 1991.
Phillips, Lisa. "Silent Partners: The Role of Unpaid Market Labor in Families." *Feminist Economics* 14, no. 2 (2008): 37–57.
Picchio, Antonella. *Social Reproduction: The Political Economy of the Labour Market*. Cambridge: Cambridge University Press, 1992.
Picchio, Antonella, ed. *Unpaid Work and the Economy: A Gender Analysis of the Standards of Living*. New York: Routledge, 2005.
Pinchbeck, Ivy. *Women Workers and the Industrial Revolution, 1750–1850*. New York: Frank Cass, 1977; first edition, London: George Routledge, 1930.
Pomata, Gianna. "Madri illegittime tra Ottocento e Novecento: storie cliniche e storie di vita." *Quaderni storici* 15, no. 44 (1980): 497–542.

———. "La storia delle donne: una questione di confine." In *Il mondo contemporaneo*, edited by Giovanni De Luna, Peppino Ortoleva, Marco Revelli, and Nicola Tranfaglia. Vol. 10: *Gli strumenti della ricerca, 2, Questioni di metodo*", pt. 2, 1434–69. Firenze: La Nuova Italia, 1983.

Poni, Carlo. "La famiglia contadina e il podere in Emilia Romagna." In Carlo Poni, *Fossi e cavedagne benedicon le campagne*, 283–356. Bologna: Il Mulino, 1982.

Porciani, Leone. "Appunti sulla schiavitù greca: il caso dei *dēmosioi* ad Atene." In *Nuove e antiche forme di schiavitù*, edited by Mauro Simonazzi and Thomas Casadei, 25–38. Napoli: Editoriale Scientifica, 2018.

———. "Schiavi pubblici ad Atene: per una discussione sul rapporto fra amministrazione e politica." In *Revisiter l'esclavage ancien: méthodologies et nouvelles approches critiques*, forthcoming.

Potter, Jane. "Valliant Heroines or Pacific Ladies? Women in War and Peace." In *The Routledge History of Women*, edited by Deborah Simonton, 259–98. New York: Routledge 2006.

Poullain, François [or Poulain de la Barre]. *De l'égalité des deux sexes, discours physique et moral où l'on voit l'importance de se défaire des préjugez*. Paris: Jean du Puis, 1673. First English translation: *The Woman as Good as the Man: Or, The Equality of Both Sexes*, translated by A. L., London: N. Brooks, 1677. New translation by Desmond M. Clarke in *The Equality of the Sexes: Three Feminist Texts of the Seventeenth Century*. Oxford: Oxford University Press, 2013.

Rogers, Rebecca. "Learning to Be Good Girls and Women: Education, Training and Schools." In *The Routledge History of Women*, edited by Deborah Simonton, 93–133. New York: Routledge 2006.

Romero-Martín, Juanjo. "Craftswomen in Times of Change: Artisan Family Strategies in Nineteenth Century Barcelona." *Mélanges de l'École française de Rome—Italie et Méditerranée modernes et contemporaines* 128, no. 1 (2016): retrieved 17 December 2017 from http://journals.openedition.org/mefrim/2445.

Rowbotham, Sheila. *Hidden from History: 300 Years of Women's Oppression and the Fight Against It*. London: Pluto Press, 1973.

Roy, Delphine. "La contribution du travail domestique non marchand au bien-être matériel des ménages: une quantification à partir de l'enquête Emploi du Temps." *Document de travail*, no F1104, Insee, March 2011.

Sabean, David W. *Property, Production, and Family in Neckarhausen, 1700–1870*. Cambridge: Cambridge University Press, 1990.

Saito, Osamu. "Historical Origins of the Male Breadwinner Household Model: Britain, Sweden and Japan." *Japan Labor Review* 11, no. 4 (2014): 5–20.

Sarasúa, Carmen. "Leaving Home to Help the Family? Male and Female Temporary Migrants in Eighteenth- and Nineteenth-Century Spain." In *Women, Gender and Labour Migration: Historical and Global Perspectives*, edited by Pamela Sharpe, 29–59. New York: Routledge, 2001.

Sarti, Raffaella. "Servire al femminile, servire al maschile nella Bologna sette-ottocentesca." In *Operaie, serve, maestre, impiegate*, edited by Paola Nava, 237–64. Torino: Rosenberg & Sellier, 1992.

———. *Europe at Home: Family and Material Culture, 1500–1800*. New Haven, CT: Yale University Press, 2002. English translation, by Allan Cameron, of *Vita di casa: abitare, mangiare, vestire nell'Europa moderna*. Roma-Bari: Laterza, 1999.

———. "Oltre il gender? Un percorso tra recenti studi italiani di storia economico-sociale." In *A che punto è la storia delle donne in Italia*, edited by Anna Rossi-Doria, 93–144. Roma: Viella, 2003.

———. "Who Are Servants? Defining Domestic Service in Western Europe (16th–21st Centuries)." In *Proceedings of the Servant Project*, edited by Suzy Pasleau and Isabelle Schopp, with Raffaella Sarti, 2:3–59. Liège: Éditions de l'Université de Liège, 2005. Retrieved 17 December 2017 from http://www.uniurb.it/sarti/Raffaella_Sarti_Who_are_servants_Proceedings_of_the_Servant_Project.pdf.

———. "Historians, Social Scientists, Servants, and Domestic Workers: Fifty Years of Research on Domestic and Care Work." *International Review of Social History* 59, no. 2 (2014): 279–314. Also published in *Towards a Global History of Domestic and Caregiving Workers*, edited by Dirk Hoerder, Elise van Nederveen Meerkerk, and Silke Neunsinger, 25–60. Leiden, Brill, 2015.

———. "Ländliche Hauslandschaften in Europa in einer Langzeitperspektive." In *Das Haus in der Geschichte Europas: Ein Handbuch*, edited by Joachim Eibach and Inken Schmidt-Voges, together with Simone Derix, Philip Hahn, Elizabeth Harding, Margareth Lanzinger, red. Roman Bonderer, 175–94. Berlin: De Gruyter Oldenbourg, 2015.

———. *Servo e padrone, o della (in)dipendenza: un percorso da Aristotele ai nostri giorni*. Vol. I: *Teorie e dibattiti*, Series "Quaderni" of *Scienza & Politica*, Quaderno no. 2, 2015. Bologna: Alma Mater Studiorum Università di Bologna, 2015. Open-access e-book available at http://amsacta.unibo.it/4293/1/Sarti_Servo_e_Padrone_1.pdf. Retrieved 17 December 2017.

———. "Open Houses versus Closed Borders: Migrant Domestic Workers in Italy; A Gendered Perspective (1950s–2010s)." In *Gender and Migration in Italy: A Multilayered Perspective*, edited by Elisa Olivito, 39–59. Farnham-Burlington: Ashgate, 2016.

———. "Criados rurales: el caso de Italia desde una perspectiva comparada (siglos XVI al XX)." *Mundo Agrario* 18, no. 39 (2017), e065-e065: 1–32. https://doi.org/10.24215/15155994e065.

———. "Rural Life-Cycle Service: Established Interpretations and New (Surprising) Data: The Italian Case in Comparative Perspective (Sixteenth to Twentieth Centuries)." In *Servants in Rural Europe, c. 1400–1900*, edited by Jane Whittle, 227–54. Woodbridge: Boydell & Brewer, 2017).

Saurer, Edith. *Liebe und Arbeit: Geschlechterbeziehungen im 19. und 20. Jahrhundert*, edited by Margareth Lanzinger. Wien-Köln-Weimar: Böhlau, 2014.

Say, Jean Baptiste. *Traité d'économie politique, ou simple exposition de la manière dont se forment, se distribuent et se consomment les richesses*. Cinquième édition, vol. 1. Paris: Rapilly, 1826.

Schlumbohm, Jürgen. *Lebensläufe, Familien, Höfe: die Bauern und Heuerleute des Osnabrückischen Kirchspiels Belm in proto-industrieller Zeit, 1650–1860*. Göttingen: Vandenhoeck & Ruprecht, 1994.

Schmidt, Ariadne. "Women and Guilds: Corporations and Female Labour Market Participation in Early Modern Holland." *Gender & History* 21, no. 1 (2009): 170–89.

Schmidt, Ariadne, and Elise van Nederveen Meerkerk. "Reconsidering the 'First Male

Breadwinner Economy': Women's Labor Force Participation in the Netherlands, 1600–1900." *Feminist Economics* 18, no. 4 (2012): 69–96.

Schmidt, Ariadne, Isabelle Devos, and Bruno Blondé. "Introduction: Single and the City; Men and Women Alone in North-Western European Towns since the Late Middle Ages." In *Single Life and the City,* edited by Isabelle Devos, Julie De Groot, and Ariadne Schmidt, 1–24. New York: Palgrave Macmillan, 2015.

Schulz, Wiebke, Ineke Maas, and Marco H. D. van Leeuwen. "When Women Disappear from the Labour Market: Occupational Status of Dutch Women at Marriage in a Modernizing Society, 1865–1922." *History of the Family* 19, no. 4 (2014): 426–46.

Schweitzer, Silvie. *Les Femmes ont toujours travaillé: Une histoire du travail des femmes aux XIXe et XXe siècles.* Paris: Odile Jacob, 2002.

Scott, Wallach, Joan. "Statistical Representations of Work: 'The Politics of the Chamber of Commerce's Statistique de l'Industrie à Paris,' 1847–48." In *Work in France: Representations, Meaning, Organization, and Practice,* edited by Stephen Laurence Kaplan and Cynthia J. Koepp, 335–63. Ithaca, NY: Cornell University Press, 1986. Republished as "A Statistical Representation of Work: La Statistique de l'Industrie à Paris, 1847–1848," in Joan Wallach Scott, *Gender and the Politics of History,* 113–38. New York: Columbia University Press, 1988.

———. "'L'ouvrière! Mot impie, sordide . . .': Women Workers in the Discourse of French Political Economy, 1840–1860." In Joan Wallach Scott, *Gender and the Politics of History,* 138–63. New York: Columbia University Press, 1988. Original edition published in *The Historical Meanings of Work,* edited by Patrick Joyce, 119–42. Cambridge: Cambridge University Press, 1987.

———. "The Woman Worker in the Nineteenth Century." In *History of Women in the West,* edited by Georges Duby and Michelle Perrot. Vol. 4: *Emerging Feminism from Revolution to World War,* edited by Geneviève Fraisse, 399–426. Harvard: Harvard University Press, 1993. Originally published in Italian and French, translated by Arthur Goldhammer.

Shamir, Boas, and Ilan Salomon. "Work-at-Home and the Quality of Working Life." *Academy of Management Review* 10, no. 3 (1985): 455–64.

Shelton, Beth Anne, and John Daphne. "The Division of Household Labor." *Annual Review of Sociology* 22 (1996): 299–322.

Shepard, Alexandra. "Crediting Women in the Early Modern English Economy." *History Workshop Journal* 79, no. 1 (2015): 1–24.

———. *Accounting for Oneself: Worth, Status, and the Social Order in Early Modern England.* Oxford: Oxford University Press, 2015.

Simon, Jules. *L'ouvrière.* Paris, Hachette, 1861.

Simonton, Deborah. "Widows and Wenches: Single Women in Eighteenth-Century Urban Economies." In *Female Agency in the Urban Economy,* edited by Deborah Simonton and Anne Montenach, 93–115. New York: Routledge, 2013.

Simonton, Deborah, and Anne Montenach, eds. *Female Agency in the Urban Economy: Gender in European Towns, 1640–1830.* New York: Routledge, 2013.

Smith, Adam. *An Inquiry into the Nature and Causes of the Wealth of Nations* (1776). Retrieved 6 February 2016 from http://www.econlib.org/library/Smith/smWN8.html#B.II,%20Ch.3,%20Of%20the%20Accumulation%20of%20Capital,%20or%20of%20Productive%20and%20Unproductive%20Labour.

Solà, Àngels. "Apprentices, Women and Masters in the Silk Weavers' Guild of Barcelona, 1790–1840." *Mélanges de l'École française de Rome—Italie et Méditerranée modernes et contemporaines* 128, no. 1 (2016). Retrieved 17 December 2017 from http://journals.openedition.org/mefrim/2449.

Stedman Jones, Gareth. *Karl Marx: Greatness and Illusion*. Cambridge, MA: The Belknap Press of Harvard University Press, 2016.

Steinbach, Susie. "Can We Still Use 'Separate Spheres'? British History 25 Years after *Family Fortunes*." *History Compass* 10711 (2012): 826–37.

Stiglitz, Joseph, Amartya Sen, and Jean-Paul Fitoussi. *Report by the Commission on Economic Performance and Social Progress Revisited*. Paris: Sciences Po Publications, 2009.

Thomas, Keith. *The Oxford Book of Work*. Oxford: Oxford University Press, 1999.

Tilgher, Adriano. *Work: What It Has Meant to Men through the Ages*. New York: Harcourt, Brace and Co., 1930. English translation, by Dorothy Canfield Fisher, of *Homo Faber: storia del concetto di lavoro nella civiltà occidentale, analisi filosofica di concetti affini*. Roma: Libreria di scienze e lettere, 1929.

Tilly, Louise A., and Joan W. Scott. *Women, Work and the Family*. New York: Holt, Rinehart and Winston, 1978.

Toffanin, Tania. *Fabbriche invisibili: storie di donne, lavoranti a domicilio*. Verona: Ombre Corte, 2016.

Tosh, John. *A Man's Place: Masculinity and the Middle-Class Home in Victorian England*. New Haven, CT: Yale University Press, 1999.

Toupin, Louise. *Le salaire au travail ménager: Chronique d'une lutte féministe internationale (1972–1977)*. Montréal: Éditions du Remue-Ménage, 2014.

"Travail." In Centre National des Ressources Textuelles et Lexicales, Portal Lexical, Etymologie. Retrieved 17 December 2017 from http://www.cnrtl.fr/etymologie/travail.

Trésor de la Langue française informatisé (TLFI). Retrieved 6 June 2018 from http://stella.atilf.fr/Dendien/scripts/tlfiv5/advanced.exe?8;s=885769530.

van den Heuvel, Danielle. "Partners in Marriage and Business? Guilds and the Family Economy in Urban Food Markets in the Dutch Republic." *Continuity and Change* 23, no. 2 (2008): 217–36.

van den Heuvel, Danielle, and Elise van Nederveen Meerkerk. "Introduction: Partners in Business? Spousal Cooperation in Trades in Early Modern England and the Dutch Republic." *Continuity and Change* 23, no. 2 (2008): 209–16.

———. "Households, Work and Consumer Changes: The Case of Tea and Coffee Sellers in 18th-Century Leiden." *Mems Working Papers* (2014): retrieved 17 December 2017 from https://kar.kent.ac.uk/43709/.

van der Heijden, Manon, Ariadne Schmidt, and Richard Wall, eds. "Broken Families: Economic Resources and Social Networks of Women Who Head Families." Special issue of *History of the Family* 12, no. 4 (2007).

van der Heijden, Manon, Danielle van den Heuvel. "Sailors' Families and the Urban Institutional Framework in Early Modern Holland." *History of the Family* 12, no. 4 (2007): 296–309.

van der Klein, Marian. "Women, Work and the Breadwinner Ideology, from the Fifteenth to the Twentieth Century." *International Labor and Working-Class History* 58 (2000): 318–21.

van der Linden, Marcel. "Studying Attitudes to Work Worldwide, 1500–1650: Concepts, Sources, and Problems of Interpretation." *International Review of Social History* 56, S19 (2011): 25–43.

van Nederveen Meerkerk, Elise. "Segmentation in the Pre-Industrial Labour Market: Women's Work in the Dutch Textile Industry, 1581–1810." *International Review of Social History* 51, no. 2 (2006): 189–216.

———. "Couples Cooperating? Dutch Textile Workers, Family Labour and the 'Industrious Revolution,' c. 1600–1800." *Continuity and Change* 23, no. 2 (2008): 237–66.

van Nederveen Meerkerk, Elise, and Richard Paping. "Beyond the Census: Reconstructing Dutch Women's Labour Market Participation in Agriculture in the Netherlands, ca. 1830–1910," *History of the Family* 19, no. 4 (2014): 447–68.

van Nederveen Meerkerk, Elise, and Ariadne Schmidt. "Reconsidering the 'First Male Breadwinner Economy': Long-Term Trends in Female Labor Force Participation in the Netherlands, c. 1600–1900." *Feminist Economics* 18, no. 4 (2012): 69–96.

Veblen, Thorstein. *The Theory of the Leisure Class*, edited by Martha Banta. Oxford: Oxford University Press, 2009. Originally published New York: Macmillan, 1899.

Viazzo, Pier Paolo. "What's So Special about the Mediterranean? Thirty Years of Research on Household and Family in Italy." *Continuity and Change* 18, no. 1 (2003): 111–37.

Vickery, Amanda. "Golden Age to Separate Spheres? A Review of the Categories and Chronology of English Women's History." *Historical Journal* 36, no. 2 (1993), 383–414.

———. *The Gentleman's Daughter: Women's Lives in Georgian England*. New Haven, CT: Yale University Press, 1999.

Vitali, Ornello. *Aspetti dello sviluppo economico italiano alla luce della ricostruzione della popolazione attiva*. Roma: Failli, 1970.

Vives, Juan Luis. *De Subventione Pauperum sive De Humanis Necessitatibus, Libri II*, edited by Constant Matheeussen and Charles Fantazzi, with the assistance of Jeanine De Landtsheer, translated by Charles Fantazzi. Leiden: Brill, 2002.

Waring, Marilyn. *If Women Counted: A New Feminist Economics*. San Francisco: HarperCollins, 1988.

Weatherill, Lorna. *Consumer Behaviour and Material Culture in Britain 1660–1760*. New York: Routledge, 1988.

Weber, Max, *Die protestantische Ethik und der Geist des Kapitalismus*, 1904–1905. English translation: *The Protestant Ethic and the Spirit of Capitalism: With Other Writings on the Rise of the West*. New York: Oxford University Press, 2009; and *The Protestant Ethic and the Spirit of Capitalism*, translated by Talcott Parsons, with an introduction by Anthony Giddens. London: Routledge, 2001.

Whittle, Jane. "Enterprising Widows and Active Wives: Women's Unpaid Work in the Household Economy of Early Modern England." *History of the Family* 9, no. 3 (2014): 283–300.

Whittle, Jane, and Elizabeth Griffiths. *Consumption and Gender in the Early Seventeenth-Century Household: The World of Alice Le Strange*. Oxford: Oxford University Press, 2012.

Widerquist, Karl, José A. Noguera, Yannick Vanderborght, and Jurgen De Wispelaere, eds. *Basic Income: An Anthology of Contemporary Research.* Chichester: Wiley Blackwell, 2013.

Wiesner, Merry E. *Working Women in Renaissance Germany.* New Brunswick, NJ: Rutgers University Press, 1986.

———. "Guilds, Male Bonding and Women's Work in Early Modern Germany." *Gender & History* 1, no. 2 (1989): 125–37.

———. "Wandervogels Women: Journeymen's Concepts of Masculinity in Early Modern Germany." *Journal of Social History* 24, no. 4 (1991): 767–82.

———. "Gender and the Worlds of Work." In *Germany: A New Social and Economic History.* Vol. 1: *1450–1630,* edited by Bob Scribner, 209–32. New York: Arnold, 1996.

Yeates, Nicola. "Changing Places: Ireland in the International Division of Reproductive Labour." *Translocations: The Irish Migration, Race and Social Transformation Review* 1, no. 1 (2006): 5–21.

Zarri, Gabriella. "Pietà e profezia alle corti padane: le pie consigliere dei principi." In *Il Rinascimento nelle corti padane: Società e cultura,* edited by Paolo Rossi et al., 201–37. Bari: De Donato, 1977.

———. "Monasteri femminili e città (secoli XV–XVIII)." In *Storia d'Italia, Annali.* Vol. 9: *Chiesa e potere politico dal medioevo all'età contemporanea,* edited by Giorgio Chittolini and Giovanni Miccoli, 357–429. Torino: Einaudi, 1986.

Zijdeman, Richard L., Marco H. D. van Leeuwen, Danièle Rébaudo, and Jean-Pierre Pélissier. "Working Women in France, Nineteenth and Twentieth Centuries: Where, When, and Which Women Were in Work at Marriage?" *History of the Family* 19, no. 4 (2014): 537–63.

Zimmermann, Benedicte. "Work and Labor: History of the Concept." *International Encyclopedia of the Social & Behavioral Sciences* 24 (2001): 16561–65.

Zucca Micheletto, Beatrice. "Reconsidering the Southern Europe Model: Dowry, Women's Work and Marriage Patterns in Pre-Industrial Urban Italy (Turin, Second Half of the 18th Century)." *History of the Family* 16, no. 4 (2011): 354–70.

———. "Only Unpaid Labour Force? Women's and Girls' Work and Property in Family Business in Early Modern Italy." *History of the Family* 19, no. 3 (2014): 323–40.

———. "Husbands, Masculinity, Male Work and Household Economy in Eighteenth-Century Italy: The Case of Turin." *Gender & History* 27, no. 3 (2015): 752–72.

I

SETTING THE SCENE: THE FEMINIST CHALLENGES TO THE "DELABORIZATION" OF HOUSEHOLD WORK

This part focuses on the processes by which, starting from the eighteenth century, the rather broad early modern notions of work (also described in the introduction of this book) were refashioned in such a way that care work and domestic activities performed at home mainly by women were increasingly seen as something different from proper work with an economic value; rather, they were more and more considered as a natural duty, as a moral obligation, as a free gift due to love. Nancy Folbre illustrates the approaches to household work by the political economies of the United Kingdom, France, and the United States from the eighteenth century to the present. The distinction between productive and unproductive work made by Adam Smith and further reworked by many other authors was indeed crucial to the marginalization of family work from the realm of proper work. Smith and several other later thinkers did not even consider the obvious fact that unpaid family care work is crucial to ensuring the supply of labor to the market and to guarantee the very existence of present and future workers.

Despite the fact that different authors conceived the productive-unproductive dichotomy in different ways, they agreed with including unpaid carework and domestic tasks, i.e. those activities that later would be (often) defined as reproductive, with the unproductive work. Alessandra Pescarolo explains that classical economists ignored such activities and focuses precisely on the elaboration of the reproductive-productive work dichotomy, first conceived in the 1960s by Marxist feminists who tried to situate domestic activities within the Marxist theoretical framework. In fact, Marx, though disregarding domestic and care work, addressed the issue of reproductive work. He considered the part of factory work exchanged by workers for the salary necessary to guarantee their survival (the so-called "necessary work") as such, whereas he considered the other part of work, producing surplus, as productive.

The members of the Italian collective Lotta Femminista (Feminist Struggle), founded in Padua, Italy, in 1971, contended, from a Marxist perspective, that unpaid work performed by housewives was reproductive work. At the same time, they questioned the idea that domestic work was unproductive, arguing that it actually produced the "strange commodity" represented by the worker, i.e. labor power. Thanks to the collaboration between the founder of the collective, Mariarosa Dalla Costa, and the American (but UK-based) feminist Selma James, these elaborations contributed in launching the debate on domestic labor on an international level. Their book, *The Power of Women and the Subversion of the Community*, published in several European languages in the first half of the 1970s, would become a bestseller. Dalla Costa and James argued that housewives' work guaranteed the reproduction and production of labor power. Both to unveil the true nature of housework and to empower women, they maintained that housework should be paid: their book became the starting point of an international campaign for wages for housework. As stressed by Alessandra Gissi, this meant rejecting the prevailing definition of work as something existing only outside of the domestic sphere and reshaping the very notion of "worker."

Another interesting position was that of the French materialist feminist Christine Delphy, who studied in the United States and published, in English, her influential book *The Main Enemy: A Materialist Analysis of Women's Oppression* (1977). Delphy refused the distinction between production and reproduction, arguing that two different modes of production coexisted: the domestic one, based on the exploitation of women by men, and the capitalistic extra-domestic one, involving both male and female factory workers. In her view, women's oppression is primarily due to patriarchy, deriving from their position of producers exploited at home by their husbands.

But let's go back to the campaign for wages for housework. Despite its international spread and the theoretical support by professional economists, many feminists did not adhere to it, being afraid that wages for housework would make the gender division of labor even more rigid than before. These fears were not without reason: ideas on the need to pay for housework were not necessarily women friendly. As shown by Gissi, proposals of this kind had been suggested, for instance, during Italian Fascism in the 1930s.

Indeed, the idea that housework should be paid had deep roots in history, mainly, however, among activists who, as recalled by Folbre, as early as the 1870s hoped in this way to contribute to empower women. A century later, the promoters and supporters of the campaign for wages for housework called for wages to "denaturalize" housework and to contribute to a real revolution against women's oppression. The naturalization of housework was indeed an issue that in the 1960s and 1970s all feminists and women's and gender historians had to tackle.

The challenges to the conceptualization of household work as a natural obligation became more frequent over time. Only in the late twentieth century they began—among other factors—to affect the national income accounting. At stake there is not only the issue of promoting gender equality in the workplace but also the very recognition of the value of family work and care of dependents. Despite having an economic value, such work does not generate economies of scale because of its contextual and relational nature. Yet a reassessment of growth in terms of well-being rather than GDP, as noted by Pescarolo, might change the general theoretical perspective, while innovations such as 3D printers could erode the distinction between places of production and places of consumption.

CHAPTER 1

FAMILY WORK
A Policy-Relevant Intellectual History

Nancy Folbre

In December of 2008, Gov. Ed Rendell of Pennsylvania praised the appointment of Gov. Janet Napolitano of Arizona as secretary of Homeland Security, "because for that job you have to have no life. Janet has no family. Perfect. She can devote, literally, 19–20 hours a day to it." Governor Rendell did not realize his microphone was on. He later explained that he has no life either.[1]

In the twenty-first century United States, the difficulties of balancing family responsibility and paid employment permeate the experience of many men as well as most women. Cultural norms regarding the division of labor and the organization of family care are being renegotiated, but implicit gender bias remains pervasive. Gendered care responsibilities are often the primary cause of differences in men's and women's pay.

These trends help explain efforts to discourage "family responsibility employment discrimination" (or FRED) in the United States. These efforts have found specific expression in a growing body of case law that insists on gender neutrality in employer responses to employees' family constraints. They have found more general expression in campaigns to implement public policies that would require employers to provide more generous accommodation for all workers with family responsibilities and provide greater support for family care. The case for many proposed reforms goes beyond a critique of gender bias to assert the economic value of family work.

This case can be strengthened by attention to the evolution of liberal political and economic theory. In this chapter, I draw from my book

Greed, Lust, and Gender: A History of Economic Ideas to explore and explain reluctance to assign an economic value to unpaid work.[2] The first section situates this history within a current policy context, summarizing both narrow and broad definitions of family responsibility discrimination as examples of the links between gender equality and valuation of family work. The second section traces the exclusion of unpaid family work from the realm of political economy. In the seventeenth and eighteenth centuries, this work was largely relegated to the realm of nature. In the nineteenth century, it was more often situated in the realm of moral obligation. In the twentieth century, it was partially, if not wholly, relocated to the realm of consumption, and came to be seen primarily as a source of personal utility—one among many other lifestyle choices.[3]

The third section provides specific evidence of the devaluation of family work through analysis of the categories deployed in censuses and national income accounts in the English-speaking world. Despite occasional exceptions—and protests—the work of wives, mothers, and sisters within the home has been—and continues to be—poorly measured and undervalued. The fourth section returns to policy issues, describing some important episodes in recurring efforts to at least partially de-gender responsibilities for family care, which shaped early debates over minimum wage legislation and policies toward the employment of married women in the United States.

1. Family responsibility discrimination defined

Debates over family responsibility employment discrimination resemble, in some respects, earlier debates over sex discrimination. However, by calling attention to a factor closely related to but distinct from gender—family responsibility—they highlight the significance of unpaid family work. In traditional human capital models, the choice to take time out of paid employment is generally pictured as a decision to reduce investments in market-specific human capital that lower productivity, and therefore earnings. If employers have discriminatory preferences, these are likely to reduce profitability. In the long run, competition should drive such employers out of business.

In models less wedded to traditional neoclassical assumptions, women's specialization in unpaid family work may be explained as the outcome of household bargaining, and reduced demand for women by employers can be construed as a response to a signal of probable future reductions in job effort or career continuity likely to result from family commitments ("statistical discrimination"). Heterodox economists, as well as sociologists, are more likely to emphasize forms of collective action (including public policy) that shape women's bargaining power in the home and the workplace. They are also more likely to emphasize the influence of cultural norms that typically persist long after institutional means of enforcing them have weakened.

From this perspective, men have a collective interest in policies that diminish women's bargaining power in the home, just as employers have a collective interest in minimizing labor costs. Both public policies and cultural norms may enable collusion in practices of discrimination, segregation, and devaluation. Even those economically disadvantaged by such collusion may internalize norms that encourage acquiescence.

Whatever the most important factors influencing employment outcomes for women, the effects of gender per se can be distinguished from the effects of family responsibility. In the United States in particular, women without children fare better in the labor market than others (though these effects vary across the wage and income distribution). In general, children tend to have a negative effect on mothers' earnings and a positive effect on fathers' earnings.[4] Earnings alone don't tell the whole story. Many parents enjoy transfers from a spouse or other family member that represent at least partial compensation for their specialization in household work.[5] However, lack of independent access to earnings increases vulnerability to desertion or divorce and reduces bargaining power within the household.

The responsibilities of parenthood—especially motherhood—clearly affect labor supply. They also affect labor demand. Powerful evidence of demand-side discrimination against mothers derives from research conducted by sociologists Shelley Correll, Stephen Benard, and In Paik.[6] In a much-cited audit study, they sent fictional résumés and cover letters to employers advertising midlevel marketing and business job openings in a large Northeastern city newspaper. Childless women received 2.1 times as many callbacks as mothers. These researchers also provide evidence of broader devaluation of mothers' capabilities. In one experiment, about two hundred undergraduates were asked to rate paired applications for an imaginary midlevel managerial job. Both female and male students rated mothers lower on competence and commitment, recommended lower salaries for them, and judged them less worthy of promotion than childless women. By contrast, men enjoy a pay and prestige bonus for fatherhood.[7]

In the United States, it is not illegal to discriminate against parents relative to non-parents, although current case law suggests that mothers and fathers must be treated the same. As a result, gender inconsistency receives more sustained attention. In May 2007, the US Equal Opportunities Employment Commission issued official guidance on family responsibility employment discrimination, explaining circumstances under which discrimination against caregivers violates existing law:

> Sex-based stereotyping about caregiving responsibilities is not limited to childcare and includes other forms of caregiving, such as care of a sick parent or spouse. Thus, women with caregiving responsibilities may be perceived as more committed to caregiving than to their jobs and as less competent than other workers, regardless of how their caregiving responsibilities actually impact their work. Male caregivers may face the mirror image stereotype: that men are poorly suited to caregiving. As a result, men may be denied parental leave or other benefits routinely afforded their female counterparts.[8]

The explanation goes on to note that an employer does not violate existing prohibitions against disparate treatment if it "treats working mothers and working fathers in a similar unfavorable (or favorable) matter as compared to childless workers." As legal scholars Joan Williams and Nancy Segal explain in their thoughtful analysis of the "maternal wall," claims of family responsibility discrimination are framed not in terms of needs for workplace accommodation but as "reflections of gender discrimination that polices men into traditional breadwinner roles and women out of them."[9]

Williams and Segal go on to argue that cases of family responsibility discrimination, narrowly defined, point to broader problems that can only be remedied by laws prohibiting workplace discrimination against individuals with family responsibilities, guaranteeing equitable pay and benefits for part-time workers, and providing reasonable limits on mandatory overtime.[10] In some ways, this represents a distinctly American approach to work/family conflict, urging regulation of employers rather than public provision.

In any case, the notion that existing employment practices effectively discriminate against workers with family responsibilities points to gender-neutral dynamics that could, in principle, affect men as well as women. It invokes a much broader definition of discrimination than economists typically deploy, focusing on incentives to collectively minimize labor costs as well as the inertial influence of employment policies put in place when most employed workers could rely on female family members to provide family care.

The broad approach to family responsibility discrimination goes beyond consideration of employer-employee dynamics to assert the economic importance of family care. This approach has clear antecedents in the history of economic ideas *and* economic policies that sought to justify the disparate treatment of women on the grounds that gender equality would threaten the family.

2. Family work: productive or unproductive?

The aspects of family responsibility that come to the fore in discussions of family responsibility discrimination relate to the supply of unpaid labor to family care, which has both direct and indirect implications for the supply of labor to the market. Time devoted to family work is time that is indirectly rather than directly devoted to market work—it is a necessary input into the production of a future generation of wage earners, as well as maintenance of existing wage earners in the face of the depreciation wrought by aging, morbidity, and death. It is a necessary input into human capital and, more broadly, human capabilities.

The liberal political and social theory of seventeenth- and eighteenth-century Britain and France largely ignores this contribution. Both women and the family are taken as a given, predestined by the famous starting point of Hobbesian theory, "Men sprung full-grown from the earth, like mushrooms." John Locke's early version of the labor theory of value was based on the assumption that workers were not themselves "produced." That assumption was carried forward into Ricardian and, later, Marxian political economy.

The hegemonic impact of this androcentric perspective is evidenced by the virtual invisibility of those who challenged it. In *A Physical and Moral Discourse on the Equality of the Sexes, Which Shows the Importance of Getting Rid of One's Prejudices,* published in 1673, Poulain de la Barre argued that women's economic contribution to society was unfairly depreciated, noting that men training tigers, horses, monkeys, or elephants were far more generously rewarded than women training children.[11]

In the 1690s, Mary Astell poked fun at the Hobbesian mushroom metaphor and located the source of women's subordination in their caring responsibilities:

> Our more generous souls are bias'd only by the good we do to the children we breed and nurture: Daily experience reminding us, that all the gratification we can hope for from the unnatural creatures, for the almost infinite pains, anxieties, care, and assiduities to which we subject ourselves on their account, and which cannot be matched in any other state of civil society, is an ungrateful treatment of our persons, and the basest contempt of our sex in general. Such the generous offices we do them: Such the ungenerous returns they make us.[12]

Few references to these proto-feminist critics can be found in conventional histories of economic thought. Adam Smith, famously explained that "it is not from the benevolence of the baker or the butcher that we expect our dinner, but rather from his regard for his own self-interest," without noting that it was women who typically prepared the meals served at his table. Mothers, wives, and domestic servants seldom appeared in his writing, except to be labeled providers of "unproductive" services.

Mercantilist politicians, like the men in charge of recruiting soldiers, recognized the value of healthy families in creating a future labor force. Thomas Robert Malthus challenged this view, depicting population growth as a natural force that would outrun economic growth if not subjected to moral restraint and masculine self-control through delayed marriage. (Delayed marriage for women reduces fertility far more than delayed marriage for men, but Malthus assumed that men were the primary decision-makers).

Whatever wives and mothers were doing at home, they were not, according to economic theory, defraying in any way the financial contributions that husbands and fathers made to their support. Jean Baptiste Say's *Treatise of Political Economy,* published in 1801 and widely cited in the English-speaking countries as well as his native France, offered an unusually explicit explanation of the gender differences in market earnings.[13] He pointed to family responsibility as justification: a man's wages included the costs of supporting a wife and children, but a woman's wages did not.[14] Women wage earners seeking to support themselves on their own would always face competition from wives and daughters who were primarily supported by their husbands, and were therefore willing to work for a lower wage. This auxiliary supply of dependent labor would depress female wages.

Say ignored the unpaid domestic services that wives and daughters typically provided in return for their support, the limits that such unpaid work put on their supply of market labor, and married women's lack of property rights over their own earnings. Like Malthus, he also ignored the logic of a perfectly competitive market that should, in principle, penalize men as well as women for commitments to dependents. All else equal, men with children should earn the same wages as men without. An increase in the supply of men with no children should drive wages down to a floor determined by the costs of subsistence for a single worker.

The resulting equilibrium wage would suffice only to support an adult without dependents, until the shortage of labor would drive wages up again. The possibility that wages could be driven too low received no attention in a model that emphasized the adverse effects of driving wages too high. In demographic terms, fears of rapid population growth trumped fears of rapid population decline. As the demand for women factory workers grew in the early nineteenth century, however, concerns about the effect of wage employment on the supply of unpaid labor to the family became evident. A new explanation of the gender wage differential emerged, applying terms such as "duty," "responsibility," and "moral sensibility" assiduously to women.

In Britain, employers such as Andrew Ure defended the practice of hiring women, noting with satisfaction that the wages paid them were so low that they would be unlikely to neglect their "family duties."[15] Male trade unionists often exhorted women to stay home and avoid competition with them in the labor market out of solidarity with the working class. The 1836 report of the National Trades Union meeting in the United States declared that the "physical organization, the natural responsibilities, and the moral sensibility of women prove conclusively that her labors should be only of a domestic nature."[16]

Critics of the notion that women should be restricted either to domestic or to poorly paid pursuits were considered radicals. In their classic *Appeal of One Half the Human Race, Women, Against the Pretensions of the Other Half, Men, to Retain Them in Political, and Thence in Civil and Domestic Slavery,* the Irish socialist feminists William Thompson and Anna Wheeler went far beyond demands for woman suffrage to offer a critique of the emerging capitalist system.[17]

Unlike better-known socialists, like Robert Owen, Thompson and Wheeler pointed out that the labor theory of value ignored the labor devoted to the production and maintenance of laborers themselves. Competition would penalize persons who devoted themselves to the care of those too young or old or sick to care for themselves.[18] Family responsibilities would always put women at a disadvantage. "In the race of individual competition for wealth," Thompson wrote, "men have such fearful advantages over women, from superiority of strength and exertion uninterrupted by gestation, that they must probably maintain the lead in acquisition by individual effort."[19]

Hence the need for a more cooperative organization of society. Communities of cooperation could potentially benefit women more than men. Thompson offered detailed plans for redeploying domestic labor in his *Practical Directions for the Speedy and Economical Establishment of Communities on the Principles of Mutual Co-operation, United Possessions and Equality of Exertions and of the Means of Enjoyments* (1830). Robert Owen echoed many of its details in his *Book of the New Moral World* (1836), such as replacing the sexual division of labor with an age-based system (housework to be performed by children of eleven years or younger).

In France, fans of Charles Fourier and Henri de Saint-Simon endorsed similar views.[20] The most vehement critics of family responsibility discrimination were women socialists organized around a newspaper entitled *Le Tribune des Femmes.*[21] Anna Wheeler, by then spending much of her time in France, urged them on. One of their proclamations, printed in Robert Owen's magazine *The Crisis,* called attention to the paradox of feminine altruism: "We are born as free as men—their infancy is as helpless as ours, and ours as theirs. Without our tenderness, our sympathy and our care, they could never grow up to be our oppressors."[22] The founders of the *Tribune* called for a cross-class coalition of women bound by their common role as caregivers.[23]

In the United States, feminism took a more individualist direction. Yet feminist activists strongly emphasized the economics of family responsibility, asking why women who worked in the home lacked rights over the products of their labor. The Married Women's Property Acts, passed in many states after 1848, represented a straightforward extension of liberal political theory, gradually giving women control over inherited wealth and their own market earnings.[24] Legal guarantees of economic remuneration for housework and childrearing, however, remained out of reach.[25] Elizabeth Blackwell, the first woman doctor in the United States, asserted, "The theory that a wife who . . . bears her fair share of the joint burdens, is yet 'supported' by her husband has been the bane of all society."[26]

Nineteenth-century common law required that a husband support his wife, but the meaning of "support" was nowhere clearly defined, and many women were forced to beg their husbands for money.[27] In 1873, an article in *The Woman's Journal* explicitly demanded wages for housework. In 1878, the National Woman Suffrage Convention passed a resolution calling for legal recognition of women's rights to "the proceeds of her labor in the family."[28] Elizabeth Cady Stanton, Susan B. Anthony, and Mathilda Gage called more explicitly for a law guaranteeing the wife the absolute right to half the joint earnings of her and her husband.[29]

Across the Atlantic, John Stuart Mill and Harriet Taylor were less concerned with women's domestic work than with their access to wage employment, which would, they believed, improve bargaining power in the home. As they put it, "Even under the present laws respecting the property of women, a woman who contributes materially to the support of the family, cannot be treated in the same contemptuously tyrannical manner as one who, however she may toil as a domestic drudge, is a dependent on the man for subsistence."[30] Even they did not view domestic labor as a material contribution to the support of the family.

Early neoclassical theorists brought moral concerns to the fore. William Stanley Jevons, ardent advocate of laissez-faire, favored one exception to it: strict exclusion of the mothers of young children from employment in factories and workshops, with the possible exception of establishments that provided nurseries with medical supervision.[31] Like the French economist Leroy Beaulieu, he believed that maternal responsibilities for children were sufficiently sacred to warrant regulatory interference with free choice.[32]

Alfred Marshall went further, emphasizing women's moral responsibilities for family care. In his *Principles of Economics,* he explained that the employment of women was a "great gain in so far as it tends to develop their faculties; but an injury in so far as it tempts them to neglect their duty of building up a true home, and of investing their efforts in the personal capital of their children's character and abilities."[33] In an eight-page flysheet that he circulated to members of the Cambridge University Senate, he claimed that women could not match men in ability for creative research and also warned that their pursuit of a graduate degree would conflict with family duties.

He asked his readers to imagine the plight of a poor young student who learns, the night before her qualifying exams, that a family member is ill:

> However severe the illness of those dear to her, however urgent the need for her presence at home, she must keep her terms under penalty of losing recognition for her work. If she decides to go her own way, and let her family shift for themselves, she gets her honours; but her true life is impoverished and not enriched by them.[34]

Marshall also played a role in persuading the census-takers in both Britain and the United States to refer to married women lacking paid employment as "dependents."[35]

In the early twentieth century, women's entrance into institutions of higher learning was associated with greater attention to women's domestic work, both in the emerging field of home economics and in at least some economics departments. In 1929, Hazel Kyrk published *Economic Problems of the Family,* and 1934 saw the release of Margaret Reid's *Economics of Household Production.*[36] Neither book had much to say about gender inequality, but both considered the valuation of non-market work and its contribution to the economy as a whole, encouraging the implementation of time-diary surveys and alternative measures of gross domestic product.[37]

Their influence, however, proved less immediate than that of later inventors of the "new home economics," which adopted a more microeconomic perspective. Among the many contributors to this new paradigm, Gary Becker stands out for the development of a comprehensive, analytically compelling approach.[38] Especially notable are his relative lack of emphasis on gender differences and the absence of any Marshallian moralizing. Unlike some neoclassical economists, Becker seldom if ever assumes that women have different preferences than men, arguing instead that small differences in relative productivity in home and market production lead to an efficient and highly specialized gender division of labor.[39]

The new home economics provides valuable tools for the analysis of household production and bargaining among family members. It calls attention to factors that affect intra-family exchanges.[40] On the other hand, its emphasis on efficient utility maximization within the household deflects attention from the effects of collective action on institutional rules, including those that constrain choices regarding the balance between paid and unpaid work.[41]

The Beckerian emphasis on utility maximization deflects attention from material living standards. In principle, the value of household production contributes to "full income." But leisure is also included in full income, and the minimum value of all activities is measured by its opportunity cost in foregone earnings: household production and leisure are both treated as sources of utility. This subjective approach renders the resulting valuation incompatible with national accounting standards, which, based on market prices, effectively ignore the subjective satisfaction graphically represented as consumer surplus.[42] As a result, the impacts of non-market work on relative poverty rates, income inequality, and economic growth remain largely unexplored.

The new home economics also treats children (and other dependents) largely as consumer goods, yielding non-pecuniary benefits or services to their parents later in life. It ignores the benefits to society as a whole, and employers in particular, of parental contributions to human and social capital. Standard neoclassical reasoning espouses a narrow definition of "fairness" based on absence of explicit discrimination. This perspective is consistent with efforts to eliminate gender bias in accommodations for family responsibilities, but not with efforts to conceptualize and respond to a significant market failure—the difficulty of assigning a price to the significant positive externalities created by family commitments. These are the same externalities that early political economy ignored and that Stanley Jevons and Alfred Marshall believed could only be protected by moral and institutional strictures. From this broader perspective, Jevons and Marshall were wrong only insofar as they wanted to impose such strictures on women alone.

3. Unpaid work in censuses and national income accounts

A parallel story emerges from the history of efforts to quantify work in censuses and national income accounts in Britain and the United States, which reveals concerted resistance to the measurement and valuation of non-market work. Today, despite the proliferation of new data sources and methods of valuation, family work is relegated to occasional "satellite accounts" and strictly excluded from the hegemonic measure of economic success—gross domestic product.

In 1851, the Census of England and Wales, under the direction of the physician William Farr, restated the mercantilist notion (renounced by Malthus and most of his successors) that a country's most important product was its population.[43] It officially acknowledged the occupation of housewife, placing "wives, mothers and mistresses" who did not work for pay in a category by themselves, the "Fifth Class." Another class (the "Seventeenth," to be precise) was reserved for "dependents," or those supported by the community—"children, the sick and infirm, gypsies and vagrants, and certain ladies and gentlemen of independent means."[44]

By 1881, however, economists wielded more influence, and the census moved toward greater conformity with liberal political theory. Wives and other women engaged in domestic duties were explicitly placed in the "Unoccupied Class." While the text apologized for this apparent inconsistency, the nomenclatural demotion continued.[45] In 1890, a parliamentary committee was convened to consider improvements to the census, and Alfred Marshall was called to testify. Among his many reservations, he expressed dissatisfaction with the large numbers in the "Unoccupied" column and urged the committee to reduce them by adopting the German practice of describing married women as "dependents."[46] The 1891 census followed his advice.[47]

Labeling housewives "dependents" solved a number of problems at once. It reduced the number of the "Unoccupied," enhancing the national image. It validated the claim that men were more important than women to the economic life of the nation with the presumption that husbands were taking care of wives, but not vice versa; no partnership or reciprocity was implied. Finally, the notion that women were supported by men in the home helped justify paying them lower wages and restricting them to less well-paid jobs. After all, they could live on less. Some political economists, including the Scottish economist William Smart, dissented from this view, but to little effect.[48]

Australia, a major Commonwealth country, shifted its terminology in the same direction as Great Britain in 1890. Advocates of a clear emphasis on men as breadwinners won a decisive victory when it was agreed that wives would be classified as dependents unless they were employed for pay. The chief director of the New South Wales Census was convinced that women's participation in productive labor could only lower men's wages and the community's standard of living.[49] National statistics showing a low rate of female labor force participation would, he and others hoped, enhance Australia's image as a prosperous colony worthy of English investment.

The evolution of labor force measurement in the United States followed a slightly different but similar trajectory. The federal census assumed from the outset that women's work in the home should not be considered economically productive, and in 1900 it adopted the new term "breadwinner" to describe a person who earned market income. As in England and Australia, wives and daughters without paying jobs were designated "dependents." The state of Massachusetts, however, conducted its own late nineteenth-century censuses, and their categories were, at least initially, influenced by English assumptions. In 1875, housewives and unmarried women who performed housework without remuneration were included in the larger category of Domestic and Personal Office, along with subcategories for paid employment such as housekeepers, servants, nurses, and washerwomen. The introduction to the first volume made its distinction between productive and unproductive crystal clear: "The terms non-productive and unemployed are applied to all who take no part in the work of life."[50] Indeed, they were more likely to put idle gentlemen than energetic housewives into this category: The "propertied" were lumped in with the "non-productive."

Married women were not automatically assumed to be housewives. The enumerators inquired into the actual nature of work they performed. Some were described as "having nothing to do but superintend the households," and there were those who did even less than that. In the census's own words, "There are 4,786 wives of heads simply ornamental, but these amounted to less than 2 percent of the total."[51] After 1885, the state introduced some terminological changes that seemed to exclude the possibility of a purely ornamental wife, but it continued to recognize housework.[52]

That recognition ended in 1905, when housewives and houseworkers were placed in the "not gainful" class, along with scholars, students, retirees, those unemployed for twelve months, and dependents. The Domestic and Personal Service category was limited to those who received a wage or salary. This terminological shift was discussed in the 1889 report of the Massachusetts Bureau of Statistics of Labor, which anticipated William Smart's argument concerning the implicit value of unpaid domestic labor—what it could cost, were it paid for.[53]

The earliest estimates of the value of household production published in the United States applied a simple formula: take the number of married women without paid occupations and ask what they would be paid if employed as domestic servants or farm workers. A study sponsored by the National Bureau of Economic Research in 1921 estimated that the value of housewives' services had declined from 31 percent of market national income in 1909 to 25 percent in 1918.[54] A similar formula was applied in several subsequent discussions.

The eminent Simon Kuznets noted, in passing, that housewives' services in the United States could be valued at somewhat more than one-quarter of national income in 1929.[55] Colin Clark, another notable figure in the history of national income accounts, estimated their contribution at 27 percent of the gross national product of the United Kingdom in 1956.[56] Norway and Sweden offered official estimates of the value of household production in the late nineteenth and early twentieth century but, in the 1930s, moved toward conformity with the practices of other statistical offices, which excluded it.[57]

But these estimates were treated as curiosities, not as challenges to emerging national income accounting standards. As aforementioned, books by economists Hazel Kyrk and Margaret Reid summarized the results of early time-use surveys and inaugurated the new field of family and household economics. Their emphasis on family work was pursued by Kathryn Walker, who published many early studies of time use in the household.[58] Particularly important efforts to modify and expand the definition of income to include non-market work were published by John Kendrick, Robert Eisner, and Luisella Goldschmidt-Clermont and Elisabetta Pagnossin-Aligasakis.[59] Even these efforts, published in mainstream journals, failed to budge official practices.

Gradually, however, research initiated outside the economic discipline began to influence the discourse. The deployment of representative time-diary surveys such as the Multinational Comparative Time-Budget Research Project, undertaken under the direction of Alexander Szalai with support from European sponsors, revealed surprisingly high estimates of time devoted to non-market work.[60] The quantified results of these surveys countered initial claims that non-market work could not be measured and spurred the development of a new field of research on time use.

At the same time, a burgeoning international feminist movement began to assert that women's unpaid work was an important source of gender inequality. The Third U.N. World Conference on Women in Nairobi in 1985 passed a resolution to this effect.[61] New Zealand activist and policymaker Marilyn Waring made common cause with environmentalists and helped mobilize public support for implementation of time-use surveys with her widely read book, *If Women Counted*.[62] In 1995, the Fourth US World Conference on Women in Beijing extended and strengthened its recommendations for measurement of unpaid work.

These recommendations, bolstered by the efforts of women's groups in many countries, contributed to a proliferation of diary-based time-use surveys. While no explicitly comprehensive list is available, a concatenation of lists provided by the U.N. Statistics Division and the Centre for Time

Use Research at Oxford University documents slow growth from 1930 to 1989, doubling in the 1990s to thirty-six and more than doubling in the first decade of the twentieth century to eighty-seven. Between 2010 and 2013, twenty-five surveys were administered. Linear extrapolation of this number suggests that about sixty-three will be administered in the current decade, below the number for the first decade of the twenty-first century, but far higher than the 1990s.[63]

Important collections of data include the Harmonized European Time Use Survey (HETUS), the Multinational Time Use Studies (MTUS) archive at Oxford University, and the American Heritage Time Use Surveys including pioneering research by John Robinson, and the official American Time Use Survey (ATUS), collected on an annual basis since 2003. This growth has paralleled efforts to measure trends in non-market assets and ecosystem services, such as the United Nations' System of Economic-Environmental Accounting (SEEA) and the World Bank's Wealth Accounting and Valuation of Ecosystem Services (WAVES).[64]

With improved data on non-market work have come improved efforts at valuation, often through the development of "satellite accounts" that can revolve around the conventional estimates. Notable efforts include Duncan Ironmonger's estimates of gross household output in Australia, estimates of expanded GDP in the United States by Landefeld et al. and Bridgman et al. and, for OECD countries, Giannelli et al. and Miranda.[65] While important methodological problems remain, estimates such as these represent important steps toward improved valuation of family work.

This forward motion signals growing interest within the national income accounting community, a view clearly expressed by the internationally influential *Report by the Commission on Economic Performance and Social Progress Revisited*.[66] Yet the pace of change remains slow. Satellite accounts are easily disregarded, because they do not challenge or alter conventional measures of gross domestic product or its growth over time. Further, the growing interest in moving away from GDP toward more direct measures of happiness and/or human capabilities has also diverted attention from the task of improving measures of income.

4. Gender neutrality and family externalities in public policy

In retrospect, it seems that efforts to at least partially de-gender care have proved more successful than efforts to assign it greater economic value. Perhaps it is easier to enforce equal treatment of men and women than to challenge the logic of the market. Perhaps the increased focus on increasing market output reduced concerns regarding the viability of family commitments. In any case, political mobilization in support of equal rights for men and women was always forced to confront concerns that it might discourage women's family commitments—and thereby redistribute more of the costs of care to men.

For instance, the original rationale for a minimum wage grew out of concerns that, without it, male workers would be unable to support a family. Hence demands for a "male family wage" built on Say's reasoning: men should earn more because their dependent burden was greater. Concern that single women, in particular, were undercutting men's wages in the labor market led major US trade unions to support a minimum wage for women (but not for men) in the early twentieth century. Both the United Kingdom and France established minimum wages for women in the early twentieth century.

In the United States, twelve states passed mandatory minimum-wage laws for women and children between 1912 and 1920.[67] Before these were declared unconstitutional in 1923, they provoked considerable debate. Critics of wage-earning women insisted that no minimum was necessary because most worked only for "pin money," an extra but unnecessary bit of income. At the other end of the political spectrum, the boldest feminists argued that women should earn enough to support dependents of their own.

Mary Van Kleeck, head of a government agency that would shortly become the Women's Bureau, argued that men and women worked together to support dependent children, and older daughters were fully as responsible as older sons for contributions to this end. A fierce advocate of equal pay for equal work, Van Kleeck opposed efforts to set a female minimum wage at a level lower than the minimum wage for men. Sophonisba Breckinridge of the University of Chicago School of Social Work also called attention to women's need for higher earnings. Marshaling data from the decennial censuses as well as the Bureau of Labor Statistics budget surveys, she documented the number of married women contributing income to their families, concluding that "no safe line can be drawn between the sexes on the basis of the support of dependents."[68]

When federal minimum wage legislation was passed in 1935, it did not differentiate by gender (though several important female occupations including domestic service and home care were initially excluded). On the other hand, recurrent efforts to raise the nominal value of the minimum wage in the face of inflation began to highlight its potential negative impact on employment more than its relevance to family care of dependents.

The term "family wage" dropped out of sight, though the concerns it embodied lived on in the concept of a "living wage."[69] In their earliest stages, living wage campaigns set desirable wages standards based on how much a man would need to support a wife and two children; in recent years, however, budget standards have been redefined based on the needs of households with two earners, with two children, paying for childcare or households with one earner, no other adult, and two children. In other words, a "living wage" today is seldom expected to support for a stay-at-home parent.

In the early twentieth century, US proscriptions against employment of married women in public employment were widespread, providing another example of the link between gender equality and family work. As of 1928 (just before the Depression), 61 percent of school districts barred hiring of married women, and 52 percent stipulated that they could not be retained in employment. The percentages grew significantly during the Depression years, and, by 1942, the percentages were even higher.[70] Many private firms almost certainly followed suit, though trends there remain difficult to track.

At least some resistance was evident even at this stage. For instance, the federal rules put into place under the Roosevelt administration implemented similar regulations that were at least formally de-gendered: if two spouses were both employed in the civil service, one of the two would be required to resign. In practice, women were far more likely than men to resign.[71] In principle, however, the policy itself was gender neutral.

The so-called "marriage bars" were already on the way out when the Civil Rights Act of 1964 and subsequent legislation outlawed disparate treatment of women and men. Yet this legislation did nothing to alter institutional arrangements that had evolved during a period in which most men were full-time "breadwinners" and most married women were "homemakers." Public-school schedules made it difficult for both parents to work full time, and work schedules heavily penalized even short departures from full-time employment.

Such institutional arrangements, while not explicitly gender biased, effectively penalized adults who took responsibility for the family care of children and other dependents. They also helped minimize employer contributions to the cost of rearing the next generation of workers, effectively labeling family commitments a choice that parents themselves should pay for.

That women were penalized more heavily than men hardly seems incidental. However, as women's efforts to garner equal rights achieved more success later in the twentieth century, commitments to family care—or, in neoclassical parlance, preferences for providing family care—have become more costly. In this sense, family responsibility discrimination has partially displaced gender discrimination. The negative consequences can be borne by men as well as women. All else equal, nice guys as well as nice gals finish last.

5. Implications and reflections

What lessons does this story hold for current efforts to conceptualize discrimination and public policies toward family work? Like what William Darity describes as stratification economics, it calls attention to essentially non-market dynamics based on collective action.[72] Social institutions reflect the efforts of powerful groups to enhance their own bargaining power, having the effect of constraining individual choice. Feminist political economy complements stratification economics by calling attention to distributional conflict over the costs of providing for dependents.

The historical record shows that explicit forms of discrimination against women increased the supply of unpaid labor to both men and children within the family and limited competition from women in wage employment. In this sense, men represent one of what Darity terms "multiple self-interested groups" influencing economic outcomes. The story told above testifies to the impact of social norms, not just as a robust influence on economic decisions but as a *form* of discrimination. Individual decision-makers internalize culturally inscribed definitions of competence that coordinate forms of collective action that, in turn, reinforce those definitions. Family responsibilities in the United States have been only partially de-gendered. In 2012, almost a third of Americans responding to the General Social Survey agreed that "it is better for men to earn money while women tend the home."[73]

Finally, and most importantly, the story points beyond discrimination against women as a group, toward the devaluation of forms of work that are not fully rewarded either in the market or the household. The fulfillment of family and family-like work responsibilities is partially compensated by transfers of income within the family; it is also widely recognized as an important source of personal happiness. But its major economic contribution—the creation and maintenance of human capabilities essential to productive activity—remains officially invisible.

Family care creates an unpriced public good that can be exploited by the market economy but which is crucial to the maintenance of a stable social climate. In this sense, current policy efforts to reduce "care penalties" resemble efforts to reduce the greenhouse gases that are destabilizing our physical climate. They urge us to realize that the market is only a small part of a much larger and more complex economic system. They urge us to renegotiate the current distribution of the costs of family care.

Nancy Folbre is professor emerita of economics at the University of Massachusetts Amherst, United States. Her work explores the interface between political economy and feminist theory, with a focus on care work. Her publications include *Greed, Lust, and Gender: A History of Economic Ideas* (New York: Oxford University Press, 2009) and *Valuing Children* (Cambridge, MA: Harvard University Press, 2008).

Notes

1. Lee Speigel, "Rendell: Napolitano Perfect for Homeland Security Because She Has No Life," ABC News, 4 December 2008, retrieved 27 July 2015 from http://blogs.abcnews.com/politicalpunch/2008/12/rendell-napolit.html.
2. Nancy Folbre, *Greed, Lust, and Gender: A History of Economic Ideas* (New York: Oxford University Press, 2009).
3. Ibid.
4. Michelle J. Budig and Paula England, "The Wage Penalty for Motherhood," *American Sociological Review* 66, no. 2 (2001): 204–25; Jane Waldfogel, "Understanding the 'Family Gap' in Pay for Women with Children," *Journal of Economic Perspectives* 12, no. 1 (1998): 137–56; Michelle J. Budig, Joya Misra, and Irene Boeckman, "The Motherhood Penalty in Cross-National Perspective: The Importance of Work–Family Policies and Cultural Attitudes," *Social Policy* 19, no. 2 (2012): 163–93.
5. Shoshana Grossbard-Schectman, *On the Economics of Marriage* (Boulder, CO: Westview Press, 1993).
6. Shelley J. Correll, Stephen Benard, and In Paik, "Getting a Job: Is There a Motherhood Penalty?" *American Journal of Sociology* 112, no. 5 (2007): 1297–339.
7. Melissa J. Hodges and Michelle J. Budig, "Who Gets the Daddy Bonus? Organizational Hegemonic Masculinity and the Impact of Fatherhood on Earnings," *Gender and Society* 24, no. 4 (2010): 717–45.
8. United States Federal Equal Employment Opportunity Commission family discrimination guidelines, retrieved 22 December 2014 from http://www.eeoc.gov/policy/docs/caregiving.html.
9. Joan C. Williams and Nancy Segal, "Beyond the Maternal Wall: Relief for Family Caregivers Who Are Discriminated Against on the Job," *Harvard Women's Law Journal* 26 (2003): 77–162.
10. Ibid.
11. François Poulain de la Barre, *The Equality of the Sexes*, trans. Desmond M. Clarke (New York: Manchester University Press, 1990), 80.
12. Mary Astell, "The Hardships of the English Laws in Relation to Wives," in *Women in the Eighteenth Century: Constructions of Femininity*, ed. Vivien Jones (New York: Routledge, 2006), 220.
13. Evelyn L. Forget, "The Market for Virtue: Jean-Baptiste Say on Women in the Economy and Society," *The Status of Women in Classical Economic Thought*, ed. Robert Dimand and Chris Nyland (Cheltenham: Edward Elgar, 2003), 206–23.
14. Joan Wallach Scott, "L'ouvrière! Mot impie, sordide . . . Women Workers in the Discourse of French Political Economy, 1840–1860," in Joan Wallach Scott, *Gender and the Politics of History* (New York: Columbia University Press, 1988), 139–66.
15. Andrew Ure, *The Philosophy of Manufactures* (New York: Augustus M. Kelley, 1967), 475.

16. Philip Foner, *Women and the American Labor Movement: From Colonial Times to the Eve of World War I* (New York: Free Press, 1979), 54.
17. William Thompson, *Appeal of One Half the Human Race, Women, Against the Pretensions of the Other Half, Men, to Retain Them in Political, and Thence in Civil and Domestic Slavery* (London: Printed for Longman, Hurst, Rees, Orme, Brown, and Green, 1825). For more discussion of the issue of authorship of the *Appeal*, see Barbara Taylor, *Eve and the New Jerusalem* (Cambridge, MA: Harvard University Press, 1993), 22–23.
18. Thompson, *Appeal of One Half the Human Race*, 369.
19. Ibid., 373.
20. Folbre, *Greed, Lust, and Gender.*
21. James F. McMillan, *France and Women, 1789–1914* (New York: Routledge, 2000), 82. See also Evelyn Forget, "Saint-Simonian Feminism," *Feminist Economics* 7, no. 1 (2001): 79–96.
22. Richard K. P. Pankhurst, *The Saint Simonians Mill and Carlyle* (London: Lalibela Books, 1957), 109.
23. Jeanne Deroin, "Call to Women," *Feminism, Socialism, and French Romanticism*, ed. Claire Goldberg Moses and Leslie Wahl Rabine (Bloomington: Indiana University Press, 1993), 282–84.
24. Carole Shammas, "Re-Assessing the Married Women's Property Acts," *Journal of Women's History* 6, no. 1 (1994): 9–29.
25. Reva B. Siegel, "Home as Work: The First Woman's Rights Claims Concerning Wives' Household Labor, 1850–1880," *Yale Law Journal* 103 (1994): 1073–217.
26. Elizabeth Cady Stanton, *The Revolution*, 27 August 1868.
27. Siegel, "Home as Work."
28. William Leach, *True Love and Perfect Union: The Feminist Reform of Sex and Society* (New York: Basic Books, 1980), 194.
29. Siegel, "Home as Work," 1115.
30. Ibid. Mill inserted a similar phrase in the 1852 edition of his *Principles of Political Economy*, though he backed off somewhat in a later revision. Richard W. Krouse, "Patriarchal Liberalism and Beyond: From John Stuart Mill to Harriet Taylor," in *The Family in Political Thought*, ed. Jean Bethke Elshtain (Chicago: University of Chicago Press, 1982), 145–72; Gertrude Himmelfarb, *On Liberty and Liberalism: The Case of John Stuart Mill* (New York: Alfred A. Knopf, 1974).
31. William Stanley Jevons, *The Theory of Political Economy* (New York: Augustus M. Kelley, 1965), 172.
32. Michael V. White, "Following Strange Gods: Women in Jevon's Political Economy," in *Feminism and Political Economy in Victorian England*, ed. Peter Groenewegen (Aldershot: Edward Elgar, 1994), 46–78. On Leroy Beaulieu, see Mary Lynn Stewart, *Women, Work, and the French State: Labour Protection and Social Patriarchy* (Toronto: McGill-Queen's Press, 1989).
33. Alfred Marshall, *Principles of Economics*, 8th ed. (1890; London: Macmillan, 1962), 570.
34. Cited in David Reisman, *Alfred Marshall's Mission* (New York: St. Martin's Press, 1990), 210.
35. See chapter 17, "The Unproductive Housewife," in Folbre, *Greed, Lust, and Gender.*
36. Hazel Kyrk, *Economic Problems of the Family* (New York: Harper and Brothers Publishers, 1929); Margaret Reid, *Economics of Household Production* (New York: John Wiley and Sons, 1934).
37. See chapter 17, "The Unproductive Housewife," in Folbre, *Greed, Lust, and Gender.*
38. Gary S. Becker, *A Treatise on the Family*, rev. ed. (Cambridge, MA: Harvard University Press, 1993).
39. Victor Fuchs, *Women's Quest for Economic Equality* (Cambridge, MA: Harvard University Press, 1990).

40. Grossbard-Schectman, *On the Economics of Marriage*.
41. Nancy Folbre, "A Theory of the Misallocation of Time," in *Family Time: The Social Organization of Care*, eds. Nancy Folbre and Michael Bittman (New York: Routledge, 2004).
42. For more discussion, see Katharine G. Abraham and Christopher Mackie, eds., Panel to Study the Design of Nonmarket Accounts, National Research Council, *Beyond the Market: Designing Nonmarket Accounts for the United States* (Washington DC: National Research Council, 2005).
43. *1851 Census of England and Wales*, lxxxviii.
44. Celia Davies, "Making Sense of the Census in Britain and the U.S.A.: The Changing Occupational Classification and the Position of Nurses," *Sociological Review* 28, no. 3 (1980): 581–609.
45. *1881 Census of England and Wales*, 63.
46. Ibid., 66.
47. *1891 Census of England and Wales*, 58.
48. William Smart, *The Distribution of Income* (New York: The Macmillan Company, 1899), 69.
49. Desley Deacon, "Political Arithmetic: The Nineteenth Century Australian Census and the Construction of the Dependent Woman," *Signs: Journal of Women in Culture and Society* 11, no. 1 (1985): 35.
50. *Census of Massachusetts: 1875* (Boston: Albert J. Wright, 1876), xlix.
51. Ibid., 1.
52. Ibid., xxv.
53. Massachusetts Bureau of Labor Statistics, *Twentieth Annual Report of the Bureau of the Statistics of Labor* (Boston: Wright and Potter Printing Company, December 1889), 579: "To be sure, they (housewives) receive no stated salary or wage, but their work is surely worth what it would cost to have it done, supposing that the housewife, as such, did no work at all. There were 372,612 housewives in Massachusetts in 1885, and only 300,999 women engaged in all other branches of industry. If a housewife were not expected nor required to work, then for the labor of 372,612 women paid service would have to be substituted. Such a demand for labor could not be supplied by the inhabitants of the State itself. Consequently, as the labor of the housewives was absolutely necessary to allow society to exist in its present form, the housewife is certainly 'in industry.' As has been stated, she is excluded from the previous tables in this Part for conventional and arbitrary reasons alone. The housewife is as much a member of the army of workers as the clerk or cotton weaver, and too often supplements the toil of the day, 'in industry' with household duties performed at home, but outside of the 'in industry' classification."
54. Willford I. King, Wesley G. Mitchell, Frederick Macaulay, and Oswald W. Knauth, *Income in the United States, Its Amount and Distribution* (New York: Harcourt, Brace, and Co., 1921).
55. Simon Kuznets, *National Income and Its Composition* (New York: National Bureau of Economic Research, 1941), 2:431). In general, Kuznets argued against valuation of non-market work. It has been claimed that he later came to favor valuation and parted ways with the US Department of Commerce over the issue. See, for instance, the *Encyclopedia of Economics*, retrieved 9 February 2015 from http://www.econlib.org/library/Enc/bios/Kuznets.html. This claim is repeated in Patricia Cohen's *New York Times* article, "Putting a Price on Simon Kuznet's Nobel in Economics," retrieved August 2015 from http://www.nytimes.com/2015/02/25/business/putting-a-price-on-simon-kuznetss-nobel-in-economics.html. However, I have been unable to locate any primary source that substantiates this claim and therefore remain skeptical of it.
56. Colin Clark, *The National Income, 1924–31* (1932; London: Cass, 1965); Colin Clark, "The Economics of Housework," *Bulletin of the Oxford University Institute of Statistics* 20, no. 1 (1958): 205–11.

57. Iulie Aslaksen and Charlotte Koren, "Reflections on Unpaid Household Work, Economic Growth, and Consumption Possibilities," in *Counting on Marilyn Waring*, ed. Margunn Bjornhold and Ailsa McKay (Bradford, Ontario: Demeter Press, 2014), 55–87.
58. Kathryn Walker, "Time Spent in Household Work by Homemakers," *Family Economics Review* 3 (1969): 5–6
59. John W. Kendrick, "Expanding Imputed Values in the National Income and Product Accounts," *Review of Income and Wealth* 25, no. 4 (1979): 349–63; Robert Eisner, *The Total Incomes System of Accounts* (Chicago: University of Chicago Press, 1989); Luisella Goldschmidt-Clermont and Elisabetta Pagnossin-Aligasakis, "Household's Non-SNA Production: Labour Time, Value of Labour and of Product, and Contribution to Extended Private Consumption," *Review of Income and Wealth* 45, no. 3 (1999): 519–29.
60. Alexander Szalai, *The Use of Time: Daily Activities of Urban and Suburban Populations in Twelve Countries* (Berlin: Walter de Gruyter, 1973).
61. Meg Luxton, "The UN, Women, and Household Labor," *Women's Studies International Forum* 20, no. 3 (1997): 431–39.
62. Marilyn Waring. *If Women Counted: A New Feminist Economics* (New York: Harper and Row, 1988); Margunn Bjornhold and Ailsa McKay, eds., *Counting on Marilyn Waring* (Bradford, Ontario: Demeter Press, 2014).
63. UN Statistical Office, retrieved 9 February 2015 from http://unstats.un.org/unsd/demographic/sconcerns/tuse/tu3.aspx; Oxford University Centre for Time Use Research, retrieved 9 February 2015 from http://www.timeuse.org/mtus/surveys.
64. For more on the UN program, see http://unstats.un.org/unsd/envaccounting/seea.asp; for more on the World Bank program, see https://www.wavespartnership.org/en.
65. Duncan Ironmonger, "Households and the Household Economy," in *Households Work*, ed. Duncan Ironmonger (Sydney: Allen and Unwin, 1989), 3–17; J. Steven Landefeld and Stephanie H. McCulla, "Accounting for Nonmarket Household Production within a National Accounts Framework," *Review of Income and Wealth* 46, no. 3 (2000): 289–307; Steven Landefeld, Barbara M. Fraumeni, and Cindy M. Vojtech, "Accounting for Household Production: A Prototype Satellite Account Using the American Time Use Survey," *Review of Income and Wealth* 55, no. 2 (2009): 205–25; Benjamin Bridgman, Andrew Dugan, Mikhael Lal, Matthew Osborn, and Shaunda Villones, "Accounting for Household Production in the National Accounts, 1965–2010," *Survey of Current Business* (May 2012): 23–36; Gianna C. Giannelli, Lucia Mangiavacchi, and Luca Piccoli, "GDP and the Value of Family Caretaking: How Much Does Europe Care?," IZA Discussion Paper 5046, 2010, retrieved 31 May 2011 from http://ftp.iza.org/dp5046.pdf; Miranda Veerle, "Cooking, Caring, and Volunteering," OECD Social, Employment, and Migration Working Papers No. 116, 2011, retrieved August 2015 from http://www.oecd.org/officialdocuments/publicdisplaydocumentpdf/?cote=DELSA/ELSA/WD/SEMpercent282011percent291&doclanguage=en.
66. Joseph Stiglitz, Amartya Sen, and Jean-Paul Fitoussi, *Report by the Commission on Economic Performance and Social Progress Revisited* (Pais: OFCE—Centre de recherche en économie de Sciences Po, 2009), retrieved August 2015 from http://www.stiglitz-sen-fitoussi.fr/documents/rapport_anglais.pdf.
67. U.S. Women's Bureau, *State Laws Affecting Working Women*, Bulletin No. 16 (Washington, DC: Government Printing Office, 1921).
68. Sophonisba B. Breckinridge, "The Home Responsibilities of Women," *Journal of Political Economy* 31, no. 4 (1923): 535.
69. Lawrence B. Glickman, *A Living Wage: American Workers and the Making of Consumer Society* (Ithaca, NY: Cornell University Press, 1997); Alice Kessler-Harris, *A Woman's Wage: Historical Meanings and Social Consequences* (Lexington: University of Kentucky, 1990).
70. Claudia Goldin, *Understanding the Gender Gap* (New York: Oxford University Press, 1990).

71. Susan Ware, *Beyond Suffrage: Women in the New Deal* (Cambridge, MA: Harvard University Press, 1981); Lois Scharf, *To Work and to Wed* (Westport, CT: Greenwood Press, 1980).
72. William Darity Jr., "Racism and Colorism in Post-Racial Societies," in *Making Equality Count*, ed. Laurence Bond, Frances McGinnity, and Helen Russell (Dublin: Liffey Press, 2010), 113–129.
73. David A. Cotter, Joan M. Hermsen, and Reeve Vanneman, "Back on Track? The Stall and Rebound in Support for Women's New Roles in Work and Politics," Council on Contemporary Families Symposium, retrieved August 2015 from https://contemporaryfamilies.org/wp-content/uploads/2014/07/2014_Symposium_Gender_Rebound.pdf.

References

Abraham, Katherine G., and Christopher Mackie, eds., Panel to Study the Design of Nonmarket Accounts, National Research Council. *Beyond the Market: Designing Nonmarket Accounts for the United States*. Washington DC: National Research Council, 2005.

Aslaksen, Iulie, and Charlotte Koren. "Reflections on Unpaid Household Work, Economic Growth, and Consumption Possibilities." In *Counting on Marilyn Waring*, edited by Margunn Bjornhold and Ailsa McKay, 55–87. Bradford, Ontario: Demeter Press, 2014.

Astell, Mary. "The Hardships of the English Laws in Relation to Wives." In *Women in the Eighteenth Century: Constructions of Femininity*, edited by Vivien Jones, 217–25. New York: Routledge, 2006.

Becker, Gary S. *A Treatise on the Family*. Revised edition. Cambridge, MA: Harvard University Press, 1993.

Bjornhold, Margunn, and Ailsa McKay, eds. *Counting on Marilyn Waring*. Bradford, Ontario: Demeter Press, 2014.

Breckinridge, Sophonisba B. "The Home Responsibilities of Women." *Journal of Political Economy* 31, no. 4 (1923): 521–43.

Bridgman, Benjamin, Andrew Dugan, Mikhael Lal, Matthew Osborn, and Shaunda Villones. "Accounting for Household Production in the National Accounts, 1965–2010." *Survey of Current Business* (May 2012): 23–36.

Budig, Michelle J., and Paula England. "The Wage Penalty for Motherhood." *American Sociological Review* 66, no. 2 (2001): 204–25.

Budig, Michelle J., Joya Misra, and Irene Boeckman. "The Motherhood Penalty in Cross-National Perspective: The Importance of Work–Family Policies and Cultural Attitudes." *Social Policy* 19, no. 2 (2012): 163–93.

Census of Massachusetts: 1875. Boston: Albert J. Wright, 1876.

Clark, Colin. *The National Income, 1924–31*. London: Cass, 1965. First published in 1932.

———. "The Economics of Housework." *Bulletin of the Oxford University Institute of Statistics* 20, no. 1 (1958): 205–11.

Cohen, Patricia. "Putting a Price on Simon Kuznet's Nobel in Economics." *New York Times*, 24 February 2015. Retrived August 2015 from http://www.nytimes.com/2015/02/25/business/putting-a-price-on-simon-kuznetss-nobel-in-economics.html.

Correll, Shelley J., Stephen Benard, and In Paik. "Getting a Job: Is There a Motherhood Penalty?" *American Journal of Sociology* 112, no. 5 (2007): 1297–339.

Cotter, David A., Joan M. Hermsen, and Reeve Vanneman. "Back on Track? The Stall and Rebound in Support for Women's New Roles in Work and Politics." Council on Contemporary Families Symposium. Retrieved August 2015 from https://contemporaryfamilies.org/wp-content/uploads/2014.

Darity, William, Jr. "Racism and Colorism in Post-Racial Societies." In *Making Equality Count: Irish and International Research Measuring Equality and Discrimination*, edited by Laurence Bond, Frances McGinnity, and Helen Russell, 113–129. Dublin: Liffey Press, 2010.

Davies, Celia. "Making Sense of the Census in Britain and the U.S.A.: The Changing Occupational Classification and the Position of Nurses." *Sociological Review* 28, no. 3 (1980): 581–609.

Deacon, Desley. "Political Arithmetic: The Nineteenth Century Australian Census and the Construction of the Dependent Woman." *Signs: Journal of Women in Culture and Society* 11, no. 1 (1985): 27–47.

Deroin, Jeanne. "Call to Women." In *Feminism, Socialism, and French Romanticism*, edited by Claire Goldberg Moses and Leslie Wahl Rabine, 282–84. Bloomington: Indiana University Press, 1993.

Eisner, Robert. *The Total Incomes System of Accounts*. Chicago: University of Chicago Press, 1989.

Folbre, Nancy. "A Theory of the Misallocation of Time." In *Family Time: The Social Organization of Care*, edited by Nancy Folbre and Michael Bittman, 7–24. New York: Routledge, 2004.

———. *Greed, Lust, and Gender: A History of Economic Ideas*. New York: Oxford University Press, 2009.

Foner, Philip. *Women and the American Labor Movement: From Colonial Times to the Eve of World War I*. New York: Free Press, 1979.

Forget, Evelyn L. "Saint-Simonian Feminism." *Feminist Economics* 7, no. 1 (2001): 79–96.

———. "The Market for Virtue: Jean-Baptiste Say on Women in the Economy and Society." In *The Status of Women in Classical Economic Thought*, edited by Robert Dimand and Chris Nyland, 206–23. Cheltenham: Edward Elgar, 2003.

Fuchs, Victor. *Women's Quest for Economic Equality*. Cambridge, MA: Harvard University Press, 1990.

Giannelli, Gianna C., Lucia Mangiavacchi, and Luca Piccoli. "GDP and the Value of Family Caretaking: How Much Does Europe Care?" IZA Discussion Paper 5046, 2010. Retrieved 16 November 2017 from http://ftp.iza.org/dp5046.pdf.

Glickman, Lawrence B. *A Living Wage: American Workers and the Making of Consumer Society*. Ithaca, NY: Cornell University Press, 1997.

Goldin, Claudia. *Understanding the Gender Gap*. New York: Oxford University Press, 1990.

Goldschmidt-Clermont, Luisella, and Elisabetta Pagnossin-Aligasakis. "Household's Non-SNA Production: Labour Time, Value of Labour and of Product, and Contribution to Extended Private Consumption." *Review of Income and Wealth* 45, no. 3 (1999): 519–29.

Grossbard-Schectman, Shoshana. *On the Economics of Marriage*. Boulder, CO: Westview Press, 1993.

Himmelfarb, Gertrude. *On Liberty and Liberalism: The Case of John Stuart Mill*. New York: Alfred A. Knopf, 1974.

Hodges, Melissa J., and Michelle J. Budig. "Who Gets the Daddy Bonus? Organizational Hegemonic Masculinity and the Impact of Fatherhood on Earnings." *Gender and Society* 24, no. 4 (2010): 717–45.

Ironmonger, Duncan. "Households and the Household Economy." In *Households Work*, edited by Duncan Ironmonger, 3–17. Sydney: Allen and Unwin, 1989.

Jevons, William Stanley. *The Theory of Political Economy*. New York: Augustus M. Kelley, 1965.

Kendrick, John W. "Expanding Imputed Values in the National Income and Product Accounts." *Review of Income and Wealth* 25, no. 4 (1979): 349–63.

Kessler-Harris, Alice. *A Woman's Wage: Historical Meanings and Social Consequences*. Lexington: University of Kentucky, 1990.

King, Willford I., Wesley G. Mitchell, Frederick Macaulay, and Oswald W. Knauth. *Income in the United States, Its Amount and Distribution*. New York: Harcourt, Brace, and Co., 1921.

Krouse, Richard K. "Patriarchal Liberalism and Beyond: From John Stuart Mill to Harriet Taylor." In *The Family in Political Thought*, edited by Jean Bethke Elshtain, 145–72. Chicago: University of Chicago Press, 1982.

Kuznets, Simon. *National Income and Its Composition*. Vol. 2. New York: National Bureau of Economic Research, 1941.

Kyrk, Hazel. *Economic Problems of the Family*. New York: Harper and Brothers Publishers, 1929.

Landefeld, J. Steven, and Stephanie H. McCulla. "Accounting for Nonmarket Household Production within a National Accounts Framework." *Review of Income and Wealth* 46, no. 3 (2000): 289–307.

Landefeld, Steven, Barbara M. Fraumeni, and Cindy M. Vojtech. "Accounting for Household Production: A Prototype Satellite Account Using the American Time Use Survey." *Review of Income and Wealth* 55, no. 2 (2009): 205–25.

Leach, William. *True Love and Perfect Union: The Feminist Reform of Sex and Society*. New York: Basic Books, 1980.

Luxton, Meg. "The UN, Women, and Household Labor." *Women's Studies International Forum* 20, no. 3 (1997): 431–39.

Marshall, Alfred. *Principles of Economics*. 8th edition. London: Macmillan, 1962. First published in 1890.

Massachusetts Bureau of Labor Statistics. *Twentieth Annual Report of the Bureau of the Statistics of Labor*. Boston: Wright and Potter Printing Company, December 1889.

McMillan, James F. *France and Women, 1789–1914*. New York: Routledge, 2000.

Pankhurst, Richard K. P. *The Saint Simonians Mill and Carlyle*. London: Lalibela Books, 1957.

Poulain de la Barre, François. *The Equality of the Sexes*. Translated by Desmond M. Clarke. New York: Manchester University Press, 1990.

Reid, Margaret. *Economics of Household Production*. New York: John Wiley and Sons, 1934.

Reisman, David. *Alfred Marshall's Mission*. New York: St. Martin's Press, 1990.
Scharf, Lois W. *To Work and to Wed*. Westport, CT: Greenwood Press, 1980.
Scott, Joan Wallach. "L'ouvrière! Mot impie, sordide . . . Women Workers in the Discourse of French Political Economy, 1840–1860." In Joan Wallach Scott, *Gender and the Politics of History*, 139–66. New York: Columbia University Press, 1988.
Shammas, Carole. "Re-Assessing the Married Women's Property Acts." *Journal of Women's History* 6, no. 1 (1994): 9–29.
Siegel, Reva B. "Home as Work: The First Woman's Rights Claims Concerning Wives' Household Labor, 1850–1880." *Yale Law Journal* 103 (1994): 1073–217.
Smart, William. *The Distribution of Income*. New York: The Macmillan Company, 1899.
Stewart, Mary Lynn. *Women, Work, and the French State: Labour Protection and Social Patriarchy*. Toronto: McGill-Queen's Press, 1989.
Stiglitz, Joseph, Amartya Sen, and Jean-Paul Fitoussi. *Report by the Commission on Economic Performance and Social Progress Revisited*. Pais: OFCE—Centre de recherche en économie de Sciences Po, 2009. Retrieved August 2015 from http://www.stiglitz-sen-fitoussi.fr/documents/rapport_anglais.pdf.
Szalai, Alexander. *The Use of Time: Daily Activities of Urban and Suburban Populations in Twelve Countries*. Berlin: Walter de Gruyter, 1973.
Thompson, William. *Appeal of One Half the Human Race, Women, Against the Pretensions of the Other Half, Men, to Retain Them in Political, and Thence in Civil and Domestic Slavery*. London: Printed for Longman, Hurst, Rees, Orme, Brown, and Green, 1825.
Ure, Andrew. *The Philosophy of Manufactures*. New York: Augustus M. Kelley, 1967.
US Women's Bureau. *State Laws Affecting Working Women*, Bulletin No. 16. Washington, DC: Government Printing Office, 1921.
Veerle, Miranda. "Cooking, Caring, and Volunteering." OECD Social, Employment, and Migration Working Papers No. 116, 2011. Retrieved August 2015 from http://www.oecd.org/officialdocuments/publicdisplaydocumentpdf/?cote=DELSA/ELSA/WD/SEM percent282011 percent291&doclanguage=en.
Waldfogel, Jane. "Understanding the 'Family Gap' in Pay for Women with Children." *Journal of Economic Perspectives* 12, no. 1 (1998): 137–56.
Walker, Kathryn. "Time Spent in Household Work by Homemakers." *Family Economics Review* 3 (1969): 5–6.
Ware, Susan. *Beyond Suffrage: Women in the New Deal*. Cambridge, MA: Harvard University Press, 1981.
Waring, Marilyn. *If Women Counted: A New Feminist Economics*. New York: Harper and Row, 1988.
White, Michael V. "Following Strange Gods: Women in Jevon's Political Economy." In *Feminism and Political Economy in Victorian England*, edited by Peter Groenewegen, 46–78. Aldershot: Edward Elgar, 1994.
Williams, Joan C., and Nancy Segal. "Beyond the Maternal Wall: Relief for Family Caregivers Who Are Discriminated Against on the Job." *Harvard Women's Law Journal* 26 (2003): 77–162.

CHAPTER 2

PRODUCTIVE AND REPRODUCTIVE WORK
Uses and Abuses of an Old Dichotomy

Alessandra Pescarolo

1. The fortune of the dichotomy in women's studies

The dichotomy between productive and reproductive work is still proposed as a toil of analysis by a number of works within the discipline of gender studies. In its literal formation, this distinction was born from the reflections on Marxist feminism in the 1960s, which sought to situate domestic work on the Marxist theoretical grid, reconstructing in an innovative way the connections between this activity and the labor carried out by factory workers.[1] The influence of this line of thought on gender studies has never completely given out[2]: the renewed economic and political strength of late twentieth-century capitalism, together with its serious social faults, has actually rekindled interest in Marxism within gender studies, relaunching the ancient debate against non-Marxist feminism, criticized[3] as culturalist,[4] radical, or liberal.[5]

Yet the concept of reproductive work has continued to circulate in a part of economic literature interested in the sexual division of labor, although with a more neutral currency and less poignancy in meaning.[6] This has been used at various times in the scientific debate by economists and sociologists far removed from Marxist theory: scholars who look at market economy openly and critically, and recognized followers of liberal feminism. In her 2004 book *Key Issues in Women's Work*, Catherine Hakim applied the concept of "reproductive work" to the caregiving activities related to raising children, placing it alongside other terms such as housework and domestic work, intended to define the remaining activities carried out by women in the house.[7] And Nancy Folbre, one of the protagonists of the critical reevaluation of feminine work, has at times used it, together with caregiving, looking after the children, and performing other tasks for the family, in juxtaposition with productive work for the market.[8] Mignon Duffy has revisited "reproductive work," underlining the "nurturing" value not only of non-paid domestic activities but also of those carried out within the home by remunerated caregivers and as services to the person outside of the home, paid by public welfare or private entrepreneurs.[9]

The crossroad success of the concept of reproductive work is, however, in part independent of a strictly economic reading: one of the reasons for its fortune is the linguistic and theoretical affinity of the idea of social reproduction, already present in Marx and central to the sociological literature that followed. The latter is an even broader and more inclusive category that, together with the theme of the workers' economic reproduction, evokes the many demographic, social, and cultural processes, which allow a society to maintain, over time, a certain structure and some degree of cohesion. A broader idea of social reproduction, partially linked to Marxist thought, has been used by many feminist scholars. Barbara Laslett and Giovanna Brenner defined it thus in 1989: "While beginning, as does Marxist theory, with necessary labor, the feminist concept of social reproduction broadens its definition to include the work of maintaining existing life and reproducing the next generation. It therefore involves more than the production as Marxist theory has defined it."[10]

In the purview of this broad and polysemic concept, the feminine contribution to "reproduction" is evoked in the first place by "biological reproduction," with its powerful and fascinating processes, which in the past were the hidden core of women's social value and the reason for patriarchal control of their bodies, based on various forms of "privatization" and ideological disempowerment. While legitimated by scientific language, the concept of biological reproduction contains, however, a mechanistic nucleus making it somewhat misleading: in actual fact, procreation uses preexisting biological materials in order to create new biological individuals.

The concept of "biological reproduction" implies, moreover, that, on the quantitative scale, the "micro" behavior of families guarantees a replacement rate of the current population consistent with the necessary threshold level on the "macro" scale. For the world population, this has been established by the United Nations at about 2.1 children per woman; but families, be it for reasons linked to their social context or for other reasons, different and personal, are bound to have more or fewer offspring. The population of women worldwide, in addition to still having a mid-rate of fertility of 2.4 children per woman, slightly higher than the theoretical rate of replacement,[11] has a much higher birthrate on account of the structure of the population in less developed countries, where fertility has declined recently and young women of childbearing age are numerous. So-called biological reproduction, therefore, profoundly transforms the quantity as well as the quality of human beings.

In spite of their mechanistic traits, the concepts of social reproduction, biological reproduction, and reproductive work have experienced a revival in the last few years in studies into the non-paid work of immigrant family assistants from non-Western countries: the fertile line of research on the global chain of caregiving has revisited these categories in a heterodox mode, attributing to the sphere of economic and social reproduction, on a global scale, an economic and political centrality never seen before.[12]

Yet do the various "reproductive" theories still make sense? Overcoming the suggestive vagueness of the concept of social reproduction and leaving the idea of "biological reproduction" to the life sciences, we want to focus in these pages only on the economic concept of reproductive work, seeking to understand if its separation from productive work is—linguistically and theoretically—useful for women in order to give value to domestic work and caregiving. More, at the end of this contribution we will take into consideration the actual perspectives of the transformation of the relationship between domestic production and production outside the home.

In order to analyze the economic dimension of the concept of reproduction, we return particularly to the meaning that has been attributed to it by Marxist feminism: a "reproductive" work not of life in a flat sense, nor of the social classes, but of something that we perceive today as much more delimited—that is the capacity to work. We would like first of all to dwell, therefore, on the feminist and Marxist category of work "reproductive" of the labor force, in turn recalling the Marxist opposite concept of productive work. Doing so, we certainly deal with old questions. In 1954, for example, liberal economist Joseph Aloy Schumpeter defined the "famous controversy" on Marxist distinction between productive and non-productive work as "a dusty museum piece."[13] And even the Marxist wave of the 1970s, which gave birth to the feminist theory of reproductive work, is half a century old. The sense of "a return to the origins" proposed in these pages is, however, linked beyond the renewed fortune of its literal acceptance, rooted in historical materialism and in Marxism, with the persistent diffusion of the general acceptance of the concept of reproductive work that survives by inertia in many of our studies.

2. Going back to the origins: the Marxian view of productive work

The concept of reproductive work does not exist in classical economics: none of the classical economists devoted their attention to caregiving activities and care for various members of the family carried out within the home. Adam Smith, as Joan Scott has powerfully written, naturalized the tasks of women.[14] Within the framework of a construction making all wealth descend from manufacturing work, subjected to the processes of the division of labor, not only were biological processes—from conception to pregnancy—but also those including precise norms and social relations—such as breastfeeding, care, house work—equated to natural resources, primary materials paid for and activated by family members working in factories with their own salary. The same thought is implicit in Marx who, moving along on the utilitarian line of thought of classical economics, attributes to the interest of capital a project of biological and social reproduction of work that coincides, in its perspective of analysis, with the life of the workers themselves. Nancy Folbre has shown with extreme clarity the full stages of this construction.[15]

When Marx talks about reproduction work, on the other hand, he does not refer to that performed by the wives of those salaried laborers but to the so-called "necessary work," that is to the first hours of work performed in the factories by the workers.[16] This part of the work is the reason for which the salary is exchanged, guaranteeing the sustenance of the workers, which is the process of simple reproduction. Meanwhile the successive work hours are the surplus labor that, transformed by the capitalist into capital, will become the basis of accumulation, also defined as expanded reproduction. The latter, in the theoretical perspective of Smith and Marx, is the only truly productive part of work, courier of development and of potential social transformations.[17] The reconversion in value of enjoyable use for the proletariat of this wealth will be possible, however, only with the defeat of capitalism. Here is a synthesized passage in which Marx presents his view[18]: "The aim of capitalist production is the surplus, not the product. The labourer's necessary labour-time, and therefore also its equivalent in the product with which it is paid for, is only necessary as long as it produces surplus-labour. Otherwise it is *un-productive* for the capitalist."

Productive work excludes beyond its borders the entire spectrum of service activities and production of merchandise that the workers acquire on the market for their own sustenance, given that work becomes productive—a function of accumulation—only in the hands of the capitalist. With this perspective, all the services acquired on the market by the workers, for example the lessons from a teacher which also increase the market value of their work, are not productive work, nor is the activity of a paid chef. Only if the lessons of a teacher or the culinary skills of the chef are acquired by a capitalist can they be considered productive. Yet unlike the work that produces merchandise by the serial methods allowed by the mechanization and the division of labor from the factory, all services that cannot be detached from the person of the laborer who performs them are of little profit and thus little meaning: these are practically irrelevant within the scope of capitalistic economics.

The separation of the worker from his instruments of production and his renewed link to machines inside the capitalist factory are the prerequisite of productive work. Not even farmers or artisans, who do not sell work to a capitalistic factory owner but rather goods to consumers, are truly productive workers.[19] Even more so with female domestic work, which, acquired by the laborer without any exchange on the market, is not a part of the productive economy: within the classic framework, this activity is invisible.

3. The roots of the idea of "reproduction"

It is as much about a powerful vertigo of abstraction as a destruction of reality that excludes from the analytical framework expectations and projects foreign to the will and interest of capital. Even the laborers' way of living thus becomes a mere dependent variable, shaped entirely to fit the needs of the capitalist. It must be remembered that Marx had in front of him a society, nineteenth-century Britain, whose industrialization was rapidly eroding the weight of rural ways of life, of production for one's own consumption, and in general of the preindustrial world; laborers from childhood worked fourteen to sixteen hours a day in factories for miserable salaries; the workers accommodation, to their detriment, did not require or allow for much cleaning, and kitchen work carried little value.[20] The models of a worker's free time at the end of the century, as for example described by Eric Hobsbawm, were yet to be affirmed[21]; Marx's pan-productionist and pan-capitalist abstraction thus seemed about to transform itself into concrete reality.

Within this framework, the Marxist concept of reproduction of the labor force was affirmed: it was the analytical precedent of that to follow on reproductive work, but it was altogether different. The workforce of the laborers did not appear within the context of the nineteenth century as a limited resource on the biological or social plane; in fact, classic economists considered workers as equivalent with respect to their human traits and their abstract productive competencies; even their possibility to generate new producers, if their salaries allowed the worker to survive, was a mechanical question and merely demographic. But neither did the demographics present problematic characteristics, from the point of view of the providers of work: the fertility rate of the population was sufficiently higher than the rate of replacement. Broadly influenced by Malthus's ideas,[22] it was, if anything, the high birthrate of poor workers that worried the leading class, for its potential to break the social order. In actual fact, the presence within the population of a massive, numerous, and unstable number of young people resulted in riots and rebellions when faced with decreased salaries and famine.

Contrary to what scholars of proto-industry reprimanded him,[23] Marx did not fail to treat the topic of the relationship between demography and capitalist development, seeing demographic growth of the most marginalized part of the proletariat as a pillar in the creation of an industrial army reserve, useful to capitalism in order to constrict salaries. In an excerpt from the first book of *Capital* he wrote:[24]

> The third category of the relative surplus population, the stagnant, forms a part of the active labor army, but with extremely irregular employment. Hence it furnishes to capital an inexhaustible reservoir of disposable labour power. . . . It recruits itself constantly from the supernumerary forces of modern industry and agriculture, and especially from those decaying branches of industry where handicraft is yielding to manufacture, manufacture to machinery. Its extent grows, as with the extent and energy of accumulation, the creation of a surplus population advances. But it forms at the same time a self-reproducing and self-perpetuating element of the working class, taking a proportionally greater part in the general increase of that class than the other elements. In fact, not only the number of births and deaths, but the absolute size of the families stand in inverse proportion to the height of wages, and therefore to the amount of means of subsistence of which the different categories of labourers dispose. This law of capitalistic society would sound absurd to savages, or even civilised colonists. It calls to mind the boundless reproduction of animals individually weak and constantly hunted down.

This metaphor, which takes the formation of the industrial reserve army back not to human behavior but to that of animal species, incomprehensible even to savages, was referred by Marx to a marginal component of the laborer population, but in perpetual competition with the central components. This allows us to understand that from the author's point of view, the reproductive services incorporated in the workforce had, in general, a limited bearing.

Marx's idea of reproduction, in and of itself incompatible with a close and analytical recognition of the care work of salaried workers' wives, was taken up again in the 1970s by various exponents of the left of Marxist inspiration, in Europe, precisely so as to analyze and evaluate women's domestic activities.

The reflection on domestic work has been precocious, and in its own way innovative, in Italy. The particular attention attributed to familial work definitely explains itself with the persistence and the development, in contemporary Italian society, of models of female domestic work that were extremely pervasive in terms of hours and very committed in terms of dedication and quality. In the early 1970s there was a specific political feminist group, Lotta Femminista (Feminist Struggle), that proposed and used the concept of reproductive work. At the end of the 1970s this category had a second flowering thanks to the scope of research on small and medium Italian businesses, coordinated by Massimo Paci.

Much more recently, a new scientific proposal for the valorization of domestic work, with no reference to the idea of reproduction, has made headway in a study by Alberto Alesina and Andrea Ichino.

It is along these three lines of research that we will concentrate in the following pages.

4. The contribution of a feminist theorist

The elaboration of Lotta Femminista, and in particular of Mariarosa Dalla Costa,[25] took shape, in the early 1960s, in Padua, a city in northern Italy. The proximity of a prestigious university and a strata of combative workers, namely those from the petrochemical industrial pole in Porto Marghera, brought many students to factory gates; the rereading of Marx's texts by some university philosophers preceded, on account of this social intertwining, the birth of Lotta Femminista. The territory of Padua reflected the economic changes and social tensions of the first industrial modernity,[26] which characterized, more generally, northern Italy. The standards of living had considerably improved with the diffusion in the 1960s of accommodation for workers equipped with electricity, gas, and the first household electrical appliances.[27] Models of fertility were changing, with the transition of the average fertility rate from two children to one,[28] and the consolidation, even among laborer families, of a model of "qualitative" fertility that concentrated the material and immaterial resources of the family on few children, paying particular attention to their education. The economic boom and the union struggles of the 1960s had moreover determined a certain improvement of salaries and the generalization of the so-called short-week contracts, of forty hours a week. Giving children a secondary education, which could guarantee them a better future than that of their parents, was by then a widespread objective in many laborer families.[29]

Even if work outside the home of mothers and wives was higher than that recorded by official data,[30] it was in the early 1960s at a historic low, while their household tasks rather intensified, adjusting to new qualitative ideals. Domestic work consisted in intense working days to attain standards of hygiene, of order, of clothing, and of nutrition far higher than in the past, in order to improve the quality of life and affirm the dignity of the members of the household. The education of sons and daughters implied not only a greater control than in the past on their playtime and daily lives but also an adaptation to the rapid changes in motion within society. The Marxist concept of reproduction of the workforce was thus taken up again by the group Lotta Femminista in a rather different context than that observed by Marx.

Lotta Femminista established a relationship of continuity and rupture with Marx's reflections. The reproductive work of the workforce, only rarely touched on by Marx, and especially with reference to the "necessary work" of the laborer to obtain a salary of sustenance, was instead identified within the production of goods and services carried out by the laborers' wives. According to Mariarosa Dalla Costa, the theoretical mind of the group,

> It is often asserted that, within the definition of wage labor, women in domestic labor are not productive. In fact precisely the opposite is true if one thinks of the enormous quantity of social services which capitalist organization transforms into privatized activity, putting them on the backs of housewives. Domestic labor is not essentially "feminine work"; a woman doesn't fulfill herself more or get less exhausted than a man from washing and cleaning. These are social services inasmuch as they serve the reproduction (of labor power). And capital, precisely by instituting its family structure, has "liberated" the man from these functions so that he is completely "free" for direct exploitation; so that he is free to "earn" enough for a woman to reproduce him as labour power. It has made men wage slaves, then, to the degree that it has succeeded in allocating these services to women in the family, and by the same process controlled the flow of women onto the labour market.[31]

How did reproductive work become productive? Even if, in the text by Dalla Costa cited above, this accountable specification is not clear, her idea was perhaps, implicitly, that the work of reproduction performed in the home by women added value not only to the necessary work of reproduction carried out in the factory by the laborers but also to the surplus labor, becoming productive even in the restricted sense proposed by Marx. The new perspective had thus the merit of inserting domestic work within the economic sphere, rather than the moral one, making visible for the first time the many hours of housework performed by women and explicitly focusing on the value of the production of essential goods and services inside the home. These material activities were realistically observed, in their exhausting intertwinement with the delicate work of psychological support to family members who faced the stress of work, study, union and political activities. *Le operaie della casa* (The Female Workers of the House), a piece of propaganda and analysis by Lotta Femminista, shed an empathetic gaze on this daily exertion.

The important contribution to the understanding of caregiving from the studies of the Paduan feminist group must therefore be recognized. Thanks to these reflections, the worth of caregiving work for the economy, and in particular for the development of capitalism, was uncovered.[32] These analyses placed in specific relief data that would be verified later by the studies on the usage of time: the abnormal hours of the familial workdays of Italian women,[33] confirmed successively by all the comparative studies.

The idea of defining as productive, as producer of surplus, the "reproductive" work of women, with a partial revision but internal to Marxist thought, had, however, in my opinion, a paradoxical aspect. It signified continuing to think only from the point of view of capital and not from that of work, notwithstanding the fact that in the 1970s women's agency was a great deal more delineated than in the past. With their housework and caregiving, the laborers' wives—whether they occupied themselves exclusively with the family or carried out additional activities outside the home—even then made the effort not only to assure the survival of the family but also to produce original values of use, creating historically new figures of workers and consumers. The contribution of these activities to the creation of prospective better lives for the whole family—for their husbands, their children, and in the end also for themselves—was obscured.

After all, the importance of housework for capital was asserted with force, but without the complete evaluation of possible alternative scenarios, which hypothesized the addition of the female work quota to that already offered by men on the market. The history of the first phase of industrial revolution reminds us instead that in this period the capitalistic exploitation of women workers reached its most extreme points, suggesting scholars describe it with the expression "sweating system."[34] Furthermore, the actual activation on the market of the female workforce evokes the reintroduction of the downward competition between male and female laborers.

The studies by Mariarosa Dalla Costa were taken up again in a simplified form in the second half of the 1970s during the experiences of Italian unionist feminism. This can be seen in the documents published in the course of 150 hours in which, in contrast to what the Paduan group had maintained, the idea that women performed reproductive work at home, distinctive from productive work carried out in factories, rebounded with the force of an article of faith.[35]

Italian gender oriented sociology, in the same years, assumed more nuanced positions: "the contemporary family—Chiara Saraceno wrote in 1976—has . . . an important economic function." Apart from cleaning house and clothing, the scholar cited the many other activities that were difficult to mechanize, underlining the importance of those of caregiving, which would become more costly if they were done outside the home.[36]

The work of Dalla Costa drew a good audience in England thanks to her political and theoretical partnership with Selma James, a militant English scholar. The categories introduced by the author were actually, in this context, a stimulus to the development of the so-called "domestic labor debate." The author who shared with greater conviction the idea that the privatized productive sphere was not just a creation of capitalism but also an indispensable premise to worker exploitation was Wally Seccombe, in an article of the *New Left Review* in 1975. Yet her intervention opened up a broad critical debate, in which some social scientists countered the materialist vision of the author, critiquing the vagueness of her use of Marxist categories on the one hand and a greater emphasis on the ideological aspects of patriarchy on the other.[37]

A different position, and one of great interest, was that of Christine Delphy, later endorsed by other scholars, who together with her became exponents of so-called "material feminism."[38] Delphy denied in no uncertain terms the distinction between production and reproduction, affirming that two different modes of production coexisted in society: on the one hand, domestic production inside the home, in which the exploitation of women derived from the patriarchal domination of men; on the other, capitalistic production, outside the home, that subjugated to its logic the male and female factory workers. Thus the social subalternity of women, instead of the encapsulation in the capitalistic accumulation of their work, derived from their position as producers, exploited and dominated at home by their own husbands. The positions of material feminism have continued to long animate the theoretical discussion of feminism, also renewing life in relation to the emergence of a poststructuralist feminism.[39]

While this debate was developing, the family continued with its transformation, accentuating its affectionate traits and relaxing traditional obligations. The processes of socialization and transmission of moral norms became more flexible in the second half of the 1970s, less conformed to predefined systems of values[40]; there was a growing aspiration of parents to raise "innovative" children capable of constructing their own path in individualized and reflective forms[41]; support for courses of instruction for sons and daughters grew. Later, with the economic crisis in the 1990s, children and parents started to include in their strategies of social mobility the integration of a poor "post-materialist" variation on traditional models, which maintained educational mobility, the improvement of scholastic standards for their children in comparison to their parents, even in the absence of a prospective for economic improvement.[42] At the same time, the time dedicated to caregiving for the elderly, although changing in form, became for demographic reasons an unavoidable component of familial work: the caregivers, whether sons or daughters, daughters-in-law, or their own spouses, in addition to being a part of the workforce, had to perform a task that was of little interest to capital: accompanying people who had left the workforce toward the end of their lives.

The attention of many scholars, in Italy and elsewhere, focused on the changes in domestic work, perfecting the idea of "caregiving." This mutation implied a significant semantic move giving space on the one hand for a valorization of caregiving as a deep and specific psychological aspect of female identity,[43] and on the other for social research on the quantitative and qualitative, productive and creative, mechanical and affectionate dimensions of caregiving and its variations, linked to the specific content of the activities; in this second perspective, caregiving was not a specific female vocation, and the caregivers were not necessarily identified with women.

5. Reproductive work in the industrial districts

The economic role of the reproduction of the workforce performed as a familial task, was, however, the center, in Italy in the 1980s, of another important line of studies: that on the Italian systems of small- and medium-size firms.[44] They took into consideration a very different context than that analyzed by the Paduan feminist group: the productive reality of the industrial districts of the Third Italy, that is in areas of small and middle-range industrial businesses in the Veneto region, in Emilia-Romagna, Tuscany, the Marches, and Umbria, peripheral in comparison to the so-called "industrial triangle" where the great industries had developed in Italy. This path of development, typically Italian, based on the industrialization of small urban centers and their rural environs, had ensured that families kept, whether in structure or function, some traits of the farmer families of the past: still tied to the land, family members often living together in multigeneration units, united along ties of patrilineal kinship. These preserved, furthermore, richer economic functions than in urban contexts, remaining involved with traditional forms of production. Women, besides still participating in fieldwork in less urbanized areas, took care of the garden and chicken coop and produced at home various objects of consumption for the family components.

This research thus also looked at the economic consequences of domestic work, but with the aim of understanding its role within the complex economic circuit, be it from the point of view of industrial businesses or from that of the workers. The domestic work of women, not calculated in the budgets of business, furnished on the one hand small- and medium-size firms of industrial districts with opportunities to pay lower, more competitive salaries; on the other hand, however, this allowed for the female laborers' families to save, protecting their own work from the fluctuations of employment.[45] Domestic work thus became a significant, and in some ways strategic, economic variable, as a prerequisite for a typical Italian path of industrialization, an alternative to that of the big factory.

Paci's group proposed, for example, for the first time a meaningful reflection on how the Italian model of a diffused economy, thanks to its ability to favor family savings, helped with the purchase of houses as part of the laborer family's property and allowed not irrelevant forms of social mobility for the workers themselves, which sometimes succeeded in transforming themselves into small entrepreneurs.

Even more than the studies of Paduan feminism, the research on small and middle industries showed how the familial work of women, even more than reproducing the workforce of family members, created new social figures with long-term effects: in that era, the lifestyles of the families of female workers and those of the urban *petite bourgeoisie,* even if not identifying with each other, were getting closer.

6. The disappearance of non-market work in mainstream economics

On the opposite current to that of classical economists, such topics were also dealt with by neoclassical, or marginalist, economic thought, which since the late nineteenth century constituted the mainstream of the political economy in the Western world. It has reevaluated the use value of products, seeing the attainment of a utility on the part of the consumer, and not just of profit for capitalistic entrepreneurs, as the drive behind the economic market. All that was produced outside the market fell, however, into a black hole in this model, too.[46] In Italy, as in Western Europe and the United States, the nineteenth- and twentieth-century censuses reflected the affirmation of this ideology, excluding women "assigned to domestic tasks" from the employed population and progressively trivializing their activities to the point of defining them as "housewives."[47]

The progressive equivalence of women assigned to care of the household with not-working people was a consequence of the theoretical hegemony of the marginalism on economic studies. Yet the important marginalist reversal of the Marxist perspective, reevaluating the use value, produced in the long term a reevaluation of family caregiving: from the 1960s onward, this important change in perspective was progressively championed by Gary Becker.[48] In the study of the recomposition of individual interests, he proposed, however, a natural difference in objectives between men and women, which carried a specialization on the typical traditional roles.[49] From here, the positions of female scholars divided: the majority, from a background in history and sociology, underlined the relationships of power, outside the market, that had historically determined the exclusion of women from the public sphere, the segregation of domestic work, and the interiorization of norms that held fast to their caregiving work; Catherine Hakim, on the contrary, brought back to the fore the preferences of the different groups of women and their choices on the amount of time devoted to domestic work and to work for the market.[50]

7. Homemade Italy: a rehabilitation

A third Italian contribution, even though it leaves to one side the idea of reproduction, has recently reasserted the economic value of domestic work and caregiving. It was two economists, Alberto Alesina and Andrea Ichino, who implicitly took up again the results of gender studies and, in the successful volume *L'Italia fatta in casa*,[51] have subscribed to the idea that domestic work constitutes, above all in Italy, a hidden wealth. The use value of domestic work has been converted into exchange value with non-billed techniques of accounting. The authors' aim is to account for the contribution of domestic work to the GDP—but this operation is also important on a symbolic level—for a reevaluation of the economic value of caregiving. It is counterintuitive that, in national Italian accounting, all forms of illegal work have recently been reevaluated as hidden components of the GDP, with their inevitable connections to criminal activities, but not the caregiving work of women.[52]

Beyond these interesting accountable and symbolic aspects, the analysis of Alesina and Ichino looks from afar, and rightly so, from the position of neoclassical economists, and not only from the nineteenth century, ignoring on the whole the "moral" disadvantages of the abandonment of caregiving work by women. This actually seems to evoke, although implicitly, an ideal sharing of the role of breadwinner between men and women. This perspective is for many aspects liberating, but it displaces attention from a deep essential fact, and that is that once taken outside the borders of the family and externalized, some aspects of caregiving, beyond the gender identity of the one who creates it for others, lose an essential part of their worth. The externalization specifically tones down or erases its "dedicated" character, non-detachable from the person who offers it. Producing or cooking something special for and with their children, inventing a new game, ordering things according to a shared ritual, offering elderly relatives recognition and care—all are aspects of family relationships between caregivers and caretakers whose disempowerment can have costs in terms of emotional well-being.

The subdivision of caregiving work among men and women is a rather equitable solution, capable of lightening the burden of work that weighs on women, preserving at the same time the affectionate and/or educational content of these relationships. A flattening of the market and a depersonalization of the flow of production, as well as of creativity and affection developed in the direct relationships among grandparents, parents, and children, can instead impoverish them. As Nancy Folbre has poignantly written, it is precisely the "invisible heart" of the affection learned and practiced in the family that sustains those processes of relations, fiduciary, of reciprocal trust, that fluidify and allow for the functioning of the "invisible hand" of the market.[53]

8. Beyond the dichotomy

What is therefore of great interest is the opportunity that work and human activities can satisfy needs and desires, create material and psychological well-being, constructing historically variable but sustainable equilibriums on economic, ethical, and emotional planes. Naturally the possibility that this will come to fruition is tied to the political and economic context, to the opportunities and resources that capitalism and the other economic actors coexisting with this, from family to the state, place at the disposal of the people. These aspects are not taken for granted and are particularly problematic in the period of the international restructuring of capitalism we are experiencing, where a world population of dimensions never seen before is forced to reckon with a technological revolution of extraordinary proportions, and apparently a labor-saving one. Rather than experiencing a transformation of laborers into a middle class, we are today in front of a general impoverishment of the latter, in the West and in the South of the world.

It is useful, however, to liberate oneself from the productive/reproductive dichotomy, to return analytically to the question of the productivity of work and its activities, understood as a continuum of productive and creative experiences that interweave and recompose two theoretically different characteristics in different ways.

On the one hand there is the production of high-quality use values, where we can include, even if the language of utility does not seem apt to describe them, dedicated relationships and affections contextual to the sphere of intimacy, connections rooted in the deepest and most personal emotions and feelings. These unique goods, produced especially in the home, have a great qualitative value, but under the quantitative aspect, they have had up until now a low level of productivity. In this context, the observation by Nancy Folbre, to whom domestic caregiving does not produce consistent economies of scale,[54] appears significant and worthy of being shared.

In this sense it is also not very clear, returning to the contribution by Alesina and Ichino but also to other important works fighting for a greater presence of women in paid jobs,[55] how the mere shift to the market of low productivity work would increase, apart from the monetary GDP, the real aggregate national product.

On the other hand, the production of depersonalized values—serialized, producible, and reproducible at ever greater distances from the final users—by interchangeable actors potentially in competition with each other persists and dislocates into new territories. Values which, thanks to the economies of scale based on the interchangeability of producers and the networks of communication outside the home, can be produced in sufficient quantities for the satisfaction of needs that tend to be universal. In this type of productive organization, in itself underutilizing human intelligence, higher productivity has been reached because human contribution has nevertheless been able to combine itself with the efficiency of technology and machines.

The need/desire for intimacy and personalized products, satisfied in general by familial caregiving, was until now, on the basis of prevalent modes of production, basically alternative to and often in conflict with that of a satisfaction en masse of homogenous basically universal needs, to which industrialization, commodification of the goods produced once by the domestic economy, and mechanization of productive processes have responded. The dichotomous view of these two spheres was common in the mainstream of economic thought; Marx, in particular, would consider children caregiving services as unproductive, even if they were outside the home and concentrated in preschool services; being still closely tied to the person that offers them, they remain unsuitable for standardization and mechanization.

Yet instead of a dichotomy, we can now see a long chain formed of many intermediary rings: goods and services that, although exchanged on the market, have value because they are intrinsic to trust and affection and subjected to processes of familiarization—among these, for example, the caregiving services of a babysitter or assistants for the elderly.[56] And we also have to recognize that preschool services, caring for more children than a mother looks after at home, may produce a certain economy of scale. Moreover, the present ever more frequently joins together the signs of a persisting past, surprising indications of the potential of science and the technological innovations to recompose and adjust the poles of the dichotomy delineated above among intimate satisfaction and economies of scale.

According to Michael Spence,[57] the 3D printer has the potential to eliminate, for example, economies of scale and the distinction in each field of production made between places of production and places of consumption. And thus we can imagine a mother and child who produce together, with the click of a mouse, a ball to play with and gym shoes. Again, communication via Skype, although it does not replace the need for more proximate and physical intimacy, conveys from a distance snippets of life situated in a context of intimacy, creating experiences of close emotional intensity. Finally, social networks themselves exercise a diffused, although controversial, function in the sphere of reciprocal acknowledgment and connection among people.

Even without launching oneself into more or less futuristic flights of fantasy, the new technological applications allow us to propose never-before-seen forms of the satisfaction of needs and desires. These interweave more contextual modes of productivity and intimacy better than in the past, with a more ample, and potentially universal, production of goods and services.[58]

In conclusion, we take as a point of departure a new reflection on work that overcomes old dichotomies, the broad and diachronic definition offered to us by Chris and Charles Tilly:

> *Work* includes any human effort adding use value to goods and services. . . . To be sure, not all effort qualifies as work; purely destructive, expressive, or consumptive acts lie outside the bound: in so far as they reduce transferable use value, we might think of them as antiwork. . . . All work involves *labor processes*: allocations of various intensities and qualities of effort among different aspects of production within specific technical conditions.[59]

9. Concluding remarks

The abstract theory of value by Smith and Marx, which limited the value of production to the sphere of factory work, was in reality focused, more than on the value of use of goods, indispensable but taken for granted, on the necessity to produce it on a grand scale, leaving in its wake the capitalist interest for profit. The objectives, in a context still characterized by a general situation of scarcity, were the increase of the quantity of material goods and the growth of wealth, via an increase in productivity.

Once a broader and more inclusive concept of work is introduced, it is nevertheless important to not lose sight of the reflection on the specificities of single occupations, evidenced on the one hand by internal characteristics and on the other by the relationship with the social and economic context in which they are situated. Within the analytical picture, we must introduce new criteria of evaluation: the content of knowledge and qualitative productivity; the intrinsic destructive potential of productive processes from the point of view of the environment; the capability of emerging technologies to make economies of scale obsolete in favor of a contextual production. Individualized, but not limited by this.

Yet we must not neglect the fact that even traditional economies of scale, derived from processes of concentration, division of labor, and mechanization, maintain their import in situations of scarcity. The hierarchical relevance of these parameters in fact changes inevitably, along with the economic context in which the social actors are immersed, in addition to their individual characteristics in terms of economic position, cultural baggage, generation, gender.

The analysis of these variations is important, yet it has often been neglected by feminist theory, with the exception of a few groups of female economists.[60] Broadening the gaze of these topics is an ineluctable step, and perhaps the tradition of studies on women can ultimately give a careful and meaningful contribution on a criterion for the evaluation of jobs rarely considered by studies: the degree of the actual utility of goods and services not only under the profile of material well-being or cultural fulfillment but also from the perspective of the primary need for affection and the recognition that, in various ways, all human beings share this.

Alessandra Pescarolo served as senior research officer in IRPET, the research office for economic planning of Regione Toscana, Italy (1979–2012). She worked in the Lelio and Lisli Basso Foundation (Rome) and was a British Academy Fellow at Birkbeck College in London. She was a founder of the Italian Society of Women Historians (SIS) and a member of the editorial board of *Genesis*. She taught Sociology and History of Labor as well as Sociology and History of the Family at the University of Florence. Her publications include *Riconversione industriale e composizione di classe* (Milano: Angeli, 1979), on engineering industry in Italy after World War I; *Il proletariato invisibile*, with Gianbruno Ravenni (Milano: Angeli, 1990), on Florence straw-hat women workers from 1820 to 1950; *Famiglie in mutamento* (Milano: Angeli, 1997), with Elisabetta Cioni, Maria Carla Meini, and Paola Tronu; *Diseguaglianze sociali e modi di vivere* (Milano: Angeli 2000), with Paola Tronu; *Storia sociale delle donne in Italia* (Roma-Bari: Laterza 2001), with Anna Bravo, Margherita Pelaja, and Lucetta Scaraffia; *I giovani fra rischi e sfide della modernità* (ed.), (Firenze: IRPET, 2010); *Di generazione in generazione: le italiane dall'Unità a oggi* (Roma: Viella, 2014), ed. with Maria T. Mori, Anna Scattigno, and Simonetta Soldani.

Notes

I would like to thank Annalisa Rosselli and Giancarlo De Vivo for discussing some of the concepts expressed on these pages with me. The responsibility for the content of the work is mine. I am also grateful to Molly Abigail Flynn for her careful translation.

1. Mariarosa Dalla Costa, *Women and the Subversion of the Community* and Selma James, *A Woman's Place* (Bristol: Falling Wall Press, 1972); This was the starting point, above all in England, of the so-called "Domestic Labor Debate," to which we will return later.
2. For a more recent update of the thoughts from the Paduan group, see Lucia Chisté, Alisa Del Re, and Edvige Forti, *Oltre il lavoro domestico: il lavoro delle donne fra produzione e riproduzione* (Milano: Feltrinelli, 1979). A re-actualization of the concept of reproductive work is in Antonella Picchio, *Social Reproduction: The Political Economy of the Labour Market* (Cambridge: Cambridge University Press, 1992). There is also a Wikipedia entry in Esperanto: "Reprodukta laboro," retrieved 15 November 2015 from https://eo.wikipedia.org/wiki/Reprodukta_laboro; on the same date two entries in English and French may be found on Wikipedia, devoted to economic reproduction and social reproduction respectively.
3. For an exhaustive survey on the debate on domestic work and the difference between social and liberal feminism, see Sylvia Walby, *Patriarchy at Work: Patriarchal and Capitalistic Relations in Employment, 1800–1984* (Malden, MA: Polity Press; 1986), chapters 1–4; Eliza Darling, "Class," in *Routledge International Encyclopedia of Women: Global Women's Issues and Knowledge*, ed. Cheris Kramarae and Dale Spender (New York: Routledge, 2004), 181–84; and Melissa White, "Class and Feminism," in Kramarae and Spender, *Routledge International Encyclopedia of Women*, 184–86.
4. Julie Torrant, *The Material Family* (New York: Springer Science & Business Media, 2012).
5. Silvia Federici, *Caliban and the Witch: Women, the Body and Primitive Accumulation* (New York: Autonomedia, 2004); Silvia Federici, *Revolution at Point Zero: Housework, Reproduction, and Feminist Struggle* (Oakland, CA: PM Press [Common Notions], 2012).
6. Mignon Duffy, in *Making Care Count: A Century of Gender, Race, and Paid Care Work* (New Brunswick, NJ: Rutgers University Press, 2011), does a good job of describing this version of the concept as theoretically "light."

7. Catherine Hakim, *Key Issues in Women's Work: Female Diversity and the Polarisation of Women* (London: The Glasshouse Press, 2004), e.g. 22 and 51.
8. Nancy Folbre, *Greed, Lust, and Gender: A History of Economic Ideas* (Oxford: Clarendon Press, 2009), 128.
9. Mignon Duffy, "Doing the Dirty Work: Gender, Race, and Reproductive Labor in Historical Perspective," *Gender & Society* 21 no. 3 (2007): 313–36.
10. Barbara Laslett and Johanna Brenner, "Gender and Social Reproduction: Historical Perspectives," *Annual Review of Sociology* 15, no. 1 (1989): 381–404.
11. United Nations, Department of Economic and Social Affairs, Population Division, *World Fertility Report 2009* (New York: United Nations, 2011).
12. Rachel Salazar Parreñas, *The Force of Domesticity: Filipina Migrants and Globalization* (New York: NYU Press, 2008); Anita I. Garey and Karen V. Hansen, eds., *At the Heart of Work and Family: Engaging the Ideas of Arlie Hochschild* (New Brunswick, NJ: Rutgers University Press, 2011); Eleonore Kofman and Parvati Raghuram, "Gender and Global Labour Migrations: Incorporating Skilled Workers," *Antipode* 38, no. 2 (2006): 282–303. Also in Italy the studies on these themes are numerous. See for example Sara Ongaro, *Le donne e la globalizzazione: domande di genere all'economia globale della ri-produzione* (Soveria Mannelli: Rubbettino, 2001), and Francesca Alice Vianello, *Migrando sole: legami transnazionali tra Ucraina e Italia* (Milano: FrancoAngeli, 2009).
13. Joseph A. Schumpeter, *History of Economic Analysis*, edited from the manuscript by Elizabeth Boody Schumpeter and with an introduction by Mark Perlman (Abingdon: Taylor & Francis e-Library, 2006), 597; first published in 1954, London: Allen & Unwin.
14. Joan W. Scott, "La travailleuse," in *Histoire des femmes en Occident, le XIXe siècle*, Tome 4, ed. Georges Duby and Michelle Perrot (Paris: Plon, 1991), 419–44.
15. Nancy Folbre, *The Invisible Heart: Economics and Family Values* (New York: The New Press, 2001).
16. Carlo Pelosi, *Marx sul lavoro produttivo e improduttivo* (Roma: Istituto della Enciclopedia italiana, 1974).
17. Ibid., 44–45.
18. Karl Marx, *Theories of Surplus-Value*, vol. IV of *Capital*; chapter IV, "Theories of Productive and Unproductive Labour," 9. *Ganilh and Ricardo on Net Revenue. Ganilh as Advocate of a Diminution of the Productive Population; Ricardo as Advocate of the Accumulation of Capital and the Growth of Productive Forces*, https://www.marxists.org/archive/marx/works/1863/theories-surplus-value/ch04.htm#s1. Other reflections on the distinction between productive and nonproductive work are contained in the same piece: Part I, 12, *Productivity of Capital: Productive and Unproductive Labour*, ibid.
19. Pelosi, *Marx sul lavoro produttivo e improduttivo*, 91.
20. Raffaella Sarti, *Europe at Home: Family and Material culture 1500–1800*, trans. Allan Cameron (New Haven, CT: Yale University Press, 2002).
21. Eric J. Hobsbawm, *Worlds of Labour: Further Studies in the History of Labour* (London: Weidenfeld and Nicolson, 1984).
22. Formulated in Thomas Robert Malthus, *An Essay on the Principle of Population, as It Affects the Future Improvement of Society with Remarks on the Speculations of Mr. Godwin, M. Condorcet, and Other Writers* (London: Printed for J. Johnson, in St. Paul's Church-Yard, 1798; © 1998, Electronic Scholarly Publishing Project, http://www.esp.org).
23. Franklin F. Mendels, "Des industries rurales à la protoindustrialization: bilan historique d'un changement de perspective," *Annales E.S.C.* 39 (1984).
24. Karl Marx, *Capital: A Critique of Political Economy*, Book One: *The Process of Production of Capital*, First published in German, 1867, vol. I, Online Version: Marx/Engels Internet Archive (marxists.org) 1995, 1999; Part VII: *The Accumulation of Capital*, ch. 25: "The General Law of Capitalist Accumulation," https://www.marxists.org/archive/marx/works/1867-c1/ch25.htm.

25. Dalla Costa, *Women and the Subversion*.
26. The period of mass industrialization here is defined as "first modernity" in contrast to that of the second modernity, begun in the 1970s; I follow the interpretative line of Ulrich Beck, *Risk Society: Towards a New Modernity* (London: Sage, 1992).
27. Enrica Asquer, *Storia intima dei ceti medi: una capitale e una periferia nell'Italia del miracolo economico* (Roma-Bari: Laterza, 2011). Patrizia Gabrielli, *Anni di novità e di grandi cose: il boom economico fra tradizione e cambiamento* (Bologna: Il Mulino, 2011).
28. Istat (Italian National Institute of Statistics), *L'Italia in 150 anni. Sommario di statistiche storiche 1861–2010* (Roma: Istat, 2011). The total birthrate for women in the Lombardy region was 2.15 in 1960 and 1.4 in 1970; in the Piedmont region, it was 2 in 1970 and 1.3 in 1980.
29. Massimo Paci, "I mutamenti della stratificazione sociale," in *Storia dell'Italia Repubblicana: la trasformazione dell'Italia: sviluppo e squilibri* (Torino: Einaudi, 1996), 697–77.
30. Anna Badino, *Tutte a casa? Donne tra migrazione e lavoro nella Torino degli anni Sessanta* (Roma: Viella, 2008).
31. Dalla Costa, *Women and the Subversion*.
32. *Le operaie della casa*, 0, 1 maggio 1975, 2.
33. Franca Bimbi, "Metafore di genere tra lavoro non pagato e lavoro pagato: il tempo nei rapporti sociali di sesso," *Polis* 3 (1995): 380–400.
34. The topic of the capitalistic exploitation of female work in the first phases of industrialization was in practice little treated in those years of Italian historiography; but in 1972 the work of Stefano Merli was published, *Proletariato di fabbrica e capitalismo industriale: Il caso italiano: 1880-1900*, vol. 1 (Firenze: La Nuova Italia, 1972). The limits of the ideas of a genetic functionality to capitalism of domestic work were discussed with clarity in 1986 by Walby, *Patriarchy at Work*.
35. Giovanna Cereseto, Anna Frisone, and Laura Varlese, *Non è un gioco da ragazze: Femminismo e sindacato: i Coordinamenti donne Flm* (Roma: Ediesse, 2009).
36. Chiara Saraceno, *Anatomia della famiglia* (Bari: Laterza, 1976), 115. The concept of reproductive work has been used in other works of Italian sociology: see for example Franca Bimbi, "Measurement, Quality and Social Changes in Reproduction Time: The Twofold Presence of Women and the Gift Economy," in Olwen Hufton, *Gender and the Use of Time = Gender et emploi du temps* (The Hague: Kluwer Law Internat, 1999), 151–72. See also Ongaro, *Le donne e la globalizzazione*.
37. Wally Seccombe, "The Housewife and Her Labour under Capitalism," *New Left Review* 83 (1974): 3–24; and Wally Seccombe, "Domestic Labour: Reply to Critics," *New Left Review* 94 (1975): 85–96. For the successive debate in the *New Left Review*, with articles by Smith and Gardiner, see Walby, *Patriarchy at Work*.
38. Christine Delphy, *The Main Enemy* (London, Women's Research and Resources Center, 1977). This line of research was taken up again later by Rosemary Hennessy, for example in *Materialist Feminism and the Politics of Discourse* (New York: Routledge 1993), and by Stevi Jackson, for example in *Women's Studies International Forum* 24, nos. 3–4 (2001): 283–93. The position of Delphy has been re-elaborated by Monique Wittig, who radicalized the constructionist idea of Delphy, who considered the binary character of sexuality not to be a biological fact, underlying the construction of gender, but intrinsic to male domination. See for example "The Category of Sex," *Feminist Issues* 2 (1982): 63–68.
39. Wittig's positions have been taken up but revised in particular by Judith Butler, *Gender Trouble: Feminism and the Subversion of Identity* (New York, Routledge, 1990); in this work the material presuppositions of sexual identity have been abandoned in favor of a Foucaultian reading.
40. On the "modern" role of the family in the monopolization of the transmission of values, transforming them into private values, see Laura Balbo, *Stato di famiglia: bisogni, privato*

e collettivo (Milano: Etas, 1976), 6. On the elasticity of this role and the sharing of it with external actors, see Franco Garelli, Augusto Palmonari, and Loredana Sciolla, *La socializzazione flessibile* (Bologna: il Mulino, 2006).

41. Ulrich Beck, Anthony Giddens, and Scott Lash, *Reflexive Modernization* (Cambridge: Polity Press, 1994).
42. Natalia Faraoni and Alessandra Pescarolo, eds., *I giovani che non lavorano e non studiano: i numeri, i percorsi, le ragioni* (IRPET-Regione Toscana: Studi per il Consiglio, 9, 2012).
43. Carol Gilligan, *In a Different Voice* (Cambridge, MA: Harvard University Press, 1982).
44. Massimo Paci, ed., *Famiglia e mercato del lavoro in un'economia periferica* (Milano: FrancoAngeli, 1979); see in particular Patrizia David, "Il lavoro domestico," in Paci *Famiglia e mercato del lavoro in un'economia periferica,* 120–46, and Paola Vinay, "La famiglia come soggetto lavorativo, Il lavoro domestico," in Paci, *Famiglia e mercato del lavoro in un'economia periferica,* 222–47.
45. See Paci, "Introduzione," *Famiglia e mercato del lavoro in un'economia periferica,* 9–70.
46. Folbre, *Greed, Lust, and Gender,* 251.
47. Silvana Patriarca, *Numbers and Nationhood: Writings Statistics in Nineteenth-Century Italy* (Cambridge: Cambridge University Press, 1996); Barbara Curli and Alessandra Pescarolo, "Genere, lavori, etichette statistiche," in *Differenze e diseguaglianze: Prospettive per gli studi di genere in Italia,* edited by Franca Bimbi (Bologna: il Mulino 2003), 65–100; Raffaella Sarti, "Promesse mancate e attese deluse: spunti di riflessione su lavoro domestico e diritti in Italia," in *Il lavoro cambia,* ed. Ariella Verrocchio and Elisabetta Vezzosi (Trieste: Edizioni Università di Trieste, 2013), 55–76, and Sarti's chapter in this book.
48. Gary Becker, *A Treatise on the Family* (Harvard, MA: Harvard University Press, 1981); about this see Folbre, *Greed, Lust, and Gender,* 288. The work of the closeness of the author on the economy of the family is described well in Gary Becker, *The Economic Way of Looking at Life,* Nobel Lecture, 9 December 1992.
49. Folbre, *Greed, Lust, and Gender,* 29.
50. Catherine Hakim, *Key Issues in Women's Work,* and *Work-Lifestyle Choices in the 21st Century: Preference Theory* (Oxford University Press, 2000).
51. The English translation of the title of the book is "Italy made at home." See Alberto Alesina and Andrea Ichino, *L'Italia fatta in casa: indagine sulla vera ricchezza degli italiani* (Milano: Mondadori, 2009).
52. This last consideration takes up again the observation by Nancy Folbre in "The Value of Household Work: An Economic History," conference *Entre maison, famille et entreprise,* 23–24 October 2014, École Française de Rome.
53. Nancy Folbre, *The Invisible Heart: Economics and Family Values* (New York: New Press, 2001), Italian trans. *Il cuore invisibile: la donna, la società, l'impresa,* preface by Cristina Bombelli (Milano: Egea, 2006). On the moral and fiduciary morals of economic exchanges, see Carlo Trigilia, "Albert Hirschman and the Socio-moral Science," *Moneta e Credito* 67, no. 266 (2014): 191–203.
54. Nancy Folbre, "Measuring Care: Gender, Empowerment and the Care Economy." *Journal of Human Development* 7, no. 2 (July 2006).
55. Maurizio Ferrera, *Il fattore D. Perché il lavoro delle donne farà crescere l'Italia* (Milano: Mondadori, 2008).
56. Parreñas, *Force of Domesticity.* More in general, see Viviana A. Zelizer, *Economic Lives: How Culture Shapes the Economy* (Princeton, NJ: Princeton University Press, 2010); Italian trans. *Vite economiche: valore di mercato e valore della persona* (Bologna: il Mulino, 2009).
57. Michael Spence, *The Next Convergence: The Future of Economic Growth in a Multispeed World* (New York: Farrar, Straus and Giroux, 2011); Italian trans. *La convergenza inevitabile: una via globale per uscire dalla crisi,* pref. E. T. Cucchiani (Roma-Bari: Laterza, 2012).
58. Zelizer, *Economic Lives.*

59. Chris Tilly and Charles Tilly, *Work Under Capitalism* (Boulder, CO: Westview Press, 1998), 22–23, quoted in Marcel van der Linden and Jan Lucassen, *Prolegomena for a Global Labour History* (Amsterdam: International Institute of Social History, 1999). The whole framework of the former essay is very significant for the development of a history of labor grounded on a broad concept of work.
60. Beyond Folbre's work, cited numerous times, we can cite in Italy an important reflection from the Italian online magazine *In/Genere*. For a proposal of focus developed on the automation and the robotization of the home, see for example *Le nostre proposte per il pink new deal, In/genere,* edited text, *In/Genere* 15/12/2011.

References

Alesina, Alberto, and Andrea Ichino. *L'Italia fatta in casa: indagine sulla vera ricchezza degli italiani.* Milano: Mondadori, 2009.
Asquer, Enrica. *Storia intima dei ceti medi: una capitale e una periferia nell'Italia del miracolo economico.* Roma-Bari: Laterza, 2011.
Badino, Anna. *Tutte a casa? Donne tra migrazione e lavoro nella Torino degli anni Sessanta.* Roma: Viella, 2008.
Balbo, Laura. *Stato di famiglia: bisogni, privato e collettivo.* Milano: Etas, 1976.
Beck, Ulrich. *Risk Society: Towards a New Modernity.* London: Sage, 1992.
Beck, Ulrich, Anthony Giddens, and Scott Lash. *Reflexive Modernization.* Cambridge: Polity Press, 1994.
Becker, Gary. *A Treatise on the Family.* Harvard, MA: Harvard University Press, 1981.
———. *The Economic Way of Looking at Life.* Nobel Lecture, 9 December 1992.
Bimbi, Franca. "Metafore di genere tra lavoro non pagato e lavoro pagato: il tempo nei rapporti sociali di sesso." *Polis* 9, no. 3 (1995): 380–400.
———. "Measurement, Quality and Social Changes in Reproduction Time: The Twofold Presence of Women and the Gift Economy." In *Gender and the Use of Time = Gender et emploi du temps,* edited by Olwen Hufton, 151–72. The Hague: Kluwer Law Internat, 1999.
Butler, Judith. *Gender Trouble: Feminism and the Subversion of Identity.* New York: Routledge, 1990.
Cereseto, Giovanna, Anna Frisone, and Laura Varlese. *Non è un gioco da ragazze: femminismo e sindacato: i Coordinamenti donne Flm.* Roma: Ediesse, 2009.
Chistè, Lucia, Alisa Del Re, and Edvige Forti. *Oltre il lavoro domestico: il lavoro delle donne fra produzione e riproduzione.* Milano: Feltrinelli, 1979.
Curli, Barbara, and Alessandra Pescarolo. "Genere, lavori, etichette statistiche." In *Differenze e diseguaglianze: prospettive per gli studi di genere in Italia,* edited by Franca Bimbi, 65–100. Bologna: il Mulino 2003.
Dalla Costa, Mariarosa. *Women and the Subversion of the Community* and Selma James, *A Woman's Place.* Bristol: Falling Wall Press, 1972.
Darling, Eliza. "Class." In *Routledge International Encyclopedia of Women: Global Women's Issues and Knowledge,* edited by Cheris Kramarae and Dale Spender, 181–84. New York: Routledge, 2004.
David, Patrizia. "Il lavoro domestico." In *Famiglia e mercato del lavoro in un'economia periferica,* edited by Massimo Paci, 120–46. Milano: FrancoAngeli, 1979.

Delphy, Christine. *The Main Enemy.* London: Women's Research and Resources Center, 1977.
Duffy, Mignon. "Doing the Dirty Work: Gender, Race, and Reproductive Labor in Historical Perspective." *Gender & Society* 21, no. 3 (2007): 313–36.
———. *Making Care Count: A Century of Gender, Race, and Paid Care Work.* New Brunswick, NJ: Rutgers University Press, 2011.
Faraoni, Natalia, and Alessandra Pescarolo, eds. *I giovani che non lavorano e non studiano: i numeri, i percorsi, le ragioni.* IRPET-Regione Toscana: Studi per il Consiglio, 9, 2012.
Federici, Silvia. *Caliban and the Witch: Women, the Body and Primitive Accumulation.* New York: Autonomedia, 2004.
———. *Revolution at Point Zero: Housework, Reproduction, and Feminist Struggle.* Oakland, CA: PM Press [Common Notions], 2012.
Ferrera, Maurizio. *Il fattore D. Perché il lavoro delle donne farà crescere l'Italia.* Milano: Mondadori, 2008.
Folbre, Nancy. *The Invisible Heart: Economics and Family Values.* New York: New Press, 2001. Italian trans. *Il cuore invisibile: la donna, la società, l'impresa.* Preface by Cristina Bombelli. Milano: Egea, 2006.
———. "Measuring Care: Gender, Empowerment and the Care Economy." *Journal of Human Development* 7, no. 2 (2006): 183–99.
———. *Greed, Lust, and Gender: A History of Economic Ideas.* Oxford: Clarendon Press, 2009.
———. "The Value of Household Work: An Economic History." Conference *Entre maison, famille et entreprise,* 23–24 October 2014, École Française de Rome, Rome.
Gabrielli, Patrizia. *Anni di novità e di grandi cose: il boom economico fra tradizione e cambiamento.* Bologna: Il Mulino, 2011.
Garelli, Franco, Augusto Palmonari, and Loredana Sciolla. *La socializzazione flessibile.* Bologna: il Mulino, 2006.
Garey, Anita I., and Karen V. Hansen, eds. *At the Heart of Work and Family: Engaging the Ideas of Arlie Hochschild.* New Brunswick, NJ: Rutgers University Press, 2011.
Gilligan, Carol. *In a Different Voice.* Cambridge, MA: Harvard University Press, 1982.
Hakim, Catherine. *Work-Lifestyle Choices in the 21st Century: Preference Theory.* Oxford: Oxford University Press, 2000.
———. *Key Issues in Women's Work: Female Diversity and the Polarisation of Women.* London: The Glasshouse Press, 2004.
Hennessy, Rosemary. *Materialist Feminism and the Politics of Discourse.* New York: Routledge 1993.
Hobsbawm, Eric J. *Worlds of Labour: Further Studies in the History of Labour.* London: Weidenfeld and Nicolson, 1984.
Istat (Italian National Institute of Statistics). *L'Italia in 150 anni. Sommario di statistiche storiche 1861–2010.* Roma: Istat, 2011.
Jackson, Stevi. "Why a Materialist Feminism Is (Still) Possible—and Necessary." *Women's Studies International Forum* 24, nos. 3–4 (2001): 283–93.

Kofman, Eleonore, and Parvati Raghuram. "Gender and Global Labour Migrations: Incorporating Skilled Workers." *Antipode* 38, no. 2 (2006): 282–303.
Laslett, Barbara, and Johanna Brenner. "Gender and Social Reproduction: Historical Perspectives." *Annual Review of Sociology* 15, no. 1 (1989): 381–404.
Le nostre proposte per il pink new deal, In/genere, edited text, In/Genere 15/12/2011.
Le operaie della casa, 0, 1 maggio 1975, 2.
Malthus, Thomas Robert. *An Essay on the Principle of Population, as It Affects the Future Improvement of Society with Remarks on the Speculations of Mr. Godwin, M. Condorcet, and Other Writers*. London: Printed for J. Johnson, in St. Paul's Church-Yard, 1798. © 1998, Electronic Scholarly Publishing Project, http://www.esp.org.
Marx, Karl. *Capital: A Critique of Political Economy*. Book One: *The Process of Production of Capital*. First published in German, 1867, vol. I, Online Version: Marx/Engels Internet Archive (marxists.org) 1995, 1999; Part VII: *The Accumulation of Capital*, Ch. 25: "The General Law of Capitalist Accumulation," https://www.marxists.org/archive/marx/works/1867-c1/ch25.htm.
———. *Theories of Surplus-Value*. Vol. IV of *Capital*; chapter IV, "Theories of Productive and Unproductive Labour."
Mendels, Franklin. "Des industries rurales à la protoindustrialization: bilan historique d'un changement de perspective." *Annales E.S.C.* 39, no. 5 (1984): 977–1008.
Merli, Stefano. *Proletariato di fabbrica e capitalismo industriale: il caso italiano: 1880–1900*. Vol. 1. Firenze: La Nuova Italia, 1972.
Ongaro, Sara. *Le donne e la globalizzazione: domande di genere all'economia globale della ri-produzione*. Soveria Mannelli: Rubbettino, 2001.
Paci, Massimo. "I mutamenti della stratificazione sociale." In *Storia dell'Italia Repubblicana: La trasformazione dell'Italia: sviluppo e squilibri*. Torino: Einaudi, 1996.
Paci, Massimo, ed. *Famiglia e mercato del lavoro in un'economia periferica*. Milano: FrancoAngeli, 1979.
Parreñas, Rachel Salazar. *The Force of Domesticity: Filipina Migrants and Globalization*. New York: NYU Press, 2008.
Patriarca, Silvana. *Numbers and Nationhood: Writings Statistics in Nineteenth-Century Italy*. Cambridge: Cambridge University Press, 1996.
Pelosi, Carlo. *Marx sul lavoro produttivo e improduttivo*. Roma: Istituto della Enciclopedia italiana, 1974.
Picchio, Antonella. *Social Reproduction: The Political Economy of the Labour Market*. Cambridge: Cambridge University Press, 1992.
"Reprodukta laboro." Retrieved 15 November 2015 from https://eo.wikipedia.org/wiki/Reprodukta_laboro.
Saraceno, Chiara. *Anatomia della famiglia*. Bari: Laterza, 1976.
Sarti, Raffaella. *Europe at Home: Family and Material Culture 1500–1800*. Translated by Allan Cameron. New Haven, CT: Yale University Press, 2002.
———. "Promesse mancate e attese deluse: spunti di riflessione su lavoro domestico e diritti in Italia." In *Il lavoro cambia*, edited by Ariella Verrocchio and Elisabetta Vezzosi, 55–76. Trieste: Edizioni Università di Trieste, 2013.
Schumpeter, Joseph A. *History of Economic Analysis*. Edited from the manuscript by Elizabeth Boody Schumpeter, with an introduction by Mark Perlman. Abing-

don: Taylor & Francis e-Library, 2006. First published in 1954, London: Allen & Unwin.
Scott, Joan W. "La travailleuse." In *Histoire des femmes en Occident, le XIXe siècle,* Tome 4, edited by Georges Duby and Michelle Perrot, 419–444. Paris: Plon, 1991.
Seccombe, Wally. "The Housewife and Her Labour under Capitalism." *New Left Review* 83 (1974): 3–24.
———. "Domestic Labour: Reply to Critics." *New Left Review* 94 (1975): 85–96.
Spence, Michael. *The Next Convergence: The Future of Economic Growth in a Multi-speed World.* New York: Farrar, Straus and Giroux, 2011. Italian trans. *La convergenza inevitabile: una via globale per uscire dalla crisi,* preface by E. T. Cucchiani. Roma-Bari: Laterza, 2012.
Tilly, Chris, and Charles Tilly. *Work Under Capitalism.* Boulder, CO: Westview Press, 1998.
Torrant, Julie. *The Material Family.* New York: Springer Science & Business Media, 2012.
Trigilia, Carlo. "Albert Hirschman and the Socio-moral Science." *Moneta e Credito* 67 no. 266 (2014): 191–203.
United Nations, Department of Economic and Social Affairs, Population Division. *World Fertility Report 2009.* New York: United Nations, 2011.
Van der Linden, Marcel, and Jan Lucassen. *Prolegomena for a Global Labour History.* Amsterdam: International Institute of Social History, 1999.
Vianello, Francesca Alice. *Migrando sole: legami transnazionali tra Ucraina e Italia.* Milano: FrancoAngeli, 2009.
Vinay, Paola. "La famiglia come soggetto lavorativo, Il lavoro domestico." In *Famiglia e mercato del lavoro in un'economia periferica,* edited by Massimo Paci, 222–47. Milano: FrancoAngeli, 1979.
Walby, Sylvia. *Patriarchy at Work: Patriarchal and Capitalistic Relations in Employment, 1800–1984.* Malden, MA: Polity Press; 1986.
White, Melissa. "Class and Feminism." In *Routledge International Encyclopedia of Women: Global Women's Issues and Knowledge,* edited by Cheris Kramarae and Dale Spender. New York: Routledge, 2004.
Wittig, Monique. "The Category of Sex." *Feminist Issues* 2 (1982): 63–68.
Zelizer, Viviana A. *Economic Lives: How Culture Shapes the Economy.* Princeton, NJ: Princeton University Press, 2010. Italian trans. *Vite economiche: valore di mercato e valore della persona.* Bologna: il Mulino, 2009.

CHAPTER 3

THE HOME AS A FACTORY
Rethinking the Debate on Housewives' Wages in Italy, 1929–1980

Alessandra Gissi

In a 1973 article titled "Ma le donne sono meno uguali degli altri" (But women are less equal than others), published in issue zero of the Italian feminist monthly magazine *Effè*, Grazia Francescato and Clara Piccone define women's work as "the labor that 'does not exist,' passed over in silence, relegated to an opaque limbo, touched by neither conscience nor history."[1] In 1976, in a brief but fundamental paper that appeared in *History Workshop*, historians Sally Alexander and Anna Davin wrote, "The working class has generally meant working men; women are the wives, mothers and daughters of working men. Domestic life is treated as a static, unchanging backcloth to the world of real historical activity; unpaid domestic labor is absent."[2] Unpaid domestic work has always been the least visible; it really is "nonexistent." Yet the work that "does not exist" has been carried out, represented, and named. Nevertheless, the history "of nitty-gritty cleaning, scrubbing, grocery shopping, clothing care—the work which has been glorified as the creative responsibility of the good woman or harshly and simply judged as 'shitwork'"[3]—concerns major political and economic transformations, but also cultural norms and the relationship between genders and their construction. Even more importantly, it concerns the process of defining the concept of citizenship in the twentieth century and the difficult balance between equality and difference. Nowadays, thanks to the discourse on women and gender history which has drastically changed the historiographical landscape, we could consider it as belonging to the past; however, housewives' wages are still a neglected topic, which has received little consideration by scholars—especially Italian historians. This is a missed opportunity, because if we place housewives' wages in a historical perspective, we see how the story of the debate is longer than the mere explosion during the 1970s. In addition, it is easy to see how many crucial issues converge: the division of labor, the redefinition of men's and women's different *natural* skills, the *essential* role of women at home, the "public" and "private" spheres and the relationship between generations, the model of welfare and the "redistribution" of profit, the monetary value of housework to the family and as an estimated contribution to the gross national product.

So, why this reticence? The undeniable complexity—and even ambiguity—of this topic could be for one reason. Progressive and conservative arguments are constantly mixed. And "both sides of the debate are also found to have sometimes pursued contradictory aims."[4] For example, the sociologist Ann Oakley, using qualitative interviews with housewives in southeastern England, reached the conclusion that support for housewives' wages has conservative ends, even when it comes from a progressive background.[5]

Another good example of this ambiguity is Weimarian Germany, where the campaign for household rationalization, which was borrowed from the United States, was aimed primarily at working-class women. Industrialists, bourgeois feminists, and Social Democratic trade union leaders, three of the most enthusiastic promoters of household rationalization, all had different, and frequently contradictory, political agendas.[6]

In Italy, the debate over housewives' wages is also marked by a karst trend, where contents change and sometimes contradict themselves.

This research—still in its initial stages—focuses on the domestic-wage debate of the 1970s when the discussion among (different) feminisms was fierce and articulated. However, it aims to trace the origins of the proposal for housewives' wages starting from the 1930s. A fascist theorization, quite far from feminism, linked housewives' wages to the enhancement and scientific organization of domestic work. This is the context in which the first contradictory proposals of wages for housewives appeared.

1. Fascist housewives

The mid-1920s in Italy were characterized by the centrality of pro-natal policy, as an unprecedented emphasis began to be placed on the role of women and the female body, exclusively with regards to procreation. Motherhood was configured as a patriotic duty. This emphasis reached its peak in the mid-1930s, when even the Catholic hierarchies adopted a lexicon that specifically linked procreation and nation together. Thus, procreation and motherhood became functions of the public sphere, and demographic power featured prominently in a crucial part of the new Penal Code of 1930, inspired by Alfredo Rocco, minister of justice from 1925 to 1932.[7]

Fascism envisaged for young brides a strict apprenticeship of household management, the so-called *economia domestica*: household accounts, control of consumption, computation of the nutritional value of foods, clean and beautiful homes. During the early 1930s, fascism began to deal with housewives with a precise political agenda in mind: to consolidate the sexual hierarchy within the family and make the most of the resources of domestic work.

In order to achieve these objectives, it was necessary to make the work of housewives emerge from the private sphere and give it social recognition as regular employment. The variously discussed (and never realized) projects to grant a salary to housewives fell within the scope of propagandistic measures put in place to acknowledge the economic importance of domestic work.

In the 1931 Census, more than six million women were classed as housewives, about half of the Italian working-age female population, though the figure of the housewife had a socially heterogeneous profile.

The housewife model developed by fascism had, however, a precise referent in women belonging to the urban middle classes, especially those of white-collar standing, while peasant women were presented with a model of domesticity different from the urban one.[8] The role of these housewives was to consolidate a new form of patriarchy based on an economically weak male figure that often conflicted with the masculine image of the regime. The good housewife was the one who respected the asymmetry of gender roles within the family and guaranteed the well-being of her husband and children with her shrewd management of family resources. Her role was also to provide the family with a respectability that distinguished the middle classes from workers and peasants.

The discourse on housewives and domestic work reflected all the ambiguities that characterized fascist policies concerning women. If, on the one hand, the housewife was asked to reproduce traditional forms of subordination, she was urged on the other to modernize household tasks, thereby changing lifestyles and family relationships.[9]

2. The new housekeeping

The Ente Nazionale Italiano per l'Organizzazione Scientifica del Lavoro (ENIOS, Italian National Committee for the Scientific Management of

Work), founded in 1926, began publishing the bimonthly magazine *Casa e Lavoro* in 1929, a periodical devoted to household-management guidelines, family training, nutrition, decoration, and hygiene. The introduction in Italy of domestic economy as a scientific discipline based on the organization of labor as applied to the household was made possible by the work of the Piedmontese Maria Diez Gasca. Having graduated with a degree specializing in occupational medicine, she introduced the concept and principles of the "rationalization of the house" in 1927, during the fourth International Congress of Domestic Economy.

The American manuals about the organization of housekeeping gained interest and circulation: in 1927 *The New Housekeeping: Efficiency Studies in Home Management* by Christine Frederick was translated into Italian by Lorenzo Tealdy, while in 1930 the magazine *Casa e Lavoro* published *Il Meccanismo della casa,* a partial translation of *Household Engineering: The Scientific Management in the Home,* also by Frederick, later translated by Maria Diez Gasca.[10] In these texts, the house is conceived as a workplace where the woman acts as a worker and, at the same time, is her own manager. Moreover, in the logic of production, an efficient use of time is closely linked to money. "The management of a house should function as the mechanism of a clock . . . in the same way the expert housewife should keep track of time with the methodical handling of duties."[11] The ideal housewife was not only a wise administrator of the family budget but also a responsible consumer.

Members of the regime, engineers, and architects theorized a scientific discipline aimed at the inexorable transformation of the masses into a broad middle class. For example, the editorial of the first issue of *Casa e Lavoro* opens with the celebration of the family: "orderly, sober, industrious [family] supported by the fascist government"[12]; this praise appeared in similar magazines, such as *Casa mia*. In a 1931 "volumetto per il popolo" (booklet for the population) titled *La casa e la donna,* written by Tilde Elena Grosso Malagricci, the short household notes were preceded by a broad section devoted to the family as a symbol of civilization and to women as the fundamental basis of the family.[13]

In fascist Italy, women had a duty to "elevate the spirit of the house."[14] The real aim was to broaden the class of the *petite bourgeoisie,* the real reservoir of consensus for the regime: hence the insistence on the value of the housewife's work. For example, in the first issues of *Casa e lavoro,* "housewives' wages" became almost a slogan.[15]

Obviously, this discourse was structured in such a way as to maintain a fundamental ambiguity between social recognition, mission, and, above all, competence and "natural" temperament. It is not by chance that statements like the following appeared in the pages of *Casa e Lavoro*:

The husband is therefore a necessity . . . what I assert . . . that [for] the woman, even the modern, emancipated one, if she can financially provide for her future . . . the husband is *trait d'union* between our house and the society in which we live. We women in general are not keen on public life. Our excessive sensitivity suffers in unremitting struggle of labor among strangers and in search of material gain. A husband, in general, deals with this. We work in the house, he works outside. Our material existence is guaranteed: he provides for us. Insurance for life, a life annuity.[16]

3. The "essential role in the family"

After the Second World War, while Italy found itself in the throes of reconstruction, the US model of the housewife-consumer, the queen of a "rational" house, seemed to establish itself as a genuine interaspirational model. However, the scenario is complex, the model itself polysemic, and the achievement of equality still a far cry away. The conquest of equality, of "equal social dignity" for women in the new Republican state, is sanctioned in the second part of article 3 of the Constitution promulgated in 1948. It also gives the state an active role in removing restrictions and obstacles to the individual development and participation of both male and female workers in the country's political life and organization.

However, the brand new Constitution—says Anna Rossi-Doria—does not accept the assertion of the individual rights of women within the family and in fact reestablishes the inferiority of women in the so-called private sphere.[17] Consequently, in spite of the full equality between the sexes guaranteed by our Constitution, there were some areas in which strong traces of the old inequalities remained: in the family, on the one hand, and in at least two other crucial areas—the courts and the army.[18]

Let us consider article 37 of the Constitution relating to the individual rights of women and the relationship between work and family: "Working women have the same rights and are entitled to equal pay for equal work. Working conditions must allow women to fulfil their essential role in the family and ensure special appropriate protection for the mother and child."[19] In sum, working women have the same rights and are entitled to equal pay for equal work, but their working conditions must allow them to fulfil their essential role in the family.

The adjective "essential" attached to "women's role in the family" clearly explains and suggests both a necessity and a predetermination. This formulation is the result of a compromise between the Catholic, and conservative, forces and the leftist, and secular, parties, but it also reflects an ambivalence inside the labor movement itself. During the 1950s, the issue of domestic wages was never explicitly recovered. More moderate proposals were advanced, which had less ideological and financial impact. In 1955, the Communist and Socialist female members of parliament wrote a bill focused on the voluntary subscriptions of insurance that would favor all women over fifty-five years of age and, more importantly, on the recognition of a life annuity to women with a family income of no more than 600,000 lire.[20] Nilde Iotti, the spokesperson who presented the bill, said,

> The reasons that led us to present the proposal, therefore, are first of all of human order, due to the sense of justice that we have for women who give their whole life and their work for the welfare of Italian families, without getting any compensation at the end of their lives. . . . All of us, moreover, realise that, in the current state of our country, it is impossible to achieve such a thing, so it was decided to set up a pension on a purely voluntary basis, and with the assumption that interested women will pay the pension contributions.[21]

In the same year, a series of bills presented by the extreme right-wing party Movimento Sociale Italiano and by the Christian Democrats asked that a pension and voluntary insurance in favor of housewives be guaranteed.[22] Although not radical, the proposal would have undermined the entire Italian welfare model. Even the Communist member of parliament Enrico Berlinguer, defending a bill in 1957 on the pension for blind civilians, was forced to admit that the passing of the bill would pave "the way to claims, for example, from housewives and elderly people without pension."[23]

Later, the so-called "economic miracle" (roughly 1958–63), a period of sustained economic growth, changed the face of the country in only five years. It was a rapid, remarkable, and disorganized transformation. It enhanced the leading sectors: mechanical, steel, chemical, and manufacturing. The substance of this transformation lies in the fact that Italy tended to be unified according to myths and patterns of consumption. The image of the working woman and—albeit still timid—consumer, gradually took shape starting from the second half of the 1950s, precisely when issues related to the work of women took an undisputed central role in the public discourse. The rapid modernization processes related to this phase of intensive industrialization, on the other hand, reinforced the idea of the family and the house as a place of peace and refuge from the outside world, in which the individual feels more and more oppressed and depersonalized. According to Gabriella Turnaturi, for example,

> Only by consolidating the family institution and elevating the private and what was happening in the home . . . one could intervene and plan other people's

daily life. The house and domestic life thus assumed new value and dignity and at the same time were "attached" and connected to society. Only women were able to guarantee this connection, and to be at the same time guarantors of the "autonomy" and importance of the private.[24]

However, precisely during the thriving economic growth of the late 1950s, many young women abandoned the farming production model to migrate to cities in search of economic independence.[25]

In the turmoil induced by the modernization of the late 1950s and of the 1960s, many aspects directly affected the lives of women and girls. While the values of the rural world faded away, social and geographical mobility and common customs and languages grew, the typical feeling of modernity spread, and women blessed refrigerators, washing machines, sanitary towels and various modernities. Young women refused to get married in the countryside; their mothers and grandmothers, who knew what it meant to be the wife of a farmer, encouraged them to migrate to the cities to work in factories and services, not to have too many children, and to be economically independent.[26]

4. Housework, bread, and roses

In Italy in the 1960s, social policies were highly deficient in terms of services to the family. The standards of housework became higher, because the urban setting increasingly involved absent husbands, while children's school years became longer. However, only the protection of working mothers had attracted political attention so far. After 1968, however, this system was deeply challenged, mainly by feminism, and the role of housewives became central again. In this context, a furious debate on domestic wages developed, which divided both the institutions that did not remain indifferent to the problem and the feminist movement itself.

However, at the end of the decade, the socially shared model of passive femininity seemed to have come to an end. The student participating in "the occupations of universities, the teacher breaking with the authoritarian model of school, the worker who striked, and began to be massively present in representative bodies such as factory-workers councils, are all examples of a female condition that could no longer be relegated into subalternity. In short, women took part in the political and cultural ruptures, in particular young women became one of the emblems of that stage."[27] Young women who questioned authoritarianism in the family, school, and university—which was the central concern in 1968–69—were often overcome by persistent gender disparities. Inaugurating a season of claims on, and a search for, individual and collective self-determination, women gradually took their distance from political parties and mass organizations and experienced alternative trajectories and modes, which could radically question the relationship between the sexes that did not seem to be properly addressed anywhere else.[28] However, the slogan that sums up the spirit of the last part of the 1960s, especially for women, is "We want bread and roses": bread, that is the issues that ignited the so-called "hot autumn" in 1969[29]; roses, representing the bold claim for a different quality of life.

In the 1970s, Italian feminism was, then, first of all, a common political practice that helped to profoundly transform the consciousness and the lives of thousands of women in each Italian region, in large and small cities, and in many villages.[30] Between 1970 and 1973, groups and collectives continually formed all over Italy. They differed in terms of cultural and ideological references—some were closer to the student movement, others more distant. In an ambivalent context, in which the political system's reaction wavered between major reform projects and the movements' repression, feminism, or rather *feminisms,* immediately gained specific traits, despite their heterogeneity. On 8 March 1972, for the first time feminists took to the streets to celebrate International Women's Day. The Roman event took place in the afternoon in Campo de' Fiori. They circulated a flyer, almost a manifesto, signed by *Gruppi femministi romani* (Roman feminist groups), whose beginning significantly defined women as the slaves of housework[31]:

> International Women's Day. The woman is still a slave! 90 or 40 hours a week of unpaid work at home and the woman is still a housewife. IF YOU ARE A WORKER tired of being the last to be hired and the first to be fired, relegated to unskilled and low-paid jobs, IF YOU ARE AN EMPLOYEE, tired of being a typist, the secretary of the boss, constantly forced to be "good looking", IF YOU ARE A TEACHER and you have realized that a career in education is the only one offered to women who have studied, IF YOU ARE UNEMPLOYED maybe with a degree or diploma and for survival are forced to do casual work such as selling detergents, baby-sitting etc. IF YOU ARE A STUDENT and you understand that it is futile to think that your life will be different from that of a mother, IF YOU ARE A MOTHER not out of your own choice and you want to decide if and when to become a mother again, IF YOU HAVE REALISED THAT YOU ARE A SEX OBJECT to men and instead you want to live your sexuality in a free and satisfactory way, IF YOU ARE FALLING into the trap of marriage because you believe that a husband can give you financial security and social prestige, IN ONE WORD: IF YOU ARE A WOMAN, let's fight together for our liberation!

Thanks especially to the theoretical and political work of Mariarosa Dalla Costa[32] and other members of Lotta Femminista (LF, Feminist Struggle), the issue of housewives' wages became crucial. This organization campaigned for a salary for housework, given its strategic importance to the capitalist economy through the reproduction of the next generation of workers and the care of the current generation with no direct cost for the state or the market. Or, as the authors of the pamphlet *New Feminist Movement* put it, "And all this work that the woman does, an average of 99.6 hours weekly, without the possibility of strikes, nor absenteeism, nor to make any demands, is done for free."[33]

This campaign, which quickly spread throughout Europe and North America, resulted in the founding of one of the first transnational social movements, Wages for Housework, and prompted a critique of the welfare state as the protector and guarantor of the sexual division of labor and the reproduction of the labor force. In the early 1970s, Mariarosa Dalla Costa, a historical figure of international feminism, together with Selma James, opened the debate on domestic work and remuneration, on the woman as its subject, and on the family as a place of production and reproduction of labor power. Domestic work was analyzed and revealed to be a hidden phase of capitalist accumulation; it was divulged that behind the closed doors of their homes, women were working; the house was a production center, the housewife was its worker. To generate and reproduce itself, the workforce, the most precious commodity for capital, required the labor of women: the realization of workers' consumption entailed female labor. The working-class housewife would be the privileged subject of the political activism of this line of feminism. In Padua in 1972, Mariarosa Dalla Costa, Selma James (London), Silvia Federici (New York), and Brigitte Galtier (Paris) formed the International Feminist Collective to promote the debate on production and reproduction and to coordinate action in several countries. Soon after that, a vast network of Wages for Housework groups and committees would be formed at an international level, with an important function.

At a 1974 conference of the Italian feminist groups held in Pinarella di Cervia on the Adriatic coast, Lotta Femminista posited as its main objective the achievement of wages for housewives.[34] The topic emerged again during the second conference, in 1975.[35]

The question was quite clear: the productive dimension of work was in the public sphere, while the reproductive one was in the private realm. The sphere of social reproduction was not considered "labor," but care. This interpretation is also to be found in Marx's theories. During the 1970s—when both the Fordist model and its opposition were in full development—feminist critique affirmed that work within the domestic walls was functional to capitalist development and challenged the notion that these processes were only "private business": they were, instead, the foundation of the economic order. Starting from the assumption that in the Fordist factory the workplace was physically determined and was based on specific relations of production and power, feminists saw this model as a paradigm that could be "exported" into a class struggle within the domestic space on the ground of social reproduction.[36] Within this framework, such a request, according to someone, led to subversion rather than to the resolution of the conflict. This was mainly due to the reflections of the Trento group Il Cerchio Spezzato [The Broken Circle], according to which household work is ascribed to the overall system of production and shifts from a "private" dimension to the social and economic fields.[37] For part of the feminist movement, however, this crystallized the division of labor along gender lines.[38] One cannot ignore the subversive implication of this approach; one must also consider the complex genealogy of domestic wages, whose first theorizations go back to the 1930s when fascism had carried out a shift—loaded with ambiguity—of domesticity from the exclusively private dimension to the dimension of the state.

5. Nature, invisibility, isolation

In a 1975 essay on the working conditions of women in Sicily, Maria Rosa Cutrufelli highlights the invisibility of the female role in the labor market: "Analysing women's labor also means, necessarily, to analyze its social role," she writes. The sexual division of roles indeed "originates from the 'natural' fact that it is the production of human beings: the fact that, ultimately, the woman is a producer of labor power, and therefore her work changes precisely in relation to the production and reproduction of this very specific commodity."[39] But this production and reproduction work is invisible: "In the capitalist era, the woman as an economic object acquires a strange feature: she becomes invisible. . . . The woman delivers free—hence invisible—labor within the domestic walls, producing children as 'nature commands'—the hidden production."[40]

The entity of the free labor provided by housewives has symbolic value in its indeterminacy. The figure of twenty billion lire offered annually as free services is the most common.[41] "Sweeping for free, cooking for free, raising children for free, all the Ritas of Italy allow the system to delete from the item 'expenses' a heap of social services it would otherwise be responsible for providing."[42]

This invisibility would be determined by the lack of a salary, and a salary would in itself eradicate the prevailing definition of work as existing only within the public sphere. Domestic work is linked by a part of feminism to the overall system of production, and yet it is represented as a pattern of isolation, as we can see in this picture (figure 3.1; figure 3.2).[43]

The housewife operates in a totally anonymous space, which is empty and bereft of any references and objects, apart from a threatening clock and a radio that brings home the news from the world in addition to advertising.[44] What we are shown, therefore, is two separate worlds: the totalizing and alienating world of the house, and the outside one. The arguments in favor of wages and the images seem to suggest that wages for housewives can stop separation, thereby eliminating this alienation.

The domestic sphere is deprived of any reference to emotions or natural inclinations. The infant's weight is balanced only by the other burden of the shopping bag.

Some Marxist feminist publications started to look at male power within the family in a dual way: "as the power to *exploit* (in the family he is the bourgeoisie, the woman is the proletariat) and to *command* (the man is the master who accumulates, appropriating the surplus value produced by the woman, he does not work at home because he is the master; the woman is expropriated, the proletarian)."[45] But more often, the husband is no longer a direct antagonist of the woman; he is absent in representations and recalls an abstract figure of a mediator between capitalism and reproduction.

In one of the interviews carried out by the journalist Lietta Tornabuoni in Padua during a meeting of Lotta Femminista, one of the participants declared, "The master of the housewife is not the husband. It's the State, the economic power." "The State?" the journalist asked:

> Of course. The State does not organize kindergartens, and women take care of children. There are no centralized social services, and the labor of women must replace them. There are no retirement homes for the elderly, and women must take care of them. There are not enough hospitals, and women have to cure the less serious diseases at home. The State saves billions on the skin of women. Let the State pay, then. Let the industrialists pay.

Tornabuoni wondered: "Should industrialists pay for labor that does not produce commodities?"

> The commodity produced by women is a human being: the worker. First, they give birth to him, feed him, raise him, and educate him; then, when he works, they make his bed, sweep the floor for him, prepare his food, wash his clothes and underwear. In this way, women produce and reproduce labor power that is consumed daily in offices and factories. When an industrialist hires someone, he does not only take a worker: he hires a couple.[46]

Figure 3.1. Daniela, "Salario alle casalinghe?" (*Effe*, no. 3 [1974]: np).

Women are the proletariat that is dispossessed of its workforce and can free itself only through sharing and "gender" collaboration. The claim of the drawing below is "Housewives of the world, unite!" Housewives as a (Marxist notion of) class act their struggle again in an anonymous, white,

The Home as a Factory

Figure 3.2. Daniela, "Salario alle casalinghe?" (*Effe*, no. 3 [1974]: np).

empty space. No sign of life, not a home scenario or familiar setting. As if they did not produce anything but their intense effort, their own alienation, their own isolation. What they get from their mutual acknowledgment is the chance to throw away pots, colanders, and brooms and run away, alone (figure 3.3).

Figure 3.3. "Salario alle casalinghe?" (*Effe*, no. 3 [1974]: 21).

6. Money, wage, pay

The individuality/community/class relationship is one of the crucial issues. In a debate hosted by feminist monthly magazine *Effe*, Rosalba Pistelli, member of the Roman feminist movement, asked, "Why an individual contract? We are millions of housewives!" Lidia Menapace, editor of the newspaper *Il Manifesto,* answered:

> The relationship is always one-to-one, housewife-State, collective bargaining is not possible . . . because you, housewife, do not have a place of aggregation such as the factory. The wages just confirm that your work is for your family, not for society. . . . therefore, is it good for the housewife to transform her work from use value to exchange value?[47]

For example, the Collettivo Femminista (Feminist Collective) of Pescara, although in line with the struggle for domestic wages called for by Lotta Femminista, believed in an ideological struggle that tended to demystify the housewife role and that should be an objective for which women would finally "get out of a centuries-long isolation within the house walls," but admitted that it might also be dangerous, because it risked becoming a purely financial claim leading to the consequent institutionalization of housewifery.[48] In 1975, the New York Wages for Housework Committee had published a red booklet entitled *Counter-Planning from the Kitchen,* edited by Silvia Federici and Nicole Cox and containing two short articles: the first, with the same title as the booklet, and another one titled "Capital and the Left." The booklet was translated into Italian three years later, in 1978. It bore the same title, showed a female symbol on a turquoise cover, which was a woman's fist holding paper money, was edited by the International Feminist Collective, and contained Silvia Federici's manifesto "Wages Against Housework."[49]

The same cover in pink/red and the same symbol had also been used for *Le operaie della casa* (The house-workers) edited by the International Feminist Collective and published in 1975 (figure 3.4).[50]

Of course the theoretical and political approach was extremely sophisticated.[51] But in the public discourse it shifted continuously: wages mean money, money means "value," in any sense. Furthermore, this financial claim seems to have had a highly symbolic rate.

Figure 3.4. Collettivo Internazionale Femminista, *Le operaie della casa* (Venezia: Marsilio, 1974). Cover of the book.

In another interview conducted by Lietta Tornabuoni, a woman vehemently maintained that "even children despise us because we have no money. My eight-year-old son told me: 'Even grandma receives an annuity and you don't.'"[52]

The housewife is aware that her housework, though necessary and useful, by "not being paid, has no value and does not confer any prestige. She does tiring and unappreciated activities, often without external friendship, she becomes increasingly dependent on the approval of her husband and children."[53]

As the drawing shows, *money* is part of one's identity and "fills" it, supports it, and strengthens it. Indeed, talking about housewives' wages means facing the ambiguous status that has plagued domestic waged labor.[54] It means to clearly state that women involved in "home production" should be paid as producers. Along with the monetary value—not easy to determine[55]—the symbolic aspect of the dichotomy paid/unpaid seems even more crucial to deconstruct the invisibility, the inevitability of female domesticity.

Furthermore, in this peculiar case—so relevant but so underestimated by modern historians[56]—the dichotomy paid/unpaid is a useful interpretative category. It brings some crucial issues to light: the notions of "production," "reproduction," and "care"; the social constructions of gender; the reshaping of "public" and "private"; equality and citizenship rights.

Alessandra Gissi is assistant professor in contemporary history, University of Naples "L'Orientale." After studies at the Universities of Rome (La Sapienza) and Amsterdam, she obtained a PhD in women's and gender history from the University of Naples "L'Orientale." Her areas of specialization include Italian and European history (history of reproductive bodies and policies in Liberal and Fascist Italy, history of midwifery, history of feminisms). She is also interested in history of intellectual migrations between the two World Wars. She has been an editor of *Genesis,* the journal of the Società Italiana delle Storiche (The Italian Association of Women Historians). Currently she is an editor of the journal *Italia Contemporanea.* Among her publications are "Reproduction" in *The Politics of Everyday Life in Fascist Italy: Outside the State?,* edited by Joshua Arthurs, Michael Ebner, and Kate Ferris (New York: Palgrave Macmillan, 2017), 99–122, and two books, *Le segrete manovre delle donne: Levatrici in Italia dall'Unità al Fascismo* (Rome: Biblink, 2006) and *Otto marzo: La Giornata internazionale delle donne in Italia* (Rome: Viella, 2010). For more details see http://docenti.unior.it/index2.php?user_id=agissi&content_id_start=1&parLingua=ENG.

Notes

1. *Effe* was founded in 1973. The monthly magazine continued to be published for the next ten years until the last number in December 1982. It had initially been directed by Adele Cambria; this responsibility was then taken on, as a cooperative, by the entire editorial staff. See efferivistafemminista.it.
2. Sally Alexander and Anna Davin, "Feminist History," *History Workshop*, no. 1 (*1976*): 4–6.
3. Nona Glazer-Malbin, "Housework," *Signs: Journal of Women in Culture and Society*, no. 4 (1976): 905.
4. Louie Traikovski, "The Housewives' Wages Debate in the 1920s Australian Press," *Journal of Australian Studies*, no. 78 (2003): 9–13.
5. Ann Oakley, *The Sociology of Housework* (London: Martin Robertson, 1974), 48. See also Ann Oakley, *Housewife* (London: Allen Lane, 1974).
6. The industrialists' ambition was that a "rationalized working-class household would enhance worker productivity, decrease wage demands, and inculcate more positive attitudes toward work and management." On the other hand, bourgeois feminists, adopting the idea of domestic rationalization to gain legitimacy for housework and housewives, sought to "empower women and to free them from the most onerous burdens of domestic drudgery." The "Social Democratic workers' movement, or at any rate its leadership, endorsed the rationalized home as enthusiastically as it endorsed rationalization more broadly. Social Democrats heralded the rationalized household as an integral part of an ill-defined but appealingly modern future. It would simultaneously improve the health and efficiency of the home, preserve a traditional sexual division of labor there, and free women to be more active in the workers' movement, albeit only in supportive roles." Mary Nolan, "'Housework Made Easy': The Taylorized Housewife in Weimar Germany's Rationalized Economy," *Feminist Studies*, no. 16 (1990): 549–77.
7. Victoria De Grazia, *How Fascism Ruled Women: Italy, 1922–1945* (Berkeley: University of California Press, 1992); Perry Willson, *Women in Twentieth-Century Italy* (New York: Palgrave Macmillan, 2010), especially chapter 4; Alessandra Gissi, "Reproduction," in *The Politics of Everyday Life in Fascist Italy: Outside the State?*, ed. Joshua Arthurs, Michael Ebner, and Kate Ferris (New York: Palgrave Macmillan, 2017): 99–122.
8. *Massaie Rurali*, a large organization with over one million members by 1939, was training women in some aspects of farming and home economics, including housekeeping, childcare, handicraft manufacturing, gardening, and beekeeping. See Perry Willson, *Peasant Women and Politics in Fascist Italy: The Massaie Rurali* (London: Routledge, 2002).
9. See Augusta Molinari, "Casalinghe," in *Dizionario del Fascismo: A–K*, ed. Victoria *De Grazia* and Sergio *Luzzatto* (Torino: Einaudi, 2002): 256–58.
10. Christine Frederick, *The New Housekeeping: Efficiency Studies in Home Management* (Garden City, NY: Doubleday, Page & Company, 1913); Christine Frederick, *Household Engineering: The Scientific Management in the Home* (Chicago: American School of Home Economics, 1915); in Italian, Christine Frederick, *La donna e la casa: il taylorismo nella vita domestica; Libro destinato a tutte le donne d'Italia, per facilitar loro i lavori della casa*, trans. Lorenzo Tealdy (Torino: C. Accame, 1927); Christine Frederick, *La casa moderna: come risparmiare tempo, fatica, denaro*, trans. Maria Diez Gasca (Roma: Edizione Enios, Tipografia delle Terme, 1933). On this topic, see Cinzia Grossi, "La 'Casalinga efficiente' stile americano nell'Italia degli anni Trenta," in *Miti Americani fra Europa ed America*, ed. Caterina Ricciardi and Sabrina Vellucci (Venezia: Mazzanti, 2008), 93–106.
11. Erminia De Benedetti, *Il nostro nido: consigli sul buon governo della casa; nozioni di economia domestica* (Palermo, Milano: Sandron, 1929), in Katrin Cosseta, *Ragione e sentimento dell'abitare: la casa e l'architettura nel pensiero femminile tra le due guerre* (Milano: FrancoAngeli, 2000), 36.

12. "Ai lettori," *Casa e Lavoro,* no. 1 (1929), 2. The reformers who proposed the so-called "taylorization" of the household maintained contacts with the international movements until the adoption by the League of Nations of sanctions against Fascist Italy in response to the invasion of Ethiopia in 1935. It is shown, among other things, by the advertising in the *Revue Internationale du Travail,* the journal of the Bureau of International du Travail.
13. Tilde Elena Grosso Malagricci, *La casa e la donna.* Volumetti per il popolo, s.l., 1931, in Mariuccia Salvati, *L'inutile salotto: l'abitazione piccolo-borghese nell'Italia fascista* (Torino: Bollati Boringhieri, 1993): 183.
14. "Editoriale," *Casa e Lavoro,* no. 2 (1932) quoted in Salvati, *L'inutile salotto,* 56.
15. Salvati, *L'inutile salotto,* 57.
16. Nerina M. Jori, "Un cuore e una capanna (se poi fosse un palazzo . . .)," *Casa e Lavoro,* no. 12 (December 1933): 333–35.
17. Anna Rossi-Doria, "Le donne sulla scena politica italiana agli inizi della Repubblica," in Anna Rossi-Doria, *Dare forma al silenzio: scritti di storia politica delle donne* (Roma: Viella, 2007): 127–208. See also Molly Tambor, *The Lost Wave: Women and Democracy in Postwar Italy* (Oxford: Oxford University Press, 2014).
18. In Italy, the entry of women into the judiciary dates back to 1963 and law n. 380; 1999 admitted Italian female citizens to the public competitions for the recruitment of officers and noncommissioned officers on active service and of other ranks on voluntary service. See Fatima Farina, *Donne nelle forze armate: il servizio militare femminile in Italia e nella Nato* (Roma: Viella, 2015).
19. Constitution of the Italian Republic, Title III, *Economic Rights and Duties,* article 37.
20. "Siano le donne italiane una grande forza di pace, di libertà e di progresso per il nostro paese," *l'Unità,* 27 September 1955, 8. In 1957, the target of a pension seemed closer; see "Le casalinghe possono avere la pensione prima delle prossime elezioni politiche," *l'Unità,* 26 October 1957.
21. Atti parlamentari, Seduta Camera dei deputati, 24 November 1955, 22220.
22. Anna Garofalo, "Massaie alla ribalta," *Nuova Repubblica,* 18 December 1955. For the Christian Democrat Party's proposal, see Atti parlamentari, Seduta Camera dei deputati, 25 November 1957, 22272.
23. Atti parlamentari, Seduta Camera dei deputati, 20 September 1957, 35281
24. Gabriella Turnaturi, "La donna fra il pubblico e il privato: la nascita della casalinga e della consumatrice," *Nuova DWF,* nos. 12–13 (1979): 8–19.
25. On this, see Anna Badino, *Tutte a casa? Donne tra migrazione e lavoro nella Torino degli anni Sessanta* (Roma: Viella, 2008).
26. Anna Bravo, *A colpi di cuore: storie del sessantotto* (Roma-Bari: Laterza, 2008): 62–63.
27. Gloria Chianese, "Storie di donne tra lavoro e sindacato," in *Mondi femminili in cento anni di sindacato* (2 vols.), ed. Gloria Chianese (Roma: Ediesse, 2008), vol. 1, 78.
28. On the history of feminism, see at least Anna Bravo and Giovanna Fiume, eds., "Anni Settanta," special issue of *Genesis* 3, no. 1 (2004); Teresa Bertilotti and Anna Scattigno, eds., *Il femminismo degli anni Settanta* (Roma: Viella 2005); Liliana Ellena and Elena Petricola, eds., "Donne di mondo: percorsi transnazionali dei femminismi," special issue of *Zapruder,* no. 13 (2007); Maud Ann Bracke, *Women and the Reinvention of the Political: Feminism in Italy, 1968–1983* (New York: Routledge, 2014); Paola Stelliferi, *Il femminismo a Roma negli anni Settanta: percorsi, esperienze e memorie dei Collettivi di quartiere* (Bologna: Bononia University Press, 2015).
29. The two-year mobilization of students and workers culminated in a massive strike wave that hit Italy in the famous "hot autumn" of 1969. Stuart J. Hilwig, *Italy and 1968: Youthful Unrest and Democratic Culture* (New York: Palgrave Macmillan, 2009); Marica Tolomelli, *L'Italia dei movimenti: politica e società nella prima Repubblica* (Roma: Carocci, 2015).
30. Anna Rossi-Doria, "Ipotesi per una storia che verrà" in Bertilotti and Scattigno, *Il femminismo degli anni Settanta,* 3.

31. Alessandra Gissi, *Otto marzo: la giornata internazionale delle donne in Italia* (Roma: Viella, 2010), 61.
32. See introduction and biographical note, appendix inventory of the Archive of Lotta Femminista (Feminist Struggle), donation by Mariarosa Dalla Costa http://www.padovanet.it/allegati/C_1_Allegati_20187_Allegato.pdf, 10 October 2015.
33. Various authors, "Nuovo Movimento Femminista," May 1973, Movimento Femminista: Documenti Autonomi, retrieved 9 January 2009 from http://www.nelvento.net/archivio/68/femm/nuovo.htm, cited in Patrick Cuninghame, "Italian Feminism, Workerism and Autonomy in the 1970s: The Struggle against Unpaid Reproductive Labour and Violence," *@mnis. Revue de civilisation Contemporaine Europes/Ameriques*, no. 8 (2008), retrieved 11 June 2018 from https://journals.openedition.org/amnis/575.
34. Fiamma Lussana, *Il movimento femminista in Italia: esperienze, storie, memorie* (Roma: Carocci, 2011): 79.
35. Ibid., 81.
36. Aida Ribero, *Una questione di libertà: il femminismo degli anni settanta* (Torino: Rosenberg & Sellier, 1999): 261–68.
37. Silvia Federici, *Wages Against Housework* (Bristol: Power of Women Collective, Falling Wall Press, 1975).
38. The debate would emerge again at the end of the 1980s within a new international division of labor, through which capitalism had restructured itself.
39. Maria Rosa Cutrufelli, *Disoccupata con onore: lavoro e condizione della donna* (Milano: Mazzotta, 1975), 11–12.
40. Maria Rosa Cutrufelli, *L'invenzione della donna: miti e tecniche di uno sfruttamento* (Milano: Mazzotta, 1977), 7–8.
41. See "Salario alle casalinghe?," *Effe*, no. 3 (1974): 20. In another case, "a magistrate in Genoa has estimated the value in 4000 lire per day," in Lietta Tornabuoni, "Salario alle casalinghe," *La Stampa*, 22 April 1973.
42. Grazia Francescato and Clara Piccone, "Ma le donne sono meno uguali degli altri," *Effe*, no. 0 (1973): 33.
43. I would like to thank Daniela Colombo, one of the founders of *Effe*, who during a beautiful conversation told me she was the author of these illustrations in collaboration with Michela Caruso.
44. Housewife: and even today: sweep, wash, wash, cook, wash the dishes, iron, iron . . .
    Radio: panel of ten leaders assembled . . . agreed to . . .
    Radio: and now Dr. Ciccarelli talks about cosmetics. This year, the mouth is no longer fashionable. Fashion and technique . . . we anticipate the physiological evolution. Scientists tell us that in a hundred years, women will have a sour face and two huge, greedy eyes. Eyes to love. Eyes to be watched by fashionable men.
    Radio: the Italian woman is cheerful and thoughtful, whimsical and tender, charming and strong-willed but most, she is fashionable and chic. She is able to enhance her charm.
    Radio: X Y Z W . . . the pleasure to live in your home
    Radio: the government has decided to remove the price freeze for the following products: pasta, milk, chicken, sugar, potatoes . . .
45. *Quarto mondo*, 1 March 1971.
46. Tornabuoni, "Salario alle casalinghe."
47. "Salario alle casalinge?," *Effe*, no. 3 (1974): 20. On the complicated collective organization, see "Lavoro domestico: inchiesta del gruppo di Modena," *Bollettino: Coordinamento emiliano per il salario al lavoro domestico*, single issue, 1976.
48. Lotta Femminista, Collettivo Femminista di Pescara, Enrica Lucarelli, Margherita Repetto, "Salario alle casalinghe?," *Effe*, no. 5 (1974): 36.
49. Silvia Federici and Nicole Cox, *Counter-Planning from the Kitchen* (New York: New York Wages for Housework Committee; Bristol: Falling Wall Press, 1975); Silvia Federici and Nicole Cox, *Contropiano dalle cucine* (Venezia: Marsilio, 1978). In 1975, Wendy Edmond

and Suzie Fleming, eds., *All Work and No Pay: Women, Housework, and the Wages Due* (Bristol: Power of Women Collective and Falling Wall Press) had also been published.
50. Collettivo Internazionale Femminista, *Le operaie della casa* (Venezia: Marsilio, 1974). This drawing is very common in self-produced printing and in feminist leaflets; see "Lavoro domestico."
51. See Deborah Ardilli, "'Contropiano dalle cucine': quarant'anni per (non) pensarci," *Nazione Indiana*, 5 September 2015, retrieved 27 July 2016 from https://www.nazioneindiana.com/2015/09/05/contropiano-dalle-cucine-quarantanni-per-non-pensarci.
52. Tornabuoni, "Salario alle casalinghe."
53. Donata Francescato, "Casalinga/La nevrosi rampante," *Effe*, no. 3 (1973): 8. This issue is devoted to a deep "analysis of housework." The front cover is a drawing of Botticelli's Venus rising from dishes and pots. See also "Salario alle casalinge?," *Effe*, no. 6 (1974): 14–38.
54. About this long-standing ambiguity, see Raffaella Sarti, *Servo e padrone, o della (in)dipendenza: un percorso da Aristotele ai nostri giorni I. Teorie e dibattiti*. "Quaderni di Scienza & Politica," no. 2 (2015) (Bologna: Alma Mater Studiorum Università di Bologna, 2015), retrieved on 11 June 2018 from http://amsacta.unibo.it/4293/1/Sarti_Servo_e_Padrone_1.pdf.
55. Nona Glazer-Malbin writes, "The components of housework are usually left undefined, so that it is not possible to assess accurately what doing housework means." Glazer-Malbin, "Housework," 908.
56. The historian Silvio Lanaro in his *Storia dell'Italia Repubblicana* (Venezia: Marsilio, 1992), 362, described Lotta Femminista (LF, Feminist Struggle) in a few words as "frigid neo-marxism," whose position "was not so shared."

References

Alexander, Sally, and Anna Davin. "Feminist History." *History Workshop*, no. 1 (1976): 4–6.
Ardilli, Deborah. "'Contropiano dalle cucine': quarant'anni per (non) pensarci." *Nazione Indiana*, 5 September 2015. Retrieved 27 July 2016 from https://www.nazioneindiana.com/2015/09/05/contropiano-dalle-cucine-quaranta nni-per-non-pensarci/.
Badino, Anna. *Tutte a casa? Donne tra migrazione e lavoro nella Torino degli anni Sessanta*. Roma: Viella, 2008.
Bertilotti, Teresa, and Anna Scattigno, eds. *Il femminismo degli anni Settanta*. Roma: Viella, 2005.
Bracke, Maud Ann. *Women and the Reinvention of the Political: Feminism in Italy, 1968–1983*. New York: Routledge, 2014.
Bravo, Anna. *A colpi di cuore: storie del sessantotto*. Roma-Bari: Laterza, 2008.
Bravo, Anna, and Giovanna Fiume, eds. "Anni Settanta," special issue of *Genesis* 3, no. 1 (2004).
Chianese, Gloria. "Storie di donne tra lavoro e sindacato." In *Mondi femminili in cento anni di sindacato* (2 vols.). Vol. 1, edited by Gloria Chianese 19–83. Roma: Ediesse, 2008.
Collettivo Internazionale Femminista. *Le operaie della casa*. Venezia: Marsilio, 1974.
Cosseta, Katrin. *Ragione e sentimento dell'abitare: la casa e l'architettura nel pensiero femminile tra le due guerre*. Milano: FrancoAngeli, 2000.
Cuninghame, Patrick. "Italian Feminism, Workerism and Autonomy in the 1970s: The Struggle against Unpaid Reproductive Labour and Violence." *@mnis. Revue*

de civilisation Contemporaine Europes/Ameriques, no. 8 (2008). Retrieved 11 June 2018 from https://journals.openedition.org/amnis/575.

Cutrufelli, Maria Rosa. *Disoccupata con onore: lavoro e condizione della donna.* Milano: Mazzotta, 1975.

———. *L'invenzione della donna: miti e tecniche di uno sfruttamento.* Milano: Mazzotta, 1977.

De Benedetti, Erminia. *Il nostro nido: consigli sul buon governo della casa; nozioni di economia domestica.* Palermo, Milano: Sandron, 1929.

De Grazia, Victoria. *How Fascism Ruled Women: Italy, 1922–1945.* Berkeley: University of California Press, 1992.

Edmond, Wendy, and Suzie Fleming, eds. *All Work and No Pay: Women, Housework, and the Wages Due.* Bristol: Power of Women Collective and Falling Wall Press, 1975.

Farina, Fatima. *Donne nelle forze armate: il servizio militare femminile in Italia e nella Nato.* Roma: Viella, 2015.

Federici, Silvia. *Wages Against Housework.* Bristol: Power of Women Collective, Falling Wall Press, 1975.

Federici, Silvia, and Nicole Cox. *Counter-Planning from the Kitchen.* New York: New York Wages for Housework Committee; Bristol: Falling Wall Press, 1975.

———. *Contropiano dalle cucine.* Venezia: Marsilio, 1978.

Francescato, Donata. "Casalinga/La nevrosi rampante." *Effe*, no. 3 (1973): 8.

Francescato, Grazia, and Clara Piccone. "Ma le donne sono meno uguali degli altri." *Effe*, no. 0 (1973): 33.

Frederick, Christine. *The New Housekeeping: Efficiency Studies in Home Management.* Garden City, NY: Doubleday, Page & Company, 1913.

———. *Household Engineering: The Scientific Management in the Home.* Chicago: American School of Home Economics, 1915.

———. *La donna e la casa: il taylorismo nella vita domestica: libro destinato a tutte le donne d'Italia, per facilitar loro i lavori della casa.* Translated by Lorenzo Tealdy. Torino: C. Accame, 1927.

———. *La casa moderna: come risparmiare tempo, fatica, denaro.* Translated by Maria Diez Gasca Roma: Edizione Enios, Tipografia delle Terme, 1933.

Garofalo, Anna. "Massaie alla ribalta." *Nuova Repubblica,* 18 December 1955.

Gissi, Alessandra. *Otto marzo: la giornata internazionale delle donne in Italia.* Roma: Viella, 2010.

———. "Reproduction." In *The Politics of Everyday Life in Fascist Italy: Outside the State?,* edited by Joshua Arthurs, Michael Ebner, and Kate Ferris, 99–122. New York: Palgrave Macmillan, 2017.

Glazer-Malbin, Nona. "Housework." *Signs: Journal of Women in Culture and Society,* no. 4 (1976): 905–22.

Grossi, Cinzia. "La 'Casalinga efficiente' stile americano nell'Italia degli anni Trenta." In *Miti Americani fra Europa ed America,* edited by Caterina Ricciardi and Sabrina Vellucci, 93–106. Venezia: Mazzanti, 2008.

Hilwig, Stuart J. *Italy and 1968: Youthful Unrest and Democratic Culture.* New York: Palgrave Macmillan, 2009.

Jori, Nerina M. "Un cuore e una capanna (se poi fosse un palazzo . . .)." *Casa e Lavoro,* no. 12 (1933): 333–35.

Lanaro, Silvio. *Storia dell'Italia Repubblicana.* Venezia: Marsilio, 1992.

"Lavoro domestico: inchiesta del gruppo di Modena." *Bollettino: Coordinamento emiliano per il salario al lavoro domestico,* single issue, 1976.

"Le casalinghe possono avere la pensione prima delle prossime elezioni politiche." *l'Unità,* 26 October 1957.

Liliana, Ellena, and Elena Petricola, eds. "Donne di mondo: percorsi transnazionali dei femminismi," special issue of *Zapruder,* no. 13 (2007).

Lotta Femminista, Collettivo Femminista di Pescara, Enrica Lucarelli and Margherita Repetto. "Salario alle casalinghe?" *Effe,* no. 5 (1974): 35–37.

Lussana, Fiamma. *Il movimento femminista in Italia: esperienze, storie, memorie.* Roma: Carocci, 2011.

Molinari, Augusta. "Casalinghe." In *Dizionario del Fascismo: A–K,* edited by Victoria De Grazia and Sergio Luzzatto, 256–58. Torino: Einaudi, 2002.

Nolan, Mary. "'Housework Made Easy': The Taylorized Housewife in Weimar Germany's Rationalized Economy." *Feminist Studies,* no. 16 (1990): 549–77.

Oakley, Ann. *Housewife.* London: Allen Lane, 1974.

———. *The Sociology of Housework.* London: Martin Robertson, 1974.

Ribero, Aida. *Una questione di libertà: il femminismo degli anni settanta.* Torino: Rosenberg & Sellier, 1999.

Rossi-Doria, Anna. "Ipotesi per una storia che verrà." In Teresa Bertilotti and Anna Scattigno, eds., *Il femminismo degli anni Settanta,* 1–23. Roma: Viella, 2005.

———. "Le donne sulla scena politica italiana agli inizi della Repubblica." In Anna Rossi-Doria, *Dare forma al silenzio: scritti di storia politica delle donne,* 127–208. Roma: Viella, 2007.

"Salario alle casalinghe?" *Effe,* no. 3 (1974): 14–22.

Salvati, Mariuccia. *L'inutile salotto: l'abitazione piccolo-borghese nell'Italia fascista.* Torino: Bollati Boringhieri, 1993.

Sarti, Raffaella. *Servo e padrone, o della (in)dipendenza: un percorso da Aristotele ai nostri giorni I. Teorie e dibattiti. Quaderni di Scienza & Politica,* no. 2 (2015) (Bologna: Alma Mater Studiorum Università di Bologna, 2015). Retrieved on 11 June 2018 from http://amsacta.unibo.it/4293/1/Sarti_Servo_e_Padrone_1.pdf.

"Siano le donne italiane una grande forza di pace, di libertà e di progresso per il nostro paese." *l'Unità,* 27 September 1955.

Stelliferi, Paola. *Il femminismo a Roma negli anni Settanta: percorsi, esperienze e memorie dei Collettivi di quartiere.* Bologna: Bononia University Press, 2015.

Tambor, Molly. *The Lost Wave: Women and Democracy in Postwar Italy.* Oxford: Oxford University Press, 2014.

Tolomelli, Marica. *L'Italia dei movimenti: politica e società nella prima Repubblica.* Roma: Carocci, 2015.

Tornabuoni, Lietta. "Salario alle casalinghe." *La Stampa,* 22 April 1973.

Traikovski, Louie. "The Housewives' Wages Debate in the 1920s Australian Press." *Journal of Australian Studies,* no. 78 (2003): 9–13.

Turnaturi, Gabriella. "La donna fra il pubblico e il privato: la nascita della casalinga e della consumatrice." *Nuova DWF,* nos. 12–13 (1979): 8–19.

Willson, Perry. *Peasant Women and Politics in Fascist Italy: The Massaie Rurali.* London: Routledge, 2002.

———. *Women in Twentieth-Century Italy.* New York: Palgrave Macmillan, 2010.

II

THE CUNNING HISTORIAN: UNVEILING AND OVERCOMING THE GENDER BIAS OF SOURCES

As shown in the introduction and in the first section, for a long time women were associated with the allegedly immutable realm of nature rather than with history. Not surprisingly, they were almost absent from historical narratives. As a consequence, asking whether they had a history was provocative rather than trivial. For those (mainly feminist) historians who nonetheless considered it obvious that women actually had a history, *how* to write their history was far from obvious. Contrary to what one might expect, sources on women turned out to be numerous and allowed historians to show that women had always worked, performing both paid and unpaid activities, at home and elsewhere. Certainly female roles had changed over times, but female paid extra-domestic labor had existed long before industrialization.

Nevertheless, sources—including allegedly gender-neutral documents such as statistics and population censuses—have proved heavily gender biased. As for work, hegemonic ideas on the proper roles for women and men greatly affected how data about the working population were collected and presented. Women, especially married ones, were often recorded only according to their marital status (for instance as "wife of") or as housewives. The meaning of such classifications was actually different in different periods. In early modern times, being a wife/housewife was a well-defined role with a recognized economic value: housewifery was seen as a type of work even though it might imply different activities according to the context, the family business, the husband's job. To find out what early modern women actually did, historians must use sources and methods allowing them to go beyond simple labels such as "housewife." This is the case with the verb-oriented method illustrated in this section by Maria Ågren. On the basis of sixteen thousand statements on work activities drawn from Swedish sources spanning from 1550 to 1799, she shows that in early modern Sweden marriage was crucial for both men and women, implying a transition to authoritative and managerial roles, especially in households with servants. Interestingly, in such a rural society with a low degree of specialization as Sweden, no category of work (except for the military) was all male or all female, and marriage was at least as important as gender in shaping one's role.

While, in early modern times, defining women as housewives and/or according to their marital status did not mean considering them as not working, things went differently in later times. In the nineteenth and early twentieth centuries, the professional classification of both women and men was no easy task for the burgeoning statistical authorities. Many people had no stable jobs, worked irregularly, and performed multiple activities. Yet the classification of women was particularly difficult. Doubts and ambiguities were often overcome by classifying women according to what was considered their proper role, i.e. as housewives, even though they also performed paid activities, sometimes even extra-domestic ones. At the same time, housewifery was increasingly seen as something different from proper work. Therefore, labeling women as housewives meant constructing them statistically as dependent and unproductive. Such an issue is dealt with in the first part by Nancy Folbre, who in the 1980s and 1990s had already unveiled the statistical construction of the unproductive housewife. Folbre shows, among other things, how, in Britain, wives, mothers, and mistresses who did not work for pay, after several changes in classifications, were eventually labeled as "dependents" (1891). The new classification offered a statistical representation in line with the breadwinner ideology, according to which the male family head provided for his wife and children, even though in fact many families would not survive without the paid or unpaid work of women and children. Similar decisions to classify wives, daughters, and more generally all family workers not engaged in paid occupations as dependents were taken in many other countries.

However, the underrepresentation of women did not only depend on the classification of housewives as non-workers or on the invisibility of women who worked unpaid in family businesses. Adult men were generally assumed to be workers by default, whereas women might be underrecorded even when they performed paid domestic or extra-domestic work. As shown by Raffaella Sarti in her chapter in this part, in 1901 Italian Census individuals were classified according to their professions, not according to their conditions: for instance, a lawyer capitalist had been classified according to his profession as a lawyer rather than his condition as a capitalist, regardless of the time he devoted to such a profession. On the contrary, if a woman had declared that she was in charge of domestic tasks and was also engaged in "secondary" activities such as spinning, weaving, sewing, or working as a temporary servant, she was classified according to her condition as a housewife (i.e., among the "people supported by the family") rather than according to her occupations, even though they were paid. In her chapter in this part, Borderías, too, illustrates—in this case for Spain—a growing tendency to classify women as housewives in censuses: while population censuses differ both because of peculiar national approaches and changes over time, they experienced a similar trend in different countries as for women's work classification, implying a growing invisibility of female labor. On the other hand, inasmuch as being a "not-working" housewife became an ideal, women themselves might hide their occupations.

The long-term analysis of female participation to the labor force based on censuses and similar sources has revealed a U-shaped trend, with female participation rates falling during the nineteenth and the first half of the twentieth centuries and then recovering after the Second World War. In the light of the aforementioned gender biases, we may wonder whether such a trend reveals actual transformation in the female participation to the labor force or rather mirrors changing ideas on women's proper roles. To find out which changes affected the structure of the labor force and the contribution of men and women to family budgets and national domestic product, it is therefore crucial to understand whether it is possible to measure women's underrepresentation in such sources. Efforts to assess their reliability seem to confirm that long-term female participation to the labor force actually had a U-shaped trend, but with participation rates significantly higher than previously calculated using original, uncorrected data.

A crucial method to assess gender biases is to cross sources written with different purposes and therefore with a different "interest" in recording or omitting women's work. In this part, the chapter by Margareth Lanzinger focuses on applications for permission to marry submitted to the Catholic authorities in nineteenth-century Tyrol by men and women who, being blood relatives or related by marriage, could marry only if they obtained a special dispensation justifying their requests. Their arguments might include detailed descriptions of women's contribution to the survival and well-being of the household, as was often the case with brothers- and sisters-in-law, who—after the death of the man's wife and the woman's sister—wanted to marry, having often been living under the same roof for several years.

In sum, "cunning" historians do not only unveil the gender biases that may affect the sources. They also find ways to overcome such biases, greatly contributing to a more accurate knowledge of our past, also necessary to understand our present and future.

CHAPTER 4

THE STATISTICAL CONSTRUCTION OF WOMEN'S WORK AND THE MALE BREADWINNER ECONOMY IN SPAIN (1856–1930)

Cristina Borderías

1. Introduction

The objective of this chapter is to analyze the concepts and categories concerning labor and the construction of the concepts of female labor in the national censuses of the population (NCP, originally, the *Censo Nacional de la Población*) and women's salaries in Spanish statistics. In the first place, I will analyze the social aspect of the concept in its dual meaning of market-based labor and domestic labor and caregiving in the families. Although the national censuses of the population have been utilized, in general, from a positivist point of view, as an accounting—more or less proper—of the population and its sociodemographic and occupational characteristics, its criteria and guidelines for registering and classifying that information and, in particular, that of the occupations, reveal their social perceptions—about individuals, citizenship, family models, work and gender relations—and contribute to their reproduction. As was shown some time ago by Joan Scott in her study about social statistics, "to take the numbers as the only reality of those statistics, however, denies the role that classification and interpretation play in the construction of reality—the reality contemporaries experienced as well as the different reality we may want to impute to their lives."[1] In actual fact, the underrecording, for example, of female activity in the population censuses cannot be read as a deficit of an underdeveloped statistical system or as a lack of resources but as a reflection of the liberal model of the sexual division of labor that assigned to men the role of production and to women that of reproduction. In the same way, the naturalization of caregiving—theoretically rooted in classical political economy—and the identification of productive work with that undertaken for the market in exchange for a salary would end with the classification of domestic work as non-productive labor.[2] The analysis of the census categories as a social representation has been the object of numerous case studies in different countries,[3] although the case of Spain has been less studied[4] and is less well-known at the international level. During industrialization, social statistics—claiming to be inheritors of "positive science"—attempted, from different ideological positions, "to base upon certain and uncontestable data the reality of the working classes." [5] Out of the vast production of statistics developed by social reformism, those relating to the living standards of the population are especially noteworthy, but, just as has occurred with the NCP, they have been used more from a positive viewpoint than as part of the social discourses. In the case of the social statistics of the mid-nineteenth century, the information about wages and working-class family budgets was not limited to "documenting with data" the reality of the daily life, but it attempted to promote "more rational models for the functioning of the domestic economies," which, far from rationalism, responded to determined ideological models about the individual, the family, and gender relations.

In Spain, wages were not a central topic of the national censuses of the population, and, in fact few of them—and none before 1924—dealt with collecting this information; furthermore, contrary to what occurred in other countries, they did not systematically record or publish wage information. Without a doubt, this was a question of the highest order for social statistics, which, by the middle of the nineteenth century—in a period marked by conflicts over the poor living conditions of the working classes—had assumed a very relevant role not only in the collection of information but also in the definition of new criteria for wage determination. These criteria defended the rationality of an economic model based on the defense of family wages for men and of "complementary" wages for women, in agreement with the new models of the sexual division of labor that assigned to men the responsibility for the economic support of their families and to women the work of social reproduction and caregiving (the "male breadwinner model"). In this way, when analyzed together, the conceptualization of work (paid and unpaid) in the population censuses, the determination of gender wages, as well as the criteria used by social statisticians for structuring the working-class family budgets shed light on the statistical construction of the new models of work, family, and domestic economies in modern Spain.

These processes of opacity and of undervaluing female labor are not, evidently, solely found in the Spanish statistical system; however, this system does have its specificities and rhythms, as we will see in the pages ahead. This chapter is divided into three sections. In the first, I analyze the statistical construction of labor through the national censuses of the population, demonstrating in what ways their criteria and categories contributed to the opacity of female labor participation, to the consideration of domestic labor as non-productive, and to considering as inactive the women who devoted themselves to it. In the second section, I analyze the role of social statistics in the configuration of a new model of domestic economy based on the "male breadwinner model," through the *Statistical Monograph* (originally titled the *Monografía Estadística*) by Ildefons Cerdà (1856) and the statistics of the Municipality of Barcelona during the first three decades of the twentieth century. The chapter ends with the hypothetical conclusion that the national statistical system and the statistics generated by social reformism were part of the new discourses about the sexual division of labor that the new liberal society would establish.

2. Female activity in the national censuses of the population: social theory and historic reality

In the pre-census period, there were, in Spain as in many other countries, many different countings of the population (questionnaires, cadastres, neighborhood tallies, etc.), its wealth, and its labor. The necessities that drove the public administration to undertake these accounts were diverse and included setting taxes, determining the recruitment of soldiers, and compiling the electoral register, which, as we will see, had a lasting influence on the underreporting of economic activity in the earliest modern censuses. The fact that during the Ancien Régime, the basic unit of statistical measure was the family and not the individual also had an enduring influence on the opacity of the labor of family members other than the head of the household.[6]

The fiscal origin of censuses and the resulting tendencies of the municipal governments and their inhabitants to hide their population and wealth was one of the principal preoccupations of those responsible for the national statistics. This was made clear in the instructions that accompanied each census and also in the prologues of the publication of results, in which the resistance of residents and local powers to a transparent declaration was repeatedly underlined. In the Royal Decree for the execution of the 1837 Census—which was never carried out—insistence was placed upon the need to shed old popular beliefs: "The people should know that now statistics are not to tax them without compensation, but to learn the causes of their difficulties and to resolve them, and to protect the free exercise of industry . . . to share public offices with equity, etc. . . ."[7] Similar observations were to be repeated throughout the different censuses undertaken during the nineteenth century. In the prologue of the publication of the 1900 Census, it was still insisted that "some Municipalities, fortunately few, warned that a population Census was to be conducted to establish the basis of contributions of certain taxes, and, persuaded that hiding the inhabitants on the general registry was in favor of the local interests they represented, have tenaciously resisted the investigative proceedings employed by this directive Centre."[8]

Owing to the inspections of the statistical service, the counting of the population improved over the first three decades of the twentieth century, but the registry of occupations and, in particular, female work was not a purely technical question. The concepts, categories, and instructions given to the municipalities and census agents were influenced by the new liberal concepts about work and gender relations. The reporting of female occupations was subject to criteria that had less to do with the activity itself than with citizen status, marital status, and dependence on the husband and head of the family.

The first census to be considered modern[9] was conducted in 1857. It was also the first in which the criteria of domiciliary registry (*empadronamiento*) was "individual and not [by] family," and in which, as such, "all the individuals whatsoever be their neighbourhood, origin or domicile" were to be recorded on the census.[10] However, this criterion was not applied extensively to the occupational registry, because this census was not based on an interest in individual activity or the productive structure but on the new fiscal regime. For this reason, only the occupation of the family member responsible for paying the tax had to be recorded:

> In the professions and trades shall be listed the person who, being or not the head of the family, supports it with their income or employment. Other individuals in the family are not listed nor appear except in cases where they exercise a profession or trade different from those in the boxes. Beyond these cases, the rest of the family disappears, working or not, employed in one or another trade and being the head of the family present or absent. For this reason, the result of the classification will not coincide with the total number of souls, but will be much lower.[11]

The shortcomings of the census led to another one being carried out three years later (1860), with the objective of improving upon the 1857 census by gathering new and more complete data; comparing it with the earlier one; deducing from the examination the greater or lesser exactness of the census-recorded relations procured by the towns; and considering the inhabitants of each province, of each town, of each isolated location not only in relation to marital status and sex, as had been done previously, but also by profession, art, or trade and education.[12]

In 1857, categories had previously been established to collect information about the occupations, although the results were never published. In 1860—with the objective of better adapting the professional taxonomy—after the collection of occupational information, thirty-nine professional groups were created: ecclesiastical; altar boys; religious institutions; public employees; army; navy; merchant navy; scholars and professors; private tutors; primary school teachers; schoolboys; schoolgirls; primary schoolchildren; secondary students; students in higher education; lawyers (barristers); scribes and notaries; solicitors; doctors and surgeons; apothecaries; veterinarians; artists; architects and master builders; agronomists and surveyors; landowners; renters; salespeople; factory owners; industrialists; railroad workers; artisans; miners; factory workers; fieldworkers; servants; paupers; deaf-mute, blind, and disabled people. The guidelines for the recording of information explicitly stated that lawyers, notaries, architects, and other professionals could be recorded as such even if they were not practicing; this is evidence of the fact that there was greater interest for knowledge of the social structure than for that of the economic structure.

In 1877, the head of the Census Office faced one of the key problems of female underreporting: the definition of the criteria of residency (*vecindad*) in the city, as it was only compulsory for residents to declare their occupation. According to the Municipal Law of 20 August 1870, reformed on 2 October 1877, "A resident is any emancipated Spaniard who resides habitually in the municipal area and is enrolled as such in the municipal registry [*padrón municipal*] while a domiciled person is the person who meets the same conditions, excepting only that of being emancipated; that is to say that to be a resident four conditions shall be met: being a Spaniard, being emancipated, residing habitually in the municipal area, and being registered as such in the municipal registry."[13] Even so, as was made clear at the time of taking the census, the municipalities had made a very heterogeneous interpretation of the standing law. As explained in the prologue of the publication of the census results,

> The Provincial and Municipal Boards understood the criteria relating to residence and domicile in different ways . . . the majority of the boards, resisting any innovation, maintained the old meaning of the word resident [*vecino*], connecting such condition to the status of "active citizen with full rights," which is to say an individual of age, head of a family with a house, with means of subsistence and of contributing to the municipal budget, elector and eligible,[14] with the exclusion of the rest of the inhabitants who, for not contributing to the alleviation of the council expenses, lacking means of subsistence, living under the roof of another family or not having formed their own can neither aspire to the position of council member nor be electors, nor enjoy the same advantages of the so-called residents.[15]

This definition excluded women, as women were not considered citizens with full civil and political rights. But there were also municipalities that applied a criterion of residency more in accord with the law, considering that "every Spaniard, male or female, having reached adult age and with a habitual residence, should be classified as a resident [*residente o vecino*]." The casuistry was very diverse because

> there were also municipalities that excluded all females; others that only included those who were emancipated through marriage, completely and equally for both sexes; still, there were municipalities that even if they recognized women as emancipated, they also considered that through marriage they came under a sort of dependence and responsibility of the husband and, as such, could not enjoy the condition of resident, but only that of domiciled person.[16]

Thus, although the traditional concept of resident was still that of the majority, this diversity highlighted the moment of sociopolitical transition opened with the Liberal Constitution of 1812. The prologue to the Census of 1877 made it clear that according to the existing laws, the distinctions between residents and domiciled people were no longer applicable:

> The marked difference between the existing law of Municipalities between residents and domiciled people is almost null as it only consists of the condition of emancipation that is acquired at the very least by age[;] and it is no longer required for residency that one be the head of a family, nor possess constant means of subsistence, nor contribute to the municipal budget, without a doubt because fundamentally it is understood that no one, upon reaching *the age of virility* fails to contribute in some way to the budget, as there is really no one who lacks the elements to live, if they are not a recognized pauper. . . . But the common opinion maintains other criteria, and generally judges that each resident represents a single household and vice-versa.[17]

However, the expression "upon reaching the age of virility" shows that the condition of resident (*residente o vecino*) was only applied to men. In the municipalities in which women were considered as domiciled people, this was a factor that contributed in a decisive way to the underreporting of occupation. This heterogeneousness does not only reduce confidence in the census but also makes comparisons between the municipal and provincial data difficult.

In the same Census of 1877, the instructions given to the census agents placed special emphasis on the recording of the occupation of the head of the family or on those whose occupation allowed for complete economic independence: "Be sure to assign a profession to every head of household because only those people who live off of the resources of the head of the household (women, children, the handicapped...) will be listed without a profession."[18] These requirements left the majority of women and also children and individuals whose work was seasonal, temporary, or poorly paid out of the registry. This also excluded those women who worked for the family business and as such did not have a trade different from that of the head of the household and did not receive an independent wage, a very frequent situation in predominantly rural Spain where manufacture was still based in small family workshops.[19] In the 1920 census instructions, it was still specified that "married women or daughters of the family who, in addition to domestic work, assist the head of the family in his industry or work, will declare their trade only if it has a fixed or daily salary paid by the head of the family"[20]; however, it did not require the same of the sons who collaborated in the family business. Until the Census of 1940, the census agents were not instructed as to the need to record the activities of all women, single and married, even if they worked part time.[21]

Another obstacle that fundamentally affected the Censuses of 1857, 1860, and 1877 was the different treatment given to masculine and feminine pluriactivity. The high proportion of individuals who declared more than one occupation and the lack of criteria for the statistical treatment of this data were the main reasons why the results of the Census of 1857 were not published:

> In the classification of the inhabitants based on their professions and trades such setbacks have been suffered—for lack of customary practice, for the resulting complication of recording an individual multiple times for various classifications in the Commission's registry sheets—and for fear that it would paralyze the working of many provinces because of or due to the doubts about these particular occurrences, it was necessary to abandon at this time such queries after repeated and useless efforts to obtain them.[22]

The following censuses continued to insist on this, as "many are those who exercise different professions and trades at the same time, none of them clearly defined or sufficient, perhaps, alone, to provide continuous employment for those that exercise them."[23] But the Census of 1877, still giving directions to the census agents to collect all the professions, introduced a criterion for the classification of the employed population. It established that "those who practice various professions shall verify all of them, beginning with that from which the most is gained," but those responsible for undertaking the information gathering received an order to take into consideration only "the main occupation."[24] Yet, in 1920, although the multiple occupations were registered, only the "main occupation" was to be counted in the census publication.[25] But according to the census authorities, when domestic chores were considered the main occupation, it was the families that did not declare any other occupation of married women.

The Census of 1970, the last undertaken during the Francoist regime, established the standing criteria used to this day, breaking with the confusion about the occupational criteria and status by requiring the declaration of employment by having, in effect, worked in said employment for a determined length of time. In that census, they also introduced the concepts of activity and inactivity, establishing equal criteria for the recording of employment by defining

> as "active" the person who, during the census week, was engaged in the production of goods and the provision of services or available to do so . . . , who, in that week, worked for at least one-third of a normal period in his or her profession or trade and those having a position in which they had previously been employed but were absent from it due to illness or injury, labor conflict, vacation or permitted absence, absence without permission or an interruption of labor due to causes such as bad weather or technical incidents.[26]

3. The statistical representation of domestic work: from the census of population to the surveys of "active population" (1860–1964)

The statistical classification of domestic work reflects the new liberal concepts that progressively reduced the concept of work/labor to that of production of goods and services for the market. Neither the Census of 1857, for which the data about professions was not published, nor that of 1860 contemplated the inclusion of domestic labor undertaken for the family among the occupational groups.[27] Nor was this done in the Censuses of 1877 or 1887, but in both cases the tables of professions included a group titled "without profession and without classification," in which the women without a declared "occupation" were listed.[28] In 1900 and 1910, following the instructions of the Chicago International Congress of Statistics (1893), the aggregate national tables of "Professions" included under the group "Other professions" the rubric "Domestic work" subdivided into two subgroups: "Family members" and "Domestic servants."[29] In 1920, the group "Family members" was excluded from the "Domestic servants" group to form one of its own, in which women who had not declared any occupation as well as those who had declared to be devoted to the work of their families and children without a profession for reason of age were also included. Thus a process of naturalization of "housework" was initiated, which took it from its consideration as real work (domestic work) to its consideration as a role/status derived from its belonging to the family. However, the fact that this transition was slow is shown in the presentation of the synthesis of data published in the statistical tables "Groups of industries and professions" of 1920, which appears in the prologue to volume 5 of the 1920 Census; despite the new taxonomy, this stated that the women who were included in the rubrics of "Family members" and "Domestic servants" were "Domestic laborers" and, in addition, formed part of the "productive" population, making it explicit that "the proportion of unproductive men (32.68 percent of all men in 1920) was higher than that of women (27.66 percent)."[30]

The later evolution of this rubric testifies to the progressive naturalization of reproductive work that would occur in 1940, when it was listed under the rubric of "Their labors" [*Sus labores*, i.e. the duties of housewives]. The Census of 1950 carried this process to its logical extreme by introducing the concept of activity and inactivity,[31] presenting separate tables for both population types; women engaged in domestic work from their families were classified as a group within the tables of "inactive" population. From 1964, the surveys of the active population (the *Encuestas de Población Activa*) increased this tendency by classifying these women directly as "non-productive" population, a concept derived from orthodox economics. It was a greater consideration of economic and social marginalization than that received in the first phases of modern statistics (table 4.1).

Thus, if the national censuses of the population contributed to the opacity or invisibility of female market and non-market work, the social statistics developed during the second half of the nineteenth century to analyze the impact of industrialization on the standards of living of the working classes and propose measures to resolve the processes of impoverishment were not alien to the new models of domesticity that were becoming extensive to the working classes in the mid-nineteenth century. Even more, they contribute to argue in favor of the economic rationality of the male breadwinner model. The Barcelona statistics contain some paradigmatic examples of this, as we will now show.

Table 4.1. Categories and classification of (unpaid) domestic work in the national population censuses.

1857/1860/ 1877/1887	1900 and 1910 tables of professions for the whole country (national data)	1900 tables of professions with aggregate data for the provinces and capitals of provinces	1920 and 1930 tables of professions (all)	1940 to 1970 tables of professions (all)
No data was published about unpaid domestic work for families. Women who were "housewives" were excluded from the statistical tables	Occupational group: "Others" Subgroup X **Domestic work** 55a) **Family members** (unpaid domestic work) 55b) Domestic servants (paid domestic work)	Occupational group 33: "Family members engaged in **unpaid domestic work** and individuals without a profession or of unknown profession"	Occupational group: "Family members" 78) **Family members** 79) Children without profession by reason of age	"Non-active population" a. Dependent people b. **Housewives** (*mujeres sus labores*)

Sources: Spanish national censuses.

4. The statistical construction of the male breadwinner economy: the *Statistical Monograph of the Working Class of Barcelona in 1856* by Ildefons Cerdà

By the mid-nineteenth century, the city of Barcelona contained 26 percent of the population of the province and 11 percent of that of Catalonia. Its very diversified industrial activity, its dynamism in commerce and service provision, and its urban growth had turned it into a pole of attraction for the work of women, who, in 1856, represented more than 40 percent of the working population. The high number of women in the urban labor market and their high mortality rates made female labor the focus of the attention of politicians, hygienists, and social theorists. This centrality was solidified in the development of different labor statistics attentive to the collection of systematic information about female labor, the structure of trades based on sex and age, male and female wages, and family budget estimates. For this reason, its information was much richer and its data more trustworthy with regards to female labor than the national census of the population.[32] Even so, its analysis highlights how the modern statistical apparatus—an instrument of the reformist policies undertaken by the liberal governments—was not only a means of understanding the potentials and material and human needs upon which the social reform programs were to be based, but it was also a mechanism for articulating the social models upon which this reform was founded: in particular—and what interests us here—the models of employment, wages, and family and of the sexual division of labor.[33] The *Statistical Monograph of the Working Class of Barcelona in 1856* done by Ildefons Cerdà,[34] in addition to being the first statistics of the working population of Barcelona, is an exemplary model of the way in which statistics implicitly configured a specific model of social organization.

In 1855, Le Play published his work in six volumes, *Ouvriers européens: Études sur les travaux, la vie domestique et la condition morale des populations ouvrières de l'Europe*. Le Play was a pioneer in the establishment of an analytical methodology based on surveys and on the use of the "family budget" for the determination of standards of living. Only one year later, engineer and urban planner Ildefons Cerdà, whose name is better known in Europe for being the creator of the renovation plans of the city of Barcelona (*l'Eixample*), elaborated his *Statistical Monograph of the Working Class of Barcelona in 1856*. Cerdà, like Le Play, belonged to that group of social scientists who, influenced by the principles of the enlightenment, tried to establish the foundation of a new social science inspired by the principles of positivism. From different ideological perspectives and using different and particular instruments of observation and measurement, both conducted a "positive" study of the working conditions and standards of living of the working classes, situating the family as the unit of economic analysis and family budgets as the instrument of said analysis.

The *Monograph* emerged in the culminating phase of industrialization as an instrument of mediation of the social-labor conflicts troubling the city of Barcelona in the mid-nineteenth century. As a member of a Mixed Commission created because of the General Strike of 1855 and charged with presenting the government with "positive and factual" information about the condition of the working classes, Cerdà presented himself to the workers' associations as a "collector and compiler of all the data and news referring to their material lives." In its first part, "Alphabetical Indicator and Census of Workers," the *Monograph* contains this data, documenting with a degree of detail unsurpassed by previous and subsequent sources the work of men and women working in 171 trades; for each one of these, it lists information related to the organization of labor, technology, gender and age composition, systems of apprenticeship/learning and qualification, distinct labor categories and working conditions (days, hours, types of contract, wages and income). According to this data, women (41 percent of the working population) worked whether they were single or married, which led Cerdà to lament "the lack of daycare centres and kindergartens, because the resources that the families were obliged to spend (when the woman worked) in the payment of a girl or old maid to attend to the housework and care of the children represented the greater part or the entirety of the wife's earnings."[35] In the second part of his work, the daily wages and annual earnings of the distinct trades were collected and systematized. According to this information, the average wages of women was 4.5 *reales* per day, three times what was paid to a girl or old maid who worked as a babysitter for the workers, a salary earned by barely 1.5 percent of the female workers of Barcelona.

In the third part of the work, Cerdà undertook the analysis of the workers' budgets, using as a tool the elaboration of a budget type that—differently from that developed by Le Play—was based on a model family consisting of a couple and two children under the age of eight.[36] Indebted to the traditions and theories of Enlightement and, in particular, to classical political economics, Cerdà conceived the biological nucleus of parents and children as the first space of sociability and economics. Inherent to this conceptualization was the notion of an order that ascribed to the father the economic responsibility and to the mother the reproduction and care of the offspring. The nuclear family was thus converted into the typological unit of consumption to which the calculation of domestic budgets referred. To this budget was added that of the single male worker living in a boarding house, considering the possibility of single living for men, but not women.

Lastly, and with the objective of "responding to the crucial need of the workers to demonstrate with incontrovertible data the difficulties which they experienced with the wages established in Barcelona," it presented the conclusions about the standards of living of the Barcelona working class by giving a list of trades with figures about the deficit or surplus, which contained data—solely for the adult male workers (leaving blank spaces in the boxes for female trades)—under two assumptions: (1) the capacity for subsistence as a single person, and (2) the capacity to support a family of four members. A fixed amount of 424 *reales* (1.57 *reales* per day) was added to the balance of the married workers' budgets in order to account for their wives' assumed contributions. This amount was justified in the following manner:

We have counted as part of the married worker's income the weekly amount of 10 *reales*[37] which it is supposed his wife earns, despite the fact that we are not ignorant of the fact that this happens only during the first year of their marriage and even then not the whole time because pregnancy and childbirth and the related domestic care work prevent the woman worker from sharing the support of the family, as it is, on the contrary, not uncommonly an occasion that increases expenses. Despite this, there were women who continued working despite pregnancy and child rearing, at times in their own house and at others in a workshop, even if the wages of the girl or old maid that took care of the household chores and of the child absorbed a large part, if not all, that the married woman earned in such circumstances.[38]

Even so, his list of wages for the different trades shows that the average female wage was three times higher. Why this difference? The answer to this question is revealed in the statistical tables corresponding to the balance of family income and expenses—where one can see that the 1.57 *reales* per day was the deficit in the average salary of a male adult worker to cover the daily needs of a family of four people. In this way, Cerdà presented the wage contribution of the wives to the family budget as a mere complement to the wages of the head of the family. It is clear that only by reducing the contribution of the wife by this proportion could it be maintained that paying a babysitter was not a rational economic option for the families. Even so, the data given by the workers' associations, published in the first part of the *Monograph*, reveals that only 1.5 percent of the female workers of Barcelona earned 1.57 *reales*. By the same measure, only 20 percent of the workers reached the "family wages." And only 45 percent could manage with the wife's contribution of 1.57 *reales*; for the rest, the work of the women was not a "mere" complement. In fact, only if this contribution was greater could it offset the deficits that Cerdà considered were affecting 320 out of the 331 trades of the Barcelona working class. For the rest, the work of the women could not be a "mere" complement. The final image produced by Cerdà in the *Monograph* is that of a labor-market structure incapable of guaranteeing the formation, subsistence, and reproduction of the working-class family, and consequently of the working class itself, as the number of trades in which wages covered the entirety of family expenses—even when considering the complementary wages of the wife—was very small.

The *Monograph* constitutes a means of expressing a reformist political project based on the demand by the male worker of a family wage that could support his family, on the defense of the nuclear family, which at that moment was more a model than a reality and on the sexual division of labor—ascribing production to men and reproduction to women. It was a project whose rationality Cerdà attempted to mathematically demonstrate by adjusting the data that was supplied by the working class to this male breadwinner model, the result of which was the underestimation of female labor and of its contribution to the family economy. With this, Cerdà supported the workers' demands that aspired to bourgeois domesticity by supposing the greatest rationality of a model of social organization that only promoted an increase in wages for adult male workers and lent arguments to the entrepreneurs to discriminate on wages based on gender.

This wage model would crystallize in the second half of the nineteenth century in the programs of the workers' associations, which placed the family wage as an aspiration of adult male workers, while they considered it sufficient for female workers to earn only a complementary wage. This distinct wage model for men and women finds, in the work of Cerdà, the first theoretical reference in Spanish social science and statistics. The surveys carried out by the Commission for Social Reform, created in 1883 with the objective of "studying all questions that are directly of interest for the improvement or welfare of the working classes, in agriculture as much as in industry and that affect the relationships between capital and labor," make clear the reach and diffusion of the concept of family wage. In the questionnaire that served as the basis of the studies carried out by the commission between 1883 and 1889, this concept is made clear. So the questions corresponding to wages (questions 64 to 77) include whether the salary is insufficient for the worker to attend to his needs and those of his family (question 69). And in those relating to the labor of women, the motivations of that work are questioned.

Its impact survived in the statistical system of the city of Barcelona during the first decades of the twentieth century, as is shown by the Censuses of Workers undertaken by the Municipal Office of Statistics in 1905, 1912, and 1917. The head of the Office of Statistics, Escudé Bartolí, explained the influence of the model established by Cerdà in the elaboration of the workers' budgets: "Allow me to share a few considerations that support this work, for which the Monograph published by I. Cerdà has been for me a luminous guide and starting point, following the same plan, varied only for circumstances of time and understanding."[39]

However, the Municipal Office of Statistics of Barcelona was especially critical of the underreporting of female activity, and it developed initiatives to improve the computation of the population of female workers. In the prologue to the Census of 1905, the head of the Statistical Office, Escudé Bartolí, made clear that a contrast existed between this model and the more pressing reality of the workers that continued to resort extensively to the work of women:

> Where the Census has the most deficiencies is in the classification of women, for the very great difficulty faced due to the resistance by the individuals concerned to declaring it on the census sheets for various reasons: first and foremost because many professions and trades are only exercised by women while they are single [unmarried] and also because the occupation is not constant or if it is, [it is such] only for brief periods. The majority of unmarried women over the age of 12 and widows exercise some profession in Barcelona, and while for the most part this does not pay a sufficient wage or salary for their subsistence, it helps support the expenses of the family.[40]

If the activity of unmarried adult women and widows was considered by Escudé as the experience of the majority, he also insisted on the high levels of married women, even when they did not declare an occupation. His observations are of particular importance with regards to domestic labor, as despite their important dimension, it is a sector that does not appear in the historiographic analyses with which we have been concerned in the first pages: "There are thousands of women who work in their own homes, especially in the manufacture of sewing articles destined mostly to the export market and this circumstance was not reflected in the census form."[41]

Again in the prologue of the monograph of 1917 it states

> that industry tends generally to utilize the labor of women because with the invention of machines, the tasks of the operators have become extraordinarily simplified to the point that one does nothing but look after the work of the machines, and in addition, the tendency is focused on the economy (containment) of wages given that the work of the women is always paid less than that of the men.[42]

Following this, and in view of the family deficits, he claimed what was considered "the minimum wage" for adult male workers, identified plainly and explicitly with the "family wage" as argued by Ildefons Cerdà. As Escudé Bartolí said about the guidelines for calculating the minimum wage,

> it should be sufficient for attending to the healthy existence of the workers . . . for the law to be formulated in such a way that it tends to be possible to determine a national real minimum wage, that is to say, wages that, translated into money, correspond to the local variations in the cost of living.

And he sought also legitimization for his proposal in the "family wage" theory developed by Webb:

> Webb considers: that the married worker, as the head of the family, should earn enough to support it; that the woman's wages, be she single or married, should be less than that of the man; that all male workers have the right to receive the

minimum wage and all female workers a minimum as well; that the salary of the male worker should be sufficient to support a family and that of the single or married woman, to support an adult. . . . The principle of assuring each worker what is necessary to support a family is not only humane but convenient for society as a whole, which needs to facilitate the means of protecting large families. . . . Competent, therefore, to determine the remuneration or minimum price of labor in proportion to the needs of the worker are the mixed councils of owners and workers. . . . In our humble view, the wages in Barcelona should be adjusted to the currently indisputable expenses for the life of a family. If at the halfway point of the past century the cost of living was a little more than 3 *pesetas* daily and 4 in 1900, today the minimum salary cannot be inferior to 10 *pesetas*. We leave as a margin of social improvement, of savings, and possible insurance, however much is contributed to the family budget by the wife and children, although we aspire to the ideal that only the father and sons over the age of 14 work outside the home and provide for the expenses of household consumption.[43]

Thus, in 1917, the municipality reproduced the theories of social reform that had assumed the family wage model and the sexual division of labor implicit in the bourgeois liberal model. Nonetheless, Escudé Bartolí was very conscious of the consequences that this model would have for women when they became the head of the family with children, crudely leaving the solution of the derived situation of poverty to public assistance:

As for unmarried male workers, Webb considers it convenient not to make wage distinctions between them and married men because of the difficulties that arise by measuring the differences. As to widowed female workers with children, there is no place for distinctions regarding those that have no offspring because public assistance can help the children of female workers in different ways. This principle has been adopted by public bodies in Germany, through wage or earning supplements in proportion to the number of children.[44]

The wage statistics published in 1917 in said monograph made patently clear that, despite the social discourse in favor of this wage model, its reach was very limited: out of the over one hundred classes and categories of journeymen workers and laborers, only four had a wage equal to the expenses of a family with an inactive wife and two children.[45] So, the reality of the workers followed a very different course from that described in the social discourses about the models of family, employment, and wages.

5. Conclusions

A systematic analysis of the national censuses of the population reveals that the relatively common idea that female labor force participation fell in the second half of the nineteenth century lacks a solid statistical basis. On the contrary, the apparent fin de siècle depression shown in the census data is a product of the widely recognized underreporting of the activity in the 1887 Census, prolonged in 1900 and extended again in 1910. In the case of the city of Barcelona, it is the higher degree of confidence in the data of the initial (1856) and final dates (1920/1930) of the period contemplated, which creates this statistical effect.[46]

Although the currently available data is inconclusive, there are many indications that suggest that the discourse of domesticity was, during this period, more an ideological model than a reflection of the reality of the majority of the working class. Accordingly, the modern statistical system, both a result of and a means of reproducing a specific social discourse about gender relations, progressively underreported female labor. This underreporting did not just affect the national censuses of the population. It was progressively seen in the municipal registries (*Padrones Municipales*) and the municipal and social statistics, at the rhythm of the attempts to expand the bourgeois discourse to the working class. The concept of female labor as complementary had become codified in Barcelona by the mid-nineteenth century in the work of Cerdà, one of the objectives of which was to question the economic rationality of a model of the family economy based on a dual wage. In the face of this, it argued on behalf of making the wages of male workers sufficient to support a family and for the dedication of the wives to the care of the household. Half a century later, when the risk of not being able to guarantee the reproduction of the working class—which originally had been blamed on high female labor force participation—had disappeared, the municipality, lending strength to the work of Cerdà, appropriated this discourse because of the reality of a city that was developing through a growing contribution of female labor and an insufficient demand for male labor, seeking its legitimacy in the international social reformism that had assumed the theoretical presuppositions of the bourgeois liberal model of the family and wages during the second half of the nineteenth century. Well aware of the effects of poverty on the women and families that depended on a female wage derived from this model, the Municipal Government of Barcelona did not hesitate in considering that the solution to these problems rested with the government and the development of public assistance. In any case, the deficit in the family budgets that the majority of the historiography has documented for the long period that we have dealt with must, in actual fact, have required different strategies from those that prevailed in said discourses, as the contemporaries had denounced. In all probability, families had to use all the resources in laboring to guarantee the survival of their members or fall back on other strategies, like cohabitating with parents, subletting, or seeking welfare assistance. The data available to date about the activity of women in Barcelona does not support, at this time, the existence of a rupture and significant reduction in the trends of female activity in the second half of the nineteenth century. Everything seems to indicate that in the context of the urban area of Barcelona, there was a tendency to continuity, in which there was a complex interplay between different factors, including the maintenance of a high, diversified, and flexible demand for female labor; low salaries for men and women; a lowering fertility rate that notably decreased family expenses and at the same time lowered the number of potentially active minors; and family and neighborhood networks that may have contributed by supporting this labor.

Cristina Borderías is full professor at the Department of History and Archaeology (Contemporary History Section) of the Universidad de Barcelona, Spain. She is a specialist in labor history and gender history. She is the director of the Grupo de Investigación de Historia del Trabajo: Trabajo, Instituciones y Género (TIG) (Research Group on Labor History: Labor, Institutions, and Gender). She was also president of the Spanish Association of Women's History (Asociación Española de Historia de las Mujeres). She is a member of the editorial board of the journals *Areas, Revista de Ciencias Sociales, Recerques,* and *Ayer.* Her more recent research focuses on the reconstruction of female labor participation rates, time uses, wages and family budgets, and consumption gender differences. Her publications on this issue include the edited volume *Género y Políticas del Trabajo en la España Contemporánea* (2007), and the following articles and chapters: "Salarios y subsistencia de las trabajadoras y los trabajadores de la España Industrial, 1849–1868" (2006); "Revisiting Women's Labor Force Participation in Catalonia (1920–1936)" (2013); "Salarios infantiles y presupuestos familiares en la Cataluña Obrera, 1856–1920" (2013); "Gender Inequalities in Family Consumption:Spain 1850–1930," coauthored with Pilar Pérez-Fuentes and Carmen Sarasúa (2010); and "Nutrición y género en la Barcelona Obrera" (2016). For further details see http://www.ub.edu/dphc/cristinaborderiasmondejar.htm.

Notes

This work was developed under Project HAR2014-57187-P, financed by the Spanish Ministry of Economy and Competitivity.

1. Joan Wallach Scott, "Statistical Representations of Work: "The Politics of the Chamber of Commerce's Statistique de l'Industrie à Paris, 1847–48," in *Work in France: Representations, Meaning, Organization, and Practice*, ed. Stephen Laurence Kaplan and Cynthia J. Koepp (Ithaca, NY: Cornell University Press, 1986), 338.
2. For the place of domestic work in classical political economics, see Joan Wallach Scott, "'L'Ouvrière! Mot Impie, Sordide . . .': Women Workers in the Discourse of French Political Economy, 1840–1860," in *The Historical Meanings of Work*, ed. Patrick Joyce (Cambridge University Press, 1987), 119–42. See also Nancy Folbre, *Greed, Lust, and Gender: A History of Economic Ideas* (Oxford: Oxford University Press, 2009), and "The Unproductive Housewife: Her Evolution in Nineteenth-Century Economic Thought," *Signs: Journal of Women in Culture and Society* 16, no. 3 (1991): 463–84. Particularly interesting for the transition between the cultural values of work in medieval times and the modern era see, Raffaella Sarti, "Promesse mancate e attese deluse: spunti di riflessione su lavoro domestico e diritti in Italia," in *Il lavoro cambia*, ed. Ariella Verrocchio and Elisabetta Vezzosi (Trieste: Eut, 2014), 55–77, also available at http://hdl.handle.net/10077/9764.
3. Catherine Hakim, "Census Reports as Documentary Evidence: The Census Commentaries 1801–1951," *Sociological Review* 28, no. 3 (1980): 551–80; Scott, "L'Ouvrière!"; Edward Higgs, "Women, Occupations and Work in the Nineteenth Century Censuses," *History Workshop*, no. 23 (1987): 59–80; Nancy Folbre and Abel Marjory, "Women's Work and Women's Households: Gender Bias in the U.S. Census," *Social Research* 56, no. 3 (1989): 545–69; Silvana Patriarca, "Gender Trouble: Women and the Making of Italy's Active Population, 1861–1936," *Journal of Modern Italian Studies* 3, no. 2 (1998): 144–63; Christian Topalov, "Une revolution dans les representations du travail: L'emergènce de la categorie statistique de population active au XIXème en France, en Grand-Bretagne et aux États-Unis," *Revue Française de Sociologie* XL, no. 3 (1999): 445–73; Raffaella Sarti, "Work and Toil: Breadwinner Ideology and Women's Work in 19th and 20th Century Italy," paper presented at the international conference *Women, Work and the Breadwinner Ideology*, Salzburg, 10–11 December 1999, available online at http://www.uniurb.it/scipol/drs_work_and_ toil.pdf; Margo Anderson, "The History of Women and the History of Statistics," *Journal of Women's History* 4, no. 1 (1992): 14–36; Alessandra Pescarolo, "Asimmetrie di genere e opacità teoriche nella costruzione statistica dell'economia di mercato," in *Il percorso storico della statistica nell'Italia unita: atti del workshop – Roma, 7 giugno 2011*, ed. Dora Marucco and Aurea Micali (Roma: Istat, 2013).
4. Pilar Pérez-Fuentes, "El trabajo de las mujeres en los siglos XIX y XX: Consideraciones metodológicas," *Arenal* 2, no. 2 (1995): 219–45; Cristina Borderías, "La transición de la actividad femenina en el mercado de trabajo barcelonés (1856–1930): Teoría social y realidad histórica en el sistema estadístico moderno," in *¿Privilegios o eficiencia? Mujeres y hombres en los mercados de trabajo*, ed. Carmen Sarasúa and Lina Gálvez (Alicante: Publicaciones de la Universidad de Alicante, 2003), 241–276; Cristina Borderías, "Revisiting Women's Labor Force Participation in Catalonia (1920–1936)," *Feminist Economics* 19, no. 4 (2013): 224–42.
5. Ildefons Cerdà, *Monografía estadística de la clase obrera en Barcelona en 1856, Teoría general de la urbanización y aplicación de sus principios y doctrinas a la reforma y ensanche de Barcelona* (Madrid, Imprenta Española, 1867).
6. During the first half of the nineteenth century, the tabulations of the population were the responsibility of the Ministry of Governance (Ministerio de Gobernación, a sort of Home Office). In 1856, the General Statistics Commission for the Kingdom was created (la Comisión de Estadística General del Reino) that, unlike what occurred in other countries, combined the undertaking of the census, the cartography for the kingdom, and the formation of the cadastre. In 1861, this commission was renamed the General Board for Statistics (Junta General de Estadística); in 1870, of the Geographic Institute (Instituto Geográfico); in 1873, of the Geographic and Statistics Institute (Instituto Geográfico y Estadístico); in

1922, of the Geographic and Cadastre Institute (Instituto Geográfico y Catastral); and in 1931, of the Geographic, Cadastre and Statistical Institute (Instituto Geográfico, Catastral y de Estadística).
7. Instituto Geográfico y Estadístico, Prologue to the National Census of the Population 1860.
8. INE, Introducción a los Resultados del Censo 1900 [Introduction to the publishing of Results of the 1900 Census].
9. The census was carried out under the government of Narváez by the recently created (1856) General Statistics Commission for the Kingdom that was to centralize all statistical work, as recommended at the I International Statistics Congress that took place in Brussels in 1853. The four basic requirements for a modern census are "nominative and individual numeration, universal territoriality, simultaneousness and periodical [execution]." The registration cards (Cedulas de Empadronamiento) collect the information for each household with regards to name, sex, age, civil status, profession, and place of birth of the residing population at the moment of carrying out the census. The cards were filled out by the head of the household except in cases when this person could not write, in which case they would be filled out by the person charged with collecting them. One must take into account an illiteracy rate that year above 70 percent. Despite the decision to carry out the census in years ending in zero and five, according to the decisions taken at the International Statistics Congresses, in Spain, the political crises determined a distinct chronology, and they were conducted in 1860, 1877, and 1900—from this last date, the census would be decennial. In Great Britain and Norway, the first modern census is from 1801; in Denmark (1834), France (1836), Belgium (1846), The Netherlands (1850), Austria (1857), Switzerland (1860), Italy (1861), Germany (1864), and Russia (1897).
10. In England, the Censuses of 1811, 1821, and 1831 gathered occupational information about the families, not about the individuals in the belief that the occupation of the head of the family determined that of its members. It was not until 1831 when a process of individualizing began, although restricted to men, except in the case of servants; see Higgs, "Women, Occupations and Work." In the United States, the Censuses of 1790, 1800, and 1810 gathered information about the family; in 1850, it began to gather the occupation of all males above the age of fifteen; see Folbre and Marjory, "Women's Work and Women's Households"; also Folbre, "Unproductive Housewife."
11. On the contrary, in France, the Census of 1851 registered with the same occupation the head of the family and his wife, considering that she also contributed to the family business. However, beginning with the Census of 1861, the work of married women was only registered if they labored outside the home. The variations in the registration criteria led to unsustainable conclusions about the evolution of the rates of female activity in France. See George Grantham, "Occupation, Marital Status and Life-Cycle Determinants of Women's Labor Force Participation in Mid-nineteenth-Century Rural France," *EHES Working Papers in Economic History* 22 (July 2012).
12. Prologue to the Census of 1860.
13. Prologue to the Census of 1877.
14. In 1877 in Spain, the rights of active and passive suffrage were male and based on property ownership. Only men over the age of twenty-five who could read and write, who were heads of family, and who paid taxes were eligible to be municipal council members or legislators. Women were excluded from both. In 1878, suffrage was available to only 5 percent of the population. In 1890, universal male suffrage was declared. Women did not gain suffrage until 1933.
15. Prologue to the Census of 1877.
16. Ibid.
17. Ibid.
18. *Gaceta de Madrid*, 4 November 1877, 379.

19. Ibid. As with other countries, the recording of market-based labor undertaken within the family unit has received similar treatment, although with a different chronology. In 1841 in England, women and children who carried out work in their family business were not recorded unless they earned wages or were registered as apprentices. Between 1851 and 1871, the census agents had instructions to register the wives of farmers, artisans, and salespeople due to the belief that they had an important role in the family economy. In 1881, they were registered as "unoccupied." See, Higgs, "Women, Occupations and Work," and Hakim, "Census Reports as Documentary Evidence."
20. *Gaceta de Madrid*, 31 October 1920, 497.
21. In the United States, instructions were given to register the occupation of married women in 1900, and in 1910 it was explicitly noted that it should not be assumed that they did not work unless this was specifically verified.
22. *Gaceta de Madrid*, 1858, 278.
23. INE, Trabajos Estadísticos de España 1860–1861, xxv.
24. In the case of Italy, the distinction between main and accessory profession was introduced in the Census of 1901. See Sarti "Work and Toil," 62.
25. In Great Britain between 1851 and 1921, all occupations were declared, placing in the first space the "main occupation"; in France, between 1851 and 1901; in the United States, the census agents had to collect only the main occupation, which is what happened in the aforementioned countries during the twentieth century.
26. Prologue to the Census of 1970.
27. The English census of 1860 recognized that the domestic work of housewives was the most important in the country and classified them all as "occupied," even though it was not remunerated labor. The same census established the category of domestic labor divided into two groups: (a) Family members (order 4) and (b) Domestic servants (order 5). From 1881 they were considered inactive. See Higgs, "Women, Occupations and Work," and Hakim, "Census Reports as Documentary Evidence."
28. In Great Britain and France, this was done a few years later: in Great Britain in 1881; in France in 1896. A more detailed review of the evolution of this rubric is available in Topalov, "Une revolution," 453–54.
29. The tables relating to the provinces and province capitals in the Censuses of 1900 and 1910 showed a different classification: the group "Personal and domestic services" is separate (Group 26) while the women who carried out domestic work for their families were assigned to Group 33, which also included individuals without a profession or of unknown profession; all the women who did not declare an occupation were included in this group.
30. The following groups were considered non-productive: Residents of hospices and hospitals, the insane and feeble; Prisoners and the incarcerated; Beggars, vagabonds, and prostitutes; Individuals without a profession, and Students. Prologue to the publication of volume V of the Census of 1920, viii.
31. The United States was the first country to introduce the concepts of active and inactive to the population census, in 1820. For more, see Topalov, "Une revolution," 465.
32. For a comparison of the data of female activity in the national censuses of the population and in the statistics of the Municipality of Barcelona, see Cristian Borderías, "Women and Work in Barcelona, 1856–1936," in *Red Barcelona: Social Protest and Labor Mobilization in the Twentieth Century*, ed. Angel Smith (London: Routledge, 2002), 142–66.
33. We fully concur with the limits of social statistics as a historical source as pointed out by Scott: "Thus collecting population statistics according to households (rather than, say, villages or places of work) reveals and constructs (while it may also call into question) a certain vision of social organization based on a particular idea of the family. At the same time, of course, it does tell us how many people inhabited a town, city or state. To take the numbers as the only reality of those statistics, however, denies the role that classification and interpretation play in the construction of reality—the reality contemporaries experienced

as well as the different reality we may want to impute to their lives." Scott, "Statistical Representations of Work," 338.
34. *La Monografía Estadística sobre la clase Obrera de Barcelona en 1856* (*Statistical Monograph of the Working Class of Barcelona in 1856*), which elaborated on the basis of information from the workers' associations of Barcelona and other municipal sources, was the work of engineer and urban planner Ildefons Cerdà and was published for the first time as an appendix to his *Teoría de la construcción de las ciudades aplicada al proyecto de reforma y ensanche de Barcelona* (Madrid: Imprenta Española, 1867) (*Theory of the Construction of Cities Applied to the Project of Reform and Extension of Barcelona*); it is also included in the more recent *Teoría de la construcción de las ciudades. Cerdà y Barcelona* (Madrid/Barcelona, Instituto Nacional de la Administración Pública/Ayuntamiento de Barcelona, 1991), 256ff.
35. *Monografía estadística de la clase obrera de Barcelona en 1856,* 581.
36. Living expenses were calculated on the basis of subsistence cost for the couple and two children for a forty-year family cycle.
37. 10 *reales* per week supposes 424 per year and 1.57 per day during 365 days per year.
38. *Monografía estadística de la clase obrera de Barcelona en 1856,* 581.
39. *Anuario Estadístico Municipal de Barcelona,* 1905, 151.
40. Ibid., 152.
41. Ibid.
42. *Anuario Estadístico Municipal de Barcelona,* 1917.
43. Ibid.
44. Ibid.
45. These were: miners working in the construction sector, tailors, silversmith-jewelers and the most qualified employees in the most prestigious shops. According to the municipal statistics, they could balance the family budget of 56.35 pesetas per week if they worked 269 days per year.
46. For a reconstruction of female activity in the city of Barcelona, see Borderías, "Women and Work in Barcelona."

References

Anderson, Margo. "The History of Women and the History of Statistics." *Journal of Women's History* 4, no. 1 (1992): 14–36.

Borderías, Cristina. "Women and Work in Barcelona, 1856–1936." In *Red Barcelona: Social Protest and Labor Mobilization in the Twentieth Century,* edited by Angel Smith, 142–66. London: Routledge, 2002.

———. "La transición de la actividad femenina en el mercado de trabajo barcelonés (1856–1930): Teoría social y realidad histórica en el sistema estadístico moderno." In *¿Privilegios o eficiencia? Mujeres y hombres en los mercados de trabajo,* edited by Carmen Sarasúa and Lina Gálvez, 241–76. Alicante: Publicaciones de la Universidad de Alicante, 2003.

———. "Revisiting Women's Labor Force Participation in Catalonia (1920–1936)." *Feminist Economics* 19, no. 4 (2013): 224–42.

Cerdà, Ildefons. *Monografía estadística de la clase obrera en Barcelona en 1856, Teoría general de la urbanización y aplicación de sus principios y doctrinas a la reforma y ensanche de Barcelona.* Madrid: Imprenta Española, 1867.

Folbre, Nancy. "The Unproductive Housewife: Her Evolution in Nineteenth-Century Economic Thought." *Signs: Journal of Women in Culture and Society* 16, no. 3 (1991): 463–84.

———. *Greed, Lust, and Gender: A History of Economic Ideas.* Oxford: Oxford University Press, 2009.
Folbre, Nancy, and Marjory Abel. "Women's Work and Women's Households: Gender Bias in the U.S. Census." *Social Research* 56, no. 3 (1989): 545–69.
Grantham, George. "Occupation, Marital Status and Life-Cycle Determinants of Women's Labor Force Participation in Mid-nineteenth-Century Rural France." *EHES Working Papers in Economic History* 22 (July 2012).
Hakim, Catherine. "Census Reports as Documentary Evidence: The Census Commentaries, 1801–1951." *Sociological Review* 28, no. 3 (1980): 551–80.
Higgs, Edward. "Women, Occupations and Work in the Nineteenth Century Censuses." *History Workshop*, no. 23 (1987): 59–80.
Patriarca, Silvana. "Gender Trouble: Women and the Making of Italy's Active Population, 1861–1936." *Journal of Modern Italian Studies* 3, no. 2 (1998): 144–63.
Pérez-Fuentes, Pilar. "El trabajo de las mujeres en los siglos XIX y XX: Consideraciones metodológicas." *Arenal* 2, no. 2 (1995): 219–45.
Pescarolo, Alessandra. "Asimmetrie di genere e opacità teoriche nella costruzione statistica dell'economia di mercato." In *Il percorso storico della statistica nell'Italia unita: atti del workshop – Roma, 7 giugno 2011*, edited by Dora Marucco and Aurea Micali, 95–108. Roma: Istat, 2013.
Sarti, Raffaella. "Work and Toil: Breadwinner Ideology and Women's Work in 19th and 20th Century Italy." Paper presented at the international conference *Women, Work and the Breadwinner Ideology*, Salzburg, 10–11 December 1999. Available online at http://www.uniurb.it/scipol/drs_work_and_ toil.pdf.
———. "Promesse mancate e attese deluse: spunti di riflessione su lavoro domestico e diritti in Italia." In *Il lavoro cambia*, edited by Ariella Verrocchio and Elisabetta Vezzosi, 55–77. Trieste: Eut, 2014. Also available at http://hdl.handle.net/10077/9764.
Scott, Joan Wallach. "Statistical Representations of Work: The Politics of the Chamber of Commerce's Statistique de l'Industrie à Paris, 1847–48." In *Work in France: Representations, Meaning, Organization, and Practice*, edited by Stephen Laurence Kaplan and Cynthia J. Koepp, 335–63. Ithaca, NY: Cornell University Press, 1986.
———. "'L'Ouvrière! Mot Impie, Sordide . . .': Women Workers in the Discourse of French Political Economy, 1840–1860." In *The Historical Meanings of Work*, edited by Patrick Joyce, 119–42. Cambridge: Cambridge University Press, 1987.
Topalov, Christian. "Une révolution dans les réprésentations du travail: L'émergence de la catégorie statistique de 'population active' au XIXème en France, en Grand-Bretagne et aux États-Unis." *Revue Française de Sociologie* XL, no. 3 (1999): 445–73.

CHAPTER 5

TOILING WOMEN, NON-WORKING HOUSEWIVES, AND LESSER CITIZENS
Statistical and Legal Constructions of Female Work and Citizenship in Italy

Raffaella Sarti

1. Introduction

"Italy is a Democratic Republic founded on work": article 1 of the Italian Constitution (1948) mirrors a concept of work as a source of rights that was developed over a long period of time. In this chapter I will analyze in a gender perspective whether the seemingly universal notion of work referred to in the first article of the Italian Constitution includes every form of work or whether, on the contrary, some activities typically performed by women, such as domestic and care work (both paid and unpaid) were (and are) excluded.

I will pay attention to the statistical construction of housewives as economically passive, and to the construction of domestic work as "non-work," i.e. on what we can define as the "delaborization" of domestic work.

I will conclude the chapter with some thoughts on the so-called feminization of work and the process by which the trend toward a kind of "ennobling of work" is currently reversing and many types of work are in a sense becoming "servile" again.

2. Conflicting notions of work

> If any Subject should wish . . . to be promoted *ex integro* to the Order of Nobles . . . the Supplicant will prove that neither he nor his father has practised a manual Craft or debased his own name or used his trademark in Craft for at least thirty years. . . . And if this person . . . once admitted to the Order of Nobles should personally exercise a Craft, prejudicial to the Nobility, either in his own Dwelling or with his Trademark, or by being employed in a Ministry or Office unbecoming to the dignity of an honest living, or to a Noble in the customs of the Country, he will immediately be struck off the Order of Nobles.[1]

This quotation is an extract from a measure taken in 1726 by the authorities in the Italian city of Bologna, then in the Papal State. It allows me to recall that, to varying degrees, the different European nobilities of the Ancien Régime considered being a rentier—or at least not practicing any "mechanical craft" personally—a feature essential (although not sufficient) to be included in their ranks, which implied enjoying rights and privileges denied to other people: in a sense, those who could afford to live without working were in a better position than those who worked.[2] "The aristocracy, the *literati* and the men in power have traditionally had contempt for those who must work. The good life was the life of leisure," one author wrote, summarizing such an attitude,[3] widespread among the early modern European élites, even though there were also differences among them according to place, time, and social group.

In early modern times, as shown in the introduction of this volume, many different notions of work did exist. In the cities, artisans usually shared a positive view of work, seen as an essential component of their individual and collective identities. In urban societies work was important for the definition of many social groups and institutions, often playing a crucial role in the access to citizenship and to the political and/or economic rights.[4]

From the late eighteenth century onward, a growing number of thinkers stressed the importance of work for the economic growth and well-being of the nation, refusing the notion of work as toil to be avoided. This view implied stigmatizing the (alleged) idleness of the aristocracy and (in part) of the clergy. The struggle against the nobility and its values, and the rising of the bourgeoisie, contributed to placing a higher value on work. "Work is sacred and is a source of Italy's wealth," the revolutionary Giuseppe Mazzini maintained in 1860, for instance.[5] Yet, work was increasingly seen not only as a welcome source of wealth but also as a source of individual dignity and rights.[6]

Italy as a united country started to exist in 1861 (as a kingdom; it would become a republic after the Second World War). In a sense, in the Kingdom of Italy, it is possible to date the beginning of the legal transformation of labor into a source of rights back to 1882. In that year, a new Code of Commerce was introduced and the franchise was extended. The new electoral law lowered voting requirements in such a way that all those who paid taxes on revenues which derived from their work as employees (and/or had a two-year primary school certificate) were enfranchised. The citizens enjoying suffrage rose from slightly over six hundred thousand to over two million, i.e. 6.9 percent of the population.[7] In short, work began "to be considered as a criterion for being included among those whose full rights were recognized."[8] The transformation of work into a source of rights proceeded slowly and irregularly[9]—Italy experienced Fascism for over twenty years.[10] However, article 1 of the Constitution of the Italian Republic, which came into force on 1 January 1948, eventually made work the very foundation of the republic itself.[11] While dealing with such a transformation, we can wonder whether every kind of work experienced such a valorization.

3. The statistical construction of the (non-working) housewife

The introduction to this volume discussed changing attitudes toward housework and home-based activities, showing that from the late eighteenth century onward they were increasingly seen by many European and American economists, statisticians, politicians, and eventually ordinary people, too, as something different from proper work. A process that could be defined as "delaborization" of home-based (mainly female) work took place.

In this chapter I will focus on the Italian case. I will first consider population censuses. Discussions on women's classification provided by census officials offer an interesting vantage point to grasp the changing attitude toward working women and the growing emphasis on the alleged female domestic destiny. These discussions and the connected decisions not only uncover ideas about women and their contribution to the economy, they also provide a statistical representation of the nation according to those ideas, and such a representation helps in turn to put those very ideas into practice: censuses not only offer a representation of society, they also contribute to shape it. It is thus not surprising that, in the last fifty years, they have been the subject of growing interest by researchers. While in a first phase the main aim was to correct "distortions,"[12] later the very construction of categories has been seen as a telling subject to be investigated.[13] The case of housewives is especially revealing.

Interestingly, the Italian term *casalinga*, corresponding to the English word "housewife," was attested as a noun in the Italian language only at the beginning of the twentieth century (earlier on it was used only as an adjective). The Italian language actually had and still has another, ancient, term to indicate housewives: *massaia*.[14] Yet, in the first Italian censuses, we cannot find either the term *massaia* or the term *casalinga*. In the tables of the 1861 census there was no specific data about housewives: only by reading the comments could one learn that the so-called *donne di casa* (another way to describe *housewives*, which literally means "women of the house") were included among people without a profession (*Popolazione senza professione*) and numbered 2,916,491.[15] Even ten years later, the census tables did not show any data about housewives, and in this case the text did not provide any information either. However, the *General Report* of the 1881 Census explained that in the 1871 Census, only 393,039 women were classified as "People attending to domestic tasks" (*Persone attendenti alle cure domestiche*), whereas some 4 million women were classified as people "Without a profession."[16]

Starting with the census of 1881, a category defined as "People attending to domestic tasks" (*Persone attendenti alle cure domestiche*[17]) was regularly included in the categories used to classify Italians according to their activities. An excerpt from the *General Report* relating to the 1881 Census illustrated the "serious difficulties" in the "classification of women by trade, especially in rural areas." In many cases,

> the mother or daughter of an innkeeper, a tailor, a hat maker or a cobbler helps her husband or father in carrying out his trade, serving the guests at the inn, sewing seams on clothes or shoes and hems on hats etc., while at the same time attending to domestic tasks; the same can be said for haberdashers and shopkeepers etc. engaged in retail trade. Besides taking care of the vegetable garden and domestic chores, the woman often takes up spinning linen, hemp, cotton and wool etc. on behalf of others in her own home. In these cases, a doubt may arise as to whether she should be classified as a housewife, that is, according to the occupation which by necessity takes up the greater part of her day, or as a gardener or spinner.[18]

The professional categories of the censuses were mainly shaped on workers with single, well-defined jobs.[19] Such categories were unsuited to classify those who performed several activities, as was the case for some men and a huge number of women who toiled at many activities: unpaid care and domestic tasks for their families; unpaid work for the family business; paid work, performed at home or elsewhere. How could they be placed in mono-professional categories? Solving the problem in one way or another led to highly different results, as illustrated by comparing the criteria adopted in 1881 and 1901 on the one hand and the results of the two censuses on the other.[20]

In 1881, women carrying out multiple activities were included among workers.[21] In 1901, the solution was a different one. The criteria adopted then represent an excellent demonstration of how ideas on the proper roles of men and women and their changes over time affect the representation of socioeconomic reality provided by censuses.[22] As explained in the *General Report*, individuals were classified "according to the profession practised, instead of according to their condition." So far, the decision was not innovative at all: the 1881 Census had followed the same pattern. Therefore, a person who had declared that he was a pensioner and a scribe had been classified as a scribe, as the state of pensioner was considered to be a condition and that of a scribe a profession; lawyer capitalists were classified among lawyers and not among capitalists, and so on.[23] "Conversely," added the reporters, "if a woman had declared that she was in charge of domestic tasks and was also engaged in secondary activities such as spinning or weaving linen or hemp or wool or doing some sewing for herself or others, it was her housekeeping charge that was considered as her main occupation." "The profession of spinner and weaver or seamstress," they explained, "appears only in the classification as an accessory profession."[24] In the same way, the women who besides attending to their families performed some paid work at home, in a factory, or as servants had been classified not as workers but in the category of the "People supported by the family" (*Persone mantenute dalla famiglia*[25]). In these cases, too, their occupations had been put "in the classification of accessory professions."[26] While in 1881 women performing multiple activities had been considered as workers, in 1901 the choice was fundamentally the opposite, especially if we consider that the data on accessory professions was not even analytically sorted in the census.[27]

Thus, over time, there was a growing tendency to classify men and women according to different criteria. When people could be classified by condition or by profession, men were always classified by profession, whereas in the case of women an ambiguous distinction was introduced, hitherto unknown, between accessory activities and major activities (in the case of men, this distinction was acknowledged only when the individual had two professions). For men, it was enough to practice any type of activity in order to be classified among what would later be defined as economically active population. Conversely, for women, carrying out other activities, even paid ones, besides care and domestic work, was no longer enough to avoid being classified as housewives, who were included among the economically passive population.[28]

Generally, at that time, proper work was increasingly associated with paid work. Yet, even this trend was gendered, and the importance of payment was not the same for men and women. Proper work was actually associated with males rather than with females, and this association was stronger, it seems, than that with remuneration. As shown below, men might be considered as workers even when they were not paid, whereas women might be considered housewives even when they performed paid activities. Work was indeed being established as an essential component in the identity of all men, while in the case of women things were much more confused and uncertain. However, after the rather contradictory experimentations of the 1860s and 1870s, women were increasingly included in the category of the "People attending to domestic tasks," i.e. people whom we would define as housewives. The housewife was becoming the typical female profile, while the worker was the typical male one. This is also confirmed by the fact that unemployed adult men (as well as elderly men no longer able to work but not formally retired and male inmates condemned to prison for less than ten or, in other periods, five years) were for a long time generally classified according to the last job they had performed, whereas unemployed women supported by their families were classified as housewives.[29]

However, this trend took some time, and for some decades the very features of the "People attending to domestic tasks" were not well-defined: surprisingly, from 1881 up to 1911, some men were classified in this category, too (men were the 0.03 percent in 1881; 1.9 percent in 1901; 1.5 percent in 1911).[30] Thereafter, this category was definitely established as a category including only women.[31] As late as 1961, it was eventually replaced by that of *Casalinga* (housewife) even though in the instructions and explanations accompanying the censuses the word *casalinga* had been used much earlier.[32] The variety of terms that could be used to define housewives, and the fact that men, too, until 1911 were among the "People attending to domestic tasks" indicate that, for quite a long time, the notion of housewife was rather blurred, and far from obvious (from the 2001 Census, some men have again started to be included in the housewives category, by then declined both in the feminine form [*casalinga*] and the masculine one [*casalingo*: a neologism, as a noun]) (table 5.1).[33] Not surprisingly, in the light of all these changes, the trend in the number of what we would define as *casalinghe* turned out to be awkward and unrealistic (figure 5.1).

Table 5.1. Classification of women whom we would define as "housewives" in the Italian population censuses.

Census	Classification of housewives (a) Italian original definition	Classification of housewives (a) English translation	Larger category including (a) Italian original definition	Larger category including (a) English translation	Men in the "housewives" category: yes/no	Volume and page
1861	[*Donne di casa*[a]]	[Women of the house[a]]	*Popolazione senza professione*	People without a profession	—	P. 106
1871	No information [*Persone attendenti alle cure domestiche*[b]]	No information [People attending to domestic tasks[b]]	No information [*Categoria 17a: 1° Personale a carico altrui 2° Popolazione senza professione*]	No information [17th category: 1. Personnel supported by others 2. People without a profession]	—	Vol. III, pp. 176–77; C1881, *Relazione generale*, p. LXIX
1881	*Attendenti alle cure domestiche*	People attending to domestic tasks	*Categoria XIX. - Senza professione. Gruppo unico:* 1. *Allievi delle università, dei licei, dei convitti e di altre scuole* 2. *Attendenti alle cure domestiche* 3. *Ricoverati negli ospizi di mendicità, ospedali, manicomi, ecc.*	19th category - People without a profession. Unique group: 1. University students, secondary-school students, boarding-schools students, pupils of any other schools 2. People attending to domestic tasks 3. People in charity hostels, hospitals, asylums, etc.	Yes	Vol. III, p. 15, pp. 668–69

1901	*Persone attendenti alle cure domestiche, donne di casa*	People attending to domestic tasks, women of the house	*Classe XXXIII. - Persone mantenute dalla famiglia:* 1. *Persone attendenti alle cure domestiche, donne di casa* 2. *Studenti, scolari, seminaristi, collegiali* 3. *Persone senza professione (disoccupate da molto tempo o inabili al lavoro)*	Class XXXIII. - People supported by their families: 1. People attending to domestic tasks, women of the house 2. Students, pupils, seminarians, school boarders 3. People without a profession (the long-term unemployed or people unable to work)	Yes	Vol. III, p. 31
1911	*Persone attendenti alle cure delle rispettive case*	People attending to the care of their homes	*Categoria 11. Condizioni non professionali:* *Proprietari, capitalisti, benestanti, redditieri* *Pensionati* *Persone attendenti alle cure delle rispettive case* *Studenti, scolari, seminaristi, collegiali* *Senza professione, disoccupati, invalidi* *Ricoverati che non lavorano* *Detenuti che non lavorano* *Mendicanti e prostitute*	Category 11. Non-professional conditions: Owners, capitalists, wealthy people, rentiers Pensioners People attending to the care of their homes Students, pupils, seminarians, school boarders People without a profession, unemployed, invalids Hospitalized persons who do not work Inmates who do not work Beggars and prostitutes	Yes	Vol. IV, pp. 30–31; vol. VII, p. 129,

(*continued*)

Table 5.1. Continued

Census	Classification of housewives (a) Italian original definition	Classification of housewives (a) English translation	Larger category including (a) Italian original definition	Larger category including (a) English translation	Men in the "housewives" category: yes/no	Volume and page
1921	*Persone attendenti alle cure domestiche*	People attending to domestic tasks	*Condizioni non professionali ... Classe 46, Sottoclasse 184 Attendenti alle cure domestiche*[c]	Non-Professional Conditions[c] ... Class 46, Subclass 184 People attending to domestic tasks[c]	No	Vol. XIX p. 188*
1931	*Persone attendenti alle cure domestiche*	People attending to their domestic affairs	*Condizioni non professionali ... Classe 54, Numero d'ordine 333, Numero convenzionale 9, Attendenti alle cure domestiche*[d]	Non-professional conditions ... Class 54, Order number 333, Conventional number 9, People attending to domestic tasks[d]	No	Vol. IV, Parte II, p. 246
1936	*Persone attendenti alle cure domestiche*	People attending to domestic tasks	*Condizioni non professionali ... Classe 72, Sottoclasse 399, Attendenti alle cure domestiche*[e]	Non-professional conditions ... Class 72, Subclass 399, People attending to domestic tasks[e]	No	Vol. IV, Parte II, pp. 66–67
1951	*Persone attendenti alle cure domestiche*	People attending to their domestic affairs	*Popolazione residente non attiva ... Attendenti alle cure domestiche*[f]	Inactive resident population ... People attending to domestic tasks[f]	No	Vol. IV, p. 78
1961	*Casalinghe*	Housewives	*Popolazione non attiva ... Casalinghe*[g]	Inactive population ... Housewives[g]	No	Vol. VI, p. 10

Year						
1971	Casalinghe	Housewives	Popolazione non attiva … Casalinghe[h]	Inactive population … Housewives[h]	No	Vol. VI, Tomo 2, p. 531; Vol. X, p. 193
1981	Casalinghe	Housewives	Popolazione non attiva Scolari e studenti Casalinghe Ritirati dal lavoro Altra condizione	Inactive population: Pupils and students Housewives Retired from work Other condition	No	Vol. II, Tomo 3, p. xxiv, pp. 307–11
1991	Casalinghe	Housewives	Popolazione non attiva: Scolari e studenti Casalinghe Ritirati dal lavoro Altri	Inactive population: Pupils and students Housewives Retired from work Others	No	*Popolazione e abitazioni, Fascicolo n azionale Italia*, p. 41, p. 173
2001	Casalinghe/i	Female and male housewives	Non forze di lavoro (studenti, casalinghe/i e ritirati dal lavoro)	Non-labor force (students, female and male housewives, retired from work)	Yes	*C2001, La condizione professionale ed il mercato del lavoro in Italia al 21 Ottobre 2001. Dati definitivi* http://dawinci .istat.it
2011	Casalinga/o	Female and male housewife	Non forze di lavoro percettore-rice di una o più pensioni per effetto di attività lavorativa precedente o di redditi da capitale Studente-ssa Casalinga-o In altra condizione	Non-labor force People receiving one or more pensions from previous employment or capital revenues Male and female student Female and male housewife Other condition	Yes	http://dati-censimento popolazione .istat.it

Sources: Italian population censuses, 1861–2011.

(*continued*)

Notes

Punctuation follows that of the original censuses.

a. The definition is not used in the tables, it is only used in the comments.

b. No information provided in the 1871 Census. The *General Report* of the 1881 Census explained that in the 1871 Census only 393,039 women were classified as "people attending to domestic tasks" (*persone attendenti alle cure domestiche*), whereas some four million women were classified as people without a profession.

c. Includes several classes (from 43 to 48) and subclasses (from 180 to 190) that are almost the same as the list of 1911. Class 46 and subclass 184 only refer to people attending to domestic tasks.

d. Class 54 only includes number 9, which in turn only includes number 333, whereas in other cases one single class includes several numbers. The category "Non- professional conditions" in this census does not include owners and rich people (capitalists, rentiers, etc.), whereas, besides housewives, it still included pensioners, pupils and students, people without a profession, invalids, hospitalized persons, inmates, beggars, and prostitutes.

e. Class 72 only includes subclass 399. In this census, capitalists, rentiers and the like are again included among non-professional conditions, and a new heading, "first-time jobseekers," appears (subclass 410).

f. The inactive resident population includes first-time jobseekers, students, people attending to domestic tasks, owners and wealthy people, pensioners, people unable to work, sick people, hospitalized people, inmates, beggars, and other non-professional conditions (prostitutes were no longer explicitly mentioned but were included among the inactive population; see *C1951*, vol. 7, *Dati generali riassuntivi* (Roma: Istat, 1958), 8.

g. The inactive population classified according to their non-professional conditions includes housewives; students; owners and rich people; clerical and religious people in non-professional conditions; sick, invalid, and hospitalized people; and other non-professional conditions. In this census (and the next ones), first-time jobseekers are classified among the active population.

h. The inactive population classified according to their non-professional conditions includes housewives; students; owners and rich people; clerical and religious people in non-professional conditions; sick, invalid, and hospitalized people; and other non-professional conditions.

The explanations of many censuses made clear how long one had to be imprisoned, hospitalized, etc., to be included in the non-working population. Since the focus of this chapter is on housewives, I have not reported such information here.

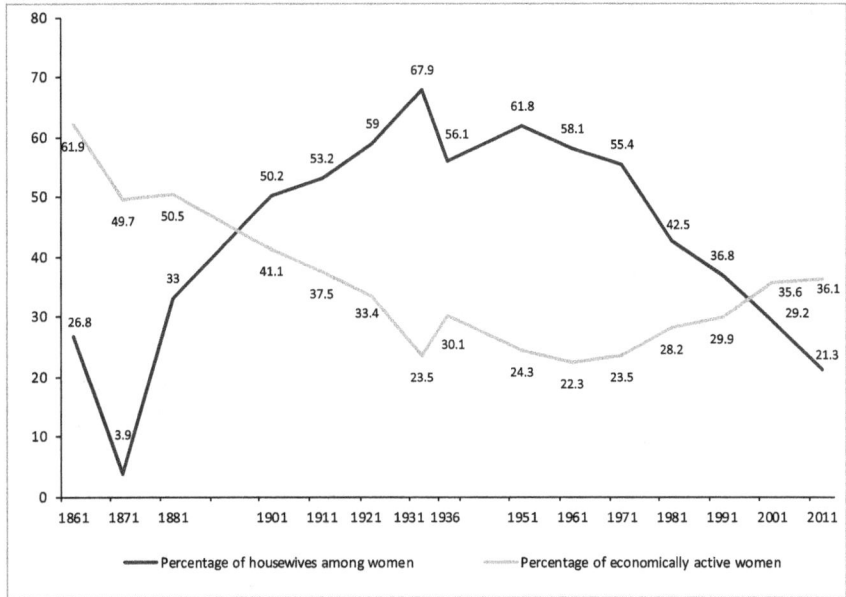

Figure 5.1. Percentages of housewives and economically active women among women, Italy, 1861–2011. Sources: Italian population censuses, 1861–2011 (original census data).

Notes:
The definition of "active population" was definitely adopted in the censuses from 1936. The figure of active women for 1861 is calculated by subtracting from the total number of women those classified in the "Proprietors" (*Possidenti*), "Poor" (*Poveri*), and "Without profession" (*Senza professione*) categories. For the year 1871, the figure is calculated by subtracting from the total number of women those included in the seventeenth category, i.e. "Personnel supported by others" (*Personale a carico altrui*) and people "Without profession" (*Senza professione*), as well as those included in the fifth category ("Property and Real Estate"). The definition of "active population" was systematically used in Italian censuses from 1936. For the censuses from 1881 to 1961, see Ornello Vitali, *Aspetti dello sviluppo economico italiano alla luce della ricostruzione della popolazione attiva* (Roma: Failli, 1970), 326–27. Data for 1961–1991 refers to economically active population in a professional condition (*Popolazione attiva in condizione professionale*), which coincides with the category of active population in previous censuses. In 2001 and 2011, such category was replaced by that of labor forces (*Forze di lavoro*), which is different because it also includes first-time jobseekers; however, a category comparable to the previous ones can be calculated.

The age groups considered are those on which professional classifications are based in each census. The classification of the population by profession includes people aged nine and over in 1881 and 1901; aged ten and over from 1911 to 1961; aged fourteen and over in 1971, 1981, and 1991; aged fifteen and over in 2001. In 1861 and 1871, the classification of the population by profession did not exclude children, if they worked; in order to calculate the percentage of active women and housewives, I have considered only the population aged ten and over.

From 1861 to 1936, the professional classification referred to the present population (*Popolazione presente*); from 1951 onward, it referred to the resident population.

The percentage of active women differs from the female activity rate, defined by Istat as the ratio between people belonging to the labor force and the population aged fifteen and over. Indeed, the active population (or active population in professional condition in the period 1961–2001) and the labor forces categories do not coincide.

As for the category of the housewives, see table 5.1.

The census officers themselves were aware of the problem. "These very serious differences . . . cannot represent a change which has taken place in occupations among the female population, but depend on different criteria followed in the classification," they wrote, comparing the data for the 1881 Census with that for 1871.[34] When, at the beginning of the twentieth century, it was decided to classify many women according to their condition—which normally meant classifying them as "People attending to domestic tasks"—the numbers of the latter increased dramatically: between 1881 and 1901, according to the census data, the percentage of housewives among all females aged nine and over jumped from 33 to 50.2 percent.[35] Again, the census reporters themselves were conscious of the fact that this (mainly) depended on the different criteria adopted in the two. Illustrating the characteristics of the category "People supported by the family" (*Persone mantenute dalla famiglia*), they wrote:

> This class concerns those people who take care of domestic tasks (mostly women), students and schoolchildren and invalids or those unemployed for a long time. In 1882, there were 4,658,086 individuals and in 1901 there were 8,355,733. The increase depended on the fact that in 1882 many women taking care of domestic tasks were classified as people without a profession; those who besides attending to their family carried out sewing or domestic spinning or weaving, or were temporary servants [*serve avventizie*], or were manufacturers [*industrianti*], were counted as seamstresses, spinners, weavers, day-laborers, or servants; whereas in 1901 these occupations were put in the classification of accessory professions.[36]

In fact, various indicators suggest that, in those years, the number of women engaged in paid extra-domestic work was diminishing, although not as dramatically as one would think by looking at the census data.[37] But it was not easy to distinguish socioeconomic changes from the cultural and ideological ones that implied new ways of classifying women's and men's activities. Already fifty years ago, Ornello Vitali tried to pinpoint only the socioeconomic changes, neutralizing the effects of different classifications. According to his corrected data, the percentages of women in the total economically active population were decreasing, but their percentages were higher than the percentages calculated from the original census data (figure 5.2). Obviously, even corrections imply a precise ideology: for instance, if they simply aim to establish the exact number of housewives, and continue to classify housewives as economically inactive population. If we consider that practically all women did (and do) some kind of housework, we can easily understand how difficult it is to establish a clear boundary between housewives and "working" women. In a sense, any criterion to distinguish "working" women from housewives is "ideological."

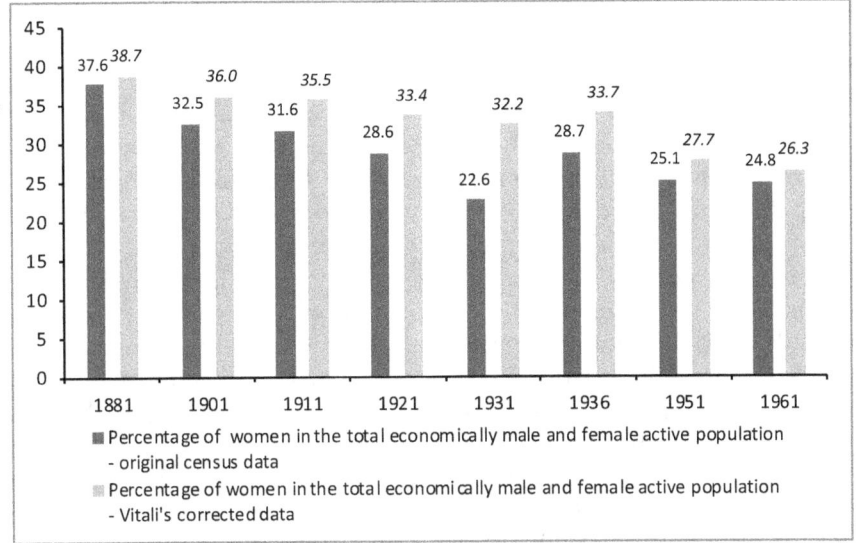

Figure 5.2. Percentage of women in the Italian male and female active population, 1881–1961. Source: Ornello Vitali, *Aspetti dello sviluppo economico italiano alla luce della ricostruzione della popolazione attiva* (Roma: Failli, 1970).

However, in the period when Italian legislation started to recognize work as a source of rights, women were less likely to be considered as proper workers. At the same time, being a housewife and "not to work" was presented as an ideal to pursue, as if—for women—work were still as debasing as it had been for centuries for the élites. Yet, while in early modern times the élites who could afford not to work enjoyed more rights than other people, in the nineteenth and twentieth centuries, rights and status were increasingly associated with work. Even more paradoxically, "non-working" housewives often actually toiled all day. However, inasmuch as some women became convinced that being a housewife and "not to work" was a privilege, they were likely to hide their occupations to census officers and to declare themselves as housewives, thus contributing to the statistical overrepresentation of housewives.

Censuses following that of 1901 also highlighted the domestic work done by women. The percentage of housewives among women aged ten years and over increased until 1931, when it reached 67.9 percent (figure 5.1). According to Vitali's calculations, as many as 2.35 million women who should be included in the active population were then classified as housewives instead.[38] Things went differently in 1936. Even though Fascism discouraged female employment,[39] in this case census officials were instructed not to classify rural women as housewives straightway, but to verify which activities they performed, because it was "absolutely indispensable" that the census showed the "actual efficiency" of the workforce employed in agriculture.[40] These instructions mirrored the strengthening of the autarchic policy launched by Fascism as a reaction to the international sanctions decreed by the League of Nations against Italy following the Italian invasion of Ethiopia. According to the autarchy program, Italy should be able to feed its population without imports, and statistical data should demonstrate the high number of people working in agriculture. After a long period during which the percentage of housewives among women was increasing and that of active women was falling, the 1936 data showed a reversal of the trend.[41] This change was therefore probably due not only to the fact that some women were replacing men fighting as soldiers in the African war but also to this different classification. Housewives, among women of working age, reduced to 56.1 percent. Yet, in 1951, they grew again to 61.8 percent, and only thereafter started to decrease, reaching 21.3 percent in 2011 (a level for the first time lower than that reported in the first Italian census) (figure 5.1).

4. Work and rights for women

As shown in the previous section, when working increasingly became a condition that granted rights, women were more and more often classified as housewives, and housewifery was growingly seen as something different from proper work, though the process was all but simple and linear. Nonetheless, this does not mean that work represented a path of access to rights only for men. Certainly, in 1882, when the electoral law was reformed, the female sex remained "an insuperable obstacle," and women continued to be disenfranchised.[42] It was the same with the reform of 1912, which introduced universal suffrage for men. But after the First World War, the huge working effort made by women during the conflict was considered by many Italians as a good reason (alongside others) for introducing new rights for them. Still, in the end, female suffrage was not introduced (and Fascism would repeal the vote for men, too).[43] Italian women would be enfranchised as late as 1945.[44] At least, however, in 1919 a law was passed that introduced juridical capacity for married women, abolishing the need for the husband's authorization, and admitted women to professions and public employment, although with important exceptions and a subsequent restrictive application.[45] In a sense, the law of 1919 started Italian women's long and tortuous journey toward equality at work, eventually sanctioned in 1977 but still unachieved.[46]

Since the beginning of the twentieth century, other regulations—"protective" ones—had addressed women workers. Within certain limits, this implied acknowledging new rights, although often formulated as prohibitions. In 1902, a law was approved on children's and women's work,[47] which established twelve years as the minimum age to start working and did not allow women of any age to work underground or minors (later all women[48]) to work overnight. The maximum workload was established to be twelve hours a day for six days a week, with one rest day weekly; compulsory (but unpaid) maternity leave was introduced. Some years later, a maternity fund was also created: both women workers and their employers had to contribute to funding it.[49] Such measures associated adult women and children, contributing to represent females as minors and weak creatures. At the same time, they aimed at protecting and encouraging working women's maternal and family functions. Both because of the ideology they conveyed and because of the increase in costs to the employer they caused, they ended up by strengthening the centrality of women's maternal and family duties, which had been so often invoked to justify their exclusion from political rights.[50] Interestingly, female activists had divergent opinions on protective measures: as early as 1898, the republican feminist Anna Maria Mozzoni and the socialist Anna Kuliscioff clashed about them. According to Mozzoni, they represented a handicap for women workers, while according to Kuliscioff they mitigated children's and women's harsh working conditions and were the welcomed premise of a better life that would also be beneficial to the class struggle.[51]

However, these measures—just as the Fascist measures that would be developed later in order to achieve the regime's demographic objectives by means of a better protection of maternity[52]—were not applied to agricultural work, nor to industrial and commercial homework, nor to that for family businesses, nor to paid domestic work.[53] Thus, while on the one hand the lawmakers aimed to limit those types of work that, being performed outside the home, patently came into competition with women's domestic roles, on the other they ignored those types of work that, although performed within the domestic sphere, could have disastrous consequences for pregnancy, childbirth, and the baby. At the same time, such measures implied recognition by the state of the importance, for the nation, of maternity and therefore of women, although these measures chained females more closely to their alleged "natural" role as mothers.[54] Even this legislation, however, confirmed that it was *extra-domestic* work that provided women with some rights, also as far as carrying out their domestic roles was concerned. Work at home, even if paid, as that performed by domestic workers or home-based industrial workers, did not grant any right to maternity protection.

Fascism would discourage girls from improving their education and would introduce several measures—known as expulsive ones—to prevent women from taking on many directive, managerial, and qualified roles, including for instance teaching history in secondary schools (*licei*), in order to limit their presence in the labor market. Fascism would definitely marginalize female workers, condemning many of them to illegal and casual work.[55] In 1931, almost 68 percent of women aged ten and over were classified in population censuses as housewives, while between 1921 and 1931 the percentage of domestic workers among economically active women jumped from 7.2 to 11.4 percent (figure 5.3). In fact, in the 1930s, because of the crisis, war, and autarchic policies, neither many families nor the nation as a whole could afford to do without women's extra-domestic work, and the Second World War would make their contribution even more crucial. In 1936, as mentioned, the extent of female agricultural work was even statistically "highlighted" and "displayed" in the population census. At that time, however, women were largely ghettoized in poorly qualified and servile occupations.

5. Domestic work is work(?)

Paid domestic work is an interesting vantage point from which to test the gendered bias and the limits of the growing association of work with rights. Within the increasingly feminized domestic sphere,[56] the unpaid work of the housewife granted almost no rights, nor did the paid work of the domestic worker. The servant condition was traditionally ambiguous. As for domestic service as an occupation in a gendered perspective, on the one hand it increasingly became a paid activity for lower-class women[57]; yet, on the other hand, its profile as proper work remained ambiguous or probably became even more so as the "unproductive" and "non-working" housewife, who was supposed to care for her family for free out of love and allegedly "natural" inclinations, emerged and strengthened. Female servants were indeed paid for carrying out the "natural" unpaid duties of wives and mothers.[58]

A note in the report of the 1901 census is particularly revealing of such a perception, making clear that the "Economically passive population" (*Popolazione economicamente passiva*) included "the people not habitually employed in any work, such as a large part of the women, the children and the elderly, and those carrying out domestic service."[59] Female domestic servants—except for "temporary" ones (*serve avventizie*), classified as economically passive housewives[60]—were actually classified as

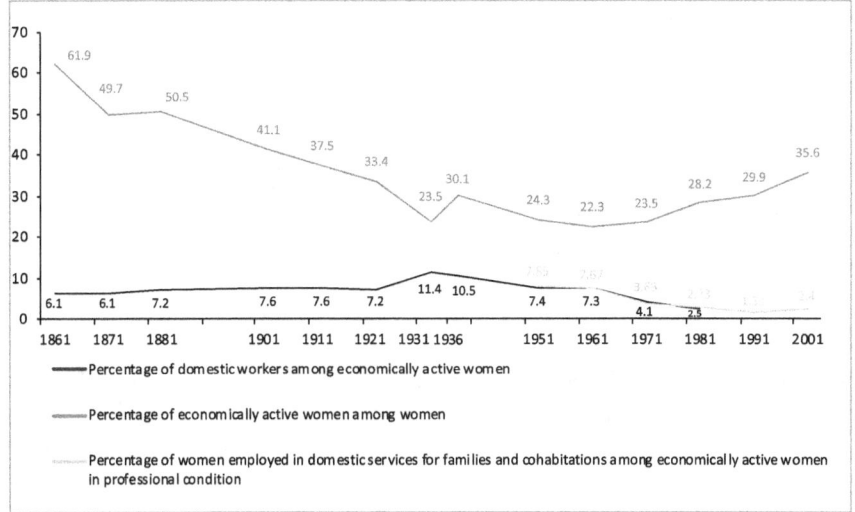

Figure 5.3. Percentage of economically active women among women and percentage of domestic workers among economically active women, Italy, 1861–2001. Sources: Italian population censuses, 1861–2011 (original census data).

Notes:
For the calculation of economically active women see figure 5.1.
On the changing classification of domestic workers, see Raffaella Sarti, "Da serva a operaia? Trasformazioni di lungo periodo del servizio domestico in Europa," *Polis: Ricerche e studi su società e politica in Italia* 19, no. 1 (2005): 91–120, appendix available at http://www.people.uniurb.it/RaffaellaSarti/Raffaella%20Sarti-Polis%202005,%20n.%201-Da%20serva%20a%20operaia%20(testo%20pubblicato%20online%20versione%20word).doc; Raffaella Sarti, "Conclusion: Domestic Service and European Identity," in *Proceedings of the Servant Project*, ed. Suzy Pasleau and Isabelle Schopp, with Raffaella Sarti (Liège: Éditions de l'Université de Liège, 2005), 5:195–284, appendix.
The 1991 census provides data at such an aggregation level that is impossible to locate domestic workers. Both for 1991 and 2001 only data *Servizi domestici presso famiglie e convivenze* ("Domestic services for families and cohabitations") are available, i.e. for families and institutions such as welfare institutions, prisons, and monasteries; such category also includes people who are not domestic workers. Nonetheless, data of such a category is used to construct a comparable series for the period 1951–2001. In the 1951 census, the category is called "Generic services" (*Servizi generici*) but coincides with that of "Domestic services for families and cohabitations" in the 1961 census. For 2011 no comparable category is available.

workers. Nonetheless, such an explanation unveils the ambiguous status of all domestics in the eyes of census officers.

Interestingly, according to authoritative jurists, a wife could be a servant only if her service was "compatible with the duties that she had toward her husband."[61] Similar statements were repeated even after the 1919 law that made married women less dependent on their husbands: as Luigi De Litala wrote in 1933, a husband had the right to "ask, *jure proprio*, as the head of the family, for the termination of the wife's work contract, if this contract should prove harmful to the fundamental duties of the married woman, that is, faithfulness, cohabitation and assistance to her husband."[62] As the duties of servants to their employers largely coincided with those of a wife to her husband, the work as a servant could clash with the family role of women even more than the modern factory jobs that worried the ruling classes. Ambiguity, however, also characterized the status of unmarried servants, especially because of the difficulty in distinguishing (in their own lives as in those of housewives) between working time and leisure, working spaces and domestic spaces.

The weak status as workers of domestics was also revealed by legislation.[63] As I have illustrated elsewhere,[64] the Italian lawmakers did not initially regulate domestic service as a particular institution. The articles of the Civil Code (1865–66) covering this matter merely stated that one of the "three major types of letting of labor and industry" was "that for which people oblige others to carry out their services" (article 1627) and that performing work could only be "for a limited period or for a determined undertaking" (article 1628).[65] The only concern was therefore that of eliminating the possible residues of personal subordination. The choice of limiting the regulation of domestic work to a few rules, subjecting it to general norms, in the end made resorting to traditions inevitable. And these traditions were based on profound and peculiar asymmetry between worker and employer. For example, servants, being accepted into the family, were expected to "follow its running and habits" and not to reveal its secrets,[66] to change residence at the "pleasure of their masters,"[67] to bear true *affectio* toward their employers,[68] to keep good conduct even beyond the domain of their work, in such a way as not to "upset the prestige of the family business." Even in 1933, the illegitimate pregnancy of a servant could thus be listed among the just causes of dismissal because it could harm "the esteem, honor and decorum of the employer and his family," whereas with factory workers it was not considered a reason for dismissal.[69]

Furthermore, domestics were excluded from most of the laws concerning work regulation or workers' protection, such as those on the work of minors and women and on the safeguard of maternity[70]; on the limitation of working hours to a maximum of eight per day and forty-eight, then forty, per week[71]; on collective wage agreements[72]; on the subjection of jurisdiction, in the case of dispute, to work tribunals established by the authorities[73]; on protection in case of involuntary unemployment; and so on[74]—the only provisions from which domestics benefited in the first forty years of the twentieth century were those of 1923 on compulsory insurance against invalidity and old age, extended in 1927 to tuberculosis.[75] Some limited regulation would be started by the Civil Code of

1942 (articles 2240–46), which introduced paid holidays and, though in limited cases, severance pay.[76] In the Kingdom of Italy, however, people working as domestics were granted almost no rights, and, by 1936, 95 percent of them were women, according to censuses (while this percentage was only 66 percent when Italy was unified).[77]

6. The Italian Republic: which citizenship for women?

As mentioned, on the 1 January 1948 the Constitution of the Italian Republic, which solemnly proclaimed that the republic itself was founded on work, became effective: it created a kind of overlap between being a worker and being a citizen. According to the data issued from the population census that took place a few years later (on 4 November 1951), only 24.3 percent of women of working age were economically active, i.e. fewer than one in four. "Women attending to domestic tasks are included in the non-professional conditions even though they occasionally or sporadically perform a working activity," the notes to the census explicated.[78] Elsewhere, this choice was explained even more clearly: "As for women attending to domestic tasks, it has to be noted that have been considered as such even those who, though carrying out a profession, craft or job, mainly carry out their activities in the home."[79] Among men, the proportion was reversed: fewer than one in four was registered as economically inactive; as many as 77 percent resulted economically active.[80] Such an imbalance announced a blatantly gender-biased citizenship at the expense of women. And, in the first years of the republic, the percentage of economically active women did not increase: on the contrary, it shrank to 22.3 percent in 1961, according to population censuses (figure 5.1).[81]

Such a trend in the years of what is known as the Italian economic miracle has prompted doubts and debates on the correctness of the data.[82] While population censuses might underestimate the number of working women, it is a fact that the large majority of women were registered as housewives; even if part of those "housewives" certainly carried out some paid activities, in most cases they surely performed irregular, precarious, casual activities that were not considered as proper work (by the census officers, their husbands, or the women themselves) and consequently were not recorded. In any case, the activities of such women—though unquestionably important or even vital for their families and for the nation as a whole—were something different from the work assumed by the constitution as the very foundation of citizenship and rights.

Furthermore, even some women officially registered as workers performed activities not often considered as proper work and were granted almost no rights, as was indeed the case with paid domestic work—about 7.5 percent of the economically active women, both in 1951 and 1961, according to the censuses, were employed as domestics (figure 5.2). However, in the 1950s and 1960s, new important rights were granted to domestic workers, such as (limited) maternity protection,[83] sickness insurance,[84] and thirteenth-month pay.[85] In 1958, an entire law was devoted to the regulation of paid domestic work (L. 2 April 1958, no. 339),[86] while, in 1969, the constitutional court would eventually declare as illegitimate the exclusion of domestic workers from collective bargaining established by article 2068 of the Civil Code: the first collective agreement would be signed in 1974.[87] In 1958, a law on home-based industrial workers was also introduced, which extended to them the same social security cover given to factory workers employed in the same sector and which regulated payment and workload (L. 13 March 1958, no. 264).[88] Women as a category were granted new rights in the labor market: particularly important were the law that allowed women to be magistrates (L. 9 February 1963, no. 66) and, later, the law on equality among women and men in the labor market (L. 9 December 1977, no. 903). On the one hand, there was growing state intervention aiming to regulate paid work performed within the domestic sphere, which slightly reduced the difference between home-based jobs and jobs performed in factories, shops, and offices. On the other hand, new opportunities of extra-domestic work opened up to women.

Yet many problems remained unsolved. Italy—despite the growing participation of women in the labor force—still has one of the lowest female activity rates in Europe.[89] Let us take the case of domestics. The 1958 law only regulated the minimum rest time and not the maximum working time, later regulated by national collective agreements, which for 2013–16 established the maximum working time, for live-ins, at as many as fifty-four hours per week (article 15). While the law prohibiting the dismissal of a pregnant worker dates back to 1929, even today the prohibition of dismissal during pregnancy and until the child has reached the age of one year is not valid in the case of domestic workers.[90] Only collective agreements have established that the workers cannot be dismissed, except for a just cause, from the beginning of pregnancy to the end of maternity leave, provided that pregnancy began after the beginning of the work contract with the employer (article 24). Other problems concern the limited rights to protection in case of illness and the low levels of pensions.[91] "Domestic work is work," was the slogan of the International Labour Organiation (ILO) campaign that in 2011 eventually led to the approval of convention 189 on decent work for domestic workers.[92] While the Italian laws on domestic work are far from being the worst ones in the world, they still present several problems, which confirms that (mainly) female employment in the domestic sphere, even paid, had and still has difficulty in being recognized as proper work, showing the gender-biased features of the transformation of work into a source of dignity and rights.

7. Feminization and servilization of work?

In the first forty years of the Italian Republic, several changes might suggest that a process was taking place, shrinking the cleavage between the opportunities offered to men and women respectively by the activities that they performed: the decrease in the number of domestic workers in the economically active population, after the peak reached in 1931; the decline in the percentage of housewives among women since 1951 and the increase in the percentage of active women after 1961, according to census data; the introduction of new rights concerning work for women in general and for women who performed paid work within the domestic sphere in particular, notably domestic workers and home-based industrial workers. It seemed that the work-based rights enjoyed by women and men were slowly becoming more similar and that Italy would eventually become the democratic republic promised by the constitution, i.e. founded on the acknowledged and dignified work of all its citizens.[93]

In a sense, as has happened with so many jobs that have lost their prestige when women have "conquered" them, the same seems to be happening with work in general—and I am speaking here of work for the market. In the last few years, new forms of paid but "atypical" jobs, different from the "proper" jobs that grant rights to workers, have emerged: these bring increasing precariousness, underemployment, and unemployment, not to mention the huge scope for the constant presence of "illegal work."

In the late 1990s, I argued that "until recently, committing oneself to reforming paid domestic work could seem almost superfluous," to the extent that paid domestic work seemed an archaic occupation destined to disappear thanks to progress and modernization, "whereas today [i.e. in the 1990s] the situation has profoundly changed: domestic service is indeed a sector destined to expand," "because of the growing life expectancy and the growing numbers of people in need of assistance; the increasing numbers of women performing extra-domestic jobs in a context of crises of the welfare state" (and with little change in men's commitment to caring for their families, I should have added); "and the growing economic and demographic imbalances between rich and poor countries."[94] Furthermore, noticing that domestic workers interviewed in a survey carried out in the 1970s turned out to be more frustrated than domestic workers interviewed in the 1990s, I suggested that this difference might be due to the worsening working conditions in the whole labor market, which made paid domestic work less "different" than it used to be. Not by chance had some scholars begun to define people performing unqualified and precarious occupations in the tertiary sector as "new servants."[95]

Since then, scholars, "metaphorically" or "realistically," more and more often speak of new servants[96] or even new slaves,[97] referring not only to the "resurgent" paid domestic workers[98] but also to workers in other sectors, especially immigrants. Sometimes these categories are also used to define more general transformations affecting work and the current conditions of (many different types of) workers.[99] Christian Marazzi may have been the first to speak of "servilization" of work.[100]

In addition to such processes of servilization of work, a recent category used to understand what is going on is that of work feminization.[101] For many people, work is increasingly flexible, intermittent, precarious, irregular, insecure, badly paid, a source of scarce or no rights, i.e. as it mainly used to be for women. This is often the case for Italians, and even more so for migrants, although being (regularly) employed—thus having proper work—allows migrants to get a residence permit.[102] Therefore, in a sense, the male and female conditions have become closer, at least in part, even though women continue to be disadvantaged. If this has happened, it is because working conditions that used to be peculiar to women more than to men are becoming increasingly ubiquitous, making work a toil granting few or no rights to larger groups of workers. More and more male and female workers are certainly asked to display with their customers caring behaviors, but often such behaviors are a matter of pure appearance, instrumental to increasing sales. Care work, despite many efforts to recognize it as crucial to society, remains undervalued, whereas, to reestablish the relationship between work and rights, it is necessary to establish a genuine caring democracy[103] giving much more importance to the work necessary to life.[104]

If Italy experiences today a profound crisis, it is due to a variety of causes and largely to phenomena that are happening on a global scale. However, the paradox of wanting to found a democratic state on work while a large share of the population—some men and the vast majority of women, according to the notion of work of the time—did not work has represented a bias with far-reaching negative consequences.

Raffaella Sarti teaches early modern history and gender history at the University of Urbino, Italy. She has also worked in Paris, Vienna, Bologna, and Murcia. She is a member of the editorial collective of *Gender & History*. Her studies address domestic service and care work; Mediterranean slavery; marriage and celibacy; family and material culture; gender and the nation; masculinity; graffiti. She is the author of approximately 150 publications in nine languages, including *Europe at Home: Family and Material Culture 1500–1800* (New Haven, CT: Yale University Press, 2002) and *Servo e padrone, o della (in)dipendenza: Un percorso da Aristotele ai nostri giorni* (Bologna: Alma Mater Studiorum Università di Bologna, 2015). She has edited "Men in a Woman's Job: Male Domestic Workers, International Migration and the Globalization of Care," with Francesca Scrinzi, special issue of *Men and Masculinities* 13, no. 1 (2010); "Men at Home: Domesticities, Authority, Emotions and Work," special issue of *Gender & History* 27, no. 3 (2015); *Familles laborieuses: Rémunération, transmission et apprentissage dans les ateliers familiaux de la fin du Moyen Âge à l'époque contemporaine en Europe*, with Anna Bellavitis and Manuela Martini, in *Mélanges de l'École française de Rome— Italie et Méditerranée modernes et contemporaines* 128, no. 1 (2016). For more details see http://www.uniurb.it/sarti/.

Notes

The research presented in this chapter started in the 1980s. For my previous contributions on the subject see below, note 13. English Revision by Clelia Boscolo. Abbreviations: Art./artt.=articolo/i (=Article, articles); Capo/cap.=capo/capitolo (=Chapter); *C1861=Censimento generale (31 dicembre 1861)* (=Population Census of 1861); *C1871=Censimento 31 dicembre 1871* (=Population Census of 1871); *C1881=Censimento della popolazione del Regno d'Italia al 31 dicembre 1881* (=Population Census of 1881); *C1901=Censimento della popolazione del Regno al 10 febbraio 1901* (=Population Census of 1901); *C1911=Censimento della Popolazione del Regno d'Italia al 10 giugno 1911* (=Population Census of 1911); *C1936=VIII Censimento generale della popolazione 21 aprile 1936-XIV* (=Population Census of 1936); *C1951=IX Censimento generale della popolazione, 4 novembre 1951* (=Population Census of 1951; D.l.=Decreto legge (a kind of law); DGS=Direzione Generale della/di Statistica (=Central Office of Statistics); Istat=Istituto Nazionale di Statistica (National Institute for Statistics); L.=Legge (=Law); MAIC= Ministero di Agricoltura, Industria e Commercio (=Ministry for Agriculture, Industry, and Trade); R.d.=Regio decreto (=Royal decree); T.u.=Testo unico (=Collection of laws).

1. *Instruzione, e metodo Da tenersi in avvenire da quei Soggetti, e da quelle Famiglie, che desiderassero essere, o reintegrate, o promosse ex integro all'Ordine Nobile...* (Bologna: Sassi, 1728), 3–5.
2. Anna Bellavitis, "'Ars mechanica' e gerarchie sociali a Venezia tra XVI e XVII secolo," in *Le technicien dans la cité en Europe occidentale, 1250–1650*, ed. Mathieu Arnoux and Pierre Monnet (Rome: École Française de Rome, 2004), 161–79.
3. Herbert Applebaum, *The Concept of Work: Ancient, Medieval, and Modern* (New York: State University of New York Press, 1992), xiii.
4. Anna Bellavitis, "Donne cittadinanza e corporazioni tra medioevo ed età moderna: ricerche in corso," in *Corpi e storia: donne e uomini dal mondo antico all'età contemporanea*, ed. Nadia Maria Filippini, Tiziana Plebani, and Anna Scattigno (Roma: Viella, 2002), 87.
5. Giuseppe Mazzini, *I doveri dell'uomo* (Torino: Morgari [Associazione Mazziniana Italiana], n.d., first published 1860), 42.

6. Lucien Febvre, "Travail: évolution d'un mot et d'une idée," *Journal de Psychologie normale et pathologique* 51, no. 1 (1948): 19–28; Maurice Godelier, "Work and Its Representations: A Research Proposal," *History Workshop Journal* 10, no. 1 (1980): 166; Patrick Joyce, "The Historical Meanings of Work: An Introduction," in *Historical Meanings of Work*, ed. Patrick Joyce (Cambridge: Cambridge University Press, 1987), 2. For more details see the introduction in this book.
7. R.d. 21/9/1882, no. 999; T.u. 22/1/1882, no. 593. Cf. Raffaele Romanelli, *Il comando impossibile: stato e società nell'Italia liberale*, 2nd ed. (Bologna: Il Mulino, 1995), 201–2. On the reform, see Paolo Pombeni, "La rappresentanza politica," in *Storia dello Stato Italiano dall'Unità ad oggi*, ed. Raffaele Romanelli (Roma: Donzelli, 1995), 87; Fulvio Cammarano, *Storia dell'Italia liberale* (2011; Roma-Bari: Laterza, 2014), 92–93.
8. Stefano Rodotà, "Le libertà e i diritti," in Romanelli, *Storia dello Stato Italiano*, 319; Stefano Rodotà, *Libertà e diritti in Italia dall'Unità ai nostri giorni* (Roma: Donzelli, 1997), 42.
9. Rodotà, "Le libertà e i diritti," 318–19.
10. Within certain limits, the process continued even during Fascism. Fascism certainly abolished many workers' rights (first of all the right to strike and trade union freedom). Yet, in exchange for the abolition of rights, wage cuts, and greater authoritarianism in employment relationships, it offered workers some advantages, from paid holidays to leisure activities; see Rodotà, "Le libertà e i diritti,," 335–36, 342–43.
11. Rodotà, "Le libertà e i diritti," 352; Paolo Barile, *Diritti dell'uomo e libertà fondamentali* (Bologna: Il Mulino, 1984), 103–4; Antonio Cantaro, *Il secolo lungo: lavoro e diritti sociali nella storia europea* (Roma: Ediesse, 2006), 68–71; Paolo Pascucci, "Il lavoro nella Costituzione," *Cultura giuridica e diritto vivente* 3 (2016): 1–15, retrieved 20 December 2017 from http://ojs.uniurb.it/index.php/cgdv/article/view/590.
12. Ornello Vitali, *La popolazione attiva in agricoltura attraverso i censimenti italiani (1881–1961)* (Roma: Failli, 1968); Ornello Vitali, *Aspetti dello sviluppo economico italiano alla luce della ricostruzione della popolazione attiva* (Roma: Failli, 1970).
13. Alessandra Pescarolo, "I mestieri femminili: continuità e spostamenti di confine nel corso dell'industrializzazione," *Memoria: rivista di storia delle donne* 10, no. 30 (1990), 55–68; Alessandra Pescarolo, "Il lavoro a domicilio femminile: economie di sussistenza in età contemporanea," in *Tra fabbrica e società: mondi operai nell'Italia del Novecento*, ed. Stefano Musso (Milano: Feltrinelli, 1999 [*Annali della Fondazione Giangiacomo Feltrinelli* 33 (1997)]), 173–95; Alessandra Pescarolo, "Il lavoro e le risorse delle donne in età contemporanea," in *Il lavoro delle donne*, ed. Angela Groppi (Roma-Bari: Laterza, 1996), 299–344, also published in *Storia sociale delle donne nell'Italia contemporanea*, ed. Anna Bravo, Margherita Pelaja, Alessandra Pescarolo, and Lucetta Scaraffia (Roma-Bari: Laterza, 2001), 127–78; Raffaella Sarti, "Dai servi alle serve: caratteristiche e implicazioni della femminilizzazione del servizio domestico tra età moderna e contemporanea," in Società Italiana delle Storiche, *Identità e appartenenza: donne e relazioni di genere dal mondo classico all'età contemporanea*, Primo Congresso delle Storiche Italiane, Rimini, 8–10 giugno 1995 (Bologna: Eurocopy, 1996), floppy disk no. 2; Silvana Patriarca, "Gender Trouble: Women and the Making of Italy's 'Active Population,' 1861–1936," *Journal of Modern Italian Studies* 3, no. 2 (1998): 144–63; Simonetta Ortaggi Cammarosano, "Industrializzazione e condizione femminile tra Otto e Novecento," in Musso, *Tra fabbrica e società*, especially 147ff; Raffaella Sarti, "Work and Toil: Breadwinner Ideology and Women's Work in 19th and 20th Century Italy," paper presented at the international conference *Women, Work and the Breadwinner Ideology*, Salzburg, 10–11 December 1999 (available at http://www.uniurb.it/scipol/drs_work_and_toil.pdf); Raffaella Sarti, *Quali diritti per "la donna"? Servizio domestico e identità di genere dalla Rivoluzione francese a oggi* (Bologna: S.I.P., 2000), available at http://www.uniurb.it/scipol/drs_quali_diritti_per_la_donna.pdf; Barbara Curli and Alessandra Pescarolo, "Genere, lavori, 'etichette statistiche': i censimenti in

una prospettiva storica," in *Differenze e diseguaglianze: prospettive per gli studi di genere in Italia*, ed. Franca Bimbi (Bologna: Il Mulino, 2003), 65–100; Patrizia Farina and Alice Mauri, "Prospettive di genere nelle statistiche dell'Italia unita," in *Il percorso storico della statistica nell'Italia unita: atti del workshop—Roma, 7 giugno 2011*, ed. Dora Marucco and Aurea Micali (Roma: Istat, 2013), 88; Alessandra Pescarolo, "Asimmetrie di genere e opacità teoriche nella costruzione statistica dell'economia di mercato," in Marucco and Micali, *Il percorso storico*, 95–108; Raffaella Sarti, "Promesse mancate e attese deluse: spunti di riflessione su lavoro domestico e diritti in Italia," in *Il lavoro cambia*, ed. Ariella Verrocchio and Elisabetta Vezzosi (Trieste: Eut, 2014), 55–77, also available at http://hdl.handle.net/10077/9764.

14. Salvatore Battaglia, *Grande dizionario della lingua italiana* (Torino: Utet, 1961–2002); Manlio Cortelazzo and Paolo Zolli, *Dizionario etimologico della lingua italiana* (Bologna: Zanichelli, 1979–1988); Fernando Palazzi and Gianfranco Folena, *Dizionario della lingua italiana* (Torino: Loescher, 1992). The term *massaia*, already used in the fourteenth century, originally meant "wife of the *massaio*," the *massaio* being a particular kind of peasant. In the twentieth century, Fascism used the term *massaia* in naming the Fascist association of agricultural women (Massaie Rurali).
15. *C1861, Popolazione. Parte I* (Firenze: Tipografia di G. Barbera, 1867), 106.
16. MAIC, DGS, *C1881, Relazione generale e confronti internazionali* (Roma: Tipografia Eredi Botta, 1885), LXIX. In *C1871*, vol. III, *Popolazione classificata per professioni, culti e infermità* principali (Roma: Regia Tipografia, 1876), 176–77, the seventeenth category included two subcategories: "Personnel supported by others" (*Personale a carico altrui*), including only a few people (women aged fifteen and over were 34,010), and people "Without profession" (*Senza professione*) including 4,429,786 women aged fifteen and over (my calculation).
17. In 1881 it was actually a subcategory of the nineteenth category, "Without profession" (*Senza professione*), which included two other categories: School pupils and Hospitalised people; see MAIC, DGS, *C1881*, vol. III, *Popolazione classificata per professioni o condizioni* (Roma: Tipografia Bodoniana, 1884).
18. MAIC, DGS, *C1881, Relazione generale*, LXVIII–LXIX.
19. In the Census of 1901, a distinction was introduced between accessory activities and major activities. It soon proved to be scarcely useful, cf. Istat, *C1936*, vol. IV—*Professioni, Parte I, Relazione* (Roma: Failli, 1939), 2, note 1. The Census of 1931 (ibid., 5) introduced the category of *Coadiuvante* (=help), still in use in the Census of 2011 (Istat, *15° Censimento generale ella popolazione e delle abitazioni. Manuale della rilevazione*, 75, 201, retrieved 20 December 2017 from http://www3.istat.it/censimenti/popolazione2011/allegati_rete_rilevazione/18_Manuale percent20della percent20Rilevazione.pdf). Rural women were often classified as *Coadiuvanti* even though they worked in the fields; see Silvia Salvatici, *Contadine dell'Italia fascista: presenze, ruoli, immagini* (Torino: Rosenberg & Sellier, 1999), 95.
20. Because of budget problems, in 1891 the census was not carried out.
21. MAIC, DGS, *C1881, Relazione generale*, LXVII; MAIC, DGS, *C1901*, vol. V, *Relazione sul metodo di esecuzione e sui risultati del censimento, raffrontati con quelli dei censimenti italiani precedenti e di censimenti esteri* (Roma: Tip. Bertero, 1904), CVII.
22. Joan Wallach Scott, "A Statistical Representation of Work: *La Statistique de l'industrie à Paris*, 1847–1848," in Joan Wallach Scott, *Gender and the Politics of History* (New York: Columbia University Press, 1988), 115: "Statistical reports exemplify the process by which visions of reality, models of social structure, were elaborated and revisited."
23. MAIC, DGS, *C1881, Relazione generale*, LXVII.
24. MAIC, DGS, *C1901*, vol. V, *Relazione*, LXXVIII.
25. In 1901, the thirty-third class, "People supported by the family" (*Persone mantenute dalla famiglia*) included three categories: "People attending to domestic tasks" (*Attendenti*

alle cure domestiche); "Students, pupils, seminarians" (*Studenti, scolari, seminaristi*); and "Long-term unemployed and people unable to work" (*Disoccupati da molto tempo o inabili al lavoro*); see *C1901*, vol. IV (Roma: Tipografia nazionale G. Bertero e C., 1904).
26. MAIC, DGS, *C1901*, vol. V, *Relazione sul metodo*, CVII.
27. According to the published data, only a limited number of persons declared to have a secondary occupation (461,142 individuals, 268,955 of which were men, and 192,187 women). Possibly only one occupation was registered at the very moment of collecting the data in the first place; see MAIC, DGS, *C1901*, vol. V, *Relazione sul metodo*, CXII.
28. MAIC, DGS, *C1901*, vol. V, *Relazione sul metodo* LXXIV.
29. Pescarolo, "Asimmetrie di genere," 99–100, 103–5.
30. MAIC, DGS, *C1881*; *C1901*; *C1911* (my calculation).
31. It should be stressed that the picture of women's work emerging from census data was also influenced by the fact that those who answered the questions about women's occupations were often not the women themselves, but their husbands or fathers.
32. MAIC, DGS, *C1901*, vol. V, *Relazione sul metodo*, LXXVII; Farina and Mauri, "Prospettive di genere," 88.
33. According to census data, men made up 0.4 percent of "housewives" in 2001, as many as 2.3 percent in 2011.
34. MAIC, DGS, *C1881*, *Relazione generale*, LXIX.
35. MAIC, DGS, *C1881*, vol. III, *Popolazione classificata per professioni o condizioni* (Roma: Tipografia Bodoniana, 1884), Tav. III, *Popolazione classificata per professioni o condizioni (esclusi i bambini fino a otto anni compiuti)*, 688–89; MAIC, DGS, *C1901*, vol. III, *Popolazione presente classificata per professioni o condizioni* (Roma: Tipografia Nazionale di G. Bertero e C., 1904), 31.
36. MAIC, DGS, *C1901*, vol. V, *Relazione*, CVII. Similar trends can be found elsewhere. For example, in the 1870 US Census, "women who took in boarders and lodgers, helped with the family farm or business, or contracted industrial homework from factories were not counted among the gainfully occupied, even though they were earning money." Moreover, in the 1900 US Census "wives and daughters without a paying job were officially designated 'dependents'"; see Nancy Folbre, "The Unproductive Housewife: Her Evolution in Nineteenth-Century Economic Thought," *Signs: Journal of Women and Culture in Society* 16, no. 3 (1991), 476–78. See also Folbre's and Borderías's chapters in this volume.
37. For instance Pescarolo, "Il lavoro e le risorse delle donne." According to data elaborated by Francesca Bettio, *The Sexual Division of Labour: The Italian Case* (Oxford: Clarendon Press, 1988), table 3.1, 51, the activity rate for women underwent a decrease in the first seventy years of the twentieth century, falling from 37.05 percent in 1901 to 18.36 percent in 1971 (there was a little reverse of the trend only between 1931 and 1936). Bettio measures the activity rate on the total female population, a choice that might produce some bias due to the changing percentages, for instance, of pupils. More recently, Istat itself has elaborated historical series of activity rates according to which women's activity rates were following: 1881: 52.0 percent; 1911: 37.2 percent; 1921: 34.2 percent; 1931: 31.6 percent; 1936: 31.1 percent; 1951: 26.0 percent; 1961: 23.2 percent; 1971: 25.1 percent; 1981: 32.9 percent; 1991: 35.0 percent; 2001: 37.6 percent; 2011: 41.8 percent; see Istat, *Serie storiche*, data and explanations available at http://seriestoriche.istat.it/fileadmin/documenti/Tavola_10.3.xls (accessed 20 December 2017).
38. Vitali, *Aspetti dello sviluppo economico italiano*, 144, 326–27.
39. Annamaria Galoppini, *Il lungo viaggio verso la parità: i diritti civili e politici delle donne dall'unità ad oggi* (Bologna: Zanichelli, 1980); Victoria De Grazia, *How Fascism Ruled Women: Italy, 1922–1945* (Berkeley: University of California Press, 1992); Perry Willson, *Women in Twentieth-Century Italy* (Palgrave Macmillan, 2010), chap. 4.
40. Istat, *C1936, Istruzioni per gli ufficiali di censimento* (Roma: Istituto poligrafico dello Stato, 1936), 23.

41. Vitali, *La popolazione attiva*, 91–92, 94, 100 on the role of the war in Ethiopia and the changed attitude of the census authorities in 1936.
42. Rodotà, "Le libertà e i diritti," 319.
43. Maria Pia Bigaran, "Il voto alle donne in Italia dal 1912 al fascismo," *Rivista di Storia Contemporanea* 16, no. 2 (1987), 240–65; Maria Pia Bigaran, "Donne e rappresentanza nel dibattito e nella legislazione tra '800 e '900," in *La sfera pubblica femminile: percorsi di storia delle donne in età contemporanea*, ed. Dianella Gagliani and Mariuccia Salvati (Bologna: Clueb, 1992), 63–71; Galoppini, *Il lungo viaggio*, 62–67, 70–91; Maria Vittoria Ballestrero, "La protezione concessa e l'eguaglianza negata: il lavoro femminile nella legislazione italiana," in Groppi, *Il lavoro delle donne*, 445–69 (in particular 458–60). On women's work during the First World War, see Anna Bravo, "Lavorare in tempo di guerra," and Laura Savelli, "Reclute dell'esercito delle retrovie: la 'nuova' manodopera femminile nell'industria di guerra, (1915–1918)," both in *Operaie, serve, maestre, impiegate*, ed. Paola Nava (Torino: Rosenberg & Sellier, 1992), 397–421 and 422–43 respectively; Barbara Curli, *Italiane al lavoro 1914–1920* (Venezia: Marsilio, 1998); Willson, *Women in Twentieth-Century Italy*, chap. 3; Giovanna Bino, "Le fragili braccia muliebri, un miracolo di energia," *Eunomia; Rivista semestrale di Storia e Politica Internazionali* 4, no. 2 (2016): 501–20.
44. D. legislativo luogotenenziale no. 23, 1/2/1945 (and d. no. 74, 10/3/ 1946 on elegibility of women); Anna Rossi-Doria, *Diventare cittadine: il voto delle donne in Italia* (Firenze: Giunti, 1996); Anna Rossi-Doria, "Italian Women Enter Politics," in *When the War Was Over: Women, War and Peace in Europe, 1940–1956*, ed. Claire Duchen and Irene Bandhauer-Schoffmann (New York: Leicester University Press, 2009), 89–101.
45. L. 17/7/1919, n. 1176.
46. L. 9/12/1977, n. 903. See, for instance, Istat, *Come cambia la vita delle donne, 2004–2014* (Roma: Istat, 2015).
47. L. 19/6/1902, no. 242, known as Legge Carcano. A previous law on children's work had not specifically addressed women (L. 11/2/1886, no. 3657, known as Legge Berti).
48. L. 7/7/1907, no. 416; l. 10/11/1907, no. 818.
49. L. 17/7/1910, no. 520.
50. Annarita Buttafuoco, *Questioni di cittadinanza: donne e diritti sociali nell'Italia liberale* (Siena: Protagon, 1997).
51. Annamaria Mozzoni, "Legislazione a difesa delle donne lavoratrici," *Avanti!*, 7 March 1898; Anna Kuliscioff, "In nome della libertà della donna—Laissez faire, laissez passer," *Avanti!*, 19 March 1898; for the two texts, see Galoppini, *Il lungo viaggio*, 30–40; Raffaella Sarti, "Lavoro in casa, lavoro fuori casa: riflessioni del tardo Ottocento e di inizio Novecento," *Economia & Lavoro* 40, no. 1 (2006): 129–46; Elda Guerra, *Storia e cultura politica delle donne* (Bologna: Archetipolibri, 2008), 110–12.
52. Especially L. 17 April 1925, no. 437 and L. 5 August 1934, no. 1347. On the importance di maternity during Fascism, see Chiara Saraceno, "Percorsi di vita femminile nella classe operaia: tra famiglia e lavoro durante il fascismo," *Memoria* 1, no. 2 (1981), 64–75; Galoppini, *Il lungo viaggio*, 128–36; De Grazia, *How Fascism Ruled Women*; Willson, *Women in Twentieth-Century Italy*, chap. 4; Ballestrero, "La protezione concessa," 461–64; Domenica La Banca, "'La creatura tipica del regime': storia dell'Opera Nazionale per la protezione della Maternità e dell'Infanzia durante il ventennio fascista (1925-43)," PhD thesis, Università degli studi di Napoli "Federico II," 2004–5; Maria Morello, *Donna, moglie e madre prolifica: l'Onmi in cinquant'anni di storia italiana* (Soveria Mannelli: Rubbettino, 2010).
53. Ballestrero, "La protezione concessa," 452–54.
54. Galoppini, *Il lungo viaggio*; Simonetta Soldani, "Strade maestre e cammini tortuosi: lo Stato liberale e la questione del lavoro femminile," in Nava, *Operaie, serve, maestre, impiegate*, 289–352; Simonetta Soldani, "Lavoro e cittadinanza nella costruzione del 'genere' femminile in Italia fra 800 e 900," in Società Italiana delle Storiche, *Identità e apparte-*

nenza, floppy disk no. 2; Pescarolo, "Il lavoro e le risorse"; Ballestrero, "La protezione concessa"; Buttafuoco, *Questioni di cittadinanza*; Maura Palazzi, *Donne sole: storia dell'altra faccia dell'Italia tra antico regime e società contemporanea* (Milano: Bruno Mondadori, 1997); Sarti, *Quali diritti per "la donna"?*; Sarti, "Work and Toil."
55. Galoppini, *Il lungo viaggio*, 106–28; Ballestrero, "La protezione concessa," 465–66; De Grazia, *How Fascism Ruled Women*; Perry Willson, *The Clokwork Factory: Women and Work in Fascist Italy* (Oxford: Clarendon Press, 1993); Salvatici, *Contadine dell'Italia fascista*; Raffaella Sarti, "La domesticité durant la période du fascisme (1922–1943)," *Sextant*, nos. 15–16 (2001): 165–202; Raffaella Sarti, "Da serva a operaia? Trasformazioni di lungo periodo del servizio domestico in Europa," *Polis: ricerche e studi su società e politica in Italia* 19, no. 1 (2005): 91–120; Raffaella Sarti, "Domestic Service: Past and Present in Southern and Northern Europe," *Gender & History* 18, no. 2 (2006): 222–45.
56. Raffaella Sarti, *Servo e padrone, o della (in)dipendenza: un percorso da Aristotele ai nostri giorni*, vol. I: *Teorie e dibattiti*, Series *Quaderni* of *Scienza & Politica*, *Quaderno* no. 2 (2015) (Bologna: Alma Mater Studiorum Università di Bologna, 2015), available at http://scienzaepolitica.unibo.it/pages/view/supplement (retrieved on 20 December 2015).
57. Raffaella Sarti, "The True Servant: Self-Definition of Male Domestics in an Italian City (Bologna, 17th–19th Centuries)," *History of the Family* 10, no. 4 (2005): 407–33; Raffaella Sarti, "Who Are Servants? Defining Domestic Service in Western Europe (16th–21st Centuries)," in *Proceedings of the Servant Project*, ed. Suzy Pasleau and Isabelle Schopp, with Raffaella Sarti (Liège: Éditions de l'Université de Liège, 2005), 2:3–59.
58. While dealing with the past, I will often speak of "domestic service" and "servants" rather than "domestic work" and "domestic workers," even though today this may not sound politically correct, because these were the terms then in use. Interestingly, in 1861 and 1871, the censuses of England and Wales included housewives and women "not otherwise described" in class 2, that is the "Domestic Class," along with paid domestic workers; see Edward Higgs, "Women, Occupations and Work in the Nineteenth Century Census," *History Workshop*, no. 23 (1987): 59–81; Folbre, "Unproductive Housewife," 471.
59. MAIC, DGS, *C1901*, vol. V, *Relazione*, LXXIV: "le persone non occupate abitualmente in qualche lavoro, come molta parte delle donne, dei fanciulli e dei vecchi, e *quelle addette al servizio domestico*" (my emphasis).
60. See above, note 36.
61. Tommaso Bruno, "Domestico," in *Il Digesto Italiano* (Torino: Utet, 1899–1902), vol. 9, part 3, 652. See also Emidio Pacifici-Mazzoni, *Codice civile italiano commentato, Trattato delle locazioni*, 2nd ed. (Firenze: Cammelli, 1872), 417–18.
62. Luigi De Litala, *Il contratto di servizio domestico e il contratto di portierato* (Roma: U.S.I.L.A., 1933), 34. See also Pietro Addeo, "Il contratto di lavoro domestico," *Diritto commerciale* s. 2, 12 (1920), 75, and Pietro Addeo, "Verso il contratto collettivo di lavoro domestico," *L'eco forense* 14 (1935), 3–7.
63. In addition to my own works, see Paolo Passaniti, "La cittadinanza sommersa: il lavoro domestico tra Otto e Novecento," *Quaderni fiorentini per la storia del pensiero giuridico moderno* 37 (2008): 233–57.
64. Sarti, "Work and Toil"; Raffaella Sarti, "Lavoro domestico e di cura: quali diritti?," in *Lavoro domestico e di cura: quali diritti?*, ed. Raffaella Sarti (Roma: Ediesse, 2010), 17–131.
65. Guido D'Amario, "Domestici (Contratto di servizio domestico)," in *Enciclopedia Giuridica Italiana* (Milano, Società Editrice Libraria, 1921), vol. 4, part 6, 521.
66. Ibid., 524.
67. De Litala, *Il contratto di servizio domestico*, 67.
68. D'Amario, "Domestici," 524.
69. De Litala, *Il contratto di servizio domestico*, 67 and 77.
70. L. 11/2/1886, no. 3657; l. 19/6/1902, no. 242; l. 7/7/1907, no. 416 and r.d.

10/11/1907, no. 818; l. 17/7/1910, no. 520; r.d.l. 15/3/1923, no. 692 e l. 17/4/1925, no. 473; r.d.l. 13/11/1924, no. 1825; r.d.l. 13/5/1929, no. 850; l. 26/4/1934, no. 653; r.d.l. 22/3/1934, no. 654 and l. 5/7/1934, no. 1347.
71. R.d.l. 15/3/1923, no. 692, art. 1, comma 2 and l. 17/4/1925, no. 473; r.d.l. 29/5/1937, no. 1768, art. 3, letter 'a' and l. 13/1/1938, no. 203.
72. R.d. 1/7/1926, no. 1130, art. 52.
73. R.d. 26/2/1928, no. 471, art. 1.
74. R.d.l. 4/10/1935, no. 1827, art. 40, 4.
75. Art. 1, comma no. 2, r.d. 30/12/1923, no. 3184; r.d. 27/10/1927, no. 2055 and r.d.l. 4/10/1935, no. 1827, art. 37; l. 6/4/1936, no. 1155.
76. Sarti, "Work and Toil"; Sarti, "Lavoro domestico e di cura."
77. Raffaella Sarti, "'Noi abbiamo visto tante città, abbiamo un'altra cultura': Servizio domestico, migrazioni e identità di genere in Italia: uno sguardo di lungo periodo," *Polis: Ricerche e studi su società e politica in Italia* 18, no. 1 (2004): 17–46.
78. *C1951*, vol. VII, *Dati generali riassuntivi* (Roma: Istat, 1958), 8.
79. *C1951*, vol. I, fascicolo 33, 8.
80. According to original census data (cf. *C1951*, vol. IV, *Professioni*, tav. 1, *Popolazione residente attiva per sesso, professione, posizione nella professione, ramo di attività economica* and tav. 10, *Popolazione residente non attiva in età di 10 anni e più per sesso, condizione e provincia*) economically active males were 14,663,427, inactive ones 4,395,593, totaling 19,059,020; according to these figures, the actives ones were 76.9 percent of the total. According to Vitali's corrections, the actives ones were 14,756,474 (*Aspetti dello sviluppo economico italiano*, 401), i.e. 77 percent of the resident male population aged ten and over.
81. On housewives in postwar Italy, see Luisa Tasca and Stuart Hilwig, "The 'Average Housewife' in Post–World War II Italy," *Journal of Women's History* 16, no. 2 (2004): 92–115.
82. Anna Badino, *Tutte a casa? Donne tra migrazione e lavoro nella Torino degli anni Sessanta* (Roma: Viella, 2008), in particular 23–62; Monica Pacini, *Donne al lavoro nella Terza Italia: San Miniato dalla ricostruzione alla società dei servizi* (Pisa: ETS, 2009); Eloisa Betti, *Il lavoro femminile nell'industria italiana: gli anni del boom economico*, "Storicamente," no. 6, 2010, http://www.storicamente.org/05_studi_ricerche/summer-school/lavoro_femminile_donne.htm.
83. L. 26/8/1950, no. 860.
84. L. 18/1/1952, no. 35.
85. L. 27/12/1953, no. 940.
86. Sarti, *Lavoro domestico e di cura: quali diritti?*
87. Ibid.; Francesco Basenghi, *Il lavoro domestico: artt. 2240–2246* (Milano: Giuffrè, 2000); Artemigia Ioli, "Dal primo contratto collettivo sul lavoro domestico ai giorni nostri," in Sarti, *Lavoro domestico e di cura: quali diritti?*, 191–204.
88. A new law on home-based industrial work would be approved in 1973 (l. 18/12/1973, no. 877). On home-based industrial work, see Tania Toffanin, *Fabbriche invisibili: storie di donne, lavoranti a domicilio* (Verona: Ombre corte, 2016).
89. In 2014 the female employment rate for the age group 15–64 was 59.6 percent in EU-28, 46.8 in Italy; see Eurostat, Gender Statistics, data up to February 2017, retrieved 20 December 2017 from http://ec.europa.eu/eurostat/statistics-explained/index.php/Gender_statistics#Labour_market.
90. D. 13/5/1929, no. 850; l. 30/12/1971, no. 1204; sentences of the constitutional court 13/2/1974, no. 27 and 15/1/1976, no. 9, 15/3/1994, no. 86.
91. On the rights of domestic workers, in addition to works mentioned in previous notes, see Daniela Gottardi, "Lavoro domestico," in *Trattato di diritto privato*, ed. Pietro Rescigno (Torino: UTET, 2004²), vol. 15, t. 1, 867–905; Claudia Alemani, "Le colf: ansie e desideri delle datrici di lavoro," *Polis* 18, no. 1 (2004), 137–66; Francesca Marinelli, "Del lavoro domestico: commento agli artt. 2240–2246 c.c.: aggiornamento," in *Codice della famiglia*,

ed. Michele Sesta (Milano: Giuffrè, 2009²), t. 2, 2253; Gisella De Simone, "I lavoratori domestici come attori della conciliazione," in *Persone, lavori, famiglie: identità e ruoli di fronte alla crisi economica*, ed. Maria Vittoria Ballestrero and Gisella De Simone (Torino: Giappichelli, 2009), 61–83; Paolo Pascucci, "La nuova disciplina della sicurezza sul lavoro del 2008/2009: una rapsodia su novità e conferme," special issue of *Working papers di Olympus*, no. 1 (2011): 1–30, retrieved 20 December 2017 from http://ojs.uniurb.it/index.php/WP-olympus/article/view/18.

92. Sarti, *Servo e padrone*, 210–11; Sabrina Marchetti, "'Domestic Work Is Work'? Condizioni lavorative delle assistenti familiari in Italia, tra finzioni e realtà," in *Viaggio nel lavoro di cura: chi sono, cosa fanno e come vivono le badanti che lavorano nelle famiglie italiane*, ed. Raffaella Maioni and Gianfranco Zucca (Roma: Ediesse, 2016), 101–23.

93. An alternative path to reduce women's weak citizenship and discrimination would obviously have been the full recognition of domestic and care work for one's family as proper work, as requested in the 1970s by some feminists campaigning for wages for housework; see Mariarosa Dalla Costa and Selma James, *Potere femminile e sovversione sociale, con "Il posto della donna" di Selma James* (Padova: Marsilio, 1972; Engl. trans. Mariarosa Dalla Costa and Selma James, *The Power of Women and the Subversion of the Community* [Bristol: Falling Wall Press, 1975]). On this issue, see the introduction to this volume, Pescarolo's and Gissi's chapters, as well as Maud A. Bracke, "Between the Transnational and the Local: Mapping the Trajectories and Contexts of the Wages for Housework Campaign in 1970s Italian Feminism," in *Women's History Review* 22, no. 4 (2013): 625–42.

94. Sarti, *Quali diritti per "la donna"?*, 19.

95. Ibid., 17.

96. Marco Rovelli, *Servi: il paese sommerso dei clandestini al lavoro* (Milano: Feltrinelli, 2009); Jacopo Storni, *Sparategli! Nuovi schiavi d'Italia* (Roma: Editori Internazionali Riuniti, 2011); Andrea Staid, *Le nostre braccia: meticciato e antropologia delle nuove schiavitù* (Milano: Agenzia X, 2011).

97. For instance, Pino Arlacchi, *Schiavi: il nuovo traffico di esseri umani* (Milano: Rizzoli, 1999); Kevin Bales, *Disposable People: New Slavery in the Global Economy* (Berkeley: University of California Press, 1999); Francesco Carchedi, Giovanni Mottura, and Enrico Pugliese, eds., *Il lavoro servile e le nuove schiavitù* (Milano: Angeli, 2003); Benedetto Bellesi and Paolo Moiola, eds., *Il prezzo del mercato: viaggio nelle nuove schiavitù* (Bologna: EMI, 2006); Tiziana Bianchini, ed., *Nuove schiavitù: fenomeni, strumenti e prospettive* (Roma: Comunità, 2006); Fabio Viti, *Schiavi, servi e dipendenti: antropologia delle forme di dipendenza personale in Africa* (Milano: Raffaello Cortina, 2007); Gianluca Ciampa, *Il delitto di riduzione o mantenimento in schiavitù o in servitù* (Napoli: Jovene, 2008); Federica Resta, *Vecchie e nuove schiavitù: dalla tratta allo sfruttamento sessuale* (Milano: Giuffrè, 2008); E. Benjamin Skinner, *A Crime So Monstrous: Face-to-Face with Modern-Day Slavery* (New York: Free Press, 2008); Francesco Carchedi, ed., *Schiavitù di ritorno: il fenomeno del lavoro gravemente sfruttato; le vittime, i servizi di protezione, i percorsi di uscita, il quadro normativo* (Rimini: Maggioli Editore, 2010); Silvia Angioli, *Schiavitù e tratta: antiche e nuove forme* (Napoli: Editoriale Scientifica, 2010), etc.

98. For instance, Cristina Morini, *La serva serve: le nuove forzate del lavoro domestico* (Roma: DeriveApprodi, 2001).

99. Giorgio Sangiorgi, *Aristocratici e servi: riflessioni sulla disuguaglianza nel lavoro* (Milano: Angeli, 2008). A pathbreaking volume was the collective book *Nuove servitù* (Roma: ManifestoLibri, 1994).

100. Christian Marazzi, *Il posto dei calzini: la svolta linguistica dell'economia e i suoi effetti sulla politica* (Torino: Bollati Boringhieri, 1999).

101. Cristina Morini, *Per amore o per forza: femminilizzazione del lavoro e biopolitiche del corpo* (Verona: Ombre Corte, 2010).

102. Sarti, *Lavoro domestico e di cura: quali diritti?*; Gianluca Bascherini and Silvia Niccolai, "Regolarizzare Mary Poppins: lavoro nello spazio domestico e qualità della cittadinanza," *Rivista del diritto della sicurezza sociale* 10, no. 3 (2010): 499–534.
103. Joan C. Tronto, *Caring Democracy: Markets, Equality, and Justice* (New York: NYU Press, 2013).
104. Roberta Altin and Elisabetta Vezzosi, "Il lavoro che serve alla vita: percorsi e contraddizioni della dimensione di cura," *Italia contemporanea*, no. 265 (2011): 657–63.

References

Addeo, Pietro. "Il contratto di lavoro domestico." *Diritto commerciale* s. 2, 12 (1920): 58–78 and 89–108.
———. "Verso il contratto collettivo di lavoro domestico." *L'eco forense* 14 (1935): 3–7.
Alemani, Claudia. "Le colf: ansie e desideri delle datrici di lavoro." *Polis* 18, no. 1 (2004): 137–66.
Altin, Roberta, and Elisabetta Vezzosi. "Il lavoro che serve alla vita: percorsi e contraddizioni della dimensione di cura." *Italia contemporanea*, no. 265 (2011): 657–63.
Angioi, Silvia. *Schiavitù e tratta: antiche e nuove forme*. Napoli: Editoriale Scientifica, 2010.
Applebaum, Herbert. *The Concept of Work: Ancient, Medieval, and Modern*. New York: State University of New York Press, 1992.
Arlacchi, Pino. *Schiavi: Il nuovo traffico di esseri umani*. Milano: Rizzoli, 1999.
Badino, Anna. *Tutte a casa? Donne tra migrazione e lavoro nella Torino degli anni Sessanta*. Roma: Viella, 2008.
Bales, Kevin. *Disposable People: New Slavery in the Global Economy*. Berkeley: University of California Press, 1999.
Ballestrero, Maria Vittoria. "La protezione concessa e l'eguaglianza negata: il lavoro femminile nella legislazione italiana." In *Il lavoro delle donne*, edited by Angela Groppi, 445–69. Roma-Bari, Laterza: 1996.
Barile, Paolo. *Diritti dell'uomo e libertà fondamentali*. Bologna: Il Mulino, 1984.
Bascherini, Gianluca, and Silvia Niccolai. "Regolarizzare Mary Poppins: lavoro nello spazio domestico e qualità della cittadinanza." *Rivista del diritto della sicurezza sociale* 10, no. 3 (2010): 499–534.
Basenghi, Francesco. *Il lavoro domestico: Artt. 2240–2246*. Milano: Giuffrè, 2000.
Battaglia, Salvatore. *Grande dizionario della lingua italiana*. Torino: Utet, 1961–2002.
Bellavitis, Anna. "Donne cittadinanza e corporazioni tra medioevo ed età moderna: ricerche in corso." In *Corpi e storia: donne e uomini dal mondo antico all'età contemporanea*, edited by Nadia Maria Filippini, Tiziana Plebani, and Anna Scattigno, 87–104. Roma: Viella, 2002.
———. "'Ars mechanica' e gerarchie sociali a Venezia tra XVI e XVII secolo." In *Le technicien dans la cité en Europe occidentale, 1250–1650*, edited by Mathieu Arnoux and Pierre Monnet, 161–79. Rome: École Française de Rome, 2004.

Bellesi, Benedetto, and Paolo Moiola, eds. *Il prezzo del mercato: viaggio nelle nuove schiavitù*. Bologna: EMI, 2006.
Betti, Eloisa. "Il lavoro femminile nell'industria italiana: gli anni del boom economico." *Storicamente*, no. 6 (2010): http://www.storicamente.org/05_studi_ricer che/summer-school/lavoro_femminile_donne.htm.
Bettio, Francesca. *The Sexual Division of Labour: The Italian Case*. Oxford: Clarendon Press, 1988.
Bianchini, Tiziana, ed. *Nuove schiavitù: fenomeni, strumenti e prospettive*. Roma: Comunità, 2006.
Bigaran, Maria Pia. "Il voto alle donne in Italia dal 1912 al fascismo." *Rivista di Storia Contemporanea* 16, no. 2 (1987): 240–65.
———. "Donne e rappresentanza nel dibattito e nella legislazione tra '800 e '900." In *La sfera pubblica femminile: percorsi di storia delle donne in età contemporanea*, in Dianella Gagliani and Mariuccia Salvati, 63–71. Bologna: Clueb, 1992.
Bino, Giovanna. "Le fragili braccia muliebri, un miracolo di energia." *Eunomia: Rivista semestrale di Storia e Politica Internazionali* 4, no. 2 (2016): 501–20.
Bracke, Maud A. "Between the Transnational and the Local: Mapping the Trajectories and Contexts of the Wages for Housework Campaign in 1970s Italian Feminism." *Women's History Review* 22, no. 4 (2013): 625–42.
Bravo, Anna. "Lavorare in tempo di guerra." In *Operaie, serve, maestre, impiegate*, edited by Paola Nava, 397–421. Torino: Rosenberg & Sellier, 1992.
Bruno, Tommaso. "Domestico." In *Il Digesto Italiano*, vol. 9, part 3, 652–54. Torino: Utet, 1899–1902.
Buttafuoco, Annarita. *Questioni di cittadinanza: donne e diritti sociali nell'Italia liberale*. Siena: Protagon, 1997.
Cammarano, Fulvio. *Storia dell'Italia liberale*. Roma-Bari: Laterza, 2014. First published in 2011.
Cantaro, Antonio. *Il secolo lungo: lavoro e diritti sociali nella storia europea*. Roma: Ediesse, 2006.
Carchedi, Francesco, ed. *Schiavitù di ritorno: il fenomeno del lavoro gravemente sfruttato; le vittime, i servizi di protezione, i percorsi di uscita, il quadro normativo*. Rimini: Maggioli Editore, 2010.
Carchedi, Francesco, Giovanni Mottura, and Enrico Pugliese, eds. *Il lavoro servile e le nuove schiavitù*. Milano: Angeli, 2003.
Ciampa, Gianluca. *Il delitto di riduzione o mantenimento in schiavitù o in servitù*. Napoli: Jovene, 2008.
Cortelazzo, Manlio, and Paolo Zolli. *Dizionario etimologico della lingua italiana*. Bologna: Zanichelli, 1979–1988.
Curli, Barbara. *Italiane al lavoro 1914–1920*. Venezia: Marsilio, 1998.
Curli, Barbara, and Alessandra Pescarolo. "Genere, lavori, 'etichette statistiche': i censimenti in una prospettiva storica." In *Differenze e diseguaglianze: prospettive per gli studi di genere in Italia*, edited by Franca Bimbi, 65–100. Bologna: Il Mulino, 2003.
Dalla Costa, Mariarosa, and Selma James. *Potere femminile e sovversione sociale, con "Il posto della donna" di Selma James*. Padova: Marsilio, 1972. Engl. trans. *The Power of Women and the Subversion of the Community*. Bristol: Falling Wall Press, 1975.

D'Amario, Guido. "Domestici (Contratto di servizio domestico)." In *Enciclopedia Giuridica Italiana*, vol. 4, part 6, 513–536. Milano: Società Editrice Libraria, 1921.
De Grazia, Victoria. *How Fascism Ruled Women: Italy, 1922–1945*. Berkeley: University of California Press, 1992.
De Litala, Luigi. *Il contratto di servizio domestico e il contratto di portierato*. Roma: U.S.I.L.A., 1933.
De Simone, Gisella. "I lavoratori domestici come attori della conciliazione." In *Persone, lavori, famiglie: identità e ruoli di fronte alla crisi economica*, edited by Maria Vittoria Ballestrero and Gisella De Simone, 61–83. Torino: Giappichelli, 2009.
Eurostat. Gender Statistics. Data up to February 2017, http://ec.europa.eu/eurostat/statistics-explained/index.php/Gender_statistics#Labour_market.
Farina, Patrizia, and Alice Mauri. "Prospettive di genere nelle statistiche dell'Italia unita." In *Il percorso storico della statistica nell'Italia unita: atti del workshop—Roma, 7 giugno 2011*, edited by Dora Marucco and Aurea Micali, 81–93. Roma: Istat, 2013.
Febvre, Lucien. "Travail: évolution d'un mot et d'une idée." *Journal de Psychologie Normale et Pathologique* 51, no. 1 (1948): 19–28.
Folbre, Nancy. "The Unproductive Housewife: Her Evolution in Nineteenth-Century Economic Thought." *Signs: Journal of Women and Culture in Society* 16, no. 3 (1991): 463–84.
Galoppini, Annamaria. *Il lungo viaggio verso la parità: i diritti civili e politici delle donne dall'unità ad oggi*. Bologna: Zanichelli, 1980.
Godelier, Maurice. "Work and Its Representations: A Research Proposal." *History Workshop Journal* 10, no. 1 (1980): 164–74.
Gottardi, Daniela. "Lavoro domestico." In *Trattato di diritto privato*, edited by Pietro Rescigno, vol. 15, t. 1. 2nd edition, 867–905. Torino: UTET, 2004.
Guerra, Elda. *Storia e cultura politica delle donne*. Bologna: Archetipolibri, 2008.
Higgs, Edward. "Women, Occupations and Work in the Nineteenth Century Census." *History Workshop*, no. 23 (1987): 59–81.
Instruzione, e metodo Da tenersi in avvenire da quei Soggetti, e da quelle Famiglie, che desiderassero essere, o reintegrate, o promosse ex integro all'Ordine Nobile . . . Bologna: Sassi, 1728.
Ioli, Artemigia. "Dal primo contratto collettivo sul lavoro domestico ai giorni nostri." In *Lavoro domestico e di cura: quali diritti?*, edited by Raffaella Sarti, 191–204. Roma: Ediesse, 2010.
Istat. *VIII Censimento generale della popolazione 21 aprile 1936–XIV*. Vol. IV: *Professioni, Parte I, Relazione*. Roma: Failli, 1939.
———. *IX Censimento generale della popolazione, 4 novembre 1951*. Vol. VII: *Dati generali riassuntivi*. Roma: Istat, 1958.
———. *15° Censimento generale ella popolazione e delle abitazioni: manuale della rilevazione*. Roma: Istat, 2011. Retrieved 20 December 2017 from http://www3.istat.it/censimenti/popolazione2011/allegati_rete_rilevazione/18_Manuale percent20della percent20Rilevazione.pdf.
———. *Come cambia la vita delle donne, 2004–2014*. Roma: Istat, 2015.
Joyce, Patrick. "The Historical Meanings of Work: An Introduction." In *Historical Meanings of Work*, edited by Patrick Joyce, 1–30. Cambridge: Cambridge University Press, 1987.

Kuliscioff, Anna. "In nome della libertà della donna—Laissez faire, laissez passer," *Avanti!*, 19 March 1898.
La Banca, Domenica. "'La creatura tipica del regime': storia dell'Opera Nazionale per la protezione della Maternità e dell'Infanzia durante il ventennio fascista (1925–43)." PhD thesis, Università degli studi di Napoli "Federico II," 2004–5.
Marazzi, Christian. *Il posto dei calzini: la svolta linguistica dell'economia e i suoi effetti sulla politica*. Torino: Bollati Boringhieri, 1999.
Marchetti, Sabrina. "'Domestic Work Is Work'? Condizioni lavorative delle assistenti familiari in Italia, tra finzioni e realtà." In *Viaggio nel lavoro di cura: chi sono, cosa fanno e come vivono le badanti che lavorano nelle famiglie italiane*, edited by Raffaella Maioni and Gianfranco Zucca, 101–23 (Roma: Ediesse, 2016).
Marinelli, Francesca. "Del lavoro domestico: commento agli artt. 2240–2246 c.c.: aggiornamento." In *Codice della famiglia*, edited by Michele Sesta, t. 2. 2nd edition, 2253. Milano: Giuffrè, 2009.
Mazzini, Giuseppe. *I doveri dell'uomo*. Torino: Morgari [Associazione Mazziniana Italiana], n.d. First edition published 1860.
Ministero di Agricoltura, Industria e Commercio. Direzione Generale della Statistica. *Censimento della popolazione del Regno d'Italia al 31 dicembre 1881*. Vol. III: *Popolazione classificata per professioni o condizioni*. Roma: Tipografia Bodoniana, 1884.
———. *Censimento della popolazione del Regno d'Italia al 31 dicembre 1881: relazione generale e confronti internazionali*. Roma: Tipografia Eredi Botta, 1885.
———. *Censimento della popolazione del Regno al 10 febbraio 1901*. Vol. III: *Popolazione presente classificata per professioni o condizioni*. Roma: Tipografia Nazionale di G. Bertero e C., 1904.
———. *Censimento della popolazione del Regno al 10 febbraio 1901*. Vol. IV. Roma: Tipografia Nazionale G. Bertero e C., 1904.
———. *Censimento della popolazione del Regno al 10 febbraio 1901*. Vol. V: *Relazione sul metodo e sui risultati del censimento, raffrontati con quelli dei censimenti italiani precedenti e dei censimenti esteri*. Roma: Tipografia Nazionale G. Bertero e C., 1904.
Morello, Maria. *Donna, moglie e madre prolifica: l'Onmi in cinquant'anni di storia italiana*. Soveria Mannelli: Rubbettino, 2010.
Morini, Cristina. *La serva serve: le nuove forzate del lavoro domestico*. Roma: DeriveApprodi, 2001.
———. *Per amore o per forza: femminilizzazione del lavoro e biopolitiche del corpo*. Verona: Ombre Corte, 2010.
Mozzoni, Annamaria. "Legislazione a difesa delle donne lavoratrici." *Avanti!*, 7 March 1898.
Nuove servitù. Roma: ManifestoLibri, 1994.
Ortaggi Cammarosano, Simonetta. "Industrializzazione e condizione femminile tra Otto e Novecento." In *Tra fabbrica e società: mondi operai nell'Italia del Novecento*, edited by Stefano Musso, 109–71. Milano: Feltrinelli, 1999 [*Annali della Fondazione Giangiacomo Feltrinelli* 33 (1997)].
Pacifici-Mazzoni, Emidio. *Codice civile italiano commentato, Trattato delle locazioni*. 2nd edition. Firenze: Cammelli, 1872.
Pacini, Monica. *Donne al lavoro nella Terza Italia: San Miniato dalla ricostruzione alla società dei servizi*. Pisa: ETS, 2009.

Palazzi, Fernando, and Gianfranco Folena. *Dizionario della lingua italiana*. Torino: Loescher, 1992.
Palazzi, Maura. *Donne sole: storia dell'altra faccia dell'Italia tra antico regime e società contemporanea*. Milano: Bruno Mondadori, 1997.
Pascucci, Paolo. "La nuova disciplina della sicurezza sul lavoro del 2008/2009: una rapsodia su novità e conferme." Special issue of *Working papers di Olympus*, no. 1 (2011): 1–30, http://ojs.uniurb.it/index.php/WP-olympus/article/view/18.
———. "Il lavoro nella Costituzione." *Cultura giuridica e diritto vivente* 3 (2016): 1–15. Retrieved 20 December 2017 from http://ojs.uniurb.it/index.php/cgdv/article/view/590.
Passaniti, Paolo. "La cittadinanza sommersa: il lavoro domestico tra Otto e Novecento." *Quaderni fiorentini per la storia del pensiero giuridico moderno* 37 (2008): 233–57.
Patriarca, Silvana. "Gender Trouble: Women and the Making of Italy's 'Active Population,' 1861–1936." *Journal of Modern Italian Studies* 3, no. 2 (1998): 144–63.
Pescarolo, Alessandra. "I mestieri femminili: continuità e spostamenti di confine nel corso dell'industrializzazione." *Memoria. Rivista di storia delle donne* 10, no. 30 (1990): 55–68
———. "Il lavoro e le risorse delle donne in età contemporanea." In *Il lavoro delle donne*, edited by Angela Groppi, 299–344. Roma-Bari: Laterza, 1996. Also published in *Storia sociale delle donne nell'Italia contemporanea*, edited by Anna Bravo, Margherita Pelaja, Alessandra Pescarolo and Lucetta Scaraffia, 127–78 (Roma-Bari: Laterza, 2001).
———. "Il lavoro a domicilio femminile: economie di sussistenza in età contemporanea." In *Tra fabbrica e società: mondi operai nell'Italia del Novecento*, edited by Stefano Musso, 173–95. Milano: Feltrinelli, 1999 [*Annali della Fondazione Giangiacomo Feltrinelli* 33 (1997)].
———. "Asimmetrie di genere e opacità teoriche nella costruzione statistica dell'economia di mercato." In *Il percorso storico della statistica nell'Italia unita: atti del workshop—Roma, 7 giugno 2011*, edited by Dora Marucco and Aurea Micali, 95–108. Roma: Istat, 2013.
Pombeni, Paolo. "La rappresentanza politica." In *Storia dello Stato Italiano dall'Unità ad oggi*, edited by Raffaele Romanelli, 73–124. Roma: Donzelli, 1995.
Resta, Federica. *Vecchie e nuove schiavitù: dalla tratta allo sfruttamento sessuale*. Milano: Giuffrè, 2008.
Rodotà, Stefano. "Le libertà e i diritti." In *Storia dello Stato Italiano*, edited by Raffaele Romanelli, 301–63. Roma: Donzelli, 1995.
———. *Libertà e diritti in Italia dall'Unità ai nostri giorni*. Roma: Donzelli, 1997.
Romanelli, Raffaele. *Il comando impossibile: stato e società nell'Italia liberale*. 2nd edition. Bologna: Il Mulino, 1995.
Rossi-Doria, Anna. *Diventare cittadine: il voto delle donne in Italia*. Firenze: Giunti, 1996.
———. "Italian Women Enter Politics." In *When the War Was Over: Women, War and Peace in Europe, 1940–1956*, edited by Claire Duchen and Irene Bandhauer-Schoffmann, 89–101. New York: Leicester University Press, 2009.
Rovelli, Marco. *Servi: il paese sommerso dei clandestini al lavoro*. Milano: Feltrinelli, 2009.

Salvatici, Silvia. *Contadine dell'Italia fascista: presenze, ruoli, immagini*. Torino: Rosenberg & Sellier, 1999.

Sangiorgi, Giorgio. *Aristocratici e servi: riflessioni sulla disuguaglianza nel lavoro*. Milano: Angeli, 2008.

Saraceno, Chiara. "Percorsi di vita femminile nella classe operaia: tra famiglia e lavoro durante il fascismo." *Memoria* 1, no. 2 (1981): 64–75.

Sarti, Raffaella. "Dai servi alle serve: caratteristiche e implicazioni della femminilizzazione del servizio domestico tra età moderna e contemporanea." In Società Italiana delle Storiche, *Identità e appartenenza: donne e relazioni di genere dal mondo classico all'età contemporanea*, Primo Congresso delle Storiche Italiane, Rimini, 8–10 giugno 1995, floppy disk no. 2. Bologna: Eurocopy, 1996.

———. "Work and Toil: Breadwinner Ideology and Women's Work in 19th and 20th Century Italy," paper presented at the international conference *Women, Work and the Breadwinner Ideology*, Salzburg, 10–11 December 1999 (copyright Raffaella Sarti, 1999, available at http://www.uniurb.it/scipol/drs_work_and_toil.pdf).

———. *Quali diritti per "la donna"? Servizio domestico e identità di genere dalla Rivoluzione francese a oggi*. Bologna: S.I.P., 2000. Available at http://www.uniurb.it/scipol/drs_quali_diritti_per_la_donna.pdf.

———. "La domesticité durant la période du fascisme (1922–1943)." *Sextant*, nos. 15–16 (2001): 165–202.

———. "'Noi abbiamo visto tante città, abbiamo un'altra cultura': servizio domestico, migrazioni e identità di genere in Italia; uno sguardo di lungo periodo." *Polis: Ricerche e studi su società e politica in Italia* 18, no. 1 (2004): 17–46.

———. "The True Servant: Self-Definition of Male Domestics in an Italian City (Bologna, 17th–19th Centuries)." *History of the Family* 10, no. 4 (2005): 407–33.

———. "Who Are Servants? Defining Domestic Service in Western Europe (16th–21st Centuries)." In *Proceedings of the Servant Project*, edited by Suzy Pasleau and Isabelle Schopp, with Raffaella Sarti, 2:3–59. Liège: Éditions de l'Université de Liège, 2005.

———. "Conclusion: Domestic Service and European Identity." In *Proceedings of the Servant Project*, edited by Suzy Pasleau and Isabelle Schopp, with Raffaella Sarti, 5:95–284. Liège: Éditions de l'Université de Liège, 2005.

———. "Da serva a operaia? Trasformazioni di lungo periodo del servizio domestico in Europa." *Polis: ricerche e studi su società e politica in Italia* 19, no. 1 (2005): 91–120.

———. "Domestic Service: Past and Present in Southern and Northern Europe." *Gender & History* 18, no. 2 (2006): 222–45.

———. "Lavoro in casa, lavoro fuori casa: riflessioni del tardo Ottocento e di inizio Novecento." *Economia & Lavoro* 40, no. 1 (2006): 129–46.

———. "Lavoro domestico e di cura: quali diritti?" In *Lavoro domestico e di cura: quali diritti?* edited by Raffaella Sarti, 17–131. Roma: Ediesse, 2010.

———. "Promesse mancate e attese deluse: spunti di riflessione su lavoro domestico e diritti in Italia." In *Il lavoro cambia*, edited by Ariella Verrocchio and Elisabetta Vezzosi, 55–77. Trieste: Eut, 2014. Also available at http://hdl.handle.net/10077/9764.

———. *Servo e padrone, o della (in)dipendenza: un percorso da Aristotele ai nostri giorni.* Vol. I: *Teorie e dibattiti,* Series "Quaderni" of "Scienza & Politica," *Quaderno* no. 2 (2015). Bologna: Alma Mater Studiorum Università di Bologna, 2015. Available at http://scienzaepolitica.unibo.it/pages/view/supplement.

Savelli, Laura. "Reclute dell'esercito delle retrovie: la 'nuova' manodopera femminile nell'industria di guerra, (1915–1918)." In *Operaie, serve, maestre, impiegate,* edited by Paola Nava, 422–43. Torino: Rosenberg & Sellier, 1992.

Scott, Joan Wallach. "A Statistical Representation of Work: *La Statistique de l'industrie à Paris,* 1847–1848." In Joan Wallach Scott, *Gender and the Politics of History,* 113–38. New York: Columbia University Press, 1988.

Skinner, E. Benjamin. *A Crime So Monstrous: Face-to-Face with Modern-Day Slavery.* New York: Free Press, 2008.

Soldani, Simonetta. "Strade maestre e cammini tortuosi: lo Stato liberale e la questione del lavoro femminile." In *Operaie, serve, maestre, impiegate,* edited by Paola Nava, 289–352. Torino: Rosenberg & Sellier, 1992.

———. "Lavoro e cittadinanza nella costruzione del 'genere' femminile in Italia fra 800 e 900." In Società Italiana delle Storiche, *Identità e appartenenza: donne e relazioni di genere dal mondo classico all'età contemporanea,* Primo Congresso delle Storiche Italiane, Rimini, 8–10 giugno 1995, floppy disk no. 2. Bologna: Eurocopy, 1996.

Staid, Andrea. *Le nostre braccia: meticciato e antropologia delle nuove schiavitù.* Milano: Agenzia X, 2011.

Storni, Jacopo. *Sparategli! Nuovi schiavi d'Italia.* Roma: Editori Internazionali Riuniti, 2011.

Tasca, Luisa, and Stuart Hilwig. "The 'Average Housewife' in Post–World War II Italy." *Journal of Women's History* 16, no. 2 (2004): 92–115.

Toffanin, Tania. *Fabbriche invisibili: storie di donne, lavoranti a domicilio.* Verona: Ombre corte, 2016.

Tronto, Joan C. *Caring Democracy: Markets, Equality, and Justice.* New York: NYU Press, 2013.

Vitali, Ornello. *La popolazione attiva in agricoltura attraverso i censimenti italiani (1881–1961).* Roma: Failli, 1968.

———. *Aspetti dello sviluppo economico italiano alla luce della ricostruzione della popolazione attiva.* Roma: Failli, 1970.

Viti, Fabio. *Schiavi, servi e dipendenti: antropologia delle forme di dipendenza personale in Africa.* Milano: Raffaello Cortina, 2007.

Willson, Perry. *The Clokwork Factory: Women and Work in Fascist Italy.* Oxford: Clarendon Press, 1993.

———. *Women in Twentieth-Century Italy.* Palgrave Macmillan, 2010.

CHAPTER 6

THE COMPLEXITIES OF WORK
Analyzing Men's and Women's Work in the Early Modern World with the Verb-Oriented Method

Maria Ågren

1. Introduction: is closing a door a form of work?

Is the closing of a door a form of work? The spontaneous answer is probably no. But after some reflection, one realizes that if the door is the door of a henhouse, closing it may be an important part of what a rural female servant does in the evening. Moreover, to people who earn income through illegal card-playing, closing the door to prevent the police from peeping in to the room may be a necessary activity in order not to get caught—and lose income. Closing the door can be a form of work, and it can be an activity that is closely related to income-earning in a broader sense. Therefore, the closing of doors can be part of the larger history of work. But if one closes the door of one's house because it is getting cold, then it seems contrary to common sense to regard this as a form of work. The verb phrase does not in itself tell us whether we have to do with an example of work or some other form of time use. We need context.

Gender historians have often pointed out that women's work tends to become invisible if one conceptualizes "work" as activities for which payment was given and/or as activities that were officially acknowledged as work (for instance, by giving the person who performed the work a special occupational title). The conclusion has been that historians need to find other indicators of what people did to support themselves in the past, indicators that acknowledge that many, or most, forms of work have historically been unpaid and most workers untitled. In this chapter, I will present results from the Gender and Work project (GaW),[1] where an alternative indicator was used, namely verb phrases describing activities of work in the broad sense. Inspired by Sheilagh Ogilvie's work on Württemberg,[2] the verb-oriented method is based on the simple facts that historians use texts as sources and that in texts it is the job of verb phrases to describe what people do. The method thus allows the researchers to circumvent two problems: how to capture unpaid work and how to capture work by people who lack occupational titles.[3]

In the Gender and Work project, the point of departure was to study practices, the purpose of which was to secure a living for the person concerned and those near him or her. Such practices are often, but not always and not necessarily, referred to as "work" in everyday language. The three examples cited at the inception of this chapter illustrate this point: whether we think of an activity as "work" or "not work" depends on a number of factors, many of which have to do with point of view, cultural context, and power. To some observers, the opening of a door cannot reasonably qualify as work, whereas to others, the ways in which such an act is construed are of central interest to the history of work. In some contexts, labeling an activity as "work" denigrates not only the activity but also the person who performs it, whereas in other contexts, "work" is a positively charged category that people want to associate their pursuits with. In early modern Lutheran Sweden, for instance, those who did not work were branded as "time-thieves"—a concept suggesting that work was the normal and recommended way of spending one's time.[4]

The meanings of work are thus complex and contingent. It is far from straightforward how work is to be defined, and it is also difficult to decide how it can be identified in the historical sources. The verb-oriented method is not the only solution to these problems, of course, but it provides a new and complementary approach. With this method we get data on people's daily activities, regardless of whether these were remunerated or not and regardless of whether the work was highly valued at the time or not. It is a method that is particularly suitable for the study of women's work, regardless of time period, but it is also a method that is congenial for the study of pre-capitalist economies and how both men and women supported themselves in such societies.[5] When the method is applied to huge datasets, it becomes particularly strong; while the single observation can be fragmentary and hard to understand and classify, large amounts of observations allow us to discern general patterns. Finally, it is an approach that tries to break with methodological nationalisms: provided that the problems of defining "work" and classifying verb phrases are handled in the same way by scholars working on different countries, results can be established that are comparable across space and time.

2. Repertoires of practices

The work activities discussed in the following were extracted from a large number of historical sources, selected so as to cover most aspects of early modern Swedish life. The sources can be grouped into four main categories: (1) court or court-like records, (2) accounts, (3) petitions, (4) diaries. The sample is varied both chronologically (spanning from 1550 to 1799) and geographically. The sample does, however, include less data from the southern and eastern parts of early modern Sweden. In total, 16,182 activities from a period of 249 years were extracted from the sources, analyzed, and stored in a specially designed database (the GaW database).[6] On average, there are sixty-five activities per year.

The extent to which the sources yielded information on women's work differed markedly. Court records turned out to yield least: only 20 percent of activities found in court records were carried out by women. The numbers were thirty-four for accounts, thirty-five for petitions and fifty-nine for women's diaries. By contrast, the activities found in men's diaries only included 3 percent of women's activities. Clearly, who the writer was had a strong impact on what types of information were included in the diary. On average, approximately 22 percent of the 16,182 activities were performed by women—a number that says more, of course, about the sources than about the actual prevalence of women's work.[7] If activities performed by persons of unknown gender are excluded, women's share of the activities will rise to 25 percent.

As was already pointed out, the verb-oriented method is not a panacea to all the problems that a scholar runs into when she tries to map early modern work. The method is no better than the sources from which the verb phrases are culled, and historical sources always have biases. First, women's work appears less frequently in the historical sources than does men's, even when the focus is on verb phrases. Second, marital status was recorded less often for men than for women. Third, it turned out that many agricultural activities that must reasonably have been very common in early modern society do not figure prominently in the sources. This might be a general phenomenon; other researchers have also experienced it. Primary-sector work simply seems to be mentioned less often in the historical sources than other forms of work.[8]

With these biases and caveats in mind, a dataset of more than 16,000 activities must still be regarded as a very large one, and 3,612 female activities is a substantial body of evidence. How can this evidence be used, and what does it *not* lend itself to?

The scholar of modern time use works with information on what a selected group of people does throughout a full day (or other unit of time). Often, such an approach requires the people in question to cooperate: they have to write down what they did throughout the day or, at least, accept being observed by scholars who register their activities. For obvious reasons, the historian cannot proceed in this way as his/her subjects are no longer among the living and, with the possible exception of diaries there are no sources that allow the scholar to "see" what people did during a full day. Diaries are, however, rare, and they were generally, although not exclusively, kept by people from the higher echelons of society. In the Gender and Work project, the scholars collected most of the data from court (or court-like) records, gleaning every verb phrase that described practices with the purpose of supporting oneself and one's family. Available throughout the period of the study, the court records provided stability to the dataset. Nevertheless, the observations are spread in time and place. Often, we have only one or a few observations for each person. The data has the character of glimpses rather than complete descriptions of full days. The method does not, therefore, allow us to map time use in the economists' sense of the word.

What the method does allow us to do, however, is to identify *repertoires of work practice* and whether such repertoires were correlated with factors such as gender, marital status, place (rural/urban), etc. For instance, what types of work were women typically described in the sources as doing? What types of work were married women typically described as doing? In other words, how did various human properties intersect with each other and correlate with practices? Based on observations of actual early modern work, the Gender and Work project provides a first baseline for Sweden of what people did for a living.

3. Almost no categories of work were one-gender only

Grouping all 16,182 observations/work activities into sixteen categories showed that practically no category of work was one-gender only. No category was all-male or all-female, with military work as the only exception. Women were also rare among fishers and hunters, but not completely absent (table 6.1).[9]

The gender of the person performing the task was more often unknown in some categories than in others. In agriculture and forestry, around 30 percent of the observed activities lacked information on gen-

Table 6.1. All work activities grouped according to category and gender, Sweden 1550–1799 (absolute numbers).

Category	Total	Women	Men	Unknown
Administrative work	3,049	288	2,593	168
Agriculture, forestry	2,071	283	1,331	457
Care	440	216	196	28
Crafts, construction	1,532	191	1,143	198
Credit	713	122	565	26
Fishing, hunting	345	8	259	78
Food, accommodation	608	286	274	48
Managerial work	832	265	523	44
Military work	121	—	111	10
Teaching	79	7	68	4
Thefts, misappropriation	640	175	439	26
Trade	2,074	792	1,161	121
Trade in real estate	1,206	268	866	72
Transport	1,214	193	796	225
Other specified work	691	273	368	50
Unspecified work for others	567	245	305	17
TOTAL	16,182	3,612	10,998	1,572

Source: Maria Ågren, ed., *Making a Living, Making a Difference* (Oxford: Oxford University Press, 2017), 30.

der, whereas this information was missing in about 10 percent of the cases in the other categories. This phenomenon is probably a reflection of two circumstances. First, as has already been pointed out, the sources reveal particularly little about some forms of work, notably agriculture, and their general silence affects not only the descriptions of work activities but also the descriptions of those who performed such work. Second, teamwork was obviously very common in agriculture and forestry, and the sources are less likely to specify names of all the persons involved in such cases.

Looking closer at the subcategory of agricultural work—arguably the most important economic sector in early modern Europe and definitely so in Scandinavia—the pattern was the same: we found both men and women in all forms of agriculture (including animal husbandry, farming, forestry, gardening, and unspecified agricultural work). Our conclusion is that there are no clear indications of some categories of agricultural work being taboo for one gender or, in other words, exclusively gendered as either male or female. Instead, our results suggest that the gender division of agricultural work was fluid and flexible when observed on the aggregate level. This is also true for other types of work: both men and women appeared as performers of most, if not all, types of work. For instance, men did take care of children, as Linda Oja has shown,[10] and women did carry out tasks that were heavy (like carrying) or that involved the exercise of authority (like ordering others to do things).

The large volume of trade and administrative work is perhaps surprising. Partly, this is a result of what the producers of the historical sources were interested in. Much ink was spent on settling trade disputes and on administering matters of the state, and this has boosted these two categories. Many activities that fall into these categories were carried out by men who were publicly employed (bailiffs, customs officials, city councilors, etc.). But this is only one part of the explanation. In fact, ordinary people spent a lot of their time doing "everyday administration," and such time use was also recorded in the database. People went to court to accuse each other, to assert their rights, to hand in documents, to pay fees, etc. It is instructive to find that women too did these forms of administrative work. One woman requested permission to build a house, another accused somebody of illegal fishing, a third petitioned for her husband's wage, a fourth negotiated a deal, and a fifth swore an oath together with eleven other women.[11] These types of tasks have been categorized as work because it is obvious that the activities were important to people's opportunities to support themselves. They have been categorized as examples of administrative work since they had to do with asserting the rights of the household and representing the household in public.

A main result is thus that men and women did similar things for a living. There was a low degree of gender specialization in early modern Scandinavian society and a high degree of occupational pluralism or "pluriactivity." Both men and women did many different kinds of work, many of which were unpaid, and neither men nor women would, in the normal case, have occupational titles; they are referred to in the sources simply by their proper names. It is true, of course that the titles that did exist more often referred to men than to women. This is particularly clear for work in the state administration, which grew rapidly in the early modern period. However, even in the case of men with titles, the titles often give a partial and sometimes misleading picture of what they actually did to support themselves and those close to them. One of the best examples of this is probably *bonde* (peasant)—a word that today means "farmer" but that denoted social status rather than occupation in the early modern period. There are many examples to the same effect. For instance, an inspector apparently supported himself by selling beverages and food, a shoemaker distilled, and a goldsmith and a hatter both worked as private soldiers.[12]

Sometimes men and women worked alongside each other. A court case from 1662 illustrates this point. When a young woman was accused of infanticide, a female servant was called as a witness. The servant told the court that, on the day in question, she had observed the woman lying in great pains on the kitchen stove. The servant knew nothing, however, of what happened later since she had subsequently left the house to do some work in the woods along with the male servants.[13] Obviously, male and female servants worked together in the wood. Did the work of the woman consist in cooking for the men? No, not in this case, and there are more examples of women doing hard forestry work than cooking in the wood. For instance, a female servant carted timber together with her head of household, a crofter woman felled an oak, and two other women felled other sorts of trees.[14]

4. Both men and women could govern the work of others, but unmarried people seldom did

Managerial work is a type of work to which the project has paid special attention. Such work is for instance described in the sources with verbs such as "order," "assign task," "ask," and "govern." In an analysis of these verbs, Karin Hassan Jansson, Rosemarie Fiebranz, and Ann-Catrin Östman showed that both women and men performed managerial work. In fact, it seems as if women were overrepresented within this category: among those who were described as governing others, 28 percent were women, and among those who assigned tasks to others, 31 percent were women.[15] Among those who ordered others, 23 percent were women, which is in line with women's overall representation in the dataset. For instance, women could employ journeymen, fire servants, request help, have responsibility for a larder, ask servants to clean a bench, have somebody carry meat, ask a servant to be quiet, etc. The idea that women were unfit to govern is clearly contradicted by these results. In everyday life and particularly in household contexts, women were in fact conspicuous as "governors."

These results can be linked to an analysis of how the female title *hustru* (wife) was used, also based on data in the GaW database. Christopher Pihl and Maria Ågren showed that *hustru* was a semantically much more complex word in early modern society than in modern society. It did not only designate marital status (a married woman) but also a woman with capacity to govern, to assume responsibility, etc. This result is consonant with what has been shown for the English word *mistress*: before the middle of the eighteenth century, this word did not signal marital status but, among other things, "a woman who governs." Similar results have also been presented for early modern Portugal and the German-speaking area.[16] In this context, it should be pointed out, as Pirjo Markkola has done, that *husbonde* (master of household) could be used to talk about both women and men in early modern Sweden. This is how it could be used in religious discourse, and the GaW database provides additional examples of this usage.[17] Contrary to the distinction master/mistress, which was linked to the difference between male and female "governors," *husbonde* was not exclusively linked to men but seems to have been a more gender-neutral word.

Thus, the analysis of titles yields results that dovetail with and support the analysis of verb phrases. Both women and men were described as performers of managerial work and as "governors" of households, and *husbonde* could be used both about women and about men, although admittedly more frequently about men.

However, not all women and men had access to the role as head of household, and they were consequently barred from governing the work of others. The group in question consisted of unmarried people. Cristina Prytz and Hanna Östholm showed that there were clear differences between what married and unmarried women did for a living.[18] Unmarried women had a conspicuously low presence among those who traded, taught, provided housing and performed administrative and managerial work. They were also seldom seen among those who were engaged in credit transactions, and they never appeared as sellers of real estate. On the other hand, they were often observed carrying out agricultural work, transporting, and doing unspecified work for others—typically described as "serving" or "working." They were also overrepresented among those who engaged in various illegal activities. Illegal activities did not, however, constitute a large share of their total working activities. By contrast, as Sofia Ling and others showed, ever-married women were the mirror images of the unmarried ones. Married women were conspicuously active in administration and trade, engaged in the credit and real estate market, performed managerial work, and provided housing.[19]

There were exceptions to these patterns. There are examples of unmarried women who did some administrative and managerial work; they could, for instance, chastise young boys, have others do things at their request, monitor others, etc. But it is important to recognize that these examples were rare. In general, there was a strong and marked difference between unmarried and ever-married women. The main reason for this pattern is the fact that marriage gave women access to a number of resources that unmarried women seldom could harness in their daily lives. As a group, married women and widows had access to material resources that they could use to trade, to extend credit, to purchase land and to provide housing against payment. They also had access to the labor of others, and they could use this labor for their own purposes, sending people around, ordering them, assigning them tasks, etc. Finally, Swedish women had access to (informal) schooling,[20] but only the married ones were expected to teach others.

The same was probably true for unmarried men. They did not have access to the same material, human, social, legal and political resources as married men did. And, while the GaW dataset is less complete when it comes to men's marital status (see above), the results that we do have suggest that men's repertoires of practice also reflected their marital status. The differences that we see in the major work patterns suggest that marital status and household position had a significant impact on what people in general could and could not do to support themselves. Marital status seems to have been more active as a factor structuring work than was gender. This speaks volumes about the character of early modern society and the crucial role that marriage had. It does not, however, completely rule out the effect of gender.

5. Gender did have an impact

While gender does not seem to have been the only or the most important factor to explain work patterns on the aggregate level, it turns out to be highly pertinent if we delve deeper into the data on the level of concrete verbs and verb phrases. Put simply, some verb phrases were used more often about men's activities than about women's, and vice versa. If we return to the verb phrases categorized as managerial work, women were often described as *asking* others to do various things, whereas the same verb was seldom used to describe what men did. On the other hand, men were described as *ordering* others to do various things much more often than women, even if women did order others too. It is impossible to say whether these differences say anything about how men and women actually behaved, or if they reflect gendered stylistic ideals about how men and women should be described: as imperious or meek.[21]

This example illustrates an important feature of the sixteen categories used in the analysis: they include wide varieties of activities and are thus *heterogeneous*. Care, for instance, includes both phrases like "heal wound," "assist at birth," and "wash dead body" and phrases like "arrange for someone's care." Women were more often observed among those who performed the first type of work and men among those who did the second type of work. Women and men were similar in the sense that they all performed work of care, but they were different in the sense that the concrete tasks were not necessarily the same. Making the categories heterogeneous allows for an analysis that acknowledges both similarity and difference. The phrases within each category are similar—this is why they belong to the same category—yet, at the same time, they can also be radically different.[22]

The impact of gender was stronger in larger organizations than in smaller ones. At the sixteenth-century state-owned demesnes, the gender division of work was more dichotomous than at family farms.[23] The picture conveyed above of a flexible economy characterized by pluriactivity is therefore true for households and less so for the, admittedly less common, large estates. Gender was also more palpable among the elderly poor and destitute: Erik Lindberg, Sofia Ling, and Benny Jacobsson showed that old women figured more prominently among those who lived with their daughters under miserable conditions.[24]

Some verb phrases (1,572) cannot be assigned to a specific gender (see table 6.1). In about one-third of these phrases, the performer of the activity was described as "we," and most we-phrases come from the two diaries included in the dataset. The use of "we" illustrates the combined effect of gender, household position, and social status. The diary kept by a married peasant man shows him talking about the work at the farm as a collective enterprise: we sowed, we harvested. In the diary of the (first unmarried and then married) woman, who was of noble origin, she too talks about household work as a collective enterprise: we baked, we brewed. In both cases, the word "we" eclipses not only the genders of those behind the collective enterprises but their proper names and other characteristics as well. Man or woman, the head of household sometimes talked about the other members of the household as extensions of him- or herself. This linguistic usage not only hides the contributions of specific persons; at times, it may even ascribe contributions to a person who perhaps did nothing but order the others to work and then write it down in the diary.[25]

6. Open houses

Many early modern women obviously supported themselves through forms of work that have left few clear traces in the historical sources. The same must have been true for many men. As was shown above, work by subordinated members of a household is likely to have been eclipsed by the head of household, either because he/she described the work as having been carried out by "us," or because other observers (such as bailiffs) ascribed the work to the head of household.

This puts a new interpretation on the low proportion of female activities in the sources and in the GaW database. Work by women (and by subordinated members of households, for that matter) may well have taken place in public and been *visible to contemporaries*, even if they are seldom mentioned in the sources. In the interstices between households, we find many different forms of commercial activities, sometimes bordering on the illegal (selling and receiving stolen goods, etc.). We also find exchange of services (baking bread, laundering) and financial transactions (extending credit, etc.). The latter activities were often described in terms of "help" or "assistance" rather than "work" or "labor." The very high numbers for trade, especially for ever-married women, suggests that their activity spheres had a spatial dimension. Whether legal or illegal, trade in goods and in services was an important source of income for many women, and through these activities, households and individuals were connected in networks of cooperation and dependence.[26]

As Dag Lindström and others argue, we need to problematize the character of "households."[27] Neither their borders nor their internal power structures can be taken for granted. Moreover, there were other ways of organizing work than through the household. Inspired by the work of Joachim Eibach, the Gender and Work project has found it useful to interpret the findings in the light of the concept of "the open house."[28] While Eibach himself uses the term to work with sociocultural questions, it is clear that the concept is also useful in a socioeconomic context. It stresses that households were not self-sufficient monoliths but, rather, dynamic groups of people that had to be flexible to meet varying economic conditions and also ready to interact with people from other households. It is another matter that this flexibility and openness is often lost in the filter of historical sources.

7. Conclusion

This chapter has had two purposes: to reflect on the theoretical and methodological approach of the Gender and Work project and to present some of its main results. Key elements in the discussion are the definition of "work" and the concept "repertoires of practice"; the verb-oriented method, its potential and limitations; the role of heterogeneous categories; the conceptualization of households as open; the intersection of factors such as gender, marital status, social status, etc.

The analysis of verb phrases with the help of sixteen main categories of work showed that the gender division of work was not particularly dichotomous in early modern Sweden. Both men and women were observed doing work that fell into almost all categories. The degree of specialization along lines of gender was low. It makes little sense, therefore, to think in terms of separate spheres.[29] Instead, women's and men's repertoires of work practices were partly overlapping.

Yet, this conclusion must be tempered by two observations. First, even if we see many similarities between men and women on the aggregate level, on a more detailed level we find clear differences. While both men and women were present in almost all categories of work and probably carried out many tasks alongside each other, differences on the level of concrete verb phrases suggest that the tasks were not always exactly the same and did not always carry the same meaning. Second, the division of work was strongly structured by marital status, household position, and, implicitly, age. The work repertoires of unmarried people, who were often young, were radically different from that of married and widowed people. There were probably clear notions of difference between people who served and people who governed those who served, even if these differences tended to be hidden behind a language that depicted work as a collective enterprise.

A major conclusion of the GaW project is the paramount importance of marriage in early modern society. Marriage was important to both women and men because it provided them with possibilities of supporting themselves through their own work and through the work of those that they could govern. What marriage meant to early modern women was therefore radically different from what it meant, and sometimes still means, to women in certain social strata in the modern Western world (after 1800). Early modern women did not get married to be supported by their husbands. They got married to be able better to support themselves. The same was true for men: marriage improved their chances of supporting themselves too. This does not exclude that people married for love, of course, but in a larger perspective, a crucial difference between early modern society and present society consists in the economic necessity of being married.

We need to think more about these results and their implications for people's senses of identity. Did the repertoires of practice create notions of sameness between married men and married women? Did it affect their identities? In view of how much time people spent on supporting themselves and those close to them, it is not implausible that the answer is yes: married men and married women probably thought of themselves as similar, as sharing a common lot and common interests. And, conversely, they probably thought of themselves as different from unmarried people, who were often young and in a subordinate position. The closing of a door *was* often a form of work, but its precise meaning could vary: it could manifest social superiority, as when it was the mistress who closed the door, but when the task was carried out by a servant at the order of the mistress, it signaled and manifested subordination.

Maria Ågren is professor of history at Uppsala University since 2002. She is an early modernist whose research interests are situated at the intersection of social history, legal history, economic history, and gender history. She has written about credit, debt, iron production, inheritance, property, marriage, and work in the early modern world. Her monograph *Domestic Secrets: Women and Property in Sweden, 1600–1857* (Chapel Hill: University of North Carolina Press) came out in 2009, and in the same year she was appointed Wallenberg Scholar. She is the leader of the research project Gender and Work, which started in 2010 and is currently funded until 2021. She is the editor of the project volume *Making a Living, Making a Difference: Gender and Work in Early Modern European Society* (Oxford: Oxford University Press, 2017) and sole author of *The State as Master: Gender, State-Formation and Commercialisation in Urban Sweden, 1650–1780* (Manchester: Manchester University Press, 2017).

Notes

1. The project was initially funded by the Knut and Alice Wallenberg Foundation through a five-year Wallenberg Scholar grant. The database was funded by the Swedish Research Council and by the KAW Foundation. At present (2017), the research project is funded through a continuation grant from the Wallenberg Foundations, and the database is funded mainly by the Bank of Sweden Tercentenary Foundation.
2. Sheilagh Ogilvie, *A Bitter Living: Women, Markets, and Social Capital in Early Modern Germany* (New York: Oxford University Press, 2003).
3. Jane Whittle, "Enterprising Widows and Active Wives: Women's Unpaid Work in the Household Economy of Early Modern England," *History of the Family* 19, no. 3 (2014): 283–300. Cf. E. A. Wrigley, "Urban Growth and Agricultural Change: England and the Continent in the Early Modern Period," *Journal of Interdisciplinary History* 15, no. 4 (1985): 683–728. Wrigley points out that even if occupational descriptors are more easily available, the ideal would be to study people's time use, preferably as time budgets.
4. Gustav II Adolfs Constitution mot tiggare och tidztiuffuer 1624 (King Gustav II Adolf. Statutory law against beggars and time thieves, 1624).

5. Cf. the discussion in E. P. Thompson, "Time, Work-Discipline, and Industrial Capitalism," *Past & Present*, no. 38 (December 1967): 56–97. Here, Thompson describes work in peasant societies as task oriented and points out that in the early development of manufacturing industry, "many mixed occupations survived." He illustrates this point with lead miners who were also smallholders and tinners who were also fishermen.
6. The GaW database was specially designed for the project by systems analysts at the Demographic Database, Umeå University, Sweden.
7. Cf. Ogilvie, *Bitter Living*, 25. Ogilvie's dataset includes 33 percent female activities.
8. Hans-Joachim Voth, *Time and Work in England* (New York: Oxford University Press, 2000).
9. All results presented here in short form are based on the volume Maria Ågren, ed., *Making a Living, Making a Difference: Gender and Work in Early Modern European Society* (Oxford: Oxford University Press, 2017).
10. Linda Oja, "Childcare and Gender in Sweden c. 1600–1800," *Gender and History* 27 no. 1 (2015): 77–111.
11. GaW dataset, Uppsala University, cases nos. 8619, 11426, 8946, 9106, and 9635.
12. Elisabeth Gräslund Berg et al., "Praktiker som gör skillnad: om den verb-inriktade metoden," *Historisk tidskrift* 133, no. 3 (2013): 339; Jenny Grandin, "That She Looks After My Croft, for Which I Will Give My Faithful Heart: Military Service, Marriage and Local Community in Early Eighteenth-Century Sweden" (unpublished MA thesis, Uppsala University, 2015), 44.
13. GaW dataset, Uppsala University, case no. 541. Thanks to Jan Mispelaere who found the case.
14. GaW dataset, Uppsala University, case nos. 8208, 10106, and 1521.
15. Karin Hassan Jansson, Rosemarie Fiebranz, and Ann-Catrin Östman, "Constitutive Tasks: Working Practices as Hierarchy and Identity," in Ågren, *Making a Living, Making a Difference*, 127–58.
16. Christopher Pihl and Maria Ågren, "Vad var en hustru? Ett begreppshistoriskt bidrag till genushistorien," *Historisk tidskrift* 134, no. 2 (2014): 170–90. See also Amy Louise Erickson, "Mistresses and Marriage: or, a Short History of the Mrs.," *History Workshop Journal* 78 (2014): 39–57; Darlene Abreu-Ferreira, "Work and Identity in Early Modern Portugal: What Did Gender Have to Do with It?" *Journal of Social History* vol. 35, no. 4 (2002): 859–87; Merry E. Wiesner, "Spinning out Capital: Women's Work in Preindustrial Europe 1350–1750" in *Becoming Visible: Women in European History*, ed. Renate Bridenthal, Susan Mosher Stuard, and Merry E. Wiesner (Boston: Houghton Mifflin, 1998), 203–32.
17. Pirjo Markkola, "Lutheranism, Women and the History of the Welfare State in the Nordic Countries," in *På kant med historien: Studier i køn, videnskab og lidenskab tilegnet Bente Rosenbeck på hendes 60-årsdag*, ed. Karin Lützen, Annette K. Nielsen, and Niels Finn Christiansen (Copenhagen: Museum Tusculanums Forlag, 2008), 90–105; Sofia Ling, Karin Hassan Jansson, Marie Lennersand, Christopher Pihl, and Maria Ågren, "Marriage and Work: Intertwined Sources of Authority and Agency," in Ågren, *Making a Living, Making a Difference*, 80–102.
18. Cristina Prytz and Hanna Östholm, "Less Than Ideal? Making a Living Before and Outside Marriage," in Ågren, *Making a Living, Making a Difference*, 103–26.
19. Prytz and Östholm, "Less Than Ideal?"; Ling et al., "Marriage and Work."
20. Egil Johansson, "The History of Literacy in Sweden," in *Understanding Literacy in Its Historical Contexts: Socio-Cultural History and the Legacy of Egil Johansson*, ed. Harvey J. Graff, Alison Mackinnon, Bengt Sandin, and Ian Winchester (Lund: Nordic Academic Press, 2009), 28–59.
21. Hassan Jansson et al., "Constitutive Tasks."
22. Maria Ågren, "Introduction," in Ågren, *Making a Living, Making a Difference*, 1–23.

23. Christopher Pihl, *Arbete: Skillnadsskapande och försörjning i 1500-talets Sverige* (Uppsala: Studia Historica Upsaliensia, 2012).
24. For a more detailed discussion of the elderly, see Erik Lindberg, Benny Jacobsson, and Sofia Ling, "The 'Dark Side' of the Ubiquity of Work: Vulnerability and Destitution among the Elderly," in Ågren, *Making a Living, Making a Difference*, 159–77.
25. For a more detailed discussion of the diaries, see Jonas Lindström, Rosemarie Fiebranz, and Göran Rydén, "The Diversity of Work," in Ågren, *Making a Living, Making a Difference*, 24–56.
26. Maria Ågren, "Emissaries, Allies, Accomplices and Enemies: Married Women's Work in Eighteenth-Century Urban Sweden," *Urban History* 41, no. 3 (2014): 394–414. See also Anne Montenach, "Legal Trades and Black Markets: Food Trades in Lyon in the Late Seventeenth and Early Eighteenth Centuries," in *Female Agency in the Urban Economy*, ed. Deborah Simonton and Anne Montenach (New York: Routledge, 2013), 17–34, for similar results.
27. Dag Lindström, Rosemarie Fiebranz, Jonas Lindström, Jan Mispelaere, and Göran Rydén, "Working Together," in Ågren, *Making a Living, Making a Difference*, 57–79.
28. Joachim Eibach, "Das offene Haus: Kommunikative Praxis im sozialen Nahraum der europäischen Frühen Neuzeit," *Zeitschrift für Historische Forschung* 38, no. 4 (2011): 621–64.
29. This point was made for England by Amanda Vickery in 1993 and has recently been repeated in Amanda Flather, "Space, Place, and Gender: The Sexual and Spatial Division of Labor in the Early Modern Household," *History and Theory* 52, no. 3 (2013): 344–60.

References

Note on references: the main purpose of this chapter is to present results from the GaW project; therefore, the footnotes are far from exhaustive in terms of summarizing previous research. For a fuller presentation, see Maria Ågren, ed., *Making a Living, Making a Difference: Gender and Work in Early Modern European Society* (Oxford: Oxford University Press, 2017).

Abreu-Ferreira, Darlene. "Work and Identity in Early Modern Portugal: What Did Gender Have to Do with It?" *Journal of Social History* 35, no. 4 (2002): 859–87.
Ågren, Maria. "Emissaries, Allies, Accomplices and Enemies: Married Women's Work in Eighteenth-Century Urban Sweden." *Urban History* 41, no. 3 (2014): 394–414.
Ågren, Maria, ed. *Making a Living, Making a Difference: Gender and Work in Early Modern European Society*. Oxford: Oxford University Press, 2017.
Eibach, Joachim. "Das offene Haus: Kommunikative Praxis im sozialen Nahraum der europäischen Frühen Neuzeit." *Zeitschrift für Historische Forschung* 38, no. 4 (2011): 621–64.
Erickson, Amy Louise. "Mistresses and Marriage: or, a Short History of the Mrs." *History Workshop Journal* 78 (2014): 39–57.
Flather, Amanda. "Space, Place, and Gender: The Sexual and Spatial Division of Labor in the Early Modern Household." *History and Theory* 52, no. 3 (2013): 344–60.
Grandin, Jenny. "That She Looks After My Croft, for Which I Will Give My Faithful Heart: Military Service, Marriage and Local Community in Early Eighteenth-Century Sweden." Unpublished MA thesis, Uppsala University, 2015.

Gräslund Berg, Elisabeth, et al. "Praktiker som gör skillnad: om den verb-inriktade metoden." *Historisk tidskrift* 133, no. 3 (2013): 335–54.
Gustav II Adolfs Constitution mot tiggare och tidztiuffuer 1624 (King Gustav II Adolf. Statutory law against beggars and time thieves, 1624).
Jansson, Karin Hassan, Rosemarie Fiebranz, and Ann-Catrin Östman. "Constitutive Tasks: Working Practices as Hierarchy and Identity." In Ågren, *Making a Living, Making a Difference*, 127–58.
Johansson, Egil. "The History of Literacy in Sweden." In *Understanding Literacy in Its Historical Contexts: Socio-Cultural History and the Legacy of Egil Johansson*, edited by Harvey J. Graff, Alison Mackinnon, Bengt Sandin, and Ian Winchester, 28–59. Lund: Nordic Academic Press, 2009.
Lindberg, Erik, Benny Jacobsson, and Sofia Ling. "The 'Dark Side' of the Ubiquity of Work: Vulnerability and Destitution among the Elderly." In Ågren, *Making a Living, Making a Difference*, 159–77.
Lindström, Dag, Rosemarie Fiebranz, Jonas Lindström, Jan Mispelaere, and Göran Rydén. "Working Together." In Ågren, *Making a Living, Making a Difference*, 57–79.
Lindström, Jonas, Rosemarie Fiebranz, and Göran Rydén. "The Diversity of Work." In Ågren, *Making a Living, Making a Difference*, 24–56.
Ling, Sofia, Karin Hassan Jansson, Marie Lennersand, Christopher Pihl, and Maria Ågren. "Marriage and Work: Intertwined Sources of Authority and Agency." In Ågren, *Making a Living, Making a Difference*, 80–102.
Markkola, Pirjo. "Lutheranism, Women and the History of the Welfare State in the Nordic Countries." In *På kant med historien: Studier i køn, videnskab og lidenskab tilegnet Bente Rosenbeck på hendes 60-årsdag*, edited by Karin Lützen, Annette K. Nielsen, and Niels Finn Christiansen, 90–105. Copenhagen: Museum Tusculanums Forlag, 2008.
Montenach, Anne. "Legal Trades and Black Markets: Food Trades in Lyon in the Late Seventeenth and Early Eighteenth Centuries." In *Female Agency in the Urban Economy*, edited by Deborah Simonton and Anne Montenach, 17–34. New York: Routledge, 2013.
Ogilvie, Sheilagh. *A Bitter Living: Women, Markets, and Social Capital in Early Modern Germany*. New York: Oxford University Press, 2003.
Oja, Linda. "Childcare and Gender in Sweden c. 1600–1800." *Gender and History* 27, no.1 (2015): 77–111.
Pihl, Christopher. *Arbete: Skillnadsskapande och försörjning i 1500-talets Sverige*. Uppsala: Studia Historica Upsaliensia, 2012.
Pihl, Christopher, and Maria Ågren. "Vad var en hustru? Ett begreppshistoriskt bidrag till genushistorien." *Historisk tidskrift* 134, no. 2 (2014): 170–90.
Prytz, Cristina, and Hanna Östholm. "Less Than Ideal? Making a Living Before and Outside Marriage." In Ågren, *Making a Living, Making a Difference*, 103–26.
Thompson, E. P. "Time, Work-Discipline, and Industrial Capitalism." *Past & Present*, no. 38 (December 1967): 56–97.
Voth, Hans-Joachim. *Time and Work in England*. New York: Oxford University Press, 2000.

Whittle, Jane. "Enterprising Widows and Active Wives: Women's Unpaid Work in the Household Economy of Early Modern England." *History of the Family* 19, no. 3 (2014): 283–300.

Wiesner, Merry E. "Spinning out Capital: Women's Work in Preindustrial Europe 1350–1750." In *Becoming Visible: Women in European History,* edited by Renate Bridenthal, Susan Mosher Stuard, and Merry E. Wiesner, 203–32. Boston: Houghton Mifflin, 1998.

Wrigley, E. A. "Urban Growth and Agricultural Change: England and the Continent in the Early Modern Period." *Journal of Interdisciplinary History* 15, no. 4 (1985): 683–728.

CHAPTER 7

THE VISIBILITY OF WOMEN'S WORK
Logics and Contexts of Documents' Production

Margareth Lanzinger

It is uncontested that organizing labor hierarchically and putting greater value on paid work outside the household than on caregiving, childrearing, reproductive work, and, generally, work done "at home" goes back to the separation of gainful employment from household work. This was a nineteenth-century process that first affected bourgeois milieus before it turned into the dualism whose effects can still be felt today. Karin Hausen defined this process as early as the 1970s in terms of the "dissociation of work and family life."[1] In the course of this process, gender roles were naturalized, and capabilities as well as inabilities were divided into male and female, thus being ascribed or denied to men and women. As a result, "gender character" (*Geschlechtscharakter*) was conceived as an essential part of the interiority of the self. Kathleen Canning comments: "Hausen contends that the polarities of rationality-emotionality and activity-passivity became prescriptive across social, economic, geographic and religious divides in German-speaking Europe, intensifying in the course of the nineteenth century in response to women's growing demands for political and social equality, and that these ideals persisted well into the early twentieth century."[2]

The resulting "natural" division of labor is a modern phenomenon that is accompanied by the separation of "private" and "public" spheres of life and by making household work invisible or by classifying it as "services rendered out of kindness and love" as opposed to "real" work—as Gisela Bock and Barbara Duden analyzed in their pioneering article of 1977 titled "Work for Love—Love as Work."³ In contrast to these categories and with regard to the early modern period, the early 1990s saw Heide Wunder introduce the concept of "the working couple" to express the mutual interdependence of husband and wife and their work capacities.⁴ The concept of the working couple precedes the pattern of the man as breadwinner. It includes care work (albeit perceived as non-hierarchical) but is by no means limited to care work. The underlying thesis is that, while a gender-specific division of labor did indeed also exist during the early modern period, the responsibilities and work respectively assumed by men and women were in fact not defined primarily via gender as a category and key of classification but rather in terms of labor-organizational criteria and according to the values associated with specific activities and/ or according to specific requirements. Criticism of this "working-couple" concept is, for the most part, aimed at the rather harmonious image that the idea of interdependence between husband and wife might produce or evoke.⁵ And it is indeed necessary to note how this was associated with legal and social gender inequalities and their impacts on practice in everyday life.

Against this backdrop, the question arises as to whether the concept of the early modern working couple would not also be useful in describing some living environments during the nineteenth century and continuing into the twentieth, particularly in rural areas and in agrarian contexts where forms of domestic economy continued to be important, such as on small and medium-sized farms and in the common situation of pluriactivity associated with agriculture or small trades, as well as in other contexts. Another question has to do with the extent to which the acknowledgment or obscuration of work done primarily by women is a period-specific phenomenon—i.e., with the nineteenth century clearly tending more toward obscuration than the early modern period—or depends more fundamentally on each period's various specific source contexts. If the latter is the case (which is the hypothesis from which this contribution starts), then the resulting way in which women were present or absent as performers of work in the sources is not limited to the modern era, but in fact applies equally to the early modern period. That would serve to somewhat qualify the impact of the nineteenth-century privatization and naturalization narrative and suggest a more general perspective, shifted toward structures of perception and economies of attention.

Additionally, historians have pointed out how the lion's share of the work done by men likewise frequently goes undocumented in the relevant sources. In this regard, Lotte van de Pol refers to the early modern period and offers the interpretation that the activities performed did not yet conform to the defining criteria of work that applied from the nineteenth century onward, for these address salaried or wage-earning work in ways that required formal qualifications and established lifelong identities.[6] Claudia Ulbrich, too, has ascertained from her research on a rural area along the German-French border that the following also applies to the first half of the nineteenth century: "The deficiencies of the statistical records affect not only women but also men working in occupations other than the 'typical' rural ones."[7]

Even so, we may assume that hiding and neglecting competences and responsibilities affected women more strongly than men. Amy Louise Erickson, for example, says of the early eighteenth century in England: "The fact is that we still have very little idea of the occupational geography of women. . . . The problem is how to identify women's work or occupation in this period, since most of the known sources identify men by their occupation ('William Jeffreys, tanner,' for example) but women by their marital status ('Martha Custis, widow')."[8] A further problem is posed by incomplete record sets such as registries of apprentices and apprenticeship. And with reference to women, Erickson says the following of London: "The actual number practising at any time in any of the companies' trades must have been much greater than the number recorded as apprentices or taking apprentices."[9]

In light of all this, the aim of the present contribution is to discuss how we could provide a multifaceted picture of women's work and how we could make visible a broad range of women's competences and responsibilities. It should be stated up front that the quality and depth of our insights depend highly on the availability of suitable source material. This becomes particularly apparent when one brings together material from different sources referring to one and the same person.

1. From "maidservant" to "sales assistant"

The initial point of access is a type of source that has seen heavy use above all in the fields of social history and history of the family since the 1970s, namely lists of households or so-called *status animarum* (parish household lists), as well as state census data. Though a major research context for the broad-based evaluation of this material was the question as to household constellations and typologies, these sources have also been used to explore the issue of "occupations" and activities.[10] These various forms of registration have in common the fact that all persons present at a particular point in time in the villages, market towns, and cities in question were recorded according to houses and households and described in varying levels of detail: the information to be found in such entries includes positions in the household, age, family status, origins, and activities. This type of source is available for all of Europe, which allows for interregional and international comparison, which in turn is what makes such material so fascinating. But if the aim is to paint a nuanced picture of various areas of activity, especially where women's work is concerned, sources of this type can prove highly problematic in terms of both how they omit things and how they tend to specify just one main activity.

The 1833 household list of Innichen/San Candido in today's South Tirol includes the two sisters Maria and Christina Fill from Gröden/Val Gardena resident at house number 87. This house belonged to their unmarried aunt, Maria Fill, who both lived there herself and ran the village store. In 1833 and in the following years, her nieces Maria and Christina are listed as "maidservants."[11] This was a classic occupation for women, who practiced it either during a certain phase of life—usually the years prior to their marriage—or their whole lives long.[12] The simple term "maidservant" could, it should be noted, denote any number of things from a broad spectrum of activities.

The year 1838 saw Maria Fill take a husband: the merchant Joseph Bacher, who was originally from a valley near the Brenner Pass. He took over the aunt's house and store,[13] which specialized in cut fabrics, foods, and metalwares.[14] In connection with all this, a lengthy and detailed contract was drawn up to ensure the rights and financial claims of both the aunt and the two nieces.[15] Only a few years later, in January of 1843, Maria Fill died, leaving behind three small daughters. And soon thereafter, her widower Joseph Bacher desired to remarry—a typical demographic pattern.[16] His intended bride was Maria's sister Christina, his sister-in-law. Such a nuptial constellation, however, was forbidden according to both canon and state law.[17] The Catholic Church prohibited marriages between men and women who were related by blood or by marriage up to the fourth degree. This rule approved by the Lateran Council in 1215 remained in force until 1917, though some countries enacted more liberal regulations before then. This did not mean, however, that such marriages were totally impossible. It was possible, in fact to obtain a so-called "dispensation" (a Church instrument that enables to grant an exception to the rule).

During the period of time at issue here, the nineteenth century, close degrees of kinship or affinity—such as first-degree relationship by marriage, in the present case—entailed the necessity of a papal dispensation, while a bishop's dispensation sufficed for more distant degrees. By this time, wedding one's sister-in-law—i.e., the sister of a deceased wife—had become a rather common remarriage pattern for widowers, especially in the German-speaking world.[18] But according to applicable laws,

Joseph Bacher had to submit a dispensation request. Bacher's duly submitted request was rejected by the Brixen consistory in the summer of 1843, after which he made several further attempts, all of which were likewise unsuccessful: his second request was also rejected by the Brixen consistory, a third was at least forwarded to Rome, and early 1845 saw him make his fourth and final attempt.[19] One important consequence of difficult dispensation proceedings with multiple requests is the fact that the documentary material, and hence also the information contained therein, exhibits noticeably greater density. Repeat requests tended to contain ever-more-detailed depictions of concrete situations in life.[20] And in keeping with this, such documents—with their increasingly urgent formulations—facilitate insights into household and family organization as well as into the various activities of men and woman, insights far more revealing than those obtainable from entries in registers. This is demonstrated nicely by the case of Christina Fill.

After his second request (made in March of 1844) had been rejected, Joseph Bacher himself wrote a multiple-page letter of supplication in which he argued that his sister-in-law was irreplaceable at the store. Even during his marriage to her sister, she had been "of outstanding support . . . in running . . . the business" because her aunt and his deceased wife had "completely familiarized" her with running it—enabling her to do a perfect job of replacing him when he was away on business. His sister-in-law had therefore often taken charge of things there "in the frequent cases" of his "travels and other periods of absence." And following his wife's passing, he came to recognize "in its full magnitude . . . the usefulness, in fact, the indispensability" of the help provided by his sister-in-law, "in that she not only . . . willingly ran [his] household" and supported him in running his "village store" but also devoted herself to the "care and raising" of his small children "with truly motherly concern." And a woman was needed, he continued, who was not only "up to dealing with [his] household" but who could also represent him in his "retail business." So in his view, Christina Fill had all the necessary qualities for running not only the household but, above all, the store. He pointed out that "such personnel of the female sex . . . , who possess the necessary characteristics for doing such business," were very rare. Among other things, she spoke Italian.[21] Innichen is located on the border to Veneto and thus between the German- and Italian-speaking worlds, meaning that such language skills most certainly could have been relevant in business dealings. And in the letter that accompanied Bacher's second attempt, the dean of Innichen mentioned that Bacher himself did not understand the "Italian language" but that he "had to do a lot of business with the Italians who arrived by way of the Kreuzberge [Passo Monte Croce]."[22]

The responsible dean of Innichen had made every effort to support the marriage project of Joseph Bacher and Christina Fill as early as the first letter to the Brixen consistory in 1843. He emphasized that the widower needed "a skillful and suitable shop assistant [*Ladenjungfer*], and that Christina Fill [was] just the person for the job since he often had to be away from home to visit the neighboring markets where he purchased the grocery goods for his shop."[23]—At first glance, one would usually not expect a "maidservant" to have such competences.

2. Contexts and implications of source production

The various sources make one very important thing clear: all of the relevant types of documents were produced in specific administrative, social, political, cultural, and other types of contexts, with their authors pursuing certain interests and agendas by concealing/ignoring or emphasizing skills of the persons being registered or described. In some cases, it was even the very same officials who registered the local residents in the parish registers and wrote the letters of recommendation for dispensation requests and questioned the prospective couples. Both tasks were, at any rate, among the responsibilities of the local clergy. We thus see how their use of blanket terms—such as "the maid"—or specification and precise description of the activities, abilities, and responsibilities that were otherwise typically subsumed under such terms was dependent upon the situation and the task at hand. The tendency of women's work to remain invisible in statistical research is something that Claudia Ulbrich, in her study on Steinbiedersdorf, also associates with prevalent notions about and concepts of the family. She writes that women's work "is rarely mentioned in the statistical sources, which were shaped by administrative interests and based on the notion of the 'normal family' with one male head of the household responsible for feeding the family: in the middle of the nineteenth century, one seamstress, two women teachers, and one midwife appear in the occupational statistics."[24] Furthermore, one must underline what Angela Groppi mentioned at the international study week (*settimana di studio*) of the Istituto Datini in Prato back in 1990: that one can understand much more about the economic activities of women (and not only women) by investigating work independent of any predefined categories.[25] For it is not enough to simply count the number of employed women and examine the areas they worked in. Economic activities also included informal and irregular work, consumption, negotiation of transfers of goods, and last but not least things relevant to social capital in the sense of social relationships—including contacts, knowledge, and information—that could be converted into economic resources.[26]

Therefore, studies on the spectrum of activities in which women were involved have long made use of source material that is narratively structured and/or pays attention to social contexts. Peter Earle, for example, analyzed depositions from a consistory court. Of the people who appeared there, about one-third were women. All of them were asked, "How and by what meanes doe you gett your liveing and are you maintained?" The author ascertains, "The bias seems to be that female witnesses were asked and answered personal questions more often than male witnesses and, as it happens, they tended to give more interesting answers."[27] That which is viewed here as "bias" could—interpreted in a productive way—mean two things: First, that various differing cultures of description and narrative styles may have also influenced informational content. However, one must always also keep in mind the role that the person transferring oral answers into written form played in formulation when looking at texts produced in such administrative contexts. Second, it could also be structurally dependent in the sense that women were less able or willing to encapsulate their activities in nouns denoting specific occupations—due to pluriactivity, temporary jobs, involvement in shadow economies, and other factors.

Taken as a whole, court documents represent an important source for a contextualized and everyday world-relevant approach to the activities of women.[28] Far broader based is the project Gender and Work at the University of Uppsala, led by Maria Ågren: its analysis of court records is joined by the evaluation of bookkeeping records,[29] supplication letters, and diaries, above all in order to bring paid and unpaid work by women and children into view. Compared to such sources, the specific nature of dispensation requests in the close degrees lies particularly in the fact that these tend to highlight women's competencies insistently and favorably.[30] This applies in particular to those submitted during difficult periods and contexts, such as the 1830s and early 1840s were for couple constellation of brother- and sister-in-law due to a harsher papal dispensation policy. This is also the context of the ultimately unsuccessful dispensation requests of Joseph Bacher and Christina Fill.

Generally speaking, the more closely related a bride and a groom were, the richer as a historical source their dispensation requests turn out to be. Marriages between relatives of the third or fourth degree were comparably uncontroversial, so their dispensation requests were usually kept rather short. They, primarily, reported causes in formulaic terms and in Latin, which were officially accepted by canon law.[31] Among the most common reasons, we find the *aetas superadulta,* the *incompetentia aut deficientia dotis,* and the *angustia loci*: if the bride had already reached the age of twenty-four, if the bride's parents or the bride herself could not afford to bring a dowry to the marriage or could only afford a small one, and, finally, if the bride could not find in her place of residence a man at least equal in social status to whom she was not related. By contrast, at closer degrees, requests usually went into greater detail in order to build a case beyond the preexisting "canonical reasons." Above all, the administrative procedure was rather complex, inasmuch as the betrothed couples required support from different competent authorities. This implied the production of very interesting sources, still preserved by various episcopal archives. Joseph Bacher and Christina Fill's Diocese of Brixen/Bressanone was especially meticulous in maintaining records of dispensation requests for the close degrees of kinship, but only from 1831 onward.[32] From the previous decades, only registers are available that contain no more than some basic information. From 1831 to 1890, Brixen processed nearly 2,150 requests, which present a wealth of precise historical detail, including extensive accounts of the specific situations.[33]

A few marriage projects were abandoned at an early stage but, in most cases, the dispensation records consist of a series of letters and reports that involved all levels of the church structure, from the parish priest to the prince-bishop and several more in between, such as the dean responsible for a number of parishes and, as it was the case in Vorarlberg, the vicar general. If the prince-bishop's consistory of Brixen/Bressanone was prepared to support the dispensation request, it had to be sent to Rome. Depending on the situation, it was addressed either to the Dataria Apostolica or to the Holy Penitentiary—the latter, in particular, if the bride was pregnant or if the couple was very poor, as the Penitentiary was defined as an institution of grace. Additionally, local authorities and the provincial government in Innsbruck also were involved.[34] The former had to allow the marriage if it represented an economically secure livelihood for the family to be established, the latter had to grant permission to resort to the papal offices in Rome. In the event of a successful application, the provincial government had to confirm the papal document—called a *breve*—and also grant the civil dispensation according to the Austrian civil law code of 1811. The documentation normally included detailed descriptions of the cases dealt with, accompanying letters and evidence, sometimes also medical testimonies and in most cases a pre-matrimonial examination based on a comprehensive set of questions called *examen matrimoniale*. In this examination, two witnesses, the groom, and, finally, the bride had to give valid reasons for seeking a marriage at such a close degree of kinship or affinity.

While on the basis of other cases some scholars argue that dispensations were a simple formality,[35] in nineteenth-century Brixen/Bressanone the opposite was true in any case regarding papal dispensations. A high percentage of dispensation requests were unsuccessful, such as those by Joseph Bacher and Christina Fill. Applications were rejected mainly by the prince-bishop's consistory in Brixen/Bressanone, but, to a certain extent, rejections occurred in Rome as well, especially in the 1830s and 1840s. Interestingly, even though the administrative procedures were complex, expensive, and time consuming, many couples did not give up. After a rejection, they tried to get the authorization to marry again, in some cases four or five times or even more. While on the one hand such stubborn resistance shows how determined they were to become husband and wife, on the other hand their actions produced more and more detailed accounts of the reasons they considered as valid to justify a dispensation, thus offering historians extremely comprehensive sources and insights.

3. Legal and economic contexts: dispensation policy and wealth

At close degrees of kinship and affinity, more pressing grounds for a dispensation were required than at the third or fourth degrees. Assuming that marriage was especially important for women—unmarried women were considered as morally endangered and suspicious—the officially accepted reasons aimed at supporting women's chances of getting married. To prevent women from remaining single, the authorities allowed them to marry a man who was related to them by blood or by marriage. Besides the above-mentioned reasons referring to age, dowry, and the local availability of suitable grooms, the situation of widows burdened with underage children to care for was also recognized as a canonical reason.[36] For men, however, and even for widowers, there were no comparable extenuating circumstances. If the proposed marriage was particularly in their interest, then it was all the more necessary that their personal or familial plight offer sufficient supporting arguments. This "disadvantaging" of men in the canonical marriage logic can be seen especially in the case of widowers with small children—as with Joseph Bacher and Christina Fill. So it is remarkable that their dispensation request addresses Christina Fill first and foremost in terms of her indispensable business and management competencies and only then as the children's aunt, along with her role in running the household. In comparable constellations, the latter role is usually accorded the most prominence. The testimony of the competent local clergymen, of the first witness in the pre-matrimonial examination, and of Joseph Bacher in his letter of supplication are merely variations on the same content.

For instance, Joseph Bacher—even though he calls it "the main thing"—writes only at the end of his first supplication letter,

> But the main thing, and that which worries me most as a father, is the calm and inner peace of my family, the good relationship between my future spouse and my children—and the assiduous care and rearing of the latter. The common expression *stepmotherly treatment* is certainly not an empty one and most assuredly grounded in experience, as a multitude of examples unfortunately prove. And even if I should be so unfortunate as to choose unhappily in this respect, I would still be spared from accusing myself most bitterly for the rest of my life of not having made every effort to secure for my children a mother of whose good qualities, of whose love and attentiveness, I was convinced beyond a doubt based on years of observation.[37]

Favoring an aunt over the "strange" and unequivocally negative figure of the stepmother was a conventional pattern of argumentation in the dispensation requests of these decades.

The 1830s and 1840s saw marital unions at close degrees of affinity faced with a policy of extreme resistance by the papacy of Gregory XVI (1831–46). The only canonical reason for which a dispensation was granted for a marriage at the first degree of affinity was "the danger of renouncing one's true faith" (*periculum defectionis a fide*), which up to Pius IX (1846–78) made it very difficult to marry a sister- or a brother-in-law. So this, then, is the specific context in which Joseph Bacher and Christina Fill's marriage project was attempted.

Since the locally and regionally active clergy from the Brixen consistory had instructions to reject such marriage projects wherever possible, they found themselves under considerable pressure from both sides: from prospective couples, who besieged and beset them to advocate for their causes, and on the other side from the prince-bishop's consistory with its demand that they adamantly reject such requests. It was therefore in the interest of the clergymen working in the parishes and deaneries to forward only the most promising cases to the consistory, which at the same time meant that they had to provide outstandingly good arguments in favor of the marriage projects in question. So in their efforts to portray every possible positive characteristic of the prospective spouse, dispensation requests explicitly mention the various types of qualified work performed by women in order to stress their indispensability in both social and economic respects. The broad spectrum of women's activities that becomes visible in this way is owed to this specific administrative context.

On the other hand, this dispensation case plays down the serious financial issues that threatened to materialize if the marriage were not allowed to take place. In the course of the dispensation proceedings, Christina Fill indicated that she would leave the house if they were unable to marry. And legally, it was indeed the case that couples whose requests had been rejected were not allowed to continue living under the same roof.[38] Such an outcome would, in turn, cause Christina Fill to insist on payment of the monies that had been promised her contractually by her aunt. When her aunt had sold the house to Joseph Bacher, she had promised Christina Fill a third of the house's selling price as a donation. This was three hundred gulden, on which Bacher was obligated to pay interest of 4 percent as long as he had not paid out this sum to her.[39] When arguments of this type, which were of an obviously economic nature, were used in a dispensation request, it could easily work to the supplicant's disadvantage. So it is therefore quite frequently the case that wealth-related implications of marriages between close kin or relatives by marriage only show up in second requests following the rejection of a first. This means that not just what was written but also what went unmentioned was subject to a communicative strategy and can often only be discovered by consulting additional source material.

4. Social and spatial proximity

Upon closer examination, a large number of dispensation applicants' cases show a situation of social and spatial proximity.[40] Marriage plans that needed a dispensation to become effective were often hatched by in-laws who lived under the same roof. Women, then, frequently and sometimes for many years, took on the role of *Wirtschafterin*, i.e. a housekeeper responsible for managing the household. In such situations, the main reason underpinning a marriage plan was that of managing the household of a widower—who was at the same time the *Wirtschafterin*'s brother-in-law. The sister-in-law would often start to help the family before the death of her sister, providing assistance in a difficult family situation—such as lengthy illness of the married sister or the birth of a child—especially if there were very young children. So, the unmarried sister would first support and then replace the wife and mother following the death of the latter. Therefore, she knew how to run the household and was familiar with its wide range of tasks, variable according to the social milieu and the economic activity of the family, such as agriculture, trade, small business, or bourgeoisie. This implies that, alongside housework, women also performed agricultural tasks, contributed business skills, and supervised other workers.

Lorenz Zwickle, a widowed timber merchant, stressed that he did not know how to write and calculate, which was necessary for his trade, and that his bride—his deceased wife's sister—had mastered these skills along with bookkeeping and had already been running his business during his wife's illness and upon her explicit wish.[41] Johann Josef Feuerstein, an innkeeper and landowner who had a considerable trading enterprise (*ausgedehntes Handelsgeschäft*) but viewed himself primarily as an artist, argued that he had only very little time for his business and therefore needed a competent wife. His bride had been doing the accounts since her youth and had, as she well deserved, been "honored with praise and respect" over the years.[42] These cases show clearly that normative models of gender roles were not (re)produced if there was a vital interest in emphasizing women's competences and skills.

An unmarried woman who lived in the household of her sister and brother-in-law could have taken on a position similar to that of a housemaid working for food, shelter, and a modest payment—just helping with the everyday tasks. In case of need, if the married sister was ill or dying, an unmarried sister could often be driven by a sense of obligation to enter her married sister's household as support. She might move there as late as on the occasion of the married sister's death. More often, an unmarried sister may have already been a member of the household for weeks, months, or even years, and would have accepted responsibilities and done all the work that her married sister was no longer able to perform and could have become a close confidant of her married sister—in contrast to "stranger" as maidservant who changes household every year. Therefore, as Leonore Davidoff ascertained, unmarried sisters could have been a "crucial resource in running the household or, among the less well off, as an aid in the family enterprise."[43]

This was especially true in poor families. A widower of limited economic means had few chances to remarry, especially if he had several small children to care for. At the same time, due to a lack of resources, he could not afford to employ a housekeeper or an experienced housemaid. In such situations, a marriage between brother- and sister-in-law might have been the most obvious solution both as regards the running of the household and the caring for the children. In the documentation referring to such cases, women often described their choice as a sacrifice, explaining that their decision was driven by generosity, moral obligation toward their deceased sister, and their pity toward their nephews and nieces. Not surprisingly, research on England shows that the poorest households were most affected by the "marriage with a deceased wife's sister bill" that existed in

Victorian England and prohibited such unions. "If the mother died, the husband could not, as did the more affluent classes, hire a housekeeper. He had to call on a relative, usually the wife's sister. . . . A propertied Englishman could go abroad to marry his deceased wife's sister, but not so a poor man, so the existing law, it was argued, operated unfairly between classes."[44]

Therefore, marriage plans between a widower and his sister-in-law were often the outcome of a cohabitation that might have already lasted a long time. In this context, if the housekeeper became the widower's prospective bride and—if they were lucky—later on his wife, it is difficult to draw an exact line between paid and unpaid work. However, the dispensation required to get married was by no means always obtainable. In the 1830s and 1840s, under the papacy of Gregory XIII, it became very difficult to get a dispensation, especially for couples related in the first degree of affinity—like a widower and his sister-in-law. Particularly, for those applicants who lived under the same roof, the rejection of their dispensation request had serious consequences, because (following a decree of 1807) they were not only prevented to marry, but they were also forced to separate from each other.[45] Having revealed their desire to marry, they were indeed suspected after the rejection of their dispensation request to be or to become concubines; to prevent "concubinage" they had to change their living arrangement. Additional sources, such as court records, show that the law was put into practice and couples were separated by order of the competent civil authorities. At least in some cases, this measure was not effective—as the court officials complained—because the sister-in-law went back after a while, especially if she and her widowered brother-in-law already had children together.

In this context, it becomes visible that sisters-in-law who had worked as housekeepers had sometimes gone unpaid for months or even years, especially in poor households and in cases of great need. Therefore, a forced separation could also have serious financial implications: the widower would then be in debt to his sister-in-law. There are also some cases—like that of Maria Bekel—in which the sister-in-law had even lent her own money to the widower. Bekel's prospective husband Konrad Amor was a widower with five small children from his first marriage and three illegitimate children with his sister-in-law. He stated that Maria Bekel "utilized her small fortune to the greatest possible advantage of my household."[46] His debts would have long since cost him his house had it not been for his sister-in-law, who—according to general opinion—had held the property together. Such entanglement of property and assets was typical of constellations of brothers-in-law and sisters-in-law who lived together. Furthermore, in the case of separation, he would have been neither in a financial position to pay for the maintenance of the illegitimate children outside of his household nor able to employ and pay a maidservant in place of his sister-in-law as an assistant in the household.

Dispensation requests are an extremely detailed source, revealing family crises and efforts to cope with them, existential worries as well as emotional dramas. At the same time, historians have to take into account that the descriptions and arguments provided in this kind of paperwork must be considered as a communication strategy aiming at convincing the authorities to grant the dispensation by addressing and anticipating their expectations. Furthermore, the arguments and descriptions provided by the applicants were filtered and, on the one hand, embellished, and on the other condensed by several intermediaries. Several people other than the applicants were involved in writing the documents: clerical keepers of the minutes, scribes, lawyers,[47] or at least advisors.

Nonetheless, dispensation requests can offer particularly interesting insights on aspects difficult to analyze on the basis of other source material. On a closer look, the relationships between brides and grooms proved to be characterized, in many cases, not only by social and/or emotional proximity but also by spatial proximity. Women's work played a crucial role in this specific context. Compared to other sources, which, on the contrary, undervalued, hid, or even made invisible women's work, their work was highlighted and valued in the dispensation requests.[48] Furthermore, dispensation requests allow us to detect in which situations and ways social relations were activated, used, and exploited in order to guarantee the organization of work, family, and household. According to Bruno Latour's concept of the social, affinal as well as blood relationships are not primarily a matter of formalized and fixed genealogies but are situational and performative: the social is "traceable only when it's being modified."[49]

5. The aspect of the social in performance: exploring levels of agency

As a consequence, various ways of acting provided the basis for this chapter rather than linguistic codes or narrative scripts. This approach exhibits certain parallels to the "verb-oriented method" used by Maria Ågren in the project Gender and Work (1550–1800) to look at selected regions of the Kingdom of Sweden.[50] The objective of her project was to find out exactly how people "used their time with the purpose of making a living." They assumed that this method makes it possible to analyze "working life and working conditions" in societies where a large share of the work was unpaid, where individual people engaged in wide arrays of activities and frequently did not have any particular "occupational" designation, and where "occupations" or professions were not statistically documented or registered. This goes above all for the everyday work done by women and children, both paid and unpaid.

The objective of the present contribution has been to expand upon this approach and portray how such an approach is, indeed, even necessary for those time periods and regions for which serial source materials do exist. This is not only due to the fact that sources that systematically document professions or occupations tend to employ undifferentiated blanket terminology that obscures concrete activities and often exhibits a gender bias (i.e., only provides very partial information on what specific kinds of work people actually did), but also because in cases of pluriactivity, as well, professional labels are usually inadequate.

Margareth Lanzinger is professor of social and economic history at the University of Vienna, Austria. She has held positions as guest professor at the Free University of Berlin and as guest lecturer at Leibniz University of Hanover and at the University of Siegen. Her research interests are within the area of microhistory, historical anthropology, and gender history and focus especially on kinship, marriage, property, legal and administrative practices, the construction of heroes, as well as historiographic topics. She is a member of the editorial boards of *Historische Anthropologie*, *L'Homme: Europäische Zeitschrift für Feministische Geschichtswissenschaft*, and *Quaderni Storici*. Her current research project focuses on "The Role of Wealth in Defining and Constituting Kinship Spaces from 16th to the 18th Century." Her most recent publications include the monograph *Verwandtschaft: Eheverbote, kirchliche und staatliche Dispenspraxis im 18. und 19. Jahrhundert* (Wien: Böhlau, 2015). She has edited several special issues and volumes, including *The Power of the Fathers: Historical Perspectives from Ancient Rome to the Nineteenth Century* (New York: Routledge, 2015). She also edited Edith Saurer's posthumous book *Liebe und Arbeit: Geschlechterbeziehungen im 19. und 20. Jahrhundert* (Wien-Köln-Weimar: Böhlau, 2014). For more details see https://wirtschaftsgeschichte.univie.ac.at/menschen/wissenschaftliche-mitarbeiterinnen/lanzinger-margareth/.

Notes

Some of the empirical material in this chapter was also discussed in my article "Widows and Their Sisters-in-Law: Family Crises, Horizontally Organized Relationships and Affinal Relatives in the Nineteenth Century," *History of the Family*, 24 June 2016. DOI: 10.1080/1081602X.2016.1176586.

1. Karin Hausen, "Family and Role Division: The Polarisation of Sexual Stereotypes in the Nineteenth Century," in *The German Family*, ed. Richard J. Evans and W. R. Lee (London: Croom Helm, 1981); originally published in German: "Die Polarisierung der 'Geschlechtscharaktere': Eine Spiegelung der Dissoziation von Erwerbs- und Familienarbeit," in *Sozialgeschichte der Familie in der Neuzeit Europas*, ed. Werner Conze (Stuttgart: Klett, 1976).
2. Kathleen Canning, Review of *Hausen, Karin: Geschlechtergeschichte als Gesellschaftsgeschichte*. Göttingen: Vandenhoeck & Ruprecht, 2012. Retrieved 15 June 2015 from http://www.hsozkult.de/review/id/rezbuecher-18711?title=test-url-titel.
3. Gisela Bock and Barbara Duden, "Arbeit aus Liebe—Liebe als Arbeit: Zur Entstehung der Hausarbeit im Kapitalismus," in *Frauen und Wissenschaft: Beiträge zur Berliner Sommeruniversität für Frauen, Juli 1976,* ed. Gruppe Berliner Dozentinnen (Berlin: Courage-Verlag, 1977).
4. Heide Wunder, *He Is the Sun, She Is the Moon: Women in Early Modern Germany* (1992; Cambridge, MA: Harvard University Press, 1998), chap. 4, "Work and Life Become Family-Based."
5. "Although Wunder indicates the possibility of conflictual relationships in various contexts, her approach, as well, is based on a model of harmony, a model that presupposes historical subjects who align their lives with the accepted norms of estate-based society. As a result of her emphasis on togetherness and on the fact that individuals are embedded within social groups, the notion of hierarchy loses valence and a different notion of equality becomes visible, one that is more appropriate to the early modern period." Claudia Ulbrich, *Shulamit and Margarete: Power, Gender, and Religion in a Rural Society in Eighteenth-Century Europe* (Boston: Brill, 2004), 13.
6. Lotte van de Pol, "Frauenarbeit," in *Enzyklopädie der Neuzeit* (Stuttgart: Metzler, 2006), 3:1101–2.
7. Ulbrich, *Shulamit and Margarete*, 95.
8. Amy Louise Erickson, "Identifying Women's Occupations in Early Modern London," unpublished paper, presented at the ESSHC, Amsterdam, March 2006, 1. Retrieved 18 May 2015 from http://www.geog.cam.ac.uk/research/projects/occupations/abstracts/paper13.pdf.
9. Ibid., 4.
10. Peter Laslett and Richard Wall, eds., *Household and Family in Past Time* (Cambridge: Cambridge University Press, 1972); Richard Wall et al., eds., *Family Forms in Historic Europe* (Cambridge: Cambridge University Press, 1993); Josef Ehmer and Michael Mitterauer, eds., *Familienstruktur und Arbeitsorganisation in ländlichen Gesellschaften* (Wien: Böhlau, 1985). On the use of census data as basic information on occupations, see for example the volume by Marco H. D. van Leeuwen, Ineke Maas, and Andrew Miles, eds., *Marriage Choices and Class Boundaries: Social Endogamy in History; International Review of Social History, Supplement 13* (Cambridge: Cambridge University Press, 2005).
11. Stiftsarchiv (STA) Innichen/San Candido, Familienbuch 1829, house no. 87. The records of this status animarum begin with the year 1828 and, with a multiyear interruption from 1844 to 1848, extend in part up to 1850. See in this regard Margareth Lanzinger, *Das gesicherte Erbe: Heirat in lokalen und familialen Kontexten, Innichen 1700–1900* (Wien-Köln-Weimar: Böhlau 2003), 51–52; Margareth Lanzinger, "Anna Fill & Co. Wohn- und Arbeitssituation, Besitz und Vorsorge lediger Frauen in Innichen im 19. Jahrhundert," in *Der ledige Un-Wille: Zur Geschichte lediger Frauen in der Neuzeit / Norma e contrarietà: una storia del nubilato in età moderna e contemporanea*, ed. Siglinde Clementi and Alessandra Spada (Wien-Bozen: Folio, 1998).
12. Raffaella Sarti, "Who Are Servants? Defining Domestic Service in Western Europe (16th–21st Centuries)," in *Proceedings of the Servant Project*, ed. Suzy Pasleau and Isabelle Schopp, with Raffaella Sarti (Liège: Éditions de l'Université de Liège, 2005), 2:3–59;

Raffaella Sarti, "'All Masters Discourage the Marrying of Their Male Servants, and Admit Not by Any Means the Marriage of the Female': Domestic Service and Celibacy in Western Europe from the Sixteenth to the Nineteenth Century," in "Unmarried Lives," special issue of *European History Quarterly* 38, no. 3 (2008): 417–49.
13. Tiroler Landesarchiv (TLA) Innsbruck, Verfachbuch Heinfels (VBH) 1838, fol. 209–11.
14. Original: "*Schnitt-, Spezerei und Eisenwaren*" [cut fabrics, foods, and metalwares]—according to the first witness's testimony in the pre-matrimonial examination.
15. TLA Innsbruck, VBH 1838, fol. 209.
16. In Western European societies, the dominant pattern was that widowers, following the deaths of their wives, tended to remarry significantly sooner and more often than widows. See Antoinette Fauve-Chamoux, "Revisiting the Decline of Remarriage in Early-Modern Europe: The Case of Rheims in France," *History of the Family* 15, no. 3 (2010): 291; Sylvie Perrier, "La marâtre dans la France d'Ancien Régime: integration ou marginalité?," *Annales de démographie historique*, no. 2 (2006): 176–78.
17. See Michael Mitterauer, "Christianity and Endogamy," *Continuity and Change* 6, no. 3 (1991).
18. See Margareth Lanzinger, *Verwaltete Verwandtschaft: Eheverbote, kirchliche und staatliche Dispenspraxis im 18. und 19. Jahrhundert* (Wien-Köln-Weimar: Böhlau, 2015), chap. 4; Edith Saurer, "Belles-mères et beaux-fils: Au sujet du choix du partenaire en Autriche vers 1800," *Annales de démographie historique* (1998): 60.
19. Diözesanarchiv Brixen/Bressanone (DIÖAB), Konsistorialakten 1844, fasc. 5a, Römische Dispensen, no. 4.
20. For the period between 1831 and 1864, nearly 20 percent of the examined requests from the Diocese of Brixen are ones that were submitted following a previous rejection.
21. DIÖAB, Konsistorialakten 1844, fasc. 5a, Römische Dispensen, no. 4, letter dated 21 May 1844 from Joseph Bacher.
22. Ibid., letter dated 8 March 1844 from the dean of Innichen.
23. Ibid., letter dated 17 July 1843 from the dean of Innichen.
24. Ulbrich, *Shulamit und Margarete*, 95.
25. Angela Groppi, "Il lavoro delle donne: un questionario da arricchire," in *La donna nell'economia secc. XIII–XVIII*, ed. Simonetta Cavaciocchi (Firenze: Le Monnier, 1990), 149.
26. Renata Ago, "Lavoro, credito ed economia nella storiografia italiana di età moderna," *Genesis: Rivista della Società italiana delle storiche* 8, no. 1 (2009): 73–74, with regard to "Tavola rotonda finale," in *La donna nell'economia, secc. XIII–XVIII*, ed. Simonetta Cavaciocchi (Firenze: Le Monnier, 1990), 698; on this, see also "I lavori delle donne," special issue of *Memoria* (1990), as well as the recently published volume by Gabriele Jancke and Daniel Schläppi, eds., *Die Ökonomie sozialer Beziehungen: Ressourcenbewirtschaftung als Geben, Nehmen, Investieren, Verschwenden, Haushalten Horten, Vererben, Schulden* (Stuttgart: Steiner, 2015).
27. Peter Earle, "The Female Labour Market in London in the Late Seventeenth and Early Eighteenth Centuries," *Economic History Review* 42, no. 3 (1989): 330.
28. See for example Amy Louise Erickson, "Married Women's Occupations in Eighteenth-Century London," *Continuity and Change* 23, no. 2 (2008); Anne Montenach, "Legal Trade and Black Markets: Foodtrades in Lyon in the Late Seventeenth and Early Eighteenth Centuries," in *Female Agency in the Urban Economy: Gender in European Towns, 1640–1830*, ed. Anne Montenach and Deborah Simonton (New York: Routledge, 2013).
29. Rosemarie Fiebranz, Erik Lindberg, Jonas Lindström, and Maria Ågren, "Making Verbs Count: The Research Project 'Gender and Work' and Its Methodology," *Scandinavian Economic History Review* 59, no. 3 (2011): 280; Maria Ågren, ed., *Making a Living, Making a Difference: Gender and Work in Early Modern Society* (Oxford: Oxford University Press, 2017); see also Maria Ågren's contribution in this volume.

30. This research project was financed by a Hertha Firnberg Postdoctoral Fellowship (2005 to 2007) and an Elise Richter Postdoctoral Fellowship (2008 to 2011) granted by the Austrian Science Fund (FWF).
31. André Burguière, using French source material from the eighteenth century, notes that the arguments are primarily stereotypical and closely aligned with the predetermined official canonical grounds, therefore hardly allowing a qualitative evaluation or more far-reaching conclusions beyond a quantitative collection of aspects. André Burguière, "'Cher Cousin': Les usages matrimoniaux de la parenté proche dans la France du 18e siècle," *Annales Histoire, Sciences Sociales* 52, no. 6 (1997): 1346–47. The same applies to the third- and fourth-degree dispensation requests of the Diocese of Brixen.
32. The Diocese of Brixen includes Vorarlberg and a large part of historical Tirol (present-day Austrian North Tirol and Italian South Tirol), excluding the areas belonging to the Dioceses of Trento and Salzburg. According to the ecclesiastic "census of souls," the Brixen diocese was home to approximately 355,000 inhabitants in 1829 and 400,000 inhabitants toward the end of the nineteenth century. See Catalogus personarum ecclesiasticarum Dioecesis Brixinensis ad initium anni MCCCCXXXI, vol. 22 (Brixen: Weger, 1831), 352; Schematismus der Säcular- und Regular-Geistlichkeit der Diözese Brixen, 1892, vol. 76 (Brixen: Weger, 1892), 230. The diocese was divided into twenty-six, later on twenty-eight, deaneries. These were the units of administration by the Church, each under the leadership of a dean.
33. Due to the completeness and the chronological order in the archives of the Diocese of Brixen, in contrast to the other archives used, it was possible to create a database. For the overall study, this material is complemented by samples taken from the neighboring Dioceses of Chur, Salzburg, and Trento. Lanzinger, *Verwaltete Verwandtschaft*.
34. With first regulations passed by Empress Maria Theresia in the 1770s and with the Marriage Patent of 1783 issued by Joseph II, in Austria the state interfered on a massive scale in matrimonial matters—up to then almost exclusively a church domain—including marriage impediments and the associated administrative procedures. See Margareth Lanzinger, "Staatliches und kirchliches Recht in Konkurrenz: Verwandtenehen und Dispenspraxis im Tirol des ausgehenden 18. Jahrhunderts," *Geschichte und Region / Storia e regione* 20, no. 2 (2011); Margareth Lanzinger, "Mariages entre parents, l'économie de mariage et le 'bien commun': La politique de dispense de l'Etat dans l'Autriche de l'Ancien Régime finissant," in *Construire les liens de famille dans l'Europe moderne*, ed. Anna Bellavitis, Laura Casella, and Dorith Raines (Mont Saint Aignan: Presses Universitaires de Rouen et du Havre, 2013).
35. David Warren Sabean, "Kinship and Class Dynamics in Nineteenth-Century Europe," in *Kinship in Europe: Approaches to Long-Term Development (1300–1900)*, ed. David Warren Sabean, Simon Teuscher, and Jon Mathieu (New York: Berghahn Books, 2007): 310–11.
36. See Edith Saurer, "Stiefmütter und Stiefsöhne: Endogamieverbote zwischen kanonischem und zivilem Recht am Beispiel Österreichs (1790–1850)," in *Frauen in der Geschichte des Rechts: Von der Frühen Neuzeit bis zur Gegenwart*, ed. Ute Gerhard (Munich: Beck, 1997), 356–57.
37. DIÖAB, Konsistorialakten 1844, fasc. 5a, Römische Dispensen, no. 4, letter of 21 May 1844 from Joseph Bacher, emphasised words underlined in the original.
38. In 1807, a court decree was issued that forbade further cohabitation by couples whose dispensation requests had been turned down. Hofkanzleidekret vom 9. Juli 1807, in Franz des Ersten politische Gesetze und Verordnungen für die Oesterreichischen, Böhmischen und Galizischen Erbländer, vol. 29, part 2 (Wien: k. k. Hof- und Staatsdruckerei, 1809), 16–17, no. 6.
39. TLA Innsbruck, VBI 1838, fol. 209–11, point one of the "conditions." In this case, it proved possible to reconstruct the story that followed this failed marriage project based on the data retrieved as part of a microstudy: Joseph Bacher went on to marry the daughter

of a glovemaker from the neighboring village of Toblach in 1846, while 1847 saw Christina Fill marry the widower Franz Eisendle, also a merchant, who had arrived in Innichen around the same time as Joseph Bacher and at first was a companion of his, with both of them having lived in the same house during their initial years in Innichen. Lanzinger, *Das gesicherte Erbe*, 326. In the next generation (1867), a daughter from Bacher's first marriage married a son from Eisendle's first marriage.

40. A similar situation is referred to by Margherita Pelaja, "Marriage by Exception: Marriage Dispensations and Ecclesiastical Policies in Nineteenth-Century Rome," *Journal of Modern Italian Studies* 1, no. 2 (1996): 238–40.
41. DIÖAB, Konsistorialakten 1853, fasc. 5a, Römische Dispensen, no. 5.
42. He is described by her as "gentle and kind." The dispensation was granted. DIÖAB, Konsistorialakten 1854, fasc. 5a, Römische Dispensen, no. 11.
43. Leonore Davidoff, *Thicker than Water: Siblings and Their Relations, 1780–1920* (Oxford: Oxford University Press, 2012), 154.
44. Nancy F. Anderson, "The 'Marriage with a Deceased Wife's Sister Bill' Controversy: Incest Anxiety and the Defense of Family Purity in Victorian England," *Journal of British Studies* 21, no. 2 (1982): 80–81; see also Margaret Morganroth Gullette, "The Puzzling Case of the Deceased Wife's Sister: Nineteenth-Century England Deals with a Second-Chance Plot," *Representations* 31, no. 2 (1990): 145; Polly Morris, "Incest or Survival Strategy? Plebeian Marriage within the Prohibited Degrees in Somerset, 1730–1835," *Journal of the History of Sexuality* 2, no. 2 (1991).
45. Hofkanzleidekret vom 9. Juli 1807 (see note 38).
46. DIÖAB, Konsistorialakten 1831, Fasz. 5a, Römische Dispensen, no. 6.
47. In contrast to Vienna and Lower Austria (Saurer, "Stiefmütter," 355), the diocese of Brixen saw lawyers and/or barrack-room lawyers employed only rarely. In the context of the administrative procedures, which were dominated here by the Church, such helpers were viewed as representing the more liberal civil rights that ran counter to the superiority of the Church and stricter canon law in questions of marriages between relatives. So using a lawyer could easily put the applicants at a disadvantage.
48. See Dionigi Albera's concept of the "organisation domestique" that is understood as all kinds of relations activated in connection with cohabitation, production, distribution, transmission, and reproduction. Dionigi Albera, *Au fil des générations: Terre, pouvoir et parenté dans l'Europe alpine (XIVe–XXe siècles)* (Grenoble: Presses universitaires de Grenoble, 2011), 7, 47–48.
49. Bruno Latour, *Reassembling the Social: An Introduction to Actor-Network-Theory* (Oxford: Oxford University Press, 2005), 159.
50. See http://www2.statsvet.uu.se/Default.aspx?alias=www2.statsvet.uu.se/genderandwork; Fiebranz et al., "Making Verbs Count"; Elisabeth Gräslund Berg et al., "Praktiker som gör skillnad: Om den verb-inriktade metoden," *Historisk Tidskrift* 133, no. 3 (2013).

References

Ago, Renata. "Lavoro, credito ed economia nella storiografia italiana di età moderna." *Genesis: Rivista della Società italiana delle storiche* 8, no. 1 (2009): 67–81.

Ågren, Maria, ed. *Making a Living, Making a Difference: Gender and Work in Early Modern Society*. Oxford: Oxford University Press, 2017.

Albera, Dionigi. *Au fil des générations: Terre, pouvoir et parenté dans l'Europe alpine (XIVe–XXe siècles)*. Grenoble: Presses universitaires de Grenoble, 2011.

Anderson, Nancy F. "The 'Marriage with a Deceased Wife's Sister Bill' Controversy:

Incest Anxiety and the Defense of Family Purity in Victorian England." *Journal of British Studies* 21, no. 2 (1982): 67–86.
Bock, Gisela, and Barbara Duden. "Arbeit aus Liebe—Liebe als Arbeit: Zur Entstehung der Hausarbeit im Kapitalismus." In *Frauen und Wissenschaft: Beiträge zur Berliner Sommeruniversität für Frauen, Juli 1976*, edited by Gruppe Berliner Dozentinnen, 118–99. Berlin: Courage-Verlag, 1977.
Burguière, André. "'Cher Cousin': Les usages matrimoniaux de la parenté proche dans la France du 18ᵉ siècle." *Annales Histoire, Sciences Sociales* 52, no. 6 (1997): 1339–60.
Canning, Kathleen. Review of *Hausen, Karin: Geschlechtergeschichte als Gesellschaftsgeschichte*. Göttingen: Vandenhoeck & Ruprecht, 2012. Retrieved 15 June 2015 from http://www.hsozkult.de/review/id/rezbuecher-18711?title=test-url-titel.
Catalogus personarum ecclesiasticarum Dioecesis Brixinensis ad initium anni MCCCCXXXI. Vol. 22. Brixen: Weger, 1831.
Davidoff, Leonore. *Thicker than Water: Siblings and Their Relations, 1780–1920*. Oxford: Oxford University Press, 2012.
Earle, Peter. "The Female Labour Market in London in the Late Seventeenth and Early Eighteenth Centuries." *Economic History Review* 42, no. 3 (1989): 328–53.
Ehmer, Josef, and Michael Mitterauer, eds. *Familienstruktur und Arbeitsorganisation in ländlichen Gesellschaften*. Wien: Böhlau, 1985.
Erickson, Amy Louise. "Identifying Women's Occupations in Early Modern London." Unpublished paper presented at the ESSHC, Amsterdam, March 2006, 1. Retrieved 18 May 2015 from http://www.geog.cam.ac.uk/research/projects/occupations/abstracts/paper13.pdf.
———. "Married Women's Occupations in Eighteenth-Century London." *Continuity and Change* 23, no. 2 (2008): 267–307.
Fauve-Chamoux, Antoinette. "Revisiting the Decline of Remarriage in Early-Modern Europe: the Case of Rheims in France." *History of the Family* 15, no. 3 (2010), 283–97.
Fiebranz, Rosemarie, Erik Lindberg, Jonas Lindström, and Maria Ågren. "Making Verbs Count: The Research Project 'Gender and Work' and Its Methodology." *Scandinavian Economic History Review* 59, no. 3 (2011): 273–93.
Franz des Ersten politische Gesetze und Verordnungen für die Oesterreichischen, Böhmischen und Galizischen Erbländer. Vol. 29, part 2. Wien: k. k. Hof- und Staatsdruckerei, 1809.
Gräslund Berg, Elisabeth, et al. "Praktiker som gör skillnad: Om den verb-inriktade metoden." *Historisk Tidskrift* 133, no. 3 (2013): 335–54.
Groppi, Angela. "Il lavoro delle donne: un questionario da arricchire." In *La donna nell'economia secc. XIII–XVIII*, edited by Simonetta Cavaciocchi, 143–54. Firenze: Le Monnier, 1990.
Hausen, Karin. "Family and Role Division: The Polarisation of Sexual Stereotypes in the Nineteenth Century." In *The German Family*, edited by Richard J. Evans and W. R. Lee, 51–83. London: Croom Helm, 1981; originally published in German: "Die Polarisierung der 'Geschlechtscharaktere': Eine Spiegelung der Dissoziation von Erwerbs- und Familienarbeit." In *Sozialgeschichte der Familie in der Neuzeit Europas*, edited by Werner Conze, 363–93. Stuttgart: Klett, 1976.
"I lavori delle donne," special issue of *Memoria* 30 (1990).

Jancke, Gabriele, and Daniel Schläppi, eds. *Die Ökonomie sozialer Beziehungen: Ressourcenbewirtschaftung als Geben, Nehmen, Investieren, Verschwenden, Haushalten Horten, Vererben, Schulden*. Stuttgart: Steiner, 2015.

Lanzinger, Margareth. "Anna Fill & Co. Wohn- und Arbeitssituation, Besitz und Vorsorge lediger Frauen in Innichen im 19. Jahrhundert." In *Der ledige Un-Wille: Zur Geschichte lediger Frauen in der Neuzeit / Norma e contrarietà: Una storia del nubilato in età moderna e contemporanea*, edited by Siglinde Clementi and Alessandra Spada, 67–98. Wien-Bozen: Folio, 1998.

———. *Das gesicherte Erbe: Heirat in lokalen und familialen Kontexten, Innichen 1700–1900*. Wien-Köln-Weimar: Böhlau 2003.

———. "Staatliches und kirchliches Recht in Konkurrenz: Verwandtenehen und Dispenspraxis im Tirol des ausgehenden 18. Jahrhunderts." *Geschichte und Region / Storia e regione* 20, no. 2 (2011): 73–91.

———. "Mariages entre parents, l'économie de mariage et le 'bien commun': La politique de dispense de l'Etat dans l'Autriche de l'Ancien Régime finissant." In *Construire les liens de famille dans l'Europe moderne*, edited by Anna Bellavitis, Laura Casella, and Dorith Raines, 69–83. Mont Saint Aignan: Presses Universitaires de Rouen et de Havre, 2013.

———. *Verwaltete Verwandtschaft: Eheverbote, kirchliche und staatliche Dispenspraxis im 18. und 19. Jahrhundert*. Wien-Köln-Weimar: Böhlau, 2015.

Laslett, Peter, and Richard Wall, eds. *Household and Family in Past Time*. Cambridge: Cambridge University Press, 1972.

Latour, Bruno. *Reassembling the Social: An Introduction to Actor-Network-Theory*. Oxford: Oxford University Press, 2005.

Mitterauer, Michael. "Christianity and Endogamy." *Continuity and Change* 6, no. 3 (1991): 295–333.

Montenach, Anne. "Legal Trade and Black Markets: Foodtrades in Lyon in the Late Seventeenth and Early Eighteenth Centuries." In *Female Agency in the Urban Economy: Gender in European Towns, 1640–1830*, edited by Anne Montenach and Deborah Simonton, 17–33. New York: Routledge, 2013.

Morganroth Gullette, Margaret. "The Puzzling Case of the Deceased Wife's Sister: Nineteenth-Century England Deals with a Second-Chance Plot." *Representations* 31, no. 2 (1990): 142–66.

Morris, Polly. "Incest or Survival Strategy? Plebeian Marriage within the Prohibited Degrees in Somerset, 1730–1835." *Journal of the History of Sexuality* 2, no. 2 (1991): 235–65.

Pelaja, Margherita. "Marriage by Exception: Marriage Dispensations and Ecclesiastical Policies in Nineteenth-Century Rome." *Journal of Modern Italian Studies* 1, no. 2 (1996): 223–44.

Perrier, Sylvie. "La marâtre dans la France d'Ancien Régime: integration ou marginalité?" *Annales de démographie historique*, no. 2 (2006): 171–87.

Sabean, David Warren. "Kinship and Class Dynamics in Nineteenth-Century Europe." In *Kinship in Europe: Approaches to Long-Term Development (1300–1900)*, edited by David Warren Sabean, Simon Teuscher, and Jon Mathieu, 301–13. New York: Berghahn Books, 2007.

Sarti, Raffaella. "Who Are Servants? Defining Domestic Service in Western Europe (16th–21st Centuries)." In *Proceedings of the Servant Project,* edited by Suzy

Pasleau and Isabelle Schopp, with Raffaella Sarti, 2:3–59. Liège: Éditions de l'Université de Liège, 2005.

———. "'All Masters Discourage the Marrying of Their Male Servants, and Admit Not by Any Means the Marriage of the Female': Domestic Service and Celibacy in Western Europe from the Sixteenth to the Nineteenth Century." In "Unmarried Lives," special issue of *European History Quarterly* 38, no. 3 (2008): 417–49.

Saurer, Edith. "Stiefmütter und Stiefsöhne: Endogamieverbote zwischen kanonischem und zivilem Recht am Beispiel Österreichs (1790–1850)." In *Frauen in der Geschichte des Rechts: Von der Frühen Neuzeit bis zur Gegenwart*, edited by Ute Gerhard, 345–66. München: Beck, 1997.

———. "Belles-mères et beaux-fils: Au sujet du choix du partenaire en Autriche vers 1800." *Annales de démographie historique* (1998): 59–71.

Schematismus der Säcular- und Regular-Geistlichkeit der Diözese Brixen. 1892, vol. 76. Brixen: Weger, 1892.

"Tavola rotonda finale." In *La donna nell'economia secc. XIII–XVIII*, edited by Simonetta Cavaciocchi, 689–705. Firenze: Le Monnier, 1990.

Ulbrich, Claudia. *Shulamit and Margarete: Power, Gender, and Religion in a Rural Society in Eighteenth-Century Europe*. Boston: Brill, 2004.

van de Pol, Lotte, "Frauenarbeit." In *Enzyklopädie der Neuzeit*, 3:1101–6. Stuttgart: Metzler, 2006.

van Leeuwen, Marco H. D., Ineke Maas, and Andrew Miles eds. *Marriage Choices and Class Boundaries: Social Endogamy in History; International Review of Social History, Supplement 13*. Cambridge: Cambridge University Press, 2005.

Wall, Richard, et al., eds. *Family Forms in Historic Europe*. Cambridge: Cambridge University Press, 1993.

Wunder, Heide. *He Is the Sun, She Is the Moon: Women in Early Modern Germany*. Cambridge, MA: Harvard University Press, 1998.

III

THE VALUE OF CARE AND UNPAID HOME-BASED WORK: THE ROLE OF THE LAW

Studies focusing on the medieval and early modern periods show that working within one's family normally gave people some rights to the family revenues and assets, entitling them to some form of remuneration, although in fact both the actual amount, form, and timing of such remuneration, intermingling with moral and legal norms, were often different according to age, gender, position within the family, etc. Family members were therefore involved in complex networks of gendered and generational rights and duties, solidarities and obligations, credits and debts: reducing any unwaged activities performed at home to the category of "unpaid" and free work would therefore be highly misleading.

Yet, as explained in previous chapters, from the late eighteenth century onward, the domestic sphere was increasingly considered the site of love and love-driven free activities, and these ideas were solidified in law: for instance, as explained by Maria Rosaria Marella in her chapter in this section, in Italy, the Constitution (article 29) defines the family as a "natural society" based on marriage. The 1975 Italian reform of family law has tried to overcome such a naturalization, but the recognition of the productive function of the family is still limited to the regime of the family business, according to which the family members who work for the family and/or the family business have the right to be supported according to the family's wealth and to share in the business earnings. For the rest, the dominant idea is that there is a natural obligation of solidarity among family members that excludes any economic exchanges, and the courts issue their sentences accordingly. Nonetheless, free activities done out of natural obligation are (surprisingly) valuable with market parameters in relations with a third party, the last solution being common, according to Marella, both to the common and civil law systems.

As in Italy, in France, too, the state attitude toward the regulation of home-based work has turned out to be difficult and ambiguous. The French parliament has been very slow in defining the legal status of family workers. In a country with inclusive and generous social rights, a law granting occupational status to collaborating spouses as well as social security benefits to those performing unpaid work for the family business was enacted as late as 1982 and implied pinpointing the boundaries of work that, exceeding the obligation to assist one's spouse, gives right to compensation. As illustrated by Florence Weber in her chapter, the French are legally obliged to support a family member in need (spouse, parent, child, grandparent, grandchildren, son-in-law, daughter-in-law, mother-in-law, father-in-law, but not siblings). The so-called *piété filiale* (filial devotion) is an absolute obligation: all children, independently from their relationships and economic exchanges with their parents, have an identical obligation to care for them; furthermore, the care they provide does not affect their shares of the inheritance. Yet, in two cases the law considers the reality of family relations: in 1939, a law was introduced to compensate with "deferred wages" (*salaires différés*), to be settled with a larger share of the inheritance, the children who remained with their parents working for free on their family farms. Furthermore, a judgment of 12 July 1994, by the French Supreme Court introduced the notion of unjust enrichment within family relations (*enrichissement sans cause dans les relations de famille*), which granted a larger share of inheritance to a man who cared for his elderly parents more than his sister and who had become impoverished.

These cases reveal the difficulty of distinguishing between unpaid market-oriented work performed within the family business and care work done because of love or moral obligations. It is not just state authorities, however, who have tried and try to regulate home-based labor. In her chapter, Eileen Boris illustrates how difficult it was, even within the International Labour Office, whose mainly male representatives initially considered only paid extra-domestic work as proper work, to recognize the need to also consider as such the various activities performed at home by women. Previous chapters have illustrated the statistical "invisibilization" of women's work in censuses and similar sources. The obscuring of female labor actually also affected the sources produced by the International Labour Office, even though the research and campaigns supported by this institution were and are crucial for the acknowledgment of the value of different types of home-based work. The ILO-sponsored book *Lace Makers of Narsapur: Indian Housewives Produce for the World Mar-*

ket by Maria Mies (1982), for instance, denounced the housewifization of secluded poor Christian and Hindu women who, in Andhra Pradesh, India, produced lace that yielded about 90 percent of the state's handicrafts export earnings: they were not even considered workers, despite the long hours spent in lace work. Slowly, however, especially thanks to engaged women, women's labor has moved from the periphery to the center of ILO policies: the ILO has passed important conventions, such as Convention no. 177 on home work in 1996 and Convention no. 189 on "Decent Work for Domestic Workers" in 2011, which today represent a cornerstone in the battle for decent work and fair globalization.

CHAPTER 8

REGULATING HOME LABORS
The ILO and the Feminization of Work

Eileen Boris

Writing in 1984 to the Program on Rural Women about its questionnaire on home-based workers, Andrea Singh of the New Delhi office of the International Labor Organization (ILO) reported in dismay that one of her correspondents "was of the impression that the information we wanted to collect referred to domestic servants."[1] This conflation of garment outworkers and domestic in-workers was not the first time that policymakers and politicians misread one form of home-based labor for another or sought to attach the circumstances of unpaid to paid home labors. Naturalized as women's work, home labor retained its association with wives, mothers, and daughters even after commodification or deployment for income generation.

Thirty-five years earlier, Mildred Fairchild, the chief of the ILO's Women's and Young Workers' Section in Geneva, also confronted conflation of different forms of home labor. The Director-General's office requested that she add to a proposed survey of the conditions of domestic service the issue of the economic value of women's work in the home. In response, she offered an admittedly "rather far-fetched" and imprecise attaching of unpaid housewifery onto either the ongoing study of domestic workers or the one on social services to relieve the family responsibilities of wage-earning women.[2]

A year later, R. A. Métall, the chief of the ILO's International Organizations Section in New York, asked Fairchild, a U.S. citizen and former professor of social investigation at Bryn Mawr College in Pennsylvania, to figure some way to accommodate the ILO's friends on the United

Nations (UN) Economic and Social Council with a study of "women's work in the home." Perhaps Fairchild might estimate the economic value of such labor by figuring the costs of replacement on the market or by linking estimated wages for housewives to those actually given to people employed to perform similar tasks—procedures that at the same time seemed "unscientific" to Fairchild but that a later generation of feminist economists would deploy.[3] Métall cautioned that "the philosophical and sociological considerations about the importance of women working at home and playing their part in family life would need to be brought in on the lines of the speeches of the Belgian, French and Lebanese Members in such a way that the various organisations concerned [traditional Catholic women's groups] could have the satisfaction of quoting in their periodicals excerpts which would please them." Recognizing the political nature of this request, he admitted, "I do not mean, of course, that the Office should necessarily fall for their views," to which Fairchild reacted, "Ha??"[4]

The astonishment of this trained social economist that she would generate anecdotal evidence for traditional Catholic women's groups to undermine the rationale for women's employment underscores the politics of the very knowledge produced by the ILO that historians and other scholars have relied upon for reliable data. Formed in the cauldron of worker unrest in 1919 and attached to the League of Nations, the ILO survived World War II to become a specialized agency of the UN focused on work, employment, and labor standards. Among its duties after World War II was carrying out research for other UN sections. Its internal organization—the International Labor Office (the Office) run by an elected Director-General, an annual International Labor Conference (ILC), and an elected Governing Body—resembles that of the UN itself. But the ILO is uniquely tripartite, with all committees and national delegations divided between government, worker, and employer representatives. Setting norms for the world of work, the ILC passes recommendations and treaty-like conventions that become legally binding when nations ratify them. These instruments have offered organizers an additional tool to press for legislative and legal change at the country level. The agency also has engaged in technical assistance, advising governments, unions, and NGOs on administrative, legal, educational, and other programs (such as vocational training and cooperative enterprise.)[5]

Initially, the ILO conceived of the worker as a man employed in industry, transport, agriculture, or extractive processes, most of which took place away from residential spaces. Labor standards codified conditions; they created agreed-upon rules for the arena of formal employment. Though ILO conventions were to include all workers, regardless of sex, few women appeared in covered sectors, except for textiles and plantations, and even there they were subjected to their own protections, like restrictions on night work. In ILO deliberations, the woman worker emerged as a special kind of worker who required targeted conventions that addressed bodily functions and social circumstances—such as maternity, exposure to hazardous substances, and family responsibilities—that were thought to distinguish women from men. While labor protections regulated the excesses of capitalist and colonial exploitation, women (and some classes of men) also came under cultures of protection based on perceived differences from the male industrial breadwinner amid concerns over sexuality, marriage, family, proper behavior, and dependent status (i.e., colonized and indigenous people).[6]

When it came to the woman worker, this dual agenda—universal standards and special protections—stayed with the ILO until the 1980s when it finally embraced the Convention to End Discrimination Against Women and gender mainstreaming, while ending its defense of women-only protections. However, the organization had emphasized equality discourses for decades, despite retaining a handful of women-only instruments. As Fairchild informed a committee of women trade unionists in 1952, "Thinking has been moving from primary interest shown earlier in the protection of women, to primary interest in the development of employment opportunities for women."[7] This declaration occurred after the passage of C#100 "Equal Remuneration" (1951), which the Governing Body had placed on the organization's agenda instead of standards for domestic and industrial homeworkers that labor feminists also wanted. The ILO focused on other items that appeared genderless, like "free association" and collective bargaining, but disproportionately benefited male workers, who were more likely to be in unionized occupations.

By 1965, the Consultative Committee on "Women Workers' Problems" recommended a goal that labor feminists had held from the start but ILO founders had dismissed: "an evolution of social policy directed towards obtaining similar protective standards for men and women, with as few differentials as possible," aside from maternity protection "in the broadest sense."[8] While pushing for equality between the sexes, these experts also distinguished women in industrialized countries from those in "developing" ones, the latter who still required special protections due to presumably harsher conditions, including patriarchal oppression in the family and economic underdevelopment.[9] If women stood for difference against a white European male norm, then "women in developing countries" represented "difference's other."[10] Only in 1990 was the most controversial of the old women-only protections, Night Work, revised to cover men as well (C#171).[11]

Historians have followed the same path as the ILO itself presumably did by focusing on its protective codes for the woman worker, rarely considering anti-discrimination conventions and efforts to increase employment opportunity.[12] This chapter offers another narrative by looking where the majority of the world's women have worked: the home. Present even when absent, the home haunts the making of global labor standards, hovering as a hidden but essential force as the "invisible" labor performed there makes it possible for all other work to occur, as today's domestic worker activists often remind policymakers and the public alike.[13]

In recovering the intertwined history of home labors, that is, industrial homework, domestic service, and family responsibilities, I highlight the centrality of reproductive labors to the construction of the woman worker. By reproductive labors, I mean those activities that exist as a counterpart, but also prior, to employment or income generation, what usually is considered production. Also referred to as social reproduction, such work is about the making of people through the tasks of daily life necessary to develop and sustain labor power. These activities are both material (like feeding), emotional (like love), and assimilative (like transference of norms and values), whether occurring in the family, school, church, or community.[14]

By the twenty-first century, poor women in the Global South, but also immigrants and ethnic and racial minorities in the Global North, engaged in a variety of home labors, circulating between outwork, domestic service, and unpaid family household and carework. Some also performed domestic labors in institutional settings as hospitals and schools.[15] As these women became the vanguard of an exploding informal economy, characteristics once thought of as adhering to feminized labor—part-time and irregular hours, low wages, lack of benefits, and temporary assignments outside of regulation or unionization—adhered to all kinds of work, for men as well as women, in the core industrial nations as well as the "third world."[16]

The ILO responded to these changes by seeking to incorporate the informal economy into standard-setting. Conventions covering Home Work, C#177 (1996), and Domestic Work, C#189 (2011), along with accompanying recommendations, would represent the culmination of campaigns that Fairchild and other labor feminists began after World War II. These regulations solidified, as I have explained elsewhere, only with the organizing of home-based workers themselves, personnel shifts at the ILO, transformations in international labor federations, and growth of new feminist movements.[17] Standard-setting has sought to make home labors legible as work; it has meant squeezing various forms of unpaid, care, and paid reproductive labor into categories forged with the male industrial and formal sector worker as the norm.[18]

1. The parallel fates of home work and domestic work

In passing the US-initiated "Resolution Concerning Women's Work" as a "tribute" to the wartime labors and sacrifices of women throughout the world, the delegates at the 1947 meeting of the ILC conceived home work and domestic work as part of "the problems of the employment of mothers of families" and areas for study and future action.[19] During the interwar years, the ILO often had discussed the two together, along with farm work, as forms of labor made difficult to regulate because of location. The ILC considered for inclusion in various instruments these forms of labor that it regarded almost by definition as nonstandard. But the Conference usually left them out, as with its 1936 deliberations on "holidays with pay," that is, compensated vacation time. Industrial homework appeared in more conventions, those related to wages, inspection, child labor, and social security. Trade unions and social reformers had a distinct interest in placing home work under regulation so to undermine its advantage as a source of cheap labor and thus curtail the practice. The earlier Minimum Wage-Fixing Machinery Convention (C#26, 1928), for one, specified homeworking trades as an area of concern.[20]

Few conventions included domestic workers, the notable exception being minimum age for children in nonindustrial occupations (C#33, 1932). Employer delegates regularly dismissed servants as not regular workers, viewing them as an inappropriate subject for international action. Household work had nothing to do with international commerce between nations, they insisted, although we now recognize the centrality of migration across borders to its operations. They asserted that families could not afford to pay any more and so improving wages would generate unemployment, hurting those that the ILO purported to aid.[21] Domestic work typically entered ILO deliberations obliquely as a cause of prostitution and in relation to forms of coerced or bonded labor.[22] Jobs supplying housing, like live-in service, were deemed inherently dangerous, subjecting women to sexual assault. In 1933, as its contribution to the fight against "white slavery," the ILO adopted a convention abolishing fee-charging employment agencies (C#34), justified as a measure to end abuse of women in domestic work who presumably found themselves placed in environments of sexual danger.[23]

Both types of home labors seemed to belong to a prior organization of production, one that sociologists and policymakers alike predicted would wither away with modernization.[24] That was not the case. The decrease in outwork that occurred in Europe with World War II came from a general decline in manufacturing and lack of materials; home work appeared to return in the early postwar years. During the war, women in the Global North fled domestic work for factory production; certainly the job changed from live-in to live-out in many regions afterward.[25] But in the 1950s and 1960s, commentators continued to classify household employment as a vanishing occupation just as wage-earning women sought help to cope with combining unpaid family labor with paid work. While labor feminists around the ILO's Section on Women Workers differed on whether to prohibit industrial homework, debating the possibility of extending existing labor regulation to the practice, they agreed on the need to modernize domestic service.[26]

Along with Fairchild, Frieda Miller, the director of the US Women's Bureau who belonged to the same labor feminist circles, played a major role in placing home work and domestic work on the ILO's research agenda, if not on its standard-setting one. Her involvement with both sectors suggests how home labors appeared as fit subject matter for women experts.[27] The Meeting of the Correspondence Committee on Women's Work in 1946 had recommended that the ILO conduct research on both domestic work and "the new international aspects of industrial home work (resulting from the development of transport facilities)" with the goal of finding "adequate methods of regulating" such labor. Behind this request stood questions of trade and factory conditions, as well as global competition, but the place of home in culture and society pervaded discussions.[28] So did the need to combine employment with women's unpaid family labor, which led to laments that represent an update of an earlier generation of professional women's complaints about "the servant problem." As one British expert admitted, "Women in large measure fail to recognize how much their own future as independent beings turns on finding some solution to the problem of domestic help." In improving domestic work, employers as well as household workers would benefit.[29]

By definition, the home defied regulation. As a French correspondent replied to the ILO's request for information on industrial homework, "Labour inspectors are barred from inspecting the homeworker's actual place of work by the principle of the inviolability of private domicile which French social legislation has apparently not modified to any extent."[30] Variation in practice across the globe intensified such barriers. As Miller, who sought to end home work in the United States, recognized, the line between handicraft and industrial homework was a moving one, especially when the goods produced by independent artisans and self-employed people resembled those made for an employer on "materials belonging to the employer and undertaken on order, tending to turn the home into a sweatshop."[31] This wording, from the 1946 meeting of women experts for which she served as the reporter, reiterated the common distinction between home and workshop that manufacturing in the home long appeared to defy.[32]

For cultural and social reasons, home handicraft emerged in the ILO imagination as the sector most appropriate for women in Asia and other developing areas (like the Andean region and elsewhere where indigenous people lived). Planners and promoters sought to build upon existing structures. ILO research in the early 1950s discovered that women "represent a considerable part of the productive capacity of the labour force in handicrafts." Throughout the region, urban as well as rural workers undertook pottery, lace making, spinning, weaving, and basketry. But the conditions of work were abysmal: long hours, hazardous materials, cramped quarters, and economic exploitation from middlemen.[33]

Because crafts production occurred in the household, such work posed no challenge to cultural practices that secluded women from contact with non-family. This hidden quality allowed for the obfuscation of women's labor as housework. What scholar activist Maria Mies named "housewifization" denied women the status as workers.[34] The ILO's own reports long reinforced this perception by referring to women as engaged in handicraft during "spare" time or "leisure hours," underscoring women's status as supplemental family earners or as unpaid workers in family-based cottage industries, usually on a part-time basis.[35] Such women were weighted down by childcare and housework, social customs (such as seclusion) and male dominance, illiteracy and limited education, and low status in the community. In a telling remark on the status of reproductive labor, the ILO recommended "specific measures to mitigate their handicaps."[36]

As an ILO consultant, Miller would promote home handicraft production as an employment strategy for Asian women. In 1955, she journeyed to seven Asian countries with the instruction to put "special emphasis . . . on the development of opportunities for women in handicrafts and cottage industries and on the distribution of the female labour force in industrial home work."[37] Miller was open to home-based industry under the right conditions—that is, as long as the safeguarding of labor standards took place. However, the "subsidiary role" of women as family workers in handicraft bothered her since "the higher, more esoteric and rewarding skills are carried on almost exclusively by men to whom the economic rewards go alone." With women pushed into "training for earning" programs, they generally worked with inferior materials and lacked the technical or artistic skills to gain a market niche.[38] Indeed, conditions of women's labor reflected the evils of home industry: "exploitation, over-long hours of work, health and safety hazards, as well as reduced earnings," all intensified from the home's standing outside of the labor law.[39]

Home work's dangers pervaded most discussions of handicraft. Scattered in "private" homes, unregulated and unorganized, and performed by women (often joined by their children) without other options for income, such labor was ripe for abuse. ILO staff worried how to protect handicraft workers "against exploitation by middlemen and against sweated conditions of industrial homework."[40] They sought to eliminate the middleman by developing local supplies of raw material and alternative sources of credit, pushing cooperatives that would encourage women's participation (for too often men dominated such ventures). They further advised bringing home work under national laws, even if laws could be "easily evaded."[41]

In the early post–World War II years, the ILO only researched home work and domestic work. The Director-General and Governing Board dismissed efforts to do anything else. Calling for more study delayed wrestling with proposals for international instruments. In terms of industrial homework, the Director-General felt that "it would be premature for the Office to submit this question pending the actual collection of further information," Deputy Director Jeff Rens informed Fairchild in 1947. Instead, he suggested that they publish research authorized by the Governing Body in the *International Labour Review*, the ILO's journal. Rens was signaling that the agency was not ready to act.[42] Similarly, improving the condition of work for domestic workers was a low priority compared to the question of equal remuneration, an issue that the UN desired the ILO formulate a convention on. The Governing Body would delay consideration of domestic work for years after British Labor delegates, led by Alfred Roberts and Florence Hancock of the Transport and General Workers Union, won approval in 1948 for placing deliberation on the sector on the ILC agenda in the near future. Hancock, the coauthor of the British government's "Report on Post-War Organisation of Private Domestic Employment," closely monitored the situation among delegates and strategized with Miller and Fairchild, but to no avail.[43]

Miller, the chair of the 1951 Committee of Experts on the Status and Condition of Employment of Domestic Workers, had continued to lobby for addressing domestic employment, especially as fears spread that the new wartime mobilization in Korea would further drain the supply of labor while increasing the demand for household aid. She proposed in 1949, and throughout her tenure at the Women's Bureau (a Democratic appointee, she was replaced by Eisenhower in 1953), that the United

States support a general discussion and then inclusion of domestic workers in specific conventions, as social insurance, an approach that would at least articulate basic standards. Delay, she emphasized, would make existing research out of date and would bury the issue. Though recognizing competing priorities, Miller continuously laid out the case for action to take advantage of the preparatory work that they already had accomplished.[44]

Despite an inability "to press forward" action on domestic workers, Fairchild still was "anxious to keep the question alive." She commissioned an article by Miller for the *International Labour Review*.[45] By 1953, Fairchild reported to Miller: "Because of the attitude of the Governing Body, I think the Director-General is inclined to believe that we probably cannot and should not attempt to press this subject before the conference." Latin American countries and India felt "that any attention to this question was absurd," but so did those in the industrialized West. Under budgetary limits, the Director-General was not willing to push domestic work without fuller support.[46]

In contrast to home work, domestic work was of the home, consisting of the same tasks whether done for pay or not. Some male delegates could not take household employment seriously because they associated the labor with the organization of domestic life—and the unpaid housewife. A British delegate typically argued that such workers were no longer, if they were ever, exploited. He then suggested that if the ILO would consider standards for household labor, "the most appropriate experts would be mothers with larger families rather than theorists with preconceived ideas as to how the intimate affairs of the family should be organized."[47] Even governments generally favorable to worker rights judged domestic employment as part of the problem of unpaid housework, which led Swedish delegates to lump together improved conditions for both the housewife and the employed domestic worker and recommend a woman on the basis of being a mother with five children as an employer representative to the Experts Committee.[48]

Delegates from Asia and elsewhere in the "developing" world insisted that domestic workers were "part of the family system." They asserted that "if the employer's own conditions were unsatisfactory the servant could hardly expect to be treated any more favorably" for being "part of the family," as the Chinese (Taiwanese) Government delegate claimed. "Where domestic workers were part of the family it was difficult to see how there could be a collective agreement between a family and its domestic workers," argued the Mexican Employers delegate. This "one of the family" representation also justified exclusion of domestic workers throughout the Global North.[49]

2. Family responsibilities

It wasn't only that domestic labor was like family labor. Family responsibilities disrupted employment, which served as a corollary to the claim that home work interfered with domesticity, threatening the home through disease and dirt and general unhealthful conditions. Development required women to enter production, which would lead to their liberation, many feminists would come to assert with Marxists. But working mothers required aid. In stipulating areas for the ILO to frame its deliberations on equal remuneration as early as 1947, the UN Commission on the Status of Women flagged "provision of measures to lighten the tasks that arise from women's home responsibilities, as well as the tasks relating to maternity."[50]

The ILO slowly took up that challenge in the 1950s. In 1919, one of the first conventions was "Maternity Protection" (C#3), but this excluded domestic work, home work, and agriculture until revision in 1952 (C#103), and only years later did officials speak of maternity leave as part of women's economic rights. Maternity protection included not only specified leave but also medical care and job reinstatement. Governments rather than individual employers preferably should fund such policies so to militate against raising the costs of hiring women and thus encouraging discriminatory treatment.[51]

During the Cold War, the ILO promoted measures to alleviate the "triple role of workers, mothers, and housewives" experienced by increasing numbers of women employed outside of the home in industrialized areas.[52] State socialist nations offered their public services for employed mothers as a model. But other countries, including the United States and Britain, advocated part-time work, which the UN Commission on the Status of Women asked the ILO to investigate at the same time as the ILO was reporting on handicraft and accepting home-based labor as solutions for women in the Global South to combine family labor with income generation. While home labor might allow for meeting family responsibilities, as evidenced by the overwhelming presence of women with small children, the ILO concluded as late as 2007 that "entry into home-based work is a survival strategy rather than a career choice."[53]

Four decades earlier in 1965, following the landmark report *Women in a Changing World*, the ILC passed Recommendation #123, "Women Workers with Family Responsibilities." Elizabeth Johnstone, then Coordinator of Women, Youth, and Aging, explained that to maintain women with children in the workforce "society as a whole has to adapt realistically to a new pattern of needs in their work and life."[54] The recommendation promoted childcare services and reentry training as two strategies for combining unpaid family and waged labor. The ILO sketched what feminist lawyers now call "family responsibility discrimination" as a barrier to women's equality.[55]

Nonetheless, R#123 reinforced, even as it sought to relieve, the gender division of labor. Assuming industrializing nations to be in transition from "a patriarchal, static society," the Government delegate from Cyprus urged that women's entrance into the workforce occur "without too much disruption of the traditional family structures and without detriment to a woman's responsibilities and duties vis-à-vis her family and her children." Against women's right to work, an Italian male Worker delegate posited the rights of families to women's labor and argued "for preparing and adopting efficient measures to lessen the economic necessity requiring women to seek work outside their homes." Though "the social emancipation" of women was a worthwhile goal, morality and social necessity should propel delegates to improve ILO instruments "with a view to defending the family in a developing world." The continuing emphasis on handicraft and cottage industry represented an attempt to alleviate such attitudes among member states.[56] Some consultants on women's issues recognized the dual position of women in society, holding onto continued training of girls in "the elements of home-making and home management," even as they would "prepare themselves for economic activity outside the home."[57]

Women participants at the ILC generally understood such accommodations as supplementing an equal-rights and nondiscrimination agenda even if directed only to women. But the Swedish Worker adviser appealed to gender sameness, declaring in 1965 that "responsibility for the children and the family is, in general, the same for the man as for the woman."[58] Sixteen years later, reflecting the shift to the discourse of gender equality and the move to gender mainstreaming during the UN Decade for Women, a new convention (#156) and recommendation (#165) spoke of "Workers with Family Responsibilities," including men's unpaid family work as well as women's. This articulation superseded the casting of family labor as only women's work—at least in aspirational terms. Despite claims to embrace "all categories of workers," the new instrument still concentrated on labor force participation for women in legible occupations and their performance of household and family tasks.[59] Rather than wither away from mechanization, family labors actually had intensified with enhanced norms for cleanliness and attentiveness, remaining a drain on female employment.[60]

In this context, relief for rural women in the Global South required additional effort, including access to cash income. Improving the lot of family laborers became part of the fight for world employment rather than an aspect of the struggle to end discrimination on the basis of sex—the goal that dominated women's movements in advanced industrialized nations that projected their norms as universal.[61] As Martha Loutfi of the Programme on Rural Women noted, "If one's view of economic processes and production stops at the household and does not consider the individuals inside . . . improved standards of living will be lacking." Arguing that "inequality and inequity between male and female household members have been expanding in much of the world," she proposed that the ILO take action. It wasn't just that men had greater resources, but that there was little incentive to use hard-won cash to purchase kerosene or charcoal when women still could gather wood for cooking. Providing cash to men rather than to women too often led to falling "nutritional levels . . . while wristwatches, transistor radios and bicycles (all largely utilized by men) find their way into the household," British development expert and ILO consultant Ingrid Palmer noted.[62]

Attention to this widening gender gap took place amid a continuing differentiation between the Global North and Global South and between urban and rural places. Domestic workers might replace the labor of housewives, but so could community social services and improved cooking and cleaning tools, especially for women in rural areas who had to gather fuel and water to perform home labors. Lightening domestic burdens, ILO staff insisted, would allow women to leave home for work, though countries with mores against venturing from home unaccompanied by male kin found that very notion inappropriate—making home work a respectable form of labor. With the World Employment Program in the 1970s, the ILO—and not only its units focused on women—took notice of social reproduction. It embraced the concept of "basic needs," defined as the provision of "certain minimum requirements of a family for private consumption: adequate food, shelter and clothing, as well as certain household equipment and furniture" and "essential services provided by and for the community at large, such as safe drinking water, sanitation, public transport and health, educational and cultural facilities."[63]

This emphasis made women a targeted group for meeting such a goal. Their work created the sustenance for daily life; over the next decade, ILO research on rural women would underscore this recognition of the centrality of unpaid family or reproductive labor. It wasn't enough to place women in more remunerative occupations or increase their education or expand their legal rights. Ending the overburdened quality of their lives was essential and for that to occur required "participation . . . in the direction and process of development and in its benefits, for reasons both of justice and of development," as Loutfi argued.[64] Employment might still drive development but as a means to a higher standard of living rather than an end in itself. Basic Needs required equality between women and men within the household as well as between nations, with women obtaining access to decision-making and purchasing power as well as enhanced self-provisioning.[65]

3. Turning family labor into income

The ILO certainly was not alone in efforts to generate income from women's reproductive labors. The UN Food and Agricultural Organization, for one, provided food for family consumption if women would use family lands to produce for the market as part of its World Food Program in the late 1960s and early 1970s. But so many initiatives undermined women's traditional subsistence labor by directing tools and training to men, deteriorating their economic position and undermining their status even further, as Ester Boserup first observed in 1970 and the ILO continued to reiterate. For example, the Green Revolution left some women having to pull weeds by hand, contributing to inequality among households, while other women became landless from its attributing ownership to men and recognizing only one wife where polygamy had existed. Indeed, the Green Revolution apparently increased inequality between farmers, making a few rich and pauperizing many others.[66] Similarly, "the white revolution" in India transferred dairying from poor women, who sold butter but retained skimmed buttermilk for their families, to commercial ventures run by men. These women ended up without income and with less access to no-cost nutrition.[67]

The ILO's Programme on Rural Women recognized the productive consequences of the reproductive labors of these "most forgotten participants in the economy." As Lourdes Benería, then its director, explained in 1977, "Rather than being 'marginal' participants in the stream of economic activities, they [rural women] are an 'integral' part of it." After all, "they work long hours in domestic and agricultural jobs, and . . . perform *essential* activities to the economic system, namely those related to production of foods and services, either in the fields or at home, and those related to the reproduction of the labour force."[68] But when the market intervened with "development," these necessary subsistence activities—what Loutfi termed "provision of the households' shelter, food, fuel and water, the preparation and cooking of meals, and child care"—not only were not "calculated" but lacked "value."[69] ILO development feminists recognized the diversity of poor women's labors but emphasized the necessity of improving the decision-making and overall conditions of the poorest and most rural among them. Like other women in the

UN system and feminists from Asia and throughout the Global South, they rejected the bourgeois housewife as an ideal, turning to models of consciousness-raising and empowerment that revalued women's work.[70]

Through pioneer research on "women in development" and training, cooperative, marketing, and other assistance initiatives, the Programme on Rural Women particularly sought to counter impediments toward women's advancement, but not by predetermining what better conditions meant for women. While the ILO continued to support handicraft production, feminists pushed more vigorously for "the participation and organization of poor rural women," that is, their self-employment and self-organization, to combat growing inequality and particularly the underside of outwork that became more noticeable during the last third of the twentieth century.[71] Encouraged by favorable tariff and tax policies, offshore production and home work spread beyond their historical presence in garments and textiles to include the making of additional consumer goods, electronics, and plastics. With the computer revolution, telework and home assembly of components updated the practice of clerical homework in Australia, Canada, and other "developed" nations, but also served as additional forms of offshoring from North to South and from expensive to cheaper labor markets.[72]

In the 1980s, ILO development feminists partnered with grassroots groups to improve women's lives in the informal sector, with the "new putting out system" a major project. It wasn't that these women weren't contributing a significant amount of household income—beedi (cigarette) makers in Allahabad, India, for example, earned half of all household monies, with the poorest earning an even greater percentage—but they labored long hours, and middlemen cheated them out of wages and social welfare benefits.[73] Through a series of seminars and donor-funded projects, the ILO enhanced the capabilities of rural women's organizations in India, Thailand, Pakistan, Indonesia, and Philippines, the most important being the Self-Employed Women's Association (SEWA) of Gujarat, India.[74]

SEWA became an independent women's organization of informal sector workers in the early 1980s when it broke with the then male-dominated Textile Labor Association, which objected to SEWA's non-union strategies of forming cooperatives and including own account workers (those technically self-employed even if dependent on distributors or suppliers). It pushed for coverage under social security and for welfare provisions, such as health insurance, housing, and childcare.[75] Beginning with nearly 2,000 members, its membership in 1995 had grown to about 145,000 women from various informal-sector occupations, with about 23,000 of them home-based. By 2008, it reported an "All India Membership" of nearly a million, with some 14.45 percent home-based.[76]

The United Nations Decade for Women provided an opportunity for SEWA to join a transnational women's movement, offering a feminist twist to Gandhian self-sufficiency updated for an era of structural adjustment and neoliberalism. Its secretary and chief trade union organizer Renana Jhabvala often quoted the nationalistic exhortation of Gandhi: "Women have to take *leadership* to solve the problems of the country. Women should widen their family to the whole country." Asked what to do, attendees at one SEWA leadership workshop replied, "The only way to solve the problem of rural women is through organizing." Reflecting the participatory democracy and autonomy at the center of the SEWA approach, the women insisted that "rural women have to come together and organize themselves."[77]

This focus on self-organizing was exactly what ILO development feminists were looking for. Eager to support projects that combined standard-setting with technical cooperation, they financed awareness camps for garment sewers, beedi rollers, and embroiders as a bridge between legal training and organizing. Stymied from gaining legislation for home-based workers in the Indian Parliament, SEWA sought an ILO convention as a tool for winning local social protection; it could use the ratification process to push for implementation and as the basis for legal action against miscreants. Its interests and those of feminists within the ILO's Office dovetailed.[78]

SEWA plotted a campaign for international action, helping to organize HomeNet International with British and Dutch activists, but lacked standing and power within the ILO to define the agenda.[79] Its members called for inclusion of the informal sector's self-employed in ILO actions, but "own account" workers fell out of the scope of ILO deliberations.[80] The ILC saw but refused to hear home workers. SEWA gained access to committee meetings through membership in the International Union of Food, Agricultural, Hotel, Restaurant, Catering, Tobacco and Allied Workers' Association (IUF) and indirectly the International Confederation of Trade Unions (ICTU), which had consultative NGO status at the ILO. But the employers blocked its representative from addressing the conference.[81]

To placate governments, the emerging convention and recommendation on home-based labor considered home workers as employees, asking the many nations that failed to count home workers to revise their statistics. Employers, for their part, attempted to obscure deliberations by equating industrial homeworkers with teleworkers, even though it was generally understood that the convention was to address conditions in developing nations and the informal sector.[82] Refusing to take part in deliberations over the content of the convention, Employer delegates abstained in mass during the vote in 1996. But they failed to undermine the needed quorum.[83] The rancor over the appropriateness of this action underscored the breakdown of the tripartism that had governed the ILO from the start.

4. Catching up

A decade later and nearly two decades after its gender-neutral convention on family responsibilities, the ILO acknowledged care as "the unpaid work in the family and community that is often ignored in current thinking about the economy and society." It underscored that "much of this work is done by women and is essential to the welfare not just of the young or elderly or sick but also to those in paid work. It is also often carried out alongside paid work." Building off of research commissioned by the Social Protection Division, the ILO further recognized that care work, like household employment, existed as an occupation and thus required protocols and regulations, with care workers included under social security.[84] The 1977 standards for nursing (C#149, R#157) offered a model insofar as they included the range of rights and equality of treatment of other instruments, but the care sector suffered from "discriminatory attitudes"[85]—that is, the lack of acceptance that such labor was work in the first place because of intimate and often emotional ties between care provider and receiver and because wives, mothers, and other relatives performed similar labor out of love or obligation. Earlier surveys of domestic work had included home helps, later known as home aids or home care workers, a group whose low wages stemmed from such conflations. The association with home labor and domestic service had relegated care work to low pay, casualization, and invisibility.[86] Only in 2013 did the International Labor Conference of Labor Statisticians include unpaid carework under the category "own-use production work," thus defining care as work.[87]

Convention #189, "Decent Work for Domestic Workers" (2011), marked the worthiness of monetized reproductive labor. It was conceivable because of the earlier victory of home-based pieceworkers. With the 1996 C#177 on "Home Work," the ILO for the first time valued work in the home as worthy of a labor standard of its own. Technical assistance and standard-setting on home work solidified institutional support for the informal sector, helping to redirect ILO efforts to the reproductive labor that occurs in that realm. Home work activism revealed the kind of transnational networking and coordinated strategy necessary for success within the ILO system and highlighted the importance of obtaining trade union support as an access point to the ILO deliberative process, all of which the campaign for domestic workers engaged in.[88]

The deliberations over C#189 further displayed a new model for NGO and worker engagement at the ILO. First, domestic workers maneuvered around ILO procedure to speak at the ILC. They did so by winning representation as official national delegates, but they also engaged in a politics of messaging by wearing t-shirts. They bent the rules by breaking into song and unfurling banners. They marched in the streets and held press conferences in front of the ILO. Their palpable presence stood witness to the living bodies subjected to conventions and recommendations, making it difficult for delegates who became labeled as employers of domestic workers themselves to say "No."[89] Secondly, while the campaign traveled from the local to the regional and then to the international level of struggle, it had stronger local organizations ready to press for ratifications.[90]

Names are powerful tools. A loss of words for home work led the British Government member back in 1995 to inadvertently reveal lingering conceptions that continued to link outwork to housework, productive to reproductive home labors: "Domestic services" was perhaps not the appropriate wording," he claimed, "but labour inspectors should be prevented from entering private employers' households and inspecting the conditions of domestic workers."[91] The new women who emerged from ILO campaigns to recognize their work as decent work like all other work proudly claimed the title of worker.

Today some home-based workers have gained entry into labor standards just as the standard employment contract is withering away: employers refuse to recognize workers as employees covered by wage, hour, occupational health, and social security protections and governments look the other way. Though home work and domestic worker associations and unions seek inclusion in existing labor law, they also have generated alternatives, including establishing cooperatives, shifting legal responsibility to human rights commissions, and building their own capacity for leadership and campaigning. Through organizing the whole woman and paying attention to relationships between her family and paid labor, they are waging a prolonged battle in which changing attitudes toward home labor is the first step. But whether the standard employment relation is flexible enough to combine production with reproduction in all its forms is an unfolding story.

Eileen Boris is Hull Professor and Distinguished Professor of Feminist Studies and Distinguished Professor of History, Black Studies, and Global Studies at the University of California, Santa Barbara. She writes on the home as a workplace and the racialized gendered state. Her books include the prize-winning monographs *Home to Work: Motherhood and the Politics of Industrial Homework in the United States* (New York: Cambridge University Press, 1994), and *Caring for America: Home Health Workers in the Shadow of the Welfare State,* coauthored with Jennifer Klein (New York: Oxford University Press, 2012). Among her edited collections are *Intimate Labors: Cultures, Technologies, and the Politics of Care,* coedited with Rhacel Parreñas (Stanford, CA: Stanford University Press, 2010), and *Women's ILO: Transnational Networks, Global Labour Standards, and Gender Equity,* coedited with Dorothea Hoehtker and Susan Zimmermann (Leiden and Geneva: Brill and ILO, 2018). Her current book is tentatively called *Making the Woman Worker: Precarious Labor and the Fight for Global Standards* (New York: Oxford University Press, forthcoming 2019). She is the president of the International Federation for Research in Women's History. For more details see http://www.femst.ucsb.edu/people/eileen-boris.

Notes

1. Andrea M. Singh to Zubeida Ahmad, 17 January 1984, Memo: WEP 10-4-04-018 jacket 1,ILO Archive, Geneva. Unless noted otherwise, all archival material from this location.
2. A. A. Evans to Economic Advisor, Chief of the Women's and Children's Section, Reference, "Economic Value of the Woman's Work in the Home," 5 August 1949, ILO 1-12, Jacket 1.
3. Bryce Covet, "Putting a Price Tag on Unpaid Housework," *Fortune,* 30 May 2012, retrieved 13 May 2018 from http://www.forbes.com/sites/brycecovert/2012/05/30/putting-a-price-tag-on-unpaid-housework/; Marilyn Waring, *If Women Counted: A New Feminist Economics* (New York, 1988), 8.
4. R. A. Métall to Mildred Fairchild, 8 February 1950 and 10 March 1950; Fairchild to Chief of the International Organisations Section, New York, 8 February 1940 on "Women's Work in the Home," LO 1-12, Jacket 1.
5. On the ILO, see Gerry Rodgers, Eddy Lee, Lee Sweptson, and Jasmien Van Daele, eds., *The ILO and the Quest for Social Justice, 1919–2009* (Ithaca, NY: Cornell University Press, 2009).
6. The only monograph on women and the ILO lacks adequate documentation and is descriptive: Carol Riegelman Lubin and Anne Winslow, *Social Justice for Women: The International Labor Organization and Women* (Durham, NC: Duke University Press, 1990).
7. "Report of ILO-Current Activities and Plans," Spring 1952, in WN 1-1-61, Jacket 1.
8. ILO, Meeting of Consultants on Women Workers' Problems (Geneva: 20–28 September 1965), WIN 2-1003-2, Jacket 1.
9. Elizabeth Johnstone, "Women in Economic Life: Rights and Opportunities," *Annals of the American Academy of Political and Social Science* 375, no. 1 (1968): 108; Susan Zimmermann, "Globalizing Gendered Labour Policy: International Labour Standards and the Global South, 1919–1947," in *Women's ILO: Transnational Networks, Global Labour Standards, and Gender Equity, 1919 to Present,* ed. Eileen Boris, Doroethea Hoehtker, and Susan Zimmermann (Leiden and Geneva: Brill and ILO, 2018), 227–54.

10. Eileen Boris, "Difference's Other: The ILO and 'Women in Developing Countries,'" in *The ILO and the Pacific Rim*, ed. Nelson Lichtenstein and Jill Jensen (New York and Geneva: Palgrave and ILO, 2016), 134–55.
11. Though maternity still is highlighted, the convention and recommendation refer to all workers. http://www.ilo.org/dyn/normlex/en/f?p=NORMLEXPUB:12100:0::NO::P1 2100_INSTRUMENT_ID:312316; http://www.ilo.org/dyn/normlex/en/f?p=NORM LEXPUB:12100:0::NO:12100:P12100_INSTRUMENT_ID:312516:NO.
12. Ulla Wikander, "Demands on the ILO by Internationally Organized Women in 1919," in *ILO Histories: Essays on the International Labour Organization and Its Impact on the World during the Twentieth Century*, ed. Jasmien Van Daele, Magaly Rodríguez García, Geert van Goethem, Marcel van der Linden (New York: Peter Lang, 2010), 67–89; Carol Miller, "'Geneva—the Key to Equality': Inter-war Feminists and the League of Nations," *Women's History Review* 3, no. 2 (1994): 219–45; Sandra Whitworth, "Gender, International Relations and the Case of the ILO," *Review of International Studies* 20, no. 4 (1994): 389–405; Nora Natchkova and Céline Schoeni, "L'Organisation International du Travail, les Feminists et les Réeseaux D'expertes: Les Enjeux d'une Politique Protectrice (1919–1934)," in *L'Organisation international du travail: Origine—Dévelopmmement—Avenir*, ed. Isabelle Lespinet-Moret and Vincent Viet (Rennes: Presses Universitaires de Rennes, 2011), 39–51.
13. Statement of Ms. Vicky Kanyoka, ILC, *Record of Proceedings*, 99th Session (Geneva: ILO, 2010), 8/41.
14. Heidi Hartmann, "The Unhappy Marriage of Marxism and Feminism," *Capital & Class* 3 (1979): 1–33; Leopoldina Fortunati, *Arcane of Reproduction* (Brooklyn, NY: Automedia, 1989); Lourdes Benería and Gita Sen, "Accumulation, Reproduction, and 'Women's Role in Economic Development': Boserup Revisited," *Signs: Journal of Women in Culture and Society* 7 (1981): 279–98; V. Spike Peterson, "Rewriting (Global) Political Economy as Reproductive, Productive, and Virtual (Foucauldian) Economies," *International Feminist Journal of Politics* 4, no.1 (2002): 1–30.
15. For example, see Eileen Boris and Jennifer Klein, *Caring for America: Home Health Workers in the Shadow of the Welfare State* (New York: Oxford University Press, 2012).
16. V. Spike Peterson, "Informalization, Inequalities and Global Insecurities," *International Studies Review* 12, no. 2 (2010): 244–70.
17. Eileen Boris and Jennifer Fish, "'Slaves No More': Making Global Labor Standards for Domestic Workers," *Feminist Studies* 40, no. 2 (2014): 411–43.
18. On the standard employment relation, Leah F. Vosko, *Managing the Margins: Gender, Citizenship, and the International Regulation of Precarious Employment* (New York: Oxford University Press, 2010).
19. "Resolution concerning Women's Work," 404-406; statement of Mr. Kelley, 236, both in ILC, *Record of Proceedings*, 30th Session, Geneva, 1947 (Geneva: ILO, 1948).
20. ILO *Minutes*, 77th Session of the Governing Body, 12–14 November 1936, 129; "Provisions Relating to Industrial Home Work in the Conventions of the International Labour Conference"; Elisabeth Prügl, *The Global Construction of Gender* (New York: Columbia University Press, 1999), 40–55.
21. For example, see discussion of unemployment compensation, ILC, *Record of Proceedings*, 18th Session (Geneva: ILO, 1934), 580.
22. Eileen Boris and Jennifer N. Fish, "Decent Work for Domestics: Feminist Organizing, Worker Empowerment, and the ILO," in *Towards a Global History of Domestic and Caregiving Workers*, ed. Dirk Hoerder, Elise van Nederveen Meerkerk, and Silke Neunsinger (Leiden: Brill, 2015), 530–52; Magaly Rodríguez García, "The League of Nations and the Moral Recruitment of Women," *International Review of Social History* 57 (2012): 125–26.
23. ILO, League of Nations Archives, CQS/A/19(a), "The Moral Protection of Young Women Workers," in Advisory Committee on Social Questions, Prevention of Prostitution, "Draft Report submitted by the Rapporteur," 15 May 1939, 45–77, quote at 60.

24. Lewis Coser, "Servants: The Obsolescence of an Occupation Role," *Social Forces* 52, no. 1 (1973): 31–40.
25. "Record of the Meeting of the Correspondence Committee on Women's Work," Appendix VII, ILO, *Minutes,* 99th Session of the Governing Body (Geneva: ILO, September 1946), 70–71.
26. ILO, "Meeting of Experts on Women's Work," Geneva, 11–15 December 1951, 8, WN 1002.
27. Miller and Fairchild held the same fellowship in Social Investigation and both were connected to the Consumers' League and related groups. There is no biography of Fairchild. For Miller, see Anneleise Orleck, *Common Sense and a Little Fire: Women and Working-Class Politics in the United States, 1900–1965* (Chapel Hill: University of North Carolina Press, 1995).
28. "Record of the Meeting of the Correspondence Committee on Women's Work," 72.
29. Quoted in Lucy Lethbridge, *Servants: A Downstairs View of Twentieth-Century Britain* (New York, 2013), 269.
30. "Industrial Home Work in France," esp. 13, UN1001/06.
31. "Record of the Meeting of the Correspondence Committee on Women's Work," 72; Frieda Miller to Mildred Fairchild, May 15, 1947, UN1001/06.
32. Eileen Boris, *Home to Work: Motherhood and the Politics of Industrial Homework in the United States* (New York: Cambridge University Press, 1994), 247–52.
33. ILO, Asian Advisory Committee, "Special Protective Legislation Affecting Women and Its Relation to Women's Employment in Asian Countries," 4–6, AAC/IV/D.5, 24, in WN 2/7; "Development of Opportunities for Women in Handicrafts and Cottage Industries," ILO Draft for IX Session of the Commission on the Status of Women, 28, ESC 77-8.
34. Maria Mies, *The Lace Makers of Narsapur: Indian Housewives Produce for the World Market* (London: Zed Books, 1982), 200.
35. Outline, "Development of Opportunities for Women in Handicrafts and Cottage Industries," 3, c. 1955, ESC 77-8.
36. Outline, "Development of Opportunities for Women in Handicrafts and Cottage Industries," 29.
37. "ILO Expanded Technical Assistance Programme Job Description and Details relevant to the Appointment of Experts," in Frieda Miller, ILO Personnel File P 7353 1955-1957, Jacket 1.
38. ILO, *Report to The Governments of Ceylon, India, Indonesia, Japan, Pakistan, the Philippines and Thailand on Conditions of Women's Work in Seven Asian Countries* (Geneva: ILO, 1958), 4; "Confidential" memo on trip, 4-5, Box 9, folder 192, Miller Papers, A-37, Schlesinger Library.
39. *Conditions of Women's Work in Seven Asian Countries,* 36-7. For an earlier study, "Reports and Inquiries: Conditions of Employment of Women Workers in Asia," *International Labor Review* 70 (1954): 542–56.
40. Outline, "Development of Opportunities for Women in Handicrafts and Cottage Industries," 1.
41. "Opportunities for Women in Handicrafts and Cottage Industries Progress Report prepared by the International Labour Office," for X Session, 2–4.
42. Fairchild to Miller, 15 January 1947.
43. Violet Markham and Florence Hancock, *Report on the Organization of Private Domestic Employment* (London: Ministry of Labor and National Service, 1945).
44. Frieda Miller to Edward Persons, 19 December 1952; "Proposed Statement of U.S. Position on Inclusion of Domestic Workers on 1951 Agenda for ILO," 24 May 1949, Miller to Pearson, 10 November 1950, attached, Miller to Florence Hancock Personal, 9 November 1951; Laura Dale to Miller, 6 November 1951; Cross Reference Sheet from Edward Persons, 24 October 1952; Miller to Persons, 19 October 1951; Mildred Fairchild to Frieda,

27 August 1951; Fairchild to Mary Leach, 1 January 1952; Miller to Fairchild, Personal, 27 October 1952; all in Box 68, folder "Domestic Workers;" Miller to Edward Persons, 24 October 1952, 2-3, box 66, folder "120th Meeting of the Governing Body ILO," General Correspondence, Director of U.S. Women's Bureau, RG86, National Archives, College Park, Maryland.
45. Mildred Fairchild to Frieda, 11 March 1952 in box 68, folder "Domestic Workers."
46. Fairchild to Miller, 25 April 1953, WN 1001-07.
47. *Minutes*, 112th Session of the Governing Body, 80–83.
48. Memo from S. Thorsson to Chief of Women's and Young Workers' Section, 22 February 1950 in WN 8-3-1001.
49. *Minutes*, 117th Session of the Governing Body, 1951, 32.
50. ECOSOC, Report on the Third Session of the CSW, Beirut, Lebanon, 21 March to 4 April 1949, E/1316, E/CN.6/124, 19 April 1949, "Equal Pay for Equal Work," 17–18.
51. Johnstone, "Women in Economic Life," 103.
52. Miss Jedidi, in ILC, *Record of Proceedings*, 49th Session (Geneva: ILO, 1965), 373.
53. ILO, *ABCs of Women Worker Rights and Gender Equality*, 2nd ed. (Geneva: ILO, 2007), 104.
54. Johnstone, "Women in Economic Life," 111.
55. Joan C. Williams, *Unbending Gender: Why Family and Work Conflict and What to Do about It* (New York: Oxford University Press, 2000).
56. *Record of Proceedings*, Forty-Eight Session, 469, 465, 740.
57. ILO, Meeting of Consultants on Women Workers' Problems (Geneva, 20–28 September 1965), 20, WN 2-1003-2, Jacket 1.
58. Miss Ekendahl in ibid., 383.
59. R165 at http://www.ilo.org/dyn/normlex/en/f?p=NORMLEXPUB:12100:0::NO::P12 100_INSTRUMENT_ID:312503.
60. Ruth Cowan, *More Work for Mother: The Ironies of Household Technologies from the Open Hearth to the Microwave* (New York: Basic Books, 1983).
61. *Workers with Family Responsibilities*, Report III (Part 4B) (Geneva: ILO, 1993).
62. Martha Fetherolf Loutfi, *Rural Women: Unequal Partners in Development* (Geneva: ILO, 1980), 2, 40; Palmer quoted in ibid., 50–51.
63. "Programme of Action," in International Labour Conference, 61st Session 1976 and Tripartite World Conference on Employment, Income Distribution and Social Progress and the International Division of Labour June 1976, *Australian Delegation Report* (Canberra: Australian Government, 1977), 90.
64. "Statement by the representative of the International Labor Organisation," 3, Annex I, UN Seminar on Participation of Women in Political, Economic and Social Development, Nepal, 15–22 February 1977, in UN 9-10-102, Jacket 1; Loutfi, *Rural Women*, 5.
65. Ingrid Palmer, "Rural Women and the Basic-Needs Approach to Development," *International Labour Review* 115, no. 1 (1977): 97–107.
66. Mies, *Lace Makers*, 195–203; Priti Ramamurthy, "Why Is Buying a 'Madras' Cotton Shirt a Political Act? A Feminist Commodity Chain Analysis," *Feminist Studies* 30 (2004): 734–69.
67. Ester Boserup, *Women's Role in Economic Development* (New York: St. Martin's Press, 1970); *Women Workers and the Development Process (Asia and the Pacific)*, ILO/W.7/1979, 3; Loutfi, *Rural Women*, 6, 34.
68. Lourdes Benería to Mrs. Ahmad, Mrs. Korchounova (Femmes), "Comments on 'Evaluation des Progres Intervenus dans l'Application du Principe de l'Egalite de Chances et de Traitement pour les Travailleuses Inventaire des Donnees a Rassembler,'" Minute Sheet, 6.6.77, WN-1-1-02-1000 (French without accents in the original).
69. Loutfi, *Rural Women*, 7.
70. UN, Asia and Pacific Centre for Women and Development, Expert Group Meeting on the Identification of the Basic Needs of Women of Asia and the Pacific and on the Formulation

of a Programme of Work, "Research Priorities and Considerations, Report: Part I: The Critical Needs of Women," Appendix 6 (1977), 3-4, UN, 9-10-158/168-100-1, Jacket 1.
71. Dharam Ghai and Zubeida Ahmed, "Preface," in Loutfi, *Rural Women*, iii.
72. ILO, Documents of the Meeting of Experts on the Social Protection of Homeworkers, "Social Protection of Homeworkers," Geneva, 1990, MEHW/1990/7, 7-9, and passim; for one example, Carla Freeman, *High Tech and High Heels in the Global Economy: Women, Work, and Pink-Collar Identities in the Caribbean* (Durham, NC: Duke University Press, 2000).
73. Loutfi, *Rural Women*, 21.
74. Self Employed Women's Association, "About Us," retrieved 10 June 2015 from http://www.sewa.org/About_Us_History.asp.
75. Renana Jhabvala, "SEWA's Programmes for the Organization of Home-Based Workers—India," in Ursula Huws, *Action Programmes for the Protection of Homeworkers: Ten Case Studies from Around the World* (Geneva: ILO, 1995), 20–22, 25–26.
76. "Project Description: Follow Up Activities toward an ILO Discussion on Homework," EMP 63-4-1, Jacket 1; http://www.sewa.org/About_Us_Structure.asp, accessed 17 August 2014.
77. http://www.sewa.org/About_Us_History.asp; "ILO Study Tour: Evaluation Seminar Report 19 June to 10 July 1989," 3, 7, WEP 31-0-33-3, Jacket 1.
78. Letter to Madhubala Nath from Ela Bhatt, 3/6/1994 in EMP 63-4-1, Jacket 1.
79. On HomeNet, see Annie Delaney, "Organizing Homeworkers: Women's Collective Strategies to Improve Participation and Social Change," PhD diss., School of Management, La Trobe University, June 2009, 78–97.
80. "Resolutions for UN Social Summit 1995 Proposed at SEWA General Body Meeting, 15–17 April 1994," 5–6; "Asian Regional Workshop on the ILO Convention," both in EMP 63-4-1-2, Jacket 1; ILC, "Resolution Concerning Self-Employment Promotion," *Record of Proceedings*, 77th Session, 1990 (Geneva: ILO, 1991), 7, 15
81. "Report of the Committee on Home Work: Submission and Discussion," 213–14.
82. "Report of the Committee on Home Work: Submission, Discussion and Adoption," *Record of Proceedings*, 82nd Session, 27/24; GB, "Report of the Meeting of Experts on the Social Protection of Homeworkers," Meeting of the Governing Body, 248th Session, Geneva 12–16 November 1990, III/1-2, GB 248-1—5 GB Sess. 248.
83. ILC, *Record of Proceedings*, 82nd Session, 1995 (Geneva: ILO, 1996), 252, 27/19ff; "Record of Votes," *Proceedings*, 83rd Session, 1996, 7–10.
84. Mary E. Daly, ed., *Care Work: The Quest for Security* (Geneva: ILO, 2001).
85. ILO, *ABCs of Women Worker Rights*, 28–29.
86. Boris and Klein, *Caring for America*, 53–54.
87. ILO, *Women at Work: Trends 2016* (Geneva, 2016), 19.
88. Suzanne Franzway and Mary Margaret Fonow, *Making Feminist Politics: Transnational Alliances between Women and Labor* (Urbana: University of Illinois Press, 2011); Margaret Keck and Kathryn Sikkink, *Activists beyond Borders: Advocacy Networks in International Politics* (Ithaca, NY: Cornell University Press, 1998).
89. Jennifer Fish, "Making History through Policy: A Field Report on the International Domestic Workers Movement," *International Labor and Working Class History* 88 (2015): 156–65.
90. Boris and Fish, "Slaves No More;" Merike Blodfield, *Care Work and Class: Domestic Workers' Struggle for Equal Rights in Latin America* (State College: Pennsylvania State University Press, 2012); Helen Schwenken, "From Maid to Worker," *Queries* 7, no.1 (2012): 14–21; Helen Schwenken and Elisabeth Prügl, "An ILO Convention for Domestic Workers: Contextualizing the Debate," *International Feminist Journal of Politics* 13, no. 3 (2011): 437–61; Jo Becker, *Campaigning for Justice: Human Rights and Advocacy in Practice* (Stanford, CA: Stanford University Press, 2013), 32–55.
91. "Record of Votes," *Proceedings*, 83rd Session, 1996, 20/22.

References

Becker, Jo. *Campaigning for Justice: Human Rights and Advocacy in Practice.* Palo Alto, CA: Stanford University Press, 2013.

Benería, Lourdes, and Gita Sen. "Accumulation, Reproduction, and 'Women's Role in Economic Development': Boserup Revisited." *Signs: Journal of Women in Culture and Society* 7, no. 2 (1981): 279–98.

Blodfield, Merike. *Care Work and Class: Domestic Workers' Struggle for Equal Rights in Latin America.* State College: Pennsylvania State University Press, 2012.

Boris, Eileen. *Home to Work: Motherhood and the Politics of Industrial Homework in the United States.* New York: Cambridge University Press, 1994.

———. "Difference's Other: The ILO and 'Women in Developing Countries.'" In *The ILO and the Pacific Rim,* edited by Nelson Lichtenstein and Jill Jensen, 134–55. New York and Geneva: Palgrave MacMillan and ILO, 2016.

Boris, Eileen, and Jennifer Fish. "'Slaves No More': Making Global Labor Standards for Domestic Workers." *Feminist Studies* 40, no. 2 (2014): 411–43.

———. "Decent Work for Domestics: Feminist Organizing, Worker Empowerment, and the ILO." In *Towards a Global History of Domestic and Caregiving Workers,* edited by Dirk Hoerder, Elise van Nederveen Meerkerk, and Silke Neunsinger, 530–52. Leiden: Brill, 2015.

Boris, Eileen, and Jennifer Klein. *Caring for America: Home Health Workers in the Shadow of the Welfare State.* New York: Oxford University Press, 2012.

Boserup, Ester. *Women's Role in Economic Development.* New York: St. Martin's Press, 1970.

Coser, Lewis. "Servants: The Obsolescence of an Occupation Role." *Social Forces* 52, no. 1 (1973): 31–40.

Covet, Bryce. "Putting a Price Tag on Unpaid Housework." *Fortune,* 30 May 2012. Retrieved 13 May 2018 from http://www.forbes.com/sites/brycecovert/2012/05/30/putting-a-price-tag-on-unpaid-housework/.

Cowan, Ruth. *More Work for Mother: The Ironies of Household Technologies from the Open Hearth to the Microwave.* New York: Basic Books, 1983.

Daly, Mary E., ed. *Care Work: The Quest for Security.* Geneva: ILO, 2001.

Delaney, Annie. "Organizing Homeworkers: Women's Collective Strategies to Improve Participation and Social Change." PhD diss., School of Management, La Trobe University, June 2009.

Fish, Jennifer. "Making History through Policy: A Field Report on the International Domestic Workers Movement." *International Labor and Working Class History* 88 (2015): 156–65.

Fortunati, Leopoldina. *Arcane of Reproduction: Housework, Prostitution, Labor and Capital.* Brooklyn, NY: Autonomedia, 1989.

Freeman, Carla. *High Tech and High Heels in the Global Economy: Women, Work, and Pink-Collar Identities in the Caribbean.* Durham, NC: Duke University Press, 2000.

Franzway, Suzanne, and Mary Margaret Fonow. *Making Feminist Politics: Transnational Alliances between Women and Labor.* Urbana: University of Illinois Press, 2011.

García, Magaly Rodríguez. "The League of Nations and the Moral Recruitment of Women." *International Review of Social History* 57, no. S20 (2012): 97–128.

Ghai, Dharam, and Zubeida Ahmed. "Preface." In *Rural Women: Unequal Partners in Development,* edited by Martha Loutfi, iii. Geneva: International Labour Organization, 1980.

Hartmann, Heidi. "The Unhappy Marriage of Marxism and Feminism." *Capital & Class* 3, no. 2 (1979): 1–33.

Huws, Ursula. *Action Programmes for the Protection of Homeworkers: Ten Case Studies from Around the World.* Geneva: ILO, 1995.

International Labor Conference (ILC). *Record of Proceedings,* 18th Session. Geneva: ILO, 1934.

———. *Record of Proceedings,* 30th Session, Geneva, 1947. Geneva: ILO, 1948.

———. *Record of Proceedings,* 48th Session, 1964. Geneva: ILO, 1965.

———. *Record of Proceedings,* 49th Session. Geneva: ILO, 1965.

———. *Record of Proceedings,* 77th Session, 1990. Geneva: ILO, 1991.

———. *Record of Proceedings,* 82nd Session, 1995. Geneva: ILO, 1996.

———. *Record of Proceedings,* 83rd Session, 1996. Geneva: ILO, 1997.

———. *Record of Proceedings,* 99th Session. Geneva: ILO, 2010.

ILO. *ABCs of Women Worker Rights and Gender Equality.* Geneva: ILO, 2007.

———. *Minutes.* 77th Session of the Governing Body. Geneva: ILO, 12–14 November 1936.

———. *Minutes.* 99th Session of the Governing Body. Montreal: ILO, 16, 17, 27 September 1946.

———. *Minutes.* 112th Session of the Governing Body. Geneva: ILO, June 1950.

———. *Minutes.* 117th Session of the Governing Body. Geneva: ILO, 20–23 November, 1951.

———. *Minutes.* 248th Session of the Governing Body, Geneva: ILO, 12–16, November 1990, 15–26 February 1991.

———. *Report to the Governments of Ceylon, India, Indonesia, Japan, Pakistan, the Philippines and Thailand on Conditions of Women's Work in Seven Asian Countries.* Geneva: ILO, 1958.

———. "Reports and Inquiries: Conditions of Employment of Women Workers in Asia." *International Labor Review* 70 (1954): 542–56.

———. R178-Night Work Recommendation, 1990 (No. 178). http://www.ilo.org/dyn/normlex/en/f?p=NORMLEXPUB:12100:0::NO:12100:P12100_INSTRUMENT_ID:312516:NO.

———. R165-Workers with Family Responsibilities Recommendation, 1981 (No. 165). http://www.ilo.org/dyn/normlex/en/f?p=NORMLEXPUB:12100:0::NO::P12100_INSTRUMENT_ID:312503.

———. *Women at Work: Trends 2016.* Geneva: ILO, 2016.

———. *Workers with Family Responsibilities.* Report III (Part 4B). Geneva: ILO, 1993.

Johnstone, Elizabeth. "Women in Economic Life: Rights and Opportunities." *Annals of the American Academy of Political and Social Science* 375, no. 1 (1968): 102–14.

Keck, Margaret, and Kathryn Sikkink. *Activists beyond Borders: Advocacy Networks in International Politics.* Ithaca, NY: Cornell University Press, 1998.

Lethbridge, Lucy. *Servants: A Downstairs View of Twentieth-Century Britain.* New York: Bloomsbury, 2013.

Loutfi, Martha Feherolf. *Rural Women: Unequal Partners in Development* (Geneva: ILO, 1980).
Lubin, Carol Riegelman, and Anne Winslow. *Social Justice for Women: The International Labor Organization and Women.* Durham, NC: Duke University Press, 1990.
Markham, Violet, and Florence Hancock. *Report on the Organization of Private Domestic Employment.* London: Ministry of Labor and National Service, 1945.
Mies, Maria. *The Lace Makers of Narsapur: Indian Housewives Produce for the World Market.* London: Zed Books, 1982.
Miller, Carol. "'Geneva—the Key to Equality': Inter-war Feminists and the League of Nations." *Women's History Review* 3, no. 2 (1994): 219–45.
Natchkova, Nora, and Céline Schoeni. "L'Organisation Internationale du Travail, les Féministes et les Réseaux d'Expertes: Les Enjeux d'une Politique Protectrice (1919-1934)." In *L'Organisation internationale du travail: Origine—Développement—Avenir,* edited by Isabelle Lespinet-Moret and Vincent Viet, 39–51. Rennes: Presses Universitaires de Rennes, 2011.
Orleck, Anneleise. *Common Sense and a Little Fire: Women and Working-Class Politics in the United States, 1900-1965.* Chapel Hill: University of North Carolina Press, 1995.
Palmer, Ingrid. "Rural Women and the Basic-Needs Approach to Development." *International Labour Review* 115, no. 1 (1977): 97–107.
Peterson, V. Spike. "Rewriting (Global) Political Economy as Reproductive, Productive, and Virtual (Foucauldian) Economies." *International Feminist Journal of Politics* 4, no.1 (2002): 1–30.
———. "Informalization, Inequalities and Global Insecurities." *International Studies Review* 12, no. 2 (2010): 244–70.
"Programme of Action." In International Labour Conference, 61st Session 1976 and Tripartite World Conference on Employment, Income Distribution and Social Progress and the International Division of Labour June 1976, Australian Delegation Report. Canberra: Australian Government, 1977.
Prügl, Elisabeth. *The Global Construction of Gender.* New York: Columbia University Press, 1999.
Ramamurthy, Priti. "Why Is Buying a 'Madras' Cotton Shirt a Political Act? A Feminist Commodity Chain Analysis." *Feminist Studies* 30, no. 3 (2004): 734–69.
Rodgers, Gerry, Eddy Lee, Lee Sweptson, and Jasmien Van Daele, eds. *The ILO and the Quest for Social Justice, 1919-2009.* Ithaca, NY: Cornell University Press, 2009.
Schwenken, Helen. "From Maid to Worker," *Queries* 7, no. 1 (2012): 14–21.
Schwenken, Helen, and Elisabeth Prügl. "An ILO Convention for Domestic Workers: Contextualizing the Debate." *International Feminist Journal of Politics* 13, no. 3 (2011): 437–61.
Self Employed Women's Association. "About Us." Retrieved 10 June 2015 from http://www.sewa.org/About_Us_History.asp.
Vosko, Leah F. *Managing the Margins: Gender, Citizenship, and the International Regulation of Precarious Employment.* New York: Oxford University Press, 2010.
Waring, Marilyn. *If Women Counted: A New Feminist Economics* (New York: Macmillan, 1988).

Whitworth, Sandra. "Gender, International Relations and the Case of the ILO." *Review of International Studies* 20, no. 4 (1994): 389–405.

Williams, Joan C. *Unbending Gender: Why Family and Work Conflict and What to Do about It*. New York: Oxford University Press, 2000.

Wikander, Ulla. "Demands on the ILO by Internationally Organized Women in 1919." In *ILO Histories: Essays on the International Labour Organization and Its Impact on the World during the Twentieth Century*, edited by Jasmien Van Daele, Magaly Rodríguez García, Geert van Goethem, and Marcel van der Linden, 67–89. New York: Peter Lang, 2010.

Zimmermann, Susan. "Globalizing Gendered Labour Policy: International Labour Standards and the Global South, 1919–1947." In *Women's ILO: Transnational Networks, Global Labour Standards, and Gender Equity, 1919 to Present*, edited by Eileen Boris, Doroethea Hoehtker, and Susan Zimmermann, 227–54. Leiden and Geneva: Brill and the ILO, 2018.

CHAPTER 9

FAMILY-RELATIONS LAW BETWEEN "STRATIFICATION" AND "RESISTANCE"
Housework and Family Law Exceptionalism

Maria Rosaria Marella

Stratification in the family-relations regime: a foreword

In this chapter I explore some of the results of what I name the "stratification" in family legal regime, as the phenomenon in which family relations are not, or are no longer, governed exclusively by family law but which experience an important incidence of general private law, contract law, and torts, in particular. Such phenomenon is now widely investigated under the heading "privatization of the family," and, in this framework, it has mainly stressed the growing space occupied by private autonomy in family relations. More recently (although the phenomenon is significant especially in the Italian landscape and, in part, in France and in some common-law jurisdictions), even the family immunity-in-tort principle[1] has been significantly eroded, with an increase of interspousal torts and an overlap of tort law to family law. Overall, in the regulation of family relations there is an opening to the law of the market, which does not replace family law but exists alongside it.

My assumption is that the above-described stratification is not homogeneous throughout the area covered by family law. In fact, while for some sectors this overlap of legal regimes is an acquired issue, other areas still appear to be subject to a monopoly, if not a real strong resiliency, of family law speciality or exceptionalism.[2] As a result, it seems that the special/general law dichotomy that marks the traditional depiction of family law within the legal systems plays a role within the same family law, where we can find areas that are permeable to the general law, such as contracts and torts, and areas that remain permanently out of it.

But, given that the complex (and incoherent) structure that family law tends to assume is basically self-evident—as it will appear clearer from the survey on the regulation of housework—the same cannot be said about the *quid* of this incoherence and, in particular, about the reason why some areas of family relations are firmly anchored to the family law speciality and completely kept out of general private law. The question is linked to the structural function and the ideological meaning that are attributed to family law as a special law under the private law system. It is also affected by the traditional public/private division. And although this is not the place to treat the theme of family law speciality, the political relevance that the exceptionalist approach has represented within the doctrine in the course of the time sheds light on the modes and purposes of intrafamilial housework regulation.

Family law speciality or exceptionalism underlies a certain caution or suspicion, particularly diffuse in the past, concerning the juridification of human relationships created in the family, and the degree of strength of such juridification.[3] The myth of the non-intervention of the state in the family brings about many, sometimes conflicting, perspectives. On the one hand, the narrative of the "family as an island in the sea of the law" expresses a liberal and libertarian request, which finds a strong legitimacy in the Italian constitutional formula of the family as "natural society" (article 29), in order to avoid the attempts to functionalize the family to the goals of the authoritarian state, as had happened under Fascism.[4] On the other hand, the idea of "family privacy" or "privateness," aiming at deregulation or soft regulation of family relationships, masks the disciplinary role played by the omission of regulation, which, not unlike the imposition of rules, provides the unregulated matter with a precise legal status.[5] In the case of the family, this position has historically coincided—if not in intent certainly in practice—with the strengthening of the status quo, coloring of patriarchal tints the speciality narrative.

Nowadays, it is the issue of commodification to revive the dichotomy special/general law in a new light, with the speciality of family law to be seen as a bastion against the invasion of the market logic in all the sides of social life and the increasing commodification of relationships. Here the analysis becomes more sophisticated when stressing the specificity of the areas different from the market, whether they are family, art, or education.[6] The stress is then placed on the singularity of the values that govern each social sphere; in the case of family, it is placed on the need to subtract relations based on affection, love, and care from market corruption—while once the reasons for opposing the logic of exchange and individualism of general private law were rather to safeguard the unity of the family and its hierarchical order and, with them, the intergenerational transmission of dominant values.

Finally, it is worth recalling the speculation about family law speciality developed within feminism, where the separation from market and the family privacy/public sphere opposition are represented as epiphanies of patriarchy, which still governs the household with the imposition of rigid gender roles, despite the reforms inspired by women's emancipation.[7]

As shown, the option between special and general law is not just a purely technical question, but neither has a unique political reading, being able to perform different tasks and take on different meanings. Both special and general law seem to assume, intermittently, now the face of hard law, now the one of soft law, as it happens when family law (as exceptional) is taken as paradigm of a less intense regulation of household relations, or to stem the tide of their commodification.

Inevitably, the stratification of legal regimes in the regulation of household follows a similar destiny, because the incoherence that the general and the special law compete with in regulating household relations is not such as to identify areas of discipline that can simply be read as a result of modernity and, respectively, durability or, worse, cultural backwardness. For example, the case of the new law of intrafamily torts, which cannot be largely discussed here, is so controversial that it cannot be regarded as a clear example of the evolution of the family legal regime toward modernity. Housework, as a matter apparently not legally relevant but instead a bulwark of family law exceptionalism, appears to me as an element of resilience of the patriarchal model or, more precisely as I will explain below, as the tolerated residuum of patriarchy.[8] But other readings are possible, not least the one that underlines the rhetoric of resistance to commodification.

1. Domestic sphere between hyper-juridification and deregulation: the legal irrelevance of housework

In legal systems, the speciality of family law endures but does not totally exclude general private law in regulating family and household. This circumstance, while challenging the very same family law exceptionalism—undermining its "necessariness"—also highlights the incidence of a dual level of discipline that should be taken into account in the process of investigating the family legal regime. This phenomenon of a double-level regulation occurs with regard to both personal and financial relations between spouses and is only partly justified in reclaiming the gradual family law slippage toward individualism. In fact, while it is true that, starting with the principle of equality between spouses, the new compromise between the original communitarian inspiration and the tension toward the enhancement of family members' individual personhood is the leitmotif of post–World War II family law reforms, when approaching the market rationale from within the same family law exceptionalism, the overlap of the legal tools of the market does highlight an overarching shift of family relationships with regard to the family/market dichotomy. On the one hand, family law speciality is repositioned along the path from status to contract; on the other, general private law now invades areas from which it was once excluded. In other words, a new statute of family relations suggests now that the old concept of family-community, selfless, shaped on national traditions, bearer of publicist requests, and, therefore, politically oriented,[9] never even really opposed the market logic, has not been a serious obstacle to the penetration of the latter in the regulation of many important aspects of family life. So much that many profiles of the legal regulation of the family are now attributable both to family law *and* the law of the market, marking not only the non-marginality of family law from patrimonial law but also the end of a special law monopoly. And this is without prejudice to the possible different interpretations of family law speciality, which have been mentioned above, and the diverse possible readings of the incursion of general private law among household relations.

In this scenario, however, do remain areas of resistance to privatization, by which we mean the penetration in the family regime of private law logics. This is the case of housework and care work performed by family members, the treatment of which seems even to escape a qualification in terms of legality, to be relevant at an exclusively social level. In fact, domestic work, because it is perceived as naturally gratuitous, is subtracted from the legal regime of labor; for lawyers it is just non-work, according to a setting that has instead been greatly exceeded both in sociology and economics.

Actually, housework has a legal—albeit limited—significance, but only within the logic of family law exceptionalism. This means that the rationality of market is rejected in this case, in the name of solidarity, which is conceived as the ultimate foundation of family relations: housework is inalienably free, unpaid, due to the family community by virtue of altruistic bonds and mutual aid, which are its (even legal) prerequisites. It is then clear that the apparent legal irrelevance of housework actually corresponds to a legal construction firmly founded on the dichotomy family/market and crucially dependent on its endurance.

Now, if gratuitousness is the crucial feature of housework legal status, its distribution between genders is clearly not irrelevant for the purposes of the distribution of social and economic power among family members. The rigidity in the division of roles between the sexes is deeply rooted in many cultures, with the exclusive or primary assignment to women of the burden of housework. It is a custom hard to change despite the recurrent discourse about women's emancipation. According to a recent survey carried out by Istat (Italian National Institute of Statistics), the unequal distribution of housework between sexes is already reflected in the education imparted in the family to Italian girls and boys aged fifteen to twenty years. For example, girls who occasionally perform household activities like cleaning, washing dishes, ironing, and caring of the laundry are twice, sometimes three times, more numerous their male peers. At the same time, the number of hours spent on housework by women is three to six times greater than that dedicated to it by their male partners.

Although the legal dimension of housework is often unspoken, underestimated, or ignored,[10] the thickness of its social and cultural issue is therefore rightly known. But, perhaps, it is less clear how closely the legal system is connected to the social phenomenon, determining its boundaries and suggesting its development. Never as in this case, it visibly emerges how the construction of family law as special, different, and opposite in rules and principles from general law consolidates and strengthens hierarchy among traditional roles within the family institution.

2. The family/market divide in the feminist analysis of the production/reproduction dichotomy

This link was well understood, since the early 1970s, by production/reproduction feminism, which flourished both in the Italian and in the Anglo-American materialist feminist movements. This feminist strand identifies the production/reproduction dichotomy as the foundation of the subordination of women in the family, and then in the market and the public sphere.[11] The comparison between production of goods and reproduction as production of individuals/workers, the former pertaining to men, the latter a place of marginalization and oppression of women, highlights the complementarity of family and market in capitalist societies—complementarity confirmed by the equations individual = workforce = commodity. To some extent this analysis has a certain confidence in the ability of law to produce social changes: the exclusion of women from the market and the public sphere is perceived as a collective problem that a legislator–social engineer can fix with apposite interventions, such as favoring women's access to employment and promoting permissive regulations on contraception and abortion.[12]

This explains why, in this context, it emerges a central question on the remuneration of household work as the result of an analysis of the work of women in the sphere of reproduction as "paid work to remunerate the worker," therefore productive work, although not recognized and unwaged. Wage claims—the more consistent proposal of the production/reproduction school—aim to include housework in the production cycle while providing the woman with a degree of autonomy that is a first step in the achievement of a different social role.

Above all, the wage-for-housework issue introduces an additional and crucial critical element, as far as the gratuitousness of care work done by women is such to demonstrate how the oppression of women is maintained and strengthened by a regulation of family relationships built on the construction of family law as special law, separate from the market and different from the general regulation of human relations, for it is grounded on its own rationality: the solidarity principle. The proposal represents an interesting attempt to "shuffle the cards" by undermining the family/market dichotomy, which that social (and legal) artefact is based on: housework is actually written into the logic of the capitalist division of roles and has a specific productivity that is mystified when simply regarded as a "mission," i.e. as expression of family solidarity. Wage, giving the housework an exchange value, inserts it in the production cycle with a dual effect: providing women with a minimum of economic power and a greater "social bargaining" capability and, most importantly, unmasking the ideology that lies behind the mystique of the family as place not tainted by market values.

Feminism of the early 1970s anticipates the rethinking of housework in terms of productive labor that can be found later in sociology and law and economics. In the same Anglo-American debate, for example, sociologists consider housework as part of affection and family ties—and not as productive work that contributes to satisfy the family needs—at least until Ann Oakley's seminal work, published in 1974.[13] This means that, in an ideal distribution of human activities between work and leisure, housework was ascribed to the second category, while the care role played by women in the family was mainly appreciated at the moral and psychological level, certainly not at the economic one. The change of perspective in the analysis and evaluation of housework has prompted sociologists to look much longer at the interconnections among family, labor market, consumer market, welfare, etc., whereas such an approach seems still absent in the "family legal analysis."[14]

Conversely, a similar change of perspective is clearly perceptible, in economics, in Gary Becker's famous work *A Treatise on the Family*.[15] Prerequisite for a reevaluation of housework is the critique against the economists' tendency to radically separate production from consumption, ascribing the former to businesses and the latter to families. The new approach to the economic dimension of household sheds light on how families employ goods and unpaid time for producing goods that are not allocated to the market but still have economic value. In essence, the family is no longer seen as place of mere consumption but as place of production of goods for consumption: through housework and care work, family transforms goods purchased in the market into use-value, with the aim, similar to the enterprise, to achieve utility maximization. It was inevitable that this type of analysis would have led to the establishment of a close relationship—a relationship of economic nature—between housework and the work performed in the market, and between them and the value of investments in human capital respectively addressed to one and the other: the choice between "buy" or "do," that is the decision to devote unpaid time to family instead of acquiring substitute goods or services in the market (e.g. prepared foods, housekeepers, etc.) is not (only) the result of emotional ties and family solidarity but the consequence of economic rationality, which is pursuing the most efficient solution.

Ultimately, both production/reproduction feminism and the New Home Economics exceed the traditional reconstruction of the family realm as independent and separate from the market: both emphasize the need to analyze them together in order to comprehend their dynamics; both focus on the issue of housework as a matter relating to the market.

3. The meaning of housework in the perspective of family law

The results achieved by other social sciences in the analysis of housework have not been shared so far by legal analysis. Lawyers keep on ignoring the issue, projecting it in the background of a strict family/market divide, which right here seems to find one of its pillars. This is not the case for the legal irrelevance of housework; rather, it has a limited relevance, restricted to the field of family law, assumed in its exceptionalism.

Obviously, the work carried out for the family cannot be ignored by a legal regime marked by the moral and legal equality of spouses: in Italian law, the family law reform enacted in 1975 occurs in an era when the prevailing model of family is characterized by a strict division of roles between spouses—worth mentioning "women's essential role in the household" sanctioned by article 37 of the Italian Constitution; therefore, equality must necessarily be realized through an equal consideration of the sphere of production and of reproduction. Hence one of the main steps of the reform: the adoption of joint marital property as default regime is interpreted as a means of "reward" for the housework performed by women.[16]

However, its non-mandatory character counteracts the effort, made by the 1975 Italian legislator, to approach reproduction to production. In fact, the most important recognition of housework in Italian family law is to be identified in article 143, 3 of the Civil Code (hereinafter cc): "Both spouses are required, each according to their resources and capacity of professional work or housework, to contribute to the family needs" (see also article 148, 1 cc). The explicit reference to housework is preceded by the recognition of the spouses' equality of status ("With marriage, husband and wife acquire the same rights and assume the same duties" [article 143, 1 cc]) and by the obligation of mutual cooperation in the interest of family (article 143, 2 cc), which clarifies the framework of the legal significance of housework, a framework within which spouses' equality is a prerequisite for the equality-based building of a community of "solidarity" rather than for the exercise of individual rights.[17] In this context, housework and care work stand as constituent elements of the foundations of the family patrimony regime: the obligation to contribute marks the validity of the solidarity principle on the basis of which the household community is grounded. To these purposes, the equal status assigned to professional work and housework expresses the recognition of the economic value of the contribution made through housework.[18] But this also signals the limits of housework's legal recognition, as far as the housework/care work actually done during marriage is rarely assessed as an investment in human capital and no restitution or redress can be claimed in the event of family breakdown unless a surplus in housework/care work can be proved in relation to the obligation to contribute. But such evidence is actually precluded: In fact, when can housework and care work be said to exceed the amount due to the family? What can be defined as content or limit to the obligation to contribute? Here the law confronts the problem of the complexity (and pervasiveness) of care normally provided to family members.

Such questions are critical in the determination of alimony at family breakdown. Housework—as a contribution to the formation of both spouses' common assets and the assets of each spouse—finds here another moment of relevance, but only in the framework of family law exceptionalism. The logic of contribution and solidarity is what ultimately determines the relevance of housework: investments in human capital made for the family are only remunerated in the limits of the living standard achieved by the family during marriage. If a wife's care work performed during marriage contributes to an increase in the income of her husband and to new career opportunities that take place only after the dissolution of marriage, it has no chance of being contemplated in the determination of the alimony quantum unless those gains can be considered as the "normal and expected" result of care work.[19] This is, however, an almost impossible burden of proof on the wife. It does not help to unravel the complexity of care work activities and does not move the focus from the purely internal family realm to the necessary connection between family and the market, the labor market in particular.

By contrast, the evaluation of housework takes a different substance in the discipline of family business (article 230-bis cc), where the balancing between market work and housework exceeds the logic of speciality and becomes the basis for the recognition of equal rights for family members. In fact, the family member who performs house-care-work, not differently from the one who works in the family business, has a right to maintenance, to participate in the profits generated by the business, and to the goods purchased through them, as well as to the business increases in proportion to the performed work.

In this respect, it has been observed that, unlike the provision of article 143, 3 cc which would have the ambition to produce a fair distribution between spouses of both the household expenses and the chances offered by labor market, the family business discipline has the more limited purpose of ensuring an adequate promotion of the family member employed in the reproductive sphere at the expense of the family member employed in the productive one. Therefore, such a discipline seems to fail to promote social changes, such as the introduction of a greater flexibility of roles within the family, promoting instead a status quo that ensures that the rigidity of roles is accompanied, however, by the guarantee of substantial equality.

Actually, article 230-bis cc opens the door to an assessment along the lines of productive and reproductive work, in the sense that both are rewarded according to profits and value of the family business. The law here seems to produce an osmosis between family and the market not dissimilar to that advocated by production/reproduction feminism. In either case the core of social change is in the pay of housework and care work according to market values.

However, such a perspective has a limited social impact due to the scope of applicability of article 230-bis cc. The equalization between reproductive and productive work concerns business only: it excludes both freelance activity, even if on a large scale, and the employee activity, albeit particularly qualified and demanding (e.g. top managers). Furthermore, the prevailing interpretation of the norm denies the relevance of the housework performed by those who are not included in the "legal" family, even if they are involved in the family business.

Only recently has the family business regulation been partially extended to unmarried couples. Until the new law on registered partnership, enacted in 2016 (see new article 230-ter cc), the equation production/reproduction did not work in favor of cohabiting partners. As we will see shortly, the gradual attraction of living together in the family law rationale produced in the recent past had the perverse effect of confusing the two spheres of reproductive and productive work at the expense of the latter, which in the wake of the solidarity rhetoric changes its legal status as a result of its alleged gratuitousness.

In conclusion, although article 230-bis cc is the clue of a possible treatment of housework as paid work, its impact remains marginal, so much as its role within the system. Therefore article 143, 3 cc stands as the real cornerstone of housework legal status in view of its general scope. Consequently the balance between production and reproduction, especially in relation to the division of roles between genders, is deliberately undetermined, because it is left to spouses' autonomy.

Now, can housework and care work really be the subject of an agreement between spouses? To what extent? In principle, the gender division of labor within the household should be freely negotiated by the spouses, moving from a position of equality.[20] In particular, spouses should be able to negotiate with each other the choice to focus primarily on caregiving in the family as part of the economic basis of their family ménage: this is what can be deduced from articles 143 and 144 cc, which entails the so-called agreement rule, that is the consensual—*rectius* negotiated—basis of the family project. However, a combination of social and cultural factors, as well as unfavorable and discriminatory conditions in the workplace, put many women in an objective position of disadvantage. The exercise of private autonomy that the agreement rule sets as a basis of the family institution requires not only formal equality; but the gap between the ideal family designed by the legislator and social reality implies that the "idyllic criterion of free and consensual choice may be so heavily subordinated by the 'balance of power' existing between husband and wife within the family"[21] that the ambition for equal dignity between household and productive sphere, entrusted to the mutual obligations of collaboration and contribution of the spouses (articles 143, 2 and 3 cc), is often reduced to mere "wishful thinking."

In fact, the feasibility of an agreement on housework is jeopardized not just by social hurdles but also by the very legal framework within which solidarity molds the duty of contribution of article 143, 3 cc. Here family law exceptionalism plays its crucial role by conditioning the mode and content of a possible agreement, and thus clearly marking the boundaries beyond which the logic of market is banned.

Incidentally it is worth noting that housework, because it is still perceived as the epitome of the family/market dichotomy, is treated in the same way almost everywhere in the Western legal tradition. To illustrate the limits to spouses' freedom of contract on housework, I will use an American case, *State v. Bachmann*, decided in 1994 by the Appeal Court of Minnesota.[22] In order to take advantage of a provision providing the state prison administration with the possibility to grant work permits to prisoners with a valid contract of employment, the defendant, detained in Minnesota, concludes with her husband a contract according to which husband agrees to pay her in exchange for each hour of housework that she performs over the weekend, benefiting from the aforementioned permit. Drawing on the invalidity of the agreement between husband and wife, the state contests the legitimacy of the permit. The court accepts plaintiff's argument and asserts the non-enforceability of the contract, because it has no consideration: the work performed by the wife is in fact the object of a preexisting obligation to the family resulting from marriage and from the notion of family as a community of beloveds, a place of election of solidarity-based relationships. Coherent with the legal regime of the family, what was provided in favor of the husband is already due by the wife by virtue of the marriage bond, so that the economic substance of the agreement proves purely illusory (there is no exchange under which you earn or you lose something) and the contract is invalid. The court's reasoning perfectly fits Italian law: such a contract is causeless, because housework contemplated in the agreement is already due under the obligation of article 143, 3 cc, to contribute as part of the primary family regime.

The landing point of the argument appears rather definitive: the housework performed in favor of the family can never become paid work, enter the logic of market and exchange, or be "contractualized." Solidarity here imposes a (legal) qualification in no-pecuniary terms that clashes with the economic substance of housework as productive work (see above, section 2) and denies the deep interconnection between work done inside and outside the household that frames the family conceived as an economic unit. The agreement rule, seen as a necessary complement of the basic regime of marital patrimony, is neutralized by an interpretation informed by the logic of family solidarity, in which private autonomy is ultimately reabsorbed by the mandatory statutory framework.

At this point, it is patent the distance from the logic of the family business' discipline, which firmly anchors housework to market, explicitly placing it in the production circuit. But, as we have explained, the limits of its operational impact do not allow article 230-bis cc to be made the core of the housework legal regime.

Eventually housework presents itself as the tolerated residuum of patriarchy in family law, the extreme concession that the liberal-egalitarian construction of family relationships makes to the original patriarchal institution, established on the basis of a compromise that sees, on the one hand, the triumph of the juridical equality of spouses, the sunset of marriage indissolubility, the recognition of equal dignity for legitimate and natural children, and even the success of the consensual principle in marital sex; but on the other, it sees the persistence of a reproductive sphere dramatically characterized by the gender division of labor and basically alien to freedom of contract, from which the typical bourgeois individualism of market relations remains in principle excluded.

4. Housework, investment in human capital, and family breakdown

In this framework, household and care work stand, not by chance, as a bastion of the family law speciality.

But this does not preserve their legal treatment from the pressure of those egalitarian requests that cross other areas of family law.

It is precisely from the perspective of family law exceptionalism that more recent scholarship, under the pressure of comparative law suggestions, looks for solutions that would give housework fuller recognition, aiming at remunerating "invisible capital," i.e. those investments in human capital made in favor of family life that directly or indirectly benefit career, professional success, and, ultimately, the earning capacity of the other spouse. Here is essentially adopted the perspective of the protection of the weaker spouse, normally the wife, who devotes herself to the family and in so doing renounces her possible self-fulfillment in the labor market, influenced by family needs or by career expectations lower than those of her husband. The consequences of such choices are fully manifested at the time of marriage crisis, when the spouse who has been utterly or partially devoted to care is left with insufficient resources to deal with the new situation and has to rely on the protection guaranteed by law through the post-divorce maintenance; but, in most legal systems, the structure of post-divorce alimony is not such as to reflect the economic value of the investment in human capital, for it does not aim to remunerate the care work that exceeds the obligation to contribute and has been hypothetically monetized by the other spouse. In Italian law, the parameter of quantification for alimony deployed till recently (the living standard during the marriage) was controversial and, in fact, discussed, on the one hand, because it was perceived as too burdensome for the obligor as it is due to the obligee unless she can afford the same standard of living; on the other, it was incapable of taking into account the contribution provided by the weaker spouse when the consequent improvement of the obligor's living conditions occurs only in the aftermath of marriage dissolution. The recent overruling in the case law of the Supreme Court (Corte di Cassazione)[23] has reduced the amount of the alimony due, abandoning the parameter of the standard of living during marriage, because it was judged a disproportioned burden for the obliged spouse. As a result, the contribution of housework to achieving a certain standard of living is swept out of the scenario, which now focuses only on professional work (breadwinning) on the market.

Other legal systems, however, show more flexibility in this regard. In common law, for example, post-divorce division of marital property begins to take on a more "egalitarian" connotation, where it tries to reflect the economic value of the wife's contribution to husband's professional increase and/or to the same family well-being.

Observers paid particular attention to a path-breaking decision, the English leading case *White v. White*,[24] in which the House of Lords reinterpreted a key provision of the Matrimonial Causes Act 1973, section 25, so as to establish the division of marital property in case of divorce not only on the future needs and the reasonable needs of the weaker spouse but also on the contribution, financial and not, that both spouses provided during the marriage, because, by the standard of fairness that the court interprets as correct at the present time, "there should be no bias in favour of the money-earner and against the home-maker and child-caregiver." Given that, in common law, the division of family assets is the fundamental patrimonial consequence of divorce, this departure from an exclusively subsidy mentality (the "financial needs" of section 25, Matrimonial Causes Act), mostly calibrated on criteria (reasonable requirements)—such as the standard of living achieved during marriage and the duration of marriage (very similar to the rationale and the parameters currently used in Italian law for the settlement of post-divorce alimony)—suggests to rethinking the content and function of this alimony, which should definitely serve a function of equalization.

The perspective of family law exceptionalism, along with the election of the point of view of the weaker spouse, leads here not so much to claim the full remuneration of household and care work but rather to look for a more equitable distribution of the sacrifices suffered during marriage. On the other hand, the pursuit of the former goal (although in White it had been proposed by a woman judge in the judgment of appeal) would have led to give the wife a quota of the farm business greater than the one allocated to the husband, so as to consider the contribution she made to the family as wife and mother in addition to and beyond her role as member of the farm business.[25] But this was not the vision eventually accepted by the renowned decision of the House of Lords, which also refused to embrace the equality of quotas—reflecting the equal productivity of housework and professional work—as starting point in the division of marital property.

More interestingly, therefore, appears the orientation recently started in Germany by the Supreme Court (*Bundesgerichtshof*). Still in reference to the evaluation of the contribution made by the wife to the economic well-being of the family, the *Bundesgerichtshof* strives to give a pecuniary value to unpaid housework, comparing it to the hypothetical extra-household income that the woman would have earned working full time in the market.

A different route, linked more to contract than to status, is shown by developments in the US legal system, which seems to find in the practice of the so-called premarital agreements a tool for private autonomy that allows a negotiation between the parties about the estimation of the contribution and/or sacrifice that spouses are willing to make for the family welfare and unity. Prenuptial agreement may actually be a way out from the rigidity that characterizes post-divorce alimony in Italian law. However, when the law opts for the contractual solution, it also has to take into account the difference in bargaining power between the spouses and to provide the tools to protect the weaker party.[26] For this reason the regulation of post-divorce alimony should perform a function of equalization and support the spouse with a weaker bargaining power in light of the principle according to which the parties "bargain in the shadow of the law."[27] In fact, an adequate consideration of the redistributive effects of legal rules concerning alimony and the division of marital property allows us to grasp the way in which these norms influence the position of the spouses in the face of negotiation on the consequences of divorce, determining the respective bargaining power. Bargaining in the "shadow" of a legal regime that recognizes the compensatory function of post-divorce alimony, and in so doing strengthens the position of the weaker spouses, would probably be able to better distribute between spouses both the cost of sacrifices made for the family well-being and the benefits derived from it.

However, this is not the road that leads to reverse the dominant perspective, namely to overcome the production/reproduction dichotomy and the exchange versus solidarity opposition. Family law exceptionalism is still the matrix of the legal regime of housework, even in the perspective of legal change, as far as private autonomy is the tool to identify negotiated modes to fulfill the mandatory duties of solidarity between spouses at marriage breakdown. This represents the outcome of a legal construction in which the distinctive feature of marriage is equality between spouses (see article 29, Italian Constitution); hence the regulation of the consequences of divorce, including the complementary recognition of private autonomy, is legitimate only as far as it aims at the realization of the equality principle. My account is, by contrast, that the legal status of housework is the tolerated residuum of patriarchy: therefore it intimately contradicts the constitutional principle of equality in the family and structurally prevents its full realization. At least until it is ruled according to the logic of family law exceptionalism.

5. Housework and unmarried couples, or the unpredictable drift of family solidarity

In the dialectic between status and contract, the legal regime of living together not based on marriage or other forms of legal recognition (e.g. registered partnerships) is frequently referred to as the realm of private autonomy, at least in those countries whose legal systems do not grant a status-like treatment to *de facto* cohabitation. According to this narrative, the legal status of unmarried couples represents the "contractual side" of modern family law as opposed to the discipline of the legitimate family, which is still basically founded on status. This scheme is still valid in the Italian legal system and in some common law jurisdictions (e.g. some of the United States). In reference to these experiences, the analysis of the legal treatment of housework can help to understand to what extent the logic of contract is actually operating in this area.

Well, we believe that with some caution, for example in the United States, housework is a component of the consideration that necessarily supports contractual agreements between partners in the so-called "Marvinized" regimes, i.e. in those States in which the *Marvin v. Marvin* case is recognized as precedent, thereby considering contracts between cohabitants enforceable and identifying them even in merely verbal (and even implicit) agreements.[28] In Marvin, in fact, the economic and personal sacrifice made by the "wife" in giving up her career and devoting herself to raising a family is considered by the court as the detriment that qualifies the exchange as valid under the consideration doctrine.

In reality the system of unmarried couples, if read from the angle of housework, seems to be more specifically regulated by family solidarity than by private autonomy. Again in common law, this time English common law, some aspects of the protection provided by equitable remedies to the weaker partner are strongly influenced by an understanding of housework based on solidarity. It happens that the detriment, represented by the contribution of the caregiver-partner to the family and assumed as a fundamental requirement for the recognition of an entitlement on the family house owned by the other partner, is assessed by expressly excluding all those activities that are attributable to *natural love and affection,* i.e. all those unpaid performances normally required—or expected—by family members. Courts distinguish between market-like performances, relevant to the protection, and non-market-like performances, irrelevant. In other words, the detriment deriving from the contribution to the household is what can be spent and commonly circulates in the market, while what we normally consider unpaid housework is not relevant even for the protection of the reliance engendered by living together. In fact, the legal regime governing unmarried couples is also strongly dominated by values of solidarity. Values that, within the couple, inevitably tend to assume a hierarchical connotation, so much as a hierarchical connotation pertains to the production/reproduction divide. One of the consequences of the strict division between production and reproduction in the protection of the non-owner partner is to relegate the loss of chances of career, professional success, and financial independence to the solidarity = non-market = irrelevance pattern.

In the Italian legal system, the lack of legal recognition of unmarried couples—now partly superseded by the regulation provided by the *Legge n. 76/2016*—implied the search for other solutions within the law of obligations. Italian scholarship maintained the enforceability of cohabitation arrangements since the 1980s.[29] Cohabitation agreements were deemed enforceable as long as they are consideration-grounded (*cause suffisante*). There is no doubt that a valid *causa* can be identified, for instance, in the performance of everyday housework, while detriment on the "housekeeper" can be located in the loss of professional opportunities in the labor market. Nevertheless, in case law, concerns about the protection of the weaker partners were usually addressed outside the market and beyond the boundaries of freedom of contract. Where domestic arrangements were concerned, Italian courts mostly enforced the doctrine of moral obligation (*obbligazione naturale,* article 2034 cc), where solidarity, *not* bargaining, between the partners is the operational principle. Any transfer of money or conveyance of property within the couple, whether or not for the purpose of maintenance, was interpreted as the spontaneous performance of a moral or social duty inspired by a reciprocal sense of solidarity between the partners. Consequently, there was no enforceable agreement, whatever the original intention of the parties. According to the black-letter rule, the only legal effect of this moral obligation is that the payment or the object of the performance can be retained. For example, an Italian court rejected the claim of a woman who had lent a large amount of money to her partner when he was experiencing financial troubles and who subsequently sought to retrieve the money from his heirs upon his death. The court denied that there had ever been a loan and held that the true ground for the transfer of money was the woman's sense of solidarity with her companion in the framework of their relationship; a moral rather than contractual obligation was in the background.

In most recent case law, the doctrine of the natural obligation and the doctrine of the *cause suffisante* tend to overlap in the light of the will of the parties' fulfilment. Moral duties originating from the solidarity bonds that supposedly underpin cohabitations *more uxorio* are now taken into consideration, not to overcome or subvert the contractual arrangement, but instead as the legal foundation upon which the court grounds the legitimacy of the contractual enforcement. The moral obligation now strengthens the contractual arrangement. The sale of land to the partner is therefore valid, although she did not pay the price and legal requirements for a valid gift do not occur.[30] In a most recent case, the Supreme Court endorses this interpretation while reaffirming the constitutional implications of the "de facto" family in Italian law and the importance of solidarity as the main feature of its legal regulation.[31]

Nevertheless Italian case law is strict in defining a sharp boundary between paid and unpaid work. Acts performed in the framework of a *more uxorio* relationship are held to be grounded in *affectionis vel benevolentiae causa* (that is, made "in consideration of love and affection") and should not be remunerated. In fact, unless the performer proves that a proper labor contract was established between the parties, the court will presume that because of their intimate relationship, the work was intended to be gratuitous. The exchange logic was so intensely loathed that not only housework but even professional work performed in the context of cohabitation in favor of the business of the partner was considered as natural obligation. The result was paradoxical: professional work used to be drawn into the domestic orbit, also abandoning the presumption of onerousness that in the *ius commune* characterizes labor regulation.

For example, a woman who had been working for years as a nurse in the consulting room of a doctor was held to be no longer entitled to her salary from the moment she became engaged in a *more uxorio* relationship with the doctor.[32] In the reasoning of the Supreme Court, notions of "solidarity" and "gratitude" were crucial in setting aside the presumption of paid work. In fact, the normal legal presumption was flipped in this context: in order to establish her case, the plaintiff had to prove she *was* a regular employee.

Even in more recent cases, women's work in their partners' enterprises is normally characterized as unpaid. We find the same *ratio* in the case of a woman who had been working for a long time in her partner's fish-breeding factory,[33] and in the case of a woman who not only had been working on her partner's farm, but had also lent him money.[34] In both cases, there was no remuneration and no money back; everything melts into the blob of solidarity. This order of evaluation is explicitly based on the foundation between the parties of "a community of life and interests similar to a marital relationship," so that the hospitality activity carried out at the partner's hotel over six years is to be considered gratuitous until the opposite is proven.[35] The new law enacted in 2016 partly innovated this legal regime by recognizing to the partner who works in the companion's enterprise the same rights granted to spouses. The notion of "work" in this case includes the housework performed in the family engaged in the enterprise (article 230-ter cc). But this legal regime does not extend to partners working in a professional firm or other commercial setting other than the enterprise.

The new law has also introduced the regulation of cohabitation contracts. Among the features that partners can negotiate by contract, the law lists the duty to contribute to the family ménage according to the discipline of marriage provided by article 143, 3 cc. As a default rule, this provision may be set aside by partners willing to negotiate the economic weight of housework in different terms. But, as such, the default rule tends to be attractive every time parties have no specific knowledge of the ultimate scope of the rule and its consequences. To be sure, the provision introduces the element of solidarity into the contractual scheme. It will be interesting to explore what kind of impact it will have on the actual regulation of housework.

6. Housework as production, or third-party injury to housewife's bodily integrity

As seen, civil law and common law treat housework in a similar way. Both systems are marked by the gratuitousness principle in the legitimate family and are entirely dominated by the family law logic; both are marked by the same logic also in the context of unmarried couples and are equally subjugated to the paradigm of solidarity-gratuitousness—either referred to *affectionis vel benevolaentiae causa* or to the "natural love and affection" rationale.

This can invite us to consider the conceptual deconstruction of the opposition between common law and civil law, an approach lately undertaken by comparative law, at least in its dominant addresses. But more usefully it leads us to give consideration to the feminist critique founded on the dichotomy production/reproduction, which appears to affect both common and civil law models; what is also common to them is the patriarchal basis of the family institution with its legal categories

Referring to the canons of that critical analysis and, in particular, to the deconstruction of the dichotomy that seeks to deny the production character of care work, we can now deal with a further profile of the legal regulation of housework, which has to do with its external—extra-household—significance. Here, therefore, comes the way the law reacts when an injury to health, bodily integrity, or life prevents the housewife from performing the housework as she normally used to do. Well, again, the answer seems common to the systems of common law and civil law: in relations with a third party, housework "changes its nature" and becomes economically relevant and valuable with market parameters; its loss, therefore, represents an economic loss, the presence of which allows us to recognize in it an asset held by the family as a whole. In turn, this asset is the object of an obligation, the performance of which has been prevented by the accident happened to the housewife.

The approach to the problem in Italian case law is extremely careful and analytical. Housework—reported to the figure of the housewife—is considered activity capable of economic valuation and productive of an income, although, with the work actually being gratuitous, a "figurative income."[36] However, the reduction of work capacity that comes up with the inability to carry out all household chores is considered per se an economic loss, as such to be compensated in addition to damages for the injury to bodily integrity suffered by the housewife.[37]

This orientation is definitely consolidated. For compensation purposes it is sometimes enriched by a particularly analytical approach concerning the structure of housework.

(a) Already in the 1970s, some judges feel the need to affirm "a global and generic vision of the complex activity of the housewife," an activity that "does not, as it is the case for other categories of income-producers, end in one field, but consists in very different fields: child care and child rearing, housework, management of the family business, education of children, assistance to the husband and collaboration with him in the maintenance of social relationships interesting his career."[38] From this we derive important consequences in the field of assessment of damages and, before that, the determination of the "figurative income."

If the market value of the simplest household tasks can easily be deduced from the average salary of a housekeeper, the value of the personal contribution of the housewife is also proportional to her level of education and study qualification, while her extensive role of coordination of family life, as recognized by the Italian Corte di Cassazione,[39] has a distinct economic value, even when the practical part of the housework is actually entrusted to strangers. This consideration led courts in the past to also award the family hedonic damages related to the impairment of its social life, taking into account the loss of the housewife's commitment to foster the family's social relationships, which has, albeit indirectly, patrimonial consequences on the family as a whole and the professional activity of the husband in particular.

Nowadays, the Italian law of torts has abandoned that category of hedonic damages. In the new doctrinal framework, what counts is the constitutional basis of the entitlements violated by the wrongdoer. In reference to the loss of housework ability, the constitutional basis is to be found in articles 4 and 37 of the Italian Constitution, which protect, respectively, any form of work and the rights of working women.[40] In fact, what dominates the scene is still the economic value of housework. In this sense, the Italian Corte di Cassazione further clarifies its meaning, stating that its loss deprives the family of "economic utility . . . relating to care, education and assistance"[41]; the complexity of the tasks implies—as it has been said—a measure of compensation for the family unit that cannot refer to the mere income of a housekeeper but rather to the triple of the social pension.[42]

(b) A reconfiguration of the matter has recently been shown, with regard to the subject of the compromised ability of housework, relevant for compensatory damages. First, the Corte di Cassazione has exceeded the narrow limits of the case, stating that "the radical evolution of customs no longer allows confining the issue solely to housewives, being now well possible the rise of such damages in reference to women who work in the market and also carry out household activities and in relation to men."[43] Second, the idea that housework play an economic role only in reference to the utilities gained by others (the relatives of a harmed or killed housewife), and not for those who actually perform it (the housewife herself), was finally dismissed.[44] Previously, as we have seen, household activities were considered a source of utility only for family members in favor of whom they had been carried out, particularly within the legitimate family. The issue at stake was then reconstructed by the judges as a case of tortious interference of a third party in the working activity due by law, considering the housewife as a person obliged to caretaking and her husband and children as holders of a "right toward the respective wife and mother in the scope of the family relationship."[45] The new approach allows us to recognize the economic value of housework also in favor of a single person, so that those who suffer an injury to the ability to perform home chores, such as taking care of the apartment and the laundry, cooking meals, etc., suffer not only a biological harm, which includes the impairment of their general work capacity, but also a specific economic loss.

In this light, it is difficult to maintain the principle of gratuitousness of housework performed in favor of family members outside the consideration offered by the basic marital patrimony regime (see above part 3). And this is even truer in the light of the reasoning of the Italian Corte di Cassazione, which constructs the economic loss deriving from the impairment of housework ability not only as a "consequential damage"—arising from the need to resort to maid services, laundries, restaurants, hotels, or guesthouses in extreme cases—but also as a "loss of profit" per se, in view of the productive character of housework expressly recognized by article 230-bis cc. As we know, the provision equates the work performed in the family business to housework, considering both of them the source of economic entitlements proportional to the quantity and quality of the work done. Hence the "loss of profit" following the impairment of work capacity. In the Corte di Cassazione assessment, in fact, housework seems to have passed the ford, becoming, without any doubt, "productive work"—and, I would add, productive work with its own specific and autonomous character.

Thus we are finally far from the womanly stereotypes governing case law in the 1980s, when courts refused to assess the damages claimed by the prostitute who had been bodily injured according to the evaluation of the sex work market, chastely comparing her loss of profit with the average housewife's income, in turn represented by the amount of social pension.[46] In doing so, the judges brought together, in a single stance, the two extremes of reproductive work for the family and illegal work, both equally unproductive because they are *against the public policy*. Who knows how unwittingly the court has corroborated the stereotype of the woman, "either wife or whore,"[47] along with those feminist analyses that denounce the ideological and social contiguity between the position of the wife and the figure of the prostitute on the basis of their common exclusion from the market.

Obviously, some uncertainty remains about the identification of the correct way to quantify the economic value of housework, due to the impossibility of negotiating within the family and in the market. What is clear from both the attempts made by our jurisprudence and the experience of the courts in other legal systems is that housework carried out on behalf of the family by one of its members, when considered from the outside, appears as an asset, an economic resource of the family that, if improperly compromised, should be reintegrated into its financial value. In the German experience, for example, the instance of the murder of the housewife has created a topical *Fallgruppe* (case group) in certain doctrinal creations, committed to overcome thorny problems about the conceptualization of some prejudices within the law of torts and their proper quantification. German law deploys here the *Normativer Schaden* (normative harm) notion to justify the compensatory reaction to an injury that does not produce, from the nominal viewpoint, a capital negative differential in the assets of the plaintiff, given that the housewife as such is not a wage earner or is not paid for the housework that she performs, and her death does not deprive the family of an income—at least formally. Similarly, damages assessment is entrusted to the *Fiktive Herstellungskosten* (fictitious repair cost) practice, which allows estimating the suffered injury as the salary due to the person who would substitute the killed woman in housekeeping. The special feature here is that these damages are awarded even if the family of the deceased has not actually spent a single euro to replace her with a housemaid,[48] thus highlighting that housework and care work are, ultimately, considered relevant in themselves to the family assets, or as a necessary productive component of family wealth.

The focus, correctly, comes again on the productive nature of the reproductive work done in the home, what is precisely exemplified by economists with the expression "household production." Now, not simply the recognition of a financial and compensable detriment caused by the loss of work ability but the parameters chosen for its quantification appear to be crucial in assigning the due importance to the productive character of housework. In common law, which also awards damages from the housewife's death, the obstacle represented by the gratuitousness of the housework is overcome by various tricks. A first approach analytically compares the value of the housewife's work to the sum of the prices of the single tasks she habitually carried out, as set by the market in the respective fields. This method fails to reflect the totality and complexity of the housewife's contribution, as mother and wife, on behalf of the whole family, as the above-mentioned Italian case law had tried to do by taking into account the hypothesis of a damage referred to the impairment of family's social life. A second approach seeks to address this need by quantifying damages in the same way as the salary of a housekeeper, plus the salary of a nanny-housemaid. In some cases, the presence of school-age children has advised to adopt as a parameter the salary of a primary school teacher. But even this approach has several drawbacks, because it is inherently rigid and cannot realistically reproduce the actual distribution of working time compared to the various functions regarded, with the risk to overestimate or underestimate the economic value of house-care-work. A third approach has then been proposed, directly inspired by the method of economic analysis. It compares the value of the time spent performing housework to "opportunity-costs": the time spent on household production is considered in the light of the income that the same amount of time would have earned in the market. In this way it reflects what each family member loses in terms of work outside the home and, therefore, in terms of money, to materially balance the demise of the housewife.[49] Without going into economic details, we can make two observations: the first is that this approach totally inserts the housewife into the production circuit, comparing her working time to the alternatives offered by the market (and not to the cost of housework done by a domestic servant), imagining, for the housewife, an actual interchangeability of roles between domestic sphere and production sphere. The second, closely related to the first, concerns the overcoming of gender roles also with respect to typical domestic tasks, since each component of the couple is considered potentially productive both at home and in the market. And this is a way that enables, more than the previous one, to conceive the loss of ability to work at home as a loss of economic units for both the family that benefits and those who produce it, regardless of gender and other personal circumstances like marital status and family situation.

7. Conclusion: out of family law exceptionalism; two cases

After the family law reform had entered into force, Pietro Rescigno, a prominent Italian scholar, warned against the perpetuation of "the idea of a normal extraneousness of the family to the scheme of wage labor, for the prevalence of duties of domestic collaboration," stressing that this attitude was likely to undermine the innovative efforts of the reform and particularly of the legal treatment of the work performed within the family provided by article 230-bis, whereas "the system built by the norm should affirm the opposite rule of normalcy of 'wage labor' for working relationships within the family."[50] Thirty years later, the productive function of the family, which justifies "its autonomy as an intermediate social formation,"[51] seems still misunderstood by a prevalent statutory interpretation that relegates productivity to the regime of family business, celebrating for the rest the rationale of family solidarity—and its "natural" corollary of the gratuitousness of the work done in the domestic sphere—as the cypher of the family as a legal concept.

In that context, the importance of housework for the law emerges, as we have seen, sporadically, and if the legislature seems to have set in article 143 cc the only moment of genuine concern for housework (without, however, providing for its remuneration), the interest that scholars and case law devoted to this theme mostly refers to marriage breakdown.

Following a typical argument of critical analysis, we can say that the way family law recognizes housework, as it can be deduced from the law in force, is inherently inconsistent. If, on the one hand, it is marked by the inflexibility of the basic patrimony regime set by article 143, 3 cc, which sanctions the economic and legal significance of housework as "necessary," even on an equal footing with extra-household labor, on the other it is characterized by the complete freedom of the spouses (more realistically: of the "stronger" one) in choosing the secondary so-called distributive regime, i.e. joint or separate ownership of family assets, with no regard for the fact that the joint property rule could be the main tool to reward housework. It happens that the spouses may alternatively elect—and most of them do—the property regime of separation of assets, which inevitably obscures any surplus of housework when it exceeds the obligation to contribute, leaving it devoid of economic recognition.

Therefore the legal discipline of the family ménage includes, but ultimately does not reward, housework. This discrepancy is legitimized by the system by recurring to family solidarity. But, evidently, the spouse who performs exclusively or predominantly housework is not adequately protected by the law governing the "physiology" of the household. Consequently, scholars identify the moment of the final and necessary recognition/compensation of housework in the discipline of marital crisis. As it turns out, the solution offered by Italian law is not satisfying because of the narrow welfare character of post-divorce alimony. Here the basic incoherence of the system emerges in all its evidence, with a consolidated orientation of the Corte di Cassazione against prenuptial agreements, right where the exercise of spouses' autonomy could lead to a negotiated recognition of the economic value of housework. As a result, the same production/reproduction (male/female) promise of article 143 cc is not achieved in the further development of the family legal regime.

Now, the problem of the housework legal status, although still read from the family law perspective, deserves to be rediscussed in the light of some additional data. What follows is further food for thought rather than the display of conclusive solutions.

(a) Without prejudice to the mandatory nature of the basic regime of marital patrimonial relationships, the pervasiveness of the principle of family solidarity does not justify the lack of return for housework where this is mainly provided by the spouse (the wife in most cases) who also works in the market and financially enriches—in roughly equal measure to the other spouse —family wealth. Such a case is not uncommon but places with dramatic clarity the gratuitousness of housework under the shadow of patriarchy as the "dark side" of family law exceptionalism, epitomizing a crypto-type model that permeates the so-called family solidarity, and in this way overlooks the moral and legal equality of spouses.

(b) Part of Italian scholarship is now oriented toward the negotiability of what we should otherwise see as the *essentials of marriage*, i.e. those mutual obligations imposed on wife and husband by article 143, 2 cc, as direct consequence of spouse legal status. These are non-patrimonial duties whose content is established by spouses—at least according to some scholars —on basis of the agreement rule under article 144 cc.

Now, this area of spouses' private autonomy would differ from the scope of the obligation to contribute imposed by article 143, 3 cc, and made mandatory by virtue of the provision of article 160 cc. In fact, we could not think of a mutual and total renunciation of the contribution of the spouses without denying the very idea of marriage. And this is even clearer if we think of a seemingly distant reality, which is the story of the French PACS, where, on the eve of the approval of the act, the Conseil Constitutionnel considered the obligation of the "mutual and material support" imposed to partners as mandatory, notwithstanding the freedom of contract that they enjoy in the election of the couple's property regime.

However, this is not the case for radically excluding the negotiation on how to perform the obligation to contribute. It would be paradoxical to admit the negotiability of residual non-pecuniary duties while imposing a strict compulsory regime on a pecuniary obligation, normally governed by freedom of contract. If we really want to recognize the general scope of the agreement rule of article 144 cc, we must also then admit a margin of negotiation with regard to the basic patrimony regime while complying with the provisions of article 160 cc.

With specific regard to housework, negotiating the terms of the contribution to the needs of the family may mean, for example, introducing the diachronic dimension in the agreement to define the remuneration of the surplus of housework calculated in reference to a given historical moment.

However, the most attractive alternatives in the regulation of housework lie on a different level, external to family law rationale.

The overcoming of family law exceptionalism can occur, as shown in the North American debate, on two different grounds: on the ground of general (private) law, where the need to reward the investment in human capital at family breakdown finds a (proposed) solution in the ordinary remedies for breach of contract; on the ground of public-welfare law, where care work performed in the family, properly valued in its social function, becomes the object of a compensation owed by the state.

The logical background of the first scenario is the conceptualization of marriage as a contract, in particular as a "relational contract." Adopting this approach allows us to take the marriage crisis caused by one partner as "breach of contract" and, more precisely, as the break of a long-term commitment in which "each of the parties makes investments directed to the formation of a new capital asset, which coincides with the family."[52] Based on these assumptions, the choice of the parameter according to which damages are to be settled concretely determines the model of family taken into account: namely, it defines and simultaneously reflects the roles that the spouses are supposed to assume when they get married. Consequently, expectation damages (equal to profit expectation frustrated by marriage dissolution) reflect the traditional idea of family and marriage, in which solidarity prevails and the wife is oriented to invest her energy in the care of the family rather than in the labor market. If the measure of compensation is "reliance damages," it contemplates the opportunity-costs determined by the market alternatives that have been neglected to dedicate oneself to the family, what responds to a more "individualistic" evaluation of the marriage institution. Finally, the scheme of "restitution" damages may be successful when the household commitment of one spouse has significantly contributed to the professional success of the other. In this case, the "price" of housework will be assessed on the basis of the income gained by the spouse successful in the market, and not on the basis of the value of professional opportunities missed by the plaintiff spouse.

On the terrain of public-welfare law, the overcoming of family law speciality relies on the recognition of the social value produced by taking care of one's own children. This assumption lies, on the one hand, on the conceptualization of child rearing as public good: as a commons or a service of general interest provided by parents in favor of the whole society. On the other hand, in consideration of child-raising as a long-term activity, as an obligation substantially imposed by the state to the benefit of the whole society, which requires that parents involved in care work have no way out and just have to give up a number of opportunities,[53] the whole society (or the state) must provide those parents with a financial support commensurate with the lost opportunities.

As a public good, child raising becomes a commitment not for parents alone but for the entire society. Here we appreciate a classic liberal solution, played on a fair relationship between citizens and state, and certainly not a feminist victory or a decisive step toward women's full emancipation. That is quite another thing.

However, the collective sharing of the costs of care represents an attempt to overcome the production/reproduction dichotomy outside the market and exchange logic. Therefore, it could be seen as a tactical tool to approach the goal of a truly egalitarian family, without indulging in an individualistic distortion of the family institution.

Maria Rosaria Marella is full professor of law at the University of Perugia, Italy, where she teaches private law and directs the Law Clinic on Health, Environment, and Territory. She has been research assistant in the Faculty of Law of the University of Freiburg, Germany, visiting scholar at the Max Planck Institute for Comparative and Foreign Private Law in Hamburg, Germany, and at the Harvard Law School, USA. She has been a consulting expert for the Italian government's Department for Equal Opportunities. She is editor in chief of the law review *Rivista critica del diritto privato*. Her areas of research include torts, property law, contract law and family law, feminist legal studies, European private law, and critical legal theory. Her current research focuses on the new developments in family law between status and contract, and the law of property and the tension between the private property traditional paradigm and alternative forms of ownership. She has recently published a book on family law (coauthor Giovanni Marini), *Di cosa parliamo quando parliamo di famiglia* (Roma-Bari: Laterza, 2014) and edited a volume on common goods: *Oltre il pubblico e il privato:* Per un diritto dei beni comuni (Verona: Ombre Corte 2012). Among her recent publications in English: "The Commons as a Legal Concept," *Law & Critique* 28, no. 1 (2017); "The Contractualisation of Family Law in Italy," in *Contractualisation of Family Law—Global Perspectives,* edited by Frederik Swennen (London: Springer, 2015). For more details see http://www.unipg.it/pagina-personale?matricola=003503.

Notes

1. The principle according to which family members would be one another immune from the law of torts.
2. This critical approach to family law exceptionalism is the product of my association with a group of scholars with whom I had the fortune and the honor to interact and discuss for years, in particular Janet Halley, the "founding mother" of this group, and Duncan Kennedy, whose work has inspired the whole undertaking. However, the critical analysis I develop here somehow differs from the deconstructive proposal brought about by Janet Halley and Kerry Rittich, "Critical Directions in Comparative Family Law: Genealogies and Contemporary Studies of Family Law Exceptionalism," *American Journal of Comparative Law* 58, no. 4 (2010): 753–76. The latter highlights the ideological roots of family law exceptionalism by showing the direct and indirect influence on the regulation of family relations of a broader range of legal disciplines, including labor law, taxation law, immigra-

tion law, etc., which are commonly not listed among family law sources. I totally subscribe to Halley and Rittich's account. My intent here is definitely more limited. It focuses on the core/periphery (or market/family) distinction within private law and aims to problematize that opposition.
3. Frances Olsen, "The Myth of State Intervention in the Family," *University of Michigan Journal of Law Reform*, no. 18 (1985): 835; Frances Olsen, "The Family and the Market: A Study of Ideology and Legal Reform," *Harvard Law Review* 96 (1983): 1497.
4. Fausto Caggia, Andrea Zoppini. "Art. 29," in *Commentario alla Costituzione italiana*, ed. Raffaele Bifulco, Alfonso Celotto, and Marco Olivetti, 4 vols., vol. 1: *Artt. 1-53* (Torino: Utet, 2006), 601ff.
5. As it has been pointed out with different arguments by Wesley Newcomb Hohfeld, "Some Fundamental Legal Conceptions as Applied in Judicial Reasoning," *Yale Law Journal* 23, no. 1 (1913): 16–59. The sequel is Wesley Newcomb Hohfeld, "Fundamental Legal Conceptions as Applied in Judicial Reasoning," *Yale Law Journal* 26 (1917): 710; Robert Hale, "Coercion and Distribution in a Supposedly Non-coercive state," *Political Science Quarterly* 38, no. 3 (1923): 470–94.
6. Guenter Teubner, "Ein Fall von struktureller Korruption? Die Familienbürgschaft in der Kollision unverträglicher Handlungslogiken (*BVerGE* 89, 214 ff.)," *Kritische Vierteljahresschrift für Gesetzgebung und Rechtswissenschaft (KritV)* 83, no. 3/4 (2000): 388.
7. Marella Maria Rosaria, "Le donne," in *Gli anni Settanta del diritto privato*, ed. Luca Nivarra, (Milano: Giuffrè, 2008), 341–96.
8. Duncan Kennedy, "Sexual Abuse, Sexy Dressing, and the Eroticization of Domination," in *New England Law Review* 26, no. 4 (1992): 1309–93, and now in *Sexy Dressing, etc.*, Cambridge, MA: Harvard University Press, 1993.
9. I explore this in "The Non-Subversive Function of European Private Law: The Case of Harmonization in the E.U.," *European Law Journal* 12, no. 1 (2006): 78.
10. Enrico Al Mureden, "Nuove prospettive di tutela del coniuge debole: funzione perequativa dell'assegno divorziale e famiglia destrutturata" (Milano: IPSOA, 2007), and "Le rinunce nell'interesse della famiglia e la tutela del coniuge debole tra legge e autonomia privata," *Familia*, no. 4 (2002): 991ff.
11. Juliet Mitchell, *La condizione della donna* (Torino: Einaudi, 1972).
12. Maria Rosaria Marella, "Radicalism, Resistance, and the Structures of Family Law," *Unbound* 4, no. 70 (2008): retrieved 24 November 2017 from www.legalleft.org.
13. Ann R. Oakley, *The Sociology of Housework* (Oxford: Basil Blackwell, 1974).
14. Katherine Silbaugh, "Turning Labor into Love: Housework and the Law," *Northwestern University Law Review* 91, no. 1 (1996): 15ff.
15. Gary Becker, *A Treatise on the Family*, 2nd ed. (Cambridge, MA: Harvard University Press 1981).
16. Rodolfo Sacco, "Le convenzioni matrimoniali," in *Commentario al diritto italiano della famiglia*, ed. Giorgio Cian, Giorgio Oppo, and Alberto Trabucchi, vol. 3 (Padova: Cedam, 1992): 18.
17. Angelo Falzea, "Il dovere di contribuzione nel regime patrimoniale della famiglia," *Rivista di diritto civile* 23, no. 1 (1977): 609; for an egalitarian lecture see Gilda Ferrando, "Diritti e doveri nascenti dal matrimonio," in *Giurisprudenza del diritto di famiglia: Casi e materiali*, ed. Mario Bessone, Massimo Dogliotti, and Gilda Ferrando, vol. 2, 6th ed., no. 2 (Milano: Giuffrè, 2002): 54.
18. Gilda Ferrando, "Il matrimonio," in *Trattato di diritto civile e commerciale*, ed. Antonio Cicu and Francesco Messineo, vol. V, t. 1 (Milano: Giuffrè, 2002): 89ff.
19. Corte di Cassazione, 20 March 1998, n. 2955, in *I contratti* (1998): 472.
20. Ann L. Alstott, "What We Owe to Parents," *Boston Review* (2004); Ann L. Alstott, *No Exit: What Parents Owe Their Children and What Society Owes Parents* (Oxford, New York: Oxford University Press, 2004).

21. Vincenzo Roppo, "Donne, famiglie, lavori: sopra le possibilità e i limiti del diritto di famiglia," *Politica del Diritto* 17, no. 2 (1986): 227.
22. State v. Bachmann, 521 N.W. 2d 886 (Minn. Ct. App. 1994).
23. Corte di Cassazione, 10 maggio 2017, n. 11504, in *Giurisprudenza italiana* 169, no. 6, (2017): 1299, comment by Adolfo di Majo, "Assistenza o riequilibrio negli effetti del divorzio?," *Giurisprudenza italiana* 169, no. 6 (2017): 1304–06.
24. White v. White (2000), WLR, 3, 1571.
25. Aurelia Colombi Ciacchi, "Valutazione economica del lavoro casalingo e assegno di divorzio: la svolta parallela della giurisprudenza inglese e tedesca," *Familia* (2001): 732.
26. Maria Rosaria Marella, "The Family Economy v. the Labour Market (or Housework as a Legal Issue)," in *Labour Law, Work and Family: Critical and Comparative Perspectives*, ed. Joanne Conaghan and Kerry Rittich (Oxford: Oxford University Press, 2005).
27. According to the famous image of Robert Mnookin and Lewis Kornhauser, "Bargaining in the Shadow of the Law: The Case of Divorce," *Yale Law Journal* 88, no. 5 (1979): 997.
28. See on this point Maria Rosaria Marella, "Il diritto di famiglia fra status e contratto: il caso delle convivenze non fondate sul matrimonio," in *Stare insieme: I regimi giuridici della convivenza tra status e contratto*, ed. Franco Grillini and Maria Rosaria Marella (Napoli: Jovene, 2001).
29. Francesco Gazzoni, *Dal concubinato alla famiglia di fatto* (Milano: Giuffrè, 1983).
30. *Tribunale Bologna*, 16 February 2011.
31. Corte di Cassazione, 22 January 2014, n. 1277.
32. Corte di Cassazione, 17 July 1979, n. 4221, in *Foro italiano* 102, I (1979): 2315.
33. Corte di Cassazione, 17 February 1988, n. 1701, in *Foro italiano* 111, I (1988): 2306. See also Corte di Cassazione, *Sezione Lavoro*, 14 June 1990, n. 5803.
34. *Tribunale Torino*, 24 November 1990, in *Giurisprudenza italiana* I, no. 2 (1992): 428, n. Oberto.
35. Corte di Cassazione, 14 June 1990, n. 5803. Actually, the Italian Corte di Cassazione did over time consolidate the orientation that the presumption of gratuitousness of work—even extra-household—of the partner can be overcome only when the existence of the features that usually identify an employment relationship is proven: time constraint, specific tasks, subordination to technical and functional directives, the presence of typical documentation such as work books. See Corte di Cassazione, 29 May 1991, n. 6083, in *Diritto del lavoro*, II (1991): 373.
36. Corte di Cassazione, 15 November 1996, n. 10015, in *Archivio civile* (1997): 750.
37. Among others, Corte di Cassazione, 3 November 1995, n. 11453.
38. *Tribunale Napoli*, 30 June 1977, in *Responsabilità civile e previdenza* (1978): 456.
39. Corte di Cassazione, 6 November 1997, n. 10923, in *Archivio civile* (1998): 174.
40. Corte di Cassazione, 11 December 2000, n. 15580, in *Archivio giuridico della circolazione e dei sinistri stradali* 47, (2001): 293.
41. Corte di Cassazione, 3 November 1995, n. 11453.
42. Corte di Cassazione, 10 September 1998, n. 8970.
43. Corte di Cassazione, 3 March 2005, n. 4657, in *Archivio giuridico della circolazione e dei sinistri stradali* 51, (2005): 576.
44. Corte di Cassazione, 3 March 2005, n. 4657.
45. Corte di Cassazione, 10 September 1998, n. 8970.
46. Corte di Cassazione, 1 August 1986, n. 4927, in *Foro italiano* 110, no. 10 (1987): 493.
47. Anna Maria Galoppini, *Il lungo cammino verso la parità: I diritti civili e politici delle donne dall'unità ad oggi* (Bologna: Zanichelli, 1980).
48. Maria Rosaria Marella, *La riparazione del danno in forma specifica* (Padova: Cedam, 2000).
49. Janet Yale, "The Valuation of Household Services in Wrongful Death Actions," *University of Toronto Law Journal* 34, no. 3 (1984): 283.

50. Pietro Rescigno, "Collaborazione all'impresa e lavoro nella famiglia," *Studi sassaresi* 4 (1979): 109.
51. Ibid.
52. Fausto Caggia, "Contratto, responsabilità civile e danno risarcibile da rottura del rapporto matrimoniale o di convivenza," in *La responsabilità nelle relazioni familiari*, in *Nuova giurisprudenza di diritto civile e commerciale*, ed. Michele Sesta (Torino: UTET, 2008), 371.
53. Alstott, "No Exit."

References

Al Mureden, Enrico. "Le rinunce nell'interesse della famiglia e la tutela del coniuge debole tra legge e autonomia privata," *Familia*, no. 4 (2002): 991–1028.

———. *Nuove prospettive di tutela del coniuge debole: Funzione perequativa dell'assegno divorziale e famiglia destrutturata*. Milano: IPSOA, 2007.

Alstott, Ann L. "What We Owe to Parents." *Boston Review* (2004).

———. *No Exit: What Parents Owe Their Children and What Society Owes Parents.* Oxford, New York: Oxford University Press, 2004.

Becker, Gary. *A Treatise on the Family,* 2nd edition. Cambridge, MA: Harvard University Press, 1981.

Caggia, Fausto. "Contratto, responsabilità civile e danno risarcibile da rottura del rapporto matrimoniale o di convivenza." In *La responsabilità nelle relazioni familiari*, in *Nuova giurisprudenza di diritto civile e commerciale*, edited by Michele Sesta, 354–85. Torino: Utet, 2008.

Caggia, Fausto, and Andrea Zoppini. "Art. 29." In *Commentario alla Costituzione italiana*, edited by Raffaele Bifulco, Alfonso Celotto, and Marco Olivetti. 4 vols., vol. 1: *Artt. 1-54*, 601ff. Torino: Utet, 2006.

Colombi Ciacchi, Aurelia. "Valutazione economica del lavoro casalingo e assegno di divorzio: la svolta parallela della giurisprudenza inglese e tedesca." *Familia* (2001): 732–46.

Di Majo, Adolfo. "Assistenza o riequilibrio negli effetti del divorzio?" *Giurisprudenza italiana* 169, no. 6 (2017): 1304–06.

Falzea, Angelo. "Il dovere di contribuzione nel regime patrimoniale della famiglia." *Rivista di diritto civile* 23, no. 1 (1977): 609–37.

Ferrando, Gilda. "Diritti e doveri nascenti dal matrimonio." In *Giurisprudenza del diritto di famiglia: Casi e materiali*. 2 vols., vol. 2: *Rapporti personali e patrimoniali tra coniugi, famiglia di fatto*, edited by Mario Bessone, Massimo Dogliotti, and Gilda Ferrando. 6th edition. Milano: Giuffrè, 2002.

———. "Il matrimonio." In *Trattato di diritto civile e commerciale*, edited by Antonio Cicu and Francesco Messineo. Vol. V, t. 1. Milano: Giuffrè, 2002.

Galoppini, Anna Maria. *Il lungo cammino verso la parità: I diritti civili e politici delle donne dall'unità ad oggi*. Bologna: Zanichelli, 1980.

Gazzoni, Francesco. *Dal concubinato alla famiglia di fatto*. Milano: Giuffrè, 1983.

Hale, Robert. "Coercion and Distribution in a Supposedly Non-coercive State." *Political Science Quarterly* 38, no. 3 (1923): 470–94.

Halley, Janet, and Kerry Rittich. "Critical Directions in Comparative Family Law: Genealogies and Contemporary Studies of Family Law Exceptionalism." *American Journal of Comparative Law* 58, no. 4 (2010): 753–76.

Hohfeld, Wesley Newcomb. "Some Fundamental Legal Conceptions as Applied in Judicial Reasoning." *Yale Law Journal* 23, no.1 (1913): 16–59.

———. "Fundamental Legal Conceptions as Applied in Judicial Reasoning." *Yale Law Journal* 26, no. 8 (1917): 710–70.

Kennedy, Duncan. "Sexual Abuse, Sexy Dressing, and the Eroticization of Domination." *New England Law Review* 26, no. 4 (1992): 1309–93, and now in *Sexy Dressing, etc.*, Cambridge, MA: Harvard University Press, 1993.

Marella, Maria Rosaria. *La riparazione del danno in forma specifica*. Padova: Cedam, 2000.

———. "Il diritto di famiglia fra status e contratto: il caso delle convivenze non fondate sul matrimonio." In *Stare insieme: I regimi giuridici della convivenza tra status e contratto*, edited by Franco Grillini and Maria Rosaria Marella. Napoli: Jovene, 2001.

———. "The Family Economy v. the Labour Market (or Housework as a Legal Issue)." In *Labour Law, Work and Family: Critical and Comparative Perspectives*, edited by Joanne Conaghan and Kerry Rittich, 156ff. Oxford: Oxford University Press, 2005.

———. "The Non-Subversive Function of European Private Law: The Case of Harmonization in the E.U." *European Law Journal* 12, no. 1 (2006): 78–105.

———. "Le donne." In *Gli anni Settanta del diritto privato*, edited by Luca Nivarra, 341–96. Milano: Giuffrè, 2008.

———. "Radicalism, Resistance, and the Structures of Family Law." *Unbound* 4, no. 70 (2008): 70–81. Retrieved 24 December 2017 from www.legalleft.org.

Mitchell, Juliet. *La condizione della donna*. Torino: Einaudi, 1972.

Mnookin, Robert, and Lewis Kornhauser. "Bargaining in the Shadow of the Law: The Case of Divorce." *Yale Law Journal* 88, no. 5 (1979): 950–97.

Oakley, Ann R. *The Sociology of Housework*. Oxford: Basil Blackwell, 1974.

Olsen, Frances. "The Family and the Market: A Study of Ideology and Legal Reform." *Harvard Law Review* 96, no. 7 (1983): 1497–1578.

———. "The Myth of State Intervention in the Family." *University of Michigan Journal of Law Reform*, no. 18 (1985): 835–64.

Rescigno, Pietro. "Collaborazione all'impresa e lavoro nella famiglia." *Studi Sassaresi* 4 (1979).

Roppo, Vincenzo. "Donne, famiglie, lavori: sopra le possibilità e i limiti del diritto di famiglia." *Politica e Diritto* 17, no. 2 (1986): 223–31.

Sacco, Rodolfo. "Le convenzioni matrimoniali." In *Commentario al diritto italiano della famiglia*, edited by Giorgio Cian, Giorgio Oppo, and Alberto Trabucchi. 8 vols., vol. 3: *Codice civile: Regime patrimoniale della famiglia*. Padova: Cedam, 1992.

Silbaugh, Katherine. "Turning Labor into Love: Housework and the Law." *Northwestern University Law Review* 91, no. 1 (1996): 1–86.

Teubner, Guenter. "Ein Fall von struktureller Korruption? Die Familienbürgschaft in der Kollision unverträglicher Handlungslogiken (*BVerGE* 89, 214 ff.)." *Kritische Vierteljahrsschrift für Gesetzgebung und Rechtswissenschaft (KritV)* 83, no. 3/4 (2000): 388–404.

Yale, Janet, "The Valuation of Household Services in Wrongful Death Actions." *University of Toronto Law Journal* 34, no. 3 (1984): 283–313.

CHAPTER 10

COULD FAMILY (CARE) WORK BE PAID?
From French Agricultural Inheritance Law (1939) to Legal Recognition of Excessive Filial Duty (1994)

Florence Weber

As agricultural work has been largely carried out in family contexts in France, it serves as an excellent point of departure in understanding what payment for family work means, including family care work, what forms this payment has taken in the absence of an employment contract—rare between kin and illegal between spouses—and what resistance this payment faced during the twentieth century in France.[1] Several social science disciplines study agricultural families: not only sociology,[2] but history,[3] anthropology[4] and economics, and in particular development economics. Even though family agriculture has been used as a model for considering family work "for the market," whether it be a traditional,[5] industrial,[6] or financial[7] family-run business, it can also enable payment for family carework to be considered in a domestic context,[8] particularly when there are non-professional family assets. Indeed, the logic of transmission of assets is also at work when these assets only have a symbolic[9] or emotional[10] value. This logic can be found in the case of property assets, which became widespread in the 1960s.[11] Moreover, the logic of family production, where individual work is neither quantified nor paid,[12] can be transposed, in part, to domestic production, which is also carried out in a family context and outside a salaried one, even though agricultural production is integrated *in fine* in the market economy, unlike domestic economy, which only functions in addition to, or as a substitute for, household consumption.

I will use here the example of family carework provided for dependent elderly people. We know that the general increase in life expectancy in old age goes hand in hand with an increase in an aged population suffering from physical and mental disabilities. In France, this demographic phenomenon coincided with a change in the care model for these dependent elderly people. After the development of specialized institutions (retirement and nursing homes, public and private), French social policy progressively shifted toward supporting these people at home, with the introduction of benefits aimed at paying professional carers.[13] In parallel, an increased interest was paid to the care that these people received from their family entourage, either to deplore its absence or to emphasize its importance. Research in both sociology and economics was carried out on intergenerational transfer,[14] financial flow (generally from parents and grandparents to their children or grandchildren), and different types of support (including care work help and financial support); several research projects raised a crucial question: who, among siblings, helps their parents?[15]

Having analyzed an ethnographic example, I will illustrate how agricultural work can be used as a conceptual guide: the processes, whether institutional or emotional, for designating a "principal carer" in the case of dependent elderly people can be usefully linked to the processes, whether institutional or emotional, for designating a "successor" in the case of family-run agricultural businesses. I will use French civil law as a common thread for this comparison. Indeed, jurists in the 1990s reflected on what they called "unjust enrichment in family relations" (*l'enrichissement sans cause dans les relations de famille*) to decide whether the sharing of the estate between siblings must take into account unpaid time given by one of them to care for a dependent parent, to the detriment of their own career.[16] Yet a similar question had already received a positive response in the case of agriculture in 1939. In order to take into account unpaid work granted to the agricultural operation by the child who has remained his parents' "family worker," while his siblings receive income from their paid jobs, the law calculates "deferred wages" to be recovered at the time of inheritance, in the form of a portion of the assets.[17] The comparison between this 1939 law and 1990s jurisprudence can be used as a departure point to analyze family work outside agriculture.

1. Who should pay for the nursing home? A case study

In April 2000, Mrs. Chaux, an elderly woman who had lived in the Paris region near the house that one of her sons, Daniel, and his wife lived in, moved, on his advice (he did not consult her four other children), to a nursing home following a deterioration in her condition. Several months later, as the elderly woman's pension was not enough to cover her accommodation costs, the manager of the nursing home turned to all five children to ask each one to pay one-fifth of the monthly debt contracted by their mother.[18] Besides Daniel, two of the children were married, and had lived abroad for decades; they did not feel concerned. Another lived in Paris and, without children, enjoyed a relatively comfortable retirement. The fifth child, Marcel, a retired factory worker, married with four adult children, lived in a small town in Burgundy. It was his devastated wife, Denise, who explained the situation to me. The monthly sum demanded, even though minimal, would overstretch their already very tight budget. The couple consulted both a solicitor and a social worker: Marcel had no legal recourse, he had to pay what the nursing home was demanding in the name of the "support duty" that bound him to his mother. On Denise's insistence (she was scandalized by the discovery of this legal obligation that she felt was unjustified and unfair), Marcel turned on his brother, Daniel. After a meeting between the three brothers who had remained in France, the apartment that Mrs. Chaux had lived in, and of which one of Daniel's sons was the legal owner, was rented out; this rental supplemented the woman's pension and enabled the nursing home to be paid for.

Two types of argument were used in the family dispute: the relative financial burden, related to the income and expenses of each child; the degree of emotional proximity between the mother and each of her children, which was the result of a turbulent family history and which translated, notably, into certain financial arrangements, and the way in which the decision to place her in an institution was made, as well as the choice of nursing home. The solution that was found, without legal recourse but after legal advice by all parties, takes into account both these parameters: the monthly debt to the nursing home was to be paid regularly by the rental on the apartment belonging to Daniel's son. Daniel, who was the closest, emotionally, to his mother, who always looked after her, chose the nursing home; in addition, the burden was the least heavy, relatively, for him to bear.

This story is both frequent and insightful. Frequent: each year in France, thousands of families receive a final demand for payment of the debt contracted by an elderly, widowed mother from the institution she lives in, following the decision made by one of her family members. On such an occasion, they discover a particularity of French family law: support duty by children for their parents, whatever the reality of their past and present relationships. The choice of the institution in which to house the elderly person, as long as the person is legally an adult (i.e. that they are not under guardianship or tutorship), is assumed to be the expression of the individual desire of the elderly person, even though certain members of her entourage—but not necessarily all the people concerned by support duty—have helped in the decision-making.

Insightful: the various institutions that Denise Chaux was confronted with applied an approach that did not fit her real family. Whereas the family history had been particularly turbulent and the Chaux brothers and sisters were socially very heterogeneous, neither the manager of the nursing home nor the solicitor or social worker consulted took these singularities into account. They simply invoked the legal concept of support duty and reaffirmed the unconditional moral duty of a child to its parents.

Let us go back over the family history, from the dual perspective of social reproduction and emotional bonds. The father, a skilled Parisian laborer, only transferred his social position to one of his sons, Marcel, who became a skilled laborer in a metallurgical plant in Burgundy and married the daughter of ex–market gardeners who became farmers. The four others, to varying degrees, climbed socially: one son became an executive computer scientist, another an aviation technician, the two children who were married and lived abroad lived comfortably (the son owned a garage and the daughter was an interpreter at the embassy). Such heterogeneity is not unusual. Even though statistics concerning social mobility show the frequency of social reproduction,[19] we know that this is only a general trend: moreover, in the case of upward social mobility, it is not surprising that not all siblings are systematically concerned.[20] In the case we are looking at, the manager of the nursing home demanded an equal share from each of Mrs. Chaux's children, without worrying about their various "fortunes" (in terms of assets and income, but also family expenses). This is, admittedly, an unfair decision, but even more inadmissible for Denise Chaux and her husband as she painfully recalled a particularly turbulent family history. The Chaux's five children were born between 1930 and 1947. The couple divorced in 1953 when the children were aged between six and twenty-two. The two oldest, who were adults by then, "went with their father," as they put it, while the three others "went with their mother." This brutal emotional split had material consequences. The mother, whose parents belonged to the provincial, merchant middle class, had a lasting relationship with a man who, being a museum curator, was socially superior to her ex-husband. Choosing whether to leave or stay with their mother also meant accepting this situation or not. The woman's partner, although he never married her, helped financially, enabling her to buy a house. After this man's death in 1965, the mother sold the house, helped Daniel buy a house, and bought the apartment that she put in Daniel's son's name and where she lived before moving to the nursing home when her health deteriorated.

It is this extremely unegalitarian family story that resurfaced when the nursing home turned to the children for payment. Denise, Marcel Chaux's wife, told this story to the third parties consulted—solicitor, social worker, friends—to bear witness to the "unfair" nature of such a request. But, like the nursing home managers, French family law does not subject children's support duty concerning parents to any conditions. It is an "absolute" obligation, which only takes one element into account, to the exclusion of all others: the line of descent. There are legal means, which are complicated and little-used, to break the chain of descent: contesting paternity, the legal removal of paternity or maternity, renouncing inheritance, whether positive or negative. These radical measures are little-known and rarely used. Mrs. Chaux had five children who were legally hers to the same degree and in the same way. This is the reason why the "support debt" applied to each child. How do those affected react to this legal definition of filiation?

Denise Chaux, Marcel's wife, and my main contact, simultaneously affirmed two contradictory principles: a principle of unconditional equality between siblings, which, in her eyes, results from the unconditionality of the filiation and which corresponds to the rule of sharing assets between siblings after the death of their father and mother; a principle of differentiation between siblings, which results from the family history and the difference in conditions of their current lives.

First, Denise repeats with conviction, on multiple occasions and especially when faced with cases of misunderstanding between a mother and her children, that "a mother is a mother." By this she means that, whatever the family history, and even when the mother hardly looked after her children, the line of descent is unconditional, indestructible, and absolute. The first consequence: the universal strength of this tie forbids any indifference between a mother and her children and imposes an emotional norm, consisting of obligatory attachment and suffering, a norm that is implicitly shared and recalled during critical times, illness, departures, death. The second consequence: the siblings are equal in rights and duties. The children must not be treated differently by their mother and, in return, they must not treat their mother differently. From this dual perspective, the universal nature of a bond and the demand for equality among siblings, Denise is in agreement with the law: filiation is an unconditional bond. With her own children, she watches closely to make sure that no "jealousy" develops between them, jealousy that is only a demand for equality, which she feels is justified. She is all the more sensitive to this demand for equality between children as she herself suffered, when her parents' inheritance was shared out, from the "privilege" she felt was unduly given to one of her ten brothers and sisters who had taken over the family business, in compliance with the legal principle of "deferred wages" in agriculture (see below).

At the same time, however, as was seen with her mother-in-law's debts, she claimed the legitimacy of a differentiation among siblings. She first justified this differentiation by altering her demand for equality between the children into a principle of "fairness," which takes into account the current situation of each person. Besides their professional situations, which result in different individual incomes, the various children have different expenses and resources due to their family situations, how many children they have, the professional situation of their spouses and adult children. It is therefore fair, in her eyes, that they be treated differently, not as abstract individuals but as real groups of people connected to each other and disposing of unequal incomes, to establish *a posteriori* an equality in the standard of living between the different family groups they have formed. It may be observed immediately that this principle of fairness, legally applicable in many cases (fiscal policy, "means testing," support duty), is totally absent from the legal settlement of asset inheritance.

But Denise justified the differentiation between children in another way, which radically questions the unconditional nature of filiation. She feels that the family story should be taken into account. From their birth, children are not treated in the same way, whether their parents wish it or not. First the conditions of their education are inevitably different, depending on their rank among the siblings (being born the first or having one, two, or three children before them) and their various birth dates, which means they are confronted with different states of the world (historic dates, the age of the parents, the time in the parents' professional, residential, and emotional lives). Subsequently they may experience, in some cases, intentional differences in treatment on the part of their parents: this is often an accusation made to the parents as well as the child or children who are "favored" in this way. In this case, the differences felt in the past, whether intentional or not, lead to and justify an emotional differentiation perceived as unintentional (a more or less strong bond between a certain parent and a certain child) but also a variation in the "debt" contracted by the child to their parents. The filiation then totally changes status; from an unconditional bond, it becomes a true emotion and relationship, founded on reciprocity.

From this perspective, the three Chaux children who "went with their mother" built an emotional and material relationship with her, which was very different from the other two, who lost touch with her. One can assume that with the help of her new partner, their mother helped them to gain a comfortable professional status, and we know that she gave one of them the means to buy his main home. Their support in her extreme old age would therefore be a "response" to this first transfer. On the other hand, the two oldest had to make it alone. The sharing of responsibilities that started in the 1950s has since been respected as both of the "father's children" dealt with their father's old age alone, until he died in 1993.

Both arguments used by Denise during this family crisis to justify a lower share, or none at all, from her household in the upkeep of her mother-in-law are very different in nature. Her first argument is admissible under French law. Even though the unconditionality of filiation is indeed set out in legislation ("the child, at all ages, owes honour and respect to their father and mother" [*"l'enfant, à tout âge, doit honneur et respect à ses père et mère"*], article 371 of the French Civil Code, a precept inspired by the biblical prescription "Honor thy Father and thy Mother"), with its practical consequences (duty to help and assist, support duty), brothers and sisters are not obliged to participate equally but rather "in proportion to their means" (*"à proportion de leurs ressources"*). The equality argument used by Denise could therefore be taken into account by the judges. On the other hand, her second argument seems, at first glance, unacceptable by law.

For jurists, the reality, both past and present, of family relationships cannot justify the presence or absence of help to a parent or the "amount" of this help. However, there are at least two cases where the law takes into account the reality of family relations, not to justify *a priori* behavior (as Denise did) but to compensate *a posteriori* an excessive burden. It is, on the one hand, an advantage granted by the law, at the time of inheritance, to the child who remained the "family worker" in the parents' business, since the French law of 29 July 1939 which invented the notion of "deferred wages" in agriculture and gave rise to a "professional law for agricultural families." On the other hand, it is the advantage granted by jurisprudence, at the time of inheritance, to the child who took care of his elderly and dependent parents, since the judgment of the French Supreme Court dated 12 July 1994, which applied the notion of "unjust enrichment" to family relations. In both cases, it is the notion of "family work" and its "compensation" that are at stake.

2. Support duty, unjust enrichment, and deferred wages

From a legal perspective, the question of "who helps their parents" is meaningless. As we have seen, each person must help their father and mother: this is an absolute and personal obligation that falls under "moral duty," which jurists call "filial devotion" (*piété filiale*). Moreover, there exists in French law "support duty," i.e. a legal obligation to help a family member[21] in need, which applies between spouses, between forebears and descendents (parents and children, grandparents and grandchildren), and between direct in-laws (son-in-law, daughter-in-law, mother-in-law, father-in-law). It should be noted that this support duty is reciprocal (a father must help a son in need, and conversely), that it is only applicable in case of need, and that it does not concern siblings[22] (nothing obliges a brother to help a brother in need). The mutual duty to provide assistance is either related to "direct" descendents, i.e. consanguinity, and considered natural, or related to alliance by marriage, set out in legislation, and considered contractual. The dual legal nature of kinship can be seen here,[23] through blood (descent) and through contract (marriage), to the exclusion of a third dimension of kinship, known by historians, anthropologists, and the tax administration (the "hearth tax"—*feu*—and its derivatives, among which is the "tax household"—*foyer fiscal*) but not recognized by French law: co-residence or shared life, which is the basis of the "domestic group" (household, *maisonnée* in old French[24]). In this way, de facto civil partners are not bound by reciprocal support duty, as there is no filiation or contract between them. It can moreover be noted that, when civil partnership is taken into account by the authorities (in terms of beneficiaries of social policies for example), it is not thought of as shared life but as a weak form of alliance: the partners form an almost marital "couple" and not a group of cohabitees. It can be noted finally that working-class spouses are very clearly aware of the economic dimension of their marriage, as can be seen in this "divorce announcement" found in 1984 in the local pages of a regional French newspaper: "From this day on, Mr D. is no longer accountable for his wife's debts."

For jurists, support duty is a "personal debt as it depends, on the one hand, on the family or marital relationship and, on the other hand, on the respective fortune of the parties."[25] It is not therefore a collective debt that would involve all the concerned family members[26]—e.g. all the children, debtors in the same respect nevertheless—of a mother "in need." To be even clearer, "there is no legal solidarity between children when one of them takes sole responsibility for support duty in favor of a parent in need."[27] In practice, as we have seen, nursing homes sometimes turn against all the children in equal measure, on the condition that the home is aware of them all. However, like the various health and social care institutions that deal with a "principal carer,"[28] they generally prefer to have one unique contact, whom they consider to be the representative of the family group, without worrying about the various conflicts or specificities within this group. Furthermore, these particularities of French law (that "support debt" be personal and not collective, that support duty does not apply between siblings) do not prevent the child who is debtor from appealing against his brothers and sisters. These particularities merely force the courts to invent more or less makeshift legal solutions to order repayments or compensation, in particular at the time of inheritance.

The difference between "support duty" and "filial devotion" must be noted. Support duty is both much wider—as it applies to members of the family other than parents and children, and is reciprocal—and more restricted—as it is only applicable in case of need, i.e. when a family member is "in need" or, simply, cannot pay their debts. It authorizes third-party creditors to turn against certain family members of their debtor. "Filial devotion," on the other hand, justifies a child helping his/her father and mother and forbids considering that this help be compensated in any way whatsoever. It falls under "moral duty," which involves unconditional financial gifts or "donations," characteristic of family relations but also, in some cases, friendships.

We are witnessing in France today an important evolution of family law, which is, as yet, incomplete. The constant increase in lawsuits brought during family crises (separation of civil partners, divorce or death, emancipation of a minor) forces jurists, in the absence of suitable laws, to apply the notion of "unjust enrichment," also used in the case of contracts between unrelated people, to compensate asset imbalances occurring between members of the same family. We will set aside the application of this notion of imbalance between spouses or common-law spouses, litigated when a couple separates, to limit ourselves to the question of asset imbalance between children and parents or between siblings, litigated at the time of inheritance.

Let me briefly set out French jurisprudence in the 1990s, which will enable the notion of "unjust enrichment" to be understood. On 12 July 1994, France's Supreme Court ruled in favor of Mr. F*, who requested, in opposition to his sister, to be compensated directly from the assets inherited from their parents for the time and care that he devoted to them. The legal reasoning being the following: Mr. F* wholly cared for his parents who were elderly and disabled, but not totally without resources (i.e. outside the scope of support duty), providing them with care and assistance free of charge, at the cost of professional sacrifice (which led to his impoverishment), sparing them, in this way, the cost of a nursing home (which led to their enrichment). No one contested the parents' enrichment or the relationship to the son's impoverishment. But is it "unjust"? The Court of Appeal in Aix, on 9 June 1992, dismissed Mr. F*, considering that "the sacrifices of a child for the benefit of his parents, even if they go beyond the common measure of filial devotion, correspond to the intentional execution of a personal moral duty which constitutes the cause".[29]

The French Supreme Court, on the contrary, "authorizes the unjust enrichment case in order to compensate the exemplary devotion of a child with regards to his elderly parents"[30] by delivering the following judgment, which set a legal precedent[31]: "the moral duty of a child toward his/her parents does not exclude the fact that the child may obtain compensation for the care and assistance provided, to the extent that, having exceeded the demands of filial devotion, the services freely provided resulted in an impoverishment of the child and a correlative enrichment of the parents."[32]

Beyond the legal debate on "the common measure of filial devotion" or on its excesses, such a jurisprudential innovation opens the way for compensation, taken from the inheritance, of the family carework provided to a deceased parent free of charge by one of the children. It therefore contributes to the notion of "family carework" existing legally, opening a gap in the distinction between the area of family relations, considered by law as "devotion," "moral duty," selflessness and feeling, and that of contractual relations in which "hard work deserves a fair reward," or at the very least, some compensation.

It is interesting to observe that, in the ethnographic example put forward above, everything happens as if the legal reasoning were reversed: indeed, the "principal carer" son was considered by his sister-in-law, Denise, as having in some sense been "compensated in advance," by a patrimonial privilege granted de facto and justified by the family story (his mother's help in buying a house, the apartment "put in the name of" his son), which renders inadmissible his demand of his siblings that they pay their support duty in regard to their mother. The Supreme Court seems to have integrated this method of reasoning to evaluate exchanges among family members as closely as possible. On 23 January 2001, it confirmed the judgment by the Court of Appeal in Riom (8 September 1998) which had rejected Mr. M*'s request against his sister to be compensated from the inheritance for the care and assistance that he provided for his mother. The reasoning of the judges was the following. Once again looking to establish whether the care provided "went beyond the demands of filial devotion," they evaluated the child's impoverishment. To do this, they conceded that it is legitimate to take into account "not only the charges" but also "the care provided on every level," i.e. the time spent and services rendered free of charge. However, in the case studied, the judges considered that "this care only constituted the return for the considerable advantage that Mr. M* benefitted from, by living with his wife in the family home without paying rent and in seeing himself later attributed by his mother, the available share of her assets."[33] The law set, in this way, the interpretation of an "exchange," help versus advantage, when the protagonists fight one another precisely on the question of knowing who is helping whom: the son helping his mother, but living in her home and taking on the daily care, or the mother helping her son, by providing a house, free of charge, for him to live in. The judges in this case made a decision in favor of the second interpretation. It must be noted that the cases that are of importance legally concern loving sons (excessively so?), as the daughter's filial devotion has little chance of ever seeming excessive in their own eyes. These clues feed into an ongoing process of changing emotional norms.

This legal innovation, which renders compensation imaginable for family carework provided free of charge, extends, in the domestic production of health and social care, the decree-law of 29 July 1939 introducing in the agricultural sector a "professional family law" with the notion of a "labor contract with deferred wages" (*contrat de travail à salaire différé*). This legal invention of a "tacit contract" between the head of an agricultural business and the descendent who works with him (the law of 9 July 1999 extends this advantage to the spouse of the farmer), named "family worker," allows him at the time of inheritance to be compensated by calculating a "lump sum payment" (*rémunération forfaitaire*), provided for by the law and recovered from the inheritance. As in the previous case, "unpaid work" is taken into account, which represents both an "enrichment" of the parent who is a quasi-employer (by sparing him expenses, e.g. hiring a salaried agricultural worker) and an "impoverishment" of the child who is a quasi-employee (who has no professional career and works "free of charge": it is this "loss of earnings" that economists call the "opportunity cost" of free activity). "Differed wages" can therefore be considered a response provided by the law in certain cases to a phenomenon qualified in certain other cases as "unjust enrichment" by jurisprudence.

The technique of differed wages is applied in a restrictive way: it always intervenes at the time of inheritance; it concerns the descendent (decree-law of 29 July 1939) or the spouse (law of 9 July 1999) of an agricultural business, the spouse of a retailer or an artisan (law of 31 December 1989) but not his or her descendent, and under very strict conditions (to have worked at least ten years without pay). It does not apply to "family workers" linked to the company head by other filiations (e.g. brothers, sisters, nephews, nieces, etc.). In this it can be seen that, for the lawmaker, it is not about compensating free help but, in 1939, organizing the inheritance of the family company and, in 1989 and 1999, protecting the surviving spouse. These various laws also mark the extension of the salaried work model, to which is compared the work of a son who is the family worker in 1939, then after 1989 the work of spouses who are family workers, once the salaried work of married women had become a massive phenomenon, along with divorce.

What makes the technique of "deferred wages" transposable to other cases of family enterprise (the law of 31 December 1989 actually extended it to the spouse of an artisan or a retailer), but not in the case of unpaid help for dependent parents, is the presence or absence of an enterprise. The family member who is quasi-employer, if he/she is a farmer, artisan, or retailer, acts as the company head; in the case of caring for a dependent family member, the person who is cared for acts as a "private individual." In other words, as Mélanie Monteillet-Geffroy noted, "in the case of agriculture [as in general in the case of a family business], enrichment is not for the forebear personally, but for the [productive] family assets, in which the unpaid fruit of the descendent's labor is invested. In addition, one understands that the main aim of the institution of differed wages is to restore equality between the farmer's heirs. It would be unfair if the descendent who had contributed to the business was made to share equally with his brothers and sisters assets that he had in fact made more productive."[34]

Jurists' suggestions consist of extending the technique of differed wages to spouses who have helped their husbands free of charge in other professions (liberal professions in particular), but, in the cases of care for dependent family members, of "granting a right to differed compensation for the cost of care to parents, to compensate the services provided outside the support duty context."[35] After the metaphorical use of the notion of "salary" in the case of a freelance profession where the notion of sharing capital and income could have seemed more suited, today we see the distaste in considering a "salary" for a service activity (more or less qualified care given to a dependent person) carried out between related people and the tendency to prefer the idea of "repayment of costs." Beyond considerations of support duty and moral duty, it would seem that jurists fear seeing economic logic ("hard work deserves a fair reward") contaminating family relationships, which are supposed to be founded on selflessness and devotion.[36] The argument of affection is used by some judges against requests for compensation on inheritance. Thus, on 22 June 1999, the court of Nancy refused to compensate on inheritance using the following motive "that a descendent who looked after her bedridden mother until her death could not, on the basis of unjust enrichment, ask for restorative compensation from the enrichment obtained by the deceased's assets, when her active, devoted, and regular interventions were justified by the affection that normally unites a daughter and her mother."[37]

However, research shows that the economic behavior of parents (the choice of retirement home, the choice of paid care, using unpaid family carework) varies greatly depending on the weight of property assets in the inheritance,[38] suggesting that conserving assets, even if they are unproductive but have a strong emotional and symbolic value, can play a similar role to that of maintaining the family agricultural business. Free family carework, as in agriculture, should be thought of in terms of maintaining or improving the family assets. The French policy of home care for elderly and dependent people hesitates over the link between care for dependent people and inheritance: subsidies granted by local councils for social welfare for the poor, therefore, are only "an advance on inheritance," whereas the national policy for individual services in the context of dependency has moved away from this since 2000. If paying for professional care equals squandering assets, could it not therefore be considered that unpaid family carework allows these assets to be preserved?

3. Coheirs and coproducers: the invisible spouse

It is no coincidence that my contact during the family quarrel outlined above was Mrs. Chaux's daughter-in-law and not her son. In these affairs, the children's spouses are particularly sensitive to the differences between the group of people concerned by an inheritance (the legal group of heir children) and the group of people concerned by family carework (the practical group of coproducers, to which the children's spouses, sons-in-law, and daughters-in-law belong). These spouses do not have the right to voice their opinions during the inheritance of their parents-in-law, where they are made to feel like "outsiders," whereas they inevitably contribute to the care, whether financially or materially, that their spouse provides to the father and mother. They are, for that matter, tied to their parents-in-law by support duty.

To show their importance in maintaining and keeping the family assets of their spouse, I will first recall the French phenomenon of "son-in-law marriage" (*mariage en gendre*—marrying into and living with your wife's family), that I will propose to extend to "daughter-in-law marriage" (*mariage en bru*—marrying into and living with your husband's family).[39] I will then evoke their difficulty in seeing their role acknowledged.

The term "son-in-law marriage" is borrowed from antiquity historians by agricultural family specialists to describe a marital union where the husband, of a lower social class than his wife (he is usually a salaried agricultural worker, or even the ex–salaried agricultural worker of his future father-in-law), goes to live with his parents-in-law in order to maintain their agricultural business. He is, therefore, in some way, "adopted" by them, which is only possible if he does not have a family that would keep him and "adopt" his wife. Hence the large number of children from welfare, orphans, or immigrants having broken away from their families in these "son-in-law marriages." Such a situation only occurs in the absence of a male successor; unlike a boy, a girl could rarely take over from her father as head of the business. In a classic son-in-law marriage, work in the field is ensured by the husband, authority remains in the hands of the father-in-law. I questioned the son of one of these sons-in-law: he spoke more freely about his maternal grandfather than about his father, who left little trace in the family history. The surrounding villagers had even continued, two generations on and despite the change in surname, to call the farm—and even its managers—by the name of the maternal grandfather.[40] In this way, the son-in-law is denied his name, and his very being, to the benefit of the inheritance of assets, which is between the maternal grandfather and his daughter's son.

Such a situation is far from exceptional. In 1978, the village of Crépand, in Burgundy, had five farms, three of which were large. You only had to go back to the nineteenth century to find, among the forebears of the current farms, no identical surnames. Yet these were direct successions, not sold to outsiders. But each farm had known at least one son-in-law marriage during the previous three generations.

Even though, in these cases, the importance of the son-in-law in the transmission of assets and the business is made particularly visible by the change in surname, I would suggest that there are other cases where the daughter-in-law comes to live on her parents-in-law's farm and contributes to maintaining and transmitting the assets: she plays a similar role, which is just as important. It is preferable that she does not have her own resources, like the sons-in-law of the previous cases. Otherwise she might attract her husband away to another farm or even force him to change profession. This is, for example, what happened in Crépand at the largest rented farm in the 1950s. There were three sons, but no daughter-in-law agreed to "take over" her husband's farm. The farm was therefore let go to a tenant farmer and another line of descent. When, in 1978, I interviewed one of the concerned couples, the husband explained that his wife, a teacher, was not "capable" of carrying out the work of a woman on a large dairy farm. The husband therefore went to work in a factory where he had a good career (he ended up as a foreman). His wife was reluctant to admit her responsibility in the decision to leave the farm, as she explained to me that her husband had to step aside for his brothers (which is clearly not true, as no brother took over the farm).

I therefore propose to use the expression "daughter-in-law marriage" in cases where the daughter-in-law is, to a certain extent, "adopted" by her parents-in-law and contributes to maintaining the family assets of her husband's line of descent. I will just provide one example, taken from

Nicolas Renahy's research. In a working-class family in Lacanche (Côte-d'Or, France), "the adoption of Pauline by her family-in-law," induced by her sedentary lifestyle in the village and by the fact that her husband was the only one to have remained a laborer, made her "the legatee of the Legrand family's collective memory." In her dining room, she has the "buffet inherited from her husband's grandmother. 'My mother-in-law said to me: Dédé won't have the buffet, you will.'"[41] This act puts the daughter-in-law into the line of descent, and in fact she becomes the symbolic "successor," to the detriment of the legitimate daughter, Dédé, who, for that matter, was not very interested in this inheritance due to her own social upward mobility.[42]

The issue of free family work, raised and solved in agriculture for sons who take over the family business in 1939 in France, is currently an issue outside agriculture, since a large number of elderly people depend on financial or material help from a member of their family. To know who, among the siblings, helps their parents, the process of designating a "principal carer" has to be understood, a process during which health and social care institutions, neighbors, vague or explicit forms of social control, individual "qualities," and emotional relationships intervene throughout an entire family history, enabling us to understand the internalizing of a role by a child and the "life conduct" (*Lebensführung*), to use Max Weber's term,[43] that he adopts to assume this role.

Yet, this process of designating the principal carer can usefully be compared to the process of designating the "successor" of a family business, in general the child who stays to "help" his parents, before the succession itself. A detour via the law (support duty, unjust enrichment, and differed wages) imposes itself as family norms are both, in part, instituted legally and, in part, perceived by the people concerned, and a large gap between the legal and the social norms results in many court cases that, in return, help legislation evolve. We have seen that the issue of "compensation" for a task carried out in the family context is raised differently depending on whether this task concerns a business or a private individual, depending on whether it seems "normal" or "excessive," probably also depending on the gender and professional status of the person concerned (sons of farmers were entitled to "differed wages" as early as 1939; farmers' wives only after 1999). It is only raised in times of crisis and family change. It reveals tacit arrangements that do not have to be clarified as long as things remain routine.

French agricultural families still have a lot to teach sociologists who are not agricultural specialists. The professionalization of agricultural activity in France has indeed gone through paying family work, to the detriment of extending agricultural wage systems. It could be asked if contemporary legal developments in the payment of family work in the case of care for elderly, dependent people, does not constitute an essential prerequisite to the professionalization of this care. French twentieth-century social history of agricultural modernization, the disappearance of a wage system, and the unexpected development of business forms of family agriculture must drive us to be attentive to both changes in the family care of dependent people and changes in the wage systems of the health and social care sector.[44]

Florence Weber is professor of sociology and social anthropology in France, at the Ecole Normale Supérieure, University of Research Paris Sciences & Lettres. She has worked on household economy, developing several empirical enquiries, first of all on male members of the productive household activities: see *Le travail à-côté: Etude d'ethnographie ouvrière* (Paris: Editions de l'EHESS, 1989; third edition 2009, translated into Portuguese) and *L'honneur des jardiniers: Les potagers dans la France du XXème siècle* (Paris: Belin, 1997); then on the domestic production of health, especially by women: see *Charges de famille: dépendance et parenté dans la France contemporaine*, with Séverine Gojard and Agnès Gramain (Paris: Editions La Découverte, 2003). She then developed a new line of research in anthropology of kinship (*Le Sang, le nom, le quotidien*, first published in 2005, new edition *Penser la parenté aujourd'hui: La force du quotidien* [Paris: Editions Rue d'Ulm, 2013]). In 2015 she published the *Brève histoire de l'anthropologie* (Paris: Flammarion). She is currently working on an educational series of selected works of Marcel Mauss, at the Presses Universitaires de France, as well as a collective research on social and psychological disabilities in France.

Notes

1. The present chapter is the translation of a slightly reworked version of Florence Weber, "Peut-on rémunérer l'aide familiale?," in *Charges de famille: Dépendance et parenté dans la France contemporaine*, ed. Florence Weber, Séverine Gojard, and Agnès Gramain (Paris: La Découverte, 2003), 43–67. We took into account research carried out since then in the European context, as well as the articulation between family carework and professional carework at home. On this point, see in particular Loïc Trabut and Florence Weber, "How to Make Care Work Visible? The Case of Dependence Policies in France," in *Economic Sociology of Work*, Research in the Sociology of Work, vol. 18, ed. Nina Bandelj (Bingley: Emerald Group Publishing Limited, 2009), 343–68. I am grateful to Julia McLaren, who translated this version and helped me to clarify important concepts, and to Marie-Paule Laffay for our linguistic and friendly discussions.

2. In particular, for France: Pierre Bourdieu, *Le Bal des célibataires* (Paris: Seuil, 2002); Alice Barthez, *Famille, travail et agriculture* (Paris: Économica, 1982).
3. Paul-André Rosental, "Les liens familiaux, forme historique," in *Les Solidarités familiales en questions. Entraide et transmission*, ed. Danielle Debordeaux and Pierre Strobel (Paris, LGDJ, coll. "Droit et Société," vol. 34, 2002), 107–41.
4. For a summary of French peasantry, see Georges Augustins, *Comment se perpétuer? Devenir des lignées et destins des patrimoines dans les paysanneries européennes* (Nanterre: Société d'ethnologie, 1989).
5. Bernard Zarca, "Artisanat et trajectoires sociales," *Actes de la recherche en sciences sociales* 29 (1979): 3–26.
6. Pierre-Paul Zalio, *Grandes familles de Marseille au XXe siècle* (Paris, Belin, 1999).
7. Adam Kuper, "Fraternity and Endogamy: The House of Rothschild," *Social Anthropology* 9, no. 3 (October 2001): 273–88.
8. Nancy Folbre and Michael Bittman, *Family Time: The Social Organization of Care* (New York: Routledge, 2004).
9. Guy Barbichon, "Patrimoine et pouvoir symbolique des agriculteurs dépossédés," *Études rurales* 65 (1977): 93–100.
10. Louis Assier-Andrieu, "Maison de mémoire. Structure symbolique du temps familial en Languedoc: Cucurnis," *Terrain* 9, "Habiter la maison" (October 1987): 10–33.
11. Since 1985, 60 percent of households in France own property assets (Anne Gotman, *Hériter* [Paris: PUF, 1988]).
12. Barthez, *Famille, travail et agriculture*.
13. Agnès Gramain and Jérôme Wittwer, "La prise en charge des personnes âgées dépendantes: quels enjeux économiques?," *Regards sur l'actualité* 366, La Documentation française (2010): 46–60.
14. See, for sociology, Claudine Attias-Donfut, ed., *Les Solidarités entre générations : Vieillesse, familles, État* (Paris: Nathan, coll. "Essais et Recherches," 1995). For a dialogue between economics and sociology, see *Économie et Prévision*, nos. 100–101 (1991).
15. Serge Clément, "Des enfants pour la vieillesse: formes de la fratrie et soutien aux parents âgés dans le Sud-Ouest rural français," *Social Science and Medicine* 37, no. 2 (1993): 139–51. Roméo Fontaine, Agnès Gramain, Jérôme Wittwer, "Les configurations d'aide familiales mobilisées autour des personnes âgées dépendantes en Europe," *Economie et statistique* 403–4 (2007): 97–115.
16. See on this subject the law thesis of Mélanie Monteillet-Geffroy, *Les Conditions de l'enrichissement sans cause dans les relations de famille*, Doctorat et Notariat, 2001-4, Impr. La Mouette, 2001.
17. Barthez, *Famille, travail et agriculture*; Virginie Bussat and Michel Chauvière, *Famille et codification: Le périmètre du familial dans la production des normes* (Paris: La Documentation française, 2000, coll. "Perspectives sur la justice").
18. This ethnographic account was put to images by two documentarists: Florence Weber, "A Mother Is a Mother: Family Secrets, Obligatory Maintenance and Reforming French Dependency Law," in Jean-François Dars and Anne Papillault, *Histoires courtes*, http://llx.fr/site/une-mere-cest-une-mere/.
19. Claude Thélot, *Tel père tel fils: Position sociale et origine familiale* (Paris: Dunod, 1982).
20. Bernard Zarca, "Proximités socioprofessionnelles entre germains et alliés: Une comparaison dans la moyenne durée," *Population*, 1 (1999): 37–72. Emmanuelle Crenner, Jean-Hugues Déchaux, and Nicolas Herpin, "Lien de germanité à l'âge adulte," *Revue française de sociologie* 41, no. 2 (April–June 2000): 211–39.
21. To avoid the ambiguous parent = father or mother/parent = a related person, I use the expression "family member" for the second meaning of the term, without ignoring the fact that the notion of "family" is not clear, legally.

22. Let us note that the list of those who must provide support duty is arbitrary, that it differs depending on national legislation, in Europe in particular, and that it has faced renewed developments due to recent social policies.
23. French law has a tendency to reserve the term of kin (*parenté*) for blood relatives. I follow the use of kin anthropology, for which kinship comprises three dimensions: filiation, alliance, and residence. On the importance of these questions of terminology for the difference between French- and English-language anthropologies, see Louis Dumont, *Introduction à deux théories d'anthropologie sociale* (1971; Paris: Gallimard, Tel, 1997).
24. The old French word *maisonnée* marks the possibility of a shared life without cohabitation, or remote cohabitation. This allows us to take into account nonresidential caregivers. Trabut and Weber use the term "home beyond the household" to capture these extended domestic groups in which care for a dependent person is organized outside the home, but by kin: Trabut and Weber, "How to Make Care Work Visible?" Work on migration reveals the development of a very long-distance phenomenon called "extended household" by the UN, and which I propose to call "split household."
25. "Dette personnelle puisqu'elle dépend d'une part du lien de parenté ou d'alliance et d'autre part de la fortune respective des parties." J. Frossard, "Le recours du débiteur alimentaire condamné contre les codébiteurs," Dalloz, 1957, chronique, p. 24, quoted by Monteillet-Geffroy, *L'enrichissement sans cause*, 270.
26. In principle, support duty concerns the spouse first of all, and in his absence, the father and mother, and in their absence, all the others without hierarchy.
27. Monteillet-Geffroy, *L'enrichissement sans cause*, 269.
28. For this notion of "principle caregiver," used by doctors and administrators of care for the elderly social policies, see Élisabeth Cozette, Agnès Gramain, Marie-Ève Joël, and Alain Colvez, "Qui sont les aidants?," *Gérontologie et société* 89 (1999): 35–48.
29. "Les sacrifices d'un enfant au profit de ses parents, même s'ils excèdent la mesure commune de la piété filiale, correspondent à l'exécution volontaire d'un devoir moral personnel qui en constitue la cause." Monteillet-Geffroy, *L'enrichissement sans cause*, 301.
30. "Autorise l'exercice de l'action en enrichissement sans cause afin d'indemniser le dévouement exemplaire d'un enfant à l'égard de ses vieux parents." Ibid., 1.
31. For the question of the relationship between law and jurisprudence in a country of civil law like France, see Évelyne Serverin, *De la jurisprudence en droit privé: Théorie d'une pratique* (Lyon: PUL, 1985), and "The Common Law and Civil Law Traditions," The Robbins Collection (2010), retrieved 14 June 2018 from from https://www.law.berkeley.edu/library/robbins/CommonLawCivilLawTraditions.html.
32. "Le devoir moral d'un enfant envers ses parents n'exclut pas que l'enfant puisse obtenir indemnité pour l'aide et l'assistance apportées dans la mesure où, ayant excédé les exigences de la piété filiale, les prestations librement fournies avaient réalisé un appauvrissement pour l'enfant et un enrichissement corrélatif des parents."
33. I would like to thank Katia Weidenfeld, who pointed out to me that this case used a similar line of argument to that of Denise Chaux.
34. Monteillet-Geffroy, *L'enrichissement sans cause*, 152.
35. "Consacrer un droit à remboursement différé des frais d'assistance aux parents, pour compenser les prestations fournies en dehors du cadre alimentaire." Ibid., 368.
36. For an analysis of the "hostile worlds," the world of money and interest and the world of love and "family relations," see Viviana Zelizer, "Transactions intimes," *Genèses* 42 (March 2001): 121–44. Incidentally, see how Mélanie Monteillet-Geffroy defines "family relations": this expression "includes the idea of exchanges within the family. These exchanges can be diverse, they can be monetary (financial help), exchanges of time and services (professional care, accommodation, housework, treatment)" (Monteillet-Geffroy, *L'enrichissement sans cause*, 19). The term of exchange suggests a reciprocity

(but the examples given in parentheses reveal rather a "gift" or unilateral help); it is clearly noncommercial reciprocity. For an analysis of these various notions, see Florence Weber, "Transactions marchandes, échanges rituels, relations personnelles: Une ethnographie économique après le Grand Partage," *Genèses* 41 (December 2000): 85–107; and Florence Weber, "Présentation," in Marcel Mauss, *Essai sur le don* (Paris : Presses Universitaires de France, 2012).

37. "Qu'une descendante qui s'était occupée de sa mère grabataire jusqu'à sa mort ne pouvait, sur le fondement de l'enrichissement sans cause, demander à la succession une indemnité réparatrice de l'enrichissement procuré au patrimoine du défunt, dès lors que ses interventions actives, dévouées et régulières étaient justifiées par des liens d'affection unissant normalement une fille à sa mère." Monteillet-Geffroy, *L'enrichissement sans cause*, 354.

38. Agnès Gramain, *Situation et comportements économiques des aidants des personnes âgées dépendantes: Comparaison des conjoints et des enfants*, Rapport final CNRS, programme "Santé Société," June 2001.

39. I borrow a term that was used by historians of antiquity in particular: Claudine Leduc, "Comment la donner en mariage? La mariée en pays grec," in *Histoire des femmes en Occident*, vol. 1: *L'antiquité*, ed. P. S. Pantel (Paris: Plon 1991), 259–316.

40. In Crépand, I was told, fifty years after the relevant marriage: "The Vatels, they are Gontrans," Vatel being the name of the son-in-law and Gontran that of the father-in-law (Weber, "Pour penser la parenté contemporaine," 73–106). Cases of this kind are also reported in Françoise Zonabend, *La Mémoire longue: Temps et histoire au village* (Paris: PUF, 1980).

41. Renahy Nicolas, "'Vivre et travailler au pays?' Parentèles et renouvellement des groupes ouvriers dans un village industriel bourguignon," sociology doctoral thesis, EHESS, INRA-ESR Dijon, Doc. de recherches no. 53, 1999: 77.

42. For an analysis of family relations in this light, see Céline Bessière, *De génération en génération: Arrangements de famille dans les entreprises viticoles de Cognac* (Paris: Editions Raisons d'Agir, 2010); Solène Billaud, Sibylle Gollac, Alexandra Oeser, Julie Pagis, eds., *Histoires de famille: Les récits du passé dans la parenté contemporaine* (Paris, Editions Rue d'Ulm, 2012).

43. Catherine Colliot-Thélène, *La sociologie de Max Weber* (Paris: La Découverte, coll. "Repères," 2014).

44. The Medips team has established this work program since 2000. See, in particular, Florence Weber, Loïc Trabut, and Solène Billaud, eds., *Le Salaire de la confiance: L'aide à domicile aujourd'hui* (Paris: Éditions Rue d'Ulm, 2014).

References

Assier-Andrieu, Louis. "Maison de mémoire. Structure symbolique du temps familial en Languedoc: Cucurnis." *Terrain* 9, "Habiter la maison" (October 1987): 10–33.

Attias-Donfut, Claudine, ed. *Les Solidarités entre générations: Vieillesse, familles, État*. Paris: Nathan, coll. "Essais et Recherches," 1995.

Augustins, Georges. *Comment se perpétuer? Devenir des lignées et destins des patrimoines dans les paysanneries européennes*. Nanterre: Société d'ethnologie, 1989.

Barbichon, Guy. "Patrimoine et pouvoir symbolique des agriculteurs dépossédés." *Études rurales* 65 (1977): 93–100.

Barthez, Alice. *Famille, travail et agriculture*. Paris: Économica, 1982.

Bessière, Céline. *De génération en génération: Arrangements de famille dans les entreprises viticoles de Cognac.* Paris: Editions Raisons d'Agir, 2010.

Billaud, Solène, Gollac Sibylle, Oeser Alexandra, Pagis Julie, eds. *Histoires de famille: Les récits du passé dans la parenté contemporaine.* Paris: Editions Rue d'Ulm, 2012.

Bourdieu, Pierre. *Le Bal des célibataires.* Paris: Seuil, 2002.

Bussat, Virginie, and Michel Chauvière. *Famille et codification: Le périmètre du familial dans la production des normes.* Paris: La Documentation française, 2000, coll. "Perspectives sur la justice."

Clément, Serge. "Des enfants pour la vieillesse: formes de la fratrie et soutien aux parents âgés dans le Sud-Ouest rural français." *Social Science and Medicine* 37, no. 2 (1993): 139–51.

Colliot-Thélène, Catherine. *La sociologie de Max Weber.* Paris: La Découverte, coll. "Repères," 2014.

"The Common Law and Civil Law Traditions." The Robbins Collection. Berkeley, 2010. Retrieved 14 June 2018 from https://www.law.berkeley.edu/library/robbins/CommonLawCivilLawTraditions.html.

Cozette, Élisabeth, Gramain Agnès, Joël Marie-Ève, and Colvez Alain. "Qui sont les aidants?" *Gérontologie et société* 89 (1999): 35–48.

Crenner, Emmanuelle, Déchaux Jean-Hugues, and Herpin Nicolas. "Lien de germanité à l'âge adulte." *Revue française de sociologie* 41, no. 2 (April–June 2000): 211–39.

Dumont, Louis. *Introduction à deux théories d'anthropologie sociale.* Paris: Gallimard, Tel, 1997. First published in 1971.

Économie et Prévision, nos. 100–101 (1991).

Folbre, Nancy, and Michael Bittman. *Family Time: The Social Organization of Care.* New York: Routledge, 2004.

Fontaine, Roméo, Agnès Gramain, and Jérôme Wittwer. "Les configurations d'aide familiales mobilisées autour des personnes âgées dépendantes en Europe." *Economie et statistique* 403–4 (2007): 97–115.

Gotman, Anne. *Hériter.* Paris: PUF, 1988.

Gramain, Agnès. *Situation et comportements économiques des aidants des personnes âgées dépendantes: Comparaison des conjoints et des enfants.* Rapport final CNRS, programme "Santé Société," June 2001.

Gramain, Agnès, and Jérôme Wittwer. "La prise en charge des personnes âgées dépendantes: quels enjeux économiques?" *Regards sur l'actualité* 366, La Documentation française (2010): 46–60.

Kuper Adam. "Fraternity and Endogamy: The House of Rothschild." *Social Anthropology* 9, no. 3 (October 2001): 273–88.

Leduc, Claudine. "Comment la donner en mariage? La mariée en pays grec." In *Histoire des femmes en Occident.* Vol. 1: *L'antiquité,* edited by Pauline Schmitt Pantel, 259–316. Paris: Plon, 1991.

Monteillet-Geffroy, Mélanie. *Les Conditions de l'enrichissement sans cause dans les relations de famille.* Doctorat et Notariat, 2001-4, Impr. La Mouette, 2001.

Renahy, Nicolas. "'Vivre et travailler au pays?' Parentèles et renouvellement des groupes ouvriers dans un village industriel bourguignon." Sociology doctoral thesis, EHESS, INRA-ESR Dijon, Doc. de recherches no. 53, 1999.

Rosental, Paul-André. "Les liens familiaux, forme historique." In *Les Solidarités familiales en questions: Entraide et transmission*, edited by Debordeaux Danielle and Strobel Pierre, 107–41. Paris: LGDJ, coll. "Droit et Société," vol. 34, 2002.

Serverin, Évelyne. *De la jurisprudence en droit privé: Théorie d'une pratique*. Lyon: PUL, 1985.

Thélot, Claude. *Tel père tel fils: Position sociale et origine familiale*. Paris: Dunod, 1982.

Trabut, Loïc, and Florence Weber. "How to Make Care Work Visible? The Case of Dependence Policies in France." In *Economic Sociology of Work*, Research in the Sociology of Work, vol. 18, edited by in Nina Bandelj, 343–68. Bingley: Emerald Group Publishing Limited, 2009.

Weber, Florence. "Transactions marchandes, échanges rituels, relations personnelles: Une ethnographie économique après le Grand Partage." *Genèses* 41 (December 2000): 85–107.

———. "Peut-on rémunérer l'aide familiale?" In *Charges de famille: Dépendance et parenté dans la France contemporaine*, edited by Florence Weber, Séverine Gojard, Agnès Gramain, 43–67. Paris: La Découverte, 2003.

———. "A Mother Is a Mother: Family Secrets, Obligatory Maintenance and Reforming French Dependency Law." In Jean-François Dars and Anne Papillault, *Histoires courtes*, 2011, http://llx.fr/site/une-mere-cest-une-mere/.

———. "Présentation." In Marcel Mauss, *Essai sur le don*. Paris: Presses Universitaires de France, 2012.

Weber, Florence, Loïc Trabut, Solène Billaud, eds. *Le Salaire de la confiance: L'aide à domicile aujourd'hui*. Paris: Éditions Rue d'Ulm, 2014.

Zalio, Pierre-Paul. *Grandes familles de Marseille au XXe siècle*. Paris: Belin, 1999.

Zarca, Bernard. "Artisanat et trajectoires sociales." *Actes de la recherche en sciences sociales* 29 (1979): 3–26.

———. "Proximités socioprofessionnelles entre germains et alliés: Une comparaison dans la moyenne durée." *Population* 1 (1999): 37–72.

Zelizer, Viviana. "Transactions Intimes." *Genèses* 42 (March 2001): 121–44.

Zonabend, Françoise. *La Mémoire longue: Temps et histoire au village*. Paris: PUF, 1980.

IV

CONCLUSION

CONCLUSION

CAN WE CONSTRUCT A HOLISTIC APPROACH TO WOMEN'S LABOR HISTORY OVER THE *LONGUE DURÉE*?

Laura Lee Downs

Is closing a door a form of "work?" asks Maria Ågren in the opening lines of her chapter "The Complexities of Work." Throughout this volume, each of the contributing authors grapples with the question of what work is—or, to be more precise, what kinds of tasks get counted as work (and in which circumstances)—from a variety of angles and disciplinary perspectives. Their conclusions, however divergent on the particulars, converge on one overarching point: answering this question demands that we step back and analyze the wider contexts—social, economic, legal, political—that endow everyday gestures with the meaning "work." In Ågren's study of early modern Scandinavia, closing the door behind oneself to keep the house warm, for example, would probably not have been counted as work, whereas closing the door to a henhouse would have been an important part of the work that a rural housemaid performed every evening.

Recovering the hidden labors of women demands this kind of careful contextualization, as well as sharp attention to the very different divisions of labor that structured early modern societies. This in turn entails recovering earlier, more expansive understandings of what work is, and so broadening the range and kinds of sources one uses. By suggesting that one possible definition of work is that of time use with the purpose of making a living, Maria Ågren's research allows us to reach back to times and places where the range of tasks and activities that were understood to constitute "work" were far more expansive, the division of tasks between men and women far less sharply gendered, and the labors of women fully integrated into the overall organization of social and economic life, a substantial part of which unfolded inside agricultural, artisanal, and merchant households.[1] Here, the social and economic dimensions of existence were so deeply imbricated as to be hardly distinguishable, and daily toil was the lot of all women and men save those who sprang from the most privileged élite.

The kind of empirical and conceptual work that the contributors to this volume are doing is especially important given the fact that understandings of what constitutes work have narrowed considerably, if unevenly, since the early modern period, with devastating consequences for women's position in modern and present-day labor markets. Hence, notions of what work is and of who, therefore, counts as a worker have retreated from very broad early modern understandings that ran along the lines of Ågren's time use with the purpose of making a living to the far more restrictive notion of "productive" labor for the market that is typical of modern market economies.

Yet earlier, more multivalent understandings of work did not simply give way before narrower modern ones in a simple, forward-marching chronology. Rather, the two understandings, though grounded in very different social, economic and political contexts, seem to have co-existed well into the early twentieth century, and arguably up to this day in places like Alessandra Pescarolo's "Third Italy"; a fact that reminds us of the critical importance of regional differences in shaping economic life. Indeed, if the intermingling of the social with the economic is one way of defining the early modern economy, then the early modern world clearly persisted well into the twentieth century in most parts of rural Europe and North America, as well as in that important stratum of rural and urban production that remained in the hands of artisan and craft workers.[2]

When read alongside one another, the chapters in this volume reveal the complex and variegated economic landscapes on which opposing notions of what work is, each grounded in divergent and highly gendered understandings of what counts as productive labor, have coexisted. But the range and diversity of these chapters, which cover a broad chronology from different disciplinary standpoints, also allow the reader to draw up a list of the various dichotomies—distinct but interrelated—that underpin modern notions of productive work. These include the distinction between production and reproduction; between waged and unwaged labor; between the family and the market; between systems that socialize the costs of reproduction versus those that treat those costs as an individual consumer choice/responsibility.[3] These distinctions haunt the chapters in this book, for one of the poles that anchors this collection—family business—is a site on which such distinctions blur hopelessly. It is precisely for this reason that familial enterprises constitute an excellent vantage point from which to examine the coexistence of what might, for lack of a better term, be called the early modern model, in which the social and economic dimensions of life are bound together, with a modern model that has struggled to disentangle these two dimensions of life.

1. The emergence of the productive versus unproductive labor dichotomy—a very short history

As feminist economist Nancy Folbre tells it, narrowed conceptions of labor that excluded reproductive work from the account were first articulated by John Locke, who, at the end of the seventeenth century, sought to articulate the principle that private property springs from labor inputs, giving individual men (and, in theory, women) a right to what they produce. But what of the notoriously demanding work involved in producing and raising children? This kind of work, though demanding great investments of time and effort across many years, can never be placed in the same category as the work of growing food or fashioning material objects, Locke tells us, and this for one simple, imperative reason: if children are seen to be the property of the parents who "produced" them, then they can never grow up to be those self-possessing individuals who stand at the heart of liberal political understandings. For the early theorists of a liberal political order, the labor involved in producing and raising children *had* to be understood as something else: the realization of a natural instinct, perhaps, or the fulfillment of a moral obligation. But never could such labor be conceptualized as a form of work.[4]

Locke's gendered distinction between the (domestic) labor of producing children versus the work entailed in producing things would be taken up some eighty-five years later by Adam Smith, who recast this distinction in broader, more categorical terms that placed the production of services to persons in opposition to the production of material goods within the dawning "economy of production." Political economists would henceforth define productive labor as the kind of labor that produces things which can then be exchanged or transferred to another person via the market. The labor involved in producing services, by contrast, though clearly important, was not understood to be a part of the economy of production.

Of course, the very notion of an "economy of production" was itself a novel concept whose developing contours rested, by definition, on the exclusion of service labor from the realm of production: "There is one sort of labor which adds to the value of the subject upon which it is bestowed; there is another which has no such effect," declared Smith in the second book of his *Wealth of Nations* (1776). "The former, as it produces a value, may be called productive; the latter, unproductive labor." It is worth dwelling for a moment on this phase of Smith's argument. Why and in what terms did the moral–philosopher–turned–political–economist deem service labor "unproductive"? Because the labor of a "manufacturer" (that is, factory worker) "adds, generally, to the value of the materials which he works upon, that of his own maintenance, and of his master's profit. The labor of a menial servant, on the contrary, adds to the value of nothing. . ."

By this Smith meant that the value of the servant's labor is never embodied in a good that can then be sold for profit on the market. It is, rather, embodied in the well-being of the person being served, or in the health and development of the child being raised. To Adam Smith, the conclusion seemed obvious: the master's wages, invested in a "manufacturer," cost the master, in reality, "no expense, the value of those wages being generally restored, together with a profit, in the improved value of the subject upon which his labor is bestowed. *But the maintenance of a menial servant never is restored*. A man grows rich by employing a multitude of manufacturers; he grows poor by maintaining a multitude of menial servants. The labor of the [servant] however, has its value, and deserves its reward as well," concluded Smith.[5]

Across the following century, political economists would continue to classify service labor as a *non*-productive form of work, linked to the realm of consumption (itself often coded as parasitic) rather than as an economic contribution to the profit-making realm of production.[6] By the mid-nineteenth century, Karl Marx would fold into his own labor theory of value this same distinction between "productive" labor and the allegedly non-productive work involved in producing services, most famously when he singled out the sexual division of labor as the sole non-alienating division of labor. Unlike those pernicious social divisions of labor that spring from unequal socioeconomic relations and the coercive power of rich over poor, the sexual division of labor is the only one that emerges spontaneously and naturally, he claimed.[7] One wonders just how spontaneous and natural such divisions felt to his wife, Jenny von Westphalen, who was a revolutionary thinker and activist in her own right while acting as primary caretaker of the Marxes' six surviving children.[8]

It was only at the end of the nineteenth century, with the work of Alfred Marshall, William Stanley Jevons, and Léon Walras, that economists would shift the focus from material product to subjective utility. This entailed abolishing the productive versus service labor distinction and focusing instead on the distinction between goods and services that are bought and sold versus those that remain outside the market. While Marshall, Jevons, and Walras's rethinking of neoclassical economics around the concept of subjective utility was an important reconceptualization of the field, it nonetheless hived off women's unpaid care and reproductive labors from their labors in the market and consigned the former to the non-marketized sector.

The question "What is work?" is, therefore by no means a neutral or innocent one, for the distinction between productive labor and allegedly unproductive services maps largely, if imperfectly, onto gendered divisions between private and public; between the (often unpaid) services of women and the paid labor that produces material objects for sale in the market. In addition, it is worth noting that the question "What is work?" is a strikingly modern one, for it arises as such only in the context of market economies, factory (versus familial/workshop) production, and the particular, highly gendered ways of understanding the connections among (and the frontiers separating) social, political, and economic realms that have accompanied those developments in the West. Within this modern understanding, services to persons, which have always been a vital part of social and economic life, would no longer be treated as a part of the productive life of the community, while earlier conceptions of labor as punishment (for original sin) or as redemption (medieval Christianity) would be lost. For as Raffaella Sarti has cogently observed, the French Revolution overturned those earlier understandings in the name of democracy, redefining labor as a noble contribution to life of the nation and the aristocracy's conspicuous inactivity (paired with its conspicuous consumption) as parasitic.

It is here that the highly gendered distinction between the "manly" labors of production versus the servile production of services (linked not only to domesticity but more perniciously yet to the slavish hierarchies of aristocratic society) intersected with the newly politicized valorization of labor as the positive, indeed noble condition on which (male) citizenship rested. Henceforth, productive labor would constitute one indispensable basis of active citizenship in France's republican democracies (of which there have been five thus far), as well as in the democratic rethinking of European state systems more broadly.[9]

2. Work and politics in post-1789 Europe

The larger outlines of the story that unfolds in the interstices of this book, in which family production gradually moved off the center stage of European economies without ever actually *leaving* that stage altogether, intersect in significant ways with a parallel story, told by Carole Pateman (among others) about the way that the post-1789 shift toward more horizontal and egalitarian political relationships among men (the famous "fraternal contract") was anchored in a more systematic, across-the-board domination of wives by their husbands.[10] Deeply imbricated with this shift were sharper, more unbending sexual divisions of labor and a resignification of the relationship between private/domestic and public.[11]

The Revolution's famous exclusion of women from the "fraternal contract," which replaced the patriarchal power of kings over people and fathers over sons with more or less horizontal ties of citizenship among men, can thus also be read through the lens of what might be called a "productive labor theory of citizenship"; a theory that fits a number of continental European cases (including Germany, Austria, France, and Italy) very well indeed.[12] I'm not sure it fits quite so well the very different ways that the British understand citizenship in relation to labor. For early modern Britain saw no concerted attack on the social and political weight of aristocracy comparable to those seen in revolutionary and postrevolutionary France. Among other things, this meant that British women in élite families continued to exercise political or quasi-political forms of authority throughout the eighteenth and nineteenth centuries (though nearly always in subordination to élite males), while working-class men's inclusion by gradual steps in Britain's franchise (laws of 1867, 1884, and 1918) was based less on the idea that labor is noble than on the ways that ties of economic dependency were slowly being rethought in relation to political participation. At the same time, the relationships among home and work, family and enterprise were also somewhat different in Britain, where enclosure had essentially eliminated the peasantry by the late eighteenth century, and early industrial development placed family business in a somewhat different relationship to industry across the nineteenth and early twentieth centuries.

The relationships binding social and economic hierarchies to political participation were thus rather different in Great Britain, for non-élite men as well as for women. This being said, the grounding of Britain's liberal political order in self-possessing individualism takes us back to the highly problematic relationship that women have always had to liberal individualism.[13] One only has to ask oneself "What kind of a *self-possessing* individual is a pregnant woman?" in order to have an idea of just how irreducibly problematic that relationship is. The case of Britain (but also of Europe's modern democracies, through which strands of liberal political thought are wound) also remind us of a fundamental ambiguity in liberal understandings of the individual and of the private sphere, thanks to the constant slippage in liberal political thought between the individual male and the household he is presumed to stand at the head of. If at times the term "individual" actually means a (male) individual, at others an entire household is in fact being targeted, however implicitly.

The gendered politics of liberal individualism and of republican democracy thus traced somewhat distinct routes to women's notional exclusion from the world of work, routes that ran alongside and complemented the socioeconomic route (services/production distinction) outlined above. Together, they produced one of the central paradoxes that structured social and economic life in nineteenth- and twentieth-century Europe, namely that women, who were theoretically absent from the public world of production, were nonetheless everywhere present therein, toiling visibly in fields and gardens, workshops and cafés, factories and shops; laboring in economies that could not survive without their (underpaid) labors, yet rendered invisible by the notion that women are marginal to the world of work, especially "productive" work. The consequences of this paradox and the profound political and economic marginalization that it entailed for women are still with us today in the shape of unequal pay, ongoing occupational segregation, poorer representation of female labor in trade unions (as well as in socialist and other left-wing political movements), and shocking disparities in the place of women versus men in institutions of political and economic decision-making.

3. From participation in the "work of life" to domestic drudgery in obscurity: how working women began going missing from the census

The sheer range and variety of topics, times, and places covered in this volume allow us to revisit the long history of households as sites of production and consider the various ways that household and factory production have coexisted in the modern era, not always to the advantage of the household producers. Margareth Lanzinger and Maria Ågren thus remind us of the centrality of households as economic units in early modern economies, where rural and artisanal households, but often bourgeois ones as well, constituted so many nodal points structuring those economies. Over the nineteenth and twentieth centuries, continual shifts in the categories that structure the census, or shape and reshape family law, make it possible to map the gradual and uneven cession of early modern understandings of work to more restrictive modern ones, and to measure some of the consequences for women's relative bargaining power at home and at work.

Hence, as we move into the modern and contemporary eras we can see how, in the deeply connected fields of political economy and liberal political thought, reconsideration of the household and of ideal gender relations with regard to the emerging concept of civil society eventually led to a massive rethinking of the categories that structure the census. As Cristina Borderías, Nancy Folbre, Alessandra Pescarolo, and Raffaella Sarti have shown, this rethinking gave rise across the nineteenth century to new ways of thinking about the contours of the so-called "active" population that, sooner or later excluded household labors from the category of productive work while rendering the participation of women and young people in still widespread forms of family enterprise more difficult to count up accurately. Unsurprisingly, this produced a significant drop in married women's work that was precisely the outcome of redefining such women as dependents rather than as workers who were occupied in assuring what one Massachusetts census analyst called "the work of life."

But the progress of this new logic was far from steady. In the telling formulation of our late nineteenth-century American census analyst, for example the category of "worker" embraced all those who took part in the "work of life," be they servants, factory workers, farmers, housewives, bankers, doctors, or shopkeepers. Only the unemployed, a category that included rentiers and other idle rich, were understood to be non-productive members of society.[14] Massachusetts would not start to align its census categories with those of other American states until the 1910s, recasting household labor as "unproductive" and so marginalizing still further the labors of married women and other household workers.

This profound rethinking of what constitutes productive activity thus rendered even more systematic the underreporting of married women's economic activity, which was henceforth progressively recategorized into obscurity. But application of the new "liberal" census categories was highly uneven, which means that the disappearance of married women workers from national censuses happened earlier in some places, such as mid-nineteenth century Britain and Spain, than in others. France, for example, did not fully shift over till the census of 1954, when one million women suddenly went missing from the active labor force. It turns out they were peasant wives, still understood as economically productive workers in the last prewar census of 1936 before being dropped into the black hole of the "unoccupied" in France's first postwar census.[15]

The consequences of not counting women are not always predictable, and emerge rather differently in the tale that Alessandra Pescarolo has to tell us about the economy of the "Third Italy"—a region of small to mid-sized industrial enterprise cutting across central Italy and the Veneto that blossomed during the 1970s, 1980s, and 1990s. Pescarolo shows us how the undercounting of women's domestic labor became the linchpin of the Third Italy's economic miracle, as the domestic work of women, never included (let alone calculated) in the budget plans of small business, furnished small and medium-sized firms with opportunities to pay lower, more competitive salaries. Such creative accounting also allowed the female laborers' families to save, protecting their own work from the fluctuations of employment. Domestic work—that is to say, unpaid domestic *production*—thus became a significant, and in some ways strategic, economic variable, the basis of one typically Italian path of industrialization, and an alternative to that of the large factory. It was a strategy that rested on the complete obfuscation of married women's productive labor; their contribution to the GNP, if you will. As such, it has doubtless contributed significantly to weakening women's position in the Italian labor force today.

The centrality of women's unpaid productive labor in Italian family businesses may be one reason that the Wages for Housework movement of the 1970s gained some traction in Italy. The appeal seems obvious: the wage paid for housework services vital to the reproduction of the labor force renders visible and "accounted for" the thousands of hours per year clocked by countless wives and mothers whose time and effort is entirely consecrated to the well-being of others.[16] But as Alessandra Gissi's research makes clear, the project of rendering visible the invisible labors of housewives inevitably blends progressive and conservative arguments, as the demand to recognize the value of such services to the social and economic life of the nation too easily ends by normatively confining women to those "natural" domestic chores they are already performing in any event. In the case of Italy, moreover, such arguments had some very problematic fascist precedents that rendered this conservative/progressive mix all the more unsettling for 1970s feminists. On the one hand, many Italian feminists were caught up in the broader transnational movement to give public recognition to women's invisible and unpaid labors via the payment of a housewives' wage. On the other hand, fascist precedents from the 1920s and 1930s, grounded in Mussolini's famous "battle for births" that granted great public recognition (but precious few resources) to struggling young mothers, still loomed large in public memory. It was an ambivalent precedent at best.[17]

More profoundly, however, Western capitalist workplaces have always depended on the work of reproduction being accomplished for free. However much Western welfare states have sought to stabilize capitalism by absorbing some of the costs of social reproduction, these costs have been carefully contained within a patriarchal ideological framework that refuses point blank the idea that such transfers to families be thought of as "wages" for housework or "wages" for mothers.[18] It's one thing to assist families with many children via a payment that is attached to the father's wage, quite another to openly acknowledge that the hidden labors of wives and mothers are in fact socially necessary, that any kind of a "strike" on that front would bring to a screeching halt the world of productive labor.

It is precisely in those countries like France and Italy (or, for that matter Spain), where family business formed one vital backbone of the modern economy, that wage labor and family labor systems came into open conflict not only over the shifting categories of the census but also (and perhaps more profoundly) in the realms of family, civil, and private law. Maria Rosaria Marella analyzes these conflicts in fascinating ways that underscore the extent to which Italy (and also France, perhaps the entire continent) stand as important counterexamples to the trajectories taken in both Britain and the United States.

This is especially visible when we consider the crucial question that Nancy Folbre's analysis of recent trends in both Britain and the United States raises, namely, is it easier to enforce equal treatment of women and men than it is to challenge the logic of the market? This is clearly true in the United States, where the gulf separating rich from poor has grown with dizzying speed since the 1970s, while those same years have seen a narrowing of the gender gap, especially for those women who have few or no children. It seems to be largely true for Britain as well, according to the data gathered by Folbre. But Marella shows us how the moral/legal framework in a country like Italy has produced the opposite result. Indeed, it's been easier to challenge the absolute hegemony of market logic in a country where values of solidarity (social and familial) have long been supported by large segments of the political class (Christian Democrats, Socialists, and Communists), while family law is heavily stamped by Catholic conceptions of marriage, family solidarity, and the allegedly natural, inevitably hierarchical complementarity of male and female.

The result so far has been that highly inegalitarian forms of family solidarity in Italy are upheld by the law against a market system that is seen to be the bearer of non-humane values, and must therefore be contained. Marella's chapter shows how, time and again, Italian women bear the burden of the underlying logic of this system, which is that of sacrifice of self to the family in the name of unity and family welfare. Italy's version of family values has also produced some interesting paradoxes, Marella tells us, such as the outcomes of 1980s case law, where, in a new twist on the woman as wife or whore binary, housewives and prostitutes who had suffered bodily injury found themselves excluded from compensation for the loss of profit caused by their diminished physical capacity, with the work of prostitutes being defined as "unproductive" because it is contrary to Catholic morality, while housewives were excluded for the simple reason that their work is considered one of the obligations of family solidarity and so not subject to contract-based compensations in the event of disability.

Finally, it's worth noting that in countries like France and Italy, which have long been characterized by their two-tiered economies (family enterprise plus industrial sector), the production-versus-services distinction has major implications for understanding and counting (or not counting) the labor of younger men as well as women. This point emerges very strongly in Florence Weber's eye-opening chapter on the monetarization of family relationships via the concept of "deferred wages." This concept was first introduced into family businesses (primarily peasant farms) as part of the July 1939 revision of France's family code, which stipulated that henceforth, the child who remained on the farm as a family worker would receive material compensation for his or her investments of energy into the family patrimony.

Significantly, this compensation was conceptualized as a deferred wage no matter what form the compensation took, thus introducing into family enterprises the notion of wage labor contracts among family members; an elegant solution to one problem (the unpaid family worker) that created, in turn, numerous difficulties for the concept of family solidarity on which such enterprises have been built, with interesting and still-unfolding consequences for the ways in which duties of care are understood in contemporary France.[19]

Work on different forms of family business thus lays bare the larger social, economic, and political issues that are raised by the fact that important productive activities take place inside an institution (the family) that is seen to be blending emotion and economy in ways that have, in moral terms, come to seem highly problematic.

4. Household production, social welfare, and the democratization of marriage

Maria Ågren and Margareth Lanzinger's chapters, analyzing the wide range of tasks performed by women and men, married and unmarried people alike in early modern and nineteenth-century Europe, raise, if somewhat obliquely, the larger question of the changing status of married versus unmarried people and the very different positions that the married versus the unmarried occupied in the social hierarchies that organized such households. For in the early modern era, differences of gender seem to have been far less important than the differences of status and wealth that separated the married couple who owned the property and stood at its head, from the unmarried servants of both sexes who assisted them daily in the production of food and clothing, tools and implements, textiles and other material goods.

Some of those servants would have been children or young adolescents, sent from another family's farm or workshop to serve as apprentices in the hope that they, too, would one day enjoy the financial security necessary to marry and then found a family enterprise. Others would have been far older; lifetime servants whose poorer economic prospects excluded them from the privilege that was marriage in an early modern world of limited resources and labor-intensive household production, which often required more hands than the average family could provide.[20]

Social and economic historians have long known that the rapid expansion of wage labor that accompanied the movement of (some kinds of) production into factories across the long nineteenth century (1780s–1914) eventually made it possible for poorer women and men to marry and found a household whose expenses were covered (more or less) by their waged labor.[21] The rise of wage labor thus "democratized" marriage, giving those whose destiny was a lifetime of servitude in another person's household a potential route of access to married (or cohabiting) life and children of their own, albeit in straitened circumstances. At the heart of this postrevolutionary democratization of marriage and family life, however, lay the more systematic rule of husbands over wives, which, as Carole Pateman observed, underlay the spread of more democratic relations among men. The marriage that was slowly being democratized in post-1789 Europe would thus seem to have been a more systematically inegalitarian structure, vis-à-vis women, than was early modern marriage, a status that only those economically privileged individuals who stood to inherit something—a piece of land, a workshop, tools and the skills of the older generation—could aspire to.[22]

Serious contemplation of this fact (democratization of marriage/cohabiting via waged labor) opens out some new ways of thinking about the concerns that, sometimes explicitly, more often implicitly informed the ways in which institutions of social assistance and social protection were rethought and reshaped across the late nineteenth and early twentieth centuries. For it suggests that underpinning the progressive elaboration of welfare services in nineteenth- and twentieth-century Europe was the idea, rarely articulated as such, that marriage and childrearing are human goods that should be democratized and made available to all.

Clearly enhancing social stability was one goal of such policies, for in societies that had (in principle, at least) abandoned vertical hierarchy as the basis of social control and political order, the democratization of family life across formerly hierarchical societies would encourage young men to settle down and become productive and hardworking fathers of families. In this way, greater access to marriage would make family life the anchor and guarantee of social stability (or so the theory went), replacing hierarchy with a new source of social stability that rooted disciplined habits of work and leisure in the most intimate sentiments of men and women, fathers and mothers.

But alongside the political arguments for democratizing marriage lay a moral one claiming that adults of both sexes should be able to enjoy the unique emotional bonds of marriage and parenthood; that these were precious emotional goods that should be distributed more evenly across society. Many of the earliest forms of modern welfare service, organized in the second half of the nineteenth century, thus targeted children and their families via a broad range of welfare initiatives: family allocations, maternal and child-welfare clinics, elementary schools, neighborhood social centers, etc. These were developed with the goal of aiding poor children while transforming the impoverished and difficult marriages of their wage-laboring parents into more stable, prosperous unions through direct assistance, especially to children and their mothers. The progressive elaboration and generalization of such family-centered social assistance across the first half of the twentieth century broadened yet further access to marriage, eventually enabling the still significant percentage of Europeans who worked as servants in family-based rural and urban enterprises of one sort or another to move out of live-in service and set up households of their own.[23]

5. How women's productive labor inside the home went from normal activity to pernicious perversion of family life

As a number of chapters in this volume demonstrate, hardening divisions between the public and domestic spheres, with the former increasingly seen as the *sole* site of production and the latter as a kind of residual space of care services and (male) leisure, would eventually render women's industrial homework an especially problematic category for those who, in nineteenth- and twentieth-century Europe and the United States, sought to measure, analyze, or reform such work. For in a world where public and private, production and leisure were meant to be strictly separated, women's homework created deeply troubling category overlaps that menaced the moral significance of public-private divisions as key to securing social order. In the case of the early twentieth-century United States, for example, Eileen Boris tells us that the home was seen strictly as a place of leisure, where male workers recovered from long hours of arduous labor thanks to the unpaid services and attentions received from wives and daughters. How, then, were the market labors of those same women, carried out alongside their care work in a domestic space that was allegedly consecrated to family leisure, to be understood and classified by the census takers who sought to quantify such labor? By the social reformers who sought to regulate home work, or eliminate it altogether? By those labor activists who strove to organize those home workers and place them on an equal footing with the modal (male industrial) worker? The constant slippages between unpaid and paid domestic services and between domestic labor and home production for industry dogged these efforts, allowing exploited domestic workers to slip through the cracks, their labor unregulated because it was unseen as such.

6. Spaces of engagement, spaces of labor: family—civil society—market—state

The chapters in this volume all suggest that equality, as it was conceptualized by European liberals, raises immense problems for women, as its key concepts—individuals, equality, freedom, family, public, and private—can be expanded only with great difficulty (if at all) to include those who were excluded in the period of liberalism's construction as a political ideology and as a way of understanding the human world.[24] They further point to the fact that family business provides a privileged vantage point for rendering visible how liberal ideology links family and market, private and public, civil society and state in ways that tend to obscure the labor/exploitation of women and of young people of both sexes. I'd like to close with a few questions that this very stimulating collection raises, pointing to areas for further research:

1) Nancy Folbre asks a very important question, one that is worth repeating here: Why is there so much resistance to valuing women's unpaid care work? Her very plausible answer is that people fear the commodification of women's labors of love; they fear that the moral efficacy of those labors would be undermined and their meaning de-natured, if not nullified altogether, if such services were to be traded on the market or treated as salaried labor. But of course these services have already been partially commodified by the welfare state, even though the architects of those states took great pains to ensure that payments (like family allowances) often went to the fathers of families as a complement to their bread-

winner wage rather than to mothers in the form of a "salary" for undertaking each day the job of raising children. Post-1945 welfare states were thus careful to uphold the structures of patriarchy but also the unpaid status of mothers' labors, guaranteeing that they worked for love, not money, and that they remained economically dependent on male breadwinners. Alessandra Pescarolo and Florence Weber further underscore the dedicated nature of caregiving, pointing out that it is often non-detachable from she—or he—who offers it. It would therefore seem that the marketized and non-marketized labors of women remain completely entangled, a tendency which the ongoing marketization of care work that has accompanied the dismantling of welfare states only reinforces.

2) How race shapes the domestic labor-that-is-not-labor is particularly important to explore in the case of the United States, of course, but also in postcolonial Europe, where service labor is increasingly performed by impoverished immigrants (especially women) from formerly colonized territories.

3) Another kind of work that is—crucially—not defined as such is volunteer work, which is frequently, though not exclusively, performed by women, especially (though not exclusively) middle-class ones. The logic underlying the particular value that volunteering has in liberal societies (where it has recently become linked to citizenship in interesting, sometimes perverse ways) is strikingly similar to the logic that sees paying for care work as a dangerous undermining of what must remain labors of love.[25]

4) Folbre's chapter offers a brilliant analysis of the distributional conflicts over the costs of social reproduction. But the story she tells, based on US and British material, doesn't work for France or for Scandinavia, where much of the cost of childrearing, underwritten by the state, has been distributed far more widely across the society. In France, this was initially done in very gendered ways (for example through the Family code of 1939). More recently, such provision has taken more egalitarian forms (though gender equality still has a long way to go in France).

France is therefore an interesting intermediate case between Britain, where children have long been treated as a private good, and Scandinavia, which has progressively socialized the costs of childrearing since the 1930s and 1940s. Indeed, France has a *longer* history than Scandinavia of spreading the costs of children, as pro-natalist anxieties from the 1870s onward mixed with republican ideas about children's relationship to the republic (*mon fils ne m'appartient pas, il est à la République,* in Danton's memorable formulation) to create an atmosphere propitious to the gradual elaboration of school-centered and work-centered child welfare and childcare provisions. This is a very different origin from Scandinavia's post–World War II social democratic matrix that mixed concern for children with a growing commitment to gender equality at home and at work. Only recently have French policymakers started linking the long republican tradition of good childcare, early education, and socialized costs of children to more explicitly feminist and gender-equality goals.[26]

The chapters gathered in this volume thus suggest that we need to be looking at continental, Scandinavian, and Mediterranean economies more closely, for so much of what we know about women's labor history is based solely on Anglo-American examples. But the evidence suggests that in certain respects these two may well be the outliers. These chapters also suggest that we need to analyze critically through the lens of gender the production of sources like the census, whose utility and limits for grasping the past must be confronted directly. Finally, we also need to remember how strong the resistance to gender equality can be. For, from the perspective of those who are accustomed to privilege, the arrival of equality feels like oppression.

Laura Lee Downs is professor of history at the EUI, where she holds the chair in gender history, and is Directeur d'études at the Écoles des Hautes Études en Sciences Sociales, where she holds the chair in the comparative history of social management *(La gestion sociale: France-Angleterre, XXe siècle)*. She has published extensively on issues of gender and labor in twentieth-century Europe, on working-class childhood, and on the comparative history of social protection in Europe. She has won fellowships from the Guggenheim, Fulbright, NEH, Mellon, and Giles Whiting foundations, and her book *Manufacturing Inequality: Gender Division in the French and British Metalworking Industries, 1914–1939* (Ithaca, NY: Cornell University Press, 1995), won the Pinckney Prize for the best book in French History. She has also published widely on gender analysis and historical method, most notably in her *Writing Gender History* (London: Arnold Press, 2004; 2nd edition, revised and expanded, London: Bloomsbury Press, 2010). Her current research, on the construction of para-political spaces of social action in France, Italy, and Great Britain, 1870–present explores the ways in which European welfare states have been shaped from the bottom up through variously configured civil society mobilizations around the protection of vulnerable populations. For more details see http://www.eui.eu/DepartmentsAndCentres/History AndCivilization/People/Professors/Downs.aspx.

Notes

1. See Ågren's chapter and Maria Ågren, *Making a Living, Making a Difference: Gender and Work in Early Modern European Society* (New York: Oxford University Press, 2017), 204–5, 218. On time use studies, see Nancy Folbre's chapter in this volume.
2. The social and economic dimensions of life remain intermingled to this day, of course, but in very different ways that tend to obscure such intermingling under the sign of such binaries as private/familial versus public.
3. This latter is less of a binary than a contiuum, with most societies standing somewhere in between the two poles.
4. See Nancy Folbre's analysis of John Locke's, *Second Treatise of Government* (1690) in *Greed, Lust, and Gender: A History of Economic Ideas* (New York: Oxford University Press, 2009). The expanding transatlantic slave trade must surely have been an important context for Locke's insistent exclusion of the parental/maternal "production" of children from his labor theory of property.
5. Adam Smith, *Wealth of Nations* (1776; London: Penguin, 1974), bk. 2, chap.3, 429–30; my emphasis.
6. For an extended reflection on previous (seventeenth- to eighteenth-century) theories of production that saw service labor as an economic contribution, see Carolyn Steedman, *Labours Lost* (Cambridge: Cambridge University Press, 2009).
7. Friederich Engels and Karl Marx, *The German Ideology* (written in 1845–46, first published by David Riaaonov in 1932). Engels would later change his mind on this point. See Friederich Engels, *Origin of the Family, Private Property and the State in Light of the Researches of Lewis H. Morgan* (1884); both in Marx and Engels, *Collected Works* (London: Lawrence & Wishart, 1975).
8. Jenny Marx to Karl, 24 March 1846, Marx and Engels, *Collected Works*, 38:529. See also Harrison Fluss and Sam Miller, "The Life of Jenny Marx," *Jacobin*, February 2016, retrieved 8 August 2016 from https://www.jacobinmag.com/2016/02/jenny-karl-marx-mary-gabriel-love-and-capital/. This does not mean that Marx ignored the issue of women's weaker position in labor markets. Nor did he fail to see the central place that the reproduction of the labor force via women's unpaid services of care holds in the capitalist economy. But he never reflected systematically (let alone critically) on women's weaker bargaining position within the household or its consequences for the particular, patriarchal forms that capitalism has taken in Western Europe and North America.
9. Raffaella Sarti, "Promesse mancate e attese deluse: Spunti di riflessione su lavoro domestico e diritti in Italia," in *Il lavoro cambia*, ed. Ariella Verrocchio and Elisabetta Vezzosi (Trieste: Edizioni Università di Trieste, 2014), 55–77, and Raffaella Sarti's chapter in this volume.
10. Carole Pateman, *The Sexual Contract* (Stanford: Stanford University Press, 1988). See also Lynn Hunt, *The Family Romance of the French Revolution* (Berkeley, CA: University of California Press, 1992).
11. For a remarkable analysis of these developments in Central Europe, see Isabel Hull, *Sexuality, State, and Civil Society in Germany, 1700–1815* (Ithaca, NY: Cornell University Press, 1996).
12. Carole Pateman, "The Fraternal Social Contract," in *Civil Society and the State: New European Perspectives*, ed. John Keane (London : Verso, 1988), 101–27.
13. Which is also a component of republican democracy, if but a minor strand.
14. *Census of Massachusetts 1875* (Boston: Albert J. Wright, 1876), xlix, cited in Nancy Folbre's chapter in this volume.
15. Margaret Maruani and Monique Meron, *Un siècle de travail des femmes en France, 1901–2011* (Paris: La Découverte, 2012).

16. Here I refer to reproduction of the labor force in both senses of the term, that is, the daily reproduction of those worn-out workers who return home each evening to be restored by a mother/wife's care and feeding, but also the physical production of the next generation of workers.
17. Alessandra Gissi's chapter in this volume.
18. Susan Pedersen, *Family, Dependence and the Origins of the Welfare State: Britain and France, 1914–1945* (Cambridge: Cambridge University Press, 1993); Nancy Fraser, "Rethinking the Public Sphere: A Contribution to the Critique of Actually Existing Democracy," *Social Text* 25–26 (1990): 56–80. Perhaps we are back on the territory of John Locke's moral revulsion in the face of the idea that the labors of producing and raising children might be considered a form of work.
19. The 1939 Agricultural Inheritance Law is part of a larger revision of the French Family Code whose other provisions included a significant revision to family allowances: for the first time, a special *prime de la mère au foyer* (bonus for the stay-at-home mother) was added to the existing structure of allocations. While this was clearly a product of conservative and Catholic familialist politics, as well as pro-natalist fears about population decline, it is worth noting that traditions of married women's participation in paid labor were so strong in France that a measure intended to cut them out of market labor was unthinkable without offering those same women some kind of financial compensation. This marks a striking difference with Britain and America, where Depression-era efforts to reduce male unemployment by setting up so-called "marriage bars" or eliminating dual-earner families by declaring married women whose husbands were employed ineligible for the out-of-work donation (Britain's 1929 law on unemployment benefit) simply eliminated those women, uncompensated, from paid labor or unemployment benefit. See Laura Lee Downs, *Manufacturing Inequality: Gender Division in the French and British Metalworking Industries, 1914–1939* (Ithaca, NY: Cornell University Press, 1995).
20. On marriage as a privilege in early modern Europe, see Hull, *Sexuality, State, and Civil Society*.
21. "Factories" can include a division of labor among closely packed households in semirural towns, as Alison Light's *Common People: An English Family History without Roots* (London: Penguin, 2014) reminds us, while wage labor has long included all kinds of production carried out in rural households under the putting-out system (in which merchants furnish the raw materials and then pay wages for the finished products), as well as in urban households, where women, men, and children produce clothing, pins, cardboard boxes, etc., for industrial employers (home work, often called "sweated labor.")
22. Pateman, "The Fraternal Social Contract". See also Hull, *Sexuality, State, and Civil Society*.
23. Margot Béal, "La domesticité dans la région lyonnaise et stéphanoise; vers la constitution d'un prolétariat de services? (1848–1957)," PhD thesis, European University Institute, 2016.
24. For an acute analysis of the problems raised by trying to include women in structures of civil society and political deliberation whose very construction had been built upon their explicit, across-the-board exclusion, see Hull, *Sexuality, State, and Civil Society*.
25. Andrea Mühlebach, *The Moral Neoliberal: Welfare and Citizenship in Italy* (Chicago: University of Chicago Press, 2012).
26. On the Franco-Scandinavian comparison, see Dominique Méda and Alain Lefevre, *Faut-il brûler le modèle social français?* (Paris: Le Seuil, 2006). For an overview of current natalist policies in developed nations, East and West, see "Breaking the Baby Strike: People in Rich Countries Can be Coaxed into Having more Children," *The Economist*, 25 July 2015, retrieved on 16 July 2018 from https://www.economist.com/international/2015/07/25/breaking-the-baby-strike. See also Amy Borovoy and Kristen Ghodsee, "Decentering Agency in Feminist Theory: Recuperating the Family as a Social Project," *Women's Studies International Forum* 35 (2012): 153–65.

References

Ågren, Maria. *Making a Living, Making a Difference: Gender and Work in Early Modern European Society.* New York: Oxford University Press, 2017.

Béal, Margot. "La domesticité dans la région lyonnaise et stéphanoise; vers la constitution d'un prolétariat de services? (1848–1957)." PhD thesis, European University Institute, 2016.

Borovoy, Amy, and Kristen Ghodsee. "Decentering Agency in Feminist Theory: Recuperating the Family as a Social Project." *Women's Studies International Forum* 35 (2012): 153–65.

Downs, Laura Lee. *Manufacturing Inequality: Gender Division in the French and British Metalworking Industries, 1914–1939.* Ithaca, NY: Cornell University Press, 1995.

Folbre, Nancy. *Greed, Lust, and Gender: A History of Economic Ideas.* New York: Oxford University Press, 2009.

Fraser, Nancy. "Rethinking the Public Sphere: A Contribution to the Critique of Actually Existing Democracy." *Social Text* 25–26 (1990): 56–80

Hull, Isabel V. *Sexuality, State, and Civil Society in Germany, 1700–1815.* Ithaca, NY: Cornell University Press, 1996.

Hunt, Lynn. *The Family Romance of the French Revolution.* Berkeley: University of California Press, 1992.

Light, Alison. *Common People: An English Family History without Roots.* London: Penguin, 2014.

Maruani, Margaret, and Monique Meron. *Un siècle de travail des femmes en France, 1901–2011.* Paris: La Découverte, 2012.

Marx, Karl, and Friedrich Engels. *Collected Works.* Vol. 38. London: Lawrence & Wishart, 1975.

Méda, Dominique, and Alain Lefevre. *Faut-il brûler le modèle social français?* Paris: Le Seuil, 2006.

Mühlebach, Andrea. *The Moral Neoliberal: Welfare and Citizenship in Italy.* Chicago: University of Chicago Press, 2012.

Carole Pateman, "The Fraternal Social Contract." In *Civil Society and the State: New European Perspectives*, edited by John Keane, 101–27. London : Verso, 1988.

———. *The Sexual Contract.* Stanford: Stanford University Press, 1988.

Pedersen, Susan. *Family, Dependence and the Origins of the Welfare State: Britain and France, 1914–1945.* Cambridge: Cambridge University Press, 1993.

Sarti, Raffaella. "Promesse mancate e attese deluse: Spunti di riflessione su lavoro domestico e diritti in Italia." In *Il lavoro cambia*, edited by Ariella Verrocchio and Elisabetta Vezzosi, 55–77. Trieste: Edizioni Università di Trieste, 2014.

Smith, Adam. *Wealth of Nations.* London: Penguin, 1974. First published in 1776.

Steedman, Carolyn. *Labours Lost.* Cambridge: Cambridge University Press, 2009.

Index

ability/abilities, 248; children's, 97; for creative research, 97; to intervene on nature, 16; of law to produce social change, 299; in relation to work, 20, 64n200, 66n229, 314–17. *See also* capability/capabilities; skills

accounts, 2, 12, 45n10, 90, 98–99, 101–2, 141, 167, 228, 250–51, 254

activity/activities: economic, 3–4, 167, 248, 253, 279, 281, 356

Adam (and Eve), 9

administration: context, 249, 252; interests, 248; procedures, 250–51, 260n34, 261n47

Adriatic coast, 147

Africa, 202

age: adults, 11, 13, 170; children, 11, 176, 329, 332 (*see also* child/children); the elderly, 11, 327

Ågren, Maria, 7, 11, 13–14, 33, 162, 232, 238, 249, 256, 349–50, 355, 359

agriculture, 35, 41, 119, 178, 202, 229–31, 244, 253, 270, 278, 326–27, 331–32, 337–38, 340–41

aid: in the family enterprise, 254; home, 284; household, 276; mutual, 298; to working mothers, 278

Aix: Court of Appeal in, 334

Albera, Dionigi, 261n48

Alberti, Leon Battista, 8

Alesina, Alberto, 120, 128

Alexander, Sally, 139

alienation, 8–9, 51n48, 149, 151

Allen, Robert Carson, 28

America, 4, 356, 366n19; Latin, 277; North, 4, 147, 350, 365n8

American Heritage Time Use Surveys, 102

American Time Use Survey (ATUS), 102

Ancien Régime, 167, 189

Andean Region, 275

Andhra Pradesh, 37, 267

Anthony Brownell, Susan, 96

application: in relation to jobs, 91; for permission to marry, 37, 163, 250–51; technological, 129

apprenticeship, 141, 176, 245; apprentices, 14, 65n219, 180, 185n19, 245, 360

Arbeit. See work: *Arbeit*

arbeiten and *werken. See* work: *arbeiten* and *werken*

Arendt, Hannah, 5, 8

Ariès, Philippe, 58n140

aristocracy/aristocracies, 6–8, 189, 353–54

Arizona. *See* Napolitano, Janet (Gov. of Arizona)

Arnoux, Mathieu, 6

artisan/artisans, 28; independent, 274

arts: mechanical, 6

Asia, 275, 277, 282

assets: capital, 320; common, 302; conservation of/preservation of, 338; family, 12, 38, 265, 307, 313, 316, 318, 326, 329, 337–39; household, 53n69; imbalances, 334; inheritance, 327, 331, 334, 339; market, 102; in relation to marriage, 302; property, 255, 326, 337; separation of, 318; share of, 330, 336; transmission of, 326, 339

assistance, 236, 253, 282, 314, 333, 343n32, 343n35, 361; care and, 334–35; development of public, 181; to the husband, 206, 313; need of, 209; public, 180–81; social, 360–61; technical, 41, 270, 284; welfare, 182

assistant/assistants: to the elderly, 129; in the household, 256; to the husband, 12, 29 (*see* assistance: to the husband); immigrant family, 116; sales, 245; shop, 248; spouse

(*see* assistance: to the husband; husband/ husbands: assistance to the; spouse/ spouses: assistance between)
Astell, Mary, 93
Austen, Jane, 32
Australia, 34, 42, 99–100, 102, 282; clerical homework in, 42, 282
Austria, 184n9, 257, 260n34, 261n47, 354; civil law code of 1811, 250

babysitter, 2, 129, 176–77
Bacher, Joseph, 246–53, 260–61n39
Barbagli, Marzio, 54n84
Barcelona, 173–82; census of, 34; Censuses of Workers, 178; General Strike of 1855, 175; Mixed Commission, 175; Municipal Government, 181; Municipal Office of Statistics, 178; municipal registries *(Padrones Municipales)*, 181; Municipality of, 167; *Statistical Monograph of the Working Class of,* 174–75
basic needs, 280–81
Becker, Gary, 97–98, 126, 301
Beijing, 101
Bekel, Maria, 255
Belgium, 184n9, 270
Bellavitis, Anna, 6, 43, 48n28
Benard, Stephen, 91
Benedict, Saint, 6
Benería, Lourdes, 281
Berg, Maxine, 64n204
Berlinguer, Enrico, 144
Beruf, 7
Bible, 5; biblical curse, 6, 9
Blackwell, Elizabeth, 96
Bock, Gisela, 32, 243
Bologna, 44, 189, 210
bookkeeping records. *See* source/sources: bookkeeping records
Borderías, Cristina, 34–35, 163, 182, 356
Boris, Eileen, 19, 37, 41–42, 266, 285, 361
Boserup, Ester, 281
bourgeoisie: raising of, 189
boy/boys: chastised young, 233; and girls, 299, 339; tasks, 3
breadwinner, 24, 31, 33, 61n183, 92, 99–100, 104, 127, 162, 244, 271, 363; male, 174, 363; male breadwinner model, 166–67, 173–74, 178
breastfeeding, 16, 65n216, 117
Breckinridge, Sophonisba, 103
Brenner, Giovanna, 115

Brenner Pass, 246
Bressanone. *See* Brixen
Brewer, John, 29
Bridgman, Benjamin, 102
Brixen (Bressanone), 250–51; consistory of, 247–48, 250–52; Diocese of, 250, 259n20, 260nn31–33, 261n47
Brown, Wilmette, 21
Burguière, André, 260n31
Burgundy, 328–29; village of Crépand in, 339, 344n40
business, 5, 38, 301; competencies/skills, 251, 254; corporation, 24; earnings, 40; and family, 311, 332, 339–40; family, 2, 24, 33, 37–38, 40–41, 65n214, 161–62, 171, 184n11, 185n19, 191, 203, 206, 265–66, 303–5, 313, 315, 317, 326, 331, 337, 340–41, 351, 354, 357–59, 362; farm/agricultural, 214n36, 308, 327, 336, 338, 341; household, 35; industrial, 124–25; job openings, 91; out of, 90; people, 29; private, 147; small/medium, 24, 120, 124–25, 253, 357; state of, 40; women in, 25, 29, 40, 125, 247

Cady Stanton, Elizabeth, 96
Cambria, Adele, 155n1
Cambridge: University of, 12; University Senate of, 97
Canada: clerical homework in, 42, 282
Canning, Kathleen, 243
capability/capabilities: human, 18, 93, 102, 105; of males and females, 243; mothers', 91; of rural women's organizations, 282; social bargaining, 300; of technology to make economies obsolete, 130. *See also* ability/abilities; skills
capital, 20–22, 50, 57n122, 97, 117–19, 121–22, 124, 147, 153, 316, 320; human, 18, 45n10, 90, 93, 98, 301–2, 306, 319; invisible, 306; relation with labor, 178; sharing, 337; social, 26, 98, 248
capitalism, 9, 18, 20, 24–25, 61n183, 114, 117, 119, 122–23, 127, 149, 157n38, 357, 365n8; development of, 8, 15, 119, 122, 147
care, 3, 10, 15, 23, 39, 41, 93, 95–96, 117, 127, 139, 147, 154, 193, 235, 284, 296, 306, 327, 338; in relation to children, 92, 104, 149, 155n8, 176, 247, 252, 266, 275, 278, 281–82, 307, 313, 335, 364; costs of, 103, 320, 337; of dependents,

87; duties, 24, 359; in relation to family, 17, 23, 41, 89–90, 92–93, 97, 99, 103–5, 117, 177, 181, 300, 302, 314, 320, 334–38, 341, 366n16; in relation to gender, 89, 102; health and social, 333, 336, 340; medical, 278; paid, 3, 337; penalties, 105; services, 361; unpaid, 2–3, 38, 191, 272, 353, 365n8; value of, 2; workers, 284. *See also* work: care work
care work. *See* work: care work
caregiving, 19, 92, 96, 115, 124, 127, 307, 310, 343n24
caring, 16, 31, 41–42, 93, 129, 209–10, 254, 299, 337
caring democracy, 210
Catholicism, 7, 37, 140, 143, 163, 358–59; Church, 246; Lateran Council, 246; women's groups, 270
cause suffisante, 310–11
Census Enumerator's Books, 36
census/censuses: classification of men and women according different criteria, 192; data, 181, 200, 209, 214n31, 245; officers/officials, 34–35, 64n209, 190, 200–201, 205, 207; population, 1, 32, 34, 161, 163, 166, 168, 185n31, 190, 204, 207; population census categories, 4; statistical representation of the nation, 33, 190; women's work classification, 163
Cerchio Spezzato (il). *See* Il Cerchio Spezzato
Cerdà, Ildefons, 167, 174–79, 181, 186n34
Cesaroni, Francesca, 40
charity, 10
Chicago: International Congress of Statistics, 173; School of Social Work at University of, 103
child/children, 2, 10, 16, 39, 97–99, 115–16, 120, 127, 129, 149, 154, 171, 173, 176–77, 180, 251, 254–55, 277–79, 328–35, 338, 340, 352, 358, 360–61, 363–64; childless people/people without, 91–92, 94, 328, 358; childrearing, 96, 177, 243, 313, 320, 360, 363; and education, 13, 24, 93, 114, 120, 145, 313, 316, 364; grandchildren, 40, 266, 327, 333; illegitimate, 255–56; labor, 30, 62, 273, 351; natural, 306; and parents, 11, 14, 31, 40–41, 58n140, 94, 96, 103–4, 122, 124, 141, 143, 145, 148, 231, 252, 266, 314, 320, 328–35, 351, 365n4; raising of, 124, 148, 320, 351–52, 363, 366n18; schoolchildren, 169, 200; small,

176, 208, 247, 251, 253, 255, 278; wages of, 30–31, 34, 103; work of, 3, 19, 24, 27, 28–31, 34, 65n219, 95, 105, 118, 162, 185n19, 199n, 203–4, 249, 257, 273, 276, 332, 336, 359, 364, 366n21. *See also* care: in relation to children
childbearing/childbirth, 9, 15–16, 29, 51n49, 91, 116, 177, 203, 253, 331; pains of childbirth, 9
China: government of (Taiwan), 277
Christianity, 7, 37, 267, 353; Christ, 6; Christian world, 7
Cincinnatus, 7
citizenship, 1, 6, 8, 139, 154, 165, 189, 207, 218n93, 353–54, 363; citizens, 6, 156n18, 170, 190, 209, 320
civil law. *See* law: civil
civil society, 93, 356, 362, 364
Clark, Alice, 25
Clark, Colin, 101
Clark, Gregory, 28
class (social), 4, 6, 142, 150, 152, 255; cross-class coalition, 96; leading/ruling, 119, 206; lower, 28, 36, 204, 338; middle, 12, 24–25, 53n72, 128, 141–42, 329, 363; political, 358; social, 116, 338; struggle, 148, 150, 203; upper, 6–7; upper classes' disdain toward manual work, 6; working, 20, 23–24, 57n126, 62n184, 95, 119, 139–40, 147, 155n6, 166–67, 173–78, 181, 185n33, 333, 340, 354, 364
clergy, 7–8, 189, 248, 252
Colbert, Jean-Baptiste, 26
Cold War, 278
Colombo, Daniela, 157n43
commercial revolution, 12
commercialization, 15, 30
commodities: production of, 149; supply and demand of, 29
commodity: labor/work as, 15–17, 50, 148–49; laborer/worker as, 20, 50, 86, 147, 299; marketable, 15
common law. *See* law: common
Commonwealth, 99
Communism, 9, 144, 358
compensation, 144, 168, 313, 320, 332, 334–36, 340; contract-based, 359; exclusion from, 358; financial, 366n19; of housework, 318; material, 359; measure of, 314, 320; partial, 91; request for, 337; restorative, 337; right to, 40, 266, 337
competences, 91, 105, 142, 245, 248, 254

conduct manuals, 12
construction of domestic work as non-work, 188
consumption, 3, 10, 12, 27–30, 38, 87, 90, 118, 125, 129, 141, 144, 147, 176, 180, 182, 248, 280–81, 301, 326, 352–53; consumer/consumers, 12, 30, 98, 118, 122, 125, 142–44, 351; new consumer, 29; consumer revolution, 15, 29–30; role of women, 30
contextual production, 130
contract, 16, 22–23, 120, 153, 176, 206, 208, 246, 285, 295–96, 298, 305–6, 308–12, 319–21, 326, 333–34, 336, 354, 359
Convention to End Discrimination Against Women, 271
Copenhagen: Dottreskolen in, 12
Correll, Shelley, 91
Correspondence Committee on Women's Work, 274
court: records, 228–29, 249, 255. *See also* source/sources
Cox, Nicole, 153
crafts: mechanical, 189; urban, 6
curse that followed the original sin, 5
Custis, Martha, 245
Cutrufelli, Maria Rosa, 148

Dalla Costa, Mariarosa, 20–21, 57n126, 86, 120–23, 146–47
Darity, William, 105
Dataria Apostolica, 250
Davidoff, Leonore, 24–25, 254
Davin, Anna, 139
deferred wages. *See* wage/wages: deferred
de-industrialization, 27
De Litala, Luigi, 205
de Vries, Jan, 27–30
De Vivo, Giancarlo, 131n
delaborization, 15, 18, 188, 190
Delphy, Christine, 19, 57n122, 86, 123, 133n38
demand, 90–91, 243; for commodities, 29; consumer, 29; for equality, 330–31; for goods, 28, 30; home, 30, 62n185; for labor, 35, 91, 94, 108n53, 181–82; laws of supply and, 15
Denmark, 12, 184n9
dependent manual activities, 7
Depression, 104, 366n19
devaluation, 90–91, 105

development, 24, 61n183, 97, 101–2, 117, 119–20, 123–24, 135n59, 147, 174, 274, 278, 280–82, 326–27, 341, 343n24, 352–53; economic, 2, 6, 36, 51n48, 63–64n200; human, 50; individual, 143; underdevelopment, 271
diaries. *See* source/sources: diaries
Diez, Gasca Maria, 142
dispensation records/dispensation requests. *See* marriage: dispensation records; dispensation requests
diversity in European regions, 14
division of responsibilities/work between husband and wife. *See* marriage; work: division of responsibilities/work between husband and wife
divorce, 91, 306–9, 318, 333–34, 337; agreements in contemplation of, 308, 318; alimony, 302–3, 306–8, 318
Domestic and Personal Office, 100
Domestic and Personal Service, 100
domestic service, 3, 36, 44, 94, 103, 185n29, 204, 205n, 206, 209–10, 216n58, 269, 272, 274, 284–85, 362; British government's "Report on Post War Organisation of Private Domestic Employment", 276. *See also* work
domestic sphere, 22–23, 25, 39–40, 86, 149, 203–4, 208–9, 265, 297, 317, 361. *See also* private sphere; spheres, private and public
domestic work, 2–3, 114–15, 120–21, 124–26, 133n34, 140–41, 147–48, 171–73, 193, 204, 208, 216n58, 272–74, 276–78, 284, 298; "delaborization" of, 188; and GDP, 126; paid, 19, 38, 42, 203–4, 208–10; regulation of, 206; unpaid, 139, 174; unproductive, 20, 86, 166; and value, 116, 120, 126; and women, 96–97, 118, 120, 125–26, 173, 185n27, 185n29, 201, 273, 357. *See also* work: (domestic work) as work
domestic workers, 3, 19, 36, 39, 41, 203–4, 205n, 208–10, 216n58, 267, 269, 272–73, 276–77, 280, 284–85, 362; exclusion from most of the laws concerning work regulation, 208; weak status as workers, 206
domestic/public division, 140, 154, 243, 296–97, 353–54, 361–62, 365n2
dowry, 250–51
drugs: production and trafficking of, 2

Duden, Barbara, 243
Duffy, Mignon, 115

Earle, Peter, 249
early modern era/period, 3, 26, 32, 38, 231–32, 244, 258n5, 265, 350, 359
economically active: men, 207, 217n80; population, 192, 200, 209; women, 199–200, 204, 205n, 207–8
economically inactive: men, 207; population, 200; women, 1
economics: classical economics/classical thought, 18, 85, 117, 125, 166, 176, 353; economic theorists, 18, 96; neoclassical economics/neoclassical thought, 97–98, 104, 125, 127, 353
economy/economies: etymology, 10; as household management, 10; of scale, 87, 128–30; shadow, 249
Eibach, Joachim, 236
Eisendle, Franz, 261n39
Eisenhower, Dwight David, 276
Eisner, Robert, 101
élites, 189, 201, 350, 354
emancipation: condition of, 170; of a minor, 334; under Roman law and in other legal systems, 13; women's, 279, 297, 299, 320
Emilia-Romagna, 124
emotional norms, 330, 336
employment, 19, 91, 168, 172, 270, 272, 278, 280, 357; agencies, 273; contract, 285, 305, 326; development of employment opportunities, 271, 275; discrimination, 89–90, 92, 96; domestic, 276–77; fluctuations of, 125, 357; full-time, 104; gainful, 65n219, 243; household, 274, 277, 284; irregular, 119; manufacturing, 35; models of, 175, 180; opportunities, 25, 271–72; paid, 89–90, 97, 100; policies, 92; public, 104, 202; rates, 57n119; regular, 141; relations, 212n10, 285, 323n35; self-employment, 282; underemployment/unemployment (*see* underemployment; unemployment); waged, 23, 94, 96, 103, 105; and women, 25, 90–91, 96–97, 104, 201, 209, 217n89, 270, 273–75, 279, 300; world, 279–80
Engels, Friedrich, 62n184
England, 13, 24, 28, 30, 99–100, 123, 140, 185n19, 245, 254; Census, 33, 99, 184n10, 216n58; family life and gender roles, 24; Feminism in, 299; upper middle class in, 24; Victorian, 255; work rates in, 28
Enlightenment, 176
Entäusserung. *See* alienation; labor: as alienation (*Entäusserung*)
equal remuneration. *See* remuneration: equal
equality, 95, 139, 154, 258n5, 302–4, 308–9, 330–32, 337, 362, 364; achievement of, 143; formal, 304; full, 143; gender, 43, 66n229, 90, 92, 104, 279, 363–64; juridical, 306; political, 243; between the sexes, 93, 143, 271; between siblings, 330–31; social, 243; between spouses, 298, 301–2, 309, 319; of treatment, 284; between women and men, 208, 281; women's, 279; in the workplace, 87, 202
Erickson, Amy Louise, 245
Escudé Bartolí, Manuel, 178–80
Ethiopia, 156n12, 202
EU, 217n89; GDP of, 2
Europe, 3, 4, 6, 13–15, 19, 40, 43, 61n183, 120, 126, 147, 175, 208, 230, 243, 246, 273, 343n22, 350, 353–55, 359–61, 364, 365n8; aristocracy/nobility in, 6–7, 189 (*see also* aristocracy/aristocracies); clergy in, 7 (*see also* clergy); crisis in, 6, 12; economy of, 4, 353–54; households of, 10, 12, 14; Mediterranean, 10, 14; post-1789, 353–54, 360; postcolonial, 363
Eve (Adam and), 9

factory/factories, 4, 20–22, 24, 31, 39, 41, 62nn184–185, 63n200, 96, 118, 120–21, 125, 149, 153, 192, 214n36, 274, 312, 355, 357, 366n21; Fordist, 148; jobs, 206, 208; owners, 169; production, 274, 353, 355, 360; work, 20, 23, 31, 41, 86, 117, 123, 130, 145, 339; workers, 31, 86, 94, 114, 117, 123, 145, 169, 206, 208, 328, 352, 356
Fairchild, Mildred, 269–72, 274, 276–77
Fallgruppe, 316
family/families, 4, 10–12, 14, 19, 21–31, 34–35, 38–41, 43–44, 89–98, 101–5, 115–17, 119–27, 140–45, 147, 149, 153, 162–63, 165–68, 170–73, 175–82, 184n10–11, 184n14, 185n19, 185n29, 185n33, 186n36, 186n45, 191–93, 200, 203–4, 205n, 206–7, 209, 211, 229, 247–48, 250, 252–54, 256, 265, 269–75, 277–81, 283–85, 295–321, 321–22n1–2, 326–41, 350, 353–63,

366n19, 366n21; agricultural, 326, 332, 338, 340 (*see also* family/families: peasants' families); artisans', 11; assets, 12, 307, 316, 318, 326, 337–39; budget, 36, 142, 163, 166–67, 175, 177, 180–82, 186n45; business (*see* business: family); care work, 18, 85, 326, 341n1; code, 359, 363, 366n19; dual-earner, 14, 366n19; economy, 11, 29, 178, 181, 185n19; enterprise, 3, 12–13, 25, 254, 337, 356, 359–60; Family responsibility employment discrimination (FRED), 89–90; family-run economic activities, 3, 326–27; farm, 35, 41, 214n36, 235, 266; head of, 11, 13–14, 24, 33–35, 162, 168, 171, 177, 179–80, 184n10–11, 206; history, 4, 43–44, 131, 245; husband/wife, 11; labor (*see* labor: family); law, 39, 40, 265, 295–302, 304–9, 312, 317–21, 321, 321–22n2, 328, 330, 334, 336, 355, 358; law exceptionalism, 297–98, 302, 305–9, 317, 319, 321n2; life, 24, 243, 270, 298, 306, 314, 360–61; master/servant, 11; members, 3, 13, 38–40, 91–92, 97–98, 117, 122, 125, 167–68, 173, 185n27, 265–66, 298–99, 302–3, 310, 314–15, 317, 321n1, 328, 333–35, 337, 342n21, 359; members working *outside* their households, 14, 279; non-market work, 3; obligations, 4; parent/child, 11; peasants', 11 (*see also* family/families: agricultural families); relations, 40–41, 127, 141, 266, 295–96, 298, 300, 306, 315, 321n2, 327, 332, 334–35, 337, 343n36, 359; responsibilities, 89–96, 98, 104–5, 269, 271–72, 278–79, 284 (*see also* responsibility/responsibilities: family responsibility discrimination); situation, 253, 317, 331; solidarity, 40, 300–301, 305, 309, 317–19, 358–59; status, 13, 25, 246; wage, 103, 166, 177–80; work, 3, 41, 85, 87, 89–90, 93, 98, 101–2, 104–5, 279, 326–27, 332, 340–41; workers, 40–41, 65n214, 162, 266, 275, 327, 332, 336–37, 359
family workers. *See* family: workers
farmer, 40, 118, 125, 145, 185n19, 232, 281, 329, 336–37, 339–40, 356; independent, 7
Farr, William, 99
Fascism, 21, 87, 141, 148, 190, 201–2, 204, 212n10, 213n14, 296; autarchic policy, 202, 204; housewives, 140–41

Federici, Silvia, 21–22, 147, 153
female. *See* women
Feminism: development feminists, 281–83; Feminist Struggle (*see* Lotta Femminista); liberal, 114; Marxist, 18–19, 85, 114, 116, 149; materialistic, 19; second-wave, 22
feminization of work. *See* work: feminization of
fertility, 27, 94, 116, 119–20, 182
Feuerstein, Johann Josef, 254
Fiebranz, Rosemarie, 232
Fiktive Herstellungkosten, 316
filial devotion, 334
filiation, 330–33, 336, 343n23
Fill, Christina, 246–53, 261n39
Fill, Maria, 246
Flynn, Molly Abigail, 131n
Folbre, Nancy, 3, 16–18, 21, 33, 45n10, 85, 87, 106, 115, 117, 127–28, 162, 351, 356, 358, 362–63
Fonte, Moderata, 15
food: eating on the streets, 10; production of victuals, 11
forced work. *See* work: forced
Fordism, 147–48
Fourier, Charles, 95
France, 19, 40, 43, 85, 93–95, 103, 184n9, 184n11, 185n25, 185n28, 266, 295, 326–28, 334, 340–41, 354, 356, 358–59, 363–64, 366n19; agricultural families of, 326, 332, 340; censuses, 184n9, 184n11, 356, 358; Civil Code of, 332; Conseil Constitutionnel, 319; family code of (*see* family: code); French Revolution, 353; German-French border, 245; home-based work in, 266; household work, 85; law of, 40, 327–28, 330, 332–34, 343n23; law of 29 July 1939, 41, 332, 336; PACS, 319; policy of home care in, 338; political theory/social theory, 18, 93; postrevolutionary, 354; social legislation of, 274; social rights in, 40, 266; Supreme Court of, 41, 266, 332, 334–35
Francescato, Grazia, 139
fraternal sexual contract, 354.
Frederick, Christine, 22, 142
Friedan, Betty, 23

gainful employment. *See* employment: gainful
Galtier, Brigitte, 21, 147
Gandhi, Mohandas Karamchand, 283
gender, 11, 21, 30, 36, 38, 44, 90–91, 102–3, 123, 130, 145, 148, 150, 154,

162, 166, 176, 182, 188, 211, 228–31, 234–38, 243–44, 265, 271, 279, 317, 340, 364; ambiguities and biases—especially the gender ones—of the mainstream conceptions of work, 4; bias, 2, 4, 31–32, 89, 98, 104, 161, 163–64, 207, 209, 257; character, 243; differences, 94, 97, 182, 359; discrimination, 40, 92, 104, 178; division of labor, 21, 64n204, 86, 97, 231, 235, 237, 244, 279, 304, 306; equality, 43, 66n229, 87, 90, 92, 104, 279, 363–64; gap, 280, 358; Gender and Work project (GaW), 227–29, 232–34, 236–37, 238, 249, 256; history/historians, 4, 22–23, 32, 36, 43–44, 87, 139, 154, 182, 210, 238, 257, 364; identity, 127; inequality/ies, 97, 101, 244; men and women, 3, 10–11, 14, 23, 26, 31–32, 34–37, 39, 42, 102–4, 126–27, 161–63, 176, 178, 182, 192–93, 208–9, 227, 231–35, 237, 243–44, 246, 271, 281, 350, 358–61; neutral, 15, 32, 89, 92, 102, 104, 161, 233, 284; relations, 165–66, 168, 181, 356; roles, 24, 31, 66n229, 141, 243, 254, 297, 317; studies, 114, 126
generation: birth order, 11; parents and children, 11, 124, 127, 176, 333–34
Genesis, 5, 51n49
Geneva, 269
Genovesi, Antonio, 12, 53n72
Germany, 28, 180, 184n9, 308, 321, 354; German-French border, 245; household rationalization in, 140; law of, 316; Reformation, 13; Supreme Court of (*Bundesgerichtshof*), 308; Weimarian, 140
girl/girls: and boys, 3, 299, 339; education of, 12, 204; and housework, 176–77, 279, 299; unmarried, 13; women and, 145
Gissi, Alessandra, 21, 86, 154, 357
Glazer-Malbin Nona, 158
Global North, 272, 274, 277, 280
Global South, 272, 278–80, 282
GNP, 38, 357
God, 5, 7, 16
Goldin, Claudia, 35, 63n200
Goldschmidt-Clermont, Luisella, 101
goods, 15, 130, 236, 248, 361; acquiring, 12, 301; commodification of, 128; common, 321; consumer, 30, 42, 98, 118, 282; demand for, 30; human, 360; market, 27–28; material, 130, 351, 360; preserving, 12; price of, 35; production of, 10, 35–36, 64n206, 121–22, 172, 274, 299, 301, 351; purchase of, 29, 301, 303; and services, 10, 36, 64n206, 121–22, 129–30, 172, 353; substitute, 301; trade of, 236
Gray, Marion W., 61n183
Great Britain, 99, 184n9, 185n25, 185n28, 354, 364; British government's "Report on Post War Organisation of Private Domestic Employment", 276; censuses, 184n9, 185n25, 185n28; government of, 276, 285; liberal political order, 354; national income accounts, 98; political theory/social theory, 18, 93
Greece, 6, 57n119; Ancient, 16; language of, 5, 10
Green Revolution, 281
Gregory XIII, 255
Gregory XVI, 252
Gröden (Val Gardena), 246
Groppi, Angela, 248
gross domestic product (GDP), 2, 38–39, 87, 97, 99, 102, 126, 128; economic statistics on, 5 (*see also* statistics: economic statistics on GDP); female contribution to, 36 (*see also* women: economic contribution to GDP of)
Grosso Malagricci, Tilde Elena, 142
Gruppi femministi romani, 146
guilds, 11, 13, 25–26, 29; attitude towards women, 26; statutes, 13–14
Gujarat: Self-Employed Women's Association of (SEWA), 282

Hakim, Catherine, 114, 126
Hall, Catherine, 24–25
Halley, Janet, 321–22n2
Hancock, Florence, 276
handicraft, 38, 119, 267, 274–76, 278–79, 282
Harmonized European Time Use Survey (HETUS), 102
Hassan Jansson, Karin, 232
Hausväterliteratur, 7
Hayami, Akira, 27
Hinduism, 38, 267
history: social, 238, 245, 341
Hobbes, Thomas, 15, 18, 93
Hobsbawm, Eric, 118
Holy Penitentiary, 250
home, 2–4, 9, 13, 15–16, 20, 23–26, 29–31, 35, 39, 41–42, 57n126, 62n185, 63n200,

65n216, 65n219, 85–86, 90–91, 94–97, 99–100, 105, 108n53, 115–17, 121–23, 125, 128–29, 140–42, 144, 146–47, 149, 151, 155n6, 157n44, 161, 179–80, 184, 191–2, 203, 207, 243, 248, 265–66, 269–70, 272, 274–82, 284, 286, 307, 316–17, 327, 332–33, 336, 338, 341n1, 343n24, 354–55, 361, 364, 366n16, 366n19; chores, 315; economics, 155n8; family, 335; handicraft, 275; helps, 284; labors, 269, 272–74, 278, 280, 284–85; nursing, 327–30, 333–34; production, 154, 362; retirement, 149, 337
home work: paid industrial. *See* work: (home work) paid industrial
home work. *See* work: home work
home-based: activities, 4, 34, 38–39; production of textiles, 11, 26; productive work (unpaid, paid, hybrid, and intermediate) (*see* work: (home-based work) productive work—unpaid, paid, hybrid, and intermediate); work (*see* work: home-based work); work regulation (*see* work: (home-based work) regulation of)
Homeland Security, 89
HomeNet International, 283
Homo artifex, 16
Homo faber, 16
hospitality, 13, 312
household, 3–4, 9–14, 19, 24, 27–28, 32, 35, 37–38, 97–98, 100–102, 104–5, 108n53, 120–21, 126, 141–42, 156n12, 162–63, 170, 181, 184n9, 185n33, 231–33, 235–37, 243, 245–47, 251, 254–56, 272, 275–76, 279–82, 297–98, 301–7, 310, 314, 318, 320, 332–33, 343n24, 350, 355–56, 359–61, 366n21; activity/activities, 10, 299, 314, 341; assets, 53n69; bargaining, 90–91, 98; care work, 66; chores, 177, 313; community, 302; complex, 14; consumption, 180, 326; of day laborers, 10; economics, 101; economies, 4, 12; economy, 3, 11–12, 341; employment, 274, 277, 284; extra-household, 308, 318, 323n35; head of the, 19, 167, 171, 184n9, 232–33, 235–36, 248; independent, 14; as kin group and work group, 10; management, 10, 12, 141–42, 253; model of self-sufficient noble, 10–11; noble, 11; position, 14, 234–35, 237, 365n8; possessions, 12; preindustrial European, 10; production,

29, 36, 97–98, 100–101, 280, 316–17, 355, 359–60; rationalization of, 140, 155n6; sharecroppers', 14; as site for university teaching, 13; as site of schooling, 13; tax, 333; work, 15, 39, 85, 87, 91, 148, 235, 243, 273–74, 300, 356
househusband: *casalingo,* 193
housekeeper, 100, 253–55, 301, 310, 314, 316
housekeeping, 3, 12, 141–42, 192, 316
housemaid, 254, 316, 349
housewife/housewives, 1, 19, 23, 32–33, 38, 99–100, 108n53, 121, 140–42, 144, 149–50, 153, 155n6, 157n44, 188, 191–93, 198n, 199, 199n, 206, 216n58, 277, 313–17, 358–59; being a housewife as ideal to pursue, 23, 201; bodily integrity of, 312–13; bourgeois, 282; *casalinga* (Italian), 151, 191, 193; classification as, 34, 99, 141, 162–63, 191, 193, 200, 202, 204; classified as people without a profession, 191, 198, 200; as consumer, 143; *donna di casa* (Italian), 191; duties of, 173; good, 141; ideal, 142; in industry, 108n53; *massaia* (Italian), 191, 213n14; non-working, 162–63, 190, 201, 204; paid, 22, 141, 207; percentage of housewives among women, 200–202, 209; *persone attendenti alle cure domestiche* (Italian), 151,191, 198n; position of, 57n126; role of, 61n183, 141, 145; services of, 100–101; statistical overrepresentation of, 201; unpaid, 20, 29, 36, 64n206, 86, 108n53, 204, 269, 277; unproductive, 33, 162; wages of, 2, 21, 140, 142, 147, 149, 154, 270, 357; wife/mother as, 23, 32, 161, 278; woman/women as, 25, 32–34, 126, 146, 161–63, 193, 201–2, 204, 207; and work, 20, 22, 86, 108n53, 141, 147, 154, 204; work of, 2, 20, 22, 38, 86, 141–42, 148, 185n27, 278, 280, 316, 356, 357
housewifery, 33, 53n69, 153, 161–62, 202, 269
housewifization, 275
housework. *See* work: housework
Howell, Martha, 12
human capabilities, 18, 93, 102, 105
human capital, 18, 45n10, 63n200, 90, 93, 301–2, 306, 319
humanism, 7–8

Humphries, Jane, 61n183
husband/husbands, 12, 29, 55n93, 86, 99, 141, 143, 146, 149, 191, 202, 206–7, 214n31, 246, 255, 305–8, 329, 338–40, 366n19; absent, 145; approval/authorization of the, 154, 202; assistance to the, 206, 313–14, 337; authority of the, 13; and children, 29, 122; dead, 13; dependence on the, 168, 170, 205; division of responsibilities/work between husband and wife (*see* work: division of responsibilities/work between husband and wife); domination/rule by the, 123, 354, 360; ex-husband, 329; income of the, 96, 303; job/work of the, 14, 29, 33, 161, 314; support of the, 14, 94, 96, 237; wage of the, 231; and wife, 11–12, 14, 29, 32, 161, 206, 244, 251, 302, 304–5, 319, 360
husbandry, 53n69, 231; husbandmen, 52n63

Ichino, Andrea, 120, 126, 128
ideas on work. *See* work: ideas on
idleness, 8, 11, 189
il Cerchio Spezzato, 148
illegitimacy: illegitimate mothers, 32
illness, 7, 97, 172, 208, 253–54, 330
income: universal basic, 43, 66n229
(in)dependency: economic and legal (in)dependency, 11, 354
India, 37, 267, 277, 281–82; Parliament of, 283; Textile Labor Association, 282
Indonesia, 282
industry: development of, 30, 239n5, 354; districts of, 124–25; homework (*see* work: (home-work) industrial)
Industrial Revolution, 15, 25–27, 30–31, 61n183, 64n204, 122
industrialization, 26–28, 31–32, 61n183, 62n185, 118, 124–25, 128, 133n26, 133n34, 144, 161, 166, 173, 175, 357
Industrious Revolution, 26–30
inheritance, 41, 238, 266, 327, 330–32, 334–40, 366n19
in-law, 37, 40, 124, 163, 246–47, 249, 252–57, 257n, 266, 331–33, 335, 338–40, 344n40
Innichen (San Candido), 246–48, 261n39
inns, 10. *See also* taverns
Innsbruck, 250
Interdependence, 244

International Black Women for Wages for Housework, 21
International Congress of Domestic Economy, 142
International Feminist Collective, 21, 147, 153
International Labor Conference (ILC), 270, 273, 276, 278–79, 283, 285; Recommendation #123, 278–79
International Labor Conference of Labor Statisticians, 284
International Labor Organization (ILO), 37, 41, 65n214, 208, 266–67, 269–85; Committee of Experts on Domestic Work, 276; Consultative Committee, 271; Convention #3, 278; Convention #26, 273; Convention #33, 273; Convention #34, 273; Convention #100, 271; Convention #103, 278; Convention #149, 284; Convention #156, 279; Convention #171, 271; Convention #177, 41, 267, 272, 284; Convention #189, 41, 208, 267, 272, 284–85; Correspondence Committee on Women's Work, 274; Deputy Director, 276; Director-General, 269, 276–77; Employers, 278, 283, 285; Experts Committee, 277; Governing Board, 276; Office (the Office), 270; Programme/Program on Rural Women, 269, 280–82; Recommendation #123; Recommendation #157, 284; Recommendation #165, 279; Resolution Concerning Women's Work, 273; Social Protection Division, 284; Women's and Young Workers' Section, 269; Workers, 269–80, 283–85; World Employment Program, 280
International Labour Office (the Office). *See* International Labor Organization (ILO): Office (the Office)
International Labour Review, 276–77
International Women's Day, 146
internet, 4, 51n48
Iotti, Nilde, 144
Ironmonger, Duncan, 102
Italy: Christian Democracy, 144, 358; Civil Code of, 40, 206, 208, 302; Code of Commerce of, 190; Communism, 144, 358; Constitution of 1948, 1, 39, 143, 188, 190, 207, 209, 265, 296, 302, 309, 314; crisis in, 204, 210; economic miracle, 144, 207, 357; economically passive population, 193, 204; electoral law of

1882, 190, 202; Ente Nazionale Italiano per l'Organizzazione Scientifica del Lavoro (ENIOS), 141–42; expulsive fascist laws against women's work, 204; Feminism in, 19, 20, 86, 120, 122–25, 139–40, 145–48, 152–53, 203, 299, 357; *General Report of 1881*, 191, 198n; home-based industrial workers, 203, 208–9; home-based work in, 40, 266; hot autumn, 146; industrial triangle, 124; juridical capacity for married women, 202; Kingdom of, 190, 207; law in, 201, 208, 301, 305, 307–8, 311, 314, 318; law on equality among women and men in the labor market, 208; legal system of, 310; *Legge n. 76/2016*, 310, 312; maternity fund, 203; maternity leave, 203, 208; maternity protection, 203, 208; Movimento Sociale Italiano, 144; Penal Code of, 141; people attending to domestic tasks, 191, 193, 198n, 200; population censuses, 1, 34, 126, 141, 162, 184n9, 190–93, 198n, 199, 199n, 200–202, 204–5, 205n, 205, 207–9, 358; protective laws on women's and children's work, 203; reform of family law of 1975, 40, 265, 302; regulation of paid domestic work, 208; Republic of, 1–2, 143, 188, 190, 207, 209; Ritas of, 148; Socialism, 144, 203, 358; Supreme Court of (Corte di Cassazione), 307, 311, 314–15, 318, 323n35; Third Italy, 124, 350, 356–57; women according to the Constitution, 1, 143, 188, 207, 209, 302, 314; women in, 1, 21, 40, 53n71, 122, 157n44, 202, 358; women's admission to professions and public employment, 202; women's citizenship, 1, 207; women's enfranchisement, 202

Jacobsson, Benny, 235
James, Selma, 20–21, 57n126, 86, 123, 147
Japan, 27
Jeffreys, William, 245
Jevons, William Stanley, 96, 98, 352–53
Jhabvala, Renana, 283
Johnstone, Elizabeth (ILO Coordinator of Women, Youth, and Aging), 278
Joseph II (Emperor of Austria), 260n34
Judaism, 26

Kendrick, John, 101
Kennedy, Duncan, 321n2

kinship, 125, 246, 250–51, 257, 333, 341, 343n23
Kocka, Jürgen, 45n2
Korea, 276
Kreuzberge (Passo Monte Croce), 247
Kuliscioff, Anna, 203
Kuznets, Simon, 101, 108n55
Kyrk, Hazel, 97, 101

labor, 5, 10, 13, 15, 19, 21, 23, 27–28, 42, 44, 48n23, 50, 51n49, 85, 91–96, 108n53, 114–15, 119, 127, 129, 139, 142–43, 148–49, 165, 167, 172–76, 178, 180, 182, 190, 206, 234, 236, 243–44, 270–7, 280, 284–85, 298, 311, 321n2, 336–37, 349–53, 355, 357–60, 362–64, 366n18, 366n21; ability to, 20; as alienation (*Entäusserung*), 8–9, 51n48; child, 30–31, 273; development of the concept of the division of, 19; division of, 21, 66n229, 86, 89, 97, 117–18, 130, 140, 148, 157n38, 180, 243–44, 279, 304, 306, 349, 366n21; domestic, 20, 86, 95–96, 100, 121, 123, 139, 148, 161, 165, 167, 172, 179, 185n27, 272, 278, 351, 357, 362, 363; family, 274, 278–79, 281, 358; female, 147, 163, 165, 167, 174–75, 178, 180–82, 266, 355; force, 5, 19, 35–36, 42, 63–64n200, 94, 99–100, 116, 118, 147, 163, 180, 199n, 208, 279, 356–57, 365n8, 366n16; force participation rates, 35–36, 163, 182; forms of, 3–4, 273; glorification of, 8–9, 139; hand, 25; history of, 43, 182; home, 269, 272–74, 278, 280, 284–85; home-based, 41–42, 266, 269, 278, 283; household, 277, 318, 356; international division of reproductive, 19; *laborare* and *facere* or *fabricari*, 5–6; labor-based societies, 9; labor-power, 19–20, 86, 121, 147–49, 272; male, 30, 181; market, 18, 26, 28, 35, 91, 94–95, 103, 148, 174, 177, 185n19, 204, 208, 210, 282, 300, 303, 306, 310–11, 320, 350, 362, 365n8, 366n19; non-productive/unproductive, 17, 166–67, 351–52, 356; paid, 35, 185n27, 285, 353, 355, 362, 366n19; productive, 99, 300, 350–54, 357–58, 361; productive versus reproductive labor distinction, 86, 123, 350; products of, 5, 96; reduction of labor time, 9; reproductive, 19, 41, 147, 272, 275,

280–81, 284, 353; sexual division of, 19, 95, 114, 147, 155n6, 166–67, 175, 177, 180, 214n37, 352, 354; as social status providing access to citizenship, 8; standards, 41, 270, 272, 275, 284–85; subsistence, 281; surplus, 117; unpaid, 93–94, 100, 105, 357, 350; value of, 7, 353; wage/waged, 3, 9, 18, 23, 28, 121, 154, 279, 317, 350, 358–61, 366n21; women's, 35, 147–49, 178–79, 267, 275, 279, 281, 364. *See also* work
Landefeld, J. Steven, 102
Lanzinger, Margareth, 37, 163, 257, 260n33, 261n39, 355, 359
Laslett, Barbara, 115
Latin language, 5, 249
Latour, Bruno, 256
law/laws, 4, 15, 39–41, 50, 92, 96, 103, 119, 156n18, 169–70, 179, 202–3, 205–6, 208, 246, 255, 265–66, 276, 295–308, 310–14, 316–18, 321, 321–22nn1–2, 327, 332–37, 340, 343n23, 354, 358, 366n19; canon and state, 246, 249, 261n47; case, 89, 91, 307, 310–11, 313, 315–16, 318, 358; civil, 4, 40, 250, 266, 312–13, 327; common, 96, 295, 307, 309–10, 312–13, 316, 334; contract, 295, 321; development of the legal system, 299, 308, 318, 321, 341, 343n22; electoral, 190, 202; existing, 170; family, 39–40, 265, 295–302, 304, 306, 308–9, 312, 317–21, 321–22n2, 328, 330, 334, 336, 355, 358; labor, 276, 285, 321n2; legal constructions of female work, 188; municipal, 169; private, 295–98, 319, 321, 322n2, 358; Roman, 13; sumptuary, 12; welfare, 319–20
League of Nations, 156n12, 202, 270
Lebanon, 270
Lee Downs, Laura, 364
Le Goff, Jacques, 5–6
Leiden, 29, 60n174
leisure, 6–7, 15, 23, 25, 38, 98, 189, 206, 212n10, 275, 300, 361–62
Le Play, Pierre Guillaume Frédéric, 175–76
Leroy Beaulieu, Paul, 96
letters: cover, 91; and evidence, 250; of recommendation, 248; and reports, 250; supplication, 249, 252
Liberalism, 114, 116, 154, 166–68, 170, 172, 175, 180–81, 246, 261n47, 283, 296, 306, 320, 351, 354–56, 362–63;

liberal theorists, 18, 89, 93, 96, 99 (*see also* theorists)
Libertarianism, 296
life-cycle, 13
Lindberg, Erik, 235
Lindström, Dag, 236
Ling, Sofia, 233, 235
literati, 189
livelihood, 250
Locke, John, 18, 93, 351, 365n4, 366n18
London, 147, 245; textile crafts in, 25
long-term perspective, 4
Los Angeles: domestic workers in, 19
Lotta Femminista, 20, 86, 120–22, 146–47, 149, 153
Loutfi, Martha, 280–81
love, 19, 22–23, 39, 41, 58n140, 85, 157n44, 204, 237, 243–44, 252, 265–66, 272, 284, 296, 305, 310–12, 362–63
Luther: Lutherans, 7–8, 227

maintenance, 17–18, 93, 95, 105, 182, 256, 303, 306, 310, 313, 352
male activities, 2, 4, 30, 166, 178, 182, 184n11, 199n, 208, 236
Malthus, Thomas Robert, 94, 99, 119
Marazzi, Christian, 210
Marche, 124
Marella, Maria Rosaria, 39–40, 265–66, 321, 358
Maria Theresa/Theresia (Empress of Austria), 260n34
Marinella, Lucrezia, 11
marital status, 11–14, 32–33, 161–62, 168–69, 228–29, 233–34, 237, 247, 317; divorced men, 11; divorced women, 11; married men, 11, 180, 234, 237–38; married women, 11–13, 28–29, 32, 35, 61n174, 90, 94, 96–97, 99–100, 103–4, 161, 171–72, 176–77, 179–80, 184n11, 185n21, 202, 205–6, 229, 233–35, 237–38, 337, 356–57, 366n19; separated men, 11; separated women, 11; unmarried couples, 11, 304, 309–10, 312; unmarried single men, 11, 13, 180, 234; unmarried single women, 11, 13, 100, 103, 171, 176, 179, 233–35, 251, 254; widow/widows, 13, 179, 234, 245, 251, 259n16; widower/widowers, 246, 248, 251, 253–55, 259n16, 261n39; widowhood and impoverishment, 13

market: market/family divide, 39, 298–301, 305, 322n2; recourse to, 11; substitutes, 3, 301; work (*see* work: market)
Markham, Gervase, 52n63
Markkola, Pirjo, 233
marriage, 12–14, 29, 37, 44, 53n69, 54n84, 146, 162–63, 170, 177, 211, 234, 237–38, 246–47, 250–55, 257, 261n39, 271, 302–3, 305, 307, 309, 319–20, 333, 338–39, 344n40, 358–61; bars, 104, 366n19; as a contract, 333; crisis, 306, 318, 320; delayed, 94; democratization of, 359–60; discipline of, 312; dispensation records, 250; dispensation requests, 247–53, 255–56, 260n31, 260n38; early/late, 27; and family status, 11–14, 25, 32–33, 161–62, 168–69, 173, 228–29, 233–34, 237, 245–46, 317, 360; impediments, 260n34; Marriage Patent of 1783, 260n34 (*see also* Joseph II; Maria Theresa/Theresia); marital property, 302, 307–8; "natural society" based on, 39, 265; projects, 248, 250, 252, 260n39; remarriage, 246. *See also* husband/husbands; marital status; wife/wives
Marshall, Alfred, 97–99, 352–53
Martini, Manuela, 40, 44
Marvin v. Marvin, 309
Marx, Karl, 9, 15, 18–19, 24, 50, 62n184, 86, 115, 117–19, 121, 128, 130, 352, 365n8
Marxism: feminism, 18–19, 85, 114, 116, 149; theory, 18, 86, 114–15
Massachusetts, 100, 106, 108n53, 356; Bureau of Statistics of Labor, 100, 108n53; censuses, 100, 356
maternity protection, 203, 208, 271, 278
Mazzini, Giuseppe, 189
McKendrick, Neil, 29–30, 62n185
Méda, Dominique, 51n48
Mediterranean Sea, 10, 14, 44; economies of, 364
men, 9, 11–12, 17–18, 21, 24–26, 91–95, 99, 103–5, 122–23, 146, 157n44, 166, 170, 173, 177–78, 184n10, 184n14, 189, 193, 202, 207, 209, 214n27, 214n33, 231–34, 236, 251, 271, 275–76, 280–81, 299, 314, 350–51, 354, 360; activities of, 192, 200, 228, 231, 234, 247; adult, 24, 27, 34, 162, 193; and children, 94, 105, 231, 366n21; free, 7; and marriage, 14, 29, 94, 180, 228, 234, 237–38, 251, 360;

wages of, 89, 99, 103, 105, 121, 166, 182; and women, 3, 10–11, 13–14, 16, 30–37, 39, 42, 64n204, 86, 89, 92, 94–95, 97, 99, 102–5, 126–27, 140, 161–63, 176, 178–79, 192–93, 208–10, 227, 231–35, 237, 243–47, 271, 281, 350, 354–55, 358–61, 366n21; working, 23, 27, 33, 62n184, 103, 139, 176, 179, 192–93, 232, 235, 237, 244–45, 272, 279, 354; young, 359, 361
Menapace, Lidia, 153
merchant/merchants, 26, 246, 254, 261n39, 366n21; families, 12; households of, 12, 350; middle class, 329; navy, 169; wives of, 12
Métall, R. A., 269–70
Mexico, 277
Middle Ages/medieval, 3, 6–7, 9–10, 12–13, 15, 26, 38, 48n28, 61n183, 265, 353
Mies, Maria, 37–38, 267, 275
Mill, John Stuart, 96
Miller, Frieda, 274–77,
Minnesota, 305; Appeal Court of, 305
Miss Morland. *See* Jane Austen
model of the three-orders society—*bellatores, oratores, laboratores*, 6
modernization: economic and social modernization, 42
monastic world, 6
money, 15, 23, 142, 152, 179, 253, 255, 282, 311, 317, 363; earning, 105, 214n36, 307; as identity, 154; money-lending, 311–12; no money, 312; paper, 153; "pin money", 103; transfer of, 310–11; and wages, 152–53, 179; women and, 30, 96, 154, 214n36; work exchanged for, 16
Monteillet-Geffroy, Mélanie, 337, 343–44n36–37
more uxorio, 311
Mozzoni, Anna Maria, 203
multidisciplinary approach, 4
Multinational Comparative Time-Budget Research Project, 101
Mussolini, Benito, 357

Nairobi, 101
Nancy: Court of, 337
Nantes, 14
Napolitano, Janet (Gov. of Arizona), 89
national income accounts. *See* Great Britain: national income accounts; statistics:

national income accounts; United States: national income accounts
National Woman Suffrage Convention, 21, 96
naturalization, 22, 40, 87, 117, 166, 173, 244, 265, 269; of gender roles, 243
nature, 16, 22–23, 50, 148; dominion over, 16; forces of, 50; intervention on, 16; as man's work, 9; natural obligations, 39, 87, 265, 311; "nature commands", 148; productions of, 50; realm of, 31, 90, 161
negotium, 7
Netherlands, 28, 184n9; Holland, 12; Low Countries, 28
New Delhi: office of the Internationa Labor Organizazion (ILO) of, 269
New Home Economics, 2, 97–98, 301
New South Wales: Census, 99
New York, 147; ILO's International Organizations Section in, 269; Wages for Housework Committee of, 153
New Zealand, 101
NGO. *See* Non-Governmental Organization
nobility: noblewomen, 11–12; struggle against, 189
Non-Governmental Organization, 270, 283, 285
Normativer Schaden, 316
Norway, 101, 184n9

Oakley, Ann, 140, 300
obligation/obligations, 18, 26, 41, 266, 284, 305, 310, 313, 319–20, 330, 351; absolute, 40, 266, 330, 332; contractual, 311; to contribute, 302, 306, 318–19; family, 4, 359; legal, 40, 328, 333; moral, 40–41, 85, 90, 254, 266, 310–11, 351; mutual, 304, 319; of mutual cooperation, 302; natural, 39, 87, 265, 311; pecuniary, 319; sense of, 254; solidarities and, 39, 265; traditional, 123
occupation: occupational statistics, 248. *See also* work: statistics
Organisation for Economic Co-operation and Development (OECD), 102
office/offices, 4, 20, 22, 26, 37, 39, 41, 93, 100–101, 130, 149, 168–69, 178, 183n6, 189, 208, 250, 266, 269–70, 276, 283
Ogilvie, Sheilagh, 26, 28, 227
Oja, Linda, 231
open house, 236
ora et labora, pray and work, 6

organization (act of organizing), 13, 95, 143, 270, 282, 350; capitalist, 121; of domestic life, 277; of domestic work, 140; family, 247; of family care, 89; of household work, 15; of housekeeping, 142; of labor, 142, 176; practical, 4; of production, 128, 273; self-organization, 282; social, 95, 175, 178, 185n33, 350; of work, 256
organization/organizations (group of people), 4, 21, 44, 147, 155n8, 235, 269, 271, 281; mass, 146; rural women's, 282
original sin, 5, 353. *See also* biblical curse; curse that followed the original sin
Östholm, Hanna, 233
Östman, Ann-Catrin, 232
otium, 7
Owen, Robert, 95
Oxford: Centre for Time Use Research at University of, 102; Multinational Time Use Studies (MTUS) archive in, 102; University of, 102

pain, 5, 8–10, 15–16, 51n49, 93, 232, 329. *See also* suffering; toil
Paci, Massimo, 120
Padua, 20–21, 86, 120, 122–25, 147, 149
Pagnossin-Aligasakis, Elisabetta, 101
Paik, In, 91
Pakistan, 282
Palmer, Ingrid, 280
Papal State, 189
Paris, 12, 26, 44, 147, 210, 327–28, 341
Parreñas, Rhacel, 19
Passo Monte Croce. *See* Kreuzberge
Pateman, Carole, 354, 360
Paul, Saint, 7
payment, 176, 193, 226, 234, 253–54, 311, 326, 330, 334, 358, 362; of debt, 328; for family work, 326, 341; to housewives, 22, 357; "lump sum payment", 336; regulation of, 208; "repayment of costs", 337
Pennsylvania. *See* Rendell, Ed (Gov. of Pennsylvania)
Perrot, Michelle, 32
Pescarolo, Alessandra, 18, 85, 87, 130, 350, 356, 363
petitions. *See* source/sources: petitions
Philippines, 282
Picchio, Antonella, 21
Piccone, Clara, 139
pietè filiale, 40, 266, 333, 343n29, 343n32

Pihl, Christopher, 232
Pinarella di Cervia, 147
Pinchbeck, Ivy, 25
Pistelli, Rosalba, 152
Pius IX, 252
Plumb, John Harold, 29
pluriactivity, 171, 231, 235, 244, 249, 257
ponein and *ergazesthai*, 5
poor/poors. *See* poverty: poor/poors
Porciani, Leone, 56n104
Porto Marghera, 120
Portugal, 233
position: social, 7, 11, 329
possessions, 12–13, 95
Poullain de la Barre, François, 15, 93
poverty, 7, 10, 14, 98, 180–81; poor/poors, 7, 10, 13, 17, 23, 28, 37–38, 43, 97, 119, 199n, 209, 235, 250, 254–55, 267, 272, 281–82, 338, 352, 358, 360–61
Prato: Istituto Datini in, 248
precariousness, 207, 209–10
Prescod, Margaret, 21
present/present times, 3, 4, 23, 40, 85, 96, 108n53, 129, 164, 199n, 237, 260n32, 307, 328, 332, 350, 364
preserving goods. *See* goods: preserving
printers: 3D, 4, 87, 129
privatization, 115, 121, 123, 244, 295, 298
producers, 12, 38, 50, 86, 119, 122–23, 128, 148, 154, 231, 313, 338, 355
production, 2, 9–11, 15, 18–20, 25–28, 30–31, 35, 42, 50, 63n200, 86, 93, 95, 115–18, 127–30, 142, 145, 147–49, 154, 166, 177, 238, 261n48, 272–75, 278, 280–82, 284–85, 300–301, 306, 313, 317, 326, 350–53, 355, 359–62, 364, 366n16; capitalist, 20, 28, 117, 123; dichotomy of production/reproduction, 9, 18, 20–21, 85–86, 114, 116, 123, 128, 147–48, 154, 299–304, 308, 310, 313, 318, 320, 350; domestic, 3, 116, 123, 326, 336, 341, 357; forms/modes of, 50, 86, 123, 125, 128; of goods, 27, 30, 121, 129, 172, 299, 301, 351; household, 29, 36, 97–98, 100–101, 316–7, 359, 360, 366n21; for the market, 3, 19, 24, 28, 36, 64n206, 97, 115, 172, 281, 350
productive versus reproductive labor distinction. *See also* labor: productive versus reproductive labor distinction; work
productive work. *See* work: productive

productivity, 17, 40, 64n204, 97, 129–30, 300, 317; high, 64n204, 128; increase in, 27, 51n48, 130, 155n6; low, 64n204, 90, 128; of work, 128, 308
profession/professions, 17, 23, 34, 162–63, 168–69, 171–73, 179, 184n9, 185n24, 185n29, 185n30, 191–92, 198n, 199n, 200, 202, 207, 257, 337, 339
property, 96, 184n14, 199n, 238, 255, 257, 310, 318–19, 321, 360, 365n4; assets, 326, 337; family's, 125; joint property rule, 318; marital, 302, 307–8; private, 9, 321, 351; rights, 94; suppression of private, 9
prostitution, 2, 32, 185n30, 198n, 273, 315, 358–59
Protestant Reformation, 7–8, 13, 26. *See also* Luther: Lutherans
proto-industry, 26–27, 119
private sphere, 140–41, 143, 243, 297, 354. *See also* domestic sphere
private/public, 24, 31, 296, 327, 353, 361–62. *See also* separate spheres
Prytz, Cristina, 233
public sphere, 126, 140–41, 147–48, 243, 297, 299, 361

register/registers: Diocese of Brixen (Bressanone), 250; electoral, 167; parish, 248
Reid, Margaret, 97, 101
remuneration, 38, 115, 180, 193, 265, 336; equal, 271, 276, 278; for housework, 96, 100, 147, 300, 307, 318–19; no remuneration, 2, 100, 312
Renahy, Nicolas, 340
Rendell, Ed (Gov. of Pennsylvania), 89
Rens, Jeff, 276
rentier, 189, 198n, 356
reports: *Report by the Commission on Economic Performance and Social Progress Revisited*, 102; *Women in a Changing World report*, 278. *See also* Great Britain; International Labor Organization (ILO); Massachussetts
reproduction; 9–10, 15–16, 18, 20, 86, 115–21, 124, 126, 147, 149, 154, 166, 176–77, 181, 261n48, 281, 299–300, 350, 357, 365n8, 366n16; social, 18–19, 115–17, 147–48, 166, 272, 280, 329, 357, 363; *See also* production: dichotomy of production/reproduction

reproductive labors. *See* labor: reproductive
reproductive work. *See* work: reproductive
Rescigno, Pietro, 317
resource/resources, 127, 171, 234, 254, 280, 302, 306, 331, 334, 339, 357, 360; allocation of, 28; of domestic work, 21–22, 141; economic, 249, 316; educational, 64n200; family, 141, 176, 182, 316; immaterial, 120; lack of, 166, 254; material, 120, 234; natural, 117; political, 234; workforce as, 118
responsibility/responsibilities, 12, 14, 89–96, 105, 139, 166, 170, 183n6, 244, 248, 254, 279, 333, 339, 351; care, 89, 90, 92–93, 104; division of, 12; economic, 176; family (*see* family: responsibilities); family responsibility discrimination, 90, 92–93, 95, 104, 279; legal, 285; maternal, 96; sharing of, 332; women's, 53n72, 97, 232–33, 245, 278–79
Ricardo, David, 15, 18
Riom: Court of Appeal in, 335
Rittich, Kerry, 321–22n2
Roberts, Alfred, 276
Robinson, John, 102
robotization, 43
Rocco, Alfredo, 141
Rome, 19, 130, 154, 247, 250–51; army of Ancient, 7; Campo de' Fiori in, 146; culture of Ancient, 7; domestic workers in, 19; feminist movement in, 146, 152; law of Ancient, 13
Roosevelt, Franklin Delano, 104
Rosselli, Anna, 131n
Rossi-Doria, Anna, 143
Rouen, 26, 43
rural society, 11, 162, 258n5
Russia, 184n9

sacrifice, 254, 273, 307–9, 334, 343n29, 358
sailors, 14
Saint-Simon, Henri de, 95
San Candido. *See* Innichen
Sarti, Raffaella, 34, 42, 44, 64n209, 162, 210, 353, 356
satellite accounts. *See* statistics: satellite accounts
Say, Jean Baptiste, 18, 94
Scandinavia, 13, 230, 349, 363–64; economy of, 364; society of, 231
scarcity, 130
Schmidt, Ariadne, 28

Schumpeter, Joseph Alois, 116
Scott, Joan, 31, 117, 165, 185n33
Seccombe, Wally, 123
Second World War. *See* World War II
Segal, Nancy, 92
Self-Employment Women's Association (SEWA). *See* Gujarat
self-interest, 17, 93, 105
self-possessing individual, 351, 354
Sentuti, Annalisa, 40
separate spheres, 22–24, 31, 61n183, 237. *See also* private/public
conduct literature, 11
sermons, 11
servant/servants: condition, 204; live-in servants/live-in staff, 11, 14; maidservants, 245–46, 248, 254, 256; new servants, 210; outdoor servants, 11
service versus productive labor distinction, 243, 351–53, 355, 359
service/services, 19, 98, 100, 102, 115, 117–18, 121, 129, 145, 205n, 205, 236, 243, 273, 315, 320, 335, 337–38, 343n36, 351–53, 355, 357, 359–63; care, 129, 278, 361; civil, 104; domestic (*see* domestic service); free, 148; goods and, 10, 36, 64n206, 121–22, 129–30, 172, 281, 301, 353; housewives', 100–101; paid, 108n53; provision of, 172, 174, 280, 337; public, 42; reproductive, 119; social, 121, 148–49, 269, 280; statistical, 168; unpaid, 353, 362, 365n8; unproductive, 94
servilization of work. *See* work: servilization of
sexual contract. *See* fraternal sexual contract
sexual division of labor. *See* labor: sexual division of
shadow economies. *See* economy/economies: shadow
sharecroppers' households. *See* household: sharecroppers'
Shepard, Alex, 12
shop/shops, 4, 10, 14, 24, 29, 39, 41, 186n45, 208, 248, 355
siblings, 19, 40–41, 266, 327, 329–31, 333–35, 340
Simon, Jules, 62n185
Singh, Andrea, 269
skills, 53n69, 62n184, 146, 248, 275, 329, 360; artistic, 275; business, 254; culinary, 118; language, 247; natural, 140;

professional, 40; women's, 13, 37, 254. *See also* ability/abilities; capability/capabilities
Skype, 129
slave/slaves, 7, 121, 146, 365n4; new, 210
slave work. *See* work: slave
Smart, William, 99–100
Smith, Adam, 15, 17–18, 85, 93, 117, 130, 351–52
smuggling: of alcohol, 2; of tobacco, 2
Social Democracy, 140, 155n6, 364
social position. *See* position: social
social status. *See* status: social
Socialism, 95, 144, 203, 278, 355, 358
son/sons, 13, 40, 52n63, 103, 124, 154, 171, 180, 261n39, 327–29, 333, 335–36, 338–40, 354; education of, 121, 124
source/sources, 11, 32–37, 39, 98, 161–63, 174, 176, 197, 199, 201, 205, 227–32, 244–46, 248–51, 255–57, 349; biased, 36–38, 163–64; bookkeeping records 249; church reports, 250; comparison of, 36–37, 256; data, 98; diaries, 228–29, 235, 249; historical, 37, 185n33, 227–28, 231, 235–36, 249; material, 245, 249, 253, 256–57, 260n31; municipal sources, 186n34; petitions, 228, 231; production of, 248, 364; on women, 32, 161, 163, 236, 244, 266
Spain, 34, 163, 166–67, 171, 182, 183n9, 184n14, 356, 358; Census Office, 169; censuses, 34, 163, 165–75, 178–79, 181, 183n6, 184n9, 356, 358; Commission for Social Reform, 178; Liberal Constitution of 1812, 170; Municipal Law, 169; National Censuses of the Population (NCP), 165–67, 173–74, 181; Royal Decree for the execution of the 1837 census, 168; Surveys of the Active Population (*Encuestas de Población Activa*), 172–73; women's salaries, 165
specialization, 11, 26, 90–91, 126, 154, 162, 231, 237
Spence, Michael, 129
spheres, private and public, 23, 140, 147, 243, 361
spouse/spouses, 14, 32, 91, 124, 252, 298, 302–9, 312, 318–20, 326, 334, 336–38, 343n26; assistance between, 40, 92, 266, 309, 333; children's, 338; collaborating, 40, 266; equality of, 298, 301–2, 306, 309, 312, 319; weaker, 306–8; as workers, 29, 40, 104, 266, 302, 331, 336; working-class, 333. *See also* husband/husbands; marital status; wife/wives
State v. Bachmann, 305
statistics: construction of housewives as economically passive, 188; constructions of female work, 35, 178; discrimination in, 90; economic statistics on GDP, 5; on labor forces, 5; national income accounts, 90, 98, 101; and population censuses (records on female LFP), 32, 161; satellite accounts, 2, 102; social, 165–67, 173, 181, 185n33; sources, 248; that include unpaid domestic and care work and calculate its economic value, 2
status: social, 8, 232, 235, 237, 250
Steinbiedersdorf, 248
Stoicism, 7, 49n32
stepmother, 252
store, 246–47
suffering, 5, 330. *See also* pain; toil
sumptuary laws. *See* law: sumptuary
supplication letters. *See* letters; source/sources
supply/supplies, 15, 18, 28–29, 85, 91, 93–94, 105, 276, 282
support duty, 328–35, 337–38, 340, 343n22, 343n26
suppression of private property. *See* property: suppression of private
surplus value. *See* value: surplus
Sweden, 11, 13, 101, 228–30, 233; gender division of work in, 237; Kingdom of, 256; marriage in, 162; Reformation/Lutheran, 7, 227; sources of, 11, 162; specialization of society in, 162; women in, 234
Switzerland, 184n9
Szalai, Alexander, 101

taverns, 10–11. *See also* inns
Taylor, Harriet, 96
Taylorism, 22
Tealdy, Lorenzo, 142
temporary jobs. *See* work: temporary jobs
terminology: Australian, 99; blanket, 257; changes of, 100
Thailand, 282
theorists: political, 18, 351; social 18, 174
third state, 7
Thomas, Keith, 56n103
Thompson, Edward Palmer, 239n5
Thompson, William, 95
Tilly, Charles, 129

Tilly, Chris, 129
time: time-thieves, 7, 227; time wasted, 8
toil, 5–6, 8–9, 14–16, 96, 108n53, 114, 189, 191, 201, 210, 350, 355. *See also* pain; suffering
Tornabuoni, Lietta, 149, 154
trabajo. See work: *trabajo*
trabalho. See work: *trabalho*
Trabut, Loïc, 343n24
trade/trades, 28–29, 168–69, 171–72, 175–77, 179, 191, 231, 233, 245, 253–54, 273–74; family, 14; in goods and services, 236; slave, 365n4; small, 244; trader, 28–29, 38; trades [*corpi di mestiere*], 6; tradesmen, 18; wives and, 14
trade unions, 95, 103, 140, 271, 273, 283–85, 355; International Confederation of Trade Unions (ICTU), 283; International Union of Food, Agricultural, Hotel, Restaurant, Catering, Tobacco and Allied Workers Association (IUF), 283; National Trades Union, 95; Textile Labor Association (Gujarat, India), 282; Transport and General Workers Union, 276
transmission, 10, 123, 297, 326, 339
travail. See work: *travail*
travailler and *ouvrer*, 5
Trento, 148, 260nn32–33
trepalium, 5
tripartism, 284
Turnaturi, Gabriella, 144
Tuscany, 124
Tyrol/Tirol, 37, 163, 260n32; North, 260n32; South, 246, 260n32

Ulbrich, Claudia, 245, 248, 258n5
Ulysses, 7
Umbria, 124
underemployment, 209
unemployment, 43, 51n48, 206, 209, 273, 366n19
United Kingdom, 85, 101, 103; House of Lords, 307–8; household work in, 85; Matrimonial Causes Act of 1973, 307
United Nations (UN), 102, 115, 270, 276, 278–79, 281–82, 283, 343n24; Commission on the Status of Women, 278; Decade for Women, 279, 283; Economic and Social Council, 270; Food and Agricultural Organization, 281; Statistics Division, 101; System of Economic-Environmental Accounting (SEEA), 102; World Conference on Women, 101; World Food Program, 281
United States, 19, 21, 34, 85–86, 89–91, 95–98, 100–103, 105–6, 126, 140, 184n10, 185n21, 185n25, 185n31, 274, 278, 309, 358, 361, 363; Bureau of Labor Statistics, 103, 108n53; censuses, 97–98, 100, 126, 184n10, 185n25, 185n31, 356; Civil Rights Act of 1964; Equal Opportunities Employment Commission, 91; family responsibility employment discrimination (FRED), 89–90; Feminism in, 19–21, 86, 96, 299; GDP of, 102; General Social Survey, 105; household rationalization in, 140; household work, 85, 356; housewife-consumer model in, 143; legal system of, 308–9; married women in, 90, 97, 100, 103–4, 185n21, 356; National Bureau of Economic Research, 100; national income accounts, 98, 101; Resolution Concerning Women's Work, 273; The Married Women's Property Acts, 96; women without children, 91; Women's Bureau, 103, 274, 276
universal basic income. *See* income: universal basic
unjust enrichment, 41, 266, 327, 332, 334–37, 340
unmarried single women. *See* marital status: unmarried single women
unoccupied women. *See* women: unoccupied
unpaid and paid care- and housework, 3. *See also* work: (care work) unpaid and paid care- and housework
unpaid domestic work. *See* domestic work: unpaid
unpaid labor. *See* labor: unpaid
unpaid market work. *See* work: (unpaid work) unpaid market work
unpaid wives. *See* wife/wives: unpaid
unpaid work. *See* work: unpaid
unproductive activities, 3
unproductive work. *See* work: unproductive
U-shaped curve, 35–36, 63n200, 163
Uppsala: University of, 238, 249
Ure, Andrew, 95

vagrancy: vagrant/vagrants, 7, 33, 99
Val Gardena. *See* Gröden

value/values (economic value/values), 15–17, 20, 87, 98, 100, 103, 115, 117–18, 122, 128–30, 153–54, 281, 301–303, 316, 320, 352, 357, 363; creation of, 48n23; economic, 2, 30, 38–39, 85, 87, 89–90, 102, 126, 161, 269–70, 301–2, 306–7, 314; exchange, 126, 153, 300; of home-based activities, 39; of household production, 36, 98, 100–101; of housework, 2, 140, 308, 314–15, 317–18; labor theory of, 15, 93, 95, 352; market, 3, 35, 56n103, 118, 314; qualitative, 128; surplus, 18, 20, 56n115, 149; of time, 35, 317; of unpaid care and housework, 2; use, 125, 126, 128–29, 153, 301

value/values (principles and importance), 4, 17–19, 37, 39, 42, 87, 94, 116, 128, 145, 148, 244, 272, 296, 314, 326, 338, 352, 357, 363; cultural, 183n2; dominant, 297; family, 358; market, 300; of nobility, 189; non-humane, 358; nutritional, 141; of the rural world, 145; social, 115, 320; of solidarity, 310, 358; system of, 124; of use, 122; of work, 5–7, 15–16, 142, 154, 189, 243, 266

van de Pol, Lotte, 244
van den Heuvel, Danielle, 28, 60n174
van der Linden, Marcel, 45n1
Van Der Werf, Ysbrand, 28
Van Kleeck, Mary, 103
van Nederveen Meerkerk, Elise, 28, 60n174
Veneto, 124, 247, 356
Venice, 11
verb-oriented method, 33, 162, 227–28, 236, 256
Vitali, Ornello, 200–201
Vives, Jean Louis, 7
vocabulary of work. *See* work: vocabulary of
Voralberg, 250

wage/wages: deferred, 41, 266, 327, 331–32, 336–37, 359; to/for housewives, 2, 140, 147, 149, 270; labor (*see* labor: wage/waged); living, 103–4; minimum, 90, 103, 179–80, 273; Wages Due Lesbians organization, 21; Wages for Housework movement, 21–22, 86–87, 96, 147, 153, 218n93, 357–58
Wales: census, 33, 99, 216n58; work rates in, 28
Walker, Kathryn, 101
Walras, Léon, 352–53

Waring, Marilyn, 101
Webb, Sydney, 179–80
Weber, Florence, 40, 266, 341, 343n24, 359, 363
Weber, Max, 8, 340
Weisdorf, Jacob Louis, 28
welfare, 7, 16, 39, 42, 115, 140, 144, 178, 182, 205n, 282, 284, 300, 308, 318–20, 338, 358–61, 364; state, 8, 147, 209, 357, 362–64; post-1945 welfare state, 363
Western world, 6, 17, 43, 125, 128, 237, 277, 353
Wheeler, Anna, 95
White v. White, 307
widow / widows. *See* marital status: widow/widower
widower/widowers. *See* marital status: widower/widowers
widowhood, 13. *See also* marital status
widowhood and impoverishment. *See also* marital status
Wiesner, Merry, 26
wife/wives, 12–14, 18, 23–24, 33, 37, 39, 53n69, 62n185, 94, 96, 99–100, 104, 139, 145, 162, 176–77, 181, 184n11, 185n19, 204–5, 213n14, 232, 253–55, 281, 284, 303–9, 314–15, 318, 320, 327–28, 330, 333, 335, 338–40, 352, 354, 357; and children, 14, 29, 33, 94, 180; and daughters, 34, 94, 100, 214n36, 362; deceased, 37, 163, 246–47, 259n16; division of responsibilities/work between husband and (*see* work: division of responsibilities/work between husband and wife); as housewives, 32, 161; and husband (*see* husband/husbands: and wife); inactive, 180; as mothers, 23, 31, 308, 316, 366n16; peasant, 356; responsibilities of, 12; unpaid, 29, 36, 64n206, 269, 277; in relation to work, 28, 55n93, 90, 117, 119, 121–22, 206, 269 358. *See also* marital status
Williams, Joan, 92
Wirtschafterin, 253
women: as accountants for the family enterprise/for the household, 12–13, 25, 254; activities of, 2, 25, 30, 37, 166–67, 178, 182, 184n11, 199, 202, 207–8, 214n37, 228, 236, 252; alone, 13, 98; barred from many activities, 11, 35; classified as people supported by the family, 34, 163, 192, 200, 213n25; cross-dressing,

11; and development, 2, 19, 30–31, 36, 63–64n200, 143, 147, 271, 275, 278, 281–83; in development, 282; economic contribution to GDP of, 36; education for, 12; engaged in paid extra-domestic work, 32, 34, 41–42, 200, 266; as family heads, 13–14, 24; female labor force participation, 35, 63–64n200, 99, 181, 279; fishers, 11, 229; and guilds, 11, 13–14, 25–26, 29; hunters, 11, 229; as independent traders, 29; legal constructions of female work, 188; percentage in the total economically active population, 200–201, 209; replacing (dead, absent) men, 13, 202, 247; rural, 201, 269, 279–83; skills of, 13; unoccupied, 33, 99, 185n19, 356; as workers, 25, 31, 36, 122, 125, 142–43, 176–78, 180, 203–4, 210, 271–72, 274–75, 278, 356; as workers with family responsibilities, 89, 91–96, 104–5, 269, 271–72, 278–79; working independently from their husbands, 14

work: as alienation, 8–9, 51n48; *Arbeit* (German), 5; *arbeiten* and *werken* (German), 5; as an ascetic exercise, 6; atypical jobs, 209; in the Bible, 5; care work, 2–3, 16–19, 22, 38, 41–42, 44, 66n229, 85–86, 106, 119, 177, 188, 210, 218n93, 244, 266, 272, 284, 298, 300–304, 306–7, 313, 316–17, 319–20, 326–27, 335–38, 341n1, 343n24, 362–63; categories of, 11, 16, 116, 162, 229, 237; concurrent concepts of, 7; contempt for those who must, 189; decent work for domestic workers, 41, 208, 267, 284; definition of, 86, 148, 349; division of, 11, 13, 19, 26, 235, 237; division of responsibilities/work between husband and wife, 11–12; domestic service (*see* domestic service); as essential component in the identity of men, 193; etymology of, 5; everyday, 257; extra-domestic, 29, 32, 41–42, 62n185, 162, 200, 203, 208, 266; factory (*see* factory: work); feminization of, 42, 188, 209–10; forced, 7; full time, 2, 104, 308; glorification of, 8–9, 139; at home, 4, 123, 146, 149, 192, 203, 317; home-based work, 3–4, 37, 42, 190, 266, 269, 272, 278, 285; home work, 3, 41–42, 267, 272–78, 280, 282–85, 362, 366n21; household work, 15, 85, 87, 91, 148, 235, 243, 273–74, 300, 356; housewifery as something different from proper, 15, 33, 85, 162, 190, 202; housework, 2–3, 20–22, 36, 38–39, 86–87, 95–96, 100, 115, 117, 122, 140, 145–47, 153–54, 155n6, 158n55, 173, 176, 190, 200, 218n93, 253, 275, 277, 285, 296–320, 343n36, 357–58; according to humanists, 7–8; ideas on, 4–6, 8, 15, 20, 86–87, 126, 314, 354, 366n18; importance of work for the economic growth and well-being of the nation, 8, 189; (home work) industrial, 3, 274–75; informal work, 248; invisible / visible, 2, 27, 31, 35, 42, 118, 121, 139, 148, 226, 236, 243, 248, 256, 272, 355, 357; irregular, 33–34, 42, 119, 162, 207, 210, 248, 272; *lavoro* (Italian), 5, 141–42, 156n12, 199n; legal constructions of female, 188; manual, 6–7, 10–11, 52n63; market, 3–4, 93, 303; (unpaid work) for the market carried out within family enterprises, 3; (care work) marketization of, 363; of migrants, 116, 210, 272, 363; military, 11, 229; as mortification, 6, 9; non-market, 3, 97–98, 101–2, 125, 173; non-work, 4, 23, 34, 38, 162, 198n, 201, 204, 298; obscuration of women's, 37, 244, 266, 362; (home work) paid industrial, 3, 38; paid work, 15, 23, 38, 191–93, 204, 208–9, 243, 274, 284, 300, 304–5, 311; part time, 2, 92, 171, 272, 275, 278; positive meaning of, 7; productive, 3, 15, 18, 38, 85, 115–18, 123, 166, 300, 303–5, 315, 350, 355–56; (home-based work) productive (unpaid, paid, hybrid, and intermediate), 3; proper work as paid work, 15, 23, 193, 266; as redeeming activity, 6; as redemptive penance, 6; (home-based work) regulation of, 37, 40, 266, 273; relationship with life cycle, 13; remuneration of women's, 2, 11, 96, 100, 147, 185n27, 193, 271, 276, 278, 280, 300, 306–7, 312, 318–19; reproductive, 15, 18, 20, 86, 114–16, 117–18, 120–24, 148, 173, 243, 303, 315–16, 351; for self-consumption and care, 3, 38; as self-realization, 9; servilization of, 209–10; (housework) significance of, 313; slave, 7 (*see also* slave/ slaves); as source of dignity, 8, 189, 209; as source of rights, 8, 42, 188–90, 201–4, 207, 209–10; as source of wealth, 8, 189; statistics, 2, 5, 33–35, 99–100, 103, 162,

166–68, 172–75, 181, 202, 204, 245, 248, 257, 266, 283, 299; temporary jobs, 249; as toil to be avoided, 8, 189; *trabajo* (Spanish), 5, 182; *trabalho* (Portuguese), 5; *travail* (French), 5, 51n48, 156n12, 336; (care work) unpaid and paid care- and housework, 3; (housework) unpaid and paid care- and housework, 3; (unpaid work) unpaid market work, 3, 24, 44; unpaid work, 3, 20, 24, 34, 38–41, 86, 90, 94, 98, 101, 146, 162, 191, 204, 227, 249, 255, 266, 284, 311, 327, 336; unproductive, 15, 17–18, 85, 116, 352; vocabulary of, 5; wage-earning, 245; women's, 4, 20, 25–29, 31, 35, 37, 42, 64n204, 100, 114, 139, 163, 202–3, 214n31, 226–28, 245–46, 248, 256, 266, 269–70, 273–74, 279, 282, 312, 355–56; (unpaid work) women's and children's unpaid work for the market, 3; work for free, 31, 65n219; (domestic work) as work, 166, 188, 204, 266 (*see also* domestic work); working conditions, 50, 143, 148, 175–76, 203, 210, 256; working couple, 244; working life, 256; workplace, 24–25, 87, 91–92, 142, 148, 286, 304, 357

worker/workers, 4, 8–9, 18, 20, 22, 24, 29, 34, 38–39, 85–86, 89, 92–94, 104, 108n53, 115, 117–20, 122–23, 125, 141, 145–47, 149, 155n6, 156n29, 162, 169, 175–80, 186n34, 191–93, 201, 205–10, 212n10, 227, 254, 267, 269–73, 276–79, 282–83, 285, 299–300, 350, 356, 366n16; agricultural, 336, 338; care, 284; childless, 92; craft, 350; domestic (*see* domestic workers); factory (*see* factory: workers); family (*see* family: workers); farm, 100; female (*see* women: as workers); God as, 5; handicraft, 276; home-based, 269, 272, 284–85; home care, 284; homeworker, 271, 274, 283, 362; household, 274, 356; houseworker, 100, 153; industrial, 203, 208–9, 271–72, 283, 362; male, 22, 103, 176–81, 210, 271–72, 279, 362; married, 176–77, 179; non-worker, 34, 162; paid, 179; part-time, 92; pieceworker, 41, 284; pregnant, 208; rural, 28, 275; social, 328–30; unpaid, 35, 65n214, 275, 359; waged, 29, 181; who must or might be considered a worker, 4; women (*see* women: as workers); young, 269

World Bank: Wealth Accounting and Valuation of Ecosystem Services (WAVES), 102

World War II, 1, 35, 143, 163, 190, 204, 270, 272–73, 276, 298, 364

Wunder, Heide, 244, 258n5

Xenophon, 12

Zwickle, Lorenz, 254

International Studies in Social History

General Editor: Marcel van der Linden, International Institute of Social History, Amsterdam

Published in Association with the International Institute of Social History, Amsterdam

Published under the auspices of the International Institute of Social History, Amsterdam, this series offers transnational perspectives on labor and working-class history. For a long time, labor historians have been working within national interpretive frameworks. But interest in studies contrasting different national and regional experiences and studying cross-border interactions has been increasing in recent years. This series is designed to act as a forum for these new approaches.

Volume 1
Trade Unions, Immigration, and Immigrants in Europe 1960–1993: A Comparative Study of the Actions of Trade Unions in Seven West European Countries
Edited by Rinus Penninx and Judith Roosblad

Volume 2
Class and Other Identities: Gender, Religion, and Ethnicity in the Writing of European Labour History
Edited by Lex Heerma van Voss and Marcel van der Linden

Volume 3
Rebellious Families: Household Strategies and Collective Action in the 19th and 20th Centuries
Edited by Jan Kok

Volume 4
Experiencing Wages: Social and Cultural Aspects of Wage Forms in Europe since 1500
Edited by Peter Scholliers and Leonard Schwarz

Volume 5
The Imaginary Revolution: Parisian Students and Workers in 1968
Michael Seidman

Volume 6
Revolution and Counterrevolution: Class Struggle in a Moscow Metal Factory
Kevin Murphy

Volume 7
Miners and the State in the Ottoman Empire: The Zonguldak Coalfield, 1822–1920
Donald Quataert

Volume 8
Anarchism, Revolution and Reaction: Catalan Labor and the Crisis of the Spanish State, 1898–1923
Angel Smith

Volume 9
Sugarlandia Revisited: Sugar and Colonialism in Asia and the Americas, 1800–1940
Edited by Ulbe Bosma, Juan A. Giusti-Cordero, and G. Roger Knight

Volume 10
Alternative Exchanges: Second-Hand Circulations from the Sixteenth Century to the Present
Edited by Laurence Fontaine

Volume 11
A Social History of Spanish Labour: New Perspectives on Class, Politics, and Gender
Edited by José A. Piqueras and Vicent Sanz-Rozalén

Volume 12
Learning on the Shop Floor: Historical Perspectives on Apprenticeship
Edited by Bert De Munck, Steven L. Kaplan, and Hugo Soly

Volume 14
Central European Crossroads: Social Democracy and National Revolution in Bratislava (Pressburg), 1867–1921
Pieter C. van Duin

Volume 15
Supervision and Authority in Industry: Western European Experiences, 1830–1939
Edited by Patricia Van den Eeckhout

Volume 16
Forging Political Identity: Silk and Metal Workers in Lyon, France 1900–1939
Keith Mann

Volume 17
Gendered Money: Financial Organization in Women's Movements, 1880–1933
Pernilla Jonsson and Silke Neunsinger

Volume 18
Postcolonial Migrants and Identity Politics: Europe, Russia, Japan and the United States in Comparison
Edited by Ulbe Bosma, Jan Lucassen, and Gert Oostindie

Volume 19
Charismatic Leadership and Social Movements: The Revolutionary Power of Ordinary Men and Women
Edited by Jan Willem Stutje

Volume 20
Maternalism Reconsidered: Motherhood, Welfare and Social Policy in the Twentieth Century
Edited by Marian van der Klein, Rebecca Jo Plant, Nichole Sanders, and Lori R. Weintrob

Volume 21
Routes into the Abyss: Coping with Crises in the 1930s
Edited by Helmut Konrad and Wolfgang Maderthaner

Volume 22
Alienating Labour: Workers on the Road from Socialism to Capitalism in East Germany and Hungary
Eszter Bartha

Volume 23
Migration, Settlement and Belonging in Europe, 1500–1930s: Comparative Perspectives
Edited by Steven King and Anne Winter

Volume 24
Bondage: Labor and Rights in Eurasia from the Sixteenth to the Early Twentieth Centuries
Alessandro Stanziani

Volume 25
Bread from the Lion's Mouth: Artisans Struggling for a Livelihood in Ottoman Cities
Edited by Suraiya Faroqhi

Volume 26
The History of Labour Intermediation: Institutions and Finding Employment in the Nineteenth and Early Twentieth Centuries
Edited by Sigrid Wadauer, Thomas Buchner, and Alexander Mejstrik

Volume 27
Rescuing the Vulnerable: Poverty, Welfare and Social Ties in Modern Europe
Edited by Beate Althammer, Lutz Raphael, and Tamara Stazic-Wendt

Volume 28
Labour, Unions and Politics Under the North Star: The Nordic Countries, 1700–2000
Edited by Mary Hilson, Silke Neunsinger, and Iben Vyff

Volume 29
Laborers and Enslaved Workers: Experiences in Common in the Making of Rio de Janeiro's Working Class, 1850–1920
Marcelo Badaró Mattos

Volume 30
What Is Work? Gender at the Crossroads of Home, Family, and Business from the Early Modern Era to the Present
Edited by Raffaella Sarti, Anna Bellavitis, and Manuela Martini

www.ingramcontent.com/pod-product-compliance
Lightning Source LLC
Chambersburg PA
CBHW072141100526
44589CB00015B/2038